Curriculum and Instruction for Students with Significant Disabilities in Inclusive Settings

SECOND EDITION

Diane Lea Ryndak

University of Florida

Sandra Alper

University of Northern Iowa

Boston • New York • San Francisco
Mexico City • Montreal • Toronto • London • Madrid • Munich
Paris • Hong Kong • Singapore • Tokyo • Cape Town • Sydney

Executive Editor: *Virginia Lanigan*
Series Editorial Assistant: *Rob Champagne*
Marketing Manager: *Taryn Wahlquist*
Composition and Prepress Buyer: *Linda Cox*
Manufacturing Buyer: *JoAnne Sweeney*
Cover Administrator: *Kristina Mose-Libon*
Editorial-Production Coordinator: *Mary Beth Finch*
Editorial-Production Service: *Modern Graphics, Inc.*
Electronic Composition: *Modern Graphics, Inc.*

For related titles and support materials, visit our online catalog at www.ablongman.com.

Between the time Web site information is gathered and then published, it is not unusual for some sites to have closed. Also, the transcription of URLs can result in unintended typographical errors. The publisher would appreciate notification where these errors occur so that they may be corrected in subsequent editions.

Library of Congress Cataloging-in-Publication Data

Ryndak, Diane Lea
    Curriculum and instruction for students with significant disabilities in inclusive
  settings / Diane Lea Ryndak, Sandra Alper.
       p. cm.
    Rev. ed. of: Curriculum content for students with moderate and severe disabilities in inclusive settings. c1996.
    Includes bibliographical references and index.
    ISBN 0-205-35219-7
    1. Children with disabilities—Education—United States—Curricula. 2. Mainstreaming in education—United States. I. Alper, Sandra K. II. Ryndak, Diane Lea Curriculum content for students with moderate and severe disabilities in inclusive settings. III. Title.

LC4031 .R96 2003
371.9′046—dc21

2002026079

Printed in the United States of America

10 9 8 7 6 5 4 3 2 1   07 06 05 04 03 02

To Michael Pagels, for your love and support, which make anything possible.
To Bertha, my mother, and Seth, my son, for your love.

Contents

16   *"We Want to Go to College Too": Supporting Students with Significant Disabilities in Higher Education*
Mary Beth Doyle   **307**

17   *Individualized Positive Behavior Intervention and Support in Inclusive School Settings*
Tim Knoster   **323**

PART FIVE • *Planning, Implementing, and Evaluating Instruction in Inclusive Settings*

18 *Planning Instruction for the Diverse Classroom: Approaches that Facilitate the Inclusion of All Students Linda Davern, Roberta Schnorr, and James W. Black*   **340**

Contributors

Martin Agran, Ph.D.
Department of Special Education
Schindler Education Center
University of Northern Iowa
Cedar Falls, Iowa 50614-0601

Sandra Alper, Ph.D.
Department of Special Education
Schindler Education Center
University of Northern Iowa
Cedar Falls, Iowa 50614-0601

Felix Billingsley, Ph.D.
Experimental Education Unit
Box 357925
University of Washington
Seattle, WA 98195

James W. Black, Ph.D.
Nazareth College of Rochester
4245 East Avenue
Rochester, NY 14618

Diane M. Browder, Ph.D.
Department of Counseling, Special Education, and
   Child Development
University of North Carolina - Charlotte
9201 University City Boulevard
Charlotte, NC 28223-0001

Lisa S. Cushing
Vanderbilt University
Box 328, Peabody College
Nashville, TN 37203

Linda Davern, Ph.D.
Education Department
Sage College
Troy, NY 12180

June E. Downing, Ph.D.
California State at Northridge
#ED 1204
18111 Nordhoff Street
Northridge, CA 91330

Mary Beth Doyle, Ph.D.
St. Michael's College
One Winnoski Park
Colchester, VT 05439

Brenda Fossett
University of British Columbia
2125 Main Mall
Vancouver, BC V6T 1Z4
Canada

Lori A. Garcia
Department of Special Education
205 Stone Building
Florida State University
Tallahassee, FL 32306-4459

Jill Greene
Boston University
Department of Special Education
605 Commonwealth Avenue
Boston, MA 02215

Ginny Helwick
Division of Special Education
University of Northern Colorado
Greely, CO 80639

Lewis Jackson, Ph.D.
Division of Special Education
University of Northern Colorado
Greely, CO 80639

Craig H. Kennedy, Ph.D.
Vanderbilt University
Box 328, Peabody College
Nashville, TN 37203

Tim Knoster, Ph.D.
Exceptionality Programs
Bloomsburg University
Navy Hall
Bloomsburg, PA 17815

Donna H. Lehr, Ph.D.
Boston University
Department of Special Education
605 Commonwealth Avenue
Boston, MA 02215

Karen McCaleb
Division of Special Education
University of Northern Colorado
Greely, CO 80639

Gail McGregor, Ph.D.
University of Montana
Raval Institute on Disabilities
52 Corbin Hall
Missoula, MT 59801

Bruce M. Menchetti, Ph.D.
Department of Special Education
205 Stone Building
Florida State University
Tallahassee, FL 32306-4459

Pat Mirenda, Ph.D.
University of British Columbia
2125 Main Mall
Vancouver, BC V6T 1Z4
Canada

Michael Muldoon
Florida State Department of Education
Exceptional Student Education Division
614 Turlington Building
325 W. Gaines Street
Tallahassee, FL 32399-0400

Stephanie Powers
Boston University
Department of Special Education

605 Commonwealth Avenue
Boston, MA 02215

Paige Pullen, Ph.D.
University of Virginia
235 Ruffner Hall
PO Box 400273
Charlottesville, VA 22904-4273

Beverly Rainforth, Ph.D.
SUNY Binghamton
SEHD - Division of Education
Academic B Room 238
Vestal Parkway East
Binghamton, NY 13903

Diane Lea Ryndak, Ph.D.
University of Florida
Department of Special Education
PO Box 117050
Gainesville, FL 32611-7050

Roberta Schnorr, Ph.D.
SUNY Oswego
Department of Curriculum and Instruction
109 Poucher Hall
Oswego, NY 13126

Veronica Smith
University of British Columbia
2125 Main Mall
Vancouver, BC V6T 1Z4
Canada

Fred Spooner, Ph.D.
Department of Counseling, Special Education, and
    Child Development
University of North Carolina - Charlotte
9201 University City Boulevard
Charlotte, NC 28223

Theresa Ward, Ph.D.
College of Saint Rose
432 Western Avenue
Albany, NY 12203

Michael Wehmeyer, Ph.D.
Beach Center on Families and Disabilities
3136 Haworth Hall
University of Kansas
Lawrence, KS 66045

Preface

I know that most men, including those at ease with problems of the greatest complexity, can seldom accept even the simplest and most obvious truth if it be such as would oblige them to admit the falsity of conclusions which they have delighted in explaining to their colleagues, which they have proudly taught to others, and which they have woven, thread by thread, into the fabric of their lives.

—Leo Tolstoy

Change is never easy, especially when it involves a large number of individuals and an established system, yet change is called for when innovative practices demonstrate greater effectiveness than past services. For years the education system has provided special education and related services to students with disabilities and has systematically developed a dual-service delivery system comprised of different settings, different curricula, different services, and different service providers for students with and without disabilities. That dual system was created based upon conclusions that now are suspect due to the outcomes of inclusive educational practices.

Our experiences with the inclusion of students with significant disabilities in the general education settings they would attend if they did not have disabilities, have caused us to rethink how, when, where, and by whom educational services are provided. The speed and breadth of the growth demonstrated by students, the increase in their alertness and time on task, their demonstration of unexpected cognitive and functional abilities, and the establishment of nurturing relationships with nondisabled classmates have been eye opening and thought provoking for us, as well as many other professionals in general education, special education, and related services. Responses to these findings have included both personal and systemic change, because the inclusion of students with significant disabilities in general education calls for collaboration among all service providers. As these changes continue, we are approaching the development of one educational service delivery system that serves all students.

This book has three purposes. First, it provides a process for education teams to identify curriculum content for students with significant disabilities in inclusive general education settings, defined for this book as the educational settings each student would attend if she/he did not have disabilities. Because of the nature of general education settings and the long-term goal for students to transition into inclusive adult settings, this curriculum content identification process gives equal emphasis to functional and general education content, allowing each education team to decide if one or both emphases are appropriate for an individual student during a given academic year. This process empha-sizes the concept of access to general education curriculum embedded within the Individuals with Disabilities Education Act (IDEA) 1997. Second, this book provides in-formation on curriculum content areas traditionally included in both special education and general education curricula and examples of how the process can be used in each of those areas. Third, this book provides information about instructional strategies from the fields of both general and special education that are effective for students with significant dis-abilities within inclusive general education contexts.

The book is organized into five parts. Part I provides introductory information on students with significant disabilities (Chapter 1), their inclusion in general education set-tings (Chapter 2), and how inclusion relates to other national trends (Chapters 3 and 4). Part I also provides a historical perspective on the use of an ecological approach to identi-fying relevant functional content for instruction (Chapter 5). Part II describes the curricu-lum content identification process (Chapter 6) and the role of family members, friends, and other education team members when identifying curriculum content for a student (Chapters 7 and 8). Part III discusses content traditionally included within the general ed-ucation curriculum and the application of the curriculum content identification process in relation to those areas. For instance, Chapter 9 discusses the facilitation of skill acquisition by students with significant disabilities within general education content areas. Chapters 10, 11, and 12 provide information about skill acquisition related to oral language and lit-eracy, social relationships, and motor skills. Part IV discusses content traditionally em-bedded within special education curriculum, with no specific parallels in the general education curriculum. These include (a) the ecological domains traditionally addressed in special education programs to meet the functional needs of students with significant dis-abilities (Chapter 13), (b) the promotion of self-determination (Chapter 14), (c) transition-planning processes (Chapter 15), (d) accessing college experiences (Chapter 16), and (e) positive behavioral interventions (Chapter 17). Part V provides information related to plan-ning, implementing, and evaluating instruction in inclusive general education settings. Chapter 18 discusses planning instruction for students with significant disabilities within the process of developing instruction in general education classes. Chapter 19 provides in-formation specifically on instructional principles and practices for students with signifi-cant disabilities, and Chapter 20 provides information about adapting general education environments, materials, and instruction to meet the instructional needs of students with significant disabilities. Finally, Chapter 21 provides information about accommodating motor and sensory impairments, and Chapter 22 addresses meeting the needs of students with physical and health challenges in inclusive general education settings. In addition to this information, Appendix A includes profiles of three students, describing (a) their per-formance before they were included in general education, (b) information gathered through the use of the process, (c) their annual goals and educational program after com-pletion of the process, and (d) their performance after inclusion. For one student, this in-formation is expanded into a more complete case study.

When a task of this magnitude is undertaken, a number of people are drawn into the experience and thus share in the task completion. Knowing that we cannot possibly name each of these people, we would particularly like to acknowledge certain people and groups of people. First, we would like to thank the many colleagues who have challenged us, allowing us to expand our thoughts about inclusion, viable functional and general education curriculum content, adaptations for inclusive settings, and a viable process to allow for maximized instruction in inclusive settings. Second, we would like to acknowledge the irreplaceable efforts of many parents and other education team members who shared their insights about the process and feedback on components. Third, we would like to express our appreciation to the many students with significant disabilities who were patient as their education teams went through trial-and-error procedures, attempting to maximize the effectiveness of their educational services in inclusive settings, and whose successful pioneering efforts in inclusive settings would not be denied. Fourth, we recognize that this book would not have been completed without the efforts of numerous individuals who willingly gathered information for and proofread chapters, figures, and appendixes. Fifth, we would like to thank the reviewers of our manuscript: Arthur J. Artesani, University of Maine; Pat Rogan, Indiana University; Terry C. Shepherd, Texas A&M International University; and Barbara C. Gartin, University of Arkansas. Finally, we wish to publicly recognize the patient and diligent efforts of the people at Allyn and Bacon, whose expertise helped bring this book to fruition, especially Virginia Lanigan.

1

Students with Moderate and Severe Disabilities: Definitions and Descriptive Characteristics

Sandra Alper

Objectives

After reading this chapter, the reader will be able to:

1. Discuss issues and contradictions in developing definitions of disabilities.
2. Distinguish between taxonomies and typologies as they relate to disability labels.
3. Discuss formal and informal functions of disability definitions.
4. Describe historical definitions of mental retardation.
5. Discuss the relative positive and negative social impacts of disability definitions.
6. Describe current definitions of mental retardation and severe disabilities as published by American Association on Mental Retardation (AAMR) and The Association for Persons with Severe Handicaps (TASH).
7. Define self-determination and person-centered planning as these concepts apply to quality of life for all people.
8. Describe learning, behavioral, and sensory challenges faced by people with severe disabilities.
9. Understand and appreciate the overwhelming similarities, as opposed to differences, between people with and without disabilities labels.

Key Terms

AAMR	Issues in definitions	Self-determination
Adaptive behavior	Learning characteristics	Sensory impairments
Behavioral characteristics	Levels of support	Social construction
IDEA 1997	Moderate and severe disabilities	Taxonomies
Intellectual functioning	Person-centered planning	Typologies

The field of special education has undergone rapid and profound changes during the last decade. One of these changes relates to how we educate students with moderate to severe disabilities. These students are now educated in increasing numbers in inclusive class-rooms. Under the Individuals with Disabilities Education Act (IDEA) amendments of 1997, all students with disabilities are to be provided access to the general education curriculum. One of the biggest challenges facing special and general education teachers is how to modify the general education curriculum to meet the needs of students with significant learning and behavioral challenges, while, at the same time, to provide instruction in functional skills.

The focus of this test is on what and how to teach these students. We present approaches for developing appropriate curriculum content for students with moderate to severe disabilities. A curriculum blending process will be described that includes both functional and basic academic skills. The curriculum blending process will then be applied to a number of curriculum areas. The purpose of the first chapter is to discuss definitions and to describe characteristics of students who become labeled with moderate to severe disabilities. We will look at both historic and current definitions of this term, discuss issues in definitions, and describe characteristics of students who become labeled. We begin with descriptions of three students of different ages, all of whom were labeled with severe disabilities. These descriptions represent only a few of the many unique and varied attributes of students labeled with moderate to severe disabilities.

Jay is a secondary student (16 years of age) who was diagnosed with cerebral palsy shortly after birth. Jay has attended inclusive classes since third grade and is now in a public high school with a total enrollment of 900 students. He uses a wheelchair and communicates with an augmentative device. Jay is well-liked by his teachers and has many friends. He attended the junior-senior prom and is active in the high school soccer pep club and the Young Judeah Society in his synagogue. Jay lives at home with his parents and two younger sisters. He has had the benefit of his school district's transition program, although there were few opportunities for him to obtain competitive employment training due to lack of accessibility of job sites. He hopes to attend a postsecondary program at a community college and major in computer programming. Jay and his family are now considering residential options (for example, dorm, group home, family home, or apartment with assisted-living support) after high school graduation. His family is frustrated by the fragmented adult services that exist for students with disabilities after high school graduation.

Mark is a 10-year-old boy who was reported to have sustained closed head injuries caused by parental abuse at the age of two years. At the age of six, he was removed from his family's home by social services due to repeated reports of physical abuse, drug use and manufacturing by parents, and his increasing tendencies toward violent and aggressive behaviors. He was then placed in a state institution, due to the unavailability of foster care for children with disabilities, and particularly aggressive behaviors. At the age of eight, he was moved to a community group home where he currently lives with three other young children. Mark attends classes in a public school, but is largely segregated due to continuing episodes of aggression toward others. The school staff believes he should be moved to a more restrictive environment because of his aggressive tendencies. The staff of his group home has offered to send support members to the school to deal with any aggressive episodes, but, so far, the school has declined to bring nondistrict employees into the classrooms. Mark loves animals and video games.

   Serena is three years of age and lives with her mother, father, and a five-year-old sister. She has shown a number of significant developmental delays (relative to her chronological age) believed to be associated with her premature birth and low birth weight, including hypotonia, or poor muscle tone; poor ambulation; difficulties in early feeding; frequent awakening during the night; and lack of bladder control. Serena attends an inclusive preschool three days a week and receives home visits by staff from the school twice a week. Serena is working on communication, feeding, and bathroom skills. Although her family is very supportive, they are frustrated by lack of services and unwillingness of insurance companies to compensate for Serena's many needed services, including speech and physical therapies. Her family is very concerned about the transition from preschool to an inclusive kindergarten setting for their daughter.

The Importance of Definitions

Definitions serve many purposes. They have formal and legally defined functions and meanings. They can also play informal, but very powerful, functions as they influence the perceptions and behavior of people not labeled in regard to those who are labeled.

   Legal definitions of disabilities serve formal functions, such as defining eligibility criteria for services. For example, P.L. 105-17, The Individuals with Disabilities Act Amendments of 1997 (IDEA 1997) incorporates definitions for levels of mental retardation as specified by the American Association on Mental Retardation (AAMR). Further, IDEA 1997 mandates services for infants, toddlers, and youth with severe disabilities, such as participation in state- and district-wide assessments, alternate assessments, positive behavioral supports, access to inclusive settings and the general education curriculum, and vocational services.

   Definitions and their corresponding labels are also used as a form of shorthand to communicate about students with disabilities in official school documents, such as census reports, enrollment figures, and prevalence reports. In this capacity, they often serve as the basis for determinations about levels of state and federal financial aid to schools. They also serve as a basis for different areas of teacher licensure and certification in many states, that is, teachers are often licensed based on the disability category of the students they teach.

   Definitions can function informally, and often in negative ways, to affect perceptions, expectations, and behaviors of persons without disabilities. They may, for example, convey erroneously that all people who have the same label are exactly the same. This may lead to the mistaken assumption that all persons in the same disability category should be treated exactly the same. Definitions of disability labels can also affect expectations of what persons with a particular label can or cannot learn to do. The ability of persons with severe disabilities to learn, attend public school, make friends, live in the community, or work in competitive and meaningful jobs was doubted for many years.

Issues in Defining Disabilities

There are many controversial issues surrounding labels and definitions of disabilities. We will consider three of these issues as they pertain to students with moderate to severe disabilities. First, the distinction between taxonomies and typologies (Speece & Harry, 1997) is often blurred. Second, developing a useful and consistent definition that accurately describes students in any group is problematic because of the large variety of individual differences that exist within any group of human beings. Third, definitions and disability labels can lead to overemphasizing the disability and underemphasizing the strengths and capabilities of the person.

Speece and Harry (1997), in a discussion of disability definitions and labeling, noted the differences between taxonomies and typologies. They pointed out that, although both activities involve classification, taxonomies are based on empirical data, while typologies are largely conceptual and may be socially constructed. For example, in biological taxonomies, living organisms are identified, described, and classified according to their biological characteristics, relationships, and similarities. Thus, the great apes are considered by many scientists to be related to human beings, while some dinosaurs are believed to be the precursors of birds. There is great controversy, however, as to whether or not Attention Deficit Disorder (a topology) is a valid disorder of childhood justifying chemical intervention or simply a term used to describe very active children who are, in fact, within the range of normal developmental behavior.

Taxonomic classifications must be empirically verified for reliability and validity in order to confirm whether a particular organism does or does not fall into a particular phylum and species. Typologies, on the other hand, are conceptualized based on similar descriptive characteristics believed to be shared by a group (for example, mental retardation, learning disabilities, autism, or hyperactivity), but do not always require quantitative data. Typologies may derive meaning based on how they are interpreted by a majority of people in some segment of society at a particular point in time. That is, if a majority agrees that persons with some characteristic (for example, school failure, poverty, cultural background, homosexuality, school success, orthodox or agnostic religious views, athletic prowess, access to money, members of social and politically powerful families, or unique physical features) are intrinsically inferior or superior in any way, members of the society may develop labels and then base treatment of these groups on ill-founded information and expectations. Critics of labeling have charged for years that a disproportionate number of poor, nonwhite, nonmiddle class children become labeled and placed in special education. Jane Mercer's (1973) and Roger Hurley's (1969) classic and pioneering works documented this phenomenon. Mercer defined mental retardation as an achieved social status in a social system. Hurley described the relationship between poverty and mental retardation.

Mental retardation is linguistically influenced. It is a label that refers to a wide range of behaviors. Like other labels used to describe large groups of people, it is a convenient way to make generalizations about a large group of people. Hardman, Drew, Egan, and Wolf (1996) characterized mental retardation as both a label of fact and a "label of conjecture." As a label of fact, mental retardation must refer to observable, quantifiable, and verifiable characteristics. Conditions associated with mental retardation, such as Down syndrome, phenylketonuria, or Tay Sach's disease, can be verified through observation and medical tests. In approximately 80 to 85 percent of the cases of mental retardation, however, no known cause can be verified. In these cases, mental retardation is a label of conjecture, or hypothesis.

Interestingly, as the AAMR definitions of mental retardation have changed over the years based on Intelligence Quotient (IQ) cut off point, a particular individual may or may not have been considered to fall into the category of mental retardation. And even though we use the label of learning disabilities to refer to a certain group of school-aged students, special educators cannot agree or empirically verify the definition of this term. Some authorities (Gallagher, 1998; Sarason, 1985) have argued that disabilities are largely socially constructed, rather than valid and reliably assessed human conditions.

A second difficulty in developing reliable and valid definitions of disabilities is that there is a great deal of variation within each special education category. Although we can predict with a good degree of reliability that children labeled with severe disabilities will be likely to face significant challenges in school, we cannot predict what specific problems will be experienced or what or how to teach a child who is so labeled. This is because any two students who have the same label have many individual differences. The definitional label provides very little useful information on which to base instructional programs.

Third, Browder (2001) and Alper, Ryndak, and Schloss (2001), in discussions of alternate assessment for students with disabilities, emphasized that any particular disability definition may lead us to overinterpret or misinterpret the disability and underemphasize the capacities of the person. This can lead to designing instructional programs and making life decisions for a student based on his or her deficits rather than current strengths, preferences, and capacity to grow and learn new skills. For many years, curriculum for students with disabilities was based on assumptions about what they could *never* learn to do. Attending inclusive schools, learning new skills, living in the community, making friends, interacting with persons without disabilities, and competitive employment were all considered to be beyond the capabilities of these students.

Definitions

We will now review definitions of disabilities, starting with Biblical times and moving to the present. Because severe disabilities typically includes mental retardation, we will focus on some of the historical definitions of this term.

Some early Christians believed that persons with disabilities were holy innocents, uniquely able to communicate with God. The spread of Christianity resulted in humane treatment for persons with disabilities. An old Yiddish proverb held that "a complete fool is half a prophet." Calvin and Martin Luther, however, considered persons who were retarded to be possessed by Satan. Persons with disabilities were often considered to be witches and burned at the stake by the Puritans. Szasz (1970) chronicled the historical treatment of persons considered to be deviant, including those with disabilities.

The early part of the 20th century and the growth of psychology resulted in several definitions of mental retardation that emphasized psychological pathology, inability to learn, and criminal or dangerous tendencies. For example, Tredgold's concept of mental retardation (Tredgold & Soddy, 1956) included the following assumptions: (1) incomplete mental development beginning early in life, (2) etiology consisting of hereditary factors or disease or injury, (3) pathology centered primarily in the brain, (4) little or no hope for improvement in the condition, and (5) no significant changes in the person so afflicted could be expected.

Prior to 1959, mental retardation was widely assumed to be caused by a defect of the central nervous system, incurable, and resulting in an inability of the person to benefit from schooling (Blatt, 1987). Arbitrarily determined IQ scores were believed to predict capacity. People with IQs from 50 to 75 were categorized as *morons*, those with IQ scores between 25 and 50 were labeled *imbeciles*, and persons with IQ scores lower than 25 were termed *idiots*. These labels conveyed negativity and lowered expectations. It is not surprising that many persons so labeled were institutionalized as a form of "treatment." In one of the darkest chapters in the history of humankind, the Nazi regime, many persons with disabilities residing in institutions were killed in concentration camps because it was propagandized that they were a threat to the purity and superiority of the Aaryan race. Because of their disabilities, they were portrayed as subnormal, dangerous, and able to pass on their defective genes to any progeny. Szasz (1970) and Blatt (1987) have both described the history of injustices suffered by various groups of people who were judged to be different, and, therefore, deviant, defective, and dangerous, by the majority of their peers.

Although, the term "severe disabilities" has been defined in different ways, generally speaking, it implies a condition in which the development of skills typical for chronological age is significantly delayed (Abt Associates, 1974; Baker, 1979; Brimer, 1990; Justen, 1976; Sailor & Haring, 1977; Westling & Fox, 2000). These individuals are often challenged by significant difficulties in learning, memory, generalization of skills, communication and social skills, and/or sensory and physical development. They often require ongoing assistance from individuals without disabilities. Persons referred to as having a severe disability include those who have been classified as moderately, severely, or profoundly mentally retarded and those who have multiple disabilities, including mental retardation (Westling & Fox, 2000).

The Association for Persons with Severe Handicaps (TASH) defined the condition of severe disabilities relative to *necessary support*:

> These people include individuals of all ages who require extensive ongoing support in more than one major life activity in order to participate in integrated community settings and to enjoy a quality of life that is available to citizens with fewer or no disabilities. Support may be required for life activities such as mobility, communication, self-care, and learning as necessary for independent living, employment and self-sufficiency. (Adopted by TASH, December, 1985, revised November, 1986; reprinted in Meyer, Peck, & Brown 1991 [(cited in Westling & Fox, 2000, p. 3]).

In 1992, the AAMR characterized mental retardation—often present in persons labeled with severe disabilities—as a condition in which different levels of support are required. This is the definition according to the AAMR:

> Mental retardation refers to substantial limitations in present functioning. It is characterized by significantly subaverage intellectual functioning, existing concurrently with related lim-

itations in two or more of the following applicable adaptive skill areas: communication, self-care, home living, social skills, community use, self-direction, health and home safety, functional academics, leisure, and work. Mental retardation manifests before 18.

Four assumptions that are essential considerations in applying the definition are:

1. Valid assessment considers cultural and linguistic diversity as well as differences in communication and behavioral factors;
2. The existence of limitations in adaptive skills occurs within the context of community environments typical of the individual's age peers and is indexed to the person's individualized needs for supports;
3. Specific adaptive limitations often coexist with strengths in other adaptive skills or other personal capabilities; and
4. With appropriate supports over a sustained period, the life functioning of the person with mental retardation will generally improve. (p. 1)

Table 1.1 provides specific areas of adaptive behavior.

The AAMR no longer uses the traditional degrees of mental retardation (for example, mild, moderate, severe, or profound). Instead, an individual who is diagnosed as being mentally retarded must be described using four dimensions that provide a detailed description of the person and the environment(s) in which s/he lives (AAMR, 1992). These four dimensions are:

- Dimension I: Intellectual functioning and adaptive skills
- Dimension II: Psychological/emotional considerations
- Dimension III: Physical/health/etiology considerations
- Dimension IV: Environmental considerations

All four dimensions are used to identify strengths, challenges, and types and degrees of necessary support. The types of support possible with examples follow. The degrees of support include intermittent, limited, extensive, and pervasive. These levels of support may vary across individuals, across skill areas, and across different time periods in the life span.

Intermittent

Support is on an "as needed basis" and is characterized by episodic nature, person not always needing the support(s), or short-term supports needed during lifespan transitions (for example, job loss or an acute medical crisis). Intermittent supports may be high or low intensity when provided (AAMR, 1992).

Amy received job-coaching services through a local adult services provider after she completed high school. She was recently laid off from her electronics plant job and is now being trained for a new position in the local hospital.

Limited

This requires an intensity of supports characterized by consistency over time; time limited, but not of an intermittent nature; and may require fewer staff members and less cost than

TABLE 1.1   *Clusters and Specific Adaptive Behavior Areas*

Self-help, personal appearance	***Health care, personal welfare***
Feeding, eating, drinking	Treatment of injuries, health problems
Dressing	Prevention of health problems
Toileting	Personal safety
Grooming, hygiene	Childcare practices
Physical development	***Consumer skills***
Gross motor skills	Money handling
Fine motor skills	Purchasing
	Banking
	Budgeting
Communication	***Domestic skills***
Receptive language	Household cleaning
Expressive language	Property maintenance, repair
	Clothing care
	Kitchen skills
	Household safety
Personal, social skills	***Community orientation***
Play skills	Travel skills
Interaction skills	Use of community resources
Group participation	Telephone usage
Social amenities	Community safety
Sexual behavior	
Self-direction, responsibility	
Leisure activities	
Expression of emotions	
Cognitive functioning	***Vocational skills***
Preacademics (for example, colors)	Work habits and attitudes
Reading	Job-search skills
Writing	Work performance
Numeric functions	Social vocational behavior
Time	Work safety
Money	
Measurement	

more intense levels of support for example, time-limited employment training or transitional supports during the school to adult-provided period (AAMR, 1992).

In order to obtain competitive employment, Tim received full-time job-coaching services. After three months, the job coaching was reduced to four hours per day and then faded out completely after a total of six months. Tim is employed in the hotel industry 30 hours per week and has received very positive evaluations from his supervisor.

Extensive

Supports are characterized by regular involvement (for example, daily) in at least some environments (such as work or home) and are not time limited, for example, long-term support and long-term home living support (AAMR, 1992).

Lori was born with multiple sclerosis. She has a full-time paraprofessional with her during the school day to provide help with her tracheometry tube, eating, and toileting.

Pervasive

Supports are characterized by their constancy and high intensity, are provided across environments, and have potential life-sustaining nature. Pervasive supports typically involve more staff members and intrusiveness than do extensive or time-limited supports (AAMR, 1992).

Randy demonstrated normal development until the age of nine, when he sustained a closed head injury in an automobile accident and was in a coma for three months. He now breathes with the aid of a machine, must be fed through a stomach tube, and has had a colostomy. He seemingly does not communicate in any recognizable way with others and requires 24-hour nursing care in an extended care facility.

Persons labeled with severe disabilities share a common label, but have many different individual characteristics. The common ground among the members of this population is that their general intellectual functioning as measured by standardized tests of intelligence is lower than that exhibited by about 99 percent of the rest of the population (Westling & Fox, 2000). They need more assistance and support than others in order to live life as normally as possible, be included with persons without disabilities, and enhance quality of life.

Strengths

Students with moderate to severe disabilities, like all persons, have many unique strengths and positive attributes. It is important that we see beyond the disability and come to know and appreciate each individual. These students continue to exceed our expectations if they receive appropriate education and other needed services.

Current best practices about persons with severe disabilities emphasize the values of person and family-centered planning and self-determination in conducting assessment and developing curriculum (Agran, 1997; Browder, 2001; Wehmeyer, Agran, & Hughes, 1998). Three assumptions are paramount. First, persons with severe disabilities are capable of indicating preferences, making choices, and learning self-directed behaviors and must be allowed the opportunity to do so. We assume that students with severe disabilities, like all students, can be systematically taught the behaviors required to make choices and decisions and to monitor their own performance. Agran, Wehmeyer, and King-Sears (in press) recently developed training procedures teachers can use to teach self-determination skills.

Second, all educational planning should honor students' own preferences. Students with severe disabilities should be invited to their own Individualized Education Plan (IEP) and other planning meetings and should be provided opportunities to express their choices about what they would like to learn; what activities they want to engage in; and what they prefer for social and leisure activities, place of residence, and so on. They should have an active and significant role in charting the course of their own lives. Sadly, many persons with moderate and severe disabilities are placed in educational and residential settings based on factors such as funding, waiting lists, local policies, and so forth, with no opportunities to express personal preferences.

Third, educational planning should focus on each family's priorities and values and should be sensitive to cultural values. We must actively try to identify and consider each family's cultural priorities, living environment, family constellation, family dynamics, goals for the future, and resources (Alper, Schloss, & Schloss, 1994; Turnbull & Turnbull, 1990). Families today often reflect single-parent homes, poverty, urban, rural, and isolated areas, and homes headed by grandparents, adoptive, or foster parents. Misra (1994) provided many excellent examples of cultural group differences in families' values and goals.

Challenges in School

Two points are important to keep in mind in any discussion of characteristics of students with moderate to severe disabilities. First, each student is unique and may or may not show any of the characteristics described in the following sections. Second, as mentioned previously, we must be careful not to see only the challenges faced by these students. It is important to emphasize their unique strengths. The following description of characteristics is not meant to be comprehensive or representative of each child with the label, but rather to describe only some of the challenges commonly found in the group. For a more detailed description of characteristics associated with the label of severe disabilities, see Westling and Fox (2000).

Learning Challenges

Challenges faced in school may include slower learning rate, memory problems, difficulty in generalizing skills learned in one setting to another, and difficulty in synthesizing skills learned in isolation (for example, combining skills learned separately in reading and math to perform a functional activity such as ordering and paying for fast food). Attending to relevant aspects of a problem and observational (modeling) and incidental learning may also pose difficulties. Communication may pose a problem. Self-help skills such as eating and toileting may also have to be taught. Alper and Ryndak (1992) and Ryndak and Alper (1996) presented a detailed discussion of learning challenges faced by these students, along with suggestions for classroom interventions.

Behavioral Challenges

Difficulties may include lack of response, stereotypes (that is, repetitive but seemingly meaningless behaviors such as finger-flicking or rocking), self-abuse, or aggressive behaviors toward objects or people. These behaviors make social interactions and developing friendships very difficult. Again, it is important to remember that social skills are learned behaviors and that all persons are capable of acquiring appropriate social behaviors (Carr et al., 1999; Smith, 2001).

Physical and Sensory Impairments

Some students with moderate to severe disabilities may have physical difficulties that impair their mobility and general state of health. These include conditions such as cerebral palsy, eating disorders, growth disorders, and convulsive, cardiovascular, and respiratory disorders. Still other students may experience hearing and/or visual impairments (Sirvis, Doyle & Acouloumre, 2001). A detailed description of many of these conditions is presented in later chapters of this book.

Summary

In this chapter, we have attempted to describe the population of students who typically become labeled with the term moderate or severe disabilities. We have also tried to articulate some of the pitfalls and issues involved that make defining disabilities difficult.

We provide an overview of inclusion and other trends that have significantly influenced the education of persons with moderate and severe disabilities in the next chapter. In succeeding chapters, we present a process for blending both the academic and functional skill needs of students in order to develop appropriate curriculum content. We then apply that curriculum-blending process to a variety of different curriculum areas.

References _____

Abt Associates. (1974). *Assessment of selected resources for the severely handicapped children and youth: Vol. 1. A state of the art paper.* Cambridge, MA: Abt Associates. (ERIC Document Reproduction Service No. ED 134 614)

Agran, M. (1997). *Student-directed learning: Teaching self-determination skills.* Pacific Grove, CA: Brooks/Cole Publishing Co.

Agran, M., Wehmeyer, M., & King-Sears, M. (in press). *Teachers' guide to inclusive practices: Student-directed learning and inclusion.* Baltimore: Paul H. Brookes Publishing Co.

Alper, S., & Ryndak, D. L. (1992). Educating students with severe handicaps in regular classes. *The Elementary School Journal, 92*(3), 373–387.

Alper, S., Ryndak, D. L., & Schloss, C. N. (Eds.). (2001). *Alternate assessment of students with disabilities in inclusive settings.* Boston: Allyn & Bacon.

Alper, S., Schloss, P. J., & Schloss, C. N. (1994). *Families of students with disabilities: Consultation and advocacy.* Boston: Allyn & Bacon.

American Association on Mental Retardation (AAMR). (1992). *Mental retardation: Definition, classification, and systems of supports* (9th ed.). Washington, DC: Author.

Baker, D. (1979). Severely handicapped: Toward an inclusive definition. *AAESPH Review, 4*(1), 52–65.

Blatt, B. (1987). *The conquest of mental retardation.* Austin, TX: Pro-ED, Inc.

Brimer, R. W. (1990). *Students with severe disabilities: Current perspectives and practices.* Mountain View, CA: Mayfield.

Browder, D. M. (2001). *Curriculum and assessment for students with moderate and severe disabilities.* New York: Guilford Press.

Carr, E. G., Horner, R. H., Turnbull, A. P., Marquis, J. G.,

McLaughlin, D. M., McAtee, M. L., Smith, C. E., Ryan, K. A., Ruef, M. B., Doolabh, A., & Braddock, D. (1999). *Positive behavior support for people with developmental disabilities: A research synthesis*. Washington, DC: AAMR.

Gallagher, D. J. (1998). The scientific knowledge base of special education: Do we know what we think we know? *Exceptional Children, 64*(4), 493–502.

Hardman, M. L., Drew, C. J., Egan, M. W., & Wolf, B. (1996). *Human exceptionality: Society, school, and family* (5th ed.). Boston: Allyn & Bacon.

Hurley, R. L. (1969). *Poverty and mental retardation: A causal relationship*. New York: Vintage Books.

Individuals with Disabilities Education Act, Pub. L. No. 105-117, 20 U.S.C. § 1401 *et seq.* (1997).

Justen, J. E. (1976). Who are the severely handicapped? A problem in definition. *AAESPH Review, 1*(5), 1–11.

Mercer, J. (1973). *Labeling the mentally retarded: Clinical and social system perspectives on mental retardation*. Berkeley: University of California Press.

Meyer, L. H., Peck, C. A., & Brown, L. (Eds.). (1991). *Critical issues in the lives of people with severe disabilities*. Baltimore: Paul H. Brookes Publishing Co.

Misra, A. (1994). Partnership with multicultural families. In S. K. Alper, P. J. Schloss, & C. N. Schloss (Eds.), *Families of students with disabilities: Consultation and advocacy* (pp. 143–179). Boston: Allyn & Bacon.

Ryndak, D. L., & Alper, S. (1996). *Curriculum content for students with moderate and severe disabilities in inclusive settings*. Boston: Allyn & Bacon.

Sailor, W., & Haring, N. (1977). Some current directions in the education of the severely/multiply handicapped. *AAESPH Review, 2*(2), 67–86.

Sarason, S. B. (1985). *Psychology and mental retardation: Perspectives in change*. Austin, TX: Pro-ED, Inc.

Sirvis, B. P., Doyle, M. B., & Acouloumre, D. S. (2001). Assessment of students with physical and special health needs. In S. Alper, D. L. Ryndak, & C. N. Schloss (Eds.), *Alternate assessment of students with disabilities in inclusive settings* (pp. 273–293). Boston: Allyn & Bacon.

Smith, M. A. (2001). Functional assessment of challenging behaviors in school and community. In S. Alper, D. L. Ryndak, & C. N. Schloss (Eds.), *Alternate assessment of students with disabilities in inclusive settings* (pp. 256–272). Boston: Allyn & Bacon.

Speece, D. L., & Harry, B. (1997). Classification for children. In J. W. Lloyd, E. J. Kameenui, & D. Chard (Eds.), *Issues in educating students with disabilities* (pp. 63–73). Mahway, NJ: Lawrence Erlbaum Associates, Publishers.

Szasz, T. (1970). *The manufacture of madness: A comparative study of the inquisition and the mental health movement*. New York: Harper & Row.

Tredgold, A. F., & Soddy, K. (1956). *A textbook on mental deficiency* (9th ed.). Baltimore: Williams & Wilkins.

Turnbull, A. P., & Turnbull, H. R. (1990). *Families, professionals, and exceptionality: A special partnership*. Columbus, OH: Merrill Publishing Co.

Wehmeyer, M. L., Agran, M., & Hughes, C. (1998). *Teaching self-determination to students with disabilities: Basic skills for successful transition*. Baltimore: Paul H. Brookes Publishing Co.

Westling, D. L., & Fox, L. (2000). *Teaching students with severe disabilities* (2nd ed.). Upper Saddle River, NJ: Merrill Prentice Hall.

2

The Relationship Between Inclusion and Other Trends in Education

Sandra Alper

Objectives

After completing this chapter, the reader will be able to:

1. Define inclusion.
2. Identify some of the issues and controversies surrounding inclusion.
3. List the benefits of inclusion for students with disabilities.
4. Identify advantages of inclusion for students without disabilities.
5. Discuss similarities and differences between inclusion and normalization.
6. Describe the relationship between inclusion and deinstitutionalization.
7. Discuss how inclusion is related to the concept of least restrictive environment (LRE).
8. Articulate the similarities between mainstreaming and inclusion.
9. Discuss some of the obstacles to successful mainstreaming of students with mild disabilities that are important considerations for advocates of inclusion.
10. Discuss why many educators have called for reform in education.
11. Describe how the demands for reform in education are related to inclusion.
12. Discuss access to the general education curriculum.

Key Terms

Access to the general education curriculum	Free and appropriate education (FAPE)	Least restrictive environment (LRE)
Age-appropriate skills	Functional skills	Mainstreaming
Deinstitutionalization	Inclusion	Normalization
Educational reform	Integration	Universal design

Public Law (PL) 94-142, the Education of All Handicapped Children Act of 1975, won the right to a free and appropriate public education (FAPE) for all students, including those with the most severe disabilities. Today, a growing number of parents and educators are arguing that "appropriate" education for students with severe disabilities means receiving services within the same general educational settings as students without disabilities. Programs for students with severe disabilities have been referred to as "a stronghold of segregation" within the American educational system (McDonnell & Hardman, 1989). Although there has been an increase in the number of these students who receive services in the same schools and classrooms as their brothers and sisters and neighbors, many are still educated in separate settings and, in some cases, separate schools (Danielson & Bellamy, 1989).

Students who are typically labeled as experiencing severe disabilities have moderate to severe levels of mental retardation in addition to one or more other disabling conditions (for example, communication deficits, physical aggression, self-abusive behaviors, self-stimulating responses, seizure disorders, visual impairments, hearing impairments, or medical disabilities). The American Association on Mental Retardation (AAMR) (Luckasson et al., 1992, p. 1) defined mental retardation in the following way:

> Mental retardation refers to substantial limitations in present functioning. It is characterized by significantly subaverage intellectual functioning, existing concurrently with related limitations in two or more of the following applicable adaptive skill areas: communication, self-care, home living, social skills, community use, self-direction, health and safety, functional academics, leisure, and work. Mental retardation manifests before age 18.

The AAMR Ad Hoc Committee on Terminology and Classification further characterized mental retardation by the degree of appropriate support services needed by the individual. Thus, while individuals with severe mental retardation may need an array of support services throughout life, persons with mild mental retardation may require support services on an intermittent basis (Luckasson et al., 1992).

Students with moderate to severe disabilities encounter a number of specific learning difficulties. They learn at a significantly slower rate than other students. They have difficulty maintaining the skills they have learned and in generalizing skills learned in one situation to other situations. It is hard for them to combine skills that were initially learned individually. These students pose difficult challenges to educators. Inclusion of these students in regular classrooms is a complex process with far-reaching implications for all educators. Descriptions of two students follow.

Bryan is a fourteen-year-old boy who has been diagnosed with moderate mental retardation. He has Down syndrome. Bryan lives with his mother, father, and an older sister. He attends his neighborhood junior high school where he takes general education classes in language arts, math, science, social studies, home economics, and physical education. Bryan's general and special education teachers work as a team to develop functional skill objectives in each of his classes. His primary needs focus on learning functional academic, vocational, and domestic skills that will enable him to live and work in the community. Bryan belongs to a Boy Scout troop and enjoys attending sports activities at his school.

Maryanne is a ten-year-old girl who has been diagnosed with severe mental retardation. Her disabilities are believed to have resulted from a lack of oxygen and other complications during labor and delivery. Maryanne's mother was fifteen years old at the time, and the child was placed in foster care while still an infant. She lives in a group home with two other youngsters. Maryanne is friendly and enjoys being in class with other students. She does, however, cry and throw tantrums when frustrated. Maryanne is verbal, but her speech is difficult for others to understand. She has very poor motor coordination. Maryanne attends a general fifth grade classroom. She changes classes for art, music, and physical education. A personal aide has been assigned to her throughout the day and works closely with the special and general education elementary teachers in developing Maryanne's educational program.

Inclusion Defined

Inclusion is the term most commonly applied to the practice of educating students with moderate to severe disabilities alongside their chronological age peers without disabilities in general classrooms within their home neighborhood schools (Brown et al., 1983, 1989a, 1989b; Gartner & Lipsky, 1987; Giangreco & Putnam, 1991; Lipsky & Gartner, 1992; Stainback & Stainback, 1989; Wheeler, 1991). Inclusion includes physical integration, social integration, and access to normalized educational, recreational, and social activities that occur in school. Inclusion does not necessarily imply that all students with disabilities will spend all day everyday in a general education class or learn exactly the same things at the same mastery level as students without disabilities.

In addition to philosophical support for inclusion based on ideals of humane treatment, democracy, and equal opportunity for all persons, a legal base supports the concept. The doctrine of "separate but equal" public education programs was struck down in *Brown v. the Board of Education* in 1954. Section 504 of the Rehabilitation Act of 1973 prevents discrimination in programs that receive federal financial assistance on the basis of membership in a particular class. This means that students cannot be denied access to public education programs solely on the basis of a disability. Public Law 94-142, the Education of All Handicapped Children Act of 1975, mandated that students with disabilities be placed in the LRE, or the educational environment most like that of age peers without disabilities. This federal law further mandated that students with disabilities not be removed from the general education setting unless it is documented that they would not benefit from instruction in these settings with appropriate supports and resources.

Inclusion has significant implications for virtually every facet of public education. Our attitudes and values about the educability of *all* children, curricula, the roles of professionals from a variety of disciplines, transportation, administrative arrangements, and the very nature of teacher training programs in higher education are all affected by inclusion. There are implications for *all* students in the public schools, as well as for their parents, teachers, related service providers, and administrators. There are also implications for the community at large as more and more students with severe disabilities are provided the opportunity to grow up, go to school, work, and live in the community.

Because of its many facets and far-reaching implications, inclusion is best conceptualized as a set of practices or processes. Bates, Renzaglia, and Wehman (1981) and Williams, Fox, Thousand, and Fox (1990) identified several education practices that support inclusion. These include:

- Age-appropriate placement in general educational settings
- Age-appropriate and functional curriculum and materials
- Instruction in natural training settings outside the school
- Systematic data-based instruction
- Social integration
- Integrated therapy
- Transition planning
- Home–school partnerships
- Systematic follow-up evaluations

In addition, practices such as collaborative teaming between special and general educators, positive behavioral supports, flexible grouping options, and curriculum accommodations and adaptations are necessary components of inclusion (Ryndak, Alper, Stuart, & Clark, in press).

Many of these practices have been empirically and socially validated as best practices, or indicators of program quality (cf., Snell, 1987). We describe in the remaining chapters of this book many of these practices as they are used with students with severe disabilities in inclusive settings.

Although there is a growing base of philosophical, legal, and empirical support for inclusion (Alper & Ryndak, 1992), some educators disagree, passionately at times, on how inclusion should be implemented. One topic of debate concerns whether all students with severe disabilities should be served in inclusive settings, or if placement decisions should be made on a case-by-case basis (cf., Lieberman, 1992; Lipsky & Gartner, 1992; Stainback & Stainback, 1984; 1992; Vergason & Anderegg, 1992). Another question relates to the degree of inclusion, that is, should students with severe disabilities be served in general education classrooms for the entire school day or for only part of the day. Embedded in these controversies is the issue of choice. If a continuum of services as mandated by PL 94-142 is provided, parents retain the opportunity to choose either a more or less restricted education for their children with disabilities (Schloss, 1992).

In the remainder of this chapter, we review the advantages of inclusion for students with and without disabilities. Then we discuss the relationship between inclusion and other trends in education. This relationship is important because it can help us to understand the historical context in which inclusion evolved. It can also help us to understand and be more sensitive to the many issues and arguments that surround inclusion today.

Advantages of Inclusion

We now consider the benefits of inclusion for students with and without disabilities. It is important that educators focus on the positive aspects, rather than potential obstacles, of inclusion.

Benefits for Students with Disabilities

Alper and Ryndak (1992) reviewed literature pertaining to inclusion. They noted a number of advantages of inclusion for students with disabilities. First, spending the school day alongside classmates who do not have disabilities provides many opportunities for social interactions that would not be available in segregated settings (Sasso, Simpson, & Novak, 1985). These opportunities allow students with disabilities to improve their communication and social skills. In addition, friendships between students with and without disabilities may result. A second advantage of inclusion is that students with disabilities have appropriate models of behavior. They can observe and imitate socially acceptable behaviors of students who do not experience disabilities (Brown et al., 1983, 1989a). The third benefit of inclusion is that teachers often develop higher standards of performance for students with disabilities (Brown et al., 1989a; Snell, 1987). Both general and special educators in inclusive settings expect appropriate conduct from all students. In addition, students with disabilities are taught age-appropriate functional components of academic content, which may never be part of the curriculum in segregated settings (for example, science, social studies, and interactions with persons without disabilities.). Finally, attending inclusive schools should increase the probability that students with disabilities will continue to participate in a variety of integrated settings throughout their lives. Acquiring functional academic, social, vocational, and recreational skills should help to prepare students with disabilities to live and work in the community after they leave school.

Benefits for Students Without Disabilities

Students without disabilities have a variety of opportunities for interacting with their age peers who experience disabilities in inclusive school settings. First, they may serve as peer tutors during instructional activities (Gurry, 1984; Stainback, Stainback, & Hatcher, 1983; Slavin, as cited by Fiske, 1990). Second, they may play together during recess. Third, they may play the role of a special buddy during lunch, on the bus, or on the playground.

Critics have voiced concerns that inclusion will in some way short change students without disabilities in terms of instructional time and teacher attention. If properly implemented with appropriate resources, however, inclusion can result in several benefits for students without disabilities (Alper & Ryndak, 1992). First, these students can learn a great deal about tolerance, individual difference, and human exceptionality. Second, they learn that students with disabilities have many positive characteristics and abilities. Third, students without disabilities have the chance to learn about many of the human service professions, such as special education, speech therapy, physical therapy, recreation therapy, and vocational rehabilitation. For some, exposure to these areas may lead to career choices. Finally, inclusion offers the opportunity for students without disabilities to learn to communicate and deal effectively with a wide range of individuals. This should better prepare these students to participate fully in a pluralistic society when they are adults.

Relationship Between Inclusion and Other Trends in Education

In the remainder of this chapter we compare key elements of inclusion to other trends in education. Included are normalization, mainstreaming, integration, and access to general education curriculum.

Normalization

The philosophical basis for inclusion has its roots in the principle of normalization. This movement originated in Scandinavia in the late 1950s. Bank Mikkelson was, at that time, director of services for persons with mental retardation in Denmark. He is usually given credit for first articulating the *principle of normalization*, or allowing persons with mental retardation to experience normal lifestyles.

Bengt Nirje, executive director of the Swedish Association for Retarded Children, stated: "The normalization principle means making available to the mentally retarded patterns and conditions of everyday life which are as close as possible to the norms and patterns of mainstream society" (Kugel & Wolfensberger, 1969, p. 181). Nirje reported the minutes of a meeting held by 50 young adults with mental retardation in Malmo, Sweden, in 1970. This group talked about their lives and issued a strong statement demanding normalized residential, vocational, and recreational opportunities in the community (cited in Wolfensberger, 1983).

The normalization philosophy quickly spread throughout western Europe, Canada, and the United States. Advocates of this philosophy argued for better (that is, more normal and community-based) residential, educational, vocational, and leisure opportunities for persons with mental retardation. Wolf Wolfensberger (1972) was the primary proponent of normalization in the United States and Canada. He expanded the concept in his definition of the principle of normalization as "the utilization of means that are as culturally normative as possible in order to bring about in potentially deviant clients' behaviors that are as culturally normative as possible" (p. 87).

Deinstitutionalization

A corollary of the principle of normalization was the movement toward deinstitutionalization in the United States. Some of its chief proponents were parents and mental retardation professionals who knew firsthand of the inhumane conditions inside institutions. Dr. Burton Blatt, a renowned special educator and tireless advocate for the human and legal rights of persons with mental retardation, and Fred Kaplan, a photographer, published *Christmas in Purgatory* in 1966. This photographic essay of conditions inside institutions was later published in *Look* magazine. The startling photographs of life inside institutions horrified the American public.

Blatt and Kaplan observed and photographed children and adults tied to chairs, locked in isolation rooms and cages, wandering aimlessly with little or no supervision or meaningful activity in large and sterile dayrooms, and sleeping in rooms of wall-to-wall cribs or beds. Many of Blatt and Kaplan's photos reflected frightening similarity to conditions in the concentration camps of Nazi Germany. Burton Blatt (1969) lamented:

> There is a shame in America. Countless human beings are suffering needlessly. They are the unfortunate victims of society's irresponsibility. Still others are in anguish, for they know or suspect the truth. Wittingly, or unwittingly, they have been forced to institutionalize their loved ones into a life of degradation and horror. (p. 176)

During the next few years, repeated and shocking accounts of abuse and neglect in institutions for the mentally retarded all across America were made public. Journalists and human-service professionals uncovered and reported cruel and inhumane conditions in Willowbrook in New York, Beatrice State Hospital in Nebraska, Pennhurst in Pennsylvania, Belchertown in Massachusetts, Partlow State School in Alabama, and others (Biklen & Knoll, 1987). Parents and other advocates banded together to file class-action lawsuits designed to end the wretched conditions in institutions. More and more demands were made on state agencies to develop and fund residential family-like group homes and educational, vocational, and recreational opportunities in the community for persons with mental retardation. Federal support and financial assistance became available in the 1960s primarily as a result of the Kennedy family's firsthand experience with mental retardation and their political influence.

Relationship of Inclusion to Normalization and Deinstitutionalization

Many similarities exist between inclusion and the principle of normalization and its corollary, deinstitutionalization. They may be grouped into three basic categories: (1) similarities in philosophy, (2) similarities in implementation, and (3) similarities in outcome.

Similarities in Philosophy. Embedded in both the principle of normalization and inclusion is the idea that people with and without disabilities hold the same values. Factors that contribute to the quality of life (for example, friendships; choice; freedom; and normal rhythms of the day, week, and year) are the same for all people.

Burton Blatt (1987) eloquently articulated the values inherent in normalization and deinstitutionalization (and inclusion). He pointed out that the controversy surrounding these trends have been argued in two ways. Some authors (for example, Vergason & Anderegg, 1992) defended separate programs and services for people with and without disabilities. The basis of this position is that some persons, because of the severity of their disability, require separate programs to achieve their maximum level of functioning. (Indeed, this is the primary argument in favor of separate school settings for children with severe disabilities.) The counterpoint (Blatt, 1987) is that people are entitled to live free in natural settings, irrespective of what environment enhances their academic skills. Blatt (1987) wrote, "Abraham Lincoln did not emancipate the slaves in order to promote their school capability or vocational viability. The slaves were freed because people deserve to live free. . . . " (p. 238).

Those opposed to inclusion argued that it is just another educational fad with no empirical base. Blatt (1987) contended that issues surrounding inclusion of persons with disabilities in schools, places of work, and residences in the community are not empirical questions, but rather questions about our values. Normal settings are good by definition. They do not have to be justified by empirical studies. Do we hold the same values for all people, or is there one set of values for us and another for them?

Similarities in Implementation.   Similarities in applying the principle of normalization and inclusion in school programs are clearly evident in the Program Analysis of Service Systems (PASS 3) instrument, authored by Wolfensberger and Glenn (1975). PASS was developed to evaluate quantitatively the degree to which any human service program (for example, special education programs, group homes, nursing homes, or sheltered workshops) had implemented the principle of normalization. Although PASS can be used to evaluate a program, it can also serve as a teaching guide for those trying to implement normalization.

The PASS instrument shares several similarities with more recent guidelines regarding quality indicators of educational services for students with severe disabilities (cf., Williams et al., 1990). These shared elements include:

- Physical integration.
- Social integration.
- Emphasis on age-appropriate activities that result in acquisition of new, useful skills as opposed to activities that merely fill up the day. Physical integration is not enough. The support services required by students with disabilities must be available in the general educational settings.
- Facilities that are the same in location and appearance as those for students without disabilities.
- Normal length and rhythm of the school day for students with and without disabilities. The school day is the same length for everyone. Everyone eats lunch during the same block of time.
- References to students and programs that are respectful and dignified. For example, students with behavior disorders who are approximately ten years old are referred to as "fourth graders" rather than as "BD kids."

- Staff who have been trained in meeting the need of the students. Staff from a multitude of disciplines work together in collaborative teams in the same schools and classrooms (Rainforth, York, & MacDonald, 1992).

Similarities in Outcome The principle of normalization and the practice of inclusion are both directed at achieving the same outcome. The goal is that persons with moderate to severe disabilities will be able to grow up and live, work, and recreate in normal settings in the community. Brown and his colleagues (1989a; 1989b) argued that "segregation begets segregation." These advocates of inclusion pointed out that segregated and separate school settings do not offer students with disabilities the opportunities to learn the skills necessary to function in the community as adults. Segregated school programs do not have the same expectations, functional activities, opportunities to practice skills learned in natural settings, or normal role models as general educational settings. Brown et al. (1987) reported that students with moderate to severe disabilities in Madison, Wisconsin, who were included in general educational settings were more likely to work and live in integrated settings in the community as adults than were their counterparts who had been educated in separate settings.

Least Restrictive Environment

The Education for All Handicapped Children Act of 1975 guarantees that all students with disabilities have the right to a free and appropriate education in the LRE. PL 94-142 (1975) requires that "to the maximum extent appropriate, disabled children, including children in public or private institutions or other care facilities, are educated with children who are not disabled, and that special classes, separate schooling, or other removal of disabled children from regular education environments occur only when the nature or severity of the disabilities is such that education in regular classes with the use of supplementary aids and services cannot be achieved satisfactorily" (Sec. 612.5).

The intent of the LRE clause of PL 94-142 is that students with disabilities be educated alongside their chronological age peers who do not have disabilities. Further, special educational services should be provided in the schools the students would normally attend if they did not have disabilities (Gartner & Lipsky, 1987; Sailor et al., 1989).

Tucker (1989) observed that school systems attempting to comply with the LRE regulations of PL 94-142 have sometimes interpreted the concept too narrowly:

> Virtually everyone would agree that the word environment means more than location. Yet when paired with the term least restrictive in the application of services for students who are disabled, the term has remained almost exclusively a term of literal placement without reference to conditions or circumstances that exist in that location (p. 456).

Tucker suggested an alternative interpretation of the LRE concept based on the individual needs of the student. Within this perspective, the key question is what are the most normal conditions under which a student's needs can be met? It is important to note that the term "*conditions*" refers to the supports and supplemental aids needed and not to a specific setting. For example, a child with a hearing impairment may need a hearing aid or an oral interpreter, rather than a separate classroom.

Tucker's (1989) program-oriented concept of LRE is consistent with inclusion in at least three dimensions. First, both LRE and inclusion are directed at maintaining the student in the general educational setting:

> Is there any type of student need (i.e., a need defined by a given disability) that cannot be provided in the regular classroom, given all of the necessary support that might be required? I have asked that question many times, and the answer has always been a qualified no (p. 457).

Second, both concepts emphasize educating students with disabilities alongside their chronological age peers who do not have disabilities. Third, both LRE and inclusion assume that supplementary support personnel and services can be delivered within general educational settings (Alper & Ryndak, 1992; Rainforth et al., 1992; Tucker, 1989).

Mainstreaming

Mainstreaming refers to providing individualized special education services to students with disabilities while they remain in general educational settings for the majority of the school day. The mainstreaming movement gained momentum shortly after the passage of PL 94-142 in 1975. Initially, the emphasis was on maintaining students with mild disabilities in general education classrooms.

Kaufman, Agard, Gottlieb, and Kubic (1975) described three basic components of mainstreaming. These were integration, educational planning, and clarification of responsibilities.

Integration.   Kaufman et al. (1975) described three types of integration. *Temporal* integration is the mere physical placement of a child with disabilities in a general classroom. *Instructional* integration refers to opportunities for students with disabilities to participate in the range of instructional activities as students without disabilities, even though they may not be expected to master the same academic skills. *Social* integration means that students with disabilities are provided opportunities to interact socially and to participate in extracurricular activities with students without disabilities. Kaufman et al. argued that all three types of integration needed to occur if mainstreaming were to be successfully implemented.

Educational Planning.   Kaufman et al. (1975) pointed out that an individualized educational plan should be carefully developed for each student with a disability placed in the mainstream. This plan was to be developed by a team of general and special educators working in concert with the parents and the student. Again, the idea was emphasized that mere physical placement of the student with disabilities in the general classroom did not constitute mainstreaming.

Clarification of Responsibilities.   Kaufman et al. (1975) argued that the responsibilities of all professionals who participated in the education of a particular student with disabilities needed to be clearly specified in writing. This meant that open and direct communication and collaboration between parents and special and general educators was imperative. No individual had sole responsibility for the education of a student with disabilities placed in a mainstreamed classroom.

Birch (1974) reviewed successful mainstreaming programs across the United States. He recommended the following guidelines for implementing mainstreaming:

- The concerns of parents, special and general educators, administrators, and students about expectations for behavior in the classroom, instructional materials and methods appropriate for students with disabilities, classroom organization, and the adequacy of support services available should be dealt with before mainstreaming is implemented.
- Efforts must be made to shape and reinforce positive teacher attitudes. Attitudes associated with successful mainstreaming include the belief that all students can be educated, flexibility, acceptance of the idea that not all students have to master the same content, and willingness to communicate and collaborate with other professionals and parents.
- Inservice education is critical.
- Removing students with disabilities from the mainstream should be a last resort.
- Parents need to be informed and empowered participants in mainstreaming efforts.

Birch's comments are as germane to our discussion of inclusion today as they were to mainstreaming in 1974.

Similarities Between Mainstreaming and Inclusion

Although mainstreaming was focused on students with mild disabilities and inclusion has been directed toward students with moderate to severe disabilities, it should be apparent from the preceding discussion that the two concepts have several similarities. First, both concepts are philosophically grounded in the struggle for the extension of civil rights. Proponents of mainstreaming and those of inclusion have argued that isolation, exclusion, and separation on the basis of disability are as injurious as they are on the basis of race or sex (cf., Herlihy & Herlihy, 1980; McDonnell & Hardman, 1989). Second, mainstreaming and inclusion are both directed at placement of students with disabilities in general educational settings alongside their friends, neighbors, and sisters and brothers without disabilities. Third, both mainstreaming and inclusion share elements of implementation.

The lessons of history are important to learn, even in a field as young as special education. Many mainstreaming efforts were doomed from the outset because they involved moving students with disabilities into general classrooms without the necessary support services. Administrators, teachers, parents, and students without disabilities were neither prepared nor equipped to meet the needs of these students. Many became bitter opponents of mainstreaming as a result of faulty implementation. Faulty implementation and lack of funding have resulted in criticisms of inclusion, as well.

Integration

As we have noted, integration consists of both physical and social integration of students with and without disabilities. Social integration is a critical component in efforts to normalize and mainstream educational environments for learners with disabilities. Cullinan, Sabornie, and Crossland (1992) noted that, although students with mild disabilities have been physically integrated into general educational settings for some time now, their social integration in these settings has often been unsuccessful. These authors defined social integration as membership in a group in which a child is: "(a) socially accepted by peers, (b) has at least one reciprocal friendship, and (c) is an active and equal participant in activities performed by the peer group" (p. 340).

A common concern in implementing integration involves grouping. The formation of homogeneous ability groups of students without disabilities for instruction in academic areas such as reading and math has been debated by educators (Fiske, 1990; Slavin, 1987; Stallings, 1985; Swank, Taylor, Brady, Cooley, & Freiberg, 1989). Increasing emphasis is being placed on strategies that promote social integration by advocates of inclusion. Several innovative options for grouping students who have diverse learning and behavioral characteristics have been developed.

The use of flexible grouping has been suggested as an alternative to homogeneous ability groups. Flexible groups are fluid and dynamic. They may be formed and reformed depending on the goal to be accomplished (Harp, 1989; Unsworth, 1984).

Slavin (1987) and Stevens, Madden, Slavin, and Farnish (1987) described the use of cooperative learning groups. Students in cooperative learning groups work as a team to accomplish some common group goal. These authors cited evidence demonstrating higher achievement by students in cooperative groups than those in traditional ability groups. An example of a cooperative learning group project follows[1]:

In a fifth-grade elementary classroom, groups or "pods" of four to five children who varied in ability were formed into wagon trains. Each group was given a description of the family members they portrayed in the wagon trains. Wagon train families then worked together on a number of academic assignments related to the general theme of western expansion. Each wagon-train family earned points or "miles" for accuracy and turning in the assignments on time.

Another option for grouping students who vary widely in ability is peer tutoring (Brown et al., 1983; Good & Brophy, 1984; Gurry, 1984; Stainback & Stainback, 1989). Peer tutors who do not have disabilities can teach students with disabilities a wide array of functional academic and social interaction skills. Hofius (1990) pointed out that siblings can sometimes serve as tutors.

Strully and Strully (1989) are respected authors who also happen to be parents of a child with severe disabilities. They advocate the development of strategies that foster social integration. In particular, they emphasize the importance of the formation of friend-ships between students with and without disabilities. The author described the use of special "buddy" systems that can sometimes blossom into genuine friendships between students with and without disabilities. A student without a disability can serve as a helpful "buddy" to a student with disabilities in a variety of school and nonschool settings.

Reform in Education

The question of how to restructure schools to achieve excellence is an ongoing concern in the field of education (Brookover et al., 1978; Edmonds & Frederiksen, 1979; Robinson, 1985). School reform is a major concern today because of a number of problems facing the schools and the larger society. These problems include large numbers of students with and without disabilities who drop out or fail, high unemployment rates of persons with disabilities, the increasing need of United States (U.S.) employers for a skilled labor force to compete on a world market, violence and drugs in the schools, and high rates of pregnancies among youngsters who are ill-equipped to be parents.

Lipsky and Gartner (1992) identified three distinct phases of school reform. The first phase emphasized external factors such as higher standards for graduation, new curricula, more stringent teacher certification criteria, and continued education by teachers in service as a requirement for maintaining employment. The second phase of school reform focused on the roles played by adults in education. Parental choice, teacher empowerment, and local school-based management were all highlighted. The authors charged that neither of these attempts at school reform paid much attention to the needs of students with disabilities. Citing dismal statistics on dropout rates and levels of unemployment after graduation from special education, Lipsky and Gartner called for a third wave of reform that focuses on the needs of the student.

Lipsky and Gartner (1992) argued that meaningful and significant education reform is best measured by increases in student learning. Successful school outcomes, according to these authors, are more accurately reflected by what students learn rather than what teachers teach. They called for educational changes focused on (1) respect for all students, (2) actively engaging students in the learning process, (3) teaching students the functional skills they will need for successful postschool outcomes, (4) providing all students with the supports and instructional strategies needed for learning, and (5) making parents and the community partners in education.

The reforms called for by Lipsky and Gartner (1992) are in concert with inclusion. Their recommendations would support the education of all learners in the general education setting. These changes place accountability on adults for the learning outcomes of students, including those with moderate and severe disabilities. They imply that all students are assumed to be capable of learning. If a student is not learning, the problem is presumed to be due to an ineffective education program rather than to some psychological or behavioral impairment within the student who requires separate services. If fully implemented, the changes advocated by Lipsky and Gartner would mean an end to the dual system, or separate education of students with and without disabilities.

Promoting Access to the General Education Curriculum for Students with Mental Retardation

The 1997 amendments to the Individuals with Disabilities Education Act (IDEA) contained statutory language requiring that the Individualized Education Program (IEP) of students with disabilities include:

- A statement of how the child's disability affects the child's involvement with and progress in the general curriculum
- A statement of measurable goals to enable the child to be involved with and progress in the general curriculum
- A statement of the services, program modifications, and supports necessary for the child to be involved in and progress in the general curriculum

As a result of these stipulations, educators working with students with disabilities need to carefully consider how access to the general curriculum can be ensured.

In testimony on June 20, 1995, before the U.S. House of Representatives Subcommittee on Early Childhood, Youth, and Families (a subcommittee of the House Committee on Economic and Educational Opportunities), U.S. Secretary of Education Richard Riley stated:

> "Our second principle is to improve results for students with disabilities through higher expectations and access to the general curriculum. We know that most children work harder and do better when more is expected of them, whether it be in the classroom, doing their homework, or doing the dishes. Disabled students are no different. When we have high expectations for students with disabilities, most can achieve to challenging standards, and all can achieve more than society has historically expected. However, not all schools presently have high expectations for these students, and not all schools take responsibility for the academic progress of disabled students" (p. 5).

Clearly, the intent of the "access to the general curriculum" language is to ensure that students with disabilities are included with all students in the same system by which schools are held accountable for student progress within the context of a challenging curriculum and to raise expectations for students with disabilities (cf., Browder, 2001; Wehmeyer, Lattin & Agran, in press).

Secretary Riley's 1995 testimony before the U.S. House of Representatives subcommittee stressed six principles. These principles were:

1. IDEA should be aligned with state and local education improvement efforts.
2. Educators should have higher expectations and provide meaningful access to the general curriculum for students with disabilities.
3. Individual needs in the least restrictive environment must be addressed.
4. Families and teachers should be provided with more training and knowledge.
5. A greater emphasis on teaching and learning is necessary.
6. Early intervention efforts should be strengthened.

Universal Design

The application of principles of universal design to curriculum development has taken on great importance in attempts to provide access to the general curriculum for students with disabilities. The principles of universal design originated in the field of architecture. Universal Design principles were applied to buildings and physical environments to allow physical access to all people (Moon, Hart, Komissar, & Friedlander, 1995; Wehmeyer, Lattin, & Agran, in press).

The principles of universal design were developed to ensure that people with disabilities or people who are elderly, for example, have access to environments and products that enhance their quality of life. Attempts are made to design buildings with adequate ramps, wide enough doors, and accessible restrooms. Products are designed with simple controls and clearly understandable uses. Examples include telephones with large, lighted keypads and color-coded faucets. Because of the relationship between universal design principles and "gaining access" to environments and products, educators have attempted to use this same principle to assist in understanding how to gain access to curriculum. Researchers at the Center for Applied Special Technology (CAST) noted:

> The basic premise of universal design for learning is that a curriculum should include alternatives to make it accessible and applicable to students, teachers, and parents with different backgrounds, learning styles, abilities, and disabilities in widely varied learning contexts. The "universal" in universal design does not imply one optimal solution for everyone, but rather it underscores the need for inherently flexible, customizable content, assignments, and activities (CAST, 1998–1999).

The Individuals with Disabilities Education Acts require that all students, regardless of their abilities, be given the opportunity to participate in and make progress in the general education curriculum. Kameenui and Simmons (1999) provided examples of how a universally designed curriculum can be developed to allow access for students with disabilities. Guiding principles in applying the concept of universal design to curriculum for students with disabilities include:

- The curriculum provides multiple means of representation, allowing subject matter to be presented in alternative modes for students who learn best from visual or auditory information, or for those who need differing levels of complexity.
- The curriculum provides multiple means of expression to allow students to respond with their preferred means of control.
- The curriculum provides multiple means of engagement that allow student's interests in learning to be matched with the mode of presentation and their preferred means of expression (Kameenui & Simmons, 1999; Wehmeyer, Lattin, & Agran, in press).

Summary

In this chapter, we have described inclusion as a set of practices associated with successful learning outcomes for students with disabilities. The similarities and differences between inclusion and other trends in education were reviewed. Inclusion has roots in a rich tradition of philosophical, legal, and empirical support. Educators, parents, and advocates working to implement inclusion have historical antecedents that offer direction. The lessons learned from our previous efforts in normalization, LRE, and mainstreaming, all precursors of inclusion, are well worth reviewing. They contain suggestions that can facilitate inclusion, while helping us avoid repeating mistakes of the past.

References

Alper, S., & Ryndak, D. L. (1992). Educating students with severe handicaps in regular classroom settings. *The Elementary School journal, 92*, 373–387.

Bates, P., Renzaglia, A., & Wehman, P. (1981). Characteristics of an appropriate education for severely and profoundly handicapped students. *Education and Training in Mental Retardation, 16*, 142–149.

Biklen, D., & Knoll, J., (1987). The community imperative revisited. In R. R. Antonak & J. A. Mulick (Eds.), *Transitions in mental retardation*, Vol. 3 (pp. 1–27). Norwood, NJ: Ablex.

Birch, J. (1974). *Mainstreaming: Educable mentally retarded children in the regular classes.* Minneapolis: Leadership Training Institute/Special Education, University of Minnesota, pp. 2–3.

Blatt, B. (1969). Recommendations for institutional reform. In R. Kugel & W. Wolfensberger (Eds.), *Changing patterns in residential services for the mentally retarded* (pp. 175–177). Washington, DC: President's Committee on Mental Retardation.

Blatt, B. (1987). The community imperative and human values. In R. Antonak & J. A. Mulick (Eds.), *Transitions in mental retardation: The community imperative revisited* (pp. 237–246). Norwood, NJ: Ablex.

Blatt, B., & Kaplan, F. (1966). *Christmas in purgatory.* Boston: Allyn & Bacon.

Brookover, W. B., Schweitzer, J. H., Schneider, J. M., Beady, C. H., Flood, P. K., & Wisenbaker, J. M. (1978). Elementary school social climate and school achievement. *American Educational Research Journal, 15*(2), 301–318.

Browder, D. (2001). *Alternate assessment for students with moderate and severe disabilities.* New York: The Guilford Press.

Brown, L., Ford, A., Nisbet, J., Sweet, M., DonneUan, A., & Gruenewald, L. (1983). Opportunities available when severely handicapped students attend chronological age appropriate regular schools. *Journal of the Association for the Severe Handicapped, 8*(1), 16–24.

Brown, L., Long, E., Udvari-Solner, A., Davis, L., VanDeventer, P., Ahlgren, C., Johnson, F., Gruenewaid, L., & Jorgensen, J. (1989a). The home school: Why students with severe intellectual disabilities must attend the schools of their brothers, sisters, friends, and neighbors. *Journal of the Association for Persons with Severe Handicaps, 14*(1), 1–7.

Brown, L., Long, E., Udvari-Solner, A., Davis, L., VanDeventer, P., Ahlgren, C., Johnson, F., Gruenewald, L., & Jorgensen, J. (1989b). Should students with severe intellectual disabilities be based in regular or in special education classrooms in home schools? *Journal of the Association for Persons with Severe Handicaps, 14*(1), 8–12.

Brown, L., Rogan, P., Shiraga, B., Albright, K., Hessler, K., Bryson, F., Van Deventer, C., & Loomir, A. (1987). *A vocational follow-up evaluation of the 1984–1986 Madison Metropolitan School District graduates with severe intellectual disabilities.* Madison: University of Wisconsin and Madison Metropolitan School District.

Center for Applied Special Technology (1998–1999). The National Center on Accessing the General Curriculum [online]. Available: http://www.cast.org/initiatives/national_center.html.

Cullinan, D., Sabornie, E. J., & Crossland, C. L. (1992). Social mainstreaming of mildly handicapped students. *The Elementary School Journal, 92*, 339–351.

Danielson, L. C., & Bellamy, G. T. (1989). State variation in placement of children with handicaps in segregated environments. *Exceptional Children, 55*, 448–455.

Edmonds, R. R., & Frederiksen, J. R. (1979). *Search for effective schools: The identification and analysis of city schools that are instructionally effective for poor children.* (ERIC Document Reproduction Service No. ED 179 396).

Education of All Handicapped Children Act of 1975 (PL 94-142) 20 U.S.C. Sections 1400–1461.

Fiske, E. B. (1990, January 3). More and more educators agree that grouping students by ability is misguided. *New York Times*, p. 19.

Gartner, A., & Lipsky, D. K. (1987). Beyond special education: Toward a quality system for all students. *Harvard Educational Review, 57*(4), 367–395.

Giangreco, M. E., & Putnam, J., (1991). Supporting the education of students with severe disabilities in regular education environments. In L. H. Meyer, C. Pech, & L. Brown (Eds.), *Critical issues in the lives of persons with severe disabilities* (pp. 245–270). Baltimore: Paul H. Brookes Publishing Co.

Good, T., & Brophy, J. (1984). *Looking in classrooms* (3rd ed.). New York: Harper & Row.

Gurry, S. (1984). Peer tutoring and the severe special needs students: A model high school program. Washington, DC: U.S. Department of Education, National Institute of Education. (ERIC Document Reproduction Service No. ED 245 463).

Harp, B. (1989). What do we put in the place of ability grouping? *Reading Teacher, 42*(7), 534–535.

Herlihy, J. G., & Herlihy, M. T. (1980). Why mainstreaming? In J. G. Herlihy & M. T. Herlihy (Eds.), *Mainstreaming in the social studies* (pp. 2–7). Washington DC: National Council for the Social Studies.

Hofius, D. (1990). *Training children to promote social interactions with their mentally retarded siblings.* Unpublished manuscript, University of Missouri, Department of Special Education, Columbia, Missouri.

Individuals with Disabilities Education Act, Pub. L. No. 105-117, 20 U.S.C. § 1401 et seq. (1997).

Kameenui, E. J. & Simmons, D. C. (1999). *Toward successful inclusion of students with disabilities: The architecture of instruction.* Reston, VA: Council for Exceptional Children.

Kaufman, M., Agard J., Gottlieb, J., & Kubic, M. (1975). Mainstreaming: Toward an explication of the construct. *Focus on Exceptional Children, 7*, 1–12.

Kugel, R. B., & Wolfensberger, W. (1969). *Changing patterns in residential services for the mentally retarded.* Washington, DC: President's Committee on Mental Retardation.

Lieberman, L. M. (1992). Preserving special education . . . For those who need it. In W. Stainback & S. Stainback (Eds.), *Controversial issues confronting special education* (p. 13–25). Boston: Allyn & Bacon.

Lipsky, D. K., & Gartner, A. (1992). Achieving fall inclusion: Placing the student at the center of educational reform. In W. Stainback & S. Stainback (Eds.), *Controversial issues confronting special education* (pp. 3–12). Boston: Allyn & Bacon.

Luckasson, R., Coulter, D., Polloway, E., Reiss, S.,

Schalock, R., Snell, M., Spitalnik, D., & Stark, J., (1992). *Mental retardation. Definition, classification, and system of supports* (9th ed.). Washington, DC: American Association on Mental Retardation.

McDonnell, A. P., & Hardman, M. L. (1989). The desegregation of America's special schools. Strategies for change. *The Journal of the Association for Persons with Severe Handicaps, 14*, 68–74.

Moon, M. S., Hart, D., Komissar, C., & Friedlander, R. (1995). Making sports and recreation activities accessible: Assistive technology and other accommodation strategies. In K. F. Flippo, K. J. Inge, & M. Barcus (Eds.), *Assistive technology: A resource for school, work, and community* (pp. 223–244). Baltimore: Paul H. Brookes Publishing Co.

Rainforth, B., York, J., & MacDonald, C., (1992). *Collaborative teams for students with severe disabilities.* Baltimore: Paul H. Brookes Publishing Co.

Riley, R. (June 20, 1995). Testimony of Secretary of Education before the House Subcommittee on Early Childhood, Youth and Families on the Reauthorization of the Individuals with Disabilities Education Act (IDEA). Washington, DC: Federal Document Clearing House.

Robinson, G. (1985). *Effective schools: A summary of research.* Arlington, VA: Educational Research Service.

Ryndak, D. L., Alper, S., Stuart, C., & Clark, D. (in press). Identifying curriculum for students with severe disabilities in general education contexts. *Innovations.* Washington, DC: American Association on Mental Retardation.

Sailor, W., Anderson, J. L., Halvorsen, A. T., Doering, K., Filler, J., & Goetz, L. (1989). *The comprehensive school.* Baltimore: Paul Brookes Publishing Co.

Sasso, G. M., Simpson, R. L., & Novak, C. G. (1985). Procedures for facilitating integration of autistic children in public school settings. *Analysis and Intervention in Developmental Disabilities, 5*, 233–246.

Schloss, P. J. (1992). Mainstreaming revisited. *The Elementary School Journal, 92*, 233–244.

Slavin, R. E. (1987). *Cooperative learning: Student team. What research says to the teacher* (2nd ed.). Washington, DC: National Education Association.

Snell, M. E. (Ed.). (1987). *Systematic instruction of persons with severe handicaps* (3rd ed.). Columbus: Charles E. Merrill.

Stainback, S., & Stainback, W. (Eds.). (1992). *Curriculum considerations in inclusive classrooms: Facilitating learning for all students.* Baltimore: Paul H. Brookes Publishing Co.

Stainback, W., & Stainback, S. (1984). A rationale for the

merger of special and regular education. *Exceptional Children, 51*(2), 102–111.

Stainback, W., & Stainback, S. (1989). Practical organization strategies. In S. Stainback, W. Stainback, & M. Forest (Eds.), *Educating all students in the mainstream of regular education* (pp. 71–87). Baltimore: Paul H. Brookes.

Stainback, W, Stainback, S., & Hatcher, C. (1983). Non-handicapped peer involvement in the education of severely handicapped students. *Journal of the Association for the Severely Handicapped, 8*(1), 39–42.

Stallings, J. A. (1985). *A study of basic reading skills taught in secondary schools* (Report of Phase I findings). Menlo Park, CA: Stanford Research Institute.

Stevens, R. J., Madden, N. A., Slavin, R. E., & Farnish, A. M. (1987). Cooperative integrated reading and composition: Two field experiments. *Reading Research Quarterly, 22*, 433–454.

Strully, J., & Strully, C. (1989). Friendships as an educational goal. In S. Stainback, W. Stainback, & M. Forest (Eds.), *Educating all students in the mainstream of regular education* (pp. 59–68). Baltimore: Paul H. Brookes Publishing Co.

Swank, P. R., Taylor, R., Brady, M., Cooley, R., & Freiberg, J. (1989). Outcomes of grouping students in mainstreamed middle school classrooms. *National Association of Secondary School Principals Bulletin, 73*, 62–66.

Tucker, J. A. (1989). Less required energy: A response to Danielson and Bellamy. *Exceptional Children, 55*, 456–458.

Unsworth, J. (1984). Meeting individual needs through flexible within-class grouping of pupils. *Reading Teacher, 38*, 298–304.

Vergason, G. A., & Anderegg, M. L. (1992). Preserving the least restrictive environment. In W. Stainback & S. Stainback (Eds.), *Controversial issues confronting special education* (pp. 45–54). Boston: Allyn and Bacon.

Wehmeyer, M. L., Lattin, D. L., & Agran, M. (in press). Promoting access to the general curriculum for students with mental retardation. *Education and Training in Mental Retardation and Developmental Disabilities.*

Wheeler, J. J. (1991). *Educating students with severe disabilities in general education settings: A resource manual.* Pierre, SD: South Dakota State Department of Education, Office of Special Education.

Williams, W., Fox, T., Thousand, J., & Fox, W. (1990). Level of acceptance and implementation of best practices in the education of students with severe handicaps in Vermont. *Education and Training in Mental Retardation, 25*(2), 120–131.

Wolfensberger, W. (1972). Citizen advocacy for the handicapped, impaired, and disadvantaged: An overview. (ERIC Document Reproduction Service No. 077 169.).

Wolfensberger, W. (1983). Social role valorization: A proposed new term for the principle of normalization. *Mental Retardation, 21*, 234–239.

Wolfensberger, W., & Glenn, L. (1975). *PASS 3: Program analysis of service systems.* Toronto: National Institute on Mental Retardation.

Endnote

1. The example of the wagon train project was implemented by Mrs. Joyce Stanley in her fifth-grade classroom at Russell Boulevard School in Columbia, Missouri.

3

Standards-Based Reform and Students with Disabilities

Gail McGregor

Objectives

After completing this chapter, the reader will be able to:

1. Define the term *standards* and describe the rationale for their current prominence in the field of education.

2. Define the term *standards-based reform* and identify its three components and associated assumptions about learning.

3. Discuss the legislative basis for standards, accountability systems that include all students, and access to the general education curriculum by students with disabilities.

4. Distinguish between *standards-based* and *standards-referenced* approaches to Individualized Education Plan (IEP) development.

5. Describe strategies that enable teachers to reference IEPs for students with severe disabilities to general education standards.

Key Terms

Access	Content standards	Standards-based IEPs
Accountability	Foundational skills	Standards-based reform
Alternate assessment	Performance standards	Standards-referenced IEPs
Benchmarks		

Improving the academic performance of students in this country's public schools is both big news and big business. In the past decade, states have invested millions of dollars to develop state- and district-level curriculum standards, align their curriculum to these standards, and implement comprehensive testing programs to assess student achievement (Education Week, 2001). In some states, high stakes accountability measures have been established, linking graduation and promotion to successful performance on a test. What does this all have to do with students with disabilities? Doesn't the Individuals with Disabilities Education Act (IDEA) ensure that students with disabilities receive an education tailored to meet their individual needs? Yes, but IDEA also requires that IEP teams determine how individual students will participate in state and/or district assessment programs and how the child's disability affects their involvement and progress in the general education curriculum.

Students with disabilities represent a special population that is clearly encompassed by the standards-based reform movement. Special educators can and must be focused on developing programs of high quality instruction for students with disabilities that are anchored to the general education curriculum (Hock, 2000). This includes students with the most severe disabilities (Grisham-Brown & Kearns, 2001; Kearns, 2001). In order for this to occur, a clear understanding of the intent and components of standards-based reform is necessary. This foundation will provide a framework for understanding how IEPs can be written in such a way that they are referenced to existing standards, linking a student's individualized educational program to the general education curriculum.

The Evolution of Educational Standards

For many years, the concept of the bell-shaped curve provided a framework to interpret the substantial variation among students in their academic achievement (Thompson, Quenemoen, Thurlow, & Ysseldyke, 2001). Within this framework, educators expect many students to learn and perform at an acceptable level, some to excel far beyond the majority, and some to fail to master the general education curriculum. Thus, poor student performance is an anticipated outcome of normal student distribution, rather than a failure of the educational system. In practice, students represented in the middle and high end of the bell curve were those typically directed toward the college track, while those with less academic promise were funneled toward some type of trade.

A changing economy, a political environment in which this country's competitiveness in the world was seen to be at risk, and a growing body of research demonstrating that schools can be more effective for traditionally underachieving students (Coleman et al., 1966; Edmonds, 1982; Purkey & Smith, 1985) are several of the major forces contributing to a shift in thinking about educational practice. Many people mark the beginning of the standards movement with the 1983 publication of *A Nation at Risk* by the National Commission on Excellence in Education (NCEE). This report sharply criticized educational practice in this country, characterizing our country's performance as mediocre and our actions as "unilateral, educational disarmament" (NCEE, 1983, p. 5). Identified weaknesses in our education system were linked to the nation's safety, financial security, and economic competitiveness. This broad-based critique of public education stimulated considerable response at the federal level, with resulting impact on individual states, districts, and schools.

A national educational summit was held by then President Bush and the states' governors in 1987. At this meeting, six broad goals were established to improve this country's educational system. Although the word "standards" did not appear in the summary report of this meeting, the goals identified later became the basis for the language of *Goals 2000: Educate America Act* (P.L. No. 103–227) enacted by Congress in 1994.

Former Assistant Secretary of Education Diane Ravitch is identified as one of the chief architects of what is now called the standards movement (Marzano & Kendall, 1996). She described the rationale for educational standards by pointing out that standards are established in other walks of life when high-quality outcomes are critical. For example, standards ensure quality and safety in the food we eat, water we drink, and the air we breathe. In her words, *"Standards are created because they improve the activity of life"* (Ravitch, 1995, p. 9). A standards-based approach to education evolved as a means of addressing two identified weaknesses in our educational system: (a) the lack of a well-defined curriculum and (b) an emphasis on educational "inputs" as opposed to educational "outputs" or outcomes (Marzano, 1998).

The national educational summit of 1987 stimulated efforts to identify standards within the respective professional organizations of each major subject area (National Research Council, 1996; National Council of Teachers of English and the International Reading Association, 1996; National Council for the Social Studies, 1994; National Council of Teachers of Mathematics, 1989). Not long after these documents became available, individual states began the process of developing their own standards documents, reflecting a strong sentiment that school policy and curricula are the business of individual states rather than the federal government (Marzano, 1998). By the year 2001, all but one state had identified state standards in the major curriculum content areas, and, in many states, individual districts also had developed local standards that are aligned with state standards (Education Week, 2001).

Standards-Based Reform

Standards-based reform is the term that has been applied to the policy response emerging from the dissatisfaction with the performance of schools in this country. The premise of this reform model stands in sharp contrast to the bell curve perspective underlying earlier educational practice. Standards-based reform is based on the following assumptions about student performance:

- All children can learn.
- All children thrive in an atmosphere of high expectations about what they will learn.
- If all children are expected to learn and they have had opportunities to reach high expectations, all children can be successful (Thompson et al., 2001, p. 3).

Standards-based reform has been the prevailing paradigm of education reform for the past decade (Smith & O'Day, 1990). This paradigm reflects a general consensus that, in order to produce meaningful improvement in schools, at least three elements must be present:

1. High content *standards*
2. Use of *assessments* to measure how schools are helping students meet these standards
3. An emphasis on *accountability*, that is, holding educators and students responsible for student achievement (Nolet & McLaughlin, 2000)

Standards are general statements of what students should know or be able to do as a result of their public school education. They typically represent the framework for the general education curriculum. Standards can be further described relative to the following associated concepts (Kendall, 2001):

- *Content standards* describe what a student should know or be able to do within a particular area of study. These statements organize a subject area by dividing it into a manageable number of generally stated goals for student learning. Content standards typically represent a consensus of what educators and the community as a whole believe that schools should teach. Thus, they encompass what is generally agreed upon as the skills necessary to become a successful and contributing citizen.
- *Benchmarks* are clear descriptions of expectations for student knowledge, skills, and abilities relative to content standards. Benchmarks are established for various points along a developmental continuum in each content area, reflecting increasing sophistication of performance in a content area as a student gets older.
- *Performance standards* describe a student's current level of skill, knowledge, or ability relative to an established benchmark. These standards provide an objective measure of the degree to which content standards have been attained. Performance standards can be described in terms of an established rubric, or some other method of characterizing different degrees of sophistication relative to the mastery of content standards.

Figure 3.1 provides an example of these elements taken from the Montana Standards Framework (Montana Office of Public Instruction, 1998), visually depicting the way in which the elements are related.

Assessment encompasses a wide variety of measurement strategies designed to determine a student's educational progress. In the context of standards-based reform, this refers specifically to a student's progress in a curriculum that is aligned with the district and/or state's curriculum standards. Similarly, large-scale assessments provide a means of assessing the progress of individual schools in improving student performance relative to state standards.

Accountability refers to efforts to quantify and report results of educational improvement efforts to all stakeholder groups and the public at large. This practice is evidenced in the growing use of school report cards as a way of capturing school performance, as well as public reports that summarize data about performance indicators, such as student test scores, attendance, and dropout and graduation rates. The accountability piece of standards-based reform places the emphasis on educational outputs (that

FIGURE 3.1 *Definitions and Sample Standard, Benchmarks, and Performance Standards*[1]

> **Reading Content Standard 4**
> **Students select, read, and respond to print and nonprint material for a variety of purposes.**

Sample Benchmarks

End of Grade 4

- Students will identify a variety of purposes for reading (e.g., personal satisfaction, lifelong reading habits).
- Student will solve a problem or answer a question through reading (e.g., signs, labels, instruction).
- Students will perform tasks for a variety of purposes by reading (e.g., recipes, directions, schedules, maps, tables, charts).
- Students will read and provide oral, written, and/or artistic responses to diverse perspectives, cultures, and issues in traditional and contemporary literature.

End of Grade 8

- Students will establish and adjust the purposes for reading (e.g., personal satisfaction, lifelong reading habits, sharing and reflecting upon their reading).
- Student will read to organize and understand information and to use material to investigate a topic (e.g., reference material, manuals, public documents, newspapers, magazines, and electronic information).
- Students will read, interpret, and apply information to perform specific tasks (e.g., maps, travel books, first aid manuals, catalogs).
- Students will read, analyze, and provide oral, written, and/or artistic responses to traditional and contemporary literature.

End of Grade 12

- Students will integrate purposes for reading into daily life (e.g., personal satisfaction, lifelong reading habits, reading as a leisure activity, sharing, and reflecting upon the reading).
- Students will read to evaluate appropriate resource material for a specific task.
- Students will locate, read, analyze, and interpret material to investigate a question, topic, or issue (e.g., reference material, pamphlets, book excerpts, articles, letters, and electronic information).
- Students will read, analyze, and synthesize information to perform complex tasks for a variety of purposes (e.g., schedules, maps, instructions, consumer reports, and technical manuals).

Performance Standard Framework

Student performance is characterized as falling within one of the four levels defined below.

Advanced	This level denotes superior performance.
Proficient	This level denotes solid academic performance for each benchmark. Students reaching this level have demonstrated competency over challenging subject matter, including subject-matter knowledge, application of such knowledge to real-world situations, and analytical skills appropriate to the subject matter.
Nearing proficiency	This level denotes that the student has partial mastery or prerequisite knowledge and skills fundamental for proficient work at each benchmark.
Novice	This level denotes that the student is beginning to attain the prerequisite knowledge and skills that are fundamental for work at each benchmark.

[1]*Source*: Montana Office of Public Instruction. (1998). *Montana standards for reading.* Helena, MT: author.

is, what students learn) rather than inputs (that is, the number of hours of instruction provided, dollars spent per pupil, and so forth.) (Finn, 1990).

Standards-Based Reform for All Students: Foundations in Title I

Although the Goals 2000 legislation stimulated the development of standards, the 1994 Amendments to the Elementary and Secondary Education Act (ESEA, 1994) clearly articulate the expectation that standards-based reform is intended to encompass *all* students. Requirements relative to each component of standards-based reform are established. In order to receive funding under Title I (that is, the federal school aid program focused on the needs of poor and underachieving students), states and districts are required to develop standards. These standards must be sufficiently broad to encompass the needs of all students, including those with disabilities and those for whom English is a second language. Further, states must use assessments that are aligned with their standards to measure student progress and must report results in such a way that the performance of students by gender, racial and ethnic group, English proficiency status, migrant status, and disability can be compared to students who do not share that characteristic. Finally, accountability information must be made public. A summary of these requirements is contained in Table 3.1.

Standards-Based Reform for All Students: Foundations in IDEA

The major elements of a standards-based reform model also are evident in the most recent amendments to The Individuals with Disabilities Education Act (IDEA) (P.L. 105-17). The message of IDEA is that students with disabilities should be working within the general education curriculum framework toward the same high standards as those established for students served in the general education program (Hock, 2000). The language specifically addressing the issue of standards is highlighted in Table 3.2.

The other two elements of standards-based reform, assessment and accountability, also are prominent in the language of IDEA. Since July of 2000, the law requires *all* students with disabilities to be included in statewide assessment programs. If the testing methods associated with a state's large-scale assessment are not appropriate for some students with disabilities, typically those with the most severe disabilities, some form of alternate assessment is required to measure their performance. (See Chapter 4 in this book.) As a result of this provision, the performance of all students with disabilities is considered in examining the educational performance of individual schools. This contributes to a renewed sense of urgency that schools work to ensure that *all* students are receiving a high-quality education that is focused on the achievement of high standards. Table 3.2 contains

TABLE 3.1   *Standards-Based Reform Requirements of Title 1*

Component of Standards	Requirement of ESEA
Standards	"The emphasis on challenging content and student performance standards for all children provides a clear goal for the new Title I law: to enable children served by Title I to meet the challenging standards established by the State for all its children. States, districts, and schools are called on to break with past practice by replacing minimum standards for some children with challenging standards for all. . . . States that have developed content and performance **standards that apply to all children** must also use them for Title I purposes" (p. 1).
Assessment	"States are responsible for assessing all students in the grades being assessed. Therefore, States must provide **means to determine the achievement of students with disabilities** and limited English proficient students relative to the State's content and performance standards when standard assessment procedures do not provide this information. This may be accomplished through providing appropriate accommodations in setting, scheduling, presentation, and response formats for the standard assessment, or through developing or adopting primary-language assessments or alternate assessment procedures tied to the content and performance standards" (p. 12).
Accountability	"Raising academic standards for all students and measuring student performance to hold schools accountable for educational progress are central strategies for promoting educational excellence and equity in our schools:" (p. 2). "Assessment results must be **disaggregated** within each school and district by gender, major racial and ethnic groups, English proficiency status, migrant status, **students with disabilities as compared to students without disabilities**, and economically disadvantaged students as compared to students who are not economically disadvantaged. Disaggregated data must be included in annual school profiles:" (p. 4). "The purpose of this requirement [referring to disaggregation] is to **ensure that the progress of all student populations is annually and systematically monitored**. This is a critical step in ensuring that **all students are meeting challenging standards**" (p. 48).

Source: ESEA (1994).

the specific citations from IDEA that address these assessment and accountability elements of the standards-based reform model.

A comparison of the information contained in Tables 3.1 and 3.2 indicates a considerable overlap in the policy requirements of these two key pieces of legislation (National Center on Educational Outcomes, 2001). Thus, unlike many of the other requirements of

TABLE 3.2   *Standards-Based Reform Requirements of IDEA*

Component of Standards-Based Reform	*Requirement of IDEA Amendments of 1997 P.L. 105-17 (emphasis added)*
Standards	Research, demonstration, and practice over the past 20 years in special education and related disciplines have built a foundation of knowledge on which State and local systemic-change activities can now be based. Such research, demonstration, and practice in special education and related disciplines have demonstrated that an effective educational system now and in the future must (A) maintain **high academic standards** and clear performance goals for children with disabilities, **consistent with the standards and expectations for all students in the educational system**, and provide for appropriate and effective strategies and methods to ensure that students who are children with disabilities have maximum opportunities to achieve those standards and goals [§651(a)(5)(A)].
Access to general education curriculum	The IEP must include a statement that indicates how a child's disability affects their **involvement and progress in the general curriculum** (§601[c][5][a]).
	Measurable goals and objectives on the IEP must enable the child **to be involved in and progress in the general curriculum** while at the same time meeting the child's unique needs (§614[d][1][A][ii]).
	The IEP must include a statement of the special education, related services, and supplementary aids and services the child is to receive to attain annual goals and **to be involved and progress in the general curriculum** (§614[d][1][A][iii]).
Assessment	All **students with disabilities must be involved** in the statewide assessment system with appropriate accommodations when necessary (§614 [6][a][i]).
	States must develop **alternate assessments** for children who cannot participate in State and district-wide assessment programs (§612[a][18][A][i]).
	The IEP must describe **how a student with a disability will participate in the statewide assessment** (§614[d][1][A][vi][aa][bb]).
Accountability	States must **establish goals for the performance of children with disabilities** and every two years, publicly report on progress relative to these goals (§612[a][16][D]).
	States must report on the number of students participating in alternate assessments (§612[a}[17][B][i][ii][iii][I][II]).
	State performance reporting must include data that are aggregated (includes students with disabilities) and disaggregated (students with disabilities only) (Final Regulations, 300.139[b][1,2]).
Standards-based reform	. . . an effective educational system now and in the future must . . . (B) create a system that fully addresses the needs of all students, including children with disabilities, **by addressing the needs of children with disabilities in carrying out educational reform activities** [§651(a)(6)(B)].

IDEA, the inclusion of students with disabilities in standards-based reform efforts at the state and local levels has strong policy support from both general and special education.

Standards as a Framework for Instructional Planning for Students with Disabilities

Despite the strong policy framework that clearly articulates the expectation that students with disabilities be a part of standards-based reform efforts, several studies conducted to date indicate that teachers are unclear about how to do this (Dailey, Zantal-Wiener, & Roach, 2000; McLaughlin, 2000; Purnell & Claycomb, 2001). Although substantial differences are evident across states and districts in their approach to implementing components of a standards-based reform model, there are some general principles, derived from recent research and practice, that can guide efforts to create structures that work for students with a wide variety of needs:

1. **It is essential that special education be viewed as part of a broad range of educational services rather than as a completely separate system** (Consortium on Inclusive Schooling Practices, 1996; Lipsky & Gartner, 1997). Within such a framework, special education and other programs targeted to address the needs of specific populations (that is, Title I, English as a second language [ESL]) become the services and supports that ensure that all students have meaningful learning opportunities and access to the general education curriculum rather than separate programs that stand apart from general education (Gartner & Lipsky, 2002). This is the clear expectation articulated in the Title I legislation (ESEA, 1994) and is also consistent with the language of IDEA (IDEA, 1997).

2. **Create standards that are broad in scope and purpose** (Consortium on Inclusive Schooling Practices, 1996; Glickman, 2000). States vary considerably in their approach to writing standards in terms of the degree of specificity with which the standards are written and the range of content areas encompassed by the standards. Standards that reflect a broad scope and purpose maximize the flexibility of the curriculum, creating opportunities for instructional practices to be responsive to the diversity needs and interests of students.

3. **Use standards to focus instructional efforts and guide choices of instructional methods** (Morel, 2000). When asked in what ways standards are beneficial, teachers have identified their value in focusing instructional efforts on knowledge and skills that are most important (McLaughlin, Nolet, Him, & Henderson, 1999). Standards typically are written so as to require students to apply, demonstrate, and use specific knowledge, rather than simply demonstrate rote knowledge or retain facts. In order to achieve these deeper levels of understanding, challenging, hands-on learning experiences are necessary. As described by Klutz and Strait (2001), "The standards movement can provide teachers with a compass for crafting a rich curriculum and appropriate instruction, offering new opportunities and setting high expectations for all students in the multicultural, heterogeneous, dynamic classrooms of the 21st century" (p. 46).

4. **Use a wide range of assessment strategies to measure the progress of all students toward challenging standards** (Lopez-Reina & Bay, 1997). Because there is a strong emphasis on educational outcomes in a standards-based reform model, educators must be prepared to use a full range of strategies to measure student performance. Although standardized tests are one source of information, they often are not well-aligned with content standards and are not an effective measurement strategy for many students. Portfolios, interviews, observations, anecdotal records, journals, and questionnaires are among the assessment approaches available to measure the learning of all students effectively. In a context where this range and type of assessment is prevalent, completely different approaches to assessment are not necessary for students with severe disabilities.

5. **The concept of Universal Design for Learning (UDC) holds great promise in designing instruction and selecting materials that provide opportunities for all students to be successful** (Nolet & McLaughlin, 2000; Pasha & Cone, 2001). The concept of Universal Design was first introduced in the field of architecture as a means of designing public spaces that are accessible to all citizens. As applied to instructional design, UDC is intended to make instructional materials and practices more accessible to a wide range of students. New multimedia tools make it possible for materials to be presented and stored in an array of formats, making both alternative and multisensory approaches to instruction more readily available for students who require such forms of presentation in order to benefit from instruction. The book *Talking Walls* (Outmarch Corporation, 1999) is an example of such a product. The book is stored on a CD that can be read conventionally on a computer or can be read by text reader software that speaks and highlights the words as they are displayed. The program incorporates a glossary that can be accessed while reading the text, easy access to an electronic notetaker, and Internet links to related content and video clips. A product designed in such a way enables the teacher to easily configure the presentation of information to be responsive to individual learner needs relative to both instruction and assessment of learning outcomes.

Strategies to Link IEPs for Students with Severe Disabilities to Standards

Within such an educational context, many special educators still raise the following question: "*How can the needs of students with the most severe disabilities be met within a standards-based reform framework?*" Upon initial consideration, it would seem that best practices for the education of students with severe disabilities, evolving directly from a philosophy about curricular relevance established in 1976 (Brown, Nietupski & Hamre-Nietupski, 1976), are incompatible with the current reform environment within general education classrooms (Ford, Davern, & Schnorr, 2001). This is an easy conclusion to draw, despite the shifts that have occurred in thinking about the importance of regular class placement for students with severe disabilities (Brown et al., 1989a; Brown et al., 1989b) and the available research that clearly documents progress in the general education curriculum by students with disabilities when they are included in general education classrooms (Fisher & Frey, 2001; Ryndak, Morrison, & Sommerstein, 1999).

The strategies suggested in the remainder of this chapter are drawn from a number of recent publications that are valuable resources in this continually evolving area of policy and practice (Ford, Davern & Schnorr, 2001; Grisham-Brown & Kearns, 2001; Hock, 2000; Kearns, 2001; Nolet & McLaughlin, 2000; Thompson et al., 2001). They provide a framework for IEP development that does not place individualized programming at odds with mandates that students with disabilities have meaningful involvement in the general education curriculum.

Standards Referenced versus Standards Based

The perceived tension between individualized program planning and the use of standards can be reconciled by introducing two related concepts: *standards-based IEPs* and *standards-referenced IEPs*. Although both terms imply a link between standards and the content of an IEP, a critical difference lies in the point of the planning process at which standards come into play. As discussed by Hock (2000), a standards-based approach starts with the standards. After it has been determined which standards are appropriate for a given student, the corresponding instructional activities and associated performance outcomes are specified. In a standards-referenced model, planning starts with the individual needs of a student. After the student has been identified, it is then possible to link student-specific goals and outcomes to the general education curriculum standards. For students with severe disabilities, a standards-referenced model maintains the integrity of the program individualization guaranteed by IDEA. For many other students with disabilities, a standards-based approach may be viable.

Link Needs Identified for an Individual Student to Standards

The COACH (Giangreco, Cloninger & Iverson, 1998) is a well-known IEP planning tool based on best practices for students with severe disabilities. The COACH process is individualized, family focused, and culturally sensitive, while also grounded in an inclusive, collaborative approach to education. When using the COACH, a prioritized list of valued outcomes is identified by the family, after which additional learning outcomes that are easily referenced to the general education curriculum are identified by the entire team. Involvement in general education is supported by considering a full array of options for student participation. Table 3.3 identifies and defines these options.

The issue of standards-based reform is not specifically addressed in the current edition of the COACH (Giangreco et al., 1998). However, there is nothing that prohibits a team from extending the program-planning process by one step: linking identified priority needs for the student to the specific curricular standard(s) to which they are related. This step serves the purpose of referencing a student's needs to the prevailing curricular framework (Ford, Davern, & Schnorr, 1992), as defined by the district or state standards. Table 3.4 provides an example of priority learning needs that are taken from the COACH and their link to academic standards common to the standards framework

TABLE 3.3 *Options for Student Participation in General Education*

Type of Participation	*What Does it Look Like?*
Same	The student is able to pursue the same learning outcomes in basically the same way as his or her typical classmates. *Example: A student with severe disabilities goes to the library with her class and checks out a book on spiders for an upcoming science unit.*
Same with individualized adaptations	The student is able to pursue the same or similar learning outcomes as his or her classmates, but does so in a different way. The individualized adaptation that enables the student to participate can consist of a change in materials, the use of personal support, a change in the sequence of the activity, a change in the rules of the activity, or some other modification that supports participation. *Example: A student with severe disabilities uses a sequence of pictures to guide her through the science activity.*
Multilevel curriculum and instruction	The student pursues learning outcomes within the same curricular area as the rest of the class, but works on instructional goals at a different instructional level. *Example: A student with severe disabilities works on a simplified set of questions to complete her science assignment.*
Curriculum overlapping	The student is involved in the same lesson as classmates, but is pursuing goals and objectives from different curricular areas that are of relevance to the student. *Example: During science, the instructional focus for a student with severe disabilities is to use a vocal output communication device to respond to yes/no questions and to initiate interaction with her lab partner.*
Alternate activity	When no apparent opportunities exist for a student to participate in a lesson or activity in the general education classroom, or if the student has unique needs that cannot be addressed within the context of general education activities, alternative activities are developed to meet his or her individual needs. *Example: A student with a severe hearing loss is scheduled for community work experience during the period when the rest of the class is in chorus.*

Source: Adapted from: Giangreco, M., Cloninger, C., & Iverson, V. (1993).

in a number of states. By delineating this relationship, it is clear how a student with severe disabilities can work on skills that are both individually relevant and related to the general education curriculum.

Focus Objectives on Foundational Skills

The way in which the educational needs of a student with severe disabilities are expressed is an important consideration in developing standards-referenced IEPs. Although not considered best practice at this point in time, it is not uncommon to see IEP objectives for students with severe disabilities focused on skills that are taken out of any meaningful context

TABLE 3.4 *Linkage between Instructional Needs Based on the COACH and Subject-Matter Content Area Standards*

Instructional Goals Based on COACH[1]	Related General Education Standards
Initiates and responds to interactions by pressing selection on vocal output device	Demonstrates competence in speaking and listening as tools for learning[2]
Makes choices when given up to four options	Demonstrates competence in the general skills and strategies of the reading process[2]
Follows picture sequences to perform tasks	Demonstrates competence in the general skills and strategies of the reading process[2]
Uses calendar	Understands and applies basic properties of the concepts of measurement[2]
Makes purchases of merchandise or services	Uses basic procedures while performing the processes of computation[2]
Participates in small group activities with peers	Interacts respectfully with others, including those with whom they have differences[3]
Follows school rules/routines	Demonstrates respect for themselves and others[3]
Does assigned classroom/school job	Demonstrates dependability, productivity, and initiative[3]
Travels safely in school and community	Understands the world in spatial terms[1]

[1]Adapted from: Giangreco et al., 1998.

[2]From: Kendall, Schoch-Roberts, & Young-Reynolds, 2000.

[3]Kendall, Synder, Schintngen, Wahlquist & Marzano, 1999.

or routine. The following objective exemplifies this issue: *When given 10 items of different shapes, sizes, and colors, the student will match like items with 80% accuracy within 5 minutes for 3 consecutive days.*

A teacher reading this objective has complete freedom to create a task to assess this skill. Unfortunately, this often results in repetitive, age-inappropriate activities that are not linked to meaningful outcomes when this might, in fact, actually be a critical skill needed to perform such meaningful tasks as filling a vending machine, delivering mail to various classrooms in the school, or putting instructional materials away in their appropriate storage area in the classroom.

The concept of *foundational skills* (Ford et al., 2001) has been suggested as an effective means of expressing educational priorities for students with severe disabilities. Ford et al. (2001) describe foundational skills as those that do the following:

> . . . open doors for people. They provide the basis for interacting with people and information in a multicultural society, successfully navigating the tasks of living, solving problems, making contributions, and doing these tasks within an ethical framework.

Foundational skills can be addressed in various ways through a range of rich activities. Development in foundational skills is important for all students, and it is particularly important for students with significant disabilities (p. 217).

This same concept emerges in discussions by Grisham-Brown and Kearns (2001) and Kearns (2001), although their term for this concept is "critical skills" or "access skills." The shared assumption of these related terms is a focus on key skills that are present across a range of daily activities and routines. Educational needs expressed in such a manner offer an identifiable way for students to access or participate in standards-based curriculum activities.

Foundational Skills as a Means of Accessing the General Education Curriculum

When the needs of students with severe disabilities are expressed in terms of critical or foundational skills, well-established strategies are available to identify opportunities for these skills to be addressed within the context of the general education curriculum. As illustrated in Figures 3.2 and 3.3, the use of an activity matrix (Fox & Williams, 1991) allows a collaborative team to analyze the general education curriculum and routines to identify *when* and *how* the learning needs of a student with severe disabilities, expressed in terms of foundational skills, can be addressed within the context of the general education classroom.

While serving as a general blueprint for a student's schedule, this approach also provides valuable information that should be added to the student's IEP to reference clearly a student's program to the general education curriculum. Although IEP formats differ across districts and states, specific information about access to the general education curriculum can be provided in these areas.

Statement About Impact of Disability on Involvement in the General Curriculum

IEPs require that the number of hours a student is to spend in general education be identified. Completion of the activity matrix provides a good means of calculating this total. This process ensures that this decision is based on student needs, rather than disability label or the availability of a separate program that typically serves a particular type of student. The end result of this planning process is the identification of meaningful opportunities for involvement in the general education classroom, with access to the general education curriculum in a manner that maintains a focus on individually relevant instructional needs.

Referencing Foundational Skills to General Education Activities and Routines when Formulating Instructional Goals and Objectives

When an analysis of a student's needs is conducted relative to the general education classroom, it is possible to identify predictable and repeated opportunities for foundation skills

FIGURE 3.2 *Student Scheduling and Program Planning Matrix*

Name: _Paula_   Grade: _3_   Teacher: _Mrs. Wright_   School Year: _2001-2002_

GENERAL EDUCATION CLASS ACTIVITIES/PERIODS

Instructional Goals for Student (abbreviated from IEP)	Morning Meeting	Reading - Group Intro	Reading - Partners	Art	Recess	Science	Library	Lunch	Playground	Language Arts (spelling)	Language Arts (writing)	Recess	Social Studies
Instructional Arrangement:	LG	LG	D	SM	SM	LG/SM	LG/SM	LG	SM	LG	LG/SM	SM	LG/SM
Duration:	20 min	15 min	30 min	40 min	15 min	45 min	30 min	30 min	15 min	20 min	45 min	15 min	45 min
Initiates & responds to interactions	X	X	X	X	X	X	X	X	X		X	X	X
Make choices	X	X	X	X	X	X	X	X	X		X	X	X
Follows picture sequences	X	X	X	X	X	X				X	X		X
Participates in small groups	X	X	X	X	X	X	X		X		X	X	X
Follows routines	X	X	X	X	X	X	X	X	X	X	X	X	X
Does assigned jobs	X			X	X		X	X	X	X			
Travels safely					X			X	X			X	
Uses calendar	X												
Participation	S	S/I	ML	S/I	S	CO	CO	S	S	ML	ML	S	ML
Necessary Supports	SE	SE	SE	P	P	PA	PA	PA	P	P	PA	P	PA

Instructional Arrangement: **LG** = large grp; **SM** = small grp; **D** = dyads; **PT** = peer tutoring; **1:1** = 1 to 1; **IW** = independent work
Student Participation Options: **S** = same; **S/I** = same with individualized adaptations; **ML** = multi-level; **CO** = Curricular Overlapping
Student Support Options: **PA** = paraeducator; **SE** = special educator; **T** = therapist; **P** = peer; **AT** = assistive technology

Source: Adapted from Fox & Williams, 1991.

45

FIGURE 3.3   *Sample IEP Goal and Objectives Linked to General Education Activities and Standards[1]*

General Education Standard: Demonstrates competence in speaking and listening as tools for learning.
Annual Goal: Paula will use a multilevel vocal output device with four choices displayed at one time to express herself with peers and adults throughout the school day.

Conditions Referenced to General Education Curriculum	Behavior	Criteria
During lunch, recess, and other unstructured times of the day	Paula will make a selection on her communication device in order to make choices and interact with others.	At least twice during these activities for five consecutive days
During reading when working with a partner	Paula will use her vocal output device and/or a display of pictures to respond to questions about the story.	For one story/week for three consecutive weeks
When Paula is working in a small group in science or social studies	Paula will respond to requests and questions and will initiate interaction with other group members.	On a daily basis for five consecutive days

[1]IEP objective format adapted from Giangreco et al., 1998.

to be embedded within meaningful routines and activities. This is critical information to add to the conditions component of the short-term objectives written into a student's IEP. Figure 3.3 provides an example of this approach, referencing activities identified as a result of completing the Activity Matrix contained in Figure 3.2 and 3.3, as well as referencing the general education standards that are related to the skill.

Description of Special Education, Related Services, and Supplementary Aids and Services Necessary to be Involved in the General Curriculum

Completion of an activities matrix will allow a team to identify and summarize the range and intensity of supports necessary for a student to address his/her goals while in the general education classroom. These needs are expressed in statements about the type and amount of related services required, as well as the specific adaptations or modifications necessary to support the student's involvement in the general education classroom. Documentation of the consideration of needs in the area of assistive technology and behavior support also are part of the IEP process, bringing these particular supports to the attention of the team as they consider what is necessary to ensure access to the general education curriculum.

Standards-Based Assessment

The issue of assessment in a standards-based IEP emerges relative both to the performance criteria and measurement strategies associated with individual goals and objectives and to the required statement of participation in the statewide assessment system. At the goal and objective level, best practices for students with severe disabilities suggest that assessment based on actual performance in settings in which a skill is required is the most meaningful form of assessment. These practices are highly congruent with the varied assessment approaches recommended within the general education literature for standards-based assessment.

The means by which a student will participate in the large-scale assessment also must be addressed. This decision must be made in the context of understanding what assessment approaches are used for the general education population. For many students with severe disabilities, an alternate approach to assessment will be necessary in order to measure student performance adequately (Thurlow, Elliott, & Ysseldyke, 1998). As described in Chapter 4 of this text, the availability of this option is intended specifically to address the needs of students for whom standardized forms of assessment would not yield meaningful information.

Preparing Yourself to Develop Standards-Referenced IEPs

Thompson et al. (2001) provide some additional recommendations about steps instructional team members can take to support their efforts to develop standards-referenced IEPs. They include the following suggestions:

- **If you are not familiar with the standards framework established in your district or state, get a copy of this document**. A curriculum coordinator would be a good resource for this information. Standards also are frequently posted on district and state Web sites because they frequently were written as a result of input from a variety of stakeholders and are of interest to many in the community at large.
- **Seek out guidance documents** that may have been developed at the district and/or state level to describe how special populations (for example, students with disabilities or students served by Title I) are to be supported within the standards-based reform activities in your school (U.S. Department of Education, 1999). Consult the teachers involved in the delivery of Title I services. This type of document also might be available to staff on district and/or state Web sites.
- **Think about the standards as you describe a student's present level of performance on the IEP**. It is helpful to start thinking about the common curriculum framework that is suggested by your district/state standards, using this as a guide to organize IEP content areas and associated descriptions of performance levels. Once again, the framework of the existing standards will affect the ease of establishing these matches. Key strategies, however, are to think broadly about what is encompassed by traditional academic areas and to think about the way in which foundational skills can be linked to these areas.

Summary

Standards-based reform is a national agenda for educational improvement that is being implemented in different ways across the country. There is a clear legislative basis in both Title I and in IDEA that students with disabilities are to be included in this reform agenda. Although many special educators were not actively involved in the development of standards, it is critical that special education services be seen as a means of supporting participation and opportunities for students with disabilities to be a part of the general education classroom. Access to the curriculum can occur in ways that address meaningful and critical skills necessary for students with disabilities to develop in order to be active participants in their community. The planning strategies that help link the participation of students with severe disabilities in general education settings are not new. However, teachers need to become familiar with the standards of their district and/or state and learn to think about the skills needed by many students with severe disabilities as foundation skills that can be linked to rich curriculum opportunities in the general education classroom.

References

Brown, L., Long, E., Udvari-Solner, A., Schwarz, P., VanDeventer, P., Ahlgren, C., Johnson, F., Gruenewald, L., & Jorgensen, J. (1989a). Should students with severe intellectual disabilities be based in regular or in special education classrooms in home schools. *Journal of the Association for Persons with Severe Handicaps, 14*, 8–12.

Brown, L., Long, E., Udvari-Solner, A., Davis, L., VanDeventer, P., Ahlgren, C., Johnson, F., Gruenewald, L., & Jorgensen, J. (1989b). The home school: Why students with severe intellectual disabilities must attend the schools of their brothers, sisters, friends, and neighbors. *Journal of the Association for Persons with Severe Handicaps, 14*, 1–7.

Brown, L., Nietupski, J., & Hamre-Nietupski, S. (1976). Criterion of ultimate functioning. In A. Thomas (Ed.), *Hey, don't forget about me!* (pp. 2–15). Reston, VA: Council for Exceptional Children.

Coleman, J. S., Campbell, E. Q., Hobson, C. J., McPartland, J., Mood, A. M., Weinfeld, F. D., & York, R. L. (1966). *Equality of educational opportunity.* Washington, DC: U.S. Government Printing Office.

Consortium on Inclusive Schooling Practices. (1996). A framework for evaluating state and local policies for inclusion. *Issue Brief.* Pittsburgh, PA: Allegheny-Singer Research Institute.

Dailey, D., Zantal-Wiener, K., & Roach, V. (2000). *Reforming high school learning: The effect of the standards movement on secondary students with disabilities.* Alexandria, VA: Center for Policy Research on the Impact of General and Special Education Reform.

Edmonds, R. (1982). Programs of school improvement: An overview. *Educational Leadership, 40*(3), 4–11.

Education Week. (2001). *Quality counts 2001. A better balance: Standards, tests, and the tools to succeed.* Marion, OH: author.

Elementary and Secondary Education Act (ESEA) as Amended by the Improving America's Schools Act of 1994, P. L. 103–382.

Final Regulations for the Amendments to the Individuals with Disabilities Education Act, P.L. 105-17 (1999). Available online at *www.ideapractices. org/lawandregs.htm.*

Finn, C. E. (1990). The biggest reform of all. *Phi Delta Kappan, 71*(8), 584–592.

Fisher, D., & Frey, N. (2001). Access to the core curriculum. Critical ingredients for student success. *Remedial and Special Education, 22*(3), 148–157.

Ford, A., Davern, L., & Schnorr, R. (2001). Learners with significant disabilities. Curricular relevance in an era of standards-based reform. *Remedial and Special Education, 22*(4), 214–222.

Ford, A., Davern, L., & Schnorr, R. (1992). Inclusive education: Making sense of the curriculum. In S. Stainback & W. Stainback (Eds.), *Curriculum considerations in inclusive classrooms: Facilitating learning for all students* (pp. 37–61). Baltimore: Paul H. Brookes Publishing Co.

Fox, T. J., & Williams, W. (1991). *Implementing best practices for all students in their local school.* Burlington, VT: University of Vermont.

Gartner, A., & Lipsky, D. K. (2002). *Inclusion: A service, not a place. A whole school approach.* Port Chester, NY: DUDE Publishing.

Giangreco, M., Cloninger, C., & Iverson, V. (1993). *Choosing options and accommodations for children. A guide to planning inclusive education* (1st ed.). Baltimore: Paul H. Brookes Publishing Co.

Giangreco, M., Cloninger, C. J., & Iverson, V. S. (1998). *COACH: Choosing outcomes and accommodations for children. A guide to educational planning for students with disabilities* (2nd ed.). Baltimore: Paul H. Brookes Publishing Co.

Glickman, C. (2000). The good and bad of standards. *ASCD Education Update, 42*(4), 7.

Goals 2000: Educate America Act (1994). P.L. 103–227.

Grisham-Brown, J., & Kearns, J. F. (2001). Creating standards-based individualized education programs. In H. L. Kleinert & J. F. Kearns (Eds.), *Alternate assessment. Measuring outcomes and supports for students with disabilities* (pp. 17–28). Baltimore: Paul H. Brookes Publishing Co.

Hock, M. L. (2000). Standards, assessments, and individualized education programs. Planning for success in the general education curriculum. In R. A. Villa & J. S. Thousand (Eds.), *Restructuring for caring and effective education. Piecing the puzzle together* (2nd ed.). Baltimore: Paul H. Brookes Publishing Co.

Individuals with Disabilities Education Act (IDEA) Amendments of 1997, P.L. 105–17, 42 U.S.C. §1400 *et seq.* Available online at *www.ideapractices.org/law/IDEAMAIN.HTM.*

Kearns, J. F. (2001). Helping students with significant disabilities gain access to general curriculum standards. In H. Kleinert & J. F. Kearns (Eds.), *Alternative assessment. Measuring outcomes and supports for students with disabilities* (pp. 29–48). Baltimore: Paul H. Brookes Publishing.

Kendall, J. S. (2001). *A technical guide for revising or developing standards and benchmarks.* Aurora, CO: Mid-continent Research for Education and Learning. Available online at *www.mcrel.org.*

Kendall, J. S., Schoch-Roberts, L., & Young-Reynolds, S. (2000). *A distillation of subject-matter content for the subject areas of geography and history.* Aurora, CO: Mid-continent Research for Education and Learning.

Kendall, J. S., Snyder, C., Schintgen, M., Wahlquist, A., & Marzano, R. J. (1999). *A distillation of subject-matter content for the subject-areas of language arts, mathematics, and science.* Aurora, CO: Mid-continent Research for Education and Learning.

Klutz, P., & Strait, D. (2001). Standards for diverse learners. *Educational Leadership, 59*(1), 43–46.

Lipsky, D. K., & Gartner, A. (1997). *Inclusion and school reform. Transforming America's classrooms.* Baltimore: Paul H. Brookes Publishing Co.

Lopez-Reina, N. A., & Bay, M. (1997). Enriching assessment: Using varied assessments for diverse learners. *Teaching Exceptional Children, 29*(4), 33–37.

Marzano, R. J. (1998). *Models of standards implementation: Implications for the classroom.* Aurora, CO: Mid-continent Regional Educational Laboratory.

Marzano, R. J., & Kendall, J. S. (1996). *The fall and rise of standards-based education.* Alexandria, VA: National Association of State Boards of Education and Aurora, CO: Mid-continent Regional Educational Laboratory.

McLaughlin, M. (2000). *Reform for EVERY learner: Teachers' views on standards and students with disabilities.* Alexandria, VA: Center for Policy Research on the Impact of General and Special Education Reform.

McLaughlin, M. J., Nolet, V., Him, L. M., & Henderson, K. (1999). Integrating standards. Including all students. *Teaching Exceptional Children, 31*(3), 66–71.

Morel. (2000). *Noteworthy perspectives on implementing standards-based education.* Aurora, CO: Mid-continent Research for Education and Learning.

Montana Office of Public Instruction (1998). *Content and performance standards for reading.* Helena, MT: author. Available online at *www.metnet.state.mt.us.*

National Center on Educational Outcomes. (2001). *Crosswalk of Title I and IDEA assessment and accountability provisions for students with disabilities.* Minneapolis, MN: University of Minnesota, author. Available online at *education.umn.edu/NCEO.*

National Commission on Excellence in Education. (1983). *A nation at risk: The imperative for educational reform.* Washington, DC: U.S. Department of Education.

National Council for the Social Studies. (1994). *Expectations of excellence: Curriculum standards for social studies.* Washington, DC: Author.

National Council of Teachers of English and the International Reading Association. (1996). *Standards for the English language arts.* Urbana, IL and Newark, DE: Authors.

National Council of Teachers of Mathematics. (1989). *Curriculum and evaluation standards for school mathematics.* Reston, VA: Author.

National Research Council. (1996). *National science*

education standards. Washington, DC: National Academy Press.

Nolet, V., & McLaughlin, M. J. (2000). *Accessing the general curriculum. Including students with disabilities in standards-based reform*. Thousand Oaks, CA: Corwin Press, Inc.

Outmarch Corporation. (1999). *Talking walls. Explore world cultures through literature and multimedia* (compact disc). Redmond, WA: Author.

Pasha, B., & Cone, P. (2001). Smart from the start. The promise of universal design for learning. *Remedial and Special Education, 22*(4), 197–203.

Purkey, S., & Smith, M. (1985). School reform: The district policy implications of the effective schools literature. *The Elementary School Journal, 85*(3).

Purnell, S., & Claycomb, C. (2001). *Implementing reform. What success for all teaches us about including students with disabilities in comprehensive school restructuring*. Alexandria, VA: National Association of State Boards of Education.

Ravitch, D. (1995). *National standards in American education: A citizen's guide*. Washington, DC: Brooking Institute.

Ryndak, D. L., Morrison, A. P., & Sommerstein, L. (1999). Literacy before and after inclusion in general education settings: A case study. *Journal of the Association for Persons with Severe Handicaps, 24*(1), 5–22.

Smith, M., & O'Day, J. (1990). Systemic school reform. In S. Fuhrman & B. Malen (Eds.), *The politics of curriculum and testing*. Philadelphia: Falmer Press.

Thompson, S. J., Quenemoen, R. F., Thurlow, M. L., & Ysseldyke, J. E. (2001). *Alternate assessments for students with disabilities*. Thousand Oaks, CA: Corwin Press, Inc. and Council for Exceptional Children.

Thurlow, M. L., Elliott, J. L., & Ysseldyke, J. E. (1998). *Testing students with disabilities. Practical strategies for complying with district and state requirements*. Thousand Oaks, CA: Corwin Press.

U.S. Department of Education. (1999). Peer reviewer guidance for evaluating evidence of final assessments under Title I of the Elementary and Secondary Education Act. Washington, DC: author. Available online at *www.ed.gov/offices/OESE/cpg.doc*.

Vermont Department of Education (2000). *Vermont's framework of standards and learning opportunities*. Montpelier, VT: Author.

4

Understanding the Purpose and Process of Alternate Assessment

Diane M. Browder and Fred Spooner

Objectives

After completing this chapter, the reader will be able to:

1. Describe the Individuals with Disabilities Act (IDEA) 1997 requirement for students with disabilities to participate in statewide accountability systems or an alternate assessment.
2. Discuss the decisions states made in developing alternate assessments and identify their own state's policies.
3. Use a variety of options for documenting student progress to demonstrate performance of standards.
4. Identify ways to use alternate assessment outcomes to improve student performance.

Key Terms

Accountability systems   Portfolio-based assessment   Standards-based reform
Alternate assessment   Performance standards

Most state departments of education have frameworks of educational standards, state assessments, and accountability systems. Wolk (1998) reported that 49 states have set standards for what students should know and be able to do at various points in their school careers. The Education Commission of the States (1997) reported that almost half of all states have implemented or are planning public accountability systems.

Why is there this recent emphasis on state standards and large-scale assessments? Kleinert and Thurlow (2001) describe the three waves of education reform that brought American schools to this point. The first occurred in the 1980s when the National Commission on Education targeted setting higher educational standards for students. The emphasis at that time was on issues like having more courses, more homework, and more time in school. During a second wave that occurred in the mid 1980s, there was a call for greater federal and state support for a wide range of education initiatives with the proposal that support be given in exchange for concrete evidence of educational results. The third wave focused on having rigorous standards for all students and public documentation of progress on these standards. This led to GOALS 2000: Educate America Act of 1994 (GOALS 2000: PL 103-227, March 31, 1994). By the early 1990s, states had begun to define standards and to develop wide-scale assessments (for example, statewide testing) to measure student performance.

At first, this reform movement seemed to bypass students with disabilities, especially students with the most significant disabilities, by exempting them from these large-scale assessments. The unfortunate consequence was that students with disabilities were also bypassed in decisionmaking. In the mid-1990s, the National Center on Educational Outcomes (NCEO) called attention to the fact that large numbers of students with disabilities were excluded from state assessment and accountability systems (Erickson, Thurlow, & Thor, 1995). Their concern was that, if students were out of sight in assessment and accountability systems, they would be out of mind when policy decisions were made. One of the unfortunate side effects of exclusion from the accountability system was an increase in rates of referral to special education (Allington & McGill-Franzen, 1992). Schools also did not set high expectations for students with disabilities when their scores did not factor into accountability decisions.

Rethinking Assumptions About Educating Students with Severe Disabilities

The implementation of alternate assessment requires rethinking some of the assumptions about educating students with severe disabilities, especially those related to achievement, curriculum, and school membership. First, the purpose of alternate assessment is to provide accountability for students' performance of state standards. When implemented well, this new requirement sets high expectations for students with severe disabilities. Educators have gone through several phases of expectations for this population. Prior to the mid-1970s, expectations were sometimes low. Educators did not expect educational achievement as reflected in some of the negative terms used to describe the population. For example, terms like low functioning, trainable, and custodial were used to describe individuals with severe disabilities (Blatt & Kaplan, 1966). Haring and Pious (1976) suggest that, at best, the public attitude toward this population was apathetic in these early years of creating services. In the 1980s, many educators began to rely on the emerging behavioral methods to teach students with severe disabilities the skills believed to be prerequisites to community placements (Browder & Bambara, 2000). Skills like food preparation, housekeeping and laundry, home safety and first aid, telephone use, dining out and buying snacks, purchasing items, community mobility, and community leisure were all taught by a variety of systematic instructional procedures (Cipani & Spooner, 1994; Ryndak & Alper, 1996; Snell & Brown, 2000; Westling & Fox, 2000). By the 1990s, most educators no longer thought that students with severe disabilities should have to earn inclusive opportunities with skill acquisition (Tashie, Jorgensen, Shapiro-Barnard, Martin, & Schuh, 1996). The focus shifted to the supports needed for enhanced quality of life through person-centered planning (O'Brien, 1987; Vandercook, York, & Forest, 1989). Even as new inclusive school opportunities were created, the focus was often more on social inclusion than skill achievement.

With the new millennium, a new expectation has emerged that students will not only have inclusive opportunities, but that all students can make progress in achieving state standards. This is not a regression to 1980s thinking that students must earn inclusive opportunities, but it also is not being satisfied with a lack of achievement in these settings. The expectation now is that all students will work toward state standards.

Another area that requires rethinking is curriculum. The field of severe disabilities has also undergone some key curricular trends. In the 1970s, as programs were first created for individuals with severe disabilities, educators sometimes borrowed ideas from early childhood curriculum. By the late 1970s, L. Brown et al. (1979) had challenged the field to focus instead on functional, age-appropriate skills. As more opportunities for school inclusion emerged in the late 1980s and 1990s, professionals often focused on social inclusion. Inclusive education provided a means for students to cultivate a circle of friends (Forest & Lusthaus, 1989). As Ford, Davern, and Schnorr (2001) note, the mandate for assessment and accountability for students with significant disabilities will influence curriculum decisions for years to come. The current challenge is to determine meaningful outcomes for students to demonstrate through these assessments.

Most states' standards focus on what Vanderwood, Ysseldyke, and Thurlow (1993) have described as academic and functional literacy outcomes. In contrast, many Individualized Education Programs (IEPs) for students with severe disabilities focus on functional and social skills reflective of the most recent curriculum trends for this population. In planning alternate assessments, states have had the challenge of either creating additional, functional standards or extending standards so that they apply to all students. When states first began working on alternate assessments, many focused on functional outcomes with no link to actual state standards (Thompson & Thurlow, 2001). By 2001, nearly all states focused their alternate assessments on either functional examples of how to apply state standards or by showing direct links from functional to academic state standards. This shift toward creating links between academic and functional standards shows that most states now view access to the general curriculum and participation in alternate assessment as related requirements. As a result, alternate assessment is creating a new era of curriculum for students with severe disabilities with much stronger emphasis on skills like literacy and numeracy than in the past. As Boundy (2000) notes, if students with severe disabilities are truly to benefit from the standards-based educational reform movement, students, parents, and advocates must remain vigilant to hold states and school districts accountable. Students with severe disabilities will only benefit when all students, including those with severe disabilities, participate or begin to have access to a challenging general curriculum.

The third area that requires rethinking with alternate assessment is school membership. At one time, advocates worked toward physical inclusion of students with severe disabilities, that is, getting students into typical educational settings. Next, the focus was on social inclusion or finding ways for students to be full members of their learning environment. Professionals also worked for instructional inclusion by focusing on ways to address the IEP in the context of general education classes. Accountability is the next barrier to cross for full school membership. Will the performance of students with severe disabilities count in decisions about school accountability and resources? For example, in some states like Kentucky and North Carolina, the performance of students on the alternate assessment counts in school accountability equations that are based on student test scores. Because this performance counts, the education of students with severe disabilities is more likely to be a consideration in planning school improvement.

Criticism of Educational Accountability Systems

Not all professionals welcome the current focus on high-stakes accountability. Experts like Hilliard (2000) argue that evidence is lacking for using testing as a reform tool to improve student achievement. Most professionals would concur that *teaching*, not testing, is what promotes student learning. Accountability systems, including the alternate assessment, run the risk of competing with valuable teaching time and becoming counterproductive to student achievement. Also, when students fail to meet performance expectations, will schools invest the resources to help all students learn or blame students for low achievement? Hilliard (2000) notes that "When money and the resolve are not there, the easy thing to do is to manipulate the requirements for high-stakes standardized achievement tests and call it reform" (p. 301). Much more research is needed to determine whether accountability systems and the inclusion of students with disabilities promote student achievement. For now, educators live in an era when accountability systems are the reality of public education and the inclusion of students in these assessments is a legal requirement. The challenge in the near future is to understand this legal requirement and find ways to meet it that benefit students.

Legal Requirement of 1997 Amendments of IDEA

With the growing focus on state and local standards for education, advocates for children with disabilities have encouraged lawmakers to make sure schools are focusing on helping all students achieve these standards. The Individuals with Disabilities Education Act (IDEA) Amendments of 1997 (IDEA '97: PL 105-17, June 4, 1997) includes two important requirements to address this goal. First, IDEA 1997 mandates that all students have access to the general curriculum. The statement of the child's present level of educational performance must describe how the disability affects participation in the general curriculum. Even more significant, the IEP must include measurable annual goals to enable the child to be involved in and progress in the general curriculum. The specific wording of IDEA 1997 is that the IEP must include:

measurable annual goals, including benchmarks or short-term objectives, related to meeting the child's needs that result from the child's disability, to enable the child to be involved in and progress in the general curriculum (IDEA '97, Sec 614 (d) (1) (A) (ii)).

IDEA 1997 also requires that all students participate in national and state assessments with accommodations. Students with disabilities who are not able to participate in large-scale assessments must be given an alternate assessment. Specifically, IDEA 1997 requires that the state or local agency

(a) develops guidelines for the participation of children with disabilities in alternate assessment for those children who cannot participate in State and district-wide assessment programs; and (b) develops and beginning not later than July 1, 2000, conducts these alternate assessments (IDEA '97, Sec. 612) (a) (17) (A)).

Earlier Title I legislation also requires that students with disabilities have access to the general curriculum and be included in state and local assessments. The National Center on Educational Outcomes (2001) has summarized this Title I support with particular reference to the Elementary and Secondary Education Act as amended by the Improving America's Schools Act of 1994. Thus, both Title I and IDEA require student participation in state and district assessments and access to the general curriculum.

By July 2001, the NCEO noted that all states had developed alternate assessments (Thompson & Thurlow, 2001). Out of the 50 states, 48 had selected a specific format for the alternate assessment, whereas two were undecided. In the development of an alternate assessment protocol, all states relied on some stakeholder input, including, for example, special educators, state assessment personnel, parents, and advocates. For the most part, alternate assessments were developed to address the same standards used in the general assessments. Most states now require either a portfolio or checklist for the alternate assessment and focus on measuring the level of student skill or competence.

Understanding Your State's Approach to Alternate Assessment

States have had a wide range of responses to the requirement to provide an alternate assessment for students who do not participate in state or local testing. Some states require portfolios to document student progress; others use checklists or videotapes. In some states, teachers score their own portfolios; in others, these are scored at the state level. Even the focus of the assessment varies. In some states, the assessment is organized by functional skills; in others, the assessment is organized by the state's academic categories. This section of the chapter provides information to understand the components of the alternate assessment process, in general, with guidelines for discovering what a specific state requires. Most states have Web sites that describe their alternate assessment procedure. The NCEO also has a resource that describes states' alternate assessments (Quenemoen, Lehr, Thurlow, & Massanari, 2001). A list of these resources can be found at their Web site: *education.umn.edu/NCEO.*

Identifying the Standards, Extended Standards, and Real-Life Indicators for a State

Elliott, Ysseldyke, Thurlow, and Erickson (1998) recommend that the place to begin in developing alternate assessment is to identify the broad areas of learning that the state expects all students, both with and without disabilities, to learn. Identifying a state's standards is also the place to begin in learning about alternate assessment. The NCEO has identified six broad areas for learning by all students including Academic and Functional Literacy, Physical Health, Responsibility and Independence, Citizenship, Personal and Social Well-Being, and Satisfaction (Ysseldyke et al., 1998). Nearly all states now have specific state standards that specify learning expected for all students. These standards vary tremendously, and most focus on academic learning (Vanderwood, Ysseldyke, & Thurlow, 1993). Some states have narrow standards like performing computation in math. Others have broader standards like using concepts of math in daily problem solving. Kleinert and Thurlow (2001) note that broader standards promote the inclusion of students with disabilities. When states have more narrowly defined standards, the task of creating links for students with severe disabilities can be challenging. The first step in understanding a state's alternate assessment is to go to the state's education Web site to review existing standards.

The next step is to understand how these standards have been translated for access by students with severe cognitive disabilities. Kleinert and Thurlow (2001) describe three ways to create access to the general curriculum for students with severe disabilities that have implications for alternate assessment. The first strategy is to give students the opportunity to achieve their IEP objectives in the context of a broad array of school, home, and community environments, including the general education classroom. A second strategy is for students with severe disabilities to receive instruction in the core academic curriculum. Although students may not be expected to master all, or even most, of the math, science, or other content for their grade level, they are expected to learn some specific target information. A third strategy is to translate the content standards to target their underlying critical functions. Kleinert and Thurlow (2001) recommend the approach of Owen White (1980) of specifying the critical function of the learning standard. Rather than focusing on the form of the response (for example, writing a three-paragraph essay), the focus is on its function (for example, summarizing and communicating key information, which may be done using pictures or other assistive technology). Nearly all states have translations of their standards that are used for the alternate assessment process based on either this concept of defining the critical function of the standard or the use of functional skills. Thompson and Thurlow (2001) found that more states have moved toward translating the

Question 1:

What are my state's standards for all students? Are they broad or specific? Do they focus primarily on academics or are there standards related to community living and employment?

state's standards versus using alternative functional skills standards in the two years states have been developing their formats.

Pennsylvania is an example of a state that is basing its alternate assessment on the state's standards by translating the critical essence (Pennsylvania Alternate System of Assessment Project Leadership Team, 2001). One academic standard in mathematics for Pennsylvania relates to "numbers, number systems, and number relationships." The essence of the standard is defined as "understands quantity, uses numbers, and performs simple calculations." This critical essence is then further defined for purposes of assessment to include identifying the "skills embedded in authentic and relevant performance tasks" by "counts, matches quantity, compares quantity, demonstrates 1:1 correspondence, makes sets, understands operations, understands concept of equality, understands one, understands order, identified numerals."

In Wyoming, the translations of state standards are called "real world performance indicators" (Chatham Educational Consultants, Inc., 2001). An example of a real-world performance indicator from Wyoming in mathematics is "indicate when a cup is empty or full." States have used many different terms for these extensions of the state standards. They may be called access skills, extended standards, and performance indicators.

Other states add functional skills standards to their state standards. For example, in Delaware (Delaware Department of Education, 2000) the alternate assessment not only addresses reading and math standards, but also focuses on communication (expressive, receptive, and interactive), personal management (mobility, attending to personal needs, behavior control, domestic routines, and recreation/leisure), social skills (intrapersonal, interpersonal, and group behavior), and career vocational skills (intrapersonal, teamwork, work performance, and personal management). An example of a functional skill standard in personal management from Delaware is "initiate/complete/maintain personal care routines."

A third alternative that states have followed is to base their alternate assessment on functional skills and then define the link to the state's standards. In North Carolina, teachers document performance for community, home and personal living, vocational, and communication skills (North Carolina Department of Public Instruction, 2001). These are then being linked back to the state's "standard course of study," which has highly specific standards. For example, a sample activity in receptive communication, "give an appropriate verbal response in response to teacher greeting," is linked back to the standard course of study goal "The learner will develop and apply enabling strategies and skills to read and write." A few states continue only to focus on functional skills in their alternate assessment. For example, some skills in the personal management domain of Nebraska's alternate

Question 2:

Does my state base the alternate assessment on extensions of the state standards, on additional functional skills, or some combination of both? Does my state have a curriculum resource that offers examples of functional activities that can be used to measure state standards?

assessment include "takes medications, follows safety measures with medication, and states dangers of drugs" (Hill, Bird, & Dughman, 2000).[1]

Identifying Eligibility Criteria

Students have three options for participation in a state or local assessment: (a) participation in the typical assessment, (b) participation in the typical assessment with accommodations, or (c) participation in alternate assessment. In summarizing the legal requirements of IDEA 1997, Shriner (2000) notes that the vast majority of students, including those with disabilities, should participate in the state's general education assessments. The alternate assessment is a substitute method to gather information on performance for students who have unique curricular considerations, but should still be consistent with the goals and standards established by the state. Eligibility for the alternate assessment is an IEP team decision and is not based on the student's diagnosis.

Participation in the alternate assessment has critical implications in some high stakes states. The term *high stakes* is used for states in which student assessment scores have consequences for students and schools. For example, students who do not pass the test may not be eligible for a high school diploma. Thompson and Thurlow (2001) found that only 52 percent of students who participate in an alternate assessment are eligible for a regular high school diploma, although they may qualify for a certificate (for example, certificate of attendance) or a special education diploma. Also, the alternate assessment scores may be automatically counted as below expectations in school accountability formulas. Neither of these unfortunate consequences relate to the purpose of alternate assessment that is to promote high performance for all students. In Kentucky, students in alternate assessments can achieve high scores for performance. Research has shown that Kentucky Alternate Portfolio scores were positively related to the school's educational accountability index for all students and that these scores were improving over time (Turner, Baldwin, Kleinert, & Kearns, 2000). If the alternate assessment is developed in a way that creates incentives for high achievement for students with severe disabilities and avoids disadvantages for participation, parents and other stakeholders may find this to be a useful alternative to state and local testing. When there are disadvantages to participate (for example, student's outcome scores are considered below proficient simply for being in the alternate assessment), identifying any student as eligible may be controversial.

Format Used for Alternate Assessment

Ysseldyke and Olsen (1999) have described four primary ways to assess students' achievement of state standards, including (a) observations, (b) interview/surveys, (c) record

Question 3:

What are the specific eligibility criteria for participation in alternate assessment in my state? How does participation affect eligibility for a high school diploma? How will it affect the reporting of the student's score in accountability formulas?

reviews, and (d) tests and portfolios. In the section on improving student progress, we provide some specific ideas for direct assessment of student progress. Not all states rely on direct assessment. Interviews, surveys, and checklists are all alternatives that use indirect methods of assessment. The most popular format for the alternate assessment is a portfolio that includes evidence of student achievement (Thompson & Thurlow, 2001). Siegel-Causey and Allinder (1998) have recommended using portfolios for students with severe disabilities. Portfolios provide opportunities to record and review assessment information in functional contexts over time. Information can be gathered not only on achievement, but also on the process of learning. A portfolio can include information from a myriad of sources: functional assessments of behavior, instructional data, and medical reports. Portfolios also have disadvantages, especially when used in an accountability system, including low reliability coefficients and high costs (Parkes, 2000). Given the disadvantages of portfolios, half the states have considered other alternatives like skills checklists, an analysis of the IEP, or some other format.

Scoring and Reporting Outcomes

Earlier in this chapter, we described what is meant by high stakes accountability in which student scores may be used to make decisions about student promotion and graduation (student accountability) or school accountability. In North Carolina, a high stakes state, alternate assessment scores are entered into the school's accountability equation that determines whether the school is exemplary. In exemplary schools, teachers receive bonus pay. In this high stakes atmosphere, teachers who have demonstrated reliability for assessing these documents score portfolios at the state level. In contrast, many states do not use scores in this way. The student's teacher may be the one who scores the alternate assessment and reports the score to the district or state. IDEA 1997 requires that student scores be publicly reported. Thompson and Thurlow (2001) found that most states (74 percent) report alternate assessment scores separately from the general scores' reports. A few states do aggregate all scores including alternate assessments.

Designing Assessments that Capture Student Progress

Given the wide variety of formats states use for alternate assessment, it is not possible to describe how to complete this process in a way that meets the needs of all states. In contrast, whatever format a state uses, teachers will want to design their assessment to capture student progress. This requires defining specific, measurable skills for instruction, setting

Question 4:

What format does the state use for the alternate assessment: a portfolio? Checklist? IEP analysis? Other?

Question 5:

Who is responsible for scoring the alternate assessment in this state? How will the scores be reported: separately or aggregated with the general scores?

up data collection systems to track ongoing progress, incorporating assessment into instruction, and communicating outcomes to stakeholders or external reviewers.

Defining What Will Be Measured

The skills that students with severe disabilities will be learning need to be observable, quantifiable, and measurable. It will be important for teachers to work from broad generalizations about skills that need to be acquired to pinpointing specifically the behavior or skill in question (Alberto & Troutman, 1999; White & Haring, 1980). A movement, an action that the teacher can see, will classify the behavior or skill that is being taught. In determining the behavioral objective, the teacher needs to use the student's name that will be performing the behavior, identify the target behavior (state what the student will do), identify the conditions of the intervention, and state the criteria for acceptable performance. The targeted skill needs to be operationally defined. The act of operationalizing a behavior is a similar process to pinpointing the skill as described by White and Haring (1980). In most cases, using precise verbs in the objective increases the precision and promotes more accurate recording of behavior. Using verbs like "to count orally," "to say," or "to walk" are preferred to ambiguous action verbs like "to arrange," "to use," or "to complete," or using action verbs that are not directly observable like "to develop," "to discriminate," or "to learn."

The statement of conditions under which the behavior or skill is to occur is another critical part of the behavioral objective. For example, "Fred will cross a partially controlled intersection when the light is green." In the previous example, "when the light is green," is the condition that describes when Fred will cross the street.

Clearly stating the performance criterion is the final remaining part of the objective. In clarifying the acceptable level of performance, a minimal standard against which student action is judged is delineated. For example, the skill in question should be performed

Application:

How would you make this objective observable and measurable? "Kim will improve her communication skills." One alternative is "Kim will indicate a preference for food or drink by pressing the appropriate switch on an Intro-Talker 4 of out 5 times." What might be another alternative?

correctly six out of six times, or at 80 percent steps correct on the task analysis, or four out of five trials correct.

Given these basics of defining an observable, measurable objective, the alternate assessment process adds additional challenges. First, how will the objective be related to a state standard to be addressed in the alternate assessment? The best way to build this link is at the time of the development of the IEP. Thompson et al. (2001) note the importance of having a "standards-based IEP." A standards-based IEP is an IEP developed with standards from the general curriculum. Rather than focusing only on the students' individual needs, the team considers ways to help the student work towards state or local standards. Thompson, Quenemoen, Thurlow, and Ysseldyke (2001) recommend doing this in several ways. After identifying the state's standards and any resources on how to extend these for real-life indicators or access skills, the team identifies the student's current level of functioning with the standards in mind. The team then develops annual goals for making progress toward these standards. The team may also want to review any IEP goals that were not developed from standards to see if a link to the standards is possible. In some states, the IEP must specify this goal-to-standards link. A second look at standards not included in the IEP may also generate new ideas for annual goals.

For example, the critical essence for a set of math standards in North Carolina is to use patterns and sorting. Kevin, a middle-school student with severe multiple disabilities who is legally blind, currently has no functional math skills. His past IEP primarily focused on increasing time on task at a workstation, using object communication symbols, and following an object schedule. In considering Kevin's current level of performance on this math standard, the team notes that, although Kevin does not have number or object-sequencing skills, he has shown recognition of the sequence of events in his schedule by anticipating what comes next. They decide that it would be helpful to enhance this skill by having Kevin set up his own object schedule at the beginning of each day to show understanding of his daily sequence. They also target having him set up a pattern of work supplies after being shown a new job task. The standards-based IEP objective for this second skill for Kevin is "When shown a pattern to set up a new job task that involves 3 to 5 work pieces, Kevin will create this pattern independently with all materials correctly sequenced for 4 out of 5 days." For example, prior to wrapping silverware for a restaurant, Kevin will locate and sequence the silverware, napkins, and completion box.

Besides linking to state standards, another challenge in defining what to measure is not losing sight of the student's individual priorities. To prevent the IEP from becoming an alternate assessment plan instead of an *individualized* plan, the team can follow their usual prioritization process with considerations of the standards being a new component in this

Application:

Another critical essence reflected in several math standards in North Carolina is to *use and interpret data and graphs*. One way Kevin might do this is to self-monitor his work performance using small counting blocks to create an object bar graph. Can you think of another example?

process. Browder (2001) recommends an ecological assessment process to develop the IEP that includes reviewing prior performance, planning with the student and family, promoting self-determination, and using ecological inventories and situational assessments. The team then uses the priorities identified through these processes in reviewing the curriculum to select target skills for the IEP. By considering priorities like family and student preferences and the needs for current and future environments *first,* the development of links to the standards becomes meaningful for the student.

A second challenge is to target skills that set high expectations for the student, but also to set criteria for mastery within an IEP year. In responding to alternate assessment, professionals sometimes question how a student with complex challenges like limited physical movement or who is medically fragile can be expected to meet state standards. Browder and Martin (1986) described the challenge of developing an IEP for a student named Tommy with spastic quadriplegia who had medical complications. When they began to assess Tommy, the team had to begin by discovering any voluntary, observable response Tommy could make because it seemed that Tommy's only responses were involuntary muscle spasms. A mistake teams sometimes make in planning for students like Tommy is to define IEP goals that the professionals will do versus that the student will do. This type of goal setting expects little of students. For example, the IEP team could have written annual goals for Tommy like "tolerating having his face washed" or "brushing teeth with hand over hand guidance" or "listening to a story," none of which would require Tommy to exert any effort on his part. Instead, his teacher discovered what Tommy *could* do. He was able to click his tongue and move one hand slightly. From this, the teacher developed an IEP in which he learned to use his tongue click to communicate, make choices, and to operate switches with his hand movement. Teachers working with students like Tommy in the current era of standards-based reform can build on these responses by determining ways to link them to standards. For example, rather than only making a choice by clicking his tongue "yes," Tommy might learn to use his response to answer some specific, factual questions derived from general curriculum. He might also use switches and his choice responses to participate in general curriculum (for example, making choices in the context of a science experiment or using a switch to operate a cassette player to review a story in language arts).

The additional challenge is setting the criteria for performance. Should the student be expected to perform the response daily? Is it reasonable to expect the student to perform the

Application:

How could this passive objective be changed to an active objective: "Bob will tolerate hand over hand guidance to participate in a science lesson?" One possible change would be "In the context of a science lesson when asked 'What is this?', Bob will identify at least two objects or pictures that are key to the point of the lesson using his Touch Talker with a total of at least eight new science words mastered this quarter." Can you write a complete objective that would provide a different alternative for active participation?

response several times a day? Should the skill be generalized across settings and people? Establishing a level at which the skill is considered to be learned (that is, criteria of performance), as well as the student's ability to perform that task under different stimulus conditions (that is, generalization) are two measures that are critical to the process. In the previous example with Tommy, it would be important to specify the number of times that Tommy would activate the switch (for example, five times in succession without error or assistance) to increase the likelihood that the skill, activating the switch, was reliably in his repertoire and did not just happen by chance. It would also be important to define some measure of generalization, such as having Tommy activate the switch at the request of different people (for example, his mother or the assistant in the classroom) or having Tommy activate several types of switches, not just a Big Mac switch.

Redesigning Data Collection to Relate to Both the IEP and Alternate Assessment

Numerous resources are available on how to create data systems for students with severe disabilities (Alberto & Troutman, 1999; Browder, 2001; Snell & Brown, 2000). What is presented here are some of the ways data systems may change to meet the demands of alternate assessment requirements.

One of the important ways data systems may change is to include a self-determination focus. Browder and Lohrmann-O'Rourke (2001) describe how to promote self-determination in curriculum and assessment for students with severe disabilities. Three of their recommendations are to use preference assessment in selecting IEP skills, to include self-determination skills as IEP objectives, and to have students participate in their IEP process. Some states, like Kentucky, require documenting student involvement in the alternate assessment. Kleinert et al. (2001) give several examples of promoting self-determination that can be documented as part of an alternate assessment process. These include, for example, documenting student choicemaking and teaching students to manage their own daily schedules. These activities could be successfully accomplished by working with a buddy, using audiotapes/videotapes, or receiving systematic teacher prompting. For example, the student may select a particular item on a data collection sheet through eye gazing and then receive assistance from the teacher, the assistant in the class, or from a peer to circle the response that indicates this choice.

Another way that data collection may change is in the amount of team involvement needed. Some states require that students demonstrate performance across people or require parental input on how the skills are performed at home. Some of the recommendations given elsewhere in this book are applicable for planning this data collection. (See Chapters 6, 7, 8, 19). For example, it will be important that the whole team, including parents, help develop the IEP so that all are on the same page when it is time to document progress. The team's conversations can focus on settings and activities frequently used by the student, ensuring that the activities and settings are strategically linked to functional and general education content and determining access, likes, and need in the participation of these activities and settings. Similarly, it will be important that data sheets are developed so that multiple professionals and parents can use them.

The data collection system itself may need to be redeveloped to address criteria in the alternate assessment requirements. For example, North Carolina considers whether the student performs the skill consistently (mastery with maintenance), generalizes, and initiates. The Charlotte Alternate Assessment Model offers numerous examples of data sheets that address these criteria for student performance on their Web site: *www.UNCC.edu/aap*. Most of the data sheets available at this Web site reflect the methods of direct assessment described by Browder (2001), including task analytic assessment, repeated trial assessment, repeated opportunity assessment, frequency counts, duration recording, and cumulative recording.

An example of a specific task analysis data collection sheet from the Charlotte Alternate Assessment Model Web site is shown in Figure 4.1. This particular task analysis data collection form is designed for Joe, a student who is deaf and blind. Joe has a skill targeted in the personal home management domain for learning to pour a beverage from a thermos. As can be seen in Figure 4.1, the 12 steps for Joe's task analysis are listed on the form, along with the code for level of performance (independent through full physical); the standard; and the items of initiation, generalization, and the embedded skill of literacy. This skill is defined as an embedded skill for literacy because Joe will begin the task by selecting a cup from an object board to request a "drink" (See Figure 4.1).

Data collection systems may also change in that many alternate assessment formats require teachers to use *qualitative* as well as quantitative assessments. The data system shown in Figure 4.1, as well as others like repeated trial and frequency counts, are quantitative methods of data collection. They involve counting the students' responses in some way as they are performed. In contrast, many states use portfolios and other methods that require qualitative assessments. Salend (1998) describes some of the types of products that may be in these assessments. For example, work samples, awards and honors, cooperative learning products, and reports could all be used to assess portfolio objectives. Teachers may also need to use *rubrics* to evaluate student performance. A rubric is an established set of rules against which a product can be evaluated or scored. For example, a rubric could be developed for the student's use of a distinctive mark and name stamp for a signature. The rubric might consider criteria like legibility, proximity to the signature line, and level of assistance required to complete the signature.

Finally, teachers may need to use technology to keep up with the increased demand for data collection related to alternate assessment. Denham and Lahm (2001) have several suggestions for using technology to construct alternate portfolios. For example, single communication aids, switches of all kinds, and adaptive keyboards to create custom IntelliKeys (IntelliTools, 1996) overlays for each student to gain access to the computer may be needed.

Managing Alternate Assessment on an Ongoing Basis

A survey of teachers in the state of Kentucky revealed that they spent a significant amount of time outside of the instructional setting completing the alternate assessment portfolio required by their state. In contrast, the time spent on preparing the alternate assessment only minimally related to outcome scores (Kampfer, Horvath, Kleinert, & Kearns, 2001). The completion of alternate assessment can be an extremely time-consuming process that

FIGURE 4.1 *Task Analysis for Joe in the Domain of Personal and Home Management*

UNC CHARLOTTE ALTERNATE ASSESSMENT PROJECT

Task Analysis

Student: Joe

Portfolio: 09876543

Code:
  I   = Independent
  T   = Tactile cues
  PP = Partial physical
  FP = Full physical

Domain: Personal and Home Management

SubDomain: Home Living

Standard: During meal/break time, Joe will pour his beverage from a thermos with all steps of the task analysis correct.

Initiation: Grasp thermos without prompting.

Generalization: Variety of settings (i.e., classroom, cafeteria, work site).

Embedded Skill: Literacy (i.e., select cup from object board to request "drink").

	Dates:					
12. Stop when beverage touches fingers						
11. Pour beverage						
10. Tip beverage						
9. Grasp thermos						
8. Put finger on edge of cup						
7. Place thermal lid on table						
6. Unscrew thermal lid						
5. Grasp thermal lid						
4. Place cup on the table						
3. Unscrew cup from thermos						
2. Grasp cup						
1. Grasp thermos						
No. Independent responses:						
Where:						
With Whom:						

Anecdotal Notes:

may rob either instructional or personal time. Some school systems give teachers release time (for example, planning days) to respond to this new requirement, but, even with this planning time, the process needs to be organized to be doable in a typical school setting. Two important considerations for this organization are to follow a timeline and to incorporate alternate assessment in ongoing instruction.

In developing a timeline, teachers may want to consider a yearly calendar of goals and ways to incorporate assessment activities in the weekly schedule. The yearly calendar may target deadlines for developing data sheets, contacting parents, setting up student self-evaluation, and compiling information for school or state review. The weekly schedule will need to incorporate times to collect information on each standard to be reviewed for each student.

Collecting information on each standard will be easier if this assessment is incorporated in instruction. Clayton, Burdge, and Kleinert (2001) give six steps for embedding alternate assessment in daily instruction. These steps include (a) getting started, (b) developing data collection and monitoring sheets, (c) designing instructional strategies, (d) adapting materials, (e) embedding all of this into classroom routines, and (f) monitoring and revising the programs as necessary. In general, if data collected for the alternate assessment become part of the daily instructional routine, it will be not only more manageable, but also more meaningful for ongoing team decisions about progress.

Improving Student Performance

As is sometimes the case with students with severe disabilities, progress on performance objectives can be slow, and, in some instances, if measurement is not finely tuned or teaching is not effective, a teacher may not be able to show demonstrated change in behavior. On the other hand, in a "high stakes accountability system," it will be important to document progress. In an attempt to measure instructional gains appropriately, it is prudent to examine some key instructional variables that may affect outcomes like curriculum assess, data collections systems, and instructional effectiveness (for example, use of assistive technology, fading prompts, and student motivation).

Why Student Outcomes May Be Disappointing

Browder, Davis, Fallin, and Griffin (2001) describe six variables that may influence student outcomes on the alternate assessment. Noninstructional variables may include the technical quality of the alternate assessment; the resources available, like curriculum examples for extended standards; time to complete the assessment; and student instability, like moving school systems and medical problems. In contrast, some key instructional variables may also influence outcomes, including curriculum access, data collection systems, and instructional effectiveness. For students to achieve expected outcomes, they need to be taught the curriculum that relates to the standards, have assessment that can capture student's progress toward these standards, and have teaching that is powerful enough to achieve progress.

Did the Student Receive Instruction on Curriculum Related to the Standards?

The first question teams may want to ask when outcomes are disappointing was whether students were taught the curriculum that relates to the standards. Thousand (1986) identifies four ways students with significant disabilities can participate in general activities. Students with significant disabilities can participate in activities the same way as other students; can participate in the same activities, but at a different level in that subject than other students; can participate in the same activities, but with different educational goals that are embedded into the activities; or can participate in different activities with different goals, but related to the current classroom activities.

Kearns (2001) has adapted Thousand's (1986) suggestions to the four ways students may learn state standards and access the general curriculum. Kearns suggests that students with significant disabilities can be helped through a hierarchy that builds on previous steps: (a) access skills in the content activities, (b) incorporate the critical function, (c) use an alternate form, or (d) teach the standard as written. Part III, Chapters 9–12, and Part IV, Chapter 20, in this book describe numerous ways (for example, academic subjects, oral language and literacy development, and environment, material, and instructional modification) to access the general curriculum.

When outcomes on alternate assessment are disappointing, it may be due to the lack of definition of what the student was to do to meet state standards. As described earlier in the section on designing assessment that captures student progress, the best vehicle for clarifying what is expected is the IEP process. The team needs to consider standards when developing the goals and objectives of the IEP so that the IEP is standards-based as well as individualized.

Was Data Collection an Authentic Representation of Student Performance?

If the IEP and daily instruction have addressed state standards, another question to consider when outcomes are disappointing is whether the assessment itself is to blame. Have the methods used to assess the student captured his or her actual progress and performance? Teachers often have some flexibility in determining how to document the student's performance. One way to better capture performance is to use multiple methods to assess performance. In addition to data collection, the teacher may want to keep anecdotal notes, student work samples, pictures of the student performing skills, or video clips of performance. As Siegel-Causey and Allinder (1998) note, using multiple formats can make assessment more authentic of student performance.

In some cases, outcomes may be outstanding, but not truly representative of student performance. Because most alternate assessments formats rely heavily on teacher judgment, the possibility exists for observer bias. One consideration is to document reliability for data collection. A convenient way to judge the accuracy and repeatability of data collection is to use interrater reliability or interobserver reliability (Alberto & Troutman, 1999). In conducting interrater reliability measures, the teacher asks another individual (for example, a paraprofessional) who is trained in the procedures or instructional techniques that are being assessed to evaluate the outcomes simultaneously. If, for example, a student is being trained using a specific task analysis, the teacher and the paraprofessional both collect data while the student performs the skill. Afterward, the teacher compares the two data sheets and uses a formula to determine the agreements of the two scores compared to the total number of steps being assessed (that is, Agreements/Agreements + Disagreements X100). Typically, only about 20 percent of the observations will require a simultaneous evaluation, and agreement should be at least 80 percent. Interrater reliability adds to the believability of the data because two people are verifying that the step was performed correctly without error or assistance.

Can Teaching Incorporate More Effective Strategies?

A third consideration is the use of more effective strategies to enhance student learning of standards-based objectives. One way to enhance student performance is through the use of technology. Denham, Bennett, Edyburn, Lahm, and Kleinert (2001) suggest that assistive technology can be used to help students plan, monitor, and evaluate their own performance in the portfolio process. For example, alternative or expanded keyboards and custom overlays using IntelliTools (2000a,b) software adaptation Intellikeys can be used as ways to increase student participation and to exert greater control over their learning. Students may also be able to perform skills better using low-tech assistive technology like counting jigs, picture cues, and audiotapes.

Another consideration is to use precise methods of prompt fading and feedback so that students perform responses without teacher assistance. Several resources have described options for prompt fading including Chapter 19 in this book. Several experts have also provided reviews of some of the systematic methods of prompt fading that can be considered (Billingsley, 1998; Schuster et al., 1998; Wolery & Gast, 1984). For example, constant time delay, progressive time delay, simultaneous prompting, system of least prompts, most-to-least hierarchy, and graduated guidance are all prompting systems that have been employed effectively to provide extra stimulus cues to help a learner with significant cognitive disabilities learn functional skills (Cipani & Spooner, 1994; Snell & Brown, 2000; Westling & Fox, 2000).

Another way to make teaching more effective is to increase student motivation to achieve criteria. Incorporating student choicemaking during instruction or using materials and activities based on student preference has been shown to enhance skill performance and to decrease problem behavior (Kern et al., 1998). Some other behavioral strategies to increase motivation include the application of reinforcement schedules (Ferster & Skinner, 1957; Reynolds, 1975). Schedules of reinforcement indicate how many and what patterns of student responding will be rewarded. Briefly, there are two overarching types of schedules: (a) interval schedules and (b) ratio schedules. Interval schedules are based on the passage of time and include the categories of fixed (for example, FI 5 min) and variable intervals (for example, VI 10 min). Ratio schedules are based on the execution of a specified number of responses and include the categories of fixed (for example, FR 5) and variable (for example, VR 10). By beginning with a fixed, continuous schedule of reinforcement (for example, praise after each correct response) and fading to a variable ratio of reinforcement (for example, intermittent praise), student responding may be maintained. One of the most important types of reinforcement is which occurs in the typical setting. If performing the skill produces some desired outcome, the student is more likely to use it again. For example, if a student who is motivated by attention is able to share a work product with the teacher or learn the skill while working with a peer, performance may be enhanced. Students who are motivated by special activities may be motivated to learn skills that provide direct access to these (for example, choicemaking or matching numbers to find room for band).

Whatever strategies are used, the key is to use ongoing data to make decisions to improve instruction. This is called formative evaluation because data are used for ongoing quality enhancement of the program. Alternate assessment is sometimes viewed as a form of summative evaluation in which data are used to evaluate what has occurred. Although summative evaluation helps to determine outcome criteria like whether students have met standards, it does not create the opportunity to make changes if goals are not being met. By linking ongoing data collection to the alternate assessment, the process becomes both formative and summative. Instructional changes can be made to enhance student progress throughout the school year so that, by the end, the student achieves the expected standard.

Summary

Not since the advent of IEPs has there been a legal requirement with the potential to impact educational programs for students with severe disabilities like alternate assessment. Although the IEP addressed students' need for an individualized program, IDEA 1997 ensures that the students also receive instruction related to standards states and local school systems set for all students. Because each state has developed its own approach to alternate assessment and these formats vary widely, it is important to research the requirements for a specific state. This chapter has provided a list of five questions that can be used when searching the state's Web site or interviewing professionals to obtain information on a state's alternate assessment requirements.

Although teachers have been assessing students with severe disabilities for many years, alternate assessment may require some rethinking of these assessment procedures. In particular, data collection may need to be redeveloped to address alternate assessment criteria and broadened to include all team participants and qualitative considerations. When student outcomes are disappointing, the planning team should consider whether the student has had access to curriculum related to the standards, if assessment has been sufficient to capture student progress, and whether more effective instructional strategies would be appropriate. Alternate assessment has the potential to raise expectations for students with severe disabilities to achieve higher standards if used as a tool to define these expectations and to document achievement.

References _____

Alberto, P. A., & Troutman, A. C. (1999). *Applied behavior analysis for teachers* (5th ed.). Upper Saddle River, NJ: Prentice-Hall.

Allington, R., & McGill-Franzen, A. (1992). Unintended effects of educational reform in New York. *Educational Policy, 6*(4), 397–414.

Billingsley, F. F. (1998). Behaving independently: Considerations in fading instructor assistance. In A. Hilton & R. Ringlaben (Eds.), *Best and promising practices in developmental disabilities* (pp. 157–168). Austin, TX: Pro-ED, Inc.

Blatt, B., & Kaplan, F. (1966). *Christmas in purgatory: A photographic essary on mental retardation.* Boston: Allyn & Bacon.

Boundy, K. (2000). Including students with disabilities in standards based educational reform. *TASH Newsletter, 26*(4), 4–5, 21.

Browder, D. M. (Ed.) (2001). *Curriculum and assessment for students with moderate and severe disabilites.* New York: Guilford Press.

Browder, D. M., & Bambara, L. (2000). Home and community. In M. E. Snell & F. Brown (Eds.), *Instruction of students with severe disabilities* (5th ed.) (pp. 543–589). Upper Saddle River, NJ: Merrill.

Browder, D. M., Davis, S., Fallin, K., & Griffin, S. (2001). *Improving student outcomes on alternate assessment.* Manuscript in preparation.

Browder, D. M., & Lohrmann-O'Rourke, S. (2001). Promoting self-determination in planning and instruction. In D. Browder (Ed.), *Curriculum and assessment for students with moderate and severe disabilities* (pp. 148–178). New York: Guilford Press.

Browder, D. M., & Martin, D. K. (1986). A new curriculum for Tommy. *TEACHING Exceptional Children, 18*, 261–265.

Brown, L., Branston, M. B., Hamre-Neitupski, S., Pumpian, I., Certo, N., & Gruenewald, L. (1979). A strategy for developing chronological-age-approprite and functional curricular content for severely handicapped adolescents and young adults. *Journal of Special Education, 13*, 81–90.

Cipani, E. C., & Spooner, F. (Eds.). (1994). *Curricular and instructional approaches for persons with severe disabilities.* Boston: Allyn & Bacon.

Chatham Educational Consultants, Inc. (2000). *Wyoming comprehensive assessment system: Alternate assessment handbook.* Cheyenne, WY: Wyoming Department of Education.

Clayton J., Burdge, M., & Kleinert, H. L. (2001). Integrating alternate assessment with ongoing instruction. In H. L. Kleinert & J. F. Kearns (Eds.), *Alternate assessment: Measuring outcomes and supports for students with disabilities.* Baltimore: Paul H. Brookes Publishing Co.

Delaware Department of Education. (July, 2000). *The standards for functional life curriculum.* Dover, DE: Author.

Denham, A., Bennett, D. E., Edyburn, D. L., Lahm, E. A., & Kleinert, H. L. (2001). Implementing technology to demonstrate higher levels of learning. In H. L. Kleinert & J. F. Kearns (Eds.), *Alternate assessment: Measuring outcomes and supports for students with disabilities.* Baltimore: Paul H. Brookes Publishing Co.

Denham, A., & Lahm, E. A. (2001). Using technology to construct alternate portfolios of students with moderate and severe disabilities. *TEACHING Exceptional Children, 33*(5), 10–17.

Education Commission of the States. (1997). *Accountability: State policies.* Denver, CO: Education Commission of the States. Retrieved November 14, 2000, at *www.ecs.org/ecs/24aa.htm.*

Elliott, J., Ysseldyke, J. E., Thurlow, M. L., & Erickson, E. (1998). What about assessment and accountability? *TEACHING Exceptional Children, 31*(1), 20–27.

Erickson, R. N., Thurlow, M. L., & Thor, K. (1995). *State special education outcomes, 1994.* Minneapolis: University of Minnesota, National Center on Educational Outcomes. (ERIC Document Reproduction Service No. ED404 799).

Ferster, C. B., & Skinner, B. F. (1957). *Schedules of reinforcement.* New York: Appleton-Century-Crofts.

Ford, A., Davern, L., & Schnorr, R. (2001). Learners with significant disabilities: Curricular relevance in an era of standards-based reform. *Remedial and Special Education, 22*, 214–222.

Forest, M., & Lusthaus, E. (1989). Promoting educational quality for all students: Circles and MAPS. In S. Stainback, W. Stainback, & M. Forest (Eds.), *Education for all students in the mainstream of regular education* (pp. 43–58). Baltimore: Paul H. Brookes Publishing Co.

Goals 2000 (1994). Goals 2000: Educate America act. Retrieved July 16, 2002, at *www.ed.gov/legislation/GOALS2000/The Act/*

Haring, N. G., & Pious, C. (1976). Future directions in work with severely and profoundly handicapped persons: An overview. In N. G. Haring & L. J. Brown (Eds.), *Teaching the severely handicapped: Volume I.* New York: Grune & Stratton.

Hill, J., Bird, A., & Dughman, R. (Eds.). (2000). *An alternate assessment system for students with disabilities.* Lincoln, NE: Nebraska Department of Education.

Hilliard, A.G. (2000). Excellence in education versus high-stakes standardized testing. *Journal of Teacher Education, 51*, 293–304.

IDEA (1997). Individuals with disabilities act amendments of 1997. Retrieved July 16, 2002, at *www.ed.gov./offices/OSERS/Policy/IDEA/the_law. html.*

IntelliTools (1996). Overlay maker [Computer software]. Novato, CA: Author.

IntelliTools (2000a). IntelliKeys. [online]. Available at *www.intellitools.com/index.html.*

IntelliTools (2000b). Overlay maker. [online]. Available at *www.intellitools.com/index.html.*

Kampfer, S. H., Horvath, L. S., Kleinert, H. L., & Kearns, J. F. (2001). Teachers' perceptions of one state's alternate assessment: Implications for practice and preparation. *Exceptional Children, 67,* 361–374.

Kearns, J. F. (2001). Helping students with significant disabilities gain access to general curriculum standards. In H. L. Kleinert & J. F. Kearns (Eds.), *Alternate assessment: Measuring outcomes and supports for students with disabilities* (pp. 29–48). Baltimore: Paul H. Brookes Publishing Co.

Kern, L., Vorndran, C. M., Hilt, A., Ringdahl, J. E., Adelman, B. E., & Dunlap, G. (1998). Choice as an intervention to improve behavior: A review of the literature. *Journal of Behavioral Education, 8,* 151–169.

Kleinert, H. L., Denham, A., Gooneck, V. B., Clayton, J., Burdge, M., Kearns, J. F., et al. (2001). Systematically teaching the components of self-determination. In H. L. Kleinert & J. F. Kearns (Eds.), *Alternate assessment: Measuring outcomes and supports for students with disabilities* (pp. 93–133). Baltimore: Paul H. Brookes Publishing Co.

Kleinert, H. L., & Thurlow, M. L. (2001). An introduction to alternate assessment. In H. L. Kleinert & J. F. Kearns (Eds.), *Alternate assessment: Measuring outcomes and supports for students with disabilities* (pp. 1–12). Baltimore: Paul H. Brookes Publishing Co.

National Center on Educational Outcomes. (2001). *Crosswalk of Title 1 and IDEA assessment and accountability provisions for students with disabilities.* Minneapolis, MN: University of Minnesota, National Center on Educational Outcomes. Retrieved November 6, 2001, at *education.umn.edu/NCEO/OnlinePubs/Crosswalk .htm.*

North Carolina Department of Public Instruction (2001). *North Carolina alternate assessment portfolio.* Raleigh, NC: Author.

O'Brien, J. (1987). A guide to lifestyle planning: Using the activities catalog to integrate service and natural support systems. In B. Wilcox & G. T. Bellamy (Eds.), *A comprehensive guide to the activities catalog: An alternative curriculum for youth and adults with severe disabilities* (pp. 175–179). Baltimore: Paul H. Brookes Publishing Co.

Parkes, J. (2000). The relationship between the reliability and cost of performance assessments. *Education Policy Analysis Archives, 8*(16). Retrieved November 14, 2000, at *epaa.asu.edu/epaa/v8n16/.*

Pennsylvania Alternate System of Assessment Project Leadership Team (2001). *Pennsylvania alternate system of assessment.* Pittsburgh, PA: University of Pittsburg.

Quenemoen, R. F., Lehr, C. A., Thurlow, M. L., & Massanari, C. B. (2001). *Students with disabilities in standards-based assessment and accountability systems: Emerging issues, strategies, and recommendations* (Synthesis Report 37). Minneapolis, MN: University of Minnesota, National Center on Educational Outcomes. Retrieved *July 16, 2002* from *education.umn.edu/ nceo/OnlinePubs/Synthesis37.html.*

Reynolds, G. S. (1975). *A primer of operant conditioning.* Glenview, IL: Scott, Foresman.

Ryndak, D. L., & Alper, S. (Eds.). (1996). *Curriculum content for students with moderate and severe disabilities in inclusive settings.* Boston: Allyn & Bacon.

Salend, S. J. (1998). Using portfolios to assess student performance. *TEACHING Exceptional Children, 31*(2), 36–42.

Schuster, J. W., Morse, T. F., Ault, M. J., Doyle, P. M., Crawford, M. R., & Wolery, M. (1998). Constant time delay with chained tasks: A review of the literature. *Education and Treatment of Children, 21,* 74–106.

Shriner, J. E. (2000). Legal perspectives on school outcome assessments for students with disabilities. *Journal of Special Education, 33,* 232–239.

Siegel-Causey, E., & Allinder, R. M. (1998). Using alternate assessment for students with severe disabilities: Alignment with best practices. *Education and Training in Mental Retardation and Developmental Disabilities, 33,* 168–178.

Snell, M. E., & Brown, F. (Eds.). (2000). *Instruction of students with severe disabilities* (5th ed.). Upper Saddle River, NJ: Merrill.

Tashie, C., Jorgensen, C., Shapiro-Barnard, S., Martin, J., & Schuh, M. (1996, September). High school inclusion: Strategies barriers. *TASH Newsletter, 22*(9), 19–22.

Thompson, S., & Thurlow, M. (2001). *2001 State special education outcomes: A report on state activities at the beginning of a new decade.* Minneapolis, MN: University of Minnesota, National Center on

Educational Outcomes. Retrieved July 16, 2002, from *www.education.umn.edu/NCEO/OnlinePubs/2001StateReport.html.*

Thousand, J. (1986). *The homecoming model: Educating students who present intensive educational challenges within regular education environments.* Burlington: University of Vermont.

Turner, M. D., Baldwin, L., Kleinert, H. L., & Kearns, J. F. (2000). The relation of a statewide alternate assessment for students with severe disabilities to other measures of instructional effectiveness. *Journal of Special Education, 34,* 69–76.

Vandercook, T., York, J., & Forest, M. (1989). The McGill Action Planning System (MAPS): A strategy for building the vision. *The Journal of the Association for Persons with Severe Handicaps, 14,* 205–215.

Vanderwood, M., Ysseldyke, J. E., & Thurlow, M. L. (1993). *Consensus building: A process for selecting educational outcomes and indicators* (Outcomes and Indicators No. 2). Minneapolis: University of Minnesota, National Center on Educational Outcomes.

Westling, D. L., & Fox, L. (2000). *Teaching students with*

severe disabilities (2nd ed.). Upper Saddle River, NJ: Merrill.

White, O. R. (1980). Adaptive performance objectives: Form versus function. In W. Sailor, B. Wilcox, & L. Brown (Eds.), *Methods of instruction for severely handicapped students* (pp. 47–70). Baltimore: Paul H. Brookes Publishing Co.

White, O. R., & Haring, N. G. (1980). *Exceptional Teaching* (2nd ed.). Columbus, OH: Charles E. Merrill.

Wolery, M., & Gast, D. L. (1984). Effective and efficient procedures for the transfer of stimulus control. *Topics in Early Childhood Special Educaiton, 4,* 57–77.

Wolk, R. A. (1998). Education's high-stakes gamble. *Education Week, 18*(15), 48.

Ysseldyke, J. E., Krentz, J., Elliott, J. L., Thurlow, M. L., Erickson, R., & Moore, M. (1998). *A comprehensive framework for educational accountability for all students.* Minneapolis: University of Minnesota, National Center on Educational Outcomes.

Ysseldyke, J., & Olsen, K. (1999). Putting alternate assessments into practice: What to measure and possible sources of data. *Exceptional Children, 63,* 175–185.

Endnote

1. The authors express their gratitude to Lynn Ahlgrim-Delzell, Project Director for the Field Initiated Research Grant on Alternate Assessment at UNC Charlotte for assistance in locating these examples.

5

An Ecological Approach to Identifying Curriculum Content for Inclusive Settings

Sandra Alper

Objectives

After completing this chapter, the reader will be able to:

1. Describe those to whom the term, "*moderate to severe disabilities*," applies.
2. Describe the major learning characteristics most commonly observed in students who have disabilities.
3. Describe the developmental, preacademic skills, and functional academic skills approaches to curriculum development.
4. Discuss the major features of the ecological approach to curriculum development for learners with severe disabilities.
5. Identify curriculum domains based on natural settings.
6. Conduct task analyses of skills required in natural training settings.
7. Develop an ecological inventory.

Key Terms

Community-referenced curriculum
Curriculum
Developmentally young
Discrepancy analysis
Domain
Ecological assessment
Ecological inventory

Environment
Generalization
Learning rate
Medical model
Mental age
Preacademic
Prevocational
Readiness

Skill synthesis
Social consensus
Social validation
Subdomain
Subenvironment
Subjective validation
Task analysis

Students who have moderate to severe disabilities are a diverse, challenging, and rewarding group of individuals with whom to work. They have so many unique individual qualities that to group them all together under one diagnostic label can be misleading. Generally speaking, the term, "*moderate to severe disabilities,*" applies to children, adolescents, and adults who have been labeled moderately mentally retarded, severely and profoundly handicapped, autistic, deaf, blind, or severely emotionally disturbed. As noted in Chapter 1, these individuals usually have moderate to severe levels of intellectual impairments in addition to one or more other types of disabilities. They represent approximately 1 percent of the general population. If any generality can be made about these individuals, it is that the only characteristic they have in common is their need for support and services from others (Falvey, 1989; Sailor & Guess, 1983).

Learning Characteristics of Students with Moderate to Severe Disabilities

Students who have been labeled with moderate to severe disabilities demonstrate a number of unique learning characteristics. First, they tend to learn at a significantly slower rate than do their age peers who do not have disabilities. Zeaman and House (1963) first demonstrated that students with moderate levels of mental retardation tend to respond to new problems in a trial-and-error fashion. They take longer than their peers without disabilities to focus on the relevant stimulus dimensions of a task and find the solution. Because of this difficulty, they may learn less material (Gaylord-Ross & Holvoet, 1985).

Second, students with severe disabilities experience difficulty in maintaining the skills and knowledge they have acquired (Homer, Dunlap, & Koegel, 1988). They require frequent opportunities to practice new academic and functional skills. Curriculum must focus on skills that they need to use frequently in school, at home, and in the community.

Third, students with severe disabilities often have great difficulty in generalizing skills learned in one setting to a different situation (Haring, 1988; Stokes & Baer, 1977). A student who learns to use money to make a small purchase in the school cafeteria, for example, cannot be expected to perform the same skills in the grocery store or at McDonald's. These settings often vary along a number of dimensions, including which persons are present, cues, materials, and consequences. Difficulties in generalization experienced by students with moderate to severe disabilities makes training in natural settings, or the settings in which the skills taught are actually performed in daily life, imperative.

Finally, students with moderate to severe disabilities find it extremely hard to combine skills that have been taught separately. For example, ordering a meal in a restaurant requires reading, math, social, and communication skills. Educators cannot teach these skills separately and in different contexts and then hope that the student will be able to synthesize them when confronted with a functional task. Thus, teaching functional skills in the natural contexts in which they are performed is necessary.

After reviewing the learning characteristics of students with moderate to severe disabilities, Alper and Ryndak (1992) concluded that, despite their difficulties, there is little empirical support for educating these students in segregated settings or in artificial or simulated situations. Rather, they learn more efficiently if taught within the contexts in which they will have to function when not in school, that is, in the same settings frequented by persons without disabilities.

It should be obvious from the previous discussion that students with moderate to severe disabilities present a number of challenges for educators. The discussion now turns to identifying curriculum content for these students in inclusive settings. First, we define curriculum. Then, several traditional approaches to developing curriculum are reviewed. Finally, the ecological approach for identification of curriculum content is presented, along with several examples.

Curriculum

The term "*curriculum*" often brings to mind a purchased package of materials, objectives, and activities that guides the teacher's instruction. Rainforth, York, and Macdonald (1992) suggested that this view is too narrow, however, because it neglects the students, parents, and other providers of services to students with moderate to severe disabilities. They favored Eisner's (1979) perspective from which curriculum is viewed as a theoretical model reflecting beliefs about an appropriate scope and sequence of education.

The approach used throughout this text views curriculum as consisting of several distinct phases (cf., Snell, 1987). These phases each require instructional decisions by the educational team members. The phases, or instructional decisions, involved in curriculum development are following:

1. What outcomes are desired for the student? Outcomes appropriate for the individual student are determined by consideration of the settings in which it is desirable for a student to function after schooling. These outcomes are basically similar to those typically achieved by students without disabilities (for example, to live and work in the community, to participate in social and recreational activities with friends, or to be able to make choices about one's own life).
2. What skills must the student learn in order to achieve those outcomes? To work in the community the student needs to learn the vocational and related skills necessary to get and keep a specific job. To maintain friendships, the student needs to learn certain social and communication skills.
3. How should those skills be taught and by whom? Based on the empirical literature on best teaching practices (Falvey, 1989; Snell, 1987), what specific instructional strategies are needed for this student to learn?
4. Where should instruction take place? What training settings located in school and in the community are appropriate? The student's learning difficulties and the desired outcomes are both considered here.
5. How should the curriculum be evaluated? What skills can the student perform independently in nonschool environments? Have the outcomes been reached?

Traditional Approaches to Curriculum Development

Psychologists and educators first became aware of the learning capabilities of persons with moderate to severe disabilities in the 1960s. At that time, much of the early experimental work on operant conditioning and applied behavior analysis was conducted with participants who resided in institutions (see Mercer & Snell, 1977, for an excellent review). Before that time, persons with moderate to severe disabilities who were institutionalized were cared for but were thought to have very little ability to learn new skills.

Three traditional approaches to developing curriculum content for persons with moderate to severe disabilities in educational programs are (1) the developmental model, (2) the preacademic skills or readiness approach, and (3) the functional academic skills approach.

Developmental Model

The developmental model of curriculum was based on theories of normal child development (Gesell & Amatruda, 1947). Normal children tend to acquire gross-motor, fine-motor, perceptual, cognitive, social, and communication skills in a fairly predictable sequence (for example, most children babble before they use words and roll over and crawl before they team to walk). Using this model, normal developmental sequences of skills were taught to students with disabilities (Bricker & Bricker, 1974).

The developmental model of curriculum was also based, at least in part, on early conceptions of students with moderate to severe disabilities as eternal children. Indeed, one of the first textbooks that addressed the education of this population was entitled *Training the Developmentally Young* (Stephens, 1971).

The developmental model is essentially a norm-referenced approach based on the normal development of young children who do not have disabilities. Specific skills and the order in which to teach them are specified for the teacher. It was originally assumed that teaching these same sequences of behaviors to students with disabilities could help them to overcome many of their delayed developmental disabilities.

The developmental approach to curriculum development, while appropriate for many young children, has a number of disadvantages for students with moderate to severe disabilities. First, strict adherence to a normal pattern of skill development can preclude an individual being taught more functional skills. Rainforth, York, and Macdonald (1992) noted that some educators and therapists have spent years trying to teach the next skills in the normal developmental sequence. As a result, more useful and functional skills have not been taught because they are presumed to be too developmentally advanced.

A second disadvantage of applying the developmental model to curriculum development for students with moderate to severe disabilities is that it encourages the use of activities and materials appropriate for infants and young children, but inappropriate for adolescents and adults (Wilcox & Bellamy, 1982). This model, with its emphasis on the skills developed by normal young children, can limit the opportunity to learn more age-appropriate and functional skills required by adolescents and adults, such as vocational and community access skills. The lack of these skills can lead to perceptions of incompetence and lowered expectations for these individuals by others (Bates, Morrow, Pancsofar, & Sedlak, 1984).

Third, curricula based on normal sequences of development do not provide for teaching functional response alternatives. A number of authors have shown how tasks can be modified so that students with moderate to severe disabilities can participate (Brown et al., 1979; Falvey, 1989; Snell, 1987; Wilcox & Bellamy, 1982). For example, a student who cannot count change, read, or write can still be taught to push the cart in the supermarket, locate desired items to be purchased, and pay for them using only one-dollar bills. Rainforth, York, and Macdonald (1992) pointed out that curriculum based on normal sequences of development do not reference the functions and contexts that confront the student in daily life in the community, at home, and at school.

Basic Academic Skills Approach

Closely related to the developmental model approach to curriculum development is the basic academic skills approach. Wilcox and Bellamy (1982) described this model in detail. The basic skills approach, according to these authors, assumes that normal behavior and development are based on a group of core skills. These core skills are those typically taught to children without disabilities in the early elementary years (for example, reading, arithmetic, and written communication). Objectives such as using money, telling time, reading, and writing a story are analyzed into their component academic skills.

Wilcox and Bellamy (1982) pointed out a number of disadvantages in applying this approach to developing curriculum for students with severe disabilities. First, the curriculum is primarily concentrated on the traditional academic "three Rs." Nonacademic skills that students with disabilities need to master, such as making a bed, cooking, ordering food in a restaurant, and appropriate social skills, may be neglected. Second, the academic skills are often taught in isolation. Reading, arithmetic, and writing are often taught in separate time periods of the school day with separate materials and tasks, yet shopping for groceries requires that the student be able to perform several different skills within the same task. In addition, there is no guarantee that the student with moderate to severe disabilities will be able to generalize skills learned in isolation to the functional context in which they are actually performed in daily life. Third, the basic academic skills taught may be different from those needed by the student with disabilities to perform a functional task in a natural context. This is particularly the case in situations in which there is more than one way to perform the functional objective. For example, students learning to use money may team to count by ones, fives, tens, and so on. Making a purchase in a store, however, may be accomplished by a student with disabilities who has learned to count only one-dollar bills (Test, Howell, Burkhart, & Beroth, 1993).

Functional Curriculum

Many special educators have adopted a functional-skills approach to developing curriculum for students with severe disabilities. Within this approach, functional skills that are performed in daily life are task-analyzed into a sequence of observable and measurable responses. Tasks such as washing dishes, riding the bus, ordering a meal in a restaurant, and many other functional skills performed at home, at work, at school, and in other community settings are task-analyzed and taught.

The functional-skills approach has several advantages over developmental approaches for students who experience moderate to severe disabilities. First, the curriculum is based on functional and age-appropriate skills needed by the student in a number of school and nonschool settings within the community. Learning to perform these skills enables the student to perform more independently in a variety of settings and often raises the expectations of others who observe the student performing in a competent manner. A second advantage of the functional-skills approach is that many of the skills taught are performed by persons who do not have disabilities. Learning to perform many of the same day-to-day tasks performed by people without disabilities increases opportunities for integration and social interaction. Third, the use of task analysis as a strategy to identify specific responses to be taught facilitates individualization. A particular task may be analyzed into any number of discrete steps, based on the unique strengths and weaknesses of the student.

Rainforth, York, and Macdonald (1992) identified one major disadvantage of the functional-skills approach. According to these authors, the functional-skills approach lacks a clear organizational framework. Because there are no universal criteria for determining what skills are functional and relevant for a particular individual, the potential exists for idiosyncratic curricular content.

Alternative Terms

Two alternative terms that are related to this discussion are "functional assessment" and "life skills assessment." The term "functional assessment" has at least two other meanings in the special education literature. First, the term has been used to describe the procedure in which the function a behavior serves is identified through observations of antecedents and consequences to that behavior. This procedure is used in planning positive behavioral support. The term has also been used to refer to the process of identifying the level of mental health functioning of individuals with severe mental illness or the physical functioning of individuals with cerebral palsy (Browder, 2001). The term "life skills assessment" is related to, but may not fully characterize ecological assessment. Ecological assessment may include curriculum planning based on general education environments and academic content in addition to functional skills.

The term "ecological assessment" comes from the focus on a student's environments in conducting planning. Brown et al. (1979) used the term "ecological inventory" to describe how to generate curriculum priorities by surveying a student's current and future environments. These inventories have been primarily applied to the domains of daily living, such as the community, home, and work, but can also be applied to general education contexts (Ryndak & Alper, 1996). The term "ecological assessment" is used to refer to assessments based on these inventories.

The Ecological Inventory Approach to Identifying Curricular Content

The ecological approach to identifying curricular content for students with severe disabilities was developed in response to at least two situations. First, the more traditional models of curriculum posed a number of disadvantages for teachers and students, as previously discussed. Second, educators and parents recognized the need for curriculum revisions when the results of several follow-up studies of special education graduates were published (Frank, Sitlington, Cooper, & Cool, 1990; Hasazi et al., 1985; Mithaug, Horiuchi, & Fanning, 1985; Wehman, Kregel, & Seyfarth, 1985). These follow-up data revealed that students with disabilities were not making a successful transition from school to adult life in the community. Instead, they experienced high rates of unemployment, segregation from their chronological age peers, and, in some cases, stayed at home with no meaningful activity for long periods of time.

Educators began to discuss what outcomes for students with moderate to severe disabilities were desirable after graduation and how curriculum might be designed to meet them. Wilcox and Bellamy (1982) synthesized the literature on quality of life, the value of competence and independence, the value of work, and normalization. They proposed three dimensions with which the adult lives of persons with moderate to severe disabilities might be assessed to evaluate the success of schooling. These dimensions were (1) degree of participation in community activities and organizations, (2) degree of independence or extent of reliance upon others, and (3) productivity or the extent to which one is involved in paid and unpaid work.

Consistent with these three dimensions, Brown and his colleagues (1979) described an ecological inventory approach. Ecology refers to the interrelationships between people and the environment. The ecological approach to curriculum is unique in that it emphasizes the stimulus features of specific settings in which people are expected to function and the importance of conducting training in those settings. The term *"inventory"* refers to the process of systematically analyzing natural settings in the community, school, and at work to identify the skills needed for one to function independently in those settings.

Identifying Curriculum Through the Ecological Inventory

Lou Brown and his colleagues (1979) at the University of Wisconsin originally described the ecological approach as centered on four areas of the curriculum, or domains: community, vocation, community access, and recreation-leisure (see Falvey [1989] and Browder [2001] for an excellent discussion of curriculum development within each of these domains). The domains represent basic areas of day-to-day life for all people. York and Vandercook (1991) first recommended that school be considered a fifth domain because it represents such a substantial part of the daily lives of all children and youth.

The steps in identifying curricular content using the ecological inventory approach developed by Brown and his coworkers (1979) are the following:

1. Select the domain of choice (for example, school).
2. Identify environments within the domain in which the student needs to learn to function (for example, homeroom classroom, lunchroom, bathroom, or playground).
3. Select subenvironments that are of priority for the student (for example, the story-time area of the classroom or the cafeteria line).
4. Identify activities within each subenvironment in which the student is to be included (for example, listening to the teacher read a story and then discussing it with other students, standing in line in the cafeteria, selecting a place to sit down and eat lunch, or washing hands after using the bathroom).
5. Task-analyze the priority activities into their component skills.

Examples of ecological inventories developed for students of three different ages are shown in Figures 5.1, 5.2, and 5.3.

Second, the ecological inventory approach fosters local referencing. Many packaged curricula containing elaborate sets of objectives and activities have been published. Two problems are often present when using these programs. The skills required to ride the bus, use local recreation facilities, or shop vary from community to community. The skills necessary to use local transportation in New York City, are very different from those required in Columbia, Missouri. Even in situations where the skills needed to perform a task are the same in two different geographic areas, local standards and performance expectations may vary (Wilcox & Bellamy, 1982). The ecological approach focuses on the skills needed by students to function in settings they must frequent in their own community and neighborhood. The third major feature of the ecological inventory is that skills identified to be taught are determined to be functional and relevant through social validation (Kazdin, 1982).

FIGURE 5.1 *Ecological Inventory for Elementary School.*

Domain: Domestic

Environment: Home

Subenvironment: Bedroom

Skill: Dressing in the morning

Task Analysis:

1. Put on clean underwear.
2. Put on socks.
3. Put on shirt.
4. Put on pants.
5. Fasten pants.
6. Put on shoes.
7. Tie or fasten shoes.
8. Look in mirror to check and make sure everything's done.

FIGURE 5.2 *Ecological Inventory for Skills at the Middle School Level.*

Domain: Domestic

Environment: Home

Subenvironment: Kitchen

Skill: Make macaroni and cheese from box

Task Analysis:

1. Ask permission to make macaroni and cheese.
2. Gather materials: measuring cup, large sauce pan, box of macaroni-and-cheese dinner, stick margarine, milk, wooden spoon, drainer, and large bowl. (Egg timer optional.)
3. Using the measuring cup, measure six cups of water into large sauce pan and place on stove.
4. Turn on correct stove burner.
5. Wait until water begins to boil.
6. Pour macaroni into pot of boiling water and stir with wooden spoon until macaroni is soft. (Could use egg timer set at 7 minutes.)
7. Turn off correct burner.
8. Use hot pad to remove macaroni pot from stove and slowly pour the macaroni into the drainer.
9. Pour drained macaroni into large bowl.
10. Using the lines on the stick of margarine, measure out one-quarter cup (four lines) margarine and add to macaroni in bowl.
11. Using the measuring cup, measure out one-quarter cup milk and add to macaroni in large bowl.
12. Add contents of sauce packet to large bowl.
13. Stir with wooden spoon until all mixed.
14. Put large sauce pan, drainer, measuring cup, and spoon into dishwater.
15. Put margarine and milk back into refrigerator.

In the process of analyzing each subenvironment, activities are identified that are (a) generally believed to be important by consumers, parents, teachers, and others and (b) performed frequently by chronological age peers without disabilities in the same setting.

The process of social validation is consistent with the values of person-centered planning (Browder, 2001; O'Brien & Lovett, 1993). Although a variety of approaches are used to implement person-centered planning, they all have in common the following components:

1. The primary direction for planning comes from the individual.
2. Family members and friends are involved in planning. Personal relationships are viewed as a primary source of support to the student.
3. Planning focuses on the individual's capacities and assets versus deficits.

FIGURE 5.3   *Ecological Inventory for Skills at the High School Level.*

Domain: Vocation

Environment: Community

Subenvironment: Bus

Skill: Riding bus to work

Task Analysis:

1. Go to bus stop at designated time.
2. Wait.
3. Pay driver and get transfer ticket.
4. Find seat on bus and sit down.
5. Follow route to transfer site.
6. Pull cord to get off bus at appropriate time.
7. Transfer to other bus.
8. Give driver transfer ticket.
9. Find seat and sit down.
10. Pull cord to get off at appropriate time.

4. An emphasis is given to the settings, services, supports, and routines available in the community or school at large versus those designed for people with disabilities.
5. The planning process can tolerate uncertainty, setbacks, false starts, and disagreement.

The process of social validation of skills leads to a fourth major advantage of the ecological approach. Because skills identified to be taught are performed by people without disabilities, students with disabilities are provided with many opportunities to engage in the same activities as more competent persons. This can serve to raise the expectations of others. The competence-deviance hypothesis (Gold, 1980) holds that the more competence a person demonstrates means the more others will tolerate deviance, or differences, in that person.

Fifth, the ecological approach emphasizes access to normal settings and opportunities to interact with persons without disabilities. The benefits of integration for persons with and without disabilities are significant and were reviewed in Chapter 2.

The sixth characteristic unique to the ecological inventory approach is that it encourages the educational team, including family members, to consider future normalized environments that are desirable for the individual student. As Brown and his colleagues (1979) observed, teaching students with severe disabilities to function in natural community and school environments early in life can increase the probability that they will remain in less restrictive community settings after schooling.

Finally, the ecological approach fosters early and ongoing family involvement. The process of considering hopes, dreams, concerns, and desirable future outcomes for the student with disabilities (Forest & Lusthaus, 1987) encourages family members and others who participate in the educational team to view the student as a unique individual with strengths and assets, as well as challenges. Browder (2001) discussed at length how this approach fosters self-determination and independence.

An Application of the Ecological Inventory Approach in General Education Settings: COACH

Giangreco, Cloninger, and Iverson (1993) developed an assessment and planning tool useful in identifying curriculum content for students with disabilities in general education settings. *Choosing Options and Accommodations for Children* (COACH) was developed based on the following assumptions:

- The design of curriculum should be related to life outcomes that are valued by many people.
- Families are consumers and partners in the design of curriculum.
- Collaboration is essential in the design and delivery of quality education.
- Curriculum objectives should be developed based on priorities and outcomes valued by the family rather than professionals representing different disciplines.
- Problem-solving strategies are instrumental in the design of effective curriculum.
- Special education is appropriately conceptualized as a service rather than a physical placement.

Curriculum development as advocated by the authors of COACH uses ecological inventory strategies within a family-centered approach. COACH has proved to be a valuable asset to educators from a variety of disciplines and families as they work together to design a curriculum that results in positive outcomes for students with disabilities in school and the larger community.

Summary

In this chapter, we reviewed several traditional models of developing curricula for students with severe disabilities. We discussed a number of difficulties when these traditional models, particularly those based on normal sequences of development in young children without disabilities, are applied to curricula for students with severe disabilities. Finally, the ecological inventory approach was described. This approach is considered favorable with its emphasis on functional and age-appropriate skills required to function in a variety of home, school, vocational, recreational, and community settings. We have also seen how this approach fosters interaction between persons with and without disabilities.

References

Alper, S., & Ryndak, D. L. (1992). Educating students with severe handicaps in regular classroom settings. *The Elementary School Journal, 92,* 373–387.

Bates, P., Morrow, S. A., Pancsofar, E., & Sedlak, R. (1984). The effect of functional vs. non-functional activities on attitudes of nonhandicapped college students: What they see is what we get. *Journal of The Association for Persons with Severe Handicaps, 9*(2), 73–78.

Bricker, W., & Bricker, D. (1974). An early language strategy. In R. L. Schiefelbusch & L. Lloyd (Eds.), *Language perspectives: Acquisition, retardation, and intervention* (pp. 431–468). Baltimore: University Park Press.

Browder, D. (2001). *Curriculum and assessment for students with moderate to severe disabilities.* New York: The Guilford Press.

Brown, L., Branston, M.B., Hamre-Nietupski, A., Pumpian, I., Certo, N., & Gruenewald, L. (1979). A strategy for developing chronological age-appropriate and functional curricular content for severely handicapped adolescents and young adults. *Journal of Special Education, 13,* 81–90.

Eisner, E. W. (1979). *The education imagination: On the design and evaluation of school programs.* New York: Macmillan Publishing Co.

Falvey, M. A. (1989). *Community based curriculum: Instructional strategies for students with severe handicaps* (2nd ed.). Baltimore: Paul H. Brookes Publishing Co.

Forest, M., & Lusthaus, E. (1987). The kaleidoscope: Challenge to the cascade. In M. Forest (Ed.), *More education/integration* (pp. 1–16). Downsview, Ontario: G. Allan Roeher Institute.

Frank, A., Sitlington, P., Cooper, L., & Cool, V. (1990). Adult adjustment of recent graduates of Iowa mental disabilities programs. *Education and Training in Mental Retardation, 25,* 62–75.

Gaylord-Ross, R. J., & Holvoet, J. F. (1985). *Strategies for educating students with severe handicaps.* Boston: Little, Brown.

Gesell, A., & Amatruda, C. S. (1947). *Developmental diagnosis.* New York: Harper & Row.

Giangreco, M. F., Cloninger, C. J., & Iverson, V. S. (1993). *Choosing options and accommodations for children.* Baltimore: Paul H. Brookes Publishing Co.

Gold, M. W. (1980). *Try another way training manual.* Champaign, IL: Research Press.

Haring, N. G. (Ed.). (1988). *Generalization for students with severe handicaps: Strategies and solutions.* Seattle: University of Washington Press.

Hasazi, S., Gordon, L., Roe, C., Finck, K., Hull, M., & Salembier, G. (1985). A statewide follow-up on post high school employment and residential status of students labeled mentally retarded. *Education and Training of the Mentally Retarded, 20,* 222–234.

Homer, R. H., Dunlap, G., & Koegel, R. L. (1988). *Generalization and maintenance: Life style changes in applied settings.* Baltimore: Paul H. Brookes Publishing Co.

Kazdin, A. E. (1982). *Single-case research designs: Methods for clinical and applied settings.* New York: Oxford University Press.

Mercer, C. D. & Snell, M. E. (1977). *Learning theory research in mental retardation: Implication for teaching.* Columbus, OH: Charles E. Merrill Publishing Co.

Mithaug, D. E., Horiuchi, C., & Fanning, P. N. (1985). A report on the Colorado statewide follow-up survey of special education students. *Exceptional Children, 51*(5), 397–404.

O'Brien, J., & Lovett, H. (1993). *Finding a way toward everyday lives: The contribution of person-centered planning.* Harrisburg: Pennsylvania Office of Mental Retardation.

Rainforth, B., York J., & Macdonald, C. (1992). *Collaborative teams for students with severe disabilities.* Baltimore: Paul H. Brookes Publishing Co.

Ryndak, D. L., & Alper, S. (1996). *Curriculum for students with moderate to severe disabilities in inclusive settings.* Boston: Allyn & Bacon.

Sailor, W., & Guess, D. (1983). *Severely handicapped students: An instructional design.* Boston: Houghton Mifflin.

Snell, M. (Ed.) (1987). *Systematic instruction of persons with severe handicaps* (3rd ed.). Columbus, OH: Charles E. Merrill.

Stephens, B. (Ed.). (1971). *Training the developmentally young.* New York: John Day Co.

Stokes, T. F., & Baer, D. B. (1977). An implicit technology of generalization. *Journal of Applied Behavior Analysis, 10*(2), 349–367.

Test, D., Howell, A., Burkhart, K., & Beroth, T. (1993). The one-more-than technique as a strategy for counting money for individuals with moderate mental retardation. *Education and Training in Mental Retardation, 28,* 232–241.

Wehman, P., Kregel, J., & Seyfarth, J. (1985). Transition from school to work for individuals with severe handicaps: A follow-up study. *Journal of the Association for Persons with Severe Handicaps, 10*(3), 132–136.

Wilcox, B., & Bellamy, G. T. (1982). *Designing of high school programs for severely handicapped students.* Baltimore: Paul H. Brookes Publishing Co.

York, J., & Vandercook, T. (1991). Designing an integrated education for learners with severe disabilities through the IEP process. *Teaching Exceptional Children, 23*(2), 22–28.

Zeaman, D., & House, B. J. (1963). The role of attention in retarded discrimination teaming. In N. R. Ellis (Ed.), *Handbook of mental deficiency* (pp. 159–223). New York: McGraw-Hill.

Endnote

1. The authors would like to acknowledge the contributions of Nicole Werner and Michelle Meenahan, who developed the ecological inventories included in this chapter.

6

The Curriculum Content Identification Process: Rationale and Overview

Diane Lea Ryndak

Objectives

After reading this chapter, the reader will be able to:

1. Define access to general education and what it means for students with significant disabilities.
2. Provide a rationale for a process of identifying curriculum content that blends functional needs and general education curriculum needs.
3. List and discuss steps for identifying a student's priority functional needs.
4. List and discuss steps for identifying a student's priority general education curriculum needs.
5. Describe how to negotiate annual goals and why negotiation is appropriate.
6. Develop meaningful annual goals for inclusive general education settings.
7. Discuss the various locations in which instruction may occur and a process of identifying locations for each goal.

Key Terms

Access to general education
Blending
Community inventory
Family inventory
Discrepancy analysis

Inventory of general education
   curriculum
Inventory of general education
   settings
Negotiation

Peer inventory
Priority needs
Related services
Student performance

As discussed by McGregor in Chapter 3, the Individuals with Disabilities Education Act (IDEA) 1997 reauthorization makes the concept of access to the general education curriculum prevalent in services for students with disabilities. The law refers to this concept by stating that a student's IEP must include the following:

> . . . a statement of measurable annual goals, including benchmarks or short-term objectives, related to (i) meeting the child's needs that result from the child's disability to enable the child *to be involved and progress in the general curriculum* [emphasis added] (20 U.S.C. section 1414 [A] [ii] [I]).

It further states that the IEP must include the following:

> . . . a statement of the special education and related services and supplementary aids and services to be provided . . . and a statement of the program modifications or supports for school personnel that will be provided for the child . . . *to be involved and progress in the general curriculum* and *to participate in extracurricula and other nonacademic activities* (emphasis added) (20 U.S.C. section 1414 [A] [iii] [II]).

Any discussion of a process to identify the content of annual goals, therefore, must be embedded within the concept of access to general education. Two variables are inherent within this concept: access and general education. In their discussion of access, Ryndak and Billingsley (in press) stated:

> The American Heritage Dictionary of the English Language (2000) defined access as "the ability or right to approach, enter, exit, communicate with, or make use of [something]." Wordnet (1997) defined access as "the right to obtain or make use of or take advantage of something (as services or membership)." Thus, if two persons have access to a building, then they both are admitted into the same building on an equal basis; if they have access to materials, then they both may obtain and use the same materials on an equal basis. In relation to educational services, if two students have access to academic content (e.g., Freshman English, 5th grade science, 3rd grade mathematics), then they both are admitted to the course and have access to the same instructional opportunities (including materials, content, and activities) on an equal basis.

The second variable, general education, could have many interpretations. In light of the IDEA provision quoted previously, however, the interpretation for students with disabilities must go beyond the content delineated in state standards and benchmarks and incorporate every component of the general education experience (Halvorsen & Neary, 2001). Ryndak, Alper, Stuart, and Clark (in press) discussed four aspects of the general education experience, including curriculum content, activities, settings, and independent functioning across contexts. Because together these comprise the experiences of general education students at any given grade level, when considering the general education experiences of a general education student (for example, a sixth grader), an education team must consider all four of these aspects (see Table 6.1). For the curriculum content identification process described in this chapter, therefore, the phrase "general education" refers not only to the content standards described by states and school districts, but also to the

TABLE 6.1   *Aspects of the General Education Experience Incorporated Within the Concept of Access to General Education*

General education content	General education students at each grade level have access to the same content standards, or a core curriculum. At each grade level, students are expected to demonstrate competence related to that core curriculum by demonstrating either grade-level performance or proficiency on state or locally determined assessments. It could be appropriate for a student with severe disabilities to demonstrate competence on all, part, or none of the core curriculum content for a given grade level or unit addressed for a given grade level. To determine this, however, all of this content must be considered specifically for each student.
General education activities	The general education experience includes activities that all students have in common, including those that are the following: <ul><li>Instructional across settings (for example, in-class, in-school, and out-of-school activities)</li><li>Logistical (for example, preparation before or clean up after instructional activities)</li><li>Social (for example, interactions in the school, on school grounds, or in field-trip settings)</li><li>Extracurricular in nature (for example, club activities or sporting events)</li></ul> As a whole, this set of activities offers students opportunities to (a) acquire skills and knowledge from the general education curriculum content, (b) demonstrate skills and knowledge incorporated in the general education curriculum content, and (c) participate in common experiences that comprise school life for students of their own age and grade level. The more activities (for example, class tasks, activities in assemblies, or experiences rushing between classes) that students with significant disabilities have in common with general education classmates means the more they are able to interact with each other about those activities. In addition to participating in the actual school-related activity, such common experiences also offer opportunities for students to observe and relate to others' behaviors across activities, especially the social norms of their same-age classmates. Without such common experiences, students with significant disabilities have no access to either the educational or social norms that influence every aspect of each student's life.
General education settings	The general education experience includes settings, both in and out of school, to which students have access and in which they are expected to function. Even though some commonalities exist across years (for example, every year students must have access to a bathroom, classrooms, and school hallways), the number, type, and physical layout of settings vary every year. Because of this, each year students must learn to function and participate in the settings used by their grade level. For instance, students must learn (a) how individual classrooms are structured and organized, (b) where classrooms and other key rooms (for example, cafeteria or nurse's office) are located in the building, and (c) when and where to attend to self-care needs (for example, storing personal items or attending to personal hygiene). Ensuring access to general education curriculum, therefore, must incorporate access to the settings encountered during general education activities, as well as functional participation in those settings.

TABLE 6.1 *Continued*

Independent functioning across contexts	The general education experience includes the use of previously acquired knowledge and skills that are relevant for independent functioning across general education contexts. Such knowledge and skills could reflect (a) standards from the general education curriculum content that were acquired during previous school years (for example, writing letters) and (b) skills not traditionally included in general education curriculum standards (for example, mobility within a classroom, self-care, appropriate behavior, or communication). These skills could have been acquired either prior to, or concomitantly with, access to the general education curriculum content. In either case, the knowledge and skills continue to be relevant to the general education experience, though they now may be applied in new or more complex applications (for example, writing words and sentences or moving in a timely manner between rooms for classes during middle school). The consistent continued use of such content allows all students to function independently across general education contexts and to benefit from opportunities to learn content from general education experiences. Though a student with significant disabilities may require additional instruction on such content relevant to independent functioning across general education contexts, this instruction is critical to ensuring access to general education.

Source: Adapted from Ryndak, D. L., & Billingsley, F. (in press).

content inherent within participation in all the experiences that comprise general education life (that is, general education activities, general education settings, and independent functioning across contexts) (Ryndak et al., in press; Ryndak & Billingsley, in press).

Rationale for a Blending Process

Because the material on which a student receives instruction determines the potential benefits from educational services in the form of skills acquired for use upon leaving school, an education team has the responsibility to consider carefully all possible curriculum content when identifying annual goals for a student. The team should select content that maximizes the student's acquisition of meaningful activities and skills in both current and future environments (Brown et al., 1979a, 1979b; Mount & Zwernik, 1988; Salisbury & Vincent, 1990). The education team should pay particular attention to the development of natural support networks that will benefit the student throughout life (Fisher, Pumpian, & Sax, 1998; Hunt, Alwell, Farron-Davis, & Goetz, 1996; Janney & Snell, 1996; Kishi & Meyer, 1994. (For an in-depth discussion of natural support networks see Chapter 7.) This is a massive responsibility, and an education team cannot view the identification of curriculum content for a student as just one of many tasks that comprise their job. Rather, it is only the first of many steps that will determine the nature and extent of that person's participation in life, both as a student and as an adult.

Identifying curriculum content for a student involves a number of steps requiring decisions that are based on judgements. Because curriculum content, by definition, will vary from student to student, the team judges the relevance and importance of every activity and skill for each student. Each team member naturally bases judgements on past experiences and personal values. Although it is unlikely that multiple teams would identify the same set of curriculum content for one student, teams that hold the same values and share similar experiences tend to identify content that, when viewed in its entirely, leads to similar short- and long-term benefits for a student. The process a team uses to identify curriculum content reflects its values. Effective teams gather the best information possible in relation to the immediate and final outcomes desired for a student. These teams then formulate their *best guesses* about the activities and skills that will be most meaningful for that student in both current and future environments and provide instruction on those activities and skills during the ensuing school year.

Curriculum content for a student in inclusive settings could and should emphasize a blending of that student's functional needs and the curriculum content presented in the general education settings. By blending these needs the education team enhances the student's (1) independence in both the inclusive settings and adult life, and (2) participation in general education activities with peers. The team also allows for teaching both general education content and functional content during general education and functional activities in the classroom, the school, and the community. In this way, both general education and functional content are reinforced during instruction in various settings and activities across the day.

Blending needs necessitates a process for identifying curriculum content that would be most appropriate for a specific student to learn at that time—a process that incorporates both functional activities (including building friendships and natural support networks) and general education curriculum content. This type of process allows education teams to fulfill the intent of inclusion in general education settings and maximize the benefits of inclusion. To accomplish this, the team first must gather information about the student's participation in activities at home, at school, and in the community. Education teams use the ecological approach of identifying curriculum content described in Chapter 5 to gather information about the student's functioning within environments and across domains.

Although this content is critical for students with moderate to severe disabilities, it is insufficient when used alone to determine curriculum content for a student in inclusive settings. When an education team considers only functional curriculum content for a student, it makes three assumptions. First, it is assumed that the student cannot learn and benefit from any of the curriculum content being presented to the general education class. A number of students with moderate to severe disabilities have, in fact, demonstrated across settings knowledge they acquired along with their general education classmates (Ryndak, Morrison, & Sommerstein, 1999). Although the amount of demonstrated knowledge varies by student, students evidently are acquiring information that similar students in self-contained classes are not acquiring. Unless an education team also focuses on general education curriculum content and deliberately identifies the most relevant components of that content for the student with moderate to severe disabilities, they are leaving to chance the components on which that student actually will receive instruction. If instruction is to occur in general education settings, is it not the responsibility of the education team to carefully select for the student the most meaningful components of the curriculum content taught in those settings and focus instruction on those components?

Second, it is assumed that, by definition, partial participation in general education class activities will lead to the acquisition of relevant social skills, academic knowledge, and functional activities. Although partial participation in general education activities provides opportunities for interacting with classmates, the instruction provided during those activities will determine the degree to which these opportunities lead to skill acquisition. Instruction may take the form of antecedents (for example, cues, directions, or models) or consequences (for example, feedback on performance, reinforcement, and error correction) (see Chapter 19). In addition, the instructor may be a peer or adult. Numerous examples of effective instruction in inclusive settings have demonstrated how the presence of planned instruction leads to skill acquisition for students with significant disabilities (Gee, Graham, Goetz, Oshima, & Yoshika, 1991; Helmstetter, Peck, & Giangreco, 1994; Hunt, Staub, Alwell, & Goetz, 1994; Kennedy, Shukla, & Fryxell, 1997; Ryndak et al., 1999; Staub, Schwartz, Gallucci, & Peck, 1994). As such, instruction can flow quite naturally within the parameters of any activity. The absence of planned instruction, however, leaves to chance the amount of learning that actually occurs for a student, especially the amount of learning on predetermined components of the curriculum. If partial participation is to occur, is it not the responsibility of the education team to carefully select the part(s) of the general education activity for which the student with moderate to severe disabilities will have responsibility and to provide instruction for that student to increase the probability of success and the extent of participation?

Third, it is assumed that, because a student with moderate to severe disabilities is in a general education class, both the general education teacher and the student's classmates will understand and accept that the student is indeed a part of that class, as are the nondisabled students. Although there are limited data supporting the belief that students with disabilities who attend a general education class on a part-time basis are not truly considered part of that class (Schnorr, 1990), there is beginning to be evidence that full-time placement alone does not constitute belongingness (Jackson, Ryndak, & Billingsley, 2000; Schnorr, 1997) (see Chapter 11). Unless completely involved in the identification of relevant curriculum content, including components of the general education curriculum, general education teachers perceive that they merely are providing an environment in which the special education teacher (and possibly related services personnel) can provide their "special" instruction to their "special" student (Idol, 1993; Orelove & Sobsey, 1996, Vandercook & York, 1990; Vandercook, York, & Forest, 1989). This perception negates the intent and benefits of inclusion. This negative perception can be avoided by: (1) including the general education teacher in all planning and curriculum content identification procedures; (2) systematically considering, with the general education teacher, whether each component of the general education curriculum content is relevant for the student; and (3) carefully selecting, with the general education teacher, any relevant component of the general education curriculum for possible inclusion in the student's curriculum content. If a student with moderate to severe disabilities truly is part of a general education class, and the purpose of that class is to present information to all students and develop their skills, is it not the responsibility of the education team to include the student in every aspect of that class?

To avoid making these assumptions, the education team must consider fully both the general education setting and curriculum content when identifying content on which instruction will be provided for a student, regardless of the type and extent of the student's handicap. For each area in which information is gathered, the education team first lists all possible curriculum content that is relevant for the student and then prioritizes the content *only for that area*. The education team then reviews the prioritized lists of content for all of the areas and uses that information to develop annual goals for the student's individualized education program (IEP), which will define the emphasis of instruction for that student during the next year.

This curriculum content identification process emphasizes; (1) the role of the family and other education team members in identifying curriculum content for a student; (2) the blending of functional and general education curriculum content during instruction, and (3) the provision of instruction on both functional and general education content in general education settings, the school building, and the community. An education team uses this process as it is determining the curriculum content to be emphasized for a student during instruction. Figure 6.1 depicts the steps in this process. Because the IEP legally dictates (by the Individuals with Disabilities Education Act [IDEA]) the content that instruction *must* address, the team should complete this process before the development of the student's IEP or individualized family service plan (IFSP).

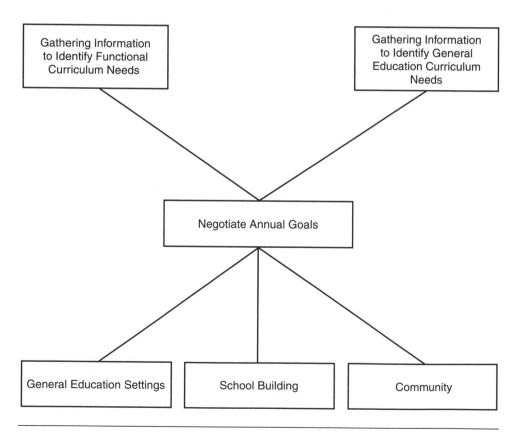

FIGURE 6.1   *Curriculum Content Identification Process Flowchart.*

Gathering Information to Identify Priority Functional Needs

As described in Chapter 5, Brown and his colleagues (1979a,b) provided a pedagogical framework for obtaining information that is useful in identifying activities and skills that are functional for a student. The curriculum content identification process described in this chapter begins by extending the use of inventories across people and settings that play a major role in that student's life. The education team uses the information obtained from these inventories to prioritize the student's functional needs for instruction in the coming school year. Inventories included in the process are family, peer, and community inventories.

In addition to using information from inventories to identify priority functional needs for a student, this section describes effective use of information from related services assessments, records, and other prior information available when determining priority functional needs. The education team reviews these with consideration for; (1) how the values they reflect correlate with the values inherent in inclusive services; and (2) how the student's described needs relate to full participation in activities at home, at school, and in the community. Finally, the process emphasizes the student's preferences in curriculum content to be addressed in instruction the next school year. Figure 6.2 summarizes the steps completed in the process to gather information to identify a student's functional needs. The steps in the process are in a specific order both in Figure 6.2 and in the following sections, but the team can complete most of these steps in any order. The family inventory should be completed first, however, because it provides valuable insight into both the student's performance in natural situations and the family's educational priorities. This information may affect how the other steps are completed.

Family Inventory

A family inventory is a tool or process education teams use to acquire information from a student's family members (Downing, 2000; Giangreco, Cloninger, & Iverson, 1998; Schwartz, 1995; Turnbull & Turnbull, 1997) that will assist in identifying the activities and skills that, when learned, would most effectively allow; (1) the student to more fully participate with their family, neighbors, and friends in activities within the home and community; and (2) the family to complete daily or weekly tasks more easily. Various approaches to gathering information from families have been developed, including Personal Future Planning, Making Action Plans (MAPS) (Menchetti & Sweeney, 1995) and the MAPS Process (Falvey, Forest, Pearpoint, & Rosenberg, 1997). Although some education teams send home a survey-type instrument for the family to complete and return, the most effective method of completing a family inventory is to interview the family in their home, using a survey-type instrument both to guide the interview and for recording responses. While this format ensures that the areas included on the instrument are addressed fully, it also allows the education team to expand the questions in areas of specific relevance for the student. In addition, the interview process itself generates more information than a written instrument alone. It allows participants to clarify comments, expand information from gen-

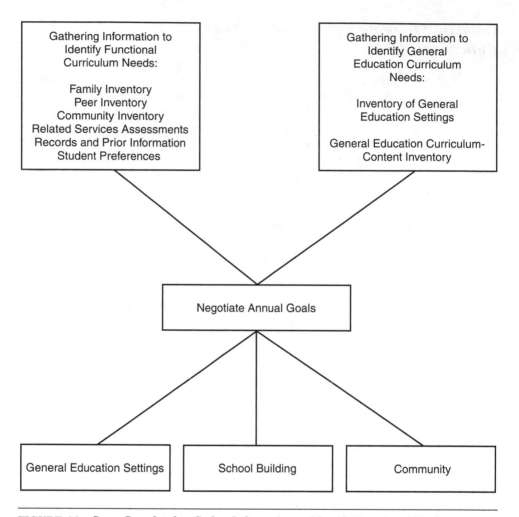

FIGURE 6.2 *Steps Completed to Gather Information to Identify Functional Needs.*

eral ideas to specific examples, enhance knowledge and understanding of a student's life, and bring into focus the family's hopes and dreams for the student.

Cohen, Agosta, Cohen, and Warren (1989) summarize some disturbing variations in family structures in the United States, including (1) the lack of legal ties between adults living together in a household, (2) no male head of household, (3) a teenage female head of household, (4) a sharp drop in household income due to divorce or separation, (5) mothers working outside the house, and (6) restructured families that include stepparents and stepchildren. In addition, the increase in households that are ethnically diverse raises culture-related issues. The interviewer considers carefully each of these variables during the completion of a family inventory. The completion of this inventory in the family's home can provide helpful insights about the student's role in the family's life, as well as the family system itself and potential needs for family support services (Cohen et al., 1989).

Although information from a family inventory can be endless and the process is at times overwhelming, the team can control the information by focusing on the purpose of the family inventory. Specifically, the family inventory should assist the education team in identifying activities and skills for inclusion in instruction during the ensuing school year. Activities and skills identified through the family inventory most effectively should allow; (1) the student to participate more fully with their family, neighbors, and friends in activities within the home and community; or (2) the family to complete daily or weekly tasks more easily. To accomplish this, there may be several areas and domains in the family inventory.

Personal Profile.   This area contains information relevant to the student across domains and environments. In addition to demographic data, information gathered includes, (1) the manner in which the student makes choices and interacts with others; (2) items, people, and activities that the student likes and dislikes; (3) physical and other management needs demonstrated by the student throughout the day; (4) health and medical concerns; and (5) issues related to ethnic diversity that affect the student's participation in inclusive settings.

Home Life.   Information is gathered about activities in which the student participates every day of the week at home, specifically including the morning routine, afternoon events, evening activities, and bedtime routine. All activities of daily living and activities in which the family participates regularly occur during these time periods. For each time period information is gathered on (1) the responsibilities completed by the student, (2) the extent of the student's participation, (3) the needs demonstrated by the student, and (4) the frequency and type of interactions in which the student engages. The team carefully considers how the student's participation in family life is influenced by ethnic diversity. Two questions consistently are asked: What could their child learn to do more independently that would help make daily life easier for the family, and for what home life activity does their child demonstrate a preference for learning?

Community Activities.   There is a wealth of information that the family can provide on a student's participation in community activities, including opportunities to participate, extent of independence during participation, interactions with family members and/or friends during participation, and desire to participate. The team collects such information in regard to the student's use of (1) recreation facilities, (2) leisure options, (3) restaurants, (4) shopping facilities, and (5) chore-related community environments (for example, banks or laundromats). In addition, the education team gathers information about how the student accesses these environments, and about options available for travel to, from, and within the environments.

Work.   Regardless of the student's age, the education team gathers information on work history, including work at home, at school, and in the community. The student's likes and dislikes in relation to jobs, working environments, job hours, and proximity of coworkers are recorded in as much detail as possible. The education team notes job-related skills (for example, staying on task, completing work independently, and interactions with authority figures) and demonstrations of the student's work ethic. Even if of primary-school age, the family can supply information on the student's job-related skills and work ethic based on performance on tasks at home and in school. As the student ages, he or she gives more detailed information on work preferences and the feasibility of specific jobs available in the home community. The feasibility of specific jobs, and the degree to which emphasis is placed on employment, may vary across families of diverse ethnic backgrounds.

General Education Curriculum.   In addition to gathering information from the family about a student's participation in life at home and in the community, the family inventory assists in focusing on the benefits from inclusion in general education settings that the family desires and foresees for the student. Although initially families generally focus on the social benefits derived from interacting with nondisabled peers of the same age, there are other benefits that inclusive settings offer for students with moderate to severe disabilities. Discussing the academic subjects, units, and desired outcomes from participating in the general education curriculum for nondisabled students assists family members in envisioning the student's participation in classroom activities. In considering a student's participation, identification of specific components of the general education curriculum that would be beneficial for the student is possible. These components may include (1) rudimentary knowledge related to content of specific units, (2) detailed knowledge related to content of one or more specific units, (3) general work skills or personal values demonstrated through partial participation in units, and (4) generalized use of functional activities within all classroom activities. The family's views of which components of the general education curriculum are the most relevant for a student both in that school year and in the future assist an education team in identifying relevant curriculum content for that student.

Future Hopes and Dreams.   Because the purpose of education is to prepare a student to function as independently as possible in both current *and* future environments, education teams must form a legitimate vision of the future environments in which the student most likely will participate. This vision must coincide and keep pace with the family's vision. For this reason, family inventories include a section that asks the family to describe their hopes and dreams for a student's future, specifically in relation to where they foresee the student living, working, being at leisure, and accessing community resources. These hopes and dreams will vary with the family's history, values, ethnic background, and socioeconomic status. The hopes and dreams are projected for three and five years into the future, as well as for after completion of the education program.

Functional Needs Priorities.   At the end of an interview for the family inventory, education team members ask the family to prioritize what they perceive the student needs to learn for participation in activities both at home and in the community. Although there may be a number of activities for possible inclusion in the student's curriculum content, the education team must determine the order of importance for these activities. Of consideration when prioritizing activities is the degree to which the activity generalizes across inclusive settings. Throughout this discussion, education team members share their perceptions of the relative importance of each functional activity and the relation of each activity to the student's current and future environments. Following this discussion, however, the emphasis should be on the family's perceptions.

General Education Priorities.   In addition to prioritizing the student's functional needs, the family also prioritizes components of general education identified as possible curriculum content for the student. Because the student has access to every aspect of general education (that is, curriculum content, activities, settings, and independent functioning), all of the content addressed across those aspects should be considered. For some students, *all* of the content will be relevant and listed as priorities; for some students, only *some* of the content will be relevant and listed as priorities. Family members should consider which components of general education the student will use most frequently across settings. By selecting those components, the team will address the student's difficulties with generalization. Again, although the education team discusses the relative importance of components of general education with the family, the focus should be on the family's priorities.

Priority Needs Inventory.   Given the two lists of priorities in functional and general education content, the family then combines the two lists, resulting in one list of the family's perceptions of priority curriculum content for the student. In developing this list, the family may choose all or some of the items from either list. In addition, they may identify needs that arise across settings. The final list of the family's priorities, therefore, may incorporate only functional activities, only components of general education, or a combination of functional activities and general education, as well as activities that occur across settings.

Peer Inventory

The importance of establishing relationships and natural support networks for students with moderate to severe disabilities demands that education teams consider curriculum content that allows each student to interact in a meaningful and effective manner with peers at school, in their community, and in their own ethnic group. To identify that curriculum content, education team members must first determine the topics about which the student's peers interact and the ways in which they interact. To accomplish this in a manner that eliminates the adults' perceptions of what is relevant to the student's peers, education teams conduct a peer inventory that includes peers both at school and in their community.

A student's peers may divulge a wealth of information covering a myriad of areas, including the following:

1. Preferred school events and weekend activities
2. Favorite leisure activities, locations, and companions
3. Current age-appropriate trends in colloquialisms, music, and styles
4. How and where to "hang out" with friends

Because being able to converse on a topic is not enough to be accepted as part of a group, the information from a peer inventory also should direct the education team toward the peer group's preferred appearances, activities, and interaction styles (Chin-Perez et al., 1986; Haring, 1991; Haring & Breen, 1989). With this information the education team can complete a discrepancy analysis (Gaylord-Ross & Browder, 1991; Hoier & Cone, 1987) between the student's appearance, participation in activities, and interaction style and that of the student's peers. This discrepancy analysis determines the activities and skills the student must acquire to increase the probability of interacting successfully with peers at school and in the community.

There are a number of formats used to conduct peer inventories at various ages. For example, at the primary level education teams have used whole language exercises, show-and-tell sessions, and art projects to obtain relevant information from students. The teams have used similar exercises at the elementary level along with surveys that require simple written or drawn responses. More sophisticated exercises are appropriate for use in middle and high schools, including more complex written surveys, video projects, essays for newspapers or school magazines, photograph essays, or computer-generated reports. Gathering information about current or potential coworkers must be quick and completed in a manner that is unobtrusive in the work setting. Although time consuming, direct observation of interactions between peers also has been effective to supplement information from a peer inventory. The formats used are irrelevant. The key is that the education team obtains information from the student's peers about the skills and knowledge that are critical for that student to acquire to increase the probability of successful and effective interaction with peers.

Upon completion of a peer inventory and possible direct observation, an education team lists the curriculum content that potentially would assist the student in participating with peers more effectively, especially across settings and peer groups. The team prioritizes the items on this list without regard to priorities from other inventories.

Community Inventory

Although the family inventory provides some information on environments and activities available in the student's home community, education teams expand on this information by going directly to that community and conducting an inventory. The purpose of a community inventory is to identify both; (1) the resources available in a student's community for living, working, and playing; and (2) the resources the student's peers frequently use, especially resources to which the student does not already have access through family activities (Brown et al., 1983). A community inventory describes the resources available within a specific range of the student's home. Figure 6.3 includes a worksheet used by some education teams to gather information for a community inventory. This information helps the education team identify activities and skills that would assist the student to participate more fully with peers in the home community. The distance from the student's home for which a community inventory is completed will vary depending upon the nature of the community (that is, urban versus rural) and the number of options appropriate and necessary for a student. For example, when attempting to identify work options within a rural home community for a student with multiple disabilities, it may be necessary to extend the

Student: Date of Inventory:

Address:

Domain:

Description of Inventory Range:

Resource	Location	Activities	Costs(s)	Clientele	Dress Code and Average Dress	Hours	Travel To and From	Accessibility

FIGURE 6.3   Community Inventory Worksheet.

range for which the community inventory is completed by several miles before finding enough feasible options to allow the student and education team choices. The range of a community inventory for the same student in an inner city, however, may not need to exceed a few blocks.

Upon completing a community inventory, the education team compares the resources available in the student's home community with the preferred activities of the student, the student's peers, and the student's family. In addition, a discrepancy analysis may determine how the student's performance in any community location differs from the performance of same-age peers. Through these comparisons, the education team identifies the community resources that would be most beneficial for the student to learn to access, thereby increasing opportunities to participate more fully with peers and family members in the community. From these resources, the education team develops a list of community resources that would be most beneficial to include in instruction for the student in the ensuing school year.

Related Services Assessments

IDEA 1997 defines related services as:

> . . . *transportation and such developmental, corrective, and other supportive services (including speech pathology and audiology services, psychological services, physical and occupational therapy, recreation, including therapeutic recreation, social work services, counseling services, including rehabilitation counseling, orientation and mobility services, and medical services, except that such medical services shall be for diagnostic purposes only) as may be required to assist a child with a disability to benefit from special education, and includes the early identification and assessment of disabling conditions in children (20 U.S. C. section 602 [22]).*

According to Rainforth, York, and Macdonald (1992):

> *The phrase* as may be required to assist a handicapped child to benefit from special education *suggests that the related services of physical and occupational therapy and speech/language pathology must both relate directly to the child's educational program and be provided in such a way that the child receives a greater benefit from the educational program than if related services were not provided. . . . both educational relevance and student benefit are addressed when therapists integrate their knowledge and skills into instruction provided in the context of routine daily activities that comprise the student's educational program, whether at school, in the community, or at home (p. 26).*

In conjunction with this interpretation, assessments on a student's needs in a related service area (for example, occupational therapy, physical therapy, or speech/language pathology) focus on the student's performance across naturally occurring environments, and the consequent need for a related service to improve the student's performance. For a student who receives educational services in inclusive settings, those environments include; (1) the general education classroom; (2) other school and community settings in which the student's class participates in activities (for example, lunchroom, library, hallway, art room, bus, locations of field trips, and playground); and (3) other school, home, and community environments identified as priority environments for instruction of either functional or general education curriculum content for that student during that school year. Giangreco et al. (1998) stated that:

> . . . *related services should be provided to enable students to pursue family-centered, discipline-free IEP goals as the focus of their educational programs, other relevant learning outcomes that provide for a well-rounded school experience, and general supports . . . (p. 9).*

Without reference to how a student demonstrates a specific need within a specific environment and how the related service will directly impact on the student's performance within that environment, an identified need becomes tangential to the student's potential educational program. IDEA, therefore, does not consider it a related service need.

If a related service assessment identifies a need for service that will improve the student's performance in specific environments, the education team discusses those needs, the activities, and environments in which those needs were identified; how the related service will improve the student's performance in those activities and environments; and the relative importance of each of those activities for the student. To assist in identifying potential functional curriculum content for inclusion in the student's education program, the education team prioritizes the activities for which the related service will improve the student's performance, emphasizing those activities that occur across settings.

Records and Prior Information

Valuable information can be gleaned from a student's records and other information from prior education services (for example, discussions with prior education team members and written products). Depending on the type of prior education services provided and the values demonstrated by those education teams, however, the information may provide varying degrees of insight into either relevant curriculum content or effective instructional strategies for the student. For instance, if there is a change in a student's placement from a self-contained class or building to a general education class, the information available from prior education teams most likely will not describe the behaviors and skills one would expect from the student in the general education class. Because the environments are dramatically different (that is, different stimuli, expectations, and consequences), the student conceivably will view the general education class as a "new" setting and will determine the appropriate behaviors to be exhibited there by observing the behaviors of others. In addition, if the prior education team's values are not consistent with those of the education team in the inclusive setting, the probability that the teams would identify similar curriculum content for the student's education program is extremely low.

For these reasons, education teams attempt to determine the values demonstrated by prior education teams by reviewing the types of services provided and the curriculum content believed to have been most critical for the student during those services. The more consistent these are with inclusive services and the values espoused by the current education team, the more informative records and other information will be. Education teams from inclusive settings review records and other information with constant attention for insight into the student's probable performance, learning style, and learning rate in the general education classroom and other naturally occurring environments in the school, home, and community. This will be the most valuable information from records when determining relevant curriculum content for the ensuing school year. From this information the education team will determine possible curriculum content and prioritize that content for possible inclusion in the student's IEP for the next school year.

Student Preferences

Any education team would be remiss if they did not identify and strongly consider a student's preferences when determining curriculum content. One of the focuses of education, after all, is to teach a student to make decisions (Helmstetter & Guess, 1987; Kennedy & Haring, 1993) based on knowledge of the options and to deal with the consequences of that decision. Initially, instruction on choice making uses information from reinforcement assessments, thus verifying that the student learns how to make choices by having at least one option that is a personal high preference (Green, Reid, Canipe, & Gardner, 1991; Green, et al., 1988; Wolery, Ault, & Doyle, 1992). Eventually, this instruction will result in students making life choices for themselves. Agran and Wehmeyer refer to this as self-determination (see Chapter 14).

When identifying a student's preferences for curriculum content to be included in instruction, therefore, it is the education team's responsibility to provide enough information to allow the student to make an informed choice between viable options. Although options for general education content during the primary and elementary years may be limited, as they are for all students, the number of options increases as a student progresses into middle school and high school and when considering instruction in the community. The number of community-based options greatly increases as the student enters middle school and high school, with time in the community and the number of activities completed in the community increasing.

As with the information gathered from the other sources listed previously, the education team prioritizes the curriculum content preferred by the student. Again, the education team should consider which of the preferences will be helpful for the student across settings and peer groups. The team will review and compare the content on this prioritized list with the content of the prioritized lists from the other sources of information as they make final decisions on curriculum content for the school year.

Gathering Information to Identify Priority General Education Needs

Thus far the education team has gathered information related only to identifying functional curriculum content that will assist a student to participate more fully in activities with peers and family members at home, in school, and in the community. In addition to this information, education teams need similar information related to identifying general education curriculum content that is relevant for the student (see Figure 6.2).

Inventory of the General Education Setting

Numerous variables about the general education setting are relevant when identifying curriculum content for a student with moderate to severe disabilities. Although a list of those variables could be endless, depending upon the specific needs of students with multiple disabilities, some variables are important for all students (see Figure 6.4). With this information, education teams can perform a discrepancy analysis between the demands of the locations and the skills currently demonstrated by the student, identifying any necessary (1) changes in physical layout (for example, amount of space between desks), (2) adaptations or additions to materials (for example, adapted utensils or writing and drawing implements or addition of switches to electrically operated equipment), (3) skills the student must acquire (for example, new class rules or use of a locker), and (4) modifications in instructional style (for example, interspersing of questions on similar content for the student during class review sessions). This information will allow the education team to determine the skills and activities that are expected of all students and, therefore, would be most beneficial for the student to acquire to participate more fully in each of the general education settings. They should note if specific skills and activities have generalized use for the student across settings. The team then can prioritize the skills and activities for later use in determining the student's actual curriculum content for the next school year.

General Education Curriculum Content Inventory

In order to identify components of the general education curriculum content that are most relevant for a student, the education team reviews the instructional units and specific

FIGURE 6.4 *General Education Setting Information.*

1. Location of various rooms (e.g., classroom, lunchroom, gym) to each other and the possible paths between those rooms
2. Areas within each room that are used for instruction (e.g., student desks, teacher desk, reading area, carpet section, small group table) and the possible paths between those areas
3. Differences in distance and ease of mobility along each path between rooms and areas within rooms
4. Location of accessible restrooms to each room
5. Location and accessibility of equipment, instructional supplies, and functional materials within each room
6. Location and method of accessing student storage areas (e.g., cloak room, locker, cubby hole) per room
7. Types of materials used during large-group, small-group, and independent instructional activities per class period
8. Class rules across instructors and rooms
9. Instructional style of each instructor

outcomes targeted per unit for the general education class. Although school districts have an established scope and sequence to their overall curriculum that is readily available, there are minor nuances to that curriculum that are specific to every teacher in a district. For example, one school district's first-grade curriculum in language arts includes a rudimentary understanding of authors and how writing styles are demonstrated in each author's books. To address this curricular area, one first-grade teacher incorporates an "author study" emphasis across three to four weeks of instruction, interweaving the content of various books by one author during reading, language experience, art, and even some math classes. Another first-grade teacher holds "author study" class sessions, comparing authors and their books in specifically structured activities.

To identify skills and activities that are most relevant for a student with moderate to severe disabilities, therefore, the education team conducts an inventory of the specific general education curriculum content to be addressed in the student's class. The team completes this by reviewing each unit completed by the general education teacher and by reviewing the outcomes that the teacher both expects and desires for the entire class. From this list of outcomes, the education team can identify the components that would be most effective in increasing the degree to which the student participates in activities in school, at home, and in the community, both that year and in the future. Figure 6.5 includes a worksheet used by some education teams during the general education curriculum content inventory. The team then prioritizes these components for future use in determining the final curriculum content for the student's next school year.

When Tony's education team needed to identify priorities from the general education curriculum content (see Appendix A), they selected the special education teacher, speech therapist, physical therapist, occupational therapist, and fifth-grade teacher as the most appropriate team members to conduct the general education curriculum content inventory because of his needs and their pivotal roles in meeting those needs. These team members met and reviewed all the curriculum content that the nondisabled fifth graders should achieve by the end of the academic year. In addition, the fifth-grade teacher discussed the academic and personal growth objectives that she would like her students to achieve by the end of the year, beyond those officially covered in the general education curriculum content. Because all three team members had at least rudimentary information about Tony, they already knew the fourth grade content he was acquiring and could envision the fifth grade content that potentially would be within his ability to acquire. In addition, they were able to relate to his family life and peer interactions, and envision the fifth-grade curriculum content that he could use most readily in those settings.

When the general education class receives instruction from more than one teacher (for example, teachers of special subject areas, such as art or physical education, or teachers of compartmentalized programs, such as language arts, science, and math), each teacher participates in completing a general education curriculum inventory. The teachers determine for each class period the outcomes and the curriculum components that would be most beneficial for the student, especially across inclusive settings and peer groups. Again, the education team then prioritizes the selected components for future use in determining the student's final curriculum content for the next school year. For Tony, the special education teacher met with the general education teacher, speech therapist, occupational therapist, and physical education instructor to complete general education curriculum content inventories.

Student:	Teacher:
Date:	Grade:
Subject:	
Unit:	

Expected Outcomes	Components Relevant for the Student	Settings and Activities for Application			
		General Education	School	Home	Community
Desired Outcomes					

FIGURE 6.5 *General Education Curriculum Content Worksheet.*

Negotiating Annual Goals

Thus far in the process, an education team has gathered information from a variety of sources and identified priority instructional needs for a student in relation to both functional and general education curriculum content. With information on prioritized needs for each inventory completed, the education team then reviews all of these lists of priorities and negotiates to identify the most relevant and critical activities and skills to emphasize for the student's instruction during the next school year.

Negotiation

Negotiation is the process of arranging for or bringing about the settlement of a matter through conference, discussion, and compromise with others (*Webster's Ninth Collegiate Dictionary*, 1991). In relation to an education team identifying the prioritized curriculum needs for a student, negotiation must incorporate true collaboration among team members. Hargreaves (cited in Ainscow, 1991) describes the need for

> . . . *true collaborative cultures that are "deep, personal and enduring. They are not," he argues, "mounted just for specific projects or events. They are not strings of one-shot deals. Cultures of collaboration rather are, constitutive of, absolutely central to, teachers' daily work." (pp. 221–222)*

Rainforth, York, and Macdonald (1992) state that "to function as a collaborative team, positive interdependence must be structured through mutually agreed upon goals, contribution to goal attainment, and celebration of goal accomplishment" (p. 206). If an education team has established a collaborative relationship built on positive interdependence, the process of negotiating the content of annual goals will reflect mutual respect for both the individual members of the team and the instructional content with which each member has expertise. Such mutual respect leads to an understanding of how acquisition of instructional content within one area affects acquisition of content in other areas.

For example, although severely physically handicapped, Tony (see Appendix A) can volitionally move his right arm to operate electronically controlled apparatus. He currently is learning to use his arm movement to identify objects and answer questions with his Introtalker, and to operate electronic equipment (i.e., pencil sharpener; tape recorder; computer) during his fifth grade class activities. In addition, Tony is learning to use his arm movement to do classroom jobs (i.e., pass out papers) (see Appendix A).

His education team understands the relationship between his physical disabilities and his need to communicate and to participate in activities that naturally occur in his fifth grade class. His annual goals, therefore, reflect this relationship and incorporate the use of his limited volitional movement with content that is both meaningful and functional for him in fifth grade activities, as well as across his other environments. The education team feels that the demonstration of better control of his volitional movement without correlation to the activities that occur in his fifth grade class would be insufficient to meet Tony's educational needs.

The negotiation process used to identify annual goals may vary across education teams, but the intent of the processes is the same. Education teams objectively review the priority curriculum content items identified during information gathering activities (for example, family inventory, student preferences inventory, and general education curriculum content inventory), understand the relevance of each item to the student's current and future life, openly and nondefensively discuss the rationale for their thoughts on each item, and reach a consensus on the items believed to be most important for inclusion on the student's IEP and for emphasis in instruction during the next school year. To accomplish this, each team member is ready to agree that a curriculum item they initially believed to be critical for the student actually is *less* critical for this year than other items. If this is not the case, the team member(s) must be able to convince other team members about the critical nature of the item through logical arguments related to the student's participation in life. The focus of discussions on a curriculum item is its relative importance to the student's participation in activities in both current and future environments, the potential generalized use of it, and the degree to which it is critical for that student during instruction in the next school year.

The education team's goal is to use the multiple lists of priorities from each domain and subject area and develop one final list of priority needs *across* them (see Figure 6.6). This final list of priorities will describe the emphasized content of instruction for the student during the next school year. Upon reviewing the prioritized needs for each of the domains and areas, the education team may find it possible to complete two activities that will simplify their negotiation process. First, one item may appear on more than one priority list, allowing the education team to consolidate the items on those lists and eliminate duplications. An example occurs in Mark's student profile (see Appendix A) when *increasing interactions* and *communication skills* are included as priorities on the family, community, peer, and general education inventories. His team used these priorities to develop annual goals #1 and #2 for Mark. Second, two or more items may be related or demonstrated during the same activity, and the education team may choose to combine these items. A similar example occurs in Tony's student profile (see Appendix A) when *increase use of adaptive switches* is included as a priority in the family inventory and *partially participate in cooking activities with a peer during home and careers class* is a priority in the general education curriculum inventory. Because these two priorities are similar, a combination of the two resulted in annual goal #4 for Tony.

After they complete these simplifying steps, the education team then reviews the remaining items to (1) determine which items are most important to include in instruction for the student during the next school year and (2) eliminate the remaining items from consideration for the next year, but hold them for consideration for the following year. The education team then lists the items selected as important for the next school year in order of priority. The team may use various methods to determine order of priority. For example, if agreement cannot be reached among all the team members, they may list items based on the number of team members that agree on its importance. If there is complete lack of agreement, the family may select one or more priorities, then the remaining team members may select the next priority, and so on. Whatever process is used, the task is to rank those items considered most relevant and critical to include in instruction for the student, giving equal consideration to family, student, and school personnel opinions. In addition, the team must give equal consideration to items that reflect both functional and general education curriculum content.

The final list of priorities for any student may reflect either (1) a combination of both functional and general education curriculum content (see student profile for Maureen in Appendix B), (2) all general education curriculum content (see student profile for Dave in Appendix A), or (3) all functional curriculum content (see student profile for Tony in

Priority Needs: Family Inventory	Priority Needs: Peer Inventory	Priority Needs: Community Inventory	Priority Needs: Related Services Assessments
Priority Needs: Records and Prior Information	Priority Needs: Student Preferences	Priority Needs: General Education Settings	Priority Needs: General Education Curriculum

Family's Priorities	Other Team Member's Priorities	Student's Preferences

Final Priorities	
1)	6)
2)	7)
3)	8)
4)	9)
5)	10)

FIGURE 6.6   *Schema for Negotiating Final List of Priorities.*

Appendix A). The intent of this process is for the education team as a whole to consider *all* relevant curriculum content for each student and to identify the most relevant and critical content for inclusion in the next year's instruction for each student.

Blending of Priority Needs Within Annual Goals

With the final list of priority items for a student, the education team then develops a feasible number of annual goals that incorporate those items. The number of annual goals developed varies per school district, education team, and student, but should be determined based upon the (1) degree to which items are critical for the student, (2) degree to which instruction can occur on multiple annual goals at one time, and (3) feasibility of providing instruction on all the content across the school year. Annual goals may, however, reflect more than one item. For instance, aside from reflecting only one curricular need (that is, one functional *or* general education curricular need), an annual goal may reflect functional *and* general education curriculum needs, more than one functional curriculum need, or more than one general education curriculum need. The key to blending items within one goal is determining the extent to which the functional activities and skills included in the items are used within the same instructional activity, as well as across activities and settings. For example, Dave's annual goal #1 addresses both the priority for improving social interaction skills across activities and participating in more activities across settings (see student profile in Appendix A).

To incorporate the guidelines found in IDEA into annual goals, as well as to delineate clearly the intent of an annual goal and to provide a specific method of measuring the degree to which a student progresses toward meeting that intent, education teams frequently develop annual goals that include the activity during which the content will be used. In addition, annual goals may include both the student's current and projected performance levels. Figure 6.7 includes two simple fill-in-the-blank worksheets education teams have used to incorporate the components into an easy-to-read format. Examples of annual goals that education teams developed using this worksheet and that incorporate these components are in the student profiles in Appendix A.

Identifying Locations for Instruction

In addition to identifying curriculum content for an annual goal, education teams determine the locations in which the student will receive instruction on, and demonstrate acquisition of, that content. Although not necessarily included within the annual goal, locations for instruction and demonstration of acquisition are important to this process for a number of reasons. First, if an education team wants a student to learn activities and skills that are functional for that student, instruction will occur in the setting(s) in which the activities and skills are needed. The team, therefore, should select locations for instruction with attention to where the student naturally will need to complete each activity and use each skill. Second, if an education team wants a student to complete an activity or use a skill in more than one setting, instruction will occur in more than one setting. The

FIGURE 6.7   *Annual Goal Development Worksheet.*

Fill in the blanks for #1:

   a)   *Student's name*
   b)   will   *increase/decrease/maintain*
   c)   *domain/area/type of skills*
   d)   during   *activity or activities*
   e)   from   *current level of performance*
   f)   to   *projected level of performance*
   g)   within one year.

or for #2:

   Student's name   will   *increase/decrease/maintain*
   domain/area/type of skills   during   *activity or activities*   from
   current level of performance   to   *projected level of performance*   within one year.

number of settings selected for instruction will be determined by the number of (1) current and future settings in which the student needs to complete each activity or use each skill; and (2) settings required for the student to generalize, as determined by the student's past acquisition and generalization rates. Third, if an education team wants a student to learn an activity or skill as quickly as possible, the number of instructional trials should be as great as possible. Whenever an event occurs, therefore, during which an activity or skill included in the student's annual goals may be incorporated, instruction on that activity or skill should occur. For all of these reasons, education teams identify the functional and general education activities during which a student will receive instruction on the identified curriculum content.

In selecting locations for instruction, education teams consider how instruction on both functional and general education curriculum content may occur either during functional or general education activities (see Figure 6.8). That is, instruction on both functional and general education curriculum content can be incorporated into general education activities in the classroom, school building, or on field trips in the community. Likewise, instruction on both functional and general education curriculum content can be incorporated into functional activities in the classroom, school building, home, or community. For example, Dave's annual goal to increase social interaction skills through engaging in reciprocal conversations can occur during instruction on both general and functional curriculum content in the classroom, the school building, his home, and the community (see his student profile in Appendix A). When both functional and general education curriculum content are blended during one instructional activity, the education team (1) maximizes the use of instructional time, (2) maximizes the probability of use of skills in settings in which those skills are needed, and (3) allows other time periods to be used for instruction on additional

Student: _____   Date: _____

Annual Goal	General Education Settings			Functional Activity Settings			
	Classroom	School Building	Field Trips	Classroom	School Building	Field Trips	Home	Community

FIGURE 6.8 *Settings for Instruction Per Annual Goal.*

content. The more that instruction can address multiple content areas, the more efficiently instructional time is used.

Summary

An education team has the responsibility to consider all possible curriculum content for each student, so as to maximize students' acquisition of activities and skills most meaningful for them in both current and future environments. In addition, the team pays particular attention to the development of students' natural support networks and the existence of ethnic diversity in each student's family. Determining the curriculum content that will comprise the education program for a student with moderate to severe disabilities entails the use of judgement when making a number of decisions, and the process used to make those decisions reflects the values held by the education team.

Education teams involved in inclusive services use a process that allows for blending functional and general education curriculum needs in annual goals and instruction. This blending necessitates a process for identifying priority needs for a student that gives equal consideration to both types of curriculum content, but selects only the most relevant content for instruction for the student during the next school year. The curriculum content identification process presented in this chapter emphasizes: (1) the role of the student, family, and other team members; (2) the blending of functional and general education curriculum content on the IEP; and (3) the provision of instruction on both functional and general education curriculum content during both general education and functional activities.

The process is based on an extension of the ecological approach for identifying functional curriculum content using (1) a family inventory, (2) a peer inventory, (3) a community inventory, (4) in vivo related services assessments, (5) records and prior information, (6) student preferences, (7) an inventory of general education settings, and (8) a general education curriculum content inventory. In completing each component of the process, the education team also identifies the priority needs for that component to be used during the negotiation of annual goals and objectives for instruction during the next school year.

Negotiation during IEP development is a process for bringing about agreement on the content on which a student will receive instruction during the next school year. True negotiation requires that a team functions in a collaborative manner across the year, in all aspects of their interactions. Each annual goal may reflect either one functional or general education curriculum need, more than one functional curriculum need, more than one general education curriculum need, or any combination of functional and general education curriculum needs. Blending needs within one goal is dependent upon the possibility of the needs being demonstrated during the same activity.

Finally, the education team identifies the location(s) in which instruction will occur on the content of each annual goal and in which the student will demonstrate acquisition of the content. The team should select locations with consideration for the occurrence of functional activities, generalized use of the skills and activities, and maximization of instructional time. The blending of instruction for functional and general education curriculum needs during the same instructional activities maximizes the impact of instruction.

References

Agran, M., & Wehmeyer, M. (2003). Promoting the self-determination of students with severe disabilities. In D. L. Ryndak & S. Alper, (Eds.), *Curriculum and instruction for students with significant disabilities in general education inclusive settings* (2nd ed.). Boston: Allyn & Bacon.

Ainscow, L. (Ed.). (1991). *Effective education for all.* London: David Fulton Publishers.

Brown, L., Branston-McLean, M. B., Baumgart, D., Vincent, L., Falvey, M., & Schroeder, J. (1979a). Using the characteristics of current and future least restrictive environments in the development of curricular content for severely handicapped students. *AAESPH Review, 4*(4), 407–424.

Brown, L., Branston, M. B., Hamre-Nietupski, S., Pumpian, I., Certo, N., & Gruenewald, L. (1979b). A strategy for developing chronological age appropriate and functional curricular content for severely handicapped adolescents and young adults. *Journal of Special Education, 13*(1), 81–90.

Brown, L., Nisbet, J., Ford, A., Sweet, M., Shiraga, B., York, J., & Loomis, R. (1983). The critical need for nonschool instruction in educational programs for severely handicapped students. *Journal of The Association for the Severely Handicapped, 8*(3), 71–77.

Chin-Perez, G., Hartman, D., Park, H. S., Sacks, S., Wershing, A., & Gaylord-Ross, R. (1986). Maximizing social contact for secondary students with severe handicaps. *Journal of The Association for Persons with Severe Handicaps, 11*(2), 118–124.

Cohen, S., Agosta, J., Cohen, J., & Warren, R. (1989). Supporting families of children with severe disabilities. *Journal of The Association for Persons with Severe Handicaps, 14*(2), 155–162.

Downing, J. E. (2000). *Including students with severe and multiple disabilities in typical classrooms.* Baltimore: Paul H. Brookes Publishing Co.

Falvey, M., Forest, M., Pearpoint, J., & Rosenberg, R. (1997). *All my life's a circle. Using the tools: Circles, MAPS, and PATHS.* Toronto, Ontario: Inclusion Press.

Federal Register, 64, 48, 1999.

Fisher, D., Pumpian, I., & Sax, C. (1998). High school students' attitudes about and recommendations for their peers with significant disabilities. *Journal of*

The Association for Persons with Severe Handicaps, 23, 272–282.

Gaylord-Ross, R., & Browder, D. (1991). Functional assessment: Dynamic and domain properties. In L. H. Meyer, C. A. Peck, & L. Brown (Eds.), *Critical issues in the lives of people with severe disabilities* (pp. 45–66). Baltimore: Paul H. Brookes.

Gee, K., Graham, N., Goetz, L., Oshima, G., & Yoshika, K. (1991). Teaching students to request the continuation of routine activities by using time delay and decreasing physical assistance in the context of chain interruption. *Journal of The Association for Persons with Severe Handicaps, 16*, 154–167.

Giangreco, M. F., Cloninger, C. J., & Iverson, V. S. (1998). *Choosing options and accommodations for children (COACH): A guide to educational planning for students with disabilities* (2nd ed.). Baltimore: Paul H. Brookes.

Green, C. W., Reid, D. H., Canipe, V. S., & Gardner, S. M. (1991). A comprehensive evaluation of reinforcer identification processes for persons with profound multiple handicaps. *Journal of Applied Behavior Analysis, 24*, 537–552.

Green, C. W., Reid, D. H., White, L. K., Halford, R. C., Brittain, D. P., & Gardner, S. M. (1988). Identifying reinforcers for persons with profound handicaps: Staff option vs. systematic assessment of preferences. *Journal of Applied Behavior Analysis, 21*, 31–44.

Halvorsen, A. T., & Neary, T. (2001). *Building inclusive schools: Tools and strategies for success.* Boston: Allyn & Bacon.

Haring, T. G. (1991). Social relationships. In L. H. Meyer, C. A. Peck, & L. Brown (Eds.), *Critical issues in the lives of people with severe disabilities* (pp. 195–217). Baltimore: Paul H. Brookes.

Haring, T. G., & Breen, C. (1989). Units of analysis of social interaction outcomes in supported employment. *Journal of The Association for Persons with Severe Handicaps, 14*(4), 255–262.

Helmstetter, E., & Guess, D. (1987). Application of the individualized curriculum sequencing model to learners with severe sensory impairments. In L. Goetz, D. Guess, & K. Stremel-Campbell (Eds.), *Innovative program design for individuals with dual sensory impairments* (pp. 255–282). Baltimore: Paul H. Brookes.

Helmstetter, E., Peck, C. A., & Giangreco, M. F. (1994). Outcomes of interactions with peers with moderate or severe disabilities: A statewide survey of high school students. *Journal of The Association for Persons with Severe Handicaps, 19*, 263–276.

Hoier, T., & Cone, J. D. (1987). Target selection of social skills for children. *Behavior Modification, 11*, 137–163.

Hunt, P., Staub, D., Alwell, M., & Goetz, L. (1994). Achievement by all students within the context of cooperative learning groups. *Journal of The Association for Persons with Severe Handicaps, 19*, 290–301.

Hunt, P., Alwell, M., Farron-Davis, F., & Goetz, L. (1996). Creating socially supportive environments for fully included students who experience multiple disabilities. *Journal of The Association for Persons with Severe Handicaps, 21*, 53–71.

Idol, L. (1993). *Special educator's consultation handbook*. Austin: Pro-Ed, Inc.

Individuals with Disabilities Education Act of 1997. Individuals with Disabilities Education Act (IDEA) Amendments of 1997, PL 105-17, 20 U.S.C. § 1400 et seq.

Individuals with Disabilities Education Act Amendments of 1997, 20 U.S.C. § 1400 *et seq.* (U.S. Government Printing Office, 1997).

Jackson, L., Ryndak, D. L., & Billingsley, F. (2000). Useful practices in inclusive education: A preliminary view of what experts in moderate and severe disabilities are saying. *Journal of The Association for Persons with Severe Handicaps, 25*(3), 129–141.

Janney, R., & Snell, M. (1996). How teachers use peer interactions to include students with moderate and severe disabilities in elementary general education classes. *Journal of The Association for Persons with Severe Handicaps, 21*, 72–80.

Kennedy, C. H., & Haring, T. G. (1993). Teaching choice making during social interactions to students with profound multiple disabilities. *Journal of Applied Behavior Analysis, 26*, 63–76.

Kennedy, C. H., Shukla, S., & Fryxell, D. (1997). Comparing the effects of educational placement on the social relationships of intermediate school students with severe disabilities. *Exceptional Children, 64*, 31–48.

Kishi, G., & Meyer, L. (1994). What children report and remember: A six-year follow-up of the effects of social contact between peers with and without severe disabilities. *Journal of The Association for Persons with Severe Handicaps, 19*, 277–289.

Menchetti, B. M., & Sweeney, M. A. (1995). *Person-centered planning: Technical assistance packet* (No. 5). Gainesville: University of Florida.

Mount, B., & Zwernik, K. (1988). *It's never too early, it's never too late: A booklet about personal futures planning*. St. Paul, MN: Metropolitan Council.

Orelove, F. P., & Sobsey, D. (1996). *Educating children with multiple disabilities: A transdisciplinary approach* (3rd ed.). Baltimore: Paul H. Brookes.

Rainforth, B., York, J., & Macdonald, C. (1992). *Collaborative teams for students with severe disabilities*. Baltimore, MD: Paul H. Brookes.

Ryndak, D. L., Alper, S., Stuart, C., & Clark, D. (in press). Identifying curriculum for students with severe disabilities in general education contexts. *AAMR Research to Practice Series: Innovations*. Washington, DC: American Association on Mental Retardation.

Ryndak, D. L., & Billingsley, F. (in press). Access to the general education curriculum. In C. Kennedy & E. Horn (Eds.), *Including students with significant disabilities: Putting research into practice*. Boston: Allyn & Bacon.

Ryndak, D. L., Morrison, A. P., & Sommerstein, L. (1999). Literacy before and after inclusion in general education settings: A case study. *Journal of The Association for Persons with Severe Handicaps, 24*, 5–22.

Salisbury, C., & Vincent, L. J. (1990). "Criterion of the next environment" and "best practices": Mainstreaming and integration 10 years later. *Topics in Early Childhood Special Education, 10*(2), 78–89.

Schnorr, R. (1990). "Peter? He comes and goes . . . ": First graders' perspectives on a part-time mainstream student. *Journal of The Association for Persons with Severe Handicaps, 15*(4), 231–240.

Schnorr, R. F. (1997). From enrollment to membership: "Belongingness" in middle and high school classes. *Journal of The Association for Persons with Severe Handicaps, 22*, 1–15.

Schwartz, I. S. (1995). Using social-validity assessments to identify meaningful outcomes for students with deaf-blindness. In N. G. Haring & L. T. Romer (Eds.), *Welcoming students who are deaf-blind into typical classrooms: Facilitating school participation, learning, and friendships* (pp. 133–142). Baltimore: Paul H. Brookes Publishing Co.

Staub, D., Schwartz, I. L., Gallucci, C., & Peck, C. A. (1994). Four portraits of friendship at an inclusive school. *Journal of The Association for Persons with Severe Handicaps, 19*, 314–325.

Turnbull, A. P., & Turnbull, H. R. (1997). *Families, professionals, and exceptionality: A special partnership (3rd ed.)*. Upper Saddle River, NJ: Merrill/Prentice-Hall.

Vandercook, T., & York, J. (1990). A team approach to

program development and support. In W. Stainback, & S. Stainback (Eds.), *Support networks for inclusive schooling: Interdependent integrated education* (pp. 95–122). Baltimore: Paul H. Brookes Publishing Co.

Vandercook, T., York, J., & Forest, M. (1989). The McGill action planning system (MAPS): A strategy for building the vision. *Journal of The Association for Persons with Severe Handicaps,* *14*(3), 205–215.

Webster's ninth collegiate dictionary (1991). Springfield, MA: Merriam-Webster.

Wolery, M., Ault, M. J., & Doyle, P. M. (1992). *Teaching students with moderate to severe disabilities: Use of response prompting strategies.* White Plains, NY: Longman.

7

Natural Support Networks: Collaborating with Family and Friends for Meaningful Education Programs in Inclusive Settings

Diane Lea Ryndak

Michael W. Muldoon

Objectives

After reading this chapter, the reader will be able to:

1. Define a natural support network and describe his/her own network.
2. Describe how and why the members of a student's natural support network should participate in the student's education program.
3. List and describe variables that affect the degree to which family members and friends participate in a student's education program.
4. Describe the role of family members and friends in the identification of curriculum content for a student's education program the next school year.
5. Describe the role of family members and friends during the implementation of instruction throughout the school year.
6. List and describe strategies for education teams to facilitate the expansion of a student's natural support network.

Key Terms _____

Jorgensen (1998) defined inclusion as the membership and full participation of individuals with disabilities in naturally occurring activities at home, at school, at work, and in the community. The nature and intent of providing such services create a situation that not only is conducive to, but also dependent upon, extensive collaboration with family members and friends in the development and implementation of a student's education program. Collaboration with family members and friends is critical because they are most knowledgeable not only about the student, but also about the settings that comprise the student's life space (Brown, Shiraga, York, Zanella, & Rogan, 1984; Giangreco, Cloninger, & Iverson, 1998) and the activities that occur in those settings. Through collaboration with these individuals, school personnel (1) identify the environments, activities, and skills most meaningful for a student's participation in everyday life and (2) facilitate the broadening of a student's natural support network. This increases the probability that the student's network will be substantial enough to support the student both during and after the educational career.

Natural Support Networks

A natural support network is the set of individuals with whom a person has ongoing interactions in everyday life, reflecting various levels of friendship, caring, support, and assistance for both parties across a variety of activities. Members of a natural support network share a mutual respect and interdependence, each receiving intrinsic benefits from interactions (Forest & Lusthaus, 1989). Although there are similarities in how individual support networks are structured, many differences also exist. For example, the manner in which a preschool student relies on a natural support network, as well as the types of support required from the network, is different from those of a premed college student, a junior-high student in the inner city, or a high-school student in a rural area. Each, however, has identified a set of individuals with whom he or she has developed a mutually supportive relationship built on friendship, caring, support, and assistance.

Jorgensen (1998) identified seven essential conditions that increase the likelihood that social connections and friendships will develop at school. They include the following:

1. Full inclusion in all aspects of school and community life;
2. Access to a means of communication at all times and classmates that understand and know how to use the system;

3. Provision of support in a way that promotes independence, interdependence, self-determination, and a reliance on natural supports;
4. Student involvement in the inclusion process and in creative problem solving;
5. Age-appropriate and respectful materials, language, expectations, and modifications;
6. Involvement of family members and school personnel in facilitating and supporting friendships and social activities; and
7. Attention to the development of a schoolwide climate of acceptance and celebration of diversity.

Although the mere presence of these essential conditions does not guarantee that individual students will develop friendships at school, they do provide a framework around which friendships are more likely to develop. Furthermore, these conditions are consistent with the definition of school inclusion for students with moderate to severe disabilities that Ryndak, Jackson, and Billingsley (2000) described.

Although the list of all possible members of a natural support network is endless, the number of actual members in a network is limited (see Figure 7.1). Sporadic interactions with numerous potential members, however, do not constitute the basis on which membership in that person's network is established. Rather, membership in a natural support network develops over time, through ongoing, purposeful, mutually beneficial interactions. Such interactions may provide any number of benefits for either or both parties. For example, the number of opportunities to socially interact or the frequency with which companionship is available during routine or special events may increase for either person. A natural support network member may become a partner for leisure activities or may provide various types of assistance (for example, physical, logistical, or emotional) that allow a person to participate in both routine and special activities. Additionally, members of a natural support network may provide various types of support. York, Giangreco, Vandercook, and Macdonald (1992) refer to four types of support that team members provide for each other.

1. Resource support—the provision of tangible material, financial resources, informational resources, or human resources to team members.

FIGURE 7.1   *Possible Members of a Natural Support Network.*

Parents	Classmates
Siblings	Coworkers
Relatives	Fellow employees
Neighbors	Employer
Family friends/extended family	Business owners
Fellow participants in community or leisure activities	Business employees
	Community workers
Members of education team	

2. Moral support—person-to-person interactions that validate the worth of people as individuals and as knowledgeable colleagues.
3. Technical support—offers of concrete strategies, methods, approaches, or ideas.
4. Evaluation support—assistance both in collecting information to monitor and adjust support and in determining the effect of support. (pp. 104–105)

Although York et al. (1992) discuss support in relation to team responsibilities and the needs of team members, the same types of support occur in relation to responsibilities of a natural support network and the needs of its members.

Members of the natural support network for a student with disabilities provide that student opportunities for interaction, companionship during leisure, assistance during activities, and support in a variety of ways. For this reason, collaboration between school personnel and network members is critical when (1) identifying both functional and general education curriculum content that is most relevant for inclusion in instruction, (2) implementing instruction, and (3) evaluating the effect of that instruction.

Identifying the Natural Support Network for a Student

Consistent with the sixth essential condition of involving family members and school personnel in facilitating friendships, Snow and Forest (1987) described a process called "circle of friends," which is used by typical peers to identify people who play certain roles in their own lives and in the life of a classmate with disabilities. This process allows students to understand the need for peers with disabilities to develop additional, nonpaid, meaningful relationships and encourages them to become part of their classmate's "circle of friends." As stated by Forest and Lusthaus (1989), the intent of this process is to assist in the development of "a network that allows for the genuine involvement of children in a friendship, caring, and support role with their peers" (p. 47). (See Chapter 11 for further information on friendship development.)

There is a similar process, for identifying members of a student's natural support network. In this process the student draws four circles in the north, south, east, and west positions with all four overlapping in the middle (see Figure 7.2). One large circle surrounds these four circles. This large circle represents all "social interaction." The four overlapping circles represent other types of benefits experienced by members of a natural support network (that is, companionship, partners for activities, assistance, and support). Note that, at the very center of this figure, all five circles overlap.

When using this process to identify members of a student's natural support network, a name is placed in the circle(s) that represents the type of benefit the *student* experiences through interactions with the person named. The only people listed, however, are those with whom the student has ongoing, purposeful, mutually beneficial interactions, resulting in various levels of friendship, caring, support, and assistance. When a name appears in more than one of the four central circles, and those circles are adjacent, that name moves to where the circles overlap. If a name is in more than two of those circles, that name moves to where all three or four circles overlap. The closer the name appears to the center of the figure indicates the more types of benefit the student experiences through interactions with the

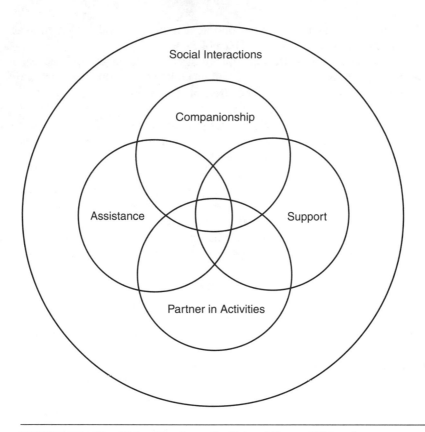

FIGURE 7.2   *Identifying Members of a Natural Support Network.*

person named. Finally, every person listed in one of the four central circles automatically appears in the large circle that represents social interaction, which automatically occurs when any of the four benefits occurs.

When peers complete this process for their own natural support network and that of a classmate with disabilities, the visual images project any discrepancy between the two networks. Follow-up discussions assist peers in realizing the degree to which classmates with disabilities must rely on others for support and assistance. If members of a natural support network are not available, their classmates must rely on people who are paid to support and assist them. To minimize the need for paid support and assistance, natural support networks for each classmate with disabilities must be extensive, and the education team should facilitate the membership of peers throughout the school years. As members join a student's natural support network, they should feel encouraged to participate in the student's education program. Completing this process can help to fulfill the seventh essential condition of developing a school-wide climate of acceptance and celebration of diversity.

Unfortunately, little is known about how to define an individual's social life and how to measure the extent to which it affects an individual's life (Malette et al., 1992).

The importance of natural support networks in both social life and education program planning, however, increasingly is being recognized (Kennedy, Horner, & Newton, 1990; Malette et al., 1992).

Cultural Diversity and Other Factors Affecting Participation of Network Members

Although the Education for Handicapped Children Act (EHA) of 1975 (PL 94-142) and its reauthorization as the Individuals with Disabilities Education Act (IDEA) of 1990 (PL 101-476) mandate the inclusion of parents in the development of a student's Individualized Education Program (IEP), the 1997 reauthorization of IDEA went a step further by indicating that parents are "expected to be equal participants along with school personnel in developing, reviewing and revising the IEP for their child." According to Salisbury and Dunst (1997), the ultimate success of meeting a student's needs will, in fact, rest on the educational system's ability to link effectively with the student's home and community.

If a student is to receive services that reflect the intent of inclusion and to experience the full benefits of inclusion, school personnel must be proactive in facilitating the involvement of parents (Shea & Bauer, 1991) and of other members of the student's natural support network. The inclusion of the student and the family on the team is especially important as parents are the primary advocates for their children. The family's commitment to the child's success extends beyond the concern for current schooling to the big picture of the child's life and future (Buswell, Schaffner, & Seyler, 1999). There is, however, a history of limited participation by parents in the development and implementation of education programs. Salisbury (1992) identifies three factors that influence the degree to which parents have been involved in education programs, and Rueda and Martinez (1992) identify three main barriers to the participation of Latino families (see Figure 7.3). Ruiz (1989) provides strategies for developing an optimal learning environment for a language-minority student. With increased focus on participation of both parents and additional network members in education programs, school personnel may want to consider these variables in relation to interaction with all network members. In addition, school personnel may want to (1) expand beyond the parents the number of members of a student's natural support network involved in the education program, (2) modify the manner of encouraging parents and other network members to participate actively, and (3) increase the extent to which information provided by parents and other network members influences the student's program.

Involvement of Family and Other Network Members in Identifying Curriculum Content

When identifying relevant curriculum content for inclusion in a student's education program, family and other network members can provide invaluable information and assistance during numerous procedures. The following sections describe three of these procedures and ways in which family and other network members proactively affect the outcome of those procedures.

FIGURE 7.3   *Factors Affecting Participation of Parents and Other Network Members in Education Programs.*

A. Communication
1. Communication is not in the primary languages of parents and other network members.
2. Professionals use jargon with which parents and other network members are not familiar.
3. Parents or other network members have intellectual or physical limitations.
4. Professionals limit communication with parents and other network members to administrative tasks.
5. Professionals and/or network members have verbal and/or nonverbal interpersonal communication skills that are ineffective.

B. Perception, Attitudes, and Values
1. Professionals demonstrate an insensitivity to differences among networks (i.e., family characteristics, cultural differences, class differences).
2. Parents and other network members are viewed as adversaries rather than partners.
3. Parents and other network members are viewed as less observant, perceptive, or intelligent than professionals.
4. Priorities and expectations of parents and other network members do not match those of professionals.
5. Professionals experience profession-related constraints (e.g., time constraints, role constraints).

C. Logistical Difficulties
1. Professionals and network members have difficulty finding mutually agreed upon times for meetings.
2. Structure of meetings minimize importance of participation of parents and other network members.

(Adapted from Salisbury [1992]. Parents as team members: Inclusive teams, collaborative outcomes. In B. Rainforth, J. York, & C. Macdonald [Eds.], *Collaborative teams for students with severe disabilities: Integrating therapy and educational services* [pp. 43–66]. Baltimore: Paul H. Brookes Publishing Co.; and Rueda & Martinez [1992]. Fiesta educativa: One community's approach to parent training in developmental disabilities for Latino families. *The Journal of The Association for Persons with Severe Handicaps, 17*[2], 95–103.)

Gathering Information

Because the purpose of education is to prepare students to be maximally independent and to participate fully in naturally occurring activities, school personnel must focus procedures related to identifying what to teach each student on determining the activities that naturally occur in each of their lives (Shea & Bauer, 1991). Only through this information can an education team identify the most meaningful content for each student. When identifying what content is most meaningful, teams must keep in mind the four essential conditions of using age-appropriate and respectful materials, language, expectations, and modifications. To accomplish this, school personnel put aside their predetermined curricula, whether based in developmental theory or activities of daily living, and systematically study the variables that are important in each student's life (see Chapter 6 for details on the procedures used to study variables).

In recent years, we have seen the development of several person-centered planning tools that have proven useful in generating a shared vision for an individual with disabilities. Having this shared vision helps team members maintain a view of the student as a person rather than a collection of deficits. Envisioning a desirable future requires knowledge of individual student characteristics, including interests, strengths, challenges, and needs (Rainforth & York-Barr, 1997). Members of a student's natural support network are the most valid source of this information and about settings and activities that are relevant for that student (Hamre-Nietupski, Nietupski, & Strathe, 1992). Vandercook, York, and Forest (1989) describe the McGill Action Planning System (MAPS) as one strategy for obtaining information from natural support network members. MAPS consists of a meeting at which seven questions are answered.

1. What is the student's history?
2. What is your dream for the student?
3. What is your nightmare?
4. Who is the student?
5. What are the student's strengths, gifts, and abilities?
6. What are the student's needs?
7. What would the student's ideal day at school look like, and what is necessary to make it happen?

Through their responses, natural support network members provide a wealth of information both about the student with disabilities and about the student's relationships with others.

Although all support network members are valuable sources of information, the logistics of obtaining equal participation by all members of a student's network are untenable. It is possible, therefore, for parents and a few other members to represent all the members of a student's support network and to participate actively in procedures that will identify the curriculum content to be included on the student's IEP for the next year. Parents and other participating network members, therefore, obtain information that is relevant to these procedures from other members of the student's network. School personnel, parents, and other participating network members then complete together a family inventory, peer inventory, community inventory, general education settings inventory, and inventory of general education curriculum content (see Chapter 6 for a discussion of these inventories).

Each parent and other network member may participate in all or some of these procedures, depending upon their intimate involvement in and knowledge of each procedure. For instance, school friends of an elementary student may participate only in the peer inventory and general education settings inventory, while intimate friends of a high-school student also may participate in the community and general education curriculum content inventories. The intent is to obtain participation from the individuals who are most involved in a student's life, and use that information to determine the most meaningful content for instruction for that student based on the student's daily life.

Negotiating Annual Goals

The second procedure in which family and other network members provide essential information and assistance is negotiation of content for annual goals (see Chapter 6 for details on negotiating annual goals). During annual goal negotiation procedures for the IEP, any education team member may become myopic, focusing on the acquisition of either isolated skills or of skills within their area of expertise, instead of the need for and use of skills within activities that are meaningful for a student in daily life. Because family and other network members are involved most intimately in the student's daily life, their assistance in refocusing the purpose of the meeting and in reaffirming the purpose of the education program being developed is essential.

There are at least three ways in which family and other network members complete these tasks. First, they ensure that discussions center on activities that occur in settings frequented by the student and that those are the basis on which functional and general education content are selected for inclusion in annual goals. When discussions digress from this focus, family and other network members step in to redirect the discussion. Second, family and other network members have the knowledge base to determine the extent to which the student will use suggested functional and general education content in daily life (Hamre-Nietupski et al., 1992). If they cannot link suggested content to specific activities in the student's naturally occurring settings (that is, general education settings, school building, home, work, or community settings), family and other network members question the content. When school personnel are unable to convince everyone of the immediate link, the education team does not include that content in the annual goals. When a link is established, family and other network members also assist in determining the relative importance of the content in comparison with other content. Third, family and other network members have the knowledge to determine when and how two or more suggested components of functional and/or general education content blend together for the student's use in daily life. This knowledge assists in minimizing the number of annual goals that need to be monitored, while maximizing the relevance of the content selected for instructional emphasis. It also assists in linking content that occurs naturally in daily settings.

Identifying Settings for Instruction

The third procedure during which family and other network members provide essential information and assistance is the identification of settings in which instruction will occur (see Chapter 6 for details on identifying settings for instruction). When discussing where instruction will occur on the content of a specific annual goal, the attention of school personnel may be limited to settings with which they immediately are familiar (that is, general education settings or school building settings) or settings that frequently are incorporated into packaged curricula (for example, kitchen, grocery store, restaurant, or restroom). Because family and other network members have first-hand knowledge of the settings frequented by the student and the additional settings to which the student has access beyond the school and traditional community settings, their collaboration in identifying instructional settings is crucial.

There are two ways in which family and other network members assist in the identification of settings for instruction. First, after agreeing on the content of an annual goal, family and other network members assist by determining all of the settings and activities in which the student can make use of the content in daily life, whether the annual goal incorporates functional or general education content. Second, during discussions of a particular setting and activity, family and other network members determine whether the student (1) likes or has the option to participate in the activity in that setting and (2) has the resources required to participate in the activity in that setting. Through this process, family and other network members verify that all instructional settings are meaningful and viable for the student.

Beyond Identifying Curriculum Content

After the education team has established the curriculum content for inclusion in the IEP, collaboration with family and other network members does not end. Family and other network members are in unique positions to continue to assist school personnel with instruction, and school personnel are in unique positions to assist family and other network members with maintaining and expanding the network itself.

Family and Other Network Members Supporting Instruction

After the initiation of instruction, family and other network members continue to interact with the student in naturally occurring settings throughout daily life. Because the content of instruction is specific for its need and use in natural settings, and because the student accesses some of those natural settings outside of the school day, family and other network members frequently are in the position to reinforce learning that is occurring at school by using instructional procedures in those natural settings (Neel & Billingsley, 1989). Although formal instruction that strictly follows procedures used in school may not be feasible or desirable to family and other network members (Idol, 1993), informal instruction at home or in the community may be possible. Informal instruction may consist of loosely following instructional procedures only at times and in situations in which the instruction will not be intrusive to the ongoing events. Parents frequently conduct informal instruction, and they use spontaneous situations as conduits for incidental learning.

This type of collaboration should be encouraged by other education team members, however, only after discussions with family and other network members who carefully consider the complex nature of the situations in which they interact with the student (Gaylord-Ross & Browder, 1991). For example, if one parent has five children to prepare for school in the morning and to interact with after school, expectations for that parent to focus on spontaneous situations for incidental learning may not be realistic. This same parent, however, may desire to focus on spontaneous situations for incidental learning after dinner when additional adult support is available. The decision to encourage such collaboration, therefore, is made on an individual basis.

Besides assisting with instruction during naturally occurring events, family and other network members also have the opportunity to observe the student's performance and participation during activities. This observation allows them to assist in (1) evaluating the degree to which the student's instruction has been effective (Gaylord-Ross & Browder, 1991), (2) identifying additional curriculum content areas that would be beneficial for the student, and (3) determining alternate instructional strategies.

Maintaining and Extending Natural Support Networks

Malette et al. (1992) state that "neither the service delivery system nor the community as a whole has a clear understanding of what defines a 'social life,' much less how to measure the extent to which it occurs" (p. 190). Newton and Horner (1993) have begun to identify strategies for developing social relationships, which are required for a social life to exist. What is clear is that natural support networks cannot develop unless potential members have opportunities to interact and develop relationships (Biklen, 1989; Stainback, Stainback, & Slavin, 1989; Strully & Strully, 1989). Schnorr (1990) described how children as young as first graders already had developed a sense of which students "belonged" in their class and which were "visitors" based on the students' full- or part-time participation in class activities. This argues convincingly for full-time participation of students with disabilities in activities with their nondisabled peers (Brown et al., 1991) if natural support networks are to develop.

In addition, many adults with disabilities do not have an extensive natural support network. They have social contacts with numerous people but few relationships that last past twelve months (Kennedy, Horner, & Newton, 1989). Even through social contacts created by secondary transition programs (Chadsey-Rusch, 1990) and employment in competitive jobs (Shafer, Rice, Metzler, & Haring, 1989), adults with disabilities seldom develop relationships that expand their natural support network.

Through their daily contact with a variety of students, school personnel are in a position to greatly influence how and when students interact with each other. Students' interactions during school hours will determine the degree and manner in which they choose to interact with each other outside of school (McDonnell, Wilcox, & Hardman, 1991). For example, if two students frequently interact socially during school hours, the chances are high that they also will interact socially outside of school when provided opportunities. Through such ongoing interactions, membership in a natural support network can develop. School personnel, therefore, can influence membership in the natural support network for specific students by providing opportunities for that student to interact with classmates (Haring, 1991; Stainback & Stainback, 1990). Although interactions may center around general education, functional, or social activities, students can learn how to support and interact effectively with each other during any type of activity. The task for school personnel is to facilitate membership in natural support networks by providing opportunities for students to interact during various types of activities.

There are a number of strategies in school (Eichinger, 1990; Staub & Hunt, 1993) and in living options programs (Newton & Horner, 1993) that provide opportunities for students to interact. As described previously, the "circle of friends" activity (Snow & Forest, 1987) can assist students of all ages to understand their classmates' needs for additional friends in their support network. This understanding alone, however, is insufficient to establish those needed friendships; opportunities to interact also are required. In many classrooms, teachers are using cooperative learning strategies across academic areas to maximize opportunities for interaction between students.

Cooperative learning strategies allow students to work in small groups, sharing responsibility for acquisition of new knowledge and for demonstration of that knowledge by each member of their group (Borich, 1992; Putnam, Rynders, Johnson, & Johnson, 1989; Schulz, Carpenter, & Turnbull, 1991). Henley, Ramsey, & Algozzine (1993) specifically define cooperative learning as "a method of structuring small groups of nondisabled and disabled students so that all the individuals achieve a learning goal through mutual planning and decision making" (p. 194). Strategies include (1) cooperative goal structuring (Johnson & Johnson, 1986), (2) jigsaw (Aronson, 1978; Slavin, 1978), (3) teams-games-tournaments (DeVries & Slavin, 1978), (4) small-group teaching (Sharon & Sharon, 1976), (5) student teams and achievement divisions (Gearheart, Weishahn, & Gearheart, 1992), (6) rap sessions (Gearheart et al., 1992), (7) team-assisted individualization (Goodman, 1990), and (8) buddy systems (Gearheart et al., 1992).

As a member of a cooperative learning group, a student with disabilities supports other group members in completing the activities necessary for acquisition and demonstration of knowledge. Likewise, the other group members provide support for the student with disabilities, ensuring the acquisition of knowledge identified for emphasis in the adapted instruction. Cooperative learning activities have been effective in enhancing interactions between students with disabilities and their nondisabled classmates (Gearheart et al., 1992; Johnson & Johnson, 1981, 1986; Johnson, Johnson, Warring, & Maruyama, 1986; Putnam et al., 1989).

At some high schools, personnel have assisted students in developing student clubs whose members facilitate the inclusion of students who are in danger of being isolated during social events. Targeted students include not only those with disabilities who receive services in inclusive settings, but also students who (1) are new to the school, (2) have English as a second language, or (3) are differentiated from the general population for other reasons. A few students may attend club activities before those activities held for the entire student body. For instance, the club may hold a pizza party/pep rally for a limited number of students before a football game. When the football game is about to begin, the students attending the club event may go as a group to the game and sit together in an assigned area. Back-to-back scheduling of events allows targeted students to become part of a smaller group of students who focus on facilitating their inclusion with peers and then move with that group to the larger event.

Summary

A natural support network is a set of individuals with whom a person has ongoing interactions that reflect various levels of friendship, caring, support, and assistance for both parties. Support networks vary in the number of members, types of relationships members share, and degree to which members rely on each other for companionship, partners during activities, assistance, and support. Providing education services in inclusive settings is conducive to, and dependent upon, collaboration with members of a student's natural support network both during development and implementation of the education program. The presence of the seven essential conditions described by Jorgensen (1998) makes it more likely that students with disabilities will develop friendships at school, increasing the potential number of members in the student's support network. School personnel depend on members' intimate knowledge of, and interest in, both the student and the settings in which that student interacts in daily life.

The use of proactive measures allows school personnel to facilitate the active participation of family and other members of a student's support network. Proactive measures help overcome barriers to their participation, such as (1) language and communication problems; (2) differences in perceptions, attitudes, and values; and (3) logistical difficulties. Particular care must be taken to accommodate for any cultural diversity that exists among members.

Once involved, family and other members of a student's support network can provide valuable information and assistance in the identification of meaningful curriculum content for the student during procedures for gathering information, negotiating annual goals, and identifying settings for instruction. During each of these procedures, family and other network members assist school personnel in maintaining the focus of discussions on the need for and use of skills within activities that are meaningful for the student. They assist by (1) ensuring that discussions focus on activities and settings frequented by the student, (2) ensuring that functional and general education content selected link directly to activities and settings frequented by the student, (3) sharing information that allows two or more suggested components of functional and general education content to be linked in activities and settings, and, therefore, in annual goals, (4) determining all of the settings and activities in which the student can make use of selected content, and (5) determining whether the student actually has access to, and either likes or needs to participate in, an activity in a particular setting.

After school personnel and natural support network members have identified curriculum content, they continue to assist each other during implementation of the education program they developed collaboratively. When feasible, family and other network members may decide to support instruction by (1) reinforcing instruction through informal instruction during spontaneous events, (2) providing feedback on the effectiveness of instruction by observing the student's performance in daily life, (3) identifying additional curriculum areas for inclusion in the student's educational program, and (4) determining alternate instructional strategies.

Finally, developing an extended natural support network for a student with disabilities is critical for long-term success in inclusive adult settings. School personnel can influence the degree of maintenance and expansion of a student's natural support network by facilitating interactions with peers at school and school events.

References

Aronson, E. (1978). *The jigsaw classroom*. Beverly Hills, CA: Sage.

Biklen, D. (1989). Making difference ordinary. In S. Stainback, W. Stainback, & M. Forest (Eds.), *Educating all students in the mainstream of regular education* (pp. 235–248). Baltimore: Paul H. Brookes.

Borich, G. D. (1992). *Effective teaching methods*. New York: Charles E. Merrill.

Brown, L., Schwarz, P., Udvari-Solner, A., Kampschroer,

E. F., Johnson, F., Jorgensen, J., & Gruenewald, L. (1991). How much time should students with severe intellectual disabilities spend in regular classrooms and elsewhere? *The Journal of The Association for Persons with Severe Handicaps, 16*(1), 39–47.

Brown, L., Shiraga, B., York, J., Zanella, K., & Rogan, P. (1984). *A life space analysis strategy for students with severe handicaps.* Madison, WI: University of Wisconsin and Madison Metropolitan School District.

Buswell, B. E., Schaffner, C. B., & Seyler, A. B. (1999). *Opening doors: Connecting students to curriculum, classmates, and learning (2nd ed.).* Colorado Springs, CO: PEAK Parent Center, Inc.

Chadsey-Rusch, J. (1990). Social interactions of secondary-aged students with severe handicaps: Implications for facilitating the transition from school to work. *The Journal of The Association for Persons with Severe Handicaps, 15*(2), 69–78.

DeVries, D. L., & Slavin, R. E. (1978). Team games tournament: A research review. *Journal of Research and Development in Education, 12*, 28–38.

Eichinger, J. (1990). Goal structure effects on social interaction. *Exceptional Children, 56*(5), 408–416.

Forest, M., & Lusthaus, E. (1989). Promoting educational equality for all students: Circles and MAPS. In S. Stainback, W. Stainback, & M. Forest (Eds.), *Educating all students in the mainstream of regular education* (pp. 43–57). Baltimore: Paul H. Brookes.

Gaylord-Ross, R., & Browder, D. (1991). Functional assessment: Dynamic and domain properties. In L. H. Meyer, C. A. Peck, & L. Brown (Eds.), *Critical issues in the lives of people with severe disabilities* (pp. 45–66). Baltimore: Paul H. Brookes.

Gearheart, B. R., Weishahn, M. W., & Gearheart, C. J. (1992). *The exceptional student in the regular classroom* (5th ed.). New York: Macmillan.

Giangreco, M. F., Cloninger, C. J., & Iverson, V. S. (1998). *Choosing options and accommodations for children (COACH): A guide to educational planning for students with disabilities* (2nd ed.). Baltimore: Paul H. Brookes.

Goodman, L. (1990). *Time and learning in the special education classroom.* Albany, NY: State University of New York Press.

Hamre-Nietupski, S., Nietupski, J., & Strathe, M. (1992). Functional life skills, academic skills, and friendship/social relationship development: What do parents of students with moderate/severe/profound disabilities value? *The Journal of The Association for Persons with Severe Handicaps, 17*(1), 53–58.

Haring, T. G. (1991). Social relationships. In L. H. Meyer, C. A. Peck, & L. Brown (Eds.), *Critical issues in the lives of persons with severe disabilities* (pp. 195–217). Baltimore: Paul H. Brookes.

Henley, M., Ramsey, R. S., & Algozzine, R. (1993). *Characteristics of and strategies for teaching students with mild disabilities.* Boston: Allyn & Bacon.

Idol, L. (1993). *Special educator's consultation handbook.* Austin: Pro-Ed. Inc.

Individuals with Disabilities Education Act (IDEA) of 1990, 20 U.S.C. 1401(a)(17).

Johnson, D. W., & Johnson, R. T. (1986). Mainstreaming and cooperative learning strategies. *Exceptional Children, 52*, 553–561.

Johnson, D. W., Johnson, R. T., Warring, D., & Maruyama, G. (1986). Different cooperative learning procedures and cross-handicap relationships. *Exceptional Children, 52*, 247–252.

Johnson, R. T., & Johnson, D. W. (1981). Building friendships between handicapped and nonhandicapped students: Effects of cooperative and individualistic instruction. *American Education Research Journal, 18*(4), 415–423.

Jorgensen, C. M. (1998). *Restructuring high schools for all students: Taking inclusion to the next level.* Baltimore, MD: Paul H. Brookes Publishing Co.

Kennedy, C. H., Horner, R. H., & Newton, S. J. (1989). Social contacts of adults with severe disabilities living in the community: A descriptive analysis of relationship patterns. *The Journal of The Association for Persons with Severe Handicaps, 14*(3), 190–196.

Kennedy, C. H., Horner, R. H., & Newton, S. J. (1990). The social networks and activity patterns of adults with severe disabilities: A correlational analysis. *The Journal of The Association for Persons with Severe Handicaps, 15*(2), 86–90.

Malette, P., Mirenda, P., Kandborg, T., Jones, P., Bunz, T., & Rogow, S. (1992). Application of a lifestyle development process for persons with severe intellectual disabilities: A case study report. *The Journal of The Association for Persons with Severe Handicaps, 17*(3), 179–191.

McDonnell, J., Wilcox, B., & Hardman, M. L. (1991). *Secondary programs for students with developmental disabilities.* Boston: Allyn & Bacon.

Neel, R. S., & Billingsley, F. F. (1989). *IMPACT: A functional curriculum handbook for students with moderate to severe disabilities.* Baltimore: Paul H. Brookes.

Newton, J. S., & Horner, R. H. (1993). Using a social guide to improve social relationships of people with severe disabilities. *The Journal of The*

Association for Persons with Severe Handicaps, 18(1), 36–45.

Putnam, J. W., Rynders, J. E., Johnson, R. T., & Johnson, D. W. (1989). Collaborative skill instruction for promoting interactions between mentally handicapped and nonhandicapped children. *Exceptional Children, 55*(6), 550–557.

Rainforth, B., & York-Barr, J. (1997). *Collaborative teams for students with severe disabilities: Integrating therapy and educational services.* Baltimore, MD: Paul H. Brookes Publishing Co.

Rainforth, B., York, J., & Macdonald, C. (1992). *Collaborative teams for students with severe disabilities: Integrating therapy and educational services.* Baltimore: Paul H. Brookes.

Rueda, R., & Martinez, I. (1992). Fiesta educativa: One community's approach to parent training in developmental disabilities for Latino families. *The Journal of The Association for Persons with Severe Handicaps, 17*(2), 95–103.

Ruiz, N. (1989). An optimal learning environment for Rosemary. *Exceptional Children, 56*(2), 130–144.

Ryndak, D. L., Jackson, L., & Billingsley, F. (2000). Defining school inclusion for students with moderate to severe disabilities: What do experts say? *Exceptionality, 8*(2), 101–116.

Salisbury, C. (1992). Parents as team members: Inclusive teams, collaborative outcomes. In B. Rainforth, J. York, & C. Macdonald (Eds.), *Collaborative teams for students with severe disabilities: Integrating therapy and educational services* (pp. 43–66). Baltimore: Paul H. Brookes.

Salisbury, C., & Dunst, C. J. (1997). Home, school, and community partnerships: Building inclusive teams. In B. Rainforth & J. York-Barr (Eds.), *Collaborative teams for students with severe disabilities: Integrating therapy and educational services* (pp. 57–87). Baltimore, MD: Paul H. Brookes.

Schnorr, R. (1990). "Peter? He comes and goes . . . ": First graders' perspectives on a part-time mainstream student. *The Journal of The Association for Persons with Severe Handicaps, 15*(4), 231–240.

Schulz, J. B., Carpenter, C. D., & Turnbull, A. P. (1991). *Mainstreaming exceptional students: A guide for classroom teachers.* Boston: Allyn & Bacon.

Shafer, M. S., Rice, M. L., Metzler, H. M. D., & Haring, M. (1989). A survey of nondisabled employee's attitudes toward supported employees with mental retardation. *The Journal of The Association for Persons with Severe Handicaps, 14*(2), 137–146.

Sharon, S., & Sharon, Y. (1976). *Small-group teaching.* Englewood Cliffs, NJ: Educational Technology.

Shea, T. M., & Bauer, A. M. (1991). *Parents and teachers of children with exceptionalities: A handbook for collaboration* (2nd ed.). Boston: Allyn & Bacon.

Slavin, R. E. (1978). Student teams and comparison among equals: Effects on academic performance and student attitudes. *Journal of Educational Psychology, 70,* 532–538.

Snow, J., & Forest, M. (1987). Circles. In M. Forest (Ed.), *More education integration* (pp. 169–176). Downsview, Ontario: G. Allen Roeher Institute.

Stainback, W., & Stainback, S. (1990). Facilitating peer supports and friendships. In W. Stainback, & S. Stainback (Eds.), *Support networks for inclusive schooling: Interdependent integrated education* (pp. 51–63). Baltimore: Paul H. Brookes.

Stainback, S., Stainback, W., & Slavin, R. (1989). Classroom organization for diversity among students. In S. Stainback, W. Stainback, & M. Forest (Eds.), *Educating all students in the mainstream of regular education* (pp. 131–142). Baltimore: Paul H. Brookes.

Staub, D., & Hunt, P. (1993). The effects of social interaction training on high school peer tutors of schoolmates with severe disabilities. *Exceptional Children, 60*(1), 41–57.

Strully, J., & Strully, C. (1989). Friendship as an educational goal. In S. Stainback, W. Stainback, & M. Forest (Eds.), *Educating all students in the mainstream of regular education* (pp. 59–68). Baltimore: Paul H. Brookes.

Vandercook, T., York, J., & Forest, M. (1989). The McGill Action Planning System (MAPS): A strategy for building the vision. *Journal of The Association for Persons with Severe Handicaps, 14*(3), 205–215.

York, J., Giangreco, M., Vandercook, T., & Macdonald, C. (1992). Integrating support personnel in the inclusive classroom. In S. Stainback, & W. Stainback (Eds.), *Curriculum considerations in inclusive classrooms: Facilitating learning for all students* (pp. 101–116). Baltimore: Paul H. Brookes.

8

Education Teams and Collaborative Teamwork in Inclusive Settings

Diane Lea Ryndak

Paige C. Pullen

Objectives

After completing this chapter, the reader will be able to:

1. Define education team.
2. List potential members of an education team and their respective areas of expertise.
3. Define collaboration.
4. Define collaborative team.
5. Describe how a collaborative education team differs from a multidisciplinary, transdisciplinary, and inter-disciplinary team.
6. Describe steps completed when developing a collaborative education team.
7. Describe ways in which a collaborative education team could divide their roles and responsibilities, en-suring that all responsibilities are covered by the team.
8. Provide examples that demonstrate collaborative education teams at work.

Key Terms

Collaboration	Interdisciplinary team	Role release
Collaborative team	Multidisciplinary team	Roles and responsibilities
Collaborative teamwork	Related services	Transdisciplinary team
Education team		

Effective education services cannot be provided in inclusive settings in isolation from the activities that naturally occur in general education classes. In addition, one person cannot provide such services; rather, effective education services in inclusive settings develop through interaction and collaboration between numerous professionals, paraprofessionals, and members of a student's natural support network (Ferguson, Meyer, Jeanchild, Jeniper, & Zingo, 1992; Giangreco, Broer, & Edelmen, 1999; Jackson, Ryndak, & Billingsley, 2000; Janney & Snell, 1997). When collaboration does not occur, a student's education services are fragmented, with instruction leading to the student's various objectives disassociated from either instruction on other objectives or instruction occurring in the general education class. Minimizing fragmentation, while maximizing effective instruction to meet identified annual goals, is the responsibility of each member of a student's education team.

Education Teams

The concept of an education team has evolved from that of a set of professionals from different disciplines "established in order to provide the best overall education and habilitation programs for a particular child" (Gaylord-Ross & Holvoet, 1985, p. 289) to a much broader concept. Thousand and Villa (1990) define a "teaching team" as

> *. . . an organizational and instructional arrangement of two or more members of the school and greater community who distribute among themselves planning, instructional, and evaluation responsibilities for the same students on a regular basis for an extended period of time (pp. 152–153).*

This broader conceptualization emphasizes the role that every team member plays in maximizing the benefits of educational activities for every student, regardless of whether that student is eligible for special education or related services. It emphasizes the necessity of team members sharing (1) their expertise with each other so that all students can benefit as a team member provides instruction, (2) the responsibility for developing educational activities that facilitate learning by all students, (3) the provision of instruction across instructional content areas, and (4) accountability for each student's acquisition of knowledge and skills across content areas, activities, and settings. As stated by Pugach and Fitzgerald, a collaborative team provides "equitable, meaningful, and effective learning for all students" (2001, p. 17). With this understanding, every team member accepts the responsibility for teaching *all* students who enter their room and caseload. Collectively, the team accepts responsibility both for students' growth, and lack of growth.

    This conceptualization of an education team eliminates the perception of any team member planning, implementing, or evaluating the effectiveness of their services in isolation from the services of other team members and highlights the importance of each team member applying expertise directly to students' needs. This conceptualization of the education team also is consistent with the definition of related services and its interpretation by Rainforth, York, and Macdonald (1992) described in Chapter 6. That is, it is consistent with their belief that the educational relevance and student benefit of related services (for example, occupational therapy, physical therapy, and speech therapy) are heightened when team members integrate their expertise into instructional activities that occur in the context of routine daily activities at school, at home, and in the community (see Chapter 6).

This emphasis on application of expertise to students' needs in natural contexts ensures that students will be more successful at learning and applying new knowledge, thus participating more fully in school, family activities, and community life. Rainforth et al. (1992) argue that, when education teams do not collaborate, they abdicate responsibility for the synthesis, application, and generalization of fragmented program components and shift that responsibility "onto the very people who require their assistance to meet daily challenges: students with severe disabilities and their families" (p. 10).

The size and composition of education teams vary, as they are dependent upon the identified needs of the students for whom that team has responsibility. For example, an education team that serves a student with multiple disabilities may include many individuals who have expertise across numerous areas because of the diversity and complexity of that student's needs. Table 8.1 includes a list of possible team members and a brief description of their traditional areas of expertise. An education team may consist of fewer members, however, when that team serves only students who do not require special education or related services or students who require only minimal special education or related service support. In these cases, the education teams do not require expertise from as many fields to serve their students.

Responsibilities of Team Members

There are four main responsibilities of each education team member. First, when planning services, members are responsible for ensuring that each student's needs are considered in a discipline-free manner, while lending the benefit of their specific expertise to that consideration. For example, during the discussion of the needs of a student with multiple disabilities, each team member has the responsibility to verify that potential instructional content will increase that student's independent functioning or partial participation in daily events at school, home, or in the community. When considering instructional content, physical therapists consider their expertise in physical development and their knowledge of that student's development in conjunction with the intent of the instructional content in relation to the student's participation at school, home, and in the community. In addition, the physical therapist raises questions that relate to the expertise of other team members, thus ensuring that the team has considered the expertise of each team member and its relation to the instructional content under consideration. In this manner, the team members share the responsibility for the team staying focused on the student's educational needs in a discipline-free manner.

Second, when implementing and evaluating the effectiveness of instruction, each team member is responsible for sharing their specific expertise with other team members and acquiring relevant information and skills from other team members. This not only maximizes the effectiveness of instructional time each team member spends with students, but also results in fewer gaps, overlaps, and contradictions (Giangreco, Cloninger, & Iverson, 1998) in educational services for any one student.

TABLE 8.1   *Possible Team Members and Areas of Expertise*

Possible Team Member	Areas of Expertise
Student with identified needs	Self-abilities, performance needs, life activities, desires, dreams, expectations
Student's natural support network (e.g., family members, peers)	Perceptions of student's abilities, performance needs, life activities, interactions with significant others, desires, dreams, expectations
Special education teachers	Methods of identifying functional needs, adaptations; curriculum content specific to special education; instructional strategies; analysis of situations, environments, and behaviors
General education teachers	Large group instructional strategies, curriculum content specific to grade level, interaction styles and content of same age peers
Special subject area educators (e.g., art teacher, wood shop teacher)	Large group instructional strategies, curriculum content and strategies specific to subject, interaction styles and content of same age peers
Content area specialists Reading specialist Math specialist	Small group instructional strategies, curriculum content and strategies specific to content area
Educational-related specialist Communication specialist Hearing specialist Vision specialist Occupational therapist Physical therapist	Discipline specific expertise, strategies for developing skills in area of expertise, especially in relation to use during activities in inclusive settings
Guidance counselor	Class options per grade level, extracurricular options per building
Employment specialist	Vocational opportunities in student's community, instructional strategies for job sites, work-related skills
Paraeducators	Awareness of student's performance across inclusive settings and subjects
Student teacher	Current instructional practices and research, link to university/college
Health professionals	Health-related effects of behavior, strategies for coping with medical needs in inclusive settings, periodic and emergency procedures
Volunteers	Fresh perceptions of student and relevance of program to real life
School or district administrator	Legal issues, policies and procedures, mechanisms for meeting building- and district-related concerns, funding mechanisms for specific materials, adaptations, or services, link to inservice training options

Third, each education team member shares the responsibility for the team functioning in a professional manner with open communication. To fulfill this responsibility each team member reviews as objectively as possible both their own behavior and the behavior of other team members, to determine whether the content and delivery manner of the interaction are both professional and open, inviting collegial dialogue across relevant topics. If a team member determines that his or her own behavior does not facilitate open collegial communication, it is that member's responsibility to modify that behavior, deal with any conflicts with other team members, and reach either a consensus or a compromise with other team members in relation to topics on which they vary. It is also his or her responsibility to assist other team members in accomplishing the same by providing objective, constructive, and meaningful feedback.

Fourth, each team member has the responsibility to provide support for fellow team members in a number of ways. For example, team members can support each other in relation to (1) obtaining and using resources (for example, people, materials, funds, or literature), (2) providing moral support (for example, listening, reinforcing, encouraging, and providing feedback), and (3) using technical knowledge (for example, developing adaptations, identifying alternate strategies, or developing instructional programs) (York, Giangreco, Vandercook, & Macdonald, 1992). Through mutual support, team members develop both more collegial and collaborative relationships and facilitate more effective instruction for all students in inclusive settings.

Addressing Cultural Diversity Among Team Members

Upon reviewing the responsibilities of education team members, it is evident that members must be aware of the cultural differences that exist among members of their team. Sue and Sue (1990) describe variables relevant to communication that differ across cultures and that affect group interaction: (1) proxemics, or personal space (for example, the physical distance between people communicating and arrangement of furniture for seating), (2) kinesics, or body movement (for example, posture, facial expression, and eye contact), (3) time orientation, and (4) paralanguage, or verbal and nonverbal vocal cues beyond words (for example, loudness, hesitations, inflections, and speed). If a team comprises members from cultural backgrounds that interpret proxemics, kinesics, time, or paralanguage use differently, and members are either oblivious to these differences or choose to ignore them, difficulties will prevail in developing collegial and collaborative relationships that facilitate effective instruction for students in inclusive settings. Effective communication will occur only when the team members identify and accommodate their own cultural differences within team interactions.

A Collaborative Team and Teamwork

There are a number of ways in which a group of individuals can function, each having their own theoretical perspective that dictates how members will interact with each other, as well as with students and family members. The following sections describe four types of teams, their theoretical perspectives, and the resultant manners of interaction.

Multidisciplinary Team

The Individuals with Disabilities Education Act (IDEA) of 1997 (PL 105-117) mandates that a set of school professionals, parents, and, whenever possible, the student with disabilities, constitute a multidisciplinary team for the purpose of implementing the evaluation, placement procedures, and development of an individualized education program (IEP) for students with disabilities. Specifically, in the 1997 reauthorization, a general education teacher must be included on the multidisciplinary team. Pfeiffer (1980) surmises that the intent of the mandate was to use a group process to provide safeguards against possible errors due to flaws in the judgements of individuals and to ensure the greatest adherence to the due process procedures outlined in the legislation. Although well-intentioned, the manner in which this mandate has been implemented has not met this probable intent. In a summary of the literature, Friend and Cook (1992) identified nine problem areas that adversely affect how teams have functioned:

1. Use of unsystematic approaches to collecting and analyzing diagnostic information.
2. Minimal parent or regular educator participation.
3. Use of a loosely construed decision-making and planning process.
4. Lack of interdisciplinary collaboration and trust.
5. Territoriality.
6. Ambiguous role definition and accountability.
7. Lack of experience and training for professionals to work together.
8. Lack of preparation in effective collaboration and team participation skills.
9. Mandatory, rather than voluntary and interested, participation (pp. 26–27).

These difficulties have led to teams of individuals from multiple disciplines that focus their interactions around the specific expertise of each member in isolation of the other members, rather than on the collective expertise of a collaborative unit (Amlund & Kardash, 1994). The personnel preparation programs for some professionals on the team emphasize a medical orientation, in which a student is viewed as a "patient" who is "sick" or "flawed" in some way, and the role of the team member is to "cure" or "fix" the student so he or she can return to the regular environment (Hanft, 1993). This medical orientation is inconsistent with the educational orientation of special and general education teachers and results in discrepant theoretical approaches to educational program development and implementation (Hanft, 1993). In most cases, educational programs that multidisciplinary teams develop can be characterized in three ways: (1) They reflect the premise that repeated isolated work on specific skills in disciplines will lead to the student's incorporation of the skills as needed during activities in natural settings, (2) they provide isolated services, or "treatment," by team members within their own areas of expertise and on separate components of a student's performance, and (3) they provide fragmented instruction focusing on isolated aspects of a student's development (for example, fine motor, gross motor, communication, and cognition).

Finally, in theory, the multidisciplinary team concept views the parent as an equal partner in the development and implementation of educational services. In practice, however, because the focus of interactions is on each professional informing the remainder of the team about information from their specific discipline in relation to the student, this negates the possibility of collaboration and minimizes the parent's participation in the team process (Amlund & Kardash, 1994).

Interdisciplinary Team

Like a multidisciplinary team, an interdisciplinary team comprises individuals from multiple disciplines who focus their expertise on the educational services for a student. The manner in which an interdisciplinary team functions, however, is different. The members of an interdisciplinary team share their expertise in relation to a student and work together to develop one cohesive program for that student (Rainforth & York-Barr, 1997). To accomplish this, team members not only share their perceptions of services within their area of expertise that would benefit the student, but also work with other team members to (1) understand other needs of the student, (2) understand how the student's needs across areas of expertise interrelate, and (3) develop one set of jointly planned goals and objectives for that student.

Transdisciplinary Team

Like multidisciplinary and interdisciplinary teams, a transdisciplinary team comprises individuals from multiple disciplines that focus their interactions around the specific expertise of each member, including school professionals, parents, and, whenever possible, the student with disabilities. A transdisciplinary team, however, has one added dimension. Members share across disciplines information and skills from their area of expertise that relate specifically to a student, resulting in team members incorporating into their services for that student information and skills from other disciplines and sharing the responsibility for services from other disciplines (Amlund & Kardash, 1994; Anderson, Hawkins, Hamilton, & Hampton, 1999; Downing, 2002; Pugach & Johnson, 2002; Rainforth & York-Barr, 1997). This practice is referred to as *role release* (Lyon & Lyon, 1980; Rainforth & York-Barr, 1997). There are four types of information shared across disciplines through role release: (1) general information on concepts and approaches related to the area of expertise, (2) specific information on practices and methods relevant to the student, (3) specific performance competencies appropriate for the student, and (4) specific interventions and methods for use with the student. In essence, various team members provide instruction across multiple areas of needs for a student to better serve that student. This allows for each team member to participate in all services on an ongoing basis and to share with other team members responsibility for the effectiveness of those services and for student growth.

In most cases educational programs developed by a transdisciplinary team reflect the premise that multiple needs of a student are interdependent and the student does not use skills in one area of development in isolation from skills in other areas of development. The team, however, focuses little attention on the settings and activities in which instruction occurs. Because of this, many educational programs developed by transdisciplinary teams do not provide instruction in naturally occurring settings, including general education classes, and in functional activities across the school and in the community.

Collaborative Team

Like a transdisciplinary team, a collaborative team comprises individuals from multiple disciplines, including school professionals, parents, and, whenever possible, the student with disabilities. The team shares across disciplines information and skills from their area of expertise that relate specifically to a student, resulting in team members incorporating into their services for that student information and skills from other disciplines and sharing the responsibility for services from other disciplines. Collaborative teams, however, are dramatically different from other teams in a number of ways. To understand these differences, let's look at components of the term "*collaborative team.*"

There are many definitions of collaboration and teamwork currently in the literature, each with definitive components. For the purposes of this book, *collaboration* is defined as *a style of problem solving by a group of equal individuals who voluntarily (1) contribute their own knowledge and skills and (2) participate in shared decisionmaking to accomplish one or more common and mutually agreed upon goals* (Friend & Cook, 1992; Rainforth et al., 1992; Thomas, Correa, & Morsink, 2001; Thousand & Villa, 1989). According to *Webster's Ninth New Collegiate Dictionary* (1991), teamwork is "work done by several associates with each doing a part but all subordinating personal prominence to the efficiency of the whole." When combining these concepts, a collaborative team could be considered a group of equal individuals who voluntarily work together in a spirit of willingness and mutual reward to problem solve and accomplish one or more common and mutually agreed upon goals by contributing their own knowledge and skills and participating in shared decisionmaking, while focusing on the efficiency of the whole team. When applied to education, the common and mutually agreed upon goal is to provide the most effective education services for a set of students, allowing each student to maximize their participation and contribution to life at school, at home, and in the community (Rainforth et al., 1992; Thousand & Villa, 1989).

Components of a Collaborative Team

There are a number of components in this definition of a collaborative team and its educational goal that differentiate this team from the transdisciplinary team and that are critical to understanding how and why a collaborative team functions. The following section describes six components of a collaborative team.

Team purpose.   First, the team's purpose for existing is linked clearly to, and defined by, the needs of each student that it serves, rather than by the training and expectations of the individual team members. Because of this, all team members put aside preconceived ideas of the services they will provide for a given student and how they will deliver those services. The education team will determine those variables in response to the student's specific needs to function and participate more fully in general education classes, in the school, at home, and in the community.

Team accomplishments.   Second, collaborative team members accept the concept that the team as a whole will either accomplish, or fail to accomplish, their goal, and that all team members have opportunities for leadership (Walther-Thomas, Korinek, McLaughlin, & Williams, 2000). With this acceptance it is clear that collaborative team members share (1) the responsibility for success and failure in meeting a student's needs at school, at home, and in the community, (2) mutual rewards with success and the ensuing satisfaction, and (3) mutual repercussions for failure and the ensuing sense of inadequacy or insufficiency. In many ways this concept and its effects on team members are consistent with those fostered with students in cooperative learning groups (Thousand & Villa, 1989).

Expanded role release.   A third distinctive component of a collaborative team is that the concept of role release takes on additional meanings. While members of transdisciplinary teams share their knowledge and skills with each other so that instruction provided by one team member incorporates content across disciplines, collaborative teams take this concept farther and actually brainstorm on (1) the necessary instruction and services for each discipline to meet a student's needs at school, at home, and in the community and (2) how to blend instruction across disciplines to meet a student's needs within naturally occurring activities in those settings. This expansion of the concept of role release demands that each team member understands the student as a whole, and how the student's skills and knowledge from one discipline interrelate with skills and knowledge in other disciplines. For example, a student included in a first-grade class may have difficulty using expressive communication skills (for example, use of augmentative communication system or speaking in two to three word phrases), gross motor skills (for example, sitting on the floor while sitting upright to attend), and fine motor skills (for example, pencil grasp and letter formation) during language arts. Rather than focusing only on the student's needs that relate to their own discipline, collaborative team members see the student in the context in which all these skills are necessary in conjunction, allowing them (1) to grasp more fully how, why, and where the student needs to use specific skills and (2) to understand better and use the knowledge and skills shared with them by other team members.

Services in natural settings.   A fourth distinctive component of a collaborative team is that services across disciplines occur in natural locations. That is, assessment procedures, direct services, and consultation services occur in the locations in which a student naturally needs to use the knowledge and skills being addressed, including general education settings, the school, the student's home, and the community. Services for which the student is pulled out of, or isolated from, those naturally occurring locations are limited to two types of services: (1) services that infringe on the student's right to privacy (for example, range of motion activities that cannot blend into naturally occurring activities) and (2) services that cannot be blended into naturally occurring activities (for example, exercises that strengthen abdominal muscles that cannot be blended into every physical education activity or into positions and mobility across the day).

Unique scheduling.   This focus on natural locations and naturally occurring activities dictates a fifth distinctive component of a collaborative team. The schedule of services allows each team member access to the student and naturally occurring activities in natural locations across the entire day. Rainforth et al. (1992) describe a block scheduling system that facilitates individual team members distributing the time they have committed to students within one class so that each team member can observe all of the students across the day within one or two weeks. This ensures that each team member can address knowledgeably any difficulty a student has encountered in relation to applying knowledge and skills from various disciplines across natural activities and locations, including the school, community, and home.

Equal partnership.   Finally, a collaborative team differs from other types of teams in the emphasis placed on the equal partnership of each team member, especially general education teachers and parents (Rainforth et al., 1992). This emphasis reflects the belief that the expertise of each team member is only relevant to a student when considered in relation to the student's functioning and participation in real life. The general education teacher has the most consistent access to the student in inclusive settings and, therefore, is most aware of the activities and locations in which the student is involved across the day, week, and school year. The parents have the most consistent access to the student after school hours both at home and in the community. Because of these unique positions, other team members are dependent on the general education teacher and parents to provide information about and insight into those real-life activities and locations. Without this information, team members lose their focus and change their purpose, ultimately resorting to functioning as a multidisciplinary or transdisciplinary team.

Benefits of Collaborative Teamwork

There are four ways of viewing the benefits of collaborative teamwork. First, collaborative teamwork can be beneficial to students with disabilities. As various team members provide instruction on goals across activities in natural contexts, the student automatically has an increased number of instructional trials throughout the day. Not only will the increased number of trials lead to faster acquisition of knowledge and skills in relation to the number of days necessary to meet criterion, but the distributed nature of those trials also will increase the efficiency of those trials, resulting in the need for fewer trials. In addition, the provision of instruction during activities in natural contexts will increase the degree to which the student actually uses skills in the activities for which they are required, rather than demonstrating the acquisition of new knowledge and skills only during artificial instructional activities. Because the activities are naturally occurring in the student's school, home, and community life, the student will maintain the skills acquired because of continued opportunities to use those skills in activities. Finally, because of the number of team members providing instruction in a large number of activities and natural contexts, the student is more likely to have generalized use of the skills learned across people, settings, and activities.

Second, because of these benefits, the student's family will benefit from collaborative teamwork in two ways. They will have (1) more information on instructional strategies and methods they can use to help their family member acquire knowledge and skills more quickly and (2) a family member who is more able to participate in family and community activities because of increased skills applied in real-life situations.

Third, collaborative teamwork can be beneficial to the nondisabled classmates of the included student. For instance, as team members provide direct services in inclusive settings, the nondisabled classmates benefit from the additional direct contact time provided by the extra personnel in the room (Ferguson, Meyer, Jeanchild, Juniper, & Zingo, 1992). In addition, the nondisabled classmates derive benefits from the indirect consultation and collaboration that occur between their general education teacher and other team members. For example, de Bettencourt (1999) found that the more time general education teachers spent with specialists who were team members, the more the general education teachers used varying instructional strategies with their class. New instructional strategies and feedback on the effectiveness of current instructional strategies are only two of the many areas in which collegial dialogue could lead to benefits for all students.

Fourth, collaborative teamwork can be beneficial to education team members through technical, moral, and problem-solving support. Benefits through technical support include the following: (1) direct assistance in the classroom for problems related to students other than the included student (Armbruster & Howe, 1985, Ferguson et al., 1992; Idol, 1993), (2) more effective use of expertise across disciplines for all students (Bauwens, Hourcade, & Friend, 1989; Rainforth & York-Barr, 1997), (3) assistance in identifying strategies for use by family members at home (Idol, 1993), and (4) increased flexibility for grouping and scheduling. Collaborative team members receive moral support through (1) feedback from other team members that provides reassurance of their own performance and objectivity, (2) recognition of reasons for self-worth and self-satisfaction (Johnson & Johnson, 1987a; Murphy, 1981, Shea & Bauer, 1991), (3) follow-through of instruction on school goals at home (Shea & Bauer, 1991), and (4) relationships built on trust, communication, and conflict resolution (Johnson & Johnson, 1999). Collaborative teams receive support in problem solving when identifying meaningful content, obtaining materials and other resources, defining specific learning or behavior problems, identifying options for intervention or instruction, implementing instruction, and evaluating the effectiveness of instruction. Thousand and Villa (1990) summarize the research literature related to benefits derived by education team members in four areas: (1) survival or power, (2) freedom, (3) sense of belonging, and (4) fun.

Developing a Collaborative Team

A collaborative team is not formed overnight. Given the nature of a collaborative team, team members require time to develop the necessary trusting and supportive relationships. There are some tasks, however, to be undertaken in order for a team to be formed and for that team to develop into a collaborative unit.

Identifying Members. When an education team is forming, the school identifies individuals to participate based on their relationship to a particular student, that student's educational needs, and the individual's area of expertise. For example, when a student who has mental retardation, physical disabilities, and communication deficits is included in fifth grade, there are some individuals who will be members of the education team because of their immediate relationship to the student (for example, the student, parents, fifth-grade general education teacher, and building principal). The fifth-grade general education teacher *must* play an active role on the team because the student's goals must ensure access to the general education curriculum (see IDEA, 1997, 20 U.S.C. 1414). Although these individuals clearly have expertise to add to the team, there are also no alternative individuals to them for meaningful participation. They are, in fact, irreplaceable.

In addition to these irreplaceable individuals, the school identifies other members based on the student's educational needs across disciplines. Affecting the educational needs of the student mentioned previously are (1) the physical development that probably requires the expertise of a physical therapist and occupational therapist, (2) the communication deficit that probably requires the expertise of a speech language pathologist or communication specialist, and (3) the mental retardation that probably requires the expertise of a special educator. Assuming this is the case, one member from each of those disciplines will join the team. Unless the district that serves the student is small, there are probably optional individuals from these disciplines who could become team members, either as employees of the district or as consultants from private agencies. Expertise from other disciplines also may be necessary for the team (for example, behavior management or medical knowledge), depending on the student's educational needs. As those needs become clear or change, members of the team will change to reflect the disciplines from which expertise is needed by the student.

In addition to core team members, support team members can serve the role of itinerants. Itinerant members would not need to be involved in a student's program on a daily basis, but would consult with the core team as needed throughout the school year (Giangreco, et al., 1998; Rainforth & York-Barr, 1997). A few examples of support team members are social workers, nurses, dieticians, orientation and mobility specialists, and psychologists (Orelove & Sobsey, 1996).

Philosophical Premises.   After the school identifies individual team members, the team must agree upon some basic philosophical premises if they are to become a collaborative team. Before agreeing on philosophical premises, however, team members require some fundamental information about the other team members. For instance, team members need to know (1) the specific expertise and experience that each member brings to the team, especially in relation to the educational needs of the student, (2) each member's philosophy in relation to the purpose of educational services, (3) each member's perception of their role within that purpose, especially in relation to the provision of direct and consultant services, and (4) each member's perception of the roles of other team members within that purpose. After the team has discussed these topics, team members can begin to determine the areas on which they agree and disagree. For the areas on which they disagree, the discussion might include (1) how the team will function given their discrepant viewpoints on the fundamental reason for the existence of an education team and/or the roles individuals play to fulfill that purpose and (2) what the team will do to resolve any discrepancies.

Another philosophical premise for discussion among team members is the type of team on which they would like to participate. Some members may not have had experience on a collaborative team; therefore, discussing the relative benefits and limitations of collaborative, multidisciplinary, transdisciplinary, and interdisciplinary teams, in relation to the fundamental purpose for the team's existence, may lead to a more mutual understanding of what a collaborative team actually is and a broader desire to function as a collaborative team.

After team members reach a consensus that they want to function in a collaborative manner, they then can begin to develop a shared mission statement. Rainforth et al. (1992) recommend that educational collaborative teams for students with severe disabilities should have at least two purposes, including support of students so they can achieve integrated life outcomes through attainment of the objectives identified in their IEPs and support for one another. Collaborative teams that serve students in inclusive settings will clarify these components further to maintain focus on (1) the performance of *all* students, across settings (that is, general education settings, school building, and community), (2) the performance of students with moderate or severe disabilities in real-life activities within naturally occurring settings, (3) the function of team members in direct and consultative roles, and (4) the development and use of effective collaboration and communication skills.

Handling the Logistics. For a team to function in a collaborative manner, the entire team must decide on a few logistical issues. For instance, no team can collaborate unless there are specific times allowed for collaboration to occur and procedures established for effective communication during and between those scheduled times. Allocated time should encompass both time for team members to provide direct and indirect services for students and time to meet with other team members to collaborate. Although some education teams have been able to build weekly or biweekly meetings into their schedules, many teams are unable to do so and have devised alternative methods for sharing expertise and information on their student observations. Some teams have opted for the special education teacher meeting with team members, preferably in small groups, but individually when necessary. The special education teacher then becomes the coordinator of information, using various methods of sharing information with the other team members. Whatever system the team develops for collaborating, each team member must feel comfortable that the team is truly collaborative and not changing to a transdisciplinary team because of scheduling difficulties.

Many school districts find it necessary to address other issues when scheduling opportunities for team members to provide effective direct and indirect services across settings. Such issues may include the manner in which related services personnel (1) acquire students on their caseload; (2) receive assignments across students, grades, and buildings; and (3) develop schedules for short intervals per student or larger intervals per class setting. In most situations, however, the degree to which related services personnel can meet the responsibilities of a collaborative team member in inclusive settings is limited unless these issues are addressed.

In addition to scheduling issues, members of a collaborative team clearly define the tasks for which they share the responsibility and determine which member will take the lead in either meeting each responsibility or coordinating the effort of team members to meet each responsibility. Table 8.2 lists tasks for which every collaborative team will have responsibility.

TABLE 8.2   *Tasks of Collaborative Teams*

IEP
Monitoring progress on IEP goals and objectives
Coordinating instruction to ensure IEP completion
Coordinating assessment procedures for developing next IEP
Collaborating to develop next IEP

Communication
Establishing form(s) of communication
Scheduling meetings
Preparing agendas
Ensuring communication occurs between all members
Communicating regularly with family members

Adaptations
Identifying when adaptations are necessary
Developing adaptations
Teaching team members to use adaptations
Ensuring appropriate use of adaptations across members

Support
Identifying need for support
Identifying available sources of necessary support
Ensuring existence of support across members

Skills
Identifying skills needed to effectively collaborate
Determining resources necessary to develop skills
Requesting resources to develop skills
Scheduling and organizing training or other method to develop skills
Ensuring acquisition and use of skills after training

IEP = Individualized education program.

Required Skills for Collaboration.   When part of a collaborative team, members clearly need expertise in their discipline area. This expertise alone, however, does not allow members to function collaboratively, because there are skills other than discipline-specific ones necessary to work collaboratively. For instance, when providing information and skills related to a discipline to team members who have limited or no background in that discipline, an effective collaborative team member will (1) explain the need for an intervention and what comprises the intervention itself, (2) demonstrate the intervention, (3) observe others implement the intervention, (4) provide corrective and reinforcing feedback, (5) monitor implementation of the intervention over time, and (6) monitor the effectiveness of the intervention and modify it when appropriate for the student (Rainforth et al., 1992). To accomplish these, team members must be supportive and approachable and be ready to provide information and answer questions in a nondefensive and nonthreatening manner. They must communicate information clearly and in an experiential manner, constantly being alert for signs of misunderstanding or confusion. The focus of information sharing, after all, is for the team to provide the most effective education for a set of students, allowing each to maximize their participation and contribution to life at school, at home, and in the community.

Beyond skills related to developing, implementing, and monitoring discipline-specific interventions, however, team members require communication and group interaction skills to function in a manner that supports the essence of collaboration, that is, interacting voluntarily as equals focusing on the efficiency of the whole team in a spirit of willingness and mutual reward to problem solve and accomplish their mutually agreed upon goals. The effectiveness of any team is dependent upon the collaborative skills of the team members, both individually and collectively. These skills cannot be assumed to exist; rather, they must be nurtured and developed (Friend, 2000). When collaborating, teams will encounter problems in meeting students' needs and in interacting effectively. Problem solving skills that collaborative teams require, therefore, include acting as a group to (1) operationally define the problem so that all members agree, (2) diagnose the problem to determine the probable cause(s), (3) formulate strategies to address the problem, given the probable cause(s), (4) select and implement the strategy of group choice, and (5) evaluate the effectiveness of the strategy on the problem.

Throughout their interactions, education teams make decisions about students' needs, interventions, and logistics. When acting collaboratively, a team makes decisions by consensus, defined as a collective opinion, or general agreement. To reach consensus, a team seeks out differences in opinion, openly discussing the underlying assumptions of each opinion. After team members have shared this information, they must make a decision without any members changing their minds only to get a decision made and without using majority votes or similar techniques to reach a decision. Reaching a consensus requires discussion until all members understand the options and agree that one of those is more appropriate at this time, though other options may be more viable at other times.

Finally, to communicate in a manner that facilitates collaboration, a team must resolve conflicts between members. Several steps can assist conflicting team members in resolving their conflict, including (1) one of the members confronting the other to acknowledge that they are, indeed, in conflict, (2) both members jointly defining the conflict, (3) openly communicating their positions and feelings in relation to the conflict, (4) openly communicating their intentions to be cooperative with each other to resolve the conflict, (5) each member putting themselves in the place of the other team member, "taking on" their perspective, (6) coordinating their efforts to negotiate in good faith, at the same time, and (7) reaching an agreement with each other. Unless team members are able to resolve conflicts in a manner that is constructive for the team, the trusting relationships that are necessary for collaboration cannot exist or endure.

In addition to discipline-specific and communication skills, a team needs group management and leadership skills to function collaboratively (Thousand & Villa, 1989). Group management skills will assist the team to be organized and function efficiently with minimal time commitment and waste of effort. Leadership skills will assist the team to accomplish tasks while maintaining positive working relationships. Care must be taken, however, that all team members have group management and leadership skills and that no one member becomes the perceived organizer or leader of the team.

Examples of Collaborative Teams at Work

There are a number of ways in which collaborative teams work together. The following examples illustrate this point and provide some visual images of how collaborative teams can function and to what this collaboration leads.

Adapting Activities from Weekly Lesson Plans

When a general education teacher completes weekly lesson plans a week ahead of time, team members have ample lead time to collaborate for the identification, development, and training related to adaptations required per lesson. One collaborative education team whose members included a general education teacher who planned over a week in advance used those lesson plans as the basis for adapting activities (Ryndak, Rainforth, & Schooley, 1993). Because of their inability to choose one mutual planning time, this team designated the special education teacher as the coordinator for information sharing. As such, the special education teacher met once a week with each team member, either singly or in small groups. During the weekly meeting with the general education teacher, that teacher shared the general education lesson plans as they were written in a weekly plan book. The two teachers discussed each of the activities planned and systematically determined how each student with a disability would participate in the activity either fully or partially and whether any of the students required an adaptation to participate. When required, they discussed the adaptation and which team member would be responsible for developing it.

For instance, when a simple curriculum or instructional strategy adaptation was necessary, the general education teacher simply made the modification while teaching. When an adaptation was necessary in the academic materials for an activity (for example, content of worksheets, words on spelling lists, or grade level of material), the special education teacher prepared those materials. When discipline-specific adaptations were required from other team members, the special education teacher took the responsibility to share the need with those members and to ensure the development of the adaptation. Such adaptations included (1) an adapted piece of equipment that allows a student with physical disabilities to participate in a specific activity (for example, equipment to allow a kindergarten student to crawl through tunnel with peers), (2) an adapted method of participation in an ongoing type of activity (for example, use of a typewriter as an alternative to most handwriting), or (3) a modification to an existing adaptation (for example, altering the communicative content on a touch talker). In these situations, the special education teacher met with the other team members whose expertise was relevant to the needed adaptation providing information on the general education activity planned and the ideas for adaptations considered with the general education teacher. They then would reach a consensus on the adaptation to be used and decided which team member would develop the adaptation by when. The team member responsible for the adaptation then took the lead, ensuring that an effective adaptation was ready for the student's use during the planned activity.

Using Generic Adaptations to Activities

A different situation occurs when a general education teacher does not plan far enough in advance for the team to discuss systematically the need for adaptations. One collaborative education team faced with this situation developed a strategy that utilized generic adaptations to activities (Ryndak et al., 1993). This team served a student with profound physical disabilities and apparent profound intellectual disabilities. This student's annual goals addressed needs such as answering yes-or-no questions with known answers, using a communication board with two items, and using switches to participate in specific activities. The team developed generic instructional plans for each annual goal and determined types of activities that were frequently used by the general education teacher. The team compared the generic instructional plans with these types of instruction, identifying which generic instructional plans could be implemented naturally during which types of instruction. Team members made modifications in the generic instructional plans as necessary to allow a better "fit" with various types of instruction. Team members then developed a process for deciding which generic instructional plan best "fit" the instructional activity selected at any moment by the general education teacher, and they used the relevant generic instructional plan.

For example, if the general education teacher decided to use a cooperative learning strategy during social studies, the student with multiple profound disabilities could participate in that activity by answering yes-or-no questions about the topic given a specific question format used by peers, or by using a switch *if* the activity included a power-driven apparatus (for example, tape player or VCR). A team member would set up the apparatus and switch, while classmates initiated the activity and asked the student yes-or-no questions when appropriate.

Exchanging Roles

One collaborative education team emphasized the sharing of instruction for all students and problem solved to identify scheduling needs and instructional activities that allowed each member to participate in each subject area across the week (Bald, 1992). This allowed every team member the opportunity to either observe, teach, or collaborate about a student in the different class periods. In addition, it allowed team members to change roles and to experience the student in activities as the other team members experienced that student. For example, during a class activity when the speech therapist was scheduled to be in the classroom, she and the general education teacher switched roles, allowing (1) the general education teacher to provide instruction in the communication needs of the student with multiple disabilities while facilitating the student's participation in the general class activity and (2) the speech therapist to provide instruction for the whole class while modeling strategies that would allow the general education teacher to maximize opportunities for the student with multiple disabilities to participate. This exchange of roles met the needs of both the general education teacher and the speech therapist without a break in the general education instructional activities.

Coteaching

A fourth way collaborative teams can work together is through coteaching. In coteaching, students and teachers are provided with direct classroom support (Walther-Thomas, Bryant, & Land, 1996) as the team plans, delivers, and evaluates instruction (Walther-Thomas, et al., 2000). The team has coordinated roles and members to provide instruction in various group settings (that is, small-group, large-group, and individual) (Rainforth & England, 2001). Four variations of coteaching include *interactive teaching, station teaching, parallel teaching*, and *alternative teaching*.

Summary

An education team comprises a student with moderate or severe disabilities and the school personnel, family members, and friends of the student who are involved in developing and implementing that student's education program. The members of an education team share the responsibility for planning, implementing, and evaluating the effectiveness of the entire education program, including both special education and related services. Across districts and buildings, education teams develop in a number of manners, resulting in either multidisciplinary, interdisciplinary, transdisciplinary, or collaborative teams. Though each approach to teaming has benefits, collaborative teaming is considered to be most effective and efficient when providing educational services for a student with moderate to severe disabilities in inclusive settings.

A collaborative education team is a group of equal individuals who voluntarily contribute their own knowledge and skills and participate in shared decisionmaking, while focusing on the efficiency of the whole team, as they work together in a spirit of willingness and mutual reward to problem solve and accomplish one or more common and mutually agreed upon goals. Their purpose is to provide the most effective education services for a set of students, allowing each student to maximize their participation and contribution to life at school, at home, and in the community.

The development of an effective collaborative team occurs over time, with conscious effort on the part of all members toward acquiring and consistently demonstrating a variety of skills beyond those in their area of expertise. These additional skills include effective communication, role release, problem solving, consensus building, conflict resolution, group management, and group leadership.

References

Amlund, J. T., & Kardash, C. M. (1994). Group approaches to consultation and advocacy. In S. K. Alper, P. J. Schloss, & C. N. Schloss (Eds.), *Families of students with disabilities:* *Consultation and advocacy.* Boston: Allyn & Bacon.

Anderson, N. B., Hawkins, J., Hamilton, R., & Hampton, J. D. (1999). Effects of transdisciplinary teaming for students with motor disabilities. *Education and Training in Mental Retardation and Developmental Disabilities, 34*, 330–341.

Bald, K. (1992). *Providing speech therapy in inclusive settings: Collaborating with team members.* Buffalo, NY: State University College at Buffalo.

Bauwens, Hourcade, & Friend. (1989). Cooperative Teaching: a model for general and special educators. *Remedial and Special Education, 10*, 17–22.

de Bettencourt, L. U. (1999). General educators' attitudes toward students with mild disabilities and their use of instructional strategies: Implications for training. *Remedial and Special Education, 20*, 27–35.

Downing, J. C. (2002). Including students with severe and multiple disabilities in typical classrooms: Practical strategies for teacher (2nd ed.). Baltimore: Paul H. Brookes Publishing Co.

Ferguson, D. L., Meyer, G., Jeanchild, L., Jeniper, L., & Zingo, J. (1992). Figuring out what to do with the grownups: How teachers make inclusion "work" for students with disabilities. *The Journal of The Association for Persons with Severe Handicaps, 17*(4), 218–226.

Friend, M. (2000). Myths and misunderstandings about professional collaboration. *Remedial and Special Education, 21*, 130–132.

Friend, M., Cook, L. (1992). *Interactions: Collaboration skills for school professionals.* New York: Longman.

Gaylord-Ross, R., & Holvoet, J. (1985). *Strategies for educating students with severe handicaps.* Boston: Little, Brown & Company.

Giangreco, M. F., Broer, S. M., & Edelmen, S. W. (1999). The tip of the iceberg: Determining whether paraprofessional support is needed for students with disabilities in inclusive settings. *Journal of The Association for Persons with Severe Handicaps, 24*(4), 281–291.

Giangreco, M. F., Cloninger, C. J., & Iverson, V. S. (1998). *Choosing options and accommodations for children (COACH): A guide to educational planning for students with disabilities.* Baltimore: Paul H. Brookes.

Hanft, B. (1993, March). *School based therapy: Effective consultation in the classroom.* Workshop presented in Rochester, New York.

IDEA 1997.

Idol, L. (1993). *Special educator's consultation handbook* (2nd ed.). Austin: Pro-ed.

Jackson, L., Ryndak, D. L., & Billingsley, F. (2000). Useful practices in inclusive education: A preliminary view of what experts in moderate to severe disabilities are saying. *Journal of The Association for Persons with Severe Handicaps, 25*(3), 129–141.

Janney, R., & Snell, M. (1997). How teachers use peer interactions to include students with moderate and severe disabilities in elementary general education classes. *Journal of The Association for Persons with Severe Handicaps, 21*(2), 72–80.

Johnson, D. W., & Johnson R. T. (1999). *Learning together and alone: Cooperative, competitive, and individualistic learning* (5th ed.). Boston: Allyn & Bacon.

Lyon, S., & Lyon, G. (1980). Team functioning and staff development: A role release approach to providing integrated educational services for severely handicapped students. *The Journal of The Association for the Severely Handicapped, 5*(3), 250–263.

Murphy, A. T. (1981). *Special children, special parents: Personal issues with handicapped children.* Englewood Cliffs, N.J.: Prentice-Hall.

Orelove, F. P., & Sabsey, D. (1996). *Educating children with multiple disabilities: A transdisciplinary approach* (3rd ed.). Baltimore: Paul H. Brookes.

Pfeiffer, S. I. (1980). The school-based interprofessional team: Recurring problems and some possible solutions. *Journal of School Psychology, 18*(4), 388–394.

Pugach, M. C., & Fitzgerald, M. A. (2001). Collaboration as deliberate curriculum decision making. In V. J. Risko & K. Bromley (Eds.). *Collaboration for Diverse Learners: Viewpoints and Practices.* Newark, DE: International Reading Association.

Pugach, M. C., & Johnson, L. J. (2002). Collaborative practitioners: Collaborative schools (2nd ed.). Denver: Love Publishing.

Rainforth, B., & England, J. L. (2001). Education teams for students with diverse needs: Structures to promote collaboration and impact. In V. J. Risko & K. Bromley (Eds.). *Collaboration for Diverse Learners: Viewpoints and Practices.* Newark, DE: International Reading Association.

Rainforth, B., York, J., & Macdonald, C. (1992). *Collaborative teams for students with severe disabilities: Integrating therapy and educational services.* Baltimore: Paul H. Brookes.

Rainforth, B., & York-Barr, J. (1997). *Collaborative teams for students with severe disabilities: Integrating therapy and educational services.* Baltimore: Paul H. Brookes Publishing Co.

Ryndak, D. L., Rainforth, B., & Schooley, R. (1993). Planning instruction for students with severe disabilities in general education settings: Two strategies for facilitating inclusion. Buffalo, NY: State University College of Buffalo.

Shea, T. M., & Bauer, A. M. (1991). *Parents and teachers of children with exceptionalities: A handbook for collaboration* (2nd ed.). Boston: Allyn & Bacon.

Sue, D. W., & Sue, D. (1990). *Counseling the culturally different: Theory and practice.* (2nd ed.). New York, Wiley.

Thomas, C. C., Correa, V. I., & Morsink, C. V. (2001). Interactive teaming: Enhancing programs for students with special needs. Upper Saddle River, NJ: Prentice-Hall.

Thousand, J., & Villa, R. (1989). Enhancing success in heterogeneous schools. In S. Stainback, W. Stainback, & M. Forest (Eds.), *Educating all students in the mainstream of regular education* (pp. 89–103). Baltimore: Paul H. Brookes.

Thousand, J., & Villa, R. (1990). Sharing expertise and responsibilities through teaching teams. In W. Stainback & S. Stainback (Eds.), *Support networks for inclusive schooling: Interdependent integrated education* (pp. 151–166). Baltimore: Paul H. Brookes Publishing Co.

Walther-Thomas, C. S., Bryant, M., & Land, S. (1996). Planning for effective coteaching: The key to successful inclusion. *Remedial and Special Education, 17,* 255–265.

Walther-Thomas, C., Korinek, L., McLaughlin, V. L., & Williams, B. T. (2000). *Collaboration for inclusive education: Developing successful programs.* Boston: Allyn & Bacon.

Webster's Ninth Collegiate Dictionary (1991). Springfield, MA: Merriam-Webster.

York, J., Giangreco, M. F., Vandercook, T., & Macdonald, C. (1992). Integrating support personnel in the inclusive classroom. In S. Stainback & W. Stainback (Eds.), *Curriculum considerations in inclusive classrooms: Facilitating learning for all students* (pp. 101–116). Baltimore: Paul H. Brookes.

9

Facilitating Skill Acquisition During General Education Academic Subjects, Electives, and Other Activities

Lewis Jackson, Karen McCaleb, and Ginny Helwick

Objectives

After reading this chapter, the reader will be able to:

1. Describe major principles and concepts associated with adapting academic lessons.
2. Identify major steps for collaboratively developing units and lessons that have adaptations built into their structure.
3. Identify major steps and procedures for creating adaptations for predeveloped academic lessons.
4. List essential materials and desk supplies for the adaptation process.
5. Discuss less-than-ideal learning situations and the role of the support specialist.
6. Show how to partition an academic lesson into steps and develop adaptations for students with varying learning capabilities and needs.

Key Terms

Accommodations	Foundational skills	Modifications
Adaptations	Levels of inclusion	Support specialist

A key to successful inclusion is to link the student with the general education curriculum by using the student's gifts, strengths, and present skill levels to achieve this linkage. Connectivity with the general education curriculum occurs concurrently with socialization and therefore must never be viewed as secondary or incidental to meeting a student's "social" goals or needs. This is because being connected to the curriculum is a pivotal step toward the kinds of authentic membership in the school or classroom that makes acquisition of social skills both meaningful and likely for the student (Jackson & Wimberley, 1993). Moreover, acceptance by peers is often mediated by whether the student is expected to learn what is perceived as essential and important by the other students, and not by mere presence in the classroom.

Ford, Davern, and Schnorr (2001) point out that "the United States has entered an era of standards-based reform in education" that is having a "significant effect on curricular guidance and foci for students with significant disabilities" (p. 215). They note that the emphasis on state content standards will necessitate "an approach to curriculum and assessment in schools" that will involve "an active integration of what has been learned in the study of individual differences with the work of the professional organizations that focus on curriculum" (p. 219).

Sapon-Shevin (1999) asserts that a student should "not have to earn his or her right to be included or struggle to maintain it. It is up to the teachers and administrators involved to make inclusion a viable possibility" (p. 4). This is how it is with immersion in the substance of the curriculum. It is the responsibility of the classroom teacher, with support from special education and other building personnel, to find ways to capitalize on the student's present capabilities as the catalyst for curriculum participation. Moreover, it is the responsibility of the special educator, collaborating with classroom teachers and others, to find ways to use the existing curriculum to address the individualized learning needs of the student who has a significant disability.

Access to, and learning from, the curriculum is made possible when teachers facilitate five interrelated levels of inclusion. These are the physical, the social, the activity, the content, and the extended level. The *physical level* refers to whether the student is present or not in the class with his or her peers. Although necessary for all other levels, physical presence is insufficient in and of itself for ensuring access to the curriculum. The *social level* refers to whether the student is connected with peers in patterns of affiliation and interaction. Social participation and involvement can significantly enhance access to, and participation in, the curriculum. The *activity level* refers to whether the student is involved and participating in the instructional and ancillary activities of the class. Activity participation, whether partial or full, is the bridge to learning within and across the curriculum, and its absence critically impacts opportunities to learn the knowledge and skills being taught to the other students. The *content level* refers to whether the student is inputting the substance of the curriculum such that information is actually learned. Content learning can be explicit (observable), measured through tests or other means, or it can be implicit, very possibly occurring but difficult to measure because of the way the disability affects the student's ability to respond. The *extended level* refers to whether the student is participating in the activities and learning that occur outside of the class, such as in doing homework or in talking to classmates about tests and assignments on the phone. Extended participation reinforces and expands the information and skills that are learned in class, ensuring that they become part of the student's repertoire.

This chapter defines, elaborates on, and gives examples of how this access can be achieved. It begins with basic principles and procedures that lay the groundwork for how educators define their roles and responsibilities. Next, processes of collaboration with general education in unit and lesson design are described. This is followed by a discussion of how previously designed lessons are adapted and a list of useful materials. The latter processes are then illustrated for three students with differing learning and support needs.

Basic Principles and Concepts

The literature is replete with recipes that promote practices for mixed-ability classes, such as strengths-based instruction (Schaffner, Buswell, O'Brien, & O'Brien, 1999), differentiating instruction (Tomlinson, Callahan, Tomchin, Eiss, Imbeau, & Landrum 1997), cooperative learning (Johnson, Johnson, Holubec, & Roy, 1984; Putnam, 1998), peer mediation strategies (Janney & Snell, 1996), co-planning and collaboration (Fuchs, Fuchs, & Bahr, 1990; Hawbaker, Balong, Buckwalter, & Runyon, 2001), thematic teaching units (Downing, 1996), and universal design (Pisha & Coyne, 2001). The evidence surrounding instruction in inclusive environments (Jackson, Ryndak, & Billingsley, 2000) suggests that practices such as these are often critical for the success of inclusive education. However, special educators have long noted that general education classrooms can be relatively hostile environments given the range of educational needs that come with students who have IEPs (Baker & Zigmond, 1990). The specter of long and grueling periods of teacher lecturing, coupled with worksheets and poorly monitored seatwork, are sometimes viewed as stark realities, anticipating a need for resource room and self-contained options for students with especially critical learning challenges.

What is perplexing about the foregoing perspective is that it frames what are essentially questionable teaching practices for all students as learning concerns for specific students, and this interpretation has historically defined the ecological and service niches of general and special educators. Because removal of students with the most difficulties reduces a concern's visibility even as it defines differential teacher roles and responsibilities, there is a sense of a problem being resolved and a valued place being affirmed for all stakeholders. However, as long as the working relationship and resource allocation processes between general and special education remain dominated by a "remove and remediate" logic, there is little impetus for changing what is essentially a larger issue affecting all students in settings in which these practices are pervasive (Jackson & Panyan, 2002).

For the practicing special educator, of course, the dilemma is more pending and immediate. It is not a question of what reforms are necessary; rather it is how to best educate a particular student without doing him or her a disservice and without losing face or position in the school community. Although advanced planning ensures proactivity in unit and lesson design, the special educator may face a need to adapt for a student "on-the-fly"; although good instructional practices reduce the need for supplemental curriculum and activity adaptations, the special educator may face a classroom in which these practices are used sparsely, reluctantly, or not at all; and, although collaboration enhances valued contributions from all stakeholders, the special educator may face a teacher who is too uncertain of his or her own skills to let others watch, too suspicious about coplanning to readily engage in it, and/or simply feels working alone is more efficient.

What must be understood is that these are not simply glaring contrasts between what ought and ought not to be in typical schools. Rather, they are unfortunate and longstanding classroom practices, and these practices impact *all* members of the school community. Hence, the optimal solution lies not in the pullout of the most obviously affected students for remediation, but rather in the development, promotion, and delivery of learning adaptations and supports that work in alignment with differing teacher styles, ecological and interpersonal contexts, and curriculum content areas.

This approach requires a set of role definitions for general and special educators that make sense when the general curriculum is the basis for instruction. General educators are viewed as content specialists with a working knowledge of practices that support their instruction; conversely, special educators are viewed as accessibility specialists with a working knowledge of additional tools and techniques for advancing the involvement and investment of specific students in the general education setting. Through the years, we have heard different names applied to these accessibility specialists, including "intervention specialists," "lead teachers," "inclusion facilitators," and "resource providers" to name a few. We, however, prefer the term "support specialist," and we will use this expression in this discussion.

Collaborating with General Educators in Unit and Lesson Design

In some situations, the support specialist is blessed with classroom teachers who assume a lead role in providing needed information in advance on unit content and lesson plans, use sound instructional practices with mixed ability groups of students, and willingly collaborate in lesson design and delivery. In such situations, the role of the support specialist becomes one of proactively and regularly detailing how the instruction can benefit and meet educational needs for specific students, helping design specific activity and material adaptations, and collaboratively scheduling the student's involvement in and supports for ongoing classroom activities.

Hawbaker et al. (2001) provide one model that can be useful for conceptualizing the task of collaborating teachers. Described as BASE, the model refers to four general processes: "Identifying the *B*ig ideas, *A*nalyzing areas of difficulty, creating *S*trategies and supports, and *E*valuating the process" (p. 25). Of special interest is the notion of the big idea. Within any given class or lesson, general education teachers can usually pinpoint for the support specialist essential content and/or processes that they view as most critical for all students. Sometimes these may be broad concepts derived from the lesson—often driven by educational standards—that can be acquired in varying ways and in varying degrees by all learners. Sometimes, skills such as critical thinking, cooperative learning, or finding resources guide the lesson design and delivery activities of the teacher. By determining in advance the learning intentions, or "big ideas" associated with a unit, lesson, or activity, the needed adaptations become more apparent.

Onosko and Jorgensen (1997) describe eight "essential elements" in the design of inclusive units, which can also be extended to individual lessons:

1. **A central problem or issue**: The unit or lesson is structured around a central issue—often framed as a question—instead of being organized around a laundry list of facts and concepts.
2. **An opening motivator**: The unit or lesson opens with an activity that entices and excites the students in relation to the intended learnings.
3. **The components are linked to the central problem or issue**: The unit or lesson activities have a demonstrable relationship with the central issue, and they are sequenced so that they contribute to each student's growing understanding of the issue.
4. **Rich array of source material**: The unit or lesson materials (books, materials, and technology) are varied and diverse, sustaining student interest and motivation.
5. **Culminating, final projects**: The unit or lesson results in one or more products that represent the fruits of each student's learning and participation. These products are shared.
6. **Varied formats**: Multiple ways of teaching are employed within and across lessons and units. These can include jigsaw activities, cooperative groups, whole group discussion, and other student arrangement and teaching style formats.
7. **Multiple and varied assessments**: Different forms of assessment are used to gauge student learning and at various points in the unit or lesson sequence.
8. **Multiple intelligences/multiple modes of student expression**: Students are encouraged to show their learning and growth through different channels, and the different channels are honored equally (see Gardner, 1993).

As noted earlier, a major issue facing educators is how to translate state content standards at different grade levels into expectations and learning outcomes for students with significant educational support needs. Ford et al. (2001) describe two procedures used by educators for developing "alternate performance indicators" that can make standards accessible. In the first procedure, the learning outcome of the standard is simplified to "find something . . . that the student can do" (p. 216). For example, a geography standard addressing the "interdependent world in which we live" (p. 216) might be addressed by having the student work with world maps and with pictures of different peoples, associating map locations with cultures and ways of life. In the second procedure, the learning outcome of the standard is redefined "so that it represents some type of functional skill" (p. 216). Using the foregoing geography example, the student might be required to learn more about his or her home community.

Ford et al. (2001) offer a third approach that they call the foundations approach. This approach emphasizes that a variety of essential skills—such as listening, speaking, reading and writing for information and understanding, and using written and oral language for self-expression—can and should be taught to all students, employing state standards for framing the educational objectives. Continuing with the geography example, the student would be engaged in the same or similar projects and activities as peers, but the focus might be on tasks that enhance ability to interact about subject content with his or her peers using an augmentative communication system. Ford et al. further comment that, although foundational skills can serve as focal points for instruction, these skills should not become "activities" in and of themselves. Put differently, students with severe disabilities should be involved in an authentic "extensive array of activities in classes such as science and social studies" (p. 217) and should not be taught foundational skills in isolation.

Adapting the Support Process for Predeveloped Lessons

Two terms that are often used for describing adaptations to an existing curriculum or lesson are *accommodations* and *modifications*. Accommodations are changes "made to the teaching or testing procedures in order to provide a student with access to information and to create an equal opportunity to demonstrate knowledge and skills" (Castagnera, Fisher, Rodifer, & Sax, 1998, p. 20). Modifications are changes "in what a student is expected to learn and/or demonstrate" as he or she works on the same subject area as "the rest of the class" (Castagnera, et al., 1998, p. 20). These two terms have descriptive utility when thinking about what is expected of the learner; however, in day-to-day practice, they are often less useful. When engaged in creating adaptations in a classroom, especially on the fly, the distinction between what is an accommodation and what is a modification quickly becomes murky. Hence, we will primarily use the term, "*adaptations*," in this chapter, which encompasses both processes.

Two systems that are helpful in developing a conceptual understanding of what is involved when creating adaptations are those of Castagnera et al. (1998) and Onosko and Jorgensen (1997). Castagnera et al. (1998) offer a breakdown of the adaptation process that focuses on the content and goals of instruction. Similar to a system developed by Giangreco, Cloninger, and Iverson (1998), their system proposes four basic kinds of adaptations that can be used separately or in various combinations. In the first kind of adaptation, "same – only less," the lesson being completed is the same as for all other students, but there are less items for the specific student to respond to. For example, the number of choices on a multiple-choice test could be reduced for the student. In the second type of adaptation, "streamlining the curriculum," the lesson "is reduced in size, breadth, or focus to emphasize key points" (Castagnera et al., 1998, p. 21). The identification of a small number of major concepts in a social studies lesson for the student to acquire relative to what is expected of other students exemplifies this adaptation. In a third type of adaptation, "same activity with infused objectives," the lesson is the same, but skills that are objectives on the IEP are expected of the student as he or she participates in the lesson. For example, the student may be expected to use an especially prepared overlay on an augmentative communication device to answer questions during a science class discussion, because increased use of the augmentative system is a goal on his or her IEP. In the fourth and final type of adaptation, "curriculum overlapping," the student works on the same assignment in two or more classes and turns in the same assignment to fulfill the expectations for those classes. For example, a student may be working in art class on drawing pictures illustrating the sequence of events from a book being studied in English class, and he or she turns in the work to fulfill requirements in both classes.

The system developed by Onosko and Jorgensen (1997) complements the Castagnera et al. (1998) system by emphasizing the support activities that go into the adaptation process. These authors describe five types of supports. First, there are people supports (for example, classmates and adults). Although care must be taken to ensure that overreliance or dependencies do not develop between the student and those providing support (Giangreco, Edelman, Luiselli, & MacFarland, 1997), people supports can encourage the kinds of interdependencies and cooperative expectations that are as much a part of learning as the content itself. Among their many examples, Onosko and Jorgensen offer these three of how classmates can provide support that is needed by another student: (1) a student "conferring" with the other student in the preparation of a written composition, (2) one student reading aloud with or to another student, and (3) one student interprets the specific signed communications of a student for a new student.

Second, there are modified materials or provisions of technology. They suggest five different ways that materials can be modified and/or technology added: (1) The student has the same materials, but interacts differently with them, such as doing a different number of math problems or reading for comprehension only parts of a book; (2) the format of the material is changed, but the information stays the same, such as when a student uses a multiple choice format to demonstrate learning that others are showing in an essay test; (3) the class materials are supplemented, such as giving the student a visual model of what to complete; (4) the class materials are substituted, such as providing reading materials on tape; and (5) technology is provided to augment a sensory or physical difficulty, such as using an enlarger to make printed material more readable.

Third, the expectations and/or performance standards can be individualized. For example, expecting a student who has difficulty grasping all of the concepts and principles of a science class can be expected to learn, instead, simplified concepts with only particular facts or applications of principles. Onosko and Jorgensen (1997) illustrate this by describing the expectations of Chris during a unit on heredity. He was expected to learn only something about how children assume characteristics of their parents, and that, if generations in the family have expressed a particular disease, there will be a certain probability of expression associated with later generations.

Fourth, the instruction can be personalized to match the learning modes and needs of particular learners in the class. Onosko and Jorgensen (1997) note that good teachers frequently word and reword their questions to check for learning and understanding in students. Other examples of this type of support include giving a student additional instructions, information, and/or structure so that he or she can complete a task being performed by the other students.

Fifth and finally, teachers can develop unique grading plans and/or evaluation criteria for particular students. Examples offered by Onosko and Jorgensen (1997) include (a) adaptations to a test's format, in item presentation method, or in item choices; (b) changes in homework expectations, such as expecting a different number of problems completed or grading an assignment using a complete/incomplete system; (c) putting more weight on criteria associated with class participation or behavior; and (d) creating a discretionary category, such as "extra credit for doing extra projects" (p. 98). Especially when based on the student's IEP, the special and general education teacher may also need to collaborate in the design of an individualized rubric for grades (A, B, C, and so forth) of work produced in class or at home.

Essential Materials and Desk Supplies

The support specialist must be equipped with a collection of tools that make it possible to create adaptations efficiently and quickly. Some of the tools that are offered here are common fare among practicing special educators and classroom teachers. However, it is our experience that many students are left fending for themselves in general education classes, partially because the supporting educators do not keep on hand, nor routinely use, a set of basic, inexpensive items that serve a range of purposes and can be applied quickly on an as-needed basis in the lesson adaptation process.

Table 9.1 provides a list of items that are invaluable and easily obtainable in schools and office supply stores, and it provides examples of how these items might be used in day-to-day practice. Other, more specialized items that should be kept on hand include the following:

- Instamatic or digital camera
- Small tape recorders, headsets, and blank tapes
- Environmental Control Unit (ECU)
- Calculators with enlarged buttons and easy-to-see liquid crystal display (LCD) screens
- Adding machine and paper rolls
- Picture symbol systems (Johnson, 1985) and Boardmaker
- Switches (for example, Big Red, jelly bean, and so forth)
- Simple and easily programmable augmentative devices, such as Big Mac and Alpha Smart

Employing the Support Process in Less-Than-Ideal Situations

Educators and parents, especially of children and youth in special education, may be inclined to view certain instructional situations as more optimal than others. However, it is instructive to recall that the majority of typical students experience a range of teaching and learning situations—some of them quite appalling by best practice standards—and they seem to emerge from their schooling experiences as reasonably educated citizens. Students with significant disabilities also need to be challenged by experiences in various learning and interpersonal contexts, and it can be a disservice to them to remove them for systematic instruction based on an opinion of inadequacy in the teaching. However, of course, students who have sensory, motor, medical, behavioral, and/or cognitive challenges will

TABLE 9.1 *Essential Materials for Routine and On-the-Fly Material Accommodations*

Items	*Description and/or Example Applications*
Pen-type liquid glue	This can be used for story sequencing and with multiple choice items (for example, child picks answer to math problem like $2 + 4 = 6$, 5, or 9, pasting the answer next to the problem).
Glue sticks	These can be used by a student who is preparing a picture collage in place of a written report.
White-out pen or bottle	Correction fluid or similar material is useful for changing or deleting items on worksheets, and so forth.
Scissors	Standard desk scissors are useful for cutting out specific items from a worksheet to delete them, change their order, or enlarge them on a copy machine.
Desk tape/dispenser	For example, single-sided tape pieces can be rolled up and used to organize picture symbols or answer cards, and the student can easily move these around.
Pencil grips	These can be commercial and/or Polyvinyl Chloride (PVC) designed. When attached to writing, marking, painting, or drawing utensils, they can increase student independence in these activities.
Dicem	This is a nonslip rubber material for keeping materials (for example, books or lunch trays) from sliding out of place. They are available in clear or colors and in various sizes. (Rubber shelf lining is an inexpensive substitute.)
Velcro	This is useful for securing and changing items on picture schedules or attaching index cards containing text or math Q&As to surfaces. (Sticky Tak can be used similarly.)
Laminating paper	This is used to cover and protect paper materials that students use every day, such as picture symbols, break cards, and so forth.
Magnified line reader	This is a durable, clear magnifier with a straight-edge line at the bottom that can be used to underline text. They are available in different sizes, but an 8-inch bar magnifier is especially useful.
Line trackers	8-inch construction paper or cardboard strips are used to underline text currently being read. They can be placed under the line being read or over previously read text, and moved down the page.
Erasable highlighters	These are like a bright highlighting marker and are available in different colors. They are used to emphasize text or other images in books or work sheets and are easily erased using an ordinary pencil eraser.

experience instructional situations that lack sufficient scaffolding to ensure learning. A skilled support specialist is especially paramount in classrooms that provide less than adequate instruction for mixed ability children and youth because they can help provide scaffolding that may benefit more than just the identified students in the class.

The support specialist must never presume that any general education curriculum content is inappropriate for a particular student, although there will certainly be classes and content that are of more interest and value to a student than other classes and content. To reiterate an important point, concerns about learning are less defined by the deficits of the student and more by the learning contexts provided by the adults. In classrooms in which information on lessons and instruction is unobtainable in advance, in which instruction is not especially good for a fair number of the students, and/or where real collaboration seems difficult to achieve, the support specialist should work with the presenting conditions to enhance the information and skill acquisition of specific learners and, ultimately, the learning of other students both present and future. The focus continues to be on the adaptation of the learning context—using the tools and techniques previously described—to provide access to the subject content, and not on fixing some characteristic of the learner. This focus certainly does not negate using more intense forms of instruction (for example, one-to-one assistance or repeated practice), but it does limit when and where such instruction occurs so that access to the knowledge and skills being taught to other students is not unduly restricted.

Illustrations

We have emphasized in previous sections that learning for students with significant disabilities must be based on state content standards and that the role of the support specialist is to enhance access to the curriculum, working in concert with the instructional style of the classroom teacher. We have offered a number of models for both designing and for adapting previously designed units, lessons, and activities. We have also provided a list of supplies that are useful for creating adaptations in advance or on the fly.

The situation in which the special educator must work with predesigned, standards-based units, lessons, and activities, creating adaptations with varying degrees of collaboration with general educators, is fairly typical in programs across the country. For this reason, the upcoming illustrations will focus on how to adapt predesigned lessons for students with significant support needs. We have selected three academic lessons representing the elementary, middle, and high school levels, respectively. We have also created three students who have very different learning abilities and support needs. We demonstrate in the upcoming sections how the learning of each of these students can be facilitated in each of these three lessons.

For purposes of this exercise, all three students will "move up" in age as we progress to different lessons, so that we can show how lessons are adapted as a student matures alongside his or her peers. The adaptations developed for each student draw on the principles and procedures described in the earlier sections, but they will reflect the kind of syntheses that a practicing teacher would be expected to demonstrate. We begin by describing the students.

The Three Students

Mark is an active, energetic boy who is very curious and loves to explore, especially when outside. His family enjoys camping throughout the United States, and they support this interest. Mark is a good listener with strong receptive skills, and he enjoys books and stories. His favorite subject is math. Mark needs to wear his glasses for optimal seeing.

Mark was diagnosed as having autism when he was two years old. Although he does not use speech, he communicates through picture symbols, gestures, vocalizations, and facial expressions. Mark is also able to read and sequence stories that are presented pictorially. Formal and informal assessment measures indicate that Mark's academic skills, though significantly below grade level, are emerging. Mark is sensitive to loud, unexpected, or high-pitched noises and sounds. He will cover his ears and show other signs of discomfort. When agitated, Mark demonstrates his emotions by screaming, running, or biting himself or others.

David is an engaging, very social young man who has many acquaintances throughout the school. His peers describe him as "a good friend." David is a Denver Bronco fan and loves to both talk about and play football with friends during recess. He enjoys school and tries hard to please his teacher. His favorite subject is music.

David has Down syndrome. His academic skills are at least two to three years below grade level, depending on content matter. He also demonstrates one to two year receptive and expressive language delays. Although his fine motor strength is sufficient, he demonstrates difficulty with fine motor planning and coordination and with holding writing utensils. David has a hard time problem solving and coping with difficult issues and situations. Transitions and changes in routine are especially hard for him.

Marissa is a sensitive young lady who loves school and enjoys interacting with her classmates. She has a keen sense of humor and is constantly smiling when around her friends. Marissa especially enjoys creative activities; her favorite subjects are music and art. She also enjoys listening to stories. Marissa has an extensive doll collection of which she is very proud. She often brings in different dolls to show to the class.

Marissa's records describe her as having a "profound" cognitive disability. She also has cerebral palsy, which significantly limits her gross motor movement and her use of her arms, hands, and legs. She uses a wheelchair for mobility, and she requires physical assistance for many tasks because of limited voluntary movement. She communicates mainly through eye gaze and facial gestures. Due to a swallowing disorder, she takes all nourishment through a g-tube.

The Lessons and Their Adaptations

The three lessons are described in the upcoming sections. Tables are used to present the recommended adaptations for the three students[1].

---

[1] A complete list of potential adaptations for the three lessons, plus additional lessons representing math and history, are available from the first author upon request.

Elementary Level Science Lesson: How Do You Describe a Peanut?   In this lesson, drawn from Sherman (2000), students work in groups and individually to observe and describe peanuts in their shells. It provides students with opportunities to practice the skills of examining, describing, classifying, and comparing tangible objects in terms of common physical properties. A typical standard from the physical sciences is that "*Students know and understand common properties, forms, and changes in matter and energy.*"

Materials: For each student, you will need one peanut (in its shell), one index card, a paper or plastic cup, and a pencil or marker. (Note: Allergies to peanuts can be quite serious, even if a person just inhales the aroma without eating them, so find out if any of your students have peanut allergies before doing this activity. In this activity, no one eats a peanut, and the peanuts remain in their shells. Use other materials if there are potential concerns.)

Procedure: Students work in groups of four or five.

1. Each group lists as many uses of a peanut as they can. Encourage them to *brainstorm*—to contribute ideas quickly, even silly ones, and to suspend judgment; include everyone's ideas.
2. Each group now gets one cup filled with eight peanuts so that there is one peanut (in its shell) for each student and a few extras, which remain in the cup. Each student chooses a peanut to observe. Students observe their peanuts, describe them, and write descriptors on the index card. (This part takes about 10 to 15 minutes.)
3. Students put the peanuts back in the cup and shake them up. Then each student finds his or her own peanut. (This takes less then five minutes.) Next, students return the peanuts to the cup, exchange index cards, and find someone else's peanut using the description (or drawing) on the index card. (This takes about five minutes.)

Assessment: Here are questions one can use with students to assess the activity when the observation phase has been completed. Students spend a few minutes answering these questions on their own, share them in their small groups, and then discuss them with the whole class.

- Were you successful in finding your own peanut? Someone else's peanut?
- If you were to describe a peanut to someone who has never seen one before, what characteristics would you use (for example, color, shape, size, texture, odor, or identifying marks)?
- As a scientist, what skills have you used to do this (for example, observation, communication, and collecting data)?

Adaptations for Mark, David, and Marissa: Table 9.2 displays some of the adaptations developed for these learners. Note that all forms of foundational skill development (for example, motor, communication, and social) occur as a function of *participation* (see Marissa, Step 2). Hence, it is important that adaptations for students vary as activities in the lesson sequence change to enhance participation-driven skill development. Of course, at any point in a lesson, there will be many adaptation possibilities, all of which could be useful. In Step 2, for example, Mark is working independently; he could

TABLE 9.2   *Individualized Adaptations for "Describing a Peanut"*

Critical Points in Lesson	Mark	David	Marissa
Step 1. Listing uses of peanut (brainstorming)	• Chooses from tailor-made word/picture symbols of uses for a peanut. • Activates/deactivates a tape recorder for class brainstorming.	• Teacher directs specific questions to him, offering him two choices.	• Uses a large switch to activate/deactivate a tape recorder to record the class's brainstorming session.
Step 2. Observing and recording a description of a peanut	• Given a distinctive peanut; works independently to draw within an outline his peanut; distinctive features are emphasized when checked by a circulating adult.	• Works with a partner, taking turns in making observations. Partner records both of their answers. It is important that both children use their senses to learn about the peanut.	• Using an index card with a big blank peanut on it, a peer finds distinguishing marks, seeks Marissa's agreement, then draws them (eye gaze, head control, and social interactions are naturally encouraged).
Step 3. Finding one's own and another student's peanut	• Mark is given his peanut by a student, and he checks its traits against those in his picture.	• The partner reads a trait from the list, and David checks to see if it is there. Together, the students decide if they have the right peanut.	• Peer reads each trait of peanut. Marissa indicates yes/no using communication board or simple, direct select two-choice device.
Assessment: Answering questions about the experience and about scientific observations and descriptions	• Answers questions about the most important features of his peanut, using word/picture symbols and his picture. • No adaptations for active listening to and acknowledging others (teacher reminders are OK).	• David and his partner answer the questions. David is responsible for making a taped record of their answers. • David answers teacher-selected questions, and the teacher writes answers down. He then uses an enlarged keyboard to copy the scribed list on the computer.	• Marissa can fully participate in answering questions about characteristics of a peanut. She uses eye gaze or switch access.

be working instead with a peer, who questions him using the descriptor checklist ("cracked or not cracked?"). Finally, note that there are lesson components that do not require specialized adaptations. During assessment activities, active listening is the same for Mark as for any other learner, and many learners benefit from teacher reminders at key points in a group or class discussion.

Middle School Science Lesson: Static and Current Electricity.   This lesson is revised from one described by Duncan (2001). There is an initial review of the structure of the atom with an emphasis on the electron, followed by a series of hands-on exercises in which properties of static electricity are explored. This is followed by a class demonstration of how electrons are involved in the conduction of electricity through a wire. Two practical applications of these principles are examined: a) The concepts of insulators and conductors are explored, and students are taught how to use a conductivity tester and b) there is a brief discussion of the improper use of electrical appliances. As a result of this lesson, students will understand how electricity is conducted through wire by electrons. Students will understand that there are two kinds of electricity: static and current. Students will know the difference between a conductor and an insulator and explain how they are used. Students will be able to explain common hazards associated with electrical appliances. A science standard that is addressed by this lesson is that "*Students know and understand common properties, forms, and changes in matter and energy; specifically, students know that energy appears in different forms, and can move (be transferred) and change (be transformed).*"

Materials: Materials needed include a ring and ring stand, a pointer, 4 feet of nylon string, 2 balloons, wool and silk pieces, yellow paper (3/8-inch × 12-inch strips), 8 feet of rope, masking tape, 2 newspaper strips (1 inch × 20 inch), plastic wrap, various examples of conductors and insulators (for example, penny, aluminum foil, pencil, glass rod, plastic rod, paper clip, ruler, or rock; small paper cup with vinegar, tap water, distilled water, distilled water with salt, distilled water with sugar), a conductivity tester, an old electric cord, and a pickle.

Procedure: The teacher first reviews previously learned concepts about the basic parts of the atom. Then the teacher explains that what makes electricity work are the electrons. Sometimes an electron flies off of one atom and connects with another. The teacher indicates that there are two basic kinds of electricity and that the class will be looking at some of the properties of these. Remaining parts of this lesson will now alternate between teacher demonstration and student hands-on application of the concepts.

1. The teacher demonstrates, in a distinct sequence, the properties of repel and attract. Tie two inflated balloons to the end of a 4-foot nylon string. Use a ring and a ring stand that has a pointer attached to the ring holder to hold the balloons. Ask the students to describe the hanging balloons at this point. Rub one balloon with a piece of silk and the other balloon with a piece of wool. Have the class observe and discuss changes that occur. On a chart or board, draw how two electrons of the same charge repel. Explain that repel means to "push away" as they saw demonstrated with the balloons. Next, follow the same procedure by rubbing one balloon with wool and one with plastic wrap. Have the class discuss what they observe. Add to the drawing on the board a second drawing that shows how

electrons attract. Explain that attract means to "come together" as they saw demonstrated with the balloons.

2. For practice, arrange students into small groups and give each group two of the precut newspaper strips. One student holds the two strips so they hang down while a second student strokes the strips lengthwise going from top to bottom each time with their thumb and forefinger. The teacher could assign additional roles to other group members such as recorder, facilitator, and so forth. The students should observe the newspaper strips flying apart. Have the students explain what they see happening using the terms "charge" and "repel."

3. Now, arrange students back into large group format. Review with students the concepts of static electricity, positive and negative charges, electron activity, and the properties of repel and attract. Check for understanding.

4. Explain how the students are now going to learn about conducting electricity. Have approximately six to eight students stand at the front of the room in a line. Tape a piece of the precut yellow paper strips to each student's arm. On each piece of yellow paper, draw a negative electron. Have the students with the papers collectively hold a rope that represents the wire. Have the students gently push each other on the back, which causes them to be propelled around the room. The teacher then explains how these are the electrons pushing each other in the wire. Then explain to the students that this represents electric current.

5. Transition to the next concept by explaining to students how conductors and insulators work in relation to an electric current. Give them a list that describes a variety of materials that could act as conductors or insulators. Using a conductivity tester, demonstrate the degree to which the item conducts electricity. Instruct students to record the results on their individual lists. Have students then make a general statement using the words "conductors" and "insulators," which synthesizes the results.

6. This final component is an extension and application of the previous concepts. The demonstration and discussion is designed to emphasize issues concerning safety with electricity. Instruct students that the following demonstration will show the dangers of electricity and that they should not try this on their own. Connect the ends of the electric cord to the pickle and plug the cord into a socket. Have the students observe and discuss what happens. The results are quite dramatic because the pickle glows, burns, and smells. Continue the discussion concerning hazards associated with electricity. For example, have students discuss why they should never use appliances in a bath or shower or why they should avoid a flooded basement.

Closure: Ask the students to describe what electrons do in static and current electricity.

Assessment: The following are assessment methods for this lesson:

- Teacher observes student understanding.
- Teacher-made quiz on conductors, insulators, and safety issue can be given.
- Write about the two kinds of electricity and how electrons respond in each one.
- Students may include a drawing. (In-class or homework assignment)

- Students bring in a collection of a preset number of items. Explain why each item is either a conductor or an insulator.

Adaptations for Mark, David, and Marissa: Table 9.3 displays some of the possible adaptations that can be used for this high-level academic lesson. We will use this lesson to make three essential points about the adaptation processes for content that is relatively abstract and difficult for many students. First, although specific characteristics of the student are considered (for example, Mark, Step 4), there is no simple one-to-one correspondence between a disability type ("autism") and the choice of adaptations; in fact, it is one of the larger misconceptions in our field that diagnostic labels provide primary information for selecting educational interventions. Experience suggests that employing such information in educational decisionmaking is far more likely to hurt the student's opportunities for learning than to shed light on ways to enhance it. Lesson adaptations must be configured to the *nature of the task in relation to the individual support needs of the learner*, not according to characteristics prescribed by a label. Second, not all learning shows itself in the face, mannerisms, actions, or responses of the student (David, Steps 4, 5, and 6). Two students, one with a disability and one without, may both be learning even if their faces are impassive or dreamy. Inversely, neither may be learning, and the reasons for their disassociation from the subject matter may be more similar than different (for example, instruction is disorganized, end-of-day fatigue, or more interesting things to think about). There is a tendency among some educators to interpret blank stares differently according to whether a student does or does not have an identified disability: The typical student is drifting while the student with a disability was never there; the typical student does not understand "this particular academic point" while the student with a disability does not understand "anything academic"; the typical student is benefiting even if he or she does not get it all while the special education student is not benefiting from the little that he or she is getting. Third and finally, adaptation of academic materials is often a trial-and-error process. Simply because an adaptation does not seem to work when first introduced and used over several sessions does not mean the student cannot benefit from the material; only that the particular adaptation, as applied, may not be especially effective. The same is true in checking for understanding and assessment. Assessment activities for Marissa, for example, may take a fair amount of trial and error before it is determined both what concepts to test and what response modalities to use.

High School Team-Building Activity: Consensus Decisionmaking.   According to Schmuck and Schmuck (1988), "Norms are shared expectations or attitudes about what are appropriate school-related procedures and behaviors" (p. 182). Because norms are stabilizers of behaviors, it is important that teachers use norm-building group activities that can enhance the focus of the students on learning. This particular norm-building lesson was derived from similarly designed lessons by Stanford (1977) and by Kagan (1990). It helps students understand that performance on a task can be improved when people work together. Students experience this by first completing a survivor checklist individually and then completing the checklist in a group with majority rule, and finally completing the same checklist with the same group using consensus. Although designed to build norms of consensus decisionmaking among groups within a classroom, the lesson addresses a standard

TABLE 9.3 *Individualized Adaptations for "Static and Current Electricity"*

Critical Points in Lesson	Mark	David	Marissa
Step 1. *Static Electricity*: Demonstrate *repel* and *attract* in large group format	• Mark assists by rubbing one balloon with wool and the other with plastic wrap.	• No adaptations necessary.	• No adaptations necessary; teacher encourages active listening.
Step 2. Hands-on practice in small groups	• Using premade word/picture cards ("charge" and "repel"), Mark explains what he sees.	• Check for understanding of concepts (charge, repel). • No adaptations needed during hands-on activity.	• With assistance, Marissa strokes paper. • With assistance, Marissa holds one of the strips.
Step 3. Review of concepts, i.e., positive and negative charges, electron activity, etc.	• No adaptations necessary. Sitting and attending to the teacher are encouraged.	• No adaptations necessary. Active listening is encouraged.	• Marissa is assisted in showing to the others *coming together and pushing away*.
Step 4. *Conducting Electricity*: Visual demonstration, using line of students	• On rope, opts whether to hold yellow paper or not. Touch, do not push; warn him in advance.	• No adaptations necessary.	• If safe, Marissa has yellow paper on wheel chair and is positioned at end of line.
Step 5. Understanding *conductors* and *insulators*	• Mark holds the tester. • Mark indicates by pointing if an item is a conductor or insulator using word cards.	• No adaptations necessary.	• Marissa indicates through eye gaze if an item is a conductor or insulator using word cards.
Step 6. Safety issues	• Mark answers specific yes/no questions about safety.	• No adaptations necessary.	• Records group's session with switch-operated tape recorder.
Closure: Ask, "What do electrons do in static and current electricity?"	• When asked, Mark points to the words *static* or *current* as teacher gives specific examples.	• David responds to specific, preplanned questions regarding electron activity.	• Using eye gaze, identifies the chart with electrons *coming together* vs. *pushing away*.

(continued)

TABLE 9.3   *Continued*

Critical Points in Lesson	Mark	David	Marissa
Assessment: Teacher observations, quiz, essay, and items from home	• Teacher-made quiz: Short, multiple-choice test that is read to him. He circles his choices. • Use individualized grading rubric.	• Teacher-made quiz: Modified quiz at David's comprehension level; Quiz is read out loud and answers are recorded on tape.	• Teacher-made quiz: Modified quiz using two-choice pictorial representations of concepts and eye-gaze responses.

related to geography: *Students understand the effects of interactions between human and physical systems and changes in meaning, use, distribution, and importance of resources: analyzing how humans perceive and react to natural hazards.*

Materials/Preparation: In advance, prepare a list of potential survival gear (for example, axe, rope, or camp stove) organized into a checklist (for examples, see Stanford [1977] pp. 194–197, or Kagan [1990] Chapter 7). Make sure that you have a verifiable answer sheet that is based on the list provided, which can be used for scoring different answers. Then prepare three copies of the survival checklist for each student. You will also need a blank chart (paper or whiteboard) that can be used to show the results from the groups. Allow about 2 hours to complete this activity, which could be on successive days.

Procedure: By way of introduction, the teacher tells the students:

"Suppose you are going on a survival trip by yourself into the high mountain country. You need to take only the gear that will contribute to your survival under extreme weather conditions. You look through your camping gear, and you have lots of things that you might take, but you only want to take that which is most important for survival. What would you take?"

1. Begin by having the students complete the worksheet independently. Emphasize to the students that working alone (without outside resources or consultation) is important for this first step. This step may be assigned as homework. Students turn in the paper to be scored by the teacher.
2. Next, have the students complete the worksheet using majority rule voting. Divide the class into odd-numbered groups of about five to seven students. Limit the time the students have to complete the activity so discussion is held to a minimum. Have groups record their final answer on one sheet. Remember to have groups identify their group name or number on the answer sheet.
3. This step explores consensus building. The students remain in the same groups, but this time answers are recorded only after the groups discuss their opinions and agree

on the answer to each item. Students are instructed to use logical reasoning and factual information to arrive at their final answers. Group members should not simply give in to the group's wishes just to make it easier to arrive at a decision, but they should also not refuse to compromise. It is important that they listen carefully to other members of the group and try to understand their ideas. The goal is complete agreement by all group members.

4. For the culminating activity, record scores on the chart in the following manner: the best individual score from a member of each group; the majority rule score; and the consensus score for each group. Return the scored individual worksheets to the students.

Assessment: Discussion questions, such as the following, can be used to assess learning:

- How were the individual scores different from the other scores?
- How did the best individual score in the group compare to the voting and consensus score in the group?
- Which method resulted in the best score: voting or consensus?
- What might be an explanation for the differences in scores?
- Compare the voting method to the consensus method.
- What were some problems the group had in reaching consensus?
- Which method did you *feel* better about?

Adaptations for Mark, David, and Marissa: Stanford (1977) asserts, "if a group is to become truly mature and productive, deliberate attention must be given to changing the students' interaction patterns from exchanges between teacher and student to exchanges among students. This involves improving both the students' listening habits and the ways in which they contribute to class activities" (p. 117). Hence, the participation adaptations shown in Table 9.4 are developed to ensure that Mark, David, and Marissa are enmeshed in the interactive processes of their respective groups. Note especially the way Marissa's participation was constructed in Steps 2 and 3.

Summary

We have defined the processes of providing an appropriate education to students with significant disabilities as ones in which general education academic lessons are adapted in relation to the capabilities and support needs of individual students. Within this perspective, general educators are viewed as content specialists, and special educators are viewed as accessibility experts. Working together, units and lessons can be developed that are intrinsically ready for learners with mixed abilities, and previously designed units and lessons can be adapted for specific learners as the need arises.

In closing, we will emphasize two points and then express a word of encouragement for those who have concerns about the changing roles of the special educator. The first point is that many of the communication, social, and motor skills typically identified as

TABLE 9.4 *Individualized Adaptations for "Consensus Decisionmaking"*

Critical Points in Lesson	Mark	David	Marissa
Step 1. Independent completion of worksheet	• Mark completes a modified survival worksheet; pictures accompany words, and the sheet has fewer items, some of which may be pretaught.	• David completes a modified survival worksheet containing only the words; he uses a picture dictionary to look up words.	• Marissa uses eye gaze to complete a modified survival worksheet containing pictures of frequently used survival gear and items unrelated to camping.
Step 2. Majority rule completion of worksheet	• Mark indicates which pictures on his worksheet identify survival gear that he thinks should be included in the final list.	• No adaptations needed.	• Marissa chooses, through eye gaze, items/picture she feels should be included. (Some of the items, of course, are also items on her Step 1 worksheet.)
Step 3. Group consensus completion of worksheet	• Mark indicates "agreement" or "disagreement" through vocalizations, gestures, or using small picture symbols.	• No adaptations needed.	• Marissa chooses the order in which to discuss the particular *items*, and the group follows her choice. When consensus is reached, a peer signals Marissa to ring a bell.
Step 4. Culminating activity: reviewing scores	• No adaptations needed.	• No adaptations needed.	• No adaptations; active listening is encouraged.
Assessment: Discussion questions	• Any discussion question can be reworded and asked in a choice fashion. ("Was the individual score lower than the consensus score?")	• No adaptations needed.	• Questions can be worded for affirmation responses, based on observations of her behavior during the lesson. "Did you like consensus building best of all?"

needs for students with severe disabilities need not be met by targeting them as goals and objectives and then providing discrete trial training over extended time periods. Rather, by developing goals and objectives related to the content of the general education curriculum and then infusing foundational motor, social, and communication skills into the learning activities and expectations made of the students, one can achieve the same kinds of learning. The risk of not doing the latter is that true access to the curriculum is unintentionally denied under the pretense that academic skills are not what this student is working on when in this class. If certain forms of academic knowledge are valued for the so-called typical students, we must make opportunities available to learners with severe disabilities to learn the same material.

The second point is that the adaptation begins where the general education teachers already are and not where we want them to be. This chapter has offered models and procedures for collaborative lesson design, and this is certainly the ideal situation. However, we have also provided and illustrated tools and techniques that can be applied to enhance the access of specific learners to specific content regardless of how instruction is approached in a particular class.

Finally, we would hope that special educators perceive their changing roles as challenges requiring foresight, skill, and time, and not as insurmountable barriers to meeting the real educational needs of students with severe disabilities. Special educators must, over time, assume leadership roles in their buildings and districts if the kinds of changes needed for the real inclusion of students with disabilities in their home communities and schools is to occur. In addition, they must come to value the learning of their students when they are with their typical peers over their own needs to have a classroom and groups of students. It is a little like watching one's children grow up. The mature parent knows when and how to let them go.

References

Baker, J. M., & Zigmond, N. (1990). Are regular education classes equipped to accommodate students with learning disabilities? *Exceptional Children, 56*, 515–526.

Castagnera, E., Fisher, D., Rodifer, K., & Sax, C. (1998). *Deciding what to teach and how to teach it: Connecting students through curriculum and instruction* (2nd ed.). Colorado Springs, CO: PEAK, Inc.

Downing, J. E. (1996). *Including students with severe and multiple disabilities in typical classrooms: Practical strategies for teachers.* Baltimore: Paul H. Brookes Publishing Co.

Duncan, R. (2001). *Electricity: Static and current.* Retrieved August 2, 2001, at *www.lessonplanspage.com/ScienceCurrentStaticElectricity68.htm*

Ford, A., Davern, L., & Schnorr, R. (2001). Learners with significant disabilities: Curricular relevance in an era of standards-based reform. *Remedial and Special Education, 22*, 214–222.

Fuchs, D., Fuchs, L. S., & Bahr, M. W. (1990). Mainstream assistance teams: A scientific basis for the art of consultation. *Exceptional Children, 57*, 128–139.

Gardner, H. (1993). *Multiple intelligences: The theory in practice.* New York: Basic Books.

Giangreco, M. F., Cloninger, C. J., & Iverson, V. S. (1998). *Choosing outcomes and accommodations for children: A guide to educational planning for students with disabilities* (2nd ed.). Baltimore: Paul H. Brookes Publishing Co.

Giangreco, M. F., Edelman, S. W., Luiselli, T. E., & MacFarland, S. Z. C. (1997). Helping or hovering? Effects of instructional assistant proximity on students with disabilities. *Exceptional Children, 64*, 7–18.

Hawbaker, B. W., Balong, M., Buckwalter, S., & Runyon,

S. (2001). Building a strong BASE of support for all students through coplanning. *Teaching Exceptional Children, 33*(4), 24–30.

Jackson, L. B., & Panyan, M. V. (2002). *Positive behavioral support in the classroom: Principles and practices*. Baltimore: Paul H. Brookes Publishing Co.

Jackson, L. B., & Wimberley, G. (1993, Nov.). *Friendship roles at different ages: A comparison between children with and without disabilities in inclusion settings*. Chicago: Association for Persons with Severe Handicaps.

Jackson, L., Ryndak, D., & Billingsley, F. (2000). Useful practices in inclusive education: A preliminary view of what experts in moderate to severe disabilities are saying. *Journal of the Association for Persons with Severe Handicaps, 25*, 129–141.

Janney, R. E., & Snell, M. E. (1996). How teachers use peer interactions to include students with moderate and severe disabilities in elementary general education classrooms. *Journal of The Association for Persons with Severe Handicaps, 21*, 72–80.

Johnson, D. W., Johnson, R. T., Holubec, E. J., & Roy, P. (1984). *Circles of learning: Cooperation in the classroom*. Alexandria, VA: ASCD.

Johnson, R. M. (1985). *The picture communication symbols (Books I & II)*. Solana Beach, CA: Mayer-Johnson.

Kagan, S. (1990). *Cooperative learning: Resources for teachers*. San Juan Capistrano, CA: Resources for Teachers.

Onosko, J. J., & Jorgensen, C. M. (1997). Unit and lesson planning in the inclusive classroom. In C. M. Jorgensen (Ed.), *Restructuring high schools for all students: Taking inclusion to the next level* (pp. 71–105). Baltimore: Paul H. Brookes Publishing Co.

Pisha, B., & Coyne, P. (2001). Smart from the start: The promise of universal design for learning. *Remedial and Special Education, 22*, 197–203.

Putnam, J. A. (Ed.). (1998). *Cooperative learning strategies and strategies for inclusion: Celebrating diversity in the classroom* (2nd ed.). Baltimore: Paul H. Brookes Publishing Co.

Sapon-Shevin, M. (1999). *Because we can change the world: A practical guide to building cooperative, inclusive classroom communities*. Boston: Allyn & Bacon.

Schaffner, C. B., Buswell, B. E., O'Brien, C. L., & O'Brien, J. (1999). Strengths: Windows into learning. In B. E. Buswell, C. B. Schaffner, & A. B. Seyler, *Opening doors: Connecting students to curriculum, classmates, and learning* (2nd ed.). Colorado Springs: PEAK, Inc.

Schmuck, R. A., & Schmuck, P. A. (1988). *Group processes in the classroom* (5th ed.). Dubuque, Iowa: Wm. C. Brown Publishers.

Sherman, S. (2000). *Science and science teaching*. Boston: Houghton Mifflin.

Stanford, G. (1977). *Developing effective classroom groups: A practical guide for teachers*. New York: Hart Publishing.

Tomlinson, C. A., Callahan, C. M., Tomchin, E. M., Eiss, N., Imbeau, M., & Landrum, M. (1997). Becoming architects of communities of learning: Addressing academic diversity in contemporary classrooms. *Exceptional Children, 63*, 269–282.

10

Facilitating Oral Language and Literacy Development During General Education Activities

Brenda Fossett, Veronica Smith,[1] and Pat Mirenda

Objectives

After reading this chapter, the reader will be able to:

1. Describe the most common modes of unaided and aided communication used by students with significant disabilities for communication and literacy.

2. List several ways general education teachers can develop talk-friendly classrooms.

3. Discuss how teachers can (a) facilitate participation in teacher-led discussions, oral presentations, and peer interactions and (b) support students to follow instructions and demonstrate increased control over language structures in general education classrooms.

4. Describe the components of early literacy instruction using the Four Blocks model, with examples of each component.

5. Describe strategies for supporting upper elementary and high school students with significant disabilities to read and write for specific purposes; develop increased knowledge of vocabulary, grammar, and literary conventions; and locate and use information from a variety of print resources.

Key Terms

Augmentative and alternative communication	Communication	Visual supports
Balanced literacy instruction	Literacy	
	Oral language	

"Language is the basis of human community. With it we inform, persuade, challenge, support, and entertain each other." (Dias, Beer, Ledwell-Brown, Pare, & Pittenger, 1992, p. 187).

Students with significant developmental disabilities are increasingly included in classrooms where oral language and literacy opportunities exist in forms that were not previously envisioned in segregated settings. In addition, important positive changes in societal and professional attitudes toward these individuals has resulted in the wide-spread availability of communication and literacy technologies that enable them to par-ticipate in inclusive, dynamic environments (Mirenda, Iacono, & Williams, 1990). The purpose of this chapter is to provide a framework for thinking about oral language and literacy development for students with developmental disabilities in inclusive classrooms and to suggest a variety of practical strategies that are appropriate for classroom teach-ers to use in this regard.

Definitions and Student Examples

In this chapter, we discuss an array of interventions for students with significant disabilities in general education classrooms. These interventions are grouped, for the sake of conve-nience, into two broad categories: those related to oral language development and those re-lated to literacy development. We use the term "oral language" to refer to behaviors that people use to communicate to others (for example, speech, facial expressions, gestures, pointing to photographs or symbols, and manual signs), as well as behaviors used to under-stand communication from others (for example, listening and watching). Although not all of these behaviors are oral per se, they are often used to process and produce communica-tions that are predominantly seen as "oral." On the other hand, we use the term "literacy" to refer to all language activities that are associated with reading and writing. Making these distinctions will enable us to deconstruct the instructional practices that serve to develop students' oral language and literacy skills in the context of "talk-friendly" classrooms that support all learners. However, we make these distinctions with an awareness that speaking, listening, reading, and writing are interrelated, and that it is only when skills in both areas are taught interactively that students' communication abilities can develop in meaningful ways.

Student Examples

At the outset, we need to acknowledge the incredible range of individual differences that exists with regard to the learning styles, learning needs, and abilities of students labeled as having significant developmental disabilities. These students come from a range of socio-cultural and language backgrounds and are educated in classrooms that differ with regard to grade level, physical arrangement, and teachers' previous experience and education. All of these factors affect exactly how the concepts we discuss in this chapter are implemented. In acknowledgement of some of this variability, we would like to introduce three students from different backgrounds who span a broad range of ages; cognitive, language, and phys-ical abilities; and grade levels. We will use these three students in this chapter to illustrate how the oral language and literacy development of individuals with a range of disabilities and from a variety of backgrounds can be supported in general education classrooms.

Lutero. Lutero is a boisterous, happy six-year-old boy who loves rap music and fast rides in his wheelchair. He attends a grade one classroom in which most of his classmates, like Lutero, are Hispanic and bilingual. He was identified at birth as having spastic quadriplegia (that is, cerebral palsy) and has no use of his legs and limited, though functional, use of his arms and hands. Lutero also has oral-motor difficulties and, despite regular speech therapy during preschool, has not developed intelligible speech. However, he has many other forms of expressive communication, including a manual sign vocabulary of approximately 20 sign approximations and a book with more than 200 Picture Communication Symbols[2] ([PCSs]; Mayer-Johnson Co., 1994) that he uses to make requests and to comment. Although Lutero is learning to communicate and read primarily in English at school, his PCSs have both English and Spanish translations so that he can use them both at school and at home. Currently, Lutero is also trying out a voice output communication aid (VOCA) because his school team and his parents hope that this will enable him to communicate and learn more effectively in the future.

Sandy. Sandy is 10-year-old girl who attends a grade four classroom in her neighborhood school in a rural town. She is an active girl who is continually on the move and who points and vocalizes to establish joint attention to objects, persons, or events. Her speech has not developed beyond vocalizations such as *Eeeee*[3] when she is excited and sounds such as *ba* and *nah* that do not appear to have specific meanings. Sandy's understanding of oral language appears to be greatly enhanced when her communication partners use real object (that is, tangible) or photographic symbols that relate to her interests and activities in the context of familiar routines. For example, when her teacher holds out her coat and says, *"Time to go outside,"* Sandy puts on the coat (with assistance from a classmate) and leaves the classroom for the playground. Sandy has also learned to activate several simple battery-operated devices to participate in educational activities with the rest of her class; these will be discussed in specific sections of the chapter.

Mitchell. Mitchell is a 15-year-old adolescent who loves to wrestle and interact physically with others. He has been labeled as having Pervasive Developmental Disorder-Not Otherwise Specified (PDD-NOS), one of the disorders on the autism spectrum. Mitchell displays many characteristics typically associated with this diagnosis, such as an insistence on rigid routines, repetitive types of play, and limited language and communication skills. Communicatively, Mitchell verbalizes a few words and short phrases, vocalizes in conjunction with pointing and gesturing, leads others to items of interest, and uses a range of PCSs to indicate items or activities that are not present. Many of his classmates have known him since kindergarten and have learned to understand his various communicative attempts. In fact, they act as translators for each new teacher until he or she gets to know Mitchell and how he communicates. He participates in school activities and benefits from the use of PCS schedules and scripted routines that sequence the steps he needs to follow to complete classroom activities.

Augmentative and Alternative Communication

Lutero, Sandy, and Mitchell all use augmentative and alternative communication (AAC) techniques to supplement or replace their speech. For example, Lutero uses a combination of both unaided and aided AAC techniques. His unaided techniques include manual signing, gestures, facial expressions, and a few vocalizations. The advantages of unaided techniques are that they are portable, readily available at no cost, and do not require any extra equipment. However, given Lutero's physical limitations, his unaided communication may be difficult to understand by communication partners who are not familiar with manual signs or with Lutero's unique execution of them. Lutero's aided communication currently includes his 200-word PCS book and the VOCA he is trying out for long-term use. Because communication through aided AAC techniques is usually quite easy for unfamiliar communication partners to understand, such techniques are often especially appropriate for inclusive classrooms. In busy classrooms in which oral language is the primary mode of communication, VOCAs also facilitate communication at a distance, enable students to gain attention in group discussions, and often act as social bridge builders because the output they provide—digitized or synthetic speech—is very similar to the oral language used by typical peers. On the other hand, aided AAC techniques can be somewhat challenging for teachers to use, are usually more expensive than unaided techniques, can break down or get lost, and must be updated regularly with the specific vocabulary words that are used in classroom lessons. Like Lutero, Sandy and Mitchell also use a combination of both unaided and aided techniques to communicate. Table 10.1 provides examples of these techniques.

From this brief description of AAC, it should be clear that all communicators, not just those with significant disabilities, use multiple techniques to communicate. We vary these techniques according to the communicative context and the skills of our communication partners. That people communicate in a variety of ways is especially important to remember when supporting children with significant disabilities, who usually benefit from a variety of AAC techniques as part of their overall communication systems.

Approaches to Oral Language and Literacy Development for Students with Disabilities

Students with significant disabilities exhibit substantial delays in communication development that make it difficult for them to express their thoughts, feelings, and ideas

TABLE 10.1 *Examples of Aided and Unaided Communication Techniques*

Aided Techniques	*Unaided Techniques*
Communication boards, books, or wallets	Speech
Pictures and line drawings	Facial expressions
VOCAs	Gestures
Computers with synthetic speech	Pointing
Writing (orthographic symbols)	Manual sign language

verbally (Falvey, 1995). This is usually due to a combination of problems in the areas of articulation (that is, pronouncing words), language use (that is, combining words in meaningful ways), language comprehension (that is, understanding the language of others), and pragmatics (that is, using language appropriately in a social and cultural context). Some students may also experience prompt dependency, passivity, or learned helplessness (Calculator, 1988). These combined problems make many students' communication attempts difficult to interpret, especially by classroom teachers who may have had little or no specific training in working with children with communication delays or disorders.

Traditional therapeutic approaches to language development for students with significant disabilities were based on the notion that speech and communication are synonymous and that increasing speech ability would automatically result in increased language and communication (Calculator, 1988). More recently, language development research has led to an increased focus on communication *per se*, in terms of both intervention targets and intervention style (Falvey, 1995). Effective communication interventions are designed to teach the language functions, forms, and contents that are likely to have the greatest impact on students' ability to function and learn in the context of natural, inclusive environments and activities (Falvey, Bishop, Grenot-Scheyer, & Coots, 1988; Halliday, 1975; McLean & Snyder-McLean, 1978). In addition, because reading and writing are integrally bound to both listening and speaking, effective literacy instruction should be designed to build on students' oral language ability and on the cultural background in which it develops and is used. Clearly, "language development is a long-term process that is interdependent with world experience and home and community language environments, attitudes, and opportunities to use and practice language" (Gambell, 1994, p. 42). Students become members of their school communities through communication and, reciprocally, their school communities provide opportunities that nurture and facilitate their oral language competence.

Developing a Talk-Friendly Classroom Climate

Only recently have the developers of educational curricula recognized the importance of oral language—both speaking and listening—as the underlying basis for literacy development across the curriculum (Ward, 1997). We now understand that talking and listening both serve two important functions in the classroom: social and intellectual. When oral language is used socially, students are able to engage in conversations and share information and ideas. Talk is also used to form relationships through language. By the same token, students' oral language skills develop in conjunction with their expanding social awareness and their ability to reflect upon and reconstruct experiences intellectually. A safe, comfortable, and relaxed atmosphere is critical for the development of oral language in the classroom and is particularly important for students whose past experiences are different from the norm. In the following sections, we consider each of these three planning and instructional aspects that support oral language development, with examples of their application in Lutero's, Sandy's, and Mitchell's classrooms.

Creating Physical Environments that Support Language Learning

If teachers are to create talk-friendly classrooms, the physical environment of the classroom must allow for flexibility with regard to grouping arrangements, so that children are provided with a range of communication opportunities. Environmental arrangement is an important strategy for promoting communication in the classroom (Halle, 1984; Haring, Neetz, Lovinger, Peck, & Semmell, 1987; Ostrosky & Kaiser, 1991).

Classroom Arrangement

Research suggests that children's behavior and learning are both influenced by the physical organization of the classroom, especially for children with significant disabilities who may not have the physical mobility or manipulation skills needed for optimal access (Light, 1997). Environmental strategies such as (a) defining the space in the room with chairs, carpets, and other furniture; (b) eliminating distractions, such as noise from people or activities; (c) clearly indicating seating arrangements; and (d) increasing accessibility to instructional materials with organization and labeling have been shown to decrease the likelihood that students will engage in problem behaviour (Staab, 1992). These strategies also appear to promote attention and task engagement and to facilitate opportunities for children to practice and generalize skills across different types of activities, settings, and people (Staab, 1992).

Lutero. Although there are times when silence is the rule in his classroom, Lutero and his classmates are encouraged to interact with one another much of the time. In order to facilitate such interaction, Ms. Carter, Lutero's grade one teacher, took some time to consider the physical arrangement of her classroom before school began in September. She realized that Lutero, who operates his power wheelchair independently, would need to be able to move around the classroom easily in order to participate in all of the learning opportunities available to his peers. Ms. Carter designated a large open corner of the classroom as a gathering place and posted the classroom schedule prominently in this area so that all of the children can refer to it when they gather for whole-class lessons, class meetings, oral presentations, or sharing times. Lutero can readily access this area in his wheelchair and at times also sits in a large bean bag chair that Ms. Carter placed there. She also set up various small group areas around the room, one of which includes a round table with chairs and a special cutout for Lutero's wheelchair and a floor area with cushions so he can sit on the floor, if necessary. The small group areas are used by five or six children at a time to play games, participate in small group discussions, or engage in group planning activities. The small group tables and chairs are also used by Lutero and his classmates when they need to work on projects or worksheets individually.

Classroom Organization

Another important element for facilitating language development involves considering the placement, use, and labeling of objects needed to mediate learning goals in the classroom. Establishing explicit organizational structures in the physical environment clarifies social and communication expectations and decreases the need for students to make decisions using social information that may be abstract, unpredictable, and/or vague (Quill, 2000). Table 10.2 provides examples of the types of organizational and labeling strategies that can be useful with students who have difficulty understanding implied social and oral language expectations.

Establishing Rules and Routines that Encourage Talk for All Learners

Establishing a psychological atmosphere in which all children feel valued and are ready to take risks is essential for initiating and maintaining productive talk in the classroom. Marzano, Pickering, and Pollock (2001) noted a sizable research literature emphasizing that students benefit from the overt teaching of strategies for planning, organizing, completing, and reflecting on content and activities. A commonly used strategy in this regard is the use of visual supports to enhance students' understanding of classroom rules and of the daily classroom schedule.

Teachers frequently incorporate the use of symbols, such as objects, pictures, photographs, and words to aid language comprehension, to facilitate students' understanding of rules and routines, and to help students to participate in social communicative

TABLE 10.2   *Supports to Assist Students to Understand Classroom Organization (Quill, 2000)*

Classroom Parameter	Strategy
Space: where to be	*Group participation*: Put group members' photographs on cards to designate tables for group work. *Individual participation*: Put students' names on desks; mark play boundaries with colored tape.
Choices: what materials to use	*Group participation*: Use different colored folders for each subject area; provide color-coded index cards listing materials needed for each activity. *Individual participation*: Label toys and materials on shelves or in transparent containers so students can use and return them independently.
Expectations: what to do	*Group participation*: Make a list of group rules and post it prominently in the classroom; assign roles to students for group activities. *Individual participation*: Ensure that activities have a clear beginning and end; use cue cards to remind students what to do and who to watch.
Transitions: when to stop and start activities	*Group participation*: Use nonverbal cues for group transitions (for example, turn the lights down and have all students raise their hands). *Individual participation*: Visually depict the current and next activity using "First, Then" and pictures of activities

interactions. Such visual supports have been referred to as "augmented input" strategies with which teachers augment the meanings of instructional events by using real objects, maps, drawings, photographs, slides, videotapes, and other media to supplement spoken descriptions (Wood, Lasker, Siegel-Causey, Beukelman, & Ball, 1998). One of the most common augmented input strategies involves the use of pictorial or written schedules that assist students to understand and follow predictable activity sequences in school settings (Wood et. al., 1998). Many types of symbols can be used to construct such schedules, depending on abilities of the student who requires this structural support.

Sandy. Sandy benefits from having a concrete representation of what will happen next in her grade four classroom. Ben, the assistant in Sandy's classroom, and Mr. Humble, her teacher, have gathered objects to act as symbols of the many activities in the class. For example, they decided that a small ball would represent the gym, a piece of carpet would represent the carpet area used for group discussions, and a book would represent the library. Every morning, Sandy and Ben order her tangible symbols (Rowland & Schweigert, 1989, 1996) in a series of boxes in Sandy's classroom (Figure 10.1). At the completion of each activity, Sandy and Ben go to the box, place the object for that activity in a "finished" compartment, and select the object for the next activity on the schedule. If a sudden change occurs in the schedule, Ben gives Sandy a special symbol—a block of wood with a red cover—that means "unusual event," which she has learned to recognize.

Mitchell. At high school, Mitchell also benefits from having a visual schedule to move independently from one classroom to the next. His high school operates on a block system, in which there are six blocks (that is, classes) in total, but only four that occur each day. Thus, each day of the week starts with a different subject. Mitchell uses a PCS display that indicates the time and sequence of activities for each day (Figure 10.2). Mitchell stores his schedule in his binder and references it independently at the close of each classroom period.

Structuring Oral Language Opportunities

There are numerous language demands in typical classrooms, and students need to be able to participate in teacher-led discussions, follow instructions, use language effectively during classroom activities to ask and answer questions, give oral presentations,

FIGURE 10.1   *Sandy's schedule box with tangible symbols representing classroom activities (courtesy of Erica Schenker, Maple Ridge, BC).*

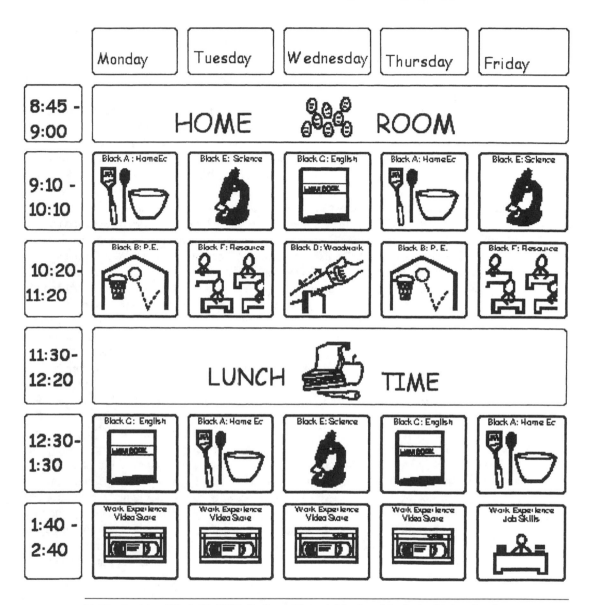

FIGURE 10.2 *Mitchell's PCS display with variable class blocks for high school.*

and participate in social interactions. Each of these is discussed in the sections that follow, with examples related to Lutero, Sandy, and Mitchell.

Participating in Teacher-Led Discussions

Most teachers are interested in encouraging students' active engagement in group lessons for at least some part of the school day. Indicators of student participation in teacher-led discussions include appropriate student responses to questions related to the content of a lesson, formulation of questions by students to clarify their understanding, and oral contributions by students to the subject under discussion. Ensuring that all students have the opportunity to participate in teacher-led discussions may require both planning and structural supports.

Lutero. In a many primary classrooms, themes are used to teach a variety of language arts skills. In Lutero's class, Ms. Carter has decided to build a theme around a children's book, *Alexander and the Terrible, Horrible, No Good, Very Bad Day* (Viorst, 1972). Her goal is that the students learn to use rich and varied language to describe events and to talk about how they feel. Her instructional plan begins with students watching a videotape of the Alexander story being read. During group discussion time following the viewing, she asks the students to provide examples and describe their own personal experiences of "no good, very bad days." Kara, the classroom assistant in Lutero's classroom, created an overlay of PCSs for Lutero to use during the discussion, on which the symbols are accompanied by both English and Spanish translations (Figure 10.3). When Ms. Carter asks the class to tell her about their most recent bad days, Lutero raises his hand, waits for Ms. Carter to select him, and then points to the relevant PCSs on his display. Lutero can also use the display later in the day to create his personal story related to the theme.

Sandy. The discussion activity that occurs weekly during group time in Sandy's classroom encourages Sandy and her classmates to make accurate predictions and ask topic-appropriate questions. Every Tuesday, Mr. Humble sends a "Clue Bag" home with one of the students. The selected student puts one or more items of interest from home in the bag and writes three clues about the items or the activities related to them. On Wednesday during group sharing time, the selected student reads the clues and the other class members try to guess the item or activity. When it is Sandy's turn to take the Clue Bag home, her parents help her select three objects—a towel, a pair of goggles, and a bathing suit—that relate to her favorite activity, swimming. They also record three clues on her Step-by-Step Communicator 75[4] (AbleNet, Inc.; Figure 10.4) so that she can "ask" her classmates to guess the items in the bag. The next day during sharing time, Sandy activates her Step-by-Step to speak and provide clues for each of her items. For example, her clue for the towel is *"You'd need a big one of these to dry a whale."* She activates the Step-by-Step to provide each of her three clues and then opens up the Clue Bag to hold up her items when one of her classmates guesses that she is talking about swimming. Sandy is learning to take turns and use her Step-by-Step Communicator in appropriate contexts during these activities.

Following Instructions

All students must be able to follow instructions from teachers and other adults in school. There are two reasons why this may be difficult. First, some students may not be aware that the teacher is speaking to them when she addresses the group. Second, they may not understand complex or abstract instructions, especially in more advanced grades where language comprehension demands increase. In order to accommodate such students, teachers may make use of visual schedules or other augmented input supports.

FIGURE 10.3 *Lutero's "terrible, horrible, no good, very bad day" PCS display for teacher-led discussion.*

Mitchell. Mitchell often encounters teachers in his high school who provide instructions that are well beyond his language level and/or who deliver information at a rapid pace, despite their best attempts to do otherwise. In Mitchell's home economics class, for example, his teacher often instructs the class as a group regarding the recipe of the day and specific cooking techniques they will need to prepare it. When Mitchell does not understand an instruction, Rajeesh, the home economics classroom assistant, prompts him to ask

FIGURE 10.4   *Sandy's Step-by-Step Communicator 75 (AbleNet, Inc.).*

---

a clarifying question by addressing the teacher or a peer, using his speech and a PCS question display (Figure 10.5). Mitchell is learning to recognize the various Wh- questions symbols as well as to ask for more information by using the *I DON'T UNDERSTAND* and *TELL ME MORE* symbols. His frustration has decreased dramatically since the beginning of the school year, and his participation in home economics class has increased, in part because he is able to understand instructions and get help when he needs it.

Demonstrating Increased Control over Language Structures

Educators are always interested in encouraging the development of language skills to enhance the sophistication and variety of students' communication. Because the language development of students with significant disabilities is frequently below that of their peers,

FIGURE 10.5   *Mitchell's PCS question display.*

specific attention is required to encourage the development of language structures during classroom activities.

   Lutero. Lutero has just started to communicate about things that he does not want to have or does not want to do. His negative communications consist of loud vocalizations, facial expressions, and sometimes body movements such as kicking his legs or abruptly moving his arms. Ms. Carter is confident that he can learn to use the signs for YES and NO in these situations and sees an opportunity to work on this language skill during a partner math activity. Lutero's partner in this activity is working on addition and subtraction by creating "number sentences" with between 1 and 10 blocks (for example, 5 + 3 = 8). Lutero's and his partner work together to decide on the number of blocks that are needed to make each part of the sentence. His partner asks Lutero *Another block?* before adding each one, and Lutero signs YES or NO in response. Ms. Carter also plans to extend Lutero's effective use of yes and no to activity choices, class discussions, and literacy activities. Lutero's problem behaviors that were used to communicate disagreement begin to subside as he learns to use appropriate language to protest more appropriately.

Giving Oral Presentations

Oral presentations require the simultaneous use of many language skills and are often very challenging for students with significant disabilities. To deliver oral presentations effectively, students need to be able to sequence ideas, speak fluently with clarity and at an acceptable volume, and provide content that is engaging to an audience. Students gain experience with these skills by recounting stories, telling real or invented narratives, reciting poems, and delivering speeches or dramatic monologues.

   Lutero. Ms. Carter plans to prepare her students to recite a nursery rhyme during the next parent-teacher event. The children are asked to choose from a selection of nursery rhymes, and Lutero selects *Mary Had a Little Lamb*. Ms. Carter helps one of Lutero's peers to record the nursery rhyme into Lutero's VOCA, and she also selects PCSs to complement the recording (see Figure 10.6). She provides several opportunities for the students to rehearse their rhymes in the classroom before the "big night"; when it's Lutero's turn to practice, Kara prompts him to point to the symbols that correspond with the sequence of the rhyme so that the VOCA will speak it out loud. Lutero anticipates the symbol sequence and waits to hear the completion of each part of the rhyme before he proceeds to the next. When Lutero presents his rhyme independently at the parent-teacher night, he demonstrates both his ability to participate in an oral presentation and to make his parents very proud.

   Sandy. Mr. Humble, Sandy's teacher, asks the students to create and participate in a dramatic representation of a book that they have read. The five students in Sandy's group decide to create a play about *Harry Potter and the Sorcerer's Stone* (Rowling, 1997). Kara, the classroom assistant, helps them select roles that will enable participation from all members of the group. They decide that three of the students will play the roles of Harry, Hermoine, and Ron, who set out in search of the sorcerer's stone. A fourth member of the group will be the narrator, who helps to tell the story so that the audience can understand the sequence of events. Sandy will play the role of Dumbledore, the wise headmaster of Hogwart's School of Wizardry, whose job it is to warn Harry, Hermoine, and Ron of the

FIGURE 10.6   Mary Had a Little Lamb *PCS overlay for Lutero's VOCA.*

many dangers they will encounter during their quest. At intervals throughout the play, the narrator delivers the line, *The children kept thinking about what Dumbledore had said . . . ,* which is Sandy's cue to press her Step-by-Step Communicator to deliver one of her prerecorded lines (for example, *"Do not venture into the third floor corridor," "You will suffer a most painful death,"* and so forth). By carefully planning the parts assigned to each student, Kara and Mr. Humble ensure that Sandy and her classmates can all participate in this exciting event to gain experience with oral presentations.

Participating in Peer Interactions

Research has indicated that, for both students with developmental disabilities and their peers, many positive social benefits can accrue as a result of placement in inclusive classrooms (Baker, Wang, & Walberg, 1994–95; Peltier, 1997; Staub & Peck, 1995). One of the most important benefits of inclusion is the opportunity to participate and interact with classmates and other students. For example, in a longitudinal case study, Ryndak, Morrison, and Sommerstein (1999) described the impact of inclusion on a student who had been placed in a segregated program for many years previously. The student presented at a local conference on inclusion and, when a moderator asked her, *What was the difference between the special class and the regular class?*, she replied, *When I was in a special class, I used to put my head down on the desk. I used to look out the door and watch the kids go by, and now they're my friends* (p. 15). Such impressive social outcomes do not just "happen," however. They require careful planning and instructional supports.

Lutero. Ms. Carter is aware that pretend play provides many opportunities for peer interaction, so she spends time every week considering the types of interactive toys that can be used in the "drama corner" of her classroom. She also programmed Lutero's VOCA with numerous statements that he can use to tell peers that he is interested and involved in playing with them, especially in the kitchen area that he particularly enjoys. Some of the statements in his VOCA include partner-focused questions (for example, *"Does it taste good?"*) and nonobligatory turns (for example, *"Mmmm, I want more"*). Lutero is eager to get his play partner's attention and enjoys the responses he gets from using these types of preprogrammed utterances, which are important for enhancing communicative competence (Light & Binger, 1998).

Sandy. During math, the students in Sandy's class are learning the multiplication tables. Mr. Humble would like Sandy to participate in math as well, so he has set up small groups of students to practice multiplication facts. Sandy participates in her math group by using a switch to activate a Dial Scan (Figure 10.7; Don Johnston, Inc.). When Sandy hits a switch, the dial scans to one of the multiplication problems that are set up around the perimeter of the unit. When the dial stops, Sandy looks at a classmate to choose who will answer the problem, while a third student checks the answer and provides feedback on it. The routine continues until all of the students have had several turns with the math problems. Many important peer interaction skills are embedded within this activity for Sandy, including turn taking, looking at others when interacting, and waiting for a communication partner complete his or her turn.

Mitchell. In high school, one of Mitchell's greatest communication challenges is learning how to use language to make and maintain friendships. When Mitchell expressed an interest in becoming friends with one of the students in his woodworking class, he and his classmate were frequently at a loss as to how to get started with conversations and what to talk about. The speech-language pathologist supporting Mitchell suggested that he be provided with a conversation book to stimulate and support social talk with peers (Beukelman & Mirenda, 1998; Hunt, Alwell, & Goetz, 1988). Conversation books contain materials such as photographs, magazine pictures, and other media representing activities that are important to the individuals who use them. Mitchell's book has many pictures of his favorite trucks and motorcycles, as well as hockey cards and family photographs, which he can use to initiate and maintain conversations with his new friend. By using his book, Mitchell is able to more readily recall past events, discuss those events more effectively, and ask questions.

Summary: Facilitating Oral Language

From the information and examples presented in this section of the chapter, it should be clear that students with significant disabilities can not only participate in the oral language activities of general education classrooms, but can also do so in ways that are meaningful and appropriate for their learning needs. Preplanning, the use of various symbol and

FIGURE 10.7   *Dial Scan (Don Johnston, Inc.) with Sandy's multiplication overlay.*

computer technologies, and a dash of creativity are the main ingredients that enable students to be successful and to develop their oral language abilities. In the next section, we provide information about literacy development and instruction with examples for Lutero, Sandy, and Mitchell, with the same goals in mind: meaningful, appropriate participation in the activities of general education classrooms.

Literacy Instruction for Students with Significant Disabilities: Past, Present, and Future

For many years, theories and research regarding literacy development in typical populations guided literacy instructional practices for students with significant disabilities. The "readiness model" of literacy instruction impacted the nature of instruction for such students, who often had difficulty acquiring the numerous prerequisite skills deemed essential for literacy development (Conners, 1992; Erickson & Koppenhaver, 1995; Kliewer & Biklen, 2001). As a result, this approach to literacy instruction "only serv[ed] to highlight students' disabilities and emphasize differences in each student's performance from that of the mainstream population" (Ryndak et al., 1999, p. 5). The many students who proved themselves to be unable to master the "necessary" prerequisite skills were thus considered ineligible for further literacy instruction.

When the curricular emphasis in the 1970s and 1980s shifted toward teaching functional life skills, students with significant disabilities were again left behind with regard to "climbing the ladder" of literacy. Often, they were "steered to . . . ladders with fewer rungs, which lead to functional or life skills reading and writing, if [they were] allowed to engage the printed word at all" (Kliewer & Biklen, 2001, p. 2). In the era of functional skills instruction, students with disabilities were typically taught to recognize sight words (for example, "enter," "exit," men," "women," "danger," and so forth) that were considered essential in order for them to be independent in community settings. Although many students were able to learn at least some sight words quite readily, they often failed to generalize this ability to noninstructional settings (Browder & Xin, 1998). In the end, the functional curriculum model—like its predecessor, the readiness model—also served to prevent many students with disabilities from acquiring literacy skills, and thus reinforced the belief that they were unable to become readers and writers.

Most recently, the pendulum has swung again, this time toward practices supported by whole language and balanced literacy theories, the use of a wide range of computer technologies, and the belief that students with disabilities can, indeed, participate meaningfully in literacy learning experiences alongside their typical peers (Kliewer & Biklen, 2001; Koppenhaver, 2000; Mirenda & Erickson, 2000). Literacy is now viewed as an interactive process that encompasses the use of listening, speaking, reading, and writing related to everyday life (Teale & Sulzby, 1986). These four components of literacy are believed to ". . . interrelate and develop both simultaneously and interactively" (Ryndak et al., 1999, p. 5). By providing learners with opportunities to develop literacy skills within classrooms that stress multiple components of literacy development, teachers can also accommodate a wide variety of learning styles. Given that "[l]anguage and literacy are simultaneously learned and are mutually beneficial processes" (Koppenhaver et al., 1995, p. 265), a literacy learning environment that is rich in meaningful communication opportunities is also essential for students across the ability range.

Literacy Instruction in an Elementary School Four Blocks Classroom

Although some researchers and practitioners continue to disagree about whether skills-based or holistic approaches to literacy learning are best (Duffy & Hoffman, 1999; Pearson, 1997), there is growing support for a balanced program of literacy instruction that emphasizes both explicit instruction of literacy-related skills and whole language approaches, especially in the early years. Patricia Cunningham and Richard Allington described such a program, the Four Blocks Model, in their book *Classrooms That Work: They Can All Read and Write* (1999). The Four Blocks of instruction include 1) self-selected reading, 2) guided reading, 3) working with words, and 4) writing.

Self-Selected Reading

At the beginning of a self-selected reading block, the classroom teacher reads aloud to children for 10 to 15 minutes to provide an appropriate model of the reading process. Children are then dismissed for individual reading and the teacher provides monitoring and instruction, as needed. During this time, the teacher may pay close attention to the extent to which students use illustrations to assist in reading text, their ability to self-correct during reading, their reading fluency, the extent to which they attempt to figure out novel words, and other early reading behaviors. Self-selected reading provides opportunities for all students to work with books at an appropriate instructional level and to receive individualized instruction related to their specific learning needs.

Lutero. During the read-aloud portion of self-selected reading, Lutero is seated on the floor with his classmates in a bean bag chair that provides him with postural support. When Ms. Carter finishes reading and begins to direct the class to assigned tables for the individualized portion of self-selected reading, Kara helps him transfer back into his wheelchair. Because it is difficult for Lutero to manipulate the books on the shelf of the classroom library, one of his friends gives him a binder of photocopied book covers so that he can chose a book. Lutero flips through the pages and selects a book that interests him by pointing to the cover picture; his friend gets the book for him from the shelf. Then, Lutero and his friend go to their assigned table.

Ms. Carter and Kara spent a lot of time early in the school year adapting the books in the classroom library so that Lutero can use them in meaningful ways. All of the books have relevant, laminated PCS symbols affixed to each page using a glue stick (such as Scotch Restickable Adhesive Glue Stick) that converts each PCS into a removable post-it note. The PCSs enable Lutero to comment about the story by pointing to relevant symbols as he and his friend read a book together.

In addition, some of the books in the classroom library have repetitive lines; those books are identified by pictures of a BIGmack®[5] (AbleNet, Inc.; see Figure 10.8) that Kara placed on their front covers. Kara printed the repetitive line for each book on an index card and attached it to the inside cover of the book with a paper clip. When Lutero chooses a repetitive line book, his classmates are able to identify it easily and have learned to record the phrase written on the index card on the BIGmack®. Because repetitive books are read frequently in the classroom, most students have memorized the repetitive lines and are able to record the phrases independently; Kara is always nearby to help if they need assistance. They have also been taught to pause whenever the line appears in the book so that Lutero can read it out loud by activating the BIGmack® with his hand.

Many of the books in the classroom library have also been adapted for use on the computer and are identified with computer symbols on their covers. Kara adapted the books using Microsoft PowerPoint software by scanning the pages into the computer and recording herself reading them out loud. When Lutero chooses to read a computerized book, his peers ask him if he'd like to read it alone or with one of them. (Not surprisingly,

FIGURE 10.8   *BIGmack® (AbleNet, Inc.).*

he usually chooses the latter.) Using the SymbiKey Computer Interface (AbleNet, Inc.) to connect his Jelly Bean Switch (AbleNet, Inc.) to the computer, Lutero turns the book's pages on the computer screen, in the same manner that an able-bodied person uses the space bar on a keyboard. Each time Lutero presses the switch, he sees a new page and hears the text being read. Later, when he meets with Ms. Carter, Lutero is also able to demonstrate his emerging word knowledge using these same books. First, Lutero selects a computerized book, and he and Ms. Carter read it together through the computer. Then, Ms. Carter turns off the computer's sound and asks Lutero questions that probe his reading comprehension abilities. For example, she might ask Lutero to *Go to the page that says "The dog chased the ball."* Lutero then activates his switch to locate the correct page, using the text and/or illustrations.

Ms. Carter also uses other strategies to monitor Lutero's emerging reading skills. For example, she writes key words on index cards from one of the books he has read and attaches the cards to a whiteboard. Then, she asks Lutero to look at words as she pronounces them (for example, *Find the word "door"*) to check his ability to identify specific words. She may also write sentences and phrases on index cards, place them on a whiteboard, and ask him to look at a specific sentence (for example, *Find the sentence that says "The bear was not happy"*). Ms. Carter is careful to check both Lutero's word identification and reading comprehension skills because she knows that ability to read single words does not necessarily ensure comprehension when those words are combined to make a sentence. Her attention to increasing Lutero's comprehension skills are paying off, and she is pleased with the number of sentences he is able to read.

Guided Reading

During guided reading, the teacher explicitly teaches specific reading strategies to the class. These include strategies such as making predictions, relating background knowledge to what is read, rereading something that doesn't make sense, self-correcting, drawing conclusions and making inferences, and summarizing what has been read. Fluent readers use these and many other strategies to construct meaning from text and to make connections between print materials and everyday experiences. Guided reading instruction can be particularly beneficial for students with disabilities who may not have the same background experiences as their typical peers, or who may experience difficulty in relating novel information to their own experiences.

Lutero. Ms. Carter uses many strategies and activities in her guided reading lessons. For example, today she is focusing on character development in a story. After reading the story of the *Three Little Pigs*, she guides the whole class in a discussion about the wolf's actions, personality, physical characteristics, and feelings at different points in the story. To do so, she has prepared four charts, one for each trait, and during class she asks students to brainstorm words in each category that describe the wolf. Before the lesson, Kara made four communication boards with PCSs relevant for each trait for Lutero to use during the class discussion. For example, the physical characteristics board contains symbols such as *TALL, STINKY*, and *UGLY*, as well as distracters such as *SHORT, CLEAN*, AND *BEAUTIFUL* (see Figure 10.9). During the lesson, as Ms. Carter leads the class to discuss each trait, Kara places the corresponding communication board on Lutero's tray. When he raises his hand to offer a suggestion by pointing to a symbol, one of his classmates reads his contribution out loud to the class.

After the group lesson, Ms. Carter asks the class to write three characteristics for each trait on a graphic organizer. Because Lutero's fine motor impairments make writing difficult, he is provided with an overlay to use on an IntelliKeys keyboard[6] (IntelliTools, Inc.) attached to the classroom computer. The overlay contains the same vocabulary words as the communication boards he used during the class. Lutero uses the IntelliKeys keyboard with his vocabulary overlay in conjunction with Writing With Symbols 2000[7] (Mayer Johnson Co.), a graphic word processor. When Lutero makes a selection by pressing a location on his overlay, the word and its corresponding symbol appear on the computer screen. After Lutero has selected all the words for his graphic organizer, he prints the word/symbol list. Kara assists him by cutting out each word and symbol combination and asks him where to place each word/symbol on the graphic organizer (see Figure 10.10).

Working with Words

The working with words component of the Four Blocks Model is designed to address two specific goals: developing students' ability to "automatically recognize and spell high-frequency words" (Cunningham & Allington, 1999, p. 223) and developing students' ability to look for and recognize common patterns found in words. These two critical goals are addressed through a variety of activities. Typically, a word wall is used daily in the classroom to focus on high-frequency words. Each Monday, the teacher adds five new words to the wall. Because the word wall is arranged alphabetically, the children learn about alphabetizing through word wall activities. When adding words to the wall, the teacher engages students in activities, such as chanting the letters in each word out loud while clapping and writing the words at their desks. After new words have been added to the wall, students may also begin a making words activity, using letter cards. After each such lesson, the teacher may also give students an activity to complete at home that evening.

Physical Characteristics

furry **pelo de animal**	beautiful **bello**	ugly **feo**
stinky **oleroso**	spotty **manchoso**	fat **gordo**
thin **delgado**	clean **limpio**	dirty **sucio**
short **corto**	tall **alto**	

FIGURE 10.9 *Lutero's* **Three Little Pigs** *PCS display for describing the wolf.*

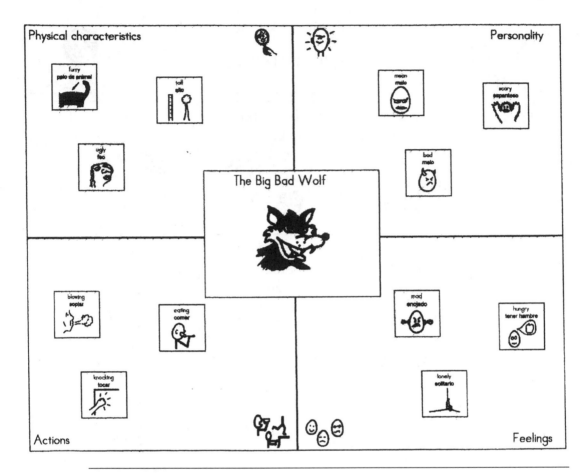

FIGURE 10.10 *Lutero's* **Three Little Pigs** *graphic organizer, created with Writing With Symbols 2000.*

Lutero. Working with words activities focus primarily on phonologic and phonemic awareness. Some might question the appropriateness of such instruction for Lutero, given that he is unable to speak. However, because Ms. Carter is aware of the importance of phonologic and phonemic awareness skills in early literacy learning, she is committed to including Lutero in these activities as much as possible. For example, during an activity in which students are asked to name words from the word wall that begin (or end) with a certain letter, Lutero is the designated judge who holds up signs that say "Yes" or "No," to provide feedback to his peers. Clearly, in order to make these judgments, Lutero is required to demonstrate his own ability to identify the target phonemes. Ms. Carter may also ask him if specific words start with a certain sound, adding occasional mistakes to assess Lutero's skills; again, he simply answers using his word cards or manual signs for yes and no.

When his classmates are manipulating letter cards to form words, Lutero works with an overlay on the computer to do the same thing. By touching various letters on the overlay, Lutero is able to compose words in the same manner as his peers. Using Writing With Symbols 2000 provides additional symbol output to support Lutero's developing sight word recognition. Lutero also enjoys sorting activities, in which students sort word cards into word families. Because he has difficulty manipulating word cards, Lutero again uses an IntelliKeys overlay on his computer, along with Writing With Symbols 2000, to sort words into various families (-at, -ot, and -it words) (see Figure 10.11).

Writing

In the Four Blocks Model, writing is taught in whole class, small group, and individual lessons. The goal of the writing block is to teach the myriad skills and strategies necessary

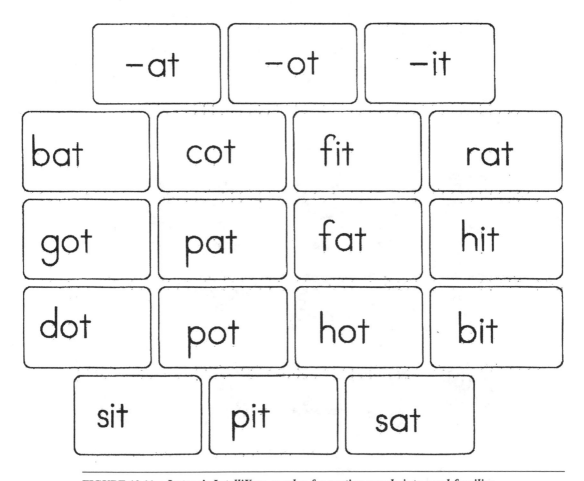

FIGURE 10.11 *Lutero's IntelliKeys overlay for sorting words into word families.*

for writing, including deciding what to write about, getting a reader's attention, writing something so that others will believe it and will want to read it, choosing appropriate words, clarifying, and editing. Specific writing conventions such as capitalization, punctuation, and so forth are also taught.

Lutero. Ms. Carter uses many strategies to develop the emerging writing abilities of her grade one students. For example, today, they are writing about a recent field trip to the pumpkin farm. Kara took digital photographs during the field trip and printed them after the class returned to school. Ms. Carter was able to predict in advance the words and sentences that would be needed for this writing activity and made a list of these for Kara so that she could produce an overlay for Lutero using Overlay Maker[8] (IntelliTools, Inc.) and Boardmaker[9] (Mayer Johnson Co.).

During a group lesson, Lutero uses his overlay to suggest words for writing about the photographs from the pumpkin patch; a classmate reads his suggestions out loud for the class. When the students are dismissed to begin writing about the field trip at their tables, Lutero and Kara move to the computer. Kara places the pumpkin patch overlay on Lutero's IntelliKeys adapted keyboard and attaches three photographs to the wall above the computer monitor. Lutero uses Writing With Symbols 2000 to write about each photograph and prints his work when he is finished (Figure 10.12). Kara then cuts each sentence into strips, holds up one sentence at a time so that Lutero can read it, and asks Lutero to look at the related photo. After Lutero identifies the correct picture, she helps him glue the sentence below it.

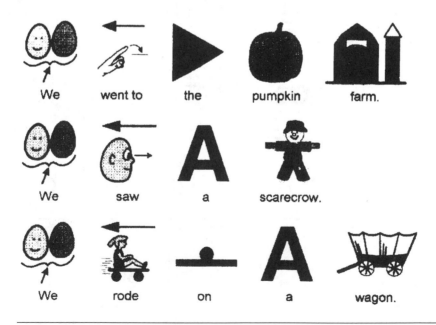

FIGURE 10.12 *Lutero's pumpkin patch sentences, created with Writing With Symbols 2000.*

Literacy Instruction in Upper Elementary and High School Classrooms

In the upper elementary grades, teachers become increasingly concerned about preparing students for high school. Students are expected to be able to read and write reasonably well, so literacy instruction usually focuses on the increased use of metacognitive strategies that are needed so that students can use text for a variety of purposes. Four of the overriding goals of literacy development in the upper grades include 1) learning to read for specific purposes; 2) developing increased knowledge of vocabulary, grammar, and literary conventions; 3) developing the ability to write for specific purposes; and 4) developing the ability to locate and use information from a variety of print resources. These goals are all designed to develop the skills that students will need as adults, regardless of their postsecondary plans. In the sections that follow, we examine each of the four literacy goals as they might apply to students with disabilities such as Sandy and Mitchell.

Reading for Specific Purposes

It is important for educators to recognize the purposes for which students will need to read in their adult lives to ensure that the necessary foundation skills are taught. This is no less the case for students with significant disabilities, including those who may not have acquired traditional literacy skills alongside their peers. As adults, these students will need reading skills to (a) understand upcoming events on a daily schedule or monthly calendar; (b) follow scripts that assist them to participate in specific activities; (c) follow directions for completing numerous daily living tasks, such as cooking and housekeeping; (d) complete various work-related activities within the community; and (e) communicate with family, friends, and community members at a distance. When considering classroom literacy instruction for students with significant disabilities, educators need to develop creative adaptations that support students to access classroom literacy instruction alongside their peers, while ensuring the development of skills that will facilitate maximum independent functioning.

Sandy. Sandy's educational team identified physical education (PE) class as one setting in which Sandy could use her reading skills for a specific purpose, namely, gathering necessary equipment before the class begins and then returning the equipment to the appropriate place when the class is finished. At the beginning of the year, Ms. Lee, the special education teacher who provides support to Sandy, took photographs of the various pieces of equipment used in PE class, mounted them on cards, and printed their names above each photo. Before each class, Sandy's PE teacher, Mr. Martino, selects photograph cards of the equipment that will be used that day and gives them to Sandy. Sandy and a classmate go to the equipment room, where her classmate hands the cards to Sandy one at a time so that she can read them, locate the related pieces of equipment, and place them in a cart. Then, Sandy and her peer wheel the cart into the gym and join the rest of the class. When the class is over, Sandy and her friend return the equipment to the equipment room; Sandy matches each item to words and symbols that are affixed to the shelves and cupboards.

Mitchell. Like Sandy, Mitchell's reading skills are still developing. However, he has acquired a small sight word vocabulary and needs support to use his emerging reading skills while continuing to learn new words. In woodworking class, Mitchell is provided with simple written instructions for his projects, using short phrases and illustrations. For example, one instruction might be "Get hammer," followed by a picture of a hammer. Mitchell has been taught to make a checkmark next to each completed step to help him remember where he is in the process. Mitchell also uses his reading skills during work experience in a video store four afternoons each week. At the video store, Mitchell uses his reading skills to return videotapes to their correct locations on the shelves. In order to accomplish this, Rajeesh placed an alphabet tape on the video cart to support Mitchell to remember the order of the letters of the alphabet. Initially, Rajeesh also needed to provide prompts to teach Mitchell to look at the first word on each videotape, locate the correct shelf section alphabetically, and then locate the matching video box to put the tape away. However, after only a few months, Rajeesh is able to remain at the front counter while Mitchell returns a full cart of videotapes to their proper places on the shelves.

Developing Vocabulary, Grammar, and Literary Conventions

As students enter the upper elementary grades, increased focus is placed on their ability to use and understand (a) increasingly sophisticated vocabulary words, (b) grammatically correct language for speaking and writing, (c) conventional spelling and punctuation, and (d) various literary conventions such as metaphors, paraphrasing, and alliteration. At the high school level, students are expected to further develop their understanding of literary conventions in relation to poetry, prose, and other forms of writing. These goals encompass both oral language and literacy development and are likely to be addressed across numerous curricular domains. In order for students with significant disabilities to be included in general education classroom activities that focus on developing such knowledge and skills, educators must be resourceful. Many language-literacy activities can provide opportunities for them to be engaged in class discussions, brainstorming sessions, and other social activities in meaningful ways.

Sandy. During writing class, Mr. Humble focuses on the use of adjectives in descriptive sentences. Because he knew that Sandy does not understand what an adjective is, he made a list of adjectives that might be included in the discussion. Ben then produced an IntelliKeys overlay with symbols for common adjectives, including *SILLY, LOUD, FUNNY,* and *HOT,* and related nouns. He shape-coded the symbols so that Sandy would be able to see which ones go together easily. In class, when it is her turn to contribute to the adjective brainstorming session, Sandy points to the symbols to make her contributions. Following this, students are asked to write ten descriptive sentences using the adjectives from the list. Sandy uses her IntelliKeys overlay to do the same activity, albeit at her own level. Instead of writing ten long sentences, Sandy writes four two-word phrases using Writing With Symbols 2000 (Figure 10.13).

Mitchell. In Mitchell's high school English class, the students have been reading *Romeo and Juliet.* Mitchell read an adapted version and watched a Hollywood movie based on the play. Now, the students are all writing essays about their perspectives concerning the

FIGURE 10.13   *Sandy's IntelliKeys shape-coded overlay for writing two-word adjective phrases.*

problems and solutions encountered in the play. Mitchell does a related activity to demonstrate his understanding of the story, using a blank story map on which he draws pictures depicting the characters, setting, plot, problems, and solutions. Mitchell labels his drawings with single words; Rajeesh provides written models of the words Mitchell is unable to spell on his own for Mitchell to copy. After he has completed his story map (Figure 10.14), Mitchell uses it to help him talk about the play with his English teacher and classmates.

Writing for Specific Purposes

As students mature, they are expected to use their writing skills for a variety of purposes: to inform, communicate, respond, and persuade. As adults, they will need to write for these purposes as well as to organize their daily lives, write checks, fill out forms, write resumes

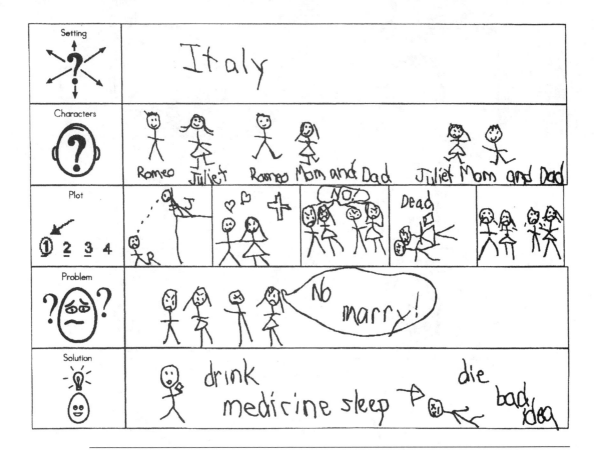

FIGURE 10.14 *Mitchell's* **Romeo and Juliet** *story map.*

and letters, and so forth. For students with significant disabilities, it is important that writing instruction be aimed at those skills that will result in increased independence in adulthood. Such skills include printing or writing legibly, using electronic media to write if fine motor skills are problematic, spelling words correctly or using spell checkers or word prediction programs, using basic conventions of writing (for example, putting spaces between words), and using appropriate words in the correct order to convey messages clearly. With these skills, students with disabilities will be better prepared to use their writing skills in community settings for social, work, and personal reasons.

Sandy. Mr. Humble has been extending the class's work related to adjectives from writing stories to writing poems. This week, the students are writing descriptive poems about the seasons for the school newsletter. Sandy was presented with a selection of four photographs depicting the four seasons of the year, and she chose "summer" as the topic for her poem. Ben then created an IntelliKeys overlay for Sandy to use to write her poem. She merely touches a symbol she wants on the overlay, and it appears on the computer screen in written form (Figure 10.15). Symbols that are both related and unrelated to the topic of summer were placed on the overlay so that Sandy has to consider each word carefully before selecting it. When she is finished writing her poem, she prints it out and submits it to the newsletter, along with the other class poems. Because Sandy is not able to read independently, she used Writing With Symbols 2000 when writing her poem, providing her with symbolized text to support her to read her own work.

Locating and Using Information from Print Resources

The ability to locate information is crucial for independence. Without this ability, one is continually dependent on others for information. As students develop their literacy skills, they are also expected to develop and improve their ability to locate information using a variety of media, including books, magazines, newspapers, and the Internet. In addition,

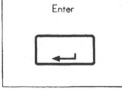

FIGURE 10.15 *Sandy's IntelliKeys overlay for writing a poem, "Summer Is . . . . "*

students are also expected to learn to use tables of content, indexes, and keyword searches to expedite the process of obtaining information. Finally, students need to be able to interpret and use information after they have located it. Most classroom teachers regularly assign individual and group research projects that provide students with opportunities to learn and practice such skills. Many of the activities associated with such projects are directly related to literacy goals for students with significant disabilities, including the ability to locate information from a variety of resources and communicate this information to others. A number of social goals that are by-products of many literacy-related activities can often be targeted as well.

Mitchell. The students in Mitchell's science class have been divided into small groups to research and write reports about endangered animals. The teacher, Mr. Harris, asks the groups to begin their research project by examining a number of resource books he has collected, selecting an endangered species, and gathering information about it. Mitchell and the other two students in his group look at several books with pictures of different animals and, after much discussion, narrow their options down to three choices. His classmates give Mitchell the final choice, and he readily points to the picture of a whale.

Next, the group discusses what they will do and who will be responsible for each task. Mitchell and a classmate volunteer to do Internet research on whale anatomy, and the other decides to gather information from the library about what whales eat and their place in the food chain. Together, they decide to make a poster of a whale and label it with the names of key body parts and sources of nutrition. Mitchell and his friend use the Internet to learn about whale anatomy on various *whale.com* sites. After they have gathered the information they need, they make a large poster of a whale and use Boardmaker to create a grid with PCSs representing the various body parts and food items. After they print the PCS grid, Mitchell cuts out the symbols individually and works with his peers to glue them onto the poster to label the whale's body parts and depict the whale's food sources. They also write statements about the purposes of the various body parts and food items. On presentation day, Mitchell points to each body part and food symbol and helps his classmates read the statements they have written (Figure 10.16).

Summary: Facilitating Literacy Instruction

This section of the chapter has highlighted only a few of the ways in which students with significant disabilities can be included in regular literacy instructional activities, even when their literacy abilities fall below those of their peers. When teachers view literacy goals as attainable, students like Lutero, Sandy, and Mitchell can all have opportunities to participate in meaningful literacy activities that incorporate peer interactions as much as possible.

Overall, it should be clear that general education classrooms offer abundant opportunities for students with significant disabilities to develop and use both oral language and literacy skills in meaningful ways. When they receive appropriate supports in these two areas, several key goals are likely to be accomplished simultaneously: (a) developing their ability to communicate, read, and write effectively; (b) providing them with opportunities to interact with typical peers in the context of classroom activities; and (c) perhaps most

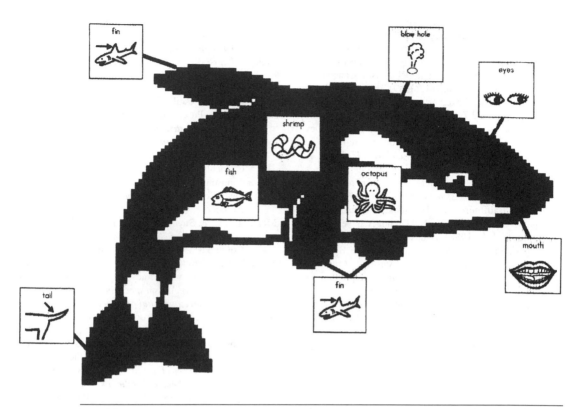

FIGURE 10.16 *Whale poster made by Mitchell and his science workgroup, depicting whale anatomy and food sources.*

important of all, enhancing self-esteem as they come to see themselves as students who are able to learn and participate in classroom and community settings.

References

Baker, E. T., Wang, M. C., & Walberg, H. J. (1994–1995). The effects of inclusion on learning. *Educational Leadership, 52,* 33–35.

Beukelman, D., & Mirenda, P. (1998). *Augmentative and alternative communication: Management of severe communication disorders in children and adults.* Baltimore: Paul H. Brookes Publishing Co.

Browder, D. M., & Xin, Y. P. (1998). A meta-analysis and review of sight word research and its implications for teaching functional reading to individuals with moderate and severe disabilities. *Journal of Special Education, 32,* 130–154.

Calculator, S. (1988). Promoting the acquisition and generalization of conversation skills by individuals with severe disabilities. *Augmentative and Alternative Communication, 4,* 94–103.

Conners, F. (1992). Reading instruction for students with moderate mental retardation: Review and analysis of research. *American Journal on Mental Retardation, 96,* 577–597.

Courtland, M. C., & Gambell, T. J. (1994). *Curriculum planning in the language arts K-12: A holistic perspective.* North York, ON: Captus Press.

Cunningham, P. M., & Allington, R. L. (1999). *Classrooms*

that work: They can all *read and write*. New York: Addison Wesley Longman.

Dias, P., Beer, A., Ledwell-Brown, J., Pare, A., & Pittenger, C. (1992). *Writing for ourselves/writing for others*. Scarborough, ON: Nelson Canada.

Duffy, G. G., & Hoffman, J. V. (1999). In pursuit of an illusion: The flawed search for a perfect method. *The Reading Teacher, 53*, 10–16.

Erickson, K. A., & Koppenhaver, D. A. (1995). Developing a literacy program for children with severe disabilities. *The Reading Teacher, 48*, 676–684.

Falvey, M. A. (1995). *Inclusive and heterogeneous schooling: Assessment, curriculum, and instruction*. Baltimore: Paul H. Brookes Publishing Co.

Falvey, M. A., Bishop, K. B., Grenot-Scheyer, M., & Coots, J. J. (1988). Issues and trends in mental retardation. In S. N. Calculator & J. L. Bedrosian (Eds.), *Communication assessment and intervention for adults with mental retardation* (pp. 45–65). Boston: College-Hill Press.

Halle, J. W. (1984). Arranging the natural environment to occasion language: Giving severely language delayed children reasons to communicate. *Seminars in Speech and Language*, 5, 185–197.

Halliday, M. A. K. (1975). *Learning how to mean*. London: Edward Arnold.

Haring, T. G., Neetz, J. A., Lovinger, L., Peck, C., & Semmell, M. I. (1987). Effects of four methods of incidental teaching procedures to create opportunities for communication. *Journal of the Association for Persons with Severe Handicaps, 72*, 218–226.

Hunt, P., Alwell, M., & Goetz, L. (1988). Acquisition of conversation skills and the reduction of inappropriate social interaction behaviors. *Journal of The Association for Persons with Severe Handicaps*, 13, 20–27.

Kliewer, C., & Biklen, D. (2001). "School's not really a place for reading": A research synthesis of the literacy lives of students with severe disabilities. *Journal of The Association for Persons with Severe Handicaps, 26*, 1–12.

Koppenhaver, D.A. (2000). Literacy in AAC: What should be written on the envelope we push? *Augmentative and Alternative Communication, 16*, 270–279.

Koppenhaver, D. A., Pierce, P. L., Steelman, J. D., & Yoder, D. E. (1995). Contexts of early literacy intervention for children with developmental disabilities. In M. Fey, J. Windsor, & S. Warren (Eds.), *Language intervention: Preschool through the elementary years* (pp. 241–276). Baltimore: Paul H. Brookes Publishing Co.

Light, J. (1997). "Let's go star fishing": Reflections on the contexts of language learning for children who use aided AAC. *Augmentative and Alternative Communication, 13*, 158–171.

Light, J. C., & Binger, C. (1998). *Building communicative competence with individuals who use augmentative and alternative communication*. Baltimore: Paul H. Brookes Publishing Co.

Marzano, R. J., Pickering, D. J., & Pollock, J. E. (2001). *Classroom instruction that works: Research based instruction for increasing student achievement*. Alexandria, VA: Association for Supervision and Curriculum Development.

Mayer-Johnson Co. (1994). *The Picture Communication Symbols combination book*. Solana Beach, CA: Author.

McLean, J. E., & Snyder-McLean, L. K. (1978). *A transactional approach to early language training*. Columbus, OH: Charles E. Merrill.

Mirenda, P., & Erickson, K. (2000). Augmentative communication and literacy. In A. Wetherby & B. Prizant (Eds.), *Autism spectrum disorders: A transactional developmental perspective* (pp. 333–367). Baltimore: Paul H. Brookes Publishing Co.

Mirenda, P., Iacono, T., & Williams, R. (1990). Communication options for persons with severe and profound disabilities: State of the art and future directions. *Journal of The Association for Persons with Severe Handicaps, 15*, 3–21.

Ostrosky, M. M., & Kaiser, A. P. (1991). Preschool classroom environments that promote communication. *Teaching Exceptional Children, 31*, 6–10.

Pearson, D. P. (1997). The politics of reading research and practice. *The Council Chronicle, 7*, 8, 24.

Peltier, G. L. (1997). The effect of inclusion on non-disabled children: A review of the research. *Contemporary Education, 68*, 234–238.

Quill, K. (2000). *Do-watch-listen-say: Social and communication intervention for children with autism*. Baltimore: Paul H. Brookes Publishing Co.

Rowland, C., & Schweigert, P. (1989). Tangible symbols: Symbolic communication for individuals with multisensory impairments. *Augmentative and Alternative Communication, 6*, 226–234.

Rowland, C., & Schweigert, P. (1996). *Tangible symbol systems* [Videorecording]. San Antonio, TX: Communication Skill Builders.

Rowling, J. K. (1997). *Harry Potter and the sorcerer's stone*. London, GB: Bloomsbury Publishing.

Ryndak, D. L., Morrison, A. P., & Sommerstein, L. (1999). Literacy prior to and after inclusion in general education settings: A case study. *Journal of The Association for Persons with Severe Handicaps, 24*, 5–22.

Staab, C. (1992). *Oral language for today's classrooms*. Markham, ON: Pippin.

Staub, D., & Peck, C. (1995). What are the outcomes for non-disabled students? *Educational Leadership, 52,* 36–41.

Teale, W. H., & Sulzby, E. (1986). *Emergent literacy: Writing and reading.* Norwood, NJ: Ablex Publishing.

Viorst, J. (1972). *Alexander and the terrible, horrible, no good, very bad day.* New York: Simon and Schuster.

von Tetzchner, S., & Hygum Jensen, M. (Eds.). (1996). *Augmentative and alternative communication:* *European perspectives.* London: Whurr Publishers.

Ward, A. (1997). *Classroom conversations: Talking and learning in elementary schools.* Toronto: ITP Nelson Canada.

Wood, L. A., Lasker, J., Siegel-Causey, E., Beukelman, D. R., & Ball, L. (1998). Input framework for augmentative and alternative communication. *Augmentative and Alternative Communication, 14,* 261–267.

Technology Resources

AbleNet, Inc. *www.ablenetinc.com/support/index.html.* Step-by-Step Communicator, BIGmack®, Symbi-Key Computer Interface, Jelly Bean Switch.

Don Johnston, Inc. *www.donjohnston.com/.* Dial Scan.

IntelliTools, Inc. *www.intellitools.com/navigation.html.* IntelliKeys, Overlay Maker.

Mayer Johnson Co. *www.mayer-johnson.com/.* Board-maker, Writing With Symbols 2000.

Endnotes

1. Authorship for the first two authors is equal; the order was determined by a coin toss.

2. Use of PCS symbols used with permission of Mayer-Johnson, Inc., The Picture Communication symbols© 1981–2002.

3. In this chapter, we adopted the conventions used by the *Augmentative and Alternative Communication* journal for transcribing interaction modalities of augmented communicators and natural speakers. These conventions were originally described by Stephen von Tetzchner and Mogens Hygum Jensen in their 1996 book, *Augmentative and Alternative Communication: European Perspectives.*

4. The Step-by-Step Communicator 75 is a digitized speech device that can accommodate any sequence of messages up to 75 seconds in total.

5. The BIGmack is a simple, digitized speech device that can record a single spoken message up to 20 seconds long.

6. IntelliKeys is a programmable alternative keyboard that plugs into any Macintosh or Windows computer. The configuration of the keyboard can be changed to accommodate specific lessons or learning needs by sliding in different paper overlays.

7. Writing With Symbols 2000 is a word-processing program that inserts PCS symbols as words are typed.

8. Overlay Maker is a software program that is used to create custom overlays for use with IntelliKeys.

9. Boardmaker is a drawing program and library of bitmapped clip art that includes PCSs. It can be used to make communication displays and VOCA overlays on a Macintosh or Windows computer.

Facilitating Social Relationships in General Education Settings

Lisa S. Cushing and Craig H. Kennedy

Objectives

After completing this chapter, the reader will be able to:

1. Discuss how social relationships can be conceptualized.
2. Understand how social relationships evolve over time.
3. Appreciate the balance between independence and interdependence.
4. Describe the appropriate roles for adults in peer-to-peer relationships.
5. Explain how peer support strategies can be used to facilitate membership.

Key Terms

Acquaintances	Peer support strategies	Social support
Friends	Social networks	
General education	Social relationships	

During the last ten years, an evolution in educators' thinking about curricular issues for students with severe disabilities has occurred (Kennedy & Horn, in press). This has resulted in a number of questions being raised regarding *what* is taught to students and *where* that curriculum content is delivered. Increasingly, researchers, practitioners, family members, and administrators are seeing the benefit of educating students with and without disabilities together. This inclusive approach to the education of students with severe disabilities is occasioning rapid progress in the development of strategies to integrate students effectively into the center of the general education system. Part of this progress is occurring in an area that was not previously considered a standard part of the curriculum, namely, how to facilitate the development of a student's *social relationships* among his or her peers. Issues emerging from efforts at improving a student's social relationships are bringing about a rethinking among professionals about what is taught in general education settings and how it is taught.

In this chapter, we will discuss how to understand and facilitate a student's social relationships in general education settings in an effort to help maximize beneficial inclusive outcomes for students with and without disabilities. Because social relationships emerge from social interactions that people have, our discussion will be closely linked to the development of social interactions. In particular, we emphasize the development of peer-to-peer interactions within the context of general education settings as a means of creating and nurturing social relationships.

Social Relationships

An important first step in facilitating social relationships is defining what is meant by the terms. In this section, we will discuss (a) what the term "social relationships" can mean and (b) how social relationships, such as friendships, develop.

Defining Social Relationships

Social relationships have two closely linked dimensions: contact patterns and subjective satisfaction. Social relationships, at their most elemental level, are based on contact patterns among people. For example, students might see each other daily in English class, or that contact may be more intermittent, such as students occasionally playing on the same team in a physical education (PE) class. Therefore, a student's social life can be viewed as the pattern of interactions he or she has with others.

Several aspects of social contact patterns are important when we discuss social relationships (Kennedy, 2001a; Newton & Horner, 1993; Staub, Peck, Gallucci, & Schwartz, 2000). One way of conceptualizing social contact patterns is shown in Figure 11.1. To start, social relationships are based on *social interactions*. A social interaction can be described as how often two students interact, how long they interact, when they interact, and so on.

When describing social relationships, another important dimension is what occurs between students when they interact. In Figure 11.1 this is referred to as *social support*. Homans (1953) has observed that, when people choose to interact over and over again, they must gain something from those interactions. These social supports include helping others (for example, loaning someone a book), exchanging information (for example, learning about a school assembly), and emotional support (for example, comforting someone when they hurt themselves).

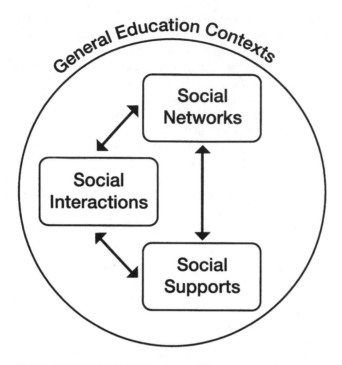

FIGURE 11.1   *A schematic approach for understanding social relationships.*

Along with social interactions and social support, we also include something called *social networks* in the definition of social relationships. A social network is the collective pattern of interaction among people. For example, three students might individually interact with each other on a daily basis, but rarely meet as a group. Although the students rarely meet as a group, they are still highly interconnected with each other.

Social interactions, social supports, and social networks occur within a *context*. Whenever we try to understand a person's social interactions, it is important to pay attention to where people interact and what they do. When we talk about social relationships in the remainder of this chapter, we will be describing them in terms of social interactions, social supports, social networks, and contexts.

There is, of course, more to social relationships than describing patterns of social interaction. The second dimension of social relationships is students' *subjective satisfaction* with their social life. Research on this topic has shown that people vary in regard to what constitutes a desirable social life. Some individuals prefer to interact with a small number of people, but interact frequently with them; others prefer to interact with a large number of people, but less frequently. With this observation noted, no ideal number of people or number of interactions define a good social life. Instead, what a particular student perceives as a satisfactory social life needs to be individually identified and evaluated.

Students' personal preferences regarding their social relationships influence how the students interpret specific relationships. One way of classifying types of social relationships is to place them on a continuum from *acquaintances* to *friends*. This distinction is important because greater importance is given to people who are friends. How students label their social relationships is a matter of personal preference. It should also be noted, however, that a person's social life is not static, but changes through time (Staub et al., 2000).

Considering these components as a whole, we begin to have a way of describing a student's social life. For a specific student, we can identify the other people with whom the individual interacts, how frequently they interact, if others are involved, where they interact, what they are doing, the types of social supports that occur, and who is perceived as a friend. Such a range of descriptors provides educators with a picture of what a student's social life is like and suggests how future supports may be arranged to facilitate and/or maintain social relationships.

How Social Relationships Develop

No one can say with certainty precisely why social relationships develop and maintain. However, a number of variables do exist that may increase the likelihood for social relationships to flourish. This basic understanding stems from researchers attempting to understand the friendship development process (for example, Kennedy, 2001a). Three basic stages to friendship development and maintenance have been identified: (a) having initial social encounters, (b) facilitating relationships through mutually preferred contexts, and (c) establishing durable relationships.

A necessary factor for social relationships to develop is that peers must have access to each other. This initial stage is often brief, just one to three interactions, and results in either the individuals spending more time with each other or a cessation of interactions. Current estimates for students with severe disabilities is that approximately 55 percent of the peers who are initially met go on to the second stage of social relationships, compared to 35 percent of interactions between two peers without disabilities (Kennedy, 2001a). One reason for such a high percentage is that many of the initial interactions are arranged through a facilitator (for example, a teacher or peer). Facilitators are likely to select peers that they believe will be successful social interaction partners. There are many ways for students and peers to meet at school. To increase the likelihood that social interactions will move beyond this initial phase, active communication and collaboration must exist between special education staff, general education personnel, families, and peers.

The second phase of social relationship development deals with establishing mutually preferred interaction contexts. After students have met, they try out different activities with each other, sometimes in new settings. Expanding on this array of opportunities provides students with chances to identify new contexts that are interesting, as well as to identify those nonpreferred contexts. This phase helps determine the future of the relationship. Such relationships either dissolve over time or move on to the third phase and become durable social relationships. Indeed, the majority of social relationships do not extend beyond the second phase, which is consistent regardless of the presence of a disability.

If relationships do extend to the third part of the social relationship process, they are often referred to as friendships. In this phase of relationship development, a stable pattern of contact emerges. Generally, students and peers establish a routine in which they have regularly scheduled opportunities to interact. For example, they may work together in English class three days a week, or they may meet every day in the same place to have lunch together. The hallmark of relationships that evolve into this status are that there is a history of successful interaction, there are rules for interacting that are mutually agreed upon, and there are mutually agreed upon opportunities to interact that occur.

Strategies to Support Social Relationships

Because a strong focus on social interactions as a core component of a student's curriculum and Individualized Education Program (IEP) is relatively new, strategies that have a research basis to support their use are only beginning to be developed. Two overlapping issues that we will discuss are *balancing independence and interdependence* and *how contexts determine appropriate social behaviors*. These two areas provide a framework for specific strategies to be implemented to facilitate social relationship development. In this section of the chapter we discuss these broader issues and then outline specific strategies that educators can use to facilitate social relationships in general education settings. These specific strategies include (a) adapting the general education curriculum, (b) using peer support strategies, (c) acquiring new skills, and (d) ensuring access to friends.

Balancing Independence and Interdependence

The growth of a relationship may be hindered due to a person's social competence. Social competence refers to a person's ability to interact effectively and to maintain social interactions. An aspect of social competence is the degree to which a person can independently engage in a set of behaviors referred to as social skills. The ability to initiate social interactions independently, maintain conversational topics, take turns, and engage in behaviors that facilitate continued interaction lead to the likelihood of a student having more social interactions. Up to very recently, special educators spent much of their time teaching individuals with severe disabilities specific social skills in an effort to prepare them for social relationships. Although skill development is important, concerns have also been raised about an overemphasis on prerequisite skills. As researchers begin to understand the nature of social interactions, they have realized that a balance should exist between independence and interdependence. Although it is important to be able to engage independently in certain behaviors, most social interactions are based to some degree on cooperation. For example, to complete a classroom assignment in science, a group project may be required necessitating different individuals working together to complete the task successfully. The nature of social relationships involves giving and receiving social supports, which inherently requires some level of interdependence among people interacting with each other.

An overemphasis on independence by educators may have established "readiness traps" (Kennedy, 2001b). If students must achieve a certain level of prerequisite skills in order to interact with students their age, students may never attain the prerequisites and thus may never be allowed access to same-aged peers. One way to combat this readiness trap is through partial participation (Ferguson & Baumgart, 1990). Partial participation acknowledges that a student with a severe disability may need a certain amount of support, but the level of support acts as a scaffold to enable the student to accomplish the task. For example, a young man with cerebral palsy may not be able to light a Bunsen burner or mix the compounds necessary to complete a chemistry experiment. However, he may be able to make the necessary calculations for mixing the chemicals and record the results of the experiment on his augmentative communication system. If participation in this class were based on independently performing each experiment, he would be deemed not ready and excluded from participating. If participation were based on interdependence, where he worked with another peer who assisted in lighting the burner and mixing the chemicals, the goal of successfully completing the chemistry experiment would be achieved.

Educators should continually strive to find a balance between developing a student's independence and facilitating interdependence. Neither set of goals is preferable to the other. Instead they are closely interrelated and are both necessary for successful social relationship development in general education settings. Educational teams should discuss what the appropriate mixture of independence and interdependence is for a particular student and provide the appropriate supports to facilitate social relationship development.

Contexts for Social Interactions

How we interact depends on where we are and with whom we are with (Schnorr, 1990). For example, two students in the hallway of a school appropriately greet each other saying "Hey, dude," but this greeting would not be appropriate if directed to a classroom teacher or principal. Another example is that a student acts differently in English class than in music class. This is due, in part, to the activities available for people to interact with, along with social expectations about what are, and what are not, appropriate behaviors for a particular classroom. Students who are deemed socially competent are able to discriminate what behaviors are appropriate for different contexts and activities. For students who have not yet learned these discriminations, it is especially important that teachers provide access to specific contexts and opportunities for practice. In school settings, there are three broad contexts within which social interactions occur: (a) classroom-based activities; (b) recess, breaks, and meal times; and (c) passing interactions.

The majority of a student's day is spent in *classroom-based activities*. Hence, these contexts become important settings for encouraging social interactions (Hunt, Alwell, Farron-Davis, & Goetz, 1996). However, what social interactions are permissible in these contexts depend on a range of variables, including the type of class activity and the grade level of the classroom. Students may have different types of social interactions when they participate in different classroom structures. For example, general education classrooms that emphasize cooperative learning strategies allow different types of peer-to-peer social interactions than classrooms that focus on individual learning activities. These differing types of arrangements significantly impact whom a student can interact with and what behaviors are appropriate to engage in.

In addition, classrooms for younger students encourage and embed appropriate social interactions within activities. Teaching children how to interact with others and play and share toys, as well as when to be quiet are typically taught as children engage in activities. By third grade, children are expected to have learned the basic rules of classroom conduct. Therefore, less time is spent promoting successful interactions, and more emphasis is placed on academics. This emphasis on academics continues to increase through middle school and high school.

The types of interactions during *recess, breaks, and mealtimes* are very different than the types of interactions observed during class time. During recess or breaks, peers engage in a range of recreational activities not appropriate in classroom settings. Often recess-based interactions are focused on a particular activity and how a student can participate in the activity. For example, if peers are playing tether ball and including a student with disabilities in the game, the interactions that individuals have will be related to how to complete the particular game.

Mealtimes are important times for students with and without disabilities. Such contexts provide natural opportunities for students to interact as they obtain, eat, and dispose of their meals. However, it is clear that many of the behaviors that are engaged in during mealtimes are different from those emitted during recess or breaks. The emphasis for adults in these contexts should be to create interaction patterns between students with severe disabilities and their peers that are consistent with the context of the social interaction.

The last type of context involves brief encounters when *transitioning* from one class to another, arriving at school, or leaving for home. The brevity of these encounters provides students with many opportunities to interact with many individuals. A student may have access to and say "Hi" to a dozen peers when going from social studies to science class. In elementary school, students may see other peers when going to lunch or returning to class from recess. In middle school and high school, students usually have five to ten minutes to get from one class to another. This provides students many opportunities to interact briefly by exchanging social greetings or by arranging to meet another peer at lunch or after school.

Peer Support Strategies

Social interactions must be encouraged and taught. Educators need to assume the role of setting up opportunities for students with severe disabilities to interact with their peers. The use of peer support strategies to facilitate classroom participation may assist in increasing the frequency and quality of social interactions. Peer support strategies involve peers without disabilities who provide direct support to a student with disabilities in a general education setting. The peer(s) serve to adapt curriculum, provide systematic instruction, and promote social participation of students with severe disabilities under the supervision of adults (Kennedy, 2001a). There are four broad steps in designing and implementing a peer support program: (a) recruiting peers, (b) identifying IEP goals, (c) facilitating access to the general education curriculum, and (d) monitoring and evaluating the peer support program.

The first step involves the recruitment of peers to act as peer supports. This step can be carried out in a number of ways (Janney & Snell, 1996; Mu, Siegel, & Allinder, in press). The educator may go to the classroom and observe those students who seem interested in working with the student with disabilities. Interest may include peers approaching the student with a disability, asking the educator questions related to the student, engaging in social support behaviors such as opening the door for the student, saying "Hello," or moving chairs to facilitate a wheelchair. In addition to the teacher observing the behavior of the peers in the presence of the student with disabilities, teachers may also ask for volunteers, provide extra credit, and/or rotate opportunities for peers to work with the student with a disability.

After the peer(s) have been selected, the teacher must identify IEP goals that the student with severe disabilities will be working on within each class. The teacher might conduct an ecological assessment of the classroom environment and assess the IEP goals that can be worked on for that particular environment. For example, in an eighth grade English class, the special educator might observe the following classroom routine:

- Students enter the classroom and sit at their desks;
- students place their homework on their desk for the teacher to collect;
- they then get out their assignment books and work on the day's assignment;
- following this, they get out their English journals and write for five minutes;
- and then the teacher provides a final five-minute question-answer session.

Using this information, the special educator could then select several IEP goals she or he thought the student with severe disabilities could work on in the English class.

The goals selected for the student might include improving communication, working on sight-word reading, using comprehension skills, and improving handwriting skills. With these goals in mind, a routine could be developed for this student that might include the following:

- Entering the classroom;
- sitting at his or her seat with peer supports;
- getting out homework;
- going to the front of the class and collecting other students' homework;
- briefly greeting each peer when homework is collected;
- returning to his or her seat;
- and, with a peer support, copying and reading words relating to the classroom assignment.

Such a routine would allow the student to participate in the class, work on multiple IEP goals, and interact frequently with peers.

The third step in the peer-support process is providing the student with severe disabilities access to the general education curriculum (see Chapter 3). This may require adaptations or modifications to the general education curriculum. Thus the peer support must be taught how to use the adaptations. For example, a peer might be taught that during English journal writing time, the peer needs to develop five words for the student with disabilities to work on. By having the peer work with the student under the supervision of a paraeducator or special education teacher, both peer and student are engaged in classwork relating to the general education curriculum.

The last step in the process is to maintain a consistent process to evaluate and monitor the success of the peer support. The peer serving as a support may have questions around the types of adaptations to make and suggestions on how to modify work or may need extra support for some other reason. This requires scheduled contact with an adult who is designated to supervise them. The ultimate goal is to provide both students with the supports necessary for them to both succeed. Monitoring may involve a check-in, as students are entering the classroom, and then checking on the student with severe disabilities and the peer support every 10 to 15 minutes.

New Skills to Facilitate Social Interactions

A great deal of educational effort focuses on how to compensate for a student's disabilities by arranging additional supports for the individual. This does not mean, however, that educators do not need to teach specific social skills (Goldstein, Kaczmarek, & English, 2001). Providing a student with disabilities the access to settings in which interactions occur allows ample opportunities to acquire new skills. There are many strategies for teaching new skills when facilitating social interactions. One such technique involves teaching students the essential skills needed to participate in an interaction, which could include interdependence skills that are required to engage in a given activity with other people. For example, having a student with severe disabilities control the mouse while surfing the Internet as a group project puts that individual at the center of the activity. Another approach is to teach students reciprocity skills during social interactions. For example, teaching a student to reply when greeted by a peer increases the probability that a longer social interaction will ensue.

Access to Highly Preferred People

A final variable that can be used to facilitate social interactions is to take into account access to highly preferred friends. The effort involved in maintaining a friendship involves a mutual understanding that the relationship is worth the effort, time, and energy necessary to maintain it. Many problems may arise when attempting to maintain friendships at school for any student. First, students may change classes. Because access to one's friends is important, changes in class schedules can inhibit or facilitate social relationships maintaining over time. Often, other opportunities for interaction must be sought out to enable the relationship to keep going. A proactive approach to identifying social interaction opportunities may help alleviate the problem of transitioning from semester to semester. If educators are aware of who are the highly preferred people for a student with severe disabilities, efforts can be taken to arrange his or her schedule so that he or she will be with friends as frequently as possible. This also becomes important when transitioning from elementary school to middle school and from middle to high school.

Additional Strategies

There are other related ways that teachers can facilitate social interactions between students with disabilities and peers without disabilities. One strategy is to use cooperative learning groups (Dugan et al., 1995; Kamps, Dugan, Potucek, & Collins, 1999). Cooperative learning groups promote a collaborative approach to learning and have been shown to increase social interaction. Another strategy teachers use to facilitate social interactions is to assign specific classroom roles (Downing, 1996; Falvey, 1995). Students may be assigned to take roll, collect papers, distribute and collect supplies, or take the lunch count. Last, teachers may provide time for socialization within the general education class. Teachers may schedule every Friday at the end of the month as "free time" for those students who successfully accomplished their work tasks. In addition to structured free time, teachers may schedule social interactions to occur prior to class or after students are finished with their work at the end of a class period.

Summary

In this chapter, we have discussed how social relationships can be operationally defined, what benefit students with severe disabilities and others received from them, and what strategies can improve a student's social life. The goals of support strategies for facilitating social relationships should be on increasing the quantity and/or quality of social interactions a student has with peers without disabilities. Interventions can also focus on teaching new social support skills and/or increasing the reciprocity of those behaviors. In addition, the student's social emeddedness in general education settings can be improved by expanding that student's social network among peers without disabilities.

By improving a student's social interactions, social supports, and social networks, a student experiences a greater degree of membership and belonging in general education settings. Strategies for facilitating these outcomes have to consider two broad issues before deciding on the specific details of a support plan. First, educators need to decide the degree to which they are going to focus students' supports on enhancing their independence and/or their interdependence. The second issue focuses on determining the types of interactions that are appropriate and desired in specific general education contexts. Focusing on these decisions first provides a framework for then generating specific support plans.

In this chapter, we have discussed several approaches for facilitating social relationships that have been demonstrated to be effective in the research literature. These interventions include peer-support strategies; social skills training; promotion of access to friendships; and the use of general education teaching strategies, such as cooperative learning, that provide the context for extended social interactions. Using these approaches helps promote improvements in a student's social interactions, social supports, and social network.

Research evidence supports general education participation for students with severe disabilities as having substantial benefits, such as (a) increased social contacts and friendships (Kennedy, Shukla, & Fryxell, 1997), (b) increased membership and belonging in school and beyond (Schnorr, 1990), (c) development and maintenance of good peer relationships (Salisbury, Galluchi, Palombaro, & Peck, 1995), (d) higher levels of happiness (Staub et al., 2000), and (e) larger social networks (Newton & Horner, 1993). By using the support strategies we have reviewed in this chapter and making use of the research literature we have cited, educators can effectively and reliably improve the social relationships their students experience.

References

Downing, J. E. (1996). *Including students with severe multiple disabilities in typical classrooms.* Baltimore: Paul H. Brookes Publishing Co.

Dugan, E., Kamps, D., Leonard, B., Watkins, N., Rheinberger, A., & Stackhaus, J. (1995). Effects of cooperative learning groups during social studies for students with autism and fourth-grade peers. *Journal of Applied Behavior Analysis, 28,* 175–188.

Falvey, M. A. (1995). *Inclusive and heterogeneous schooling: Assessment, curriculum, and instruction.* Baltimore: Paul H. Brookes Publishing Co.

Ferguson, D., & Baumgart, D. (1991). Partial participation revisited. *Journal of The Association for Persons with Severe Handicaps, 16,* 218–225.

Homans, G. C. (1953). *Social behavior as exchange.* New York: Basic Books.

Hunt, P., Alwell, M., Farron-Davis, F., & Goetz, L. (1996). Creating socially supportive environments for fully included students who experience multiple disabilities. *Journal of The Association for Persons with Severe Handicaps, 21,* 53–71.

Goldstein, H., Kaczmarek, L., & English, K. M. (2001). *Promoting social communication: Children with developmental disabilities from birth to adolescence.* Baltimore: Paul H. Brookes Publishing Co.

Janney, R. E., & Snell, M. E. (1996). How teachers use peer interactions to include students with moderate and severe disabilities in elementary general education classes. *Journal of The Association for Persons with Severe Handicaps, 21,* 72–80.

Kamps, D. M., Dugan, E., Potucek, J., & Collins, A. (1999). Effects of cross-age peer tutoring networks among students with autism and general education students. *Journal of Behavioral Education, 9,* 97–115.

Kennedy, C. H. (2001a). Promoting social-communicative interactions in adolescents. In H. Goldstein, L. Kaczmarek, & K. M. English (Eds.), *Promoting social communication: Children with developmen-* tal disabilities from birth to adolescence (pp. 307–330). Baltimore: Paul H. Brookes Publishing Co.

Kennedy, C. H. (2001b). Social interaction interventions for youth with severe disabilities should emphasize interdependence. *Mental Retardation and Developmental Disabilities Research Reviews, 7,* 122–127.

Kennedy, C. H., & Horn, E. (in press). *Including students with severe disabilities: Putting research into practice.* Boston: Allyn and Bacon.

Kennedy, C. H., Shukla, S., & Fryxell, D. (1997). Comparing the effects of educational placement on the social relationships of intermediate school students with severe disabilities. *Exceptional Children, 64,* 31–47.

Mu, K., Siegel, E. B., & Allinder, R. M. (in press). Peer interactions and sociometric status of high school students with moderate to severe disabilities in general education classrooms. *Journal of The Association for Persons with Severe Handicaps.*

Newton, J. S., & Horner, R. H. (1993). Using a social guide to improve social relationships of people with severe disabilities. *Journal of The Association for Persons with Severe Handicaps, 18,* 36–45.

Salisbury, C. L., Galluchi, C., Palombaro, M. M., & Peck, C. A. (1995). Strategies that promote social relations among elementary students with and without severe disabilities in inclusive schools. *Exceptional Children, 62,* 125–137.

Schnorr, R. (1990). Peter? He comes and goes . . . First graders' perspectives on a part-time mainstreamed student. *Journal of The Association for Persons with Severe Handicaps, 15,* 231–140.

Staub, D., Peck, C. A., Gallucci, C., & Schwartz, I. (2000). Peer relationships. In M. E. Snell, & F. Brown (Eds.), *Instruction of students with severe disabilities* (5th ed., pp. 381–409). New York: Merrill/Prentice Hall.

12

Facilitating Motor Skill Development within General Education Activities

Beverly Rainforth

Objectives

After completing this chapter, the reader will be able to:

1. Name and briefly describe four categories of motor skills according to their function.
2. Explain the importance of providing instruction on each category of motor skill in daily routines.
3. Identify opportunities to teach motor skills in everyday routines and school activities.
4. Describe similarities and differences between systematic instruction and the frames of reference used by occupational and physical therapists.
5. Describe roles and responsibilities of teachers and therapists in teaching motor skills.

Key Terms

Cerebral palsy	Mobility	Postural control
Frames of reference	Motor learning	Sensory integration/sensory
Hand use	Motor milestones	processing
Integrated therapy	Motor planning	Transfers
Microswitch	Neurodevelopmental treatment	

Physical education (PE) has been part of the educational curriculum in this country for a century, and nearly every state requires PE for its students. The Surgeon General (President's Council on Physical Fitness and Sports, September, 1999), and the National Association for Sport and Physical Education (1995) have recommended improved child and youth fitness through 30 to 45 minutes of daily physical activity. There is growing evidence that physical activity also promotes academic learning (Jensen, 2000). For the same reasons, daily physical activity is an essential element of educational programs for students with physical disabilities (President's Council on Physical Fitness and Sports, March, 1999).

Students with significant disabilities often have motor disabilities, ranging from clumsiness to delays in developing foundation motor skills, like grasping or independent sitting, to conditions like cerebral palsy that interfere with motor control. Although curriculum, instruction, and assessment for students with significant disabilities have evolved from the developmental models popular in the 1970s to ecological models, this evolution is not so evident in the area of motor skills. Thorough understanding of normal motor development does provide important guidance for planning effective instruction, but rigidly following motor milestones is abnormal and counterproductive (Campbell, 2000; Schoen & Anderson, 1999). An alternative is an ecological model for teaching motor skills, which takes into consideration principles of normal motor development and analysis of motor performance, as well as general education settings, curricula, and activities.

Planning to Teach Motor Skills in Inclusive Schools

When Individualized Education Programs (IEPs) for students with severe disabilities educated full-time in general education settings were compared with IEPs for similar students educated in special classes, the students with the most severe disabilities in inclusive education had more social, communication, and academic objectives and fewer motor objectives than comparable students in segregated programs (Hunt, Farron-Davis, Beckstead, Curtis, & Goetz, 1994). The researchers also found that less emphasis was placed on isolated foundation skills in inclusive settings, and, ideally, motor skill instruction was occurring more naturally within activity routines. Unfortunately, a study by Ott and Effgen (2000) raised serious doubts about the extent to which motor skill instruction is embedded in educational routines.

Ott and Effgen (2000) examined the frequency with which preschool children with cerebral palsy worked on gross motor skills in daily routines in segregated and integrated classes. The children selected for this study had, as part of their IEP, a physical therapy program that addressed stability (for example, maintaining upright positions), transfers (for example, moving from chair to stand), and mobility (for example, walking). The teachers and therapists worked together well as teams and were considered knowledgeable in best practices in early childhood special education. The researchers found that supported sitting was the only gross motor skill practiced frequently in either setting, and even this occurred only because children were positioned sitting in chairs so much of the day, not because of intentional instruction on maintaining upright postures. In fact, the teams rarely used the abundant opportunities to teach motor skills during daily routines, despite clear evidence of student need.

Despite more than two decades of advocacy for integrated therapy and guidance on how to implement this approach (see, for example, Rainforth & York-Barr, 1997), there continue to be few exemplars of instruction on motor skills within daily routines. We must ask whether time can be allowed for children to learn to move themselves, or if the constant rush to complete tasks and get to the next activity doesn't interfere with motor learning. Perhaps this rush limits other important learning opportunities, including opportunities for students without disabilities to use movement to enhance their learning (Jensen, 2000). Ott and Effgen's (2000) research findings support what many teachers and therapists already have experienced: Teaching motor skills in inclusive settings will occur only when instruction is carefully planned, and the necessary time is dedicated to implementation. This chapter presents an ecological approach, which demonstrates how general education settings, curricula, and activities can become the context for teaching motor skills.

An Ecological Framework for Motor Skill Instruction

Consider this common educational routine: Students arrive at class or an activity center; get materials from a desk, shelf, or cabinet; position themselves to work; complete their tasks; put materials away; and depart. This routine illustrates four general functions of motor skills: a) assuming and maintaining positions that enable participation, b) using transfers and mobility skills for transitions, c) using the hands to perform required tasks and participate in desired activities, and d) using combinations of motor skills for participation (Rainforth & York-Barr, 1997). This last category is broad and could entail the combinations of motor skills needed for tasks like carrying materials in a classroom or playing kickball during recess. The following sections offer strategies to help students fulfill these functions by teaching the corresponding motor skills: a) postural control and stability, b) transfers and mobility, c) hand use, and d) other motor participation.

Teaching Postural Control and Stability

Performance of all students, whether or not they have disabilities that affect their motor skills, is impacted by their positioning. In a study of young children with no known disabilities, Sents and Marks (1989) found significant differences in Intelligence Quotient (IQ) scores when the children took intelligence tests positioned well or positioned poorly. The only difference between the two test conditions was the size of the chairs and tables where the children worked. These findings compel every teacher to ensure that every student has access to furniture or equipment that allows their feet to rest flat on the floor or a footrest, their back and hips to reach the back of the chair, their thighs to be fully supported by the seat, and their work surface to be at midchest level.

When students have severe physical disabilities, these considerations are even more important because these students cannot adjust their own position. The condition and fit of equipment must be checked regularly. Even when equipment fits properly, however, students often end up sitting with poor posture because appropriate care has not been given to how they are placed in their seating. The student's hips are the foundation for good positioning. If a gap is left between the bottom of the hips and back of the chair, the low back gets inadequate support and curves backwards, giving a poor base to sit on, and results in the student falling forward or to the side. During the winter, when students wear bulky clothing, removing a student's coat, but failing to reposition the hips, will create the same problem. In these situations, adding head and chest supports will not improve the student's posture; the student's hips must be repositioned. Tipping the chair back (to use gravity as an aid), bending the hips, and lifting the student's shoulders slightly will usually allow the hips to slip to the back of the seat. Tightening the seat belt so it is snug across the bend in the hips will help keep the student positioned well; a loose seat belt may look comfortable, but inadvertently leads to discomfort as the student's hips slide out of position. Teachers who do not know how to position a student with physical disabilities are responsible for asking the student's occupational or physical therapist to teach them. Nothing a teacher or therapist does related to this student could be of more significance. Even when a paraprofessional works closely with a student with physical disabilities, the teacher must be prepared to meet this basic student need when the paraprofessional is not available.

Because children typically sit at school, teachers may not question the fact that students who use wheelchairs may spend most or all of their day sitting. Allowing a student with physical disabilities to sit for long periods of time is deleterious for two reasons. First, students with physical disabilities are prone to deformities, especially hip and knee flexion contractures, which are worsened by sitting for hours at a time. Stretching the joints is important to maintain joint mobility, but positioning is more effective than intermittent range-of-motion exercises. Research shows that muscles must be stretched for at least six hours a day to prevent deformities completely (Tardieu, Lespargot, Tabary, & Bret, 1988), but being positioned in standing for 30 minutes decreased spasticity and increased active movement in children with cerebral palsy (Tremblay, Malouin, Richards, & Dumas, 1990). Some school personnel don't consider changing a student's position an educational need, but students with physical disabilities have the same need for, and right to, physical activity as other students (President's Council on Physical Fitness and Sports, March, 1999). Furthermore, staying in one position too long causes discomfort, and discomfort interferes with learning. (See Chapter 22 for other health concerns related to positioning.) Finally, changes in position are necessary for students to develop the postural control and stability needed to participate fully in their educational program. To address these needs, planning for inclusion of students with physical disabilities across general education contexts should include a positioning plan.

Rhiannon is an 11-year-old girl with multiple disabilities, including severe cerebral palsy affecting her whole body. She needs an adapted chair to maintain a sitting position and has spent the majority of her school day in a wheelchair or an adapted classroom chair. As Rhiannon's team planned for her to be included in fifth grade, they worked on a positioning plan that fit with the fifth grade daily schedule. The following questions were used as a guide:

- What positions do peers without disabilities use when they engage in each general education activity?
- What positions allow for proximity to peers across general education activities?
- Which positions allow easy view of and access to materials and equipment used in general education activities?
- Which positions allow or promote the movement needed to perform critical tasks in general education settings?
- What positions encourage further development of postural control and stability?
- What positions provide alternatives to overused postures or equipment?
- If positioning equipment is required, is it unobtrusive, cosmetically acceptable, and not physically isolating?
- Is the positioning equipment safe and easy to handle?
- Is the equipment selected and modified to match individual needs?
- Is the equipment available in or easily transported to each general education setting and other natural environments (for example, home or community)?
- What personnel (for example, therapists, teachers, classmates, or parent volunteers) are needed and available to help the student change position? (Adapted from Rainforth & York-Barr, 1997, pp. 219–220)

When these questions were considered, Rhiannon's team agreed that she spends too much time sitting and would benefit from using a stander for a portion of the day.

In Rhiannon's fifth grade classroom, reading and math often involve center activities, so peers stand and move around, offering natural opportunities for Rhiannon to be in her stander. Although the classroom is crowded with tables and desks, the stander takes about the same amount of space as Rhiannon's wheelchair, so the equipment seems manageable. The tray on the stander is big enough so Rhiannon's group can work together around her tray, or the tray can be removed, and they can work together at a table. The angle of the stander can be adjusted easily to correspond with her endurance. The special education teacher or a therapist can be available to help the paraprofessional transfer Rhiannon to and from the stander. Another naturally occurring opportunity to use a stander is PE class, when peers without disabilities typically are standing, rather than sitting. In addition, Rhiannon's stander can be transported to and moved around the gym easily, has sufficient stability to be safe in that environment, and opens up new possibilities for her participation in PE. People who can be enlisted to help Rhiannon transfer to the stander include her paraprofessional, general education teacher, special education teacher, therapists, and the PE teacher (if Rhiannon arrives before class starts).

When students are more mobile, teams still need to consider the quality of their positioning. Daniel is a seven-year-old boy with developmental delays. During morning meeting and free time in his first grade classroom, he sits on the floor with his class-mates. Because he has poor trunk and hip stability, he prefers to "W-sit" (that is, both knees bent and rotated inward, with his feet alongside his hips), which gives him a wide base of support (see Figure 12.1). Unfortunately, the position limits further development of his postural stability while it damages his knee joints and allows shortening of mus-cles around the hip and knee joints. As alternatives, Daniel's team considered long

FIGURE 12.1   *Daniel (left) and friend playing with blocks. Note that Daniel "W-sits" with his feet on either side of his hips, while his friend sits lightly on his heels.*

sitting, ring sitting, and sidesitting. Daniel's leg muscles already are so tight that he cannot sit properly with his legs straight out in front of him (that is, long sitting). With help getting into other positions, Daniel can tailor sit (that is, with his legs folded in front of him) or side sit (that is, with both knees folded to one side). These positions are good for the morning meeting, when the children sit fairly still, but these positions do not work well for playing on the floor.

The team noticed that peers without disabilities use several positions as they play. For example, peers sit *on* their heels (not *between* their heels) to stack building blocks (see Figure 12.1). From this position, they move onto hands and knees to reach for more blocks and then kneel to make a taller stack. Daniel can use all of these positions, too, when an adult positions his feet closer together, under his hips, and guides him at his hips. Daniel can sit on his heels briefly, and, as peers encourage him to play, an adult guides Daniel's hips to move forward onto hands and knees, back to sitting on his heels, and up to kneeling. Guiding Daniel through these positions prevents prolonged W-sitting and helps him develop better coordination and balance. Daniel is starting to kneel independently, but he still balances by making a wide base of support with his knees (see Figure 12.2). During free time, Daniel will both receive motor instruction and experiment with independent

FIGURE 12.2 *Daniel kneeling with a friend. Note how he keeps a wide base of support with his knees.*

movement as required to learn new motor skills and to ensure their maintenance and generalization (Larin, 2000).

Teaching Transfers and Mobility

Transfers are changes in position, like standing up from the floor, sitting down from standing, and moving from a wheelchair to a toilet. Mobility refers to ways of traveling within a room, building, or the community, which could include rolling, crawling on hands and knees, walking, pushing a wheelchair, riding a bicycle, and negotiating stairs or curbs. Adults with physical disabilities typically use two or more forms of mobility and use different forms in different settings (York, 1989). For example, someone might crawl in their bedroom or bathroom at home, stand and walk a few steps in the kitchen, and use a wheelchair to get around the community. Because different forms of mobility have different energy demands, mobility demands can affect the academic performance of students with physical disabilities (Franks, Palisano, & Darbee, 1991; Park, Park, & Kim, 2001). Therefore, it is important to consider multiple forms of mobility for students with physical disabilities. Transfers that correspond with mobility must also be taught.

When deciding what form of mobility and transfers to teach a student, team decisions can be guided by the following questions:

- What forms of mobility and transfers allow or promote access to important settings and activities, including the full range of general education contexts at school and family life in the community?
- What forms of mobility and transfers allow for proximity to peers without disabilities at school and in the community?
- What forms of mobility and transfers encourage further development of motor skills, including coordination and endurance?
- What forms of mobility and transfers are efficient, leaving the student with enough time and energy to participate in critical activities at the desired destination?
- If equipment is required for mobility and transfers, is it safe, easy to handle, durable, reliable, and cosmetically acceptable to the user, peers, and society?
- Is the equipment selected carefully and then modified as necessary to meet individual needs?
- Who is available to help the student with mobility and transfers in general education settings, in the community, and at home?

For Rhiannon, a power wheelchair is her primary form of mobility for home, school, and community. Although it has increased her independence at school, driving independently from one classroom to another is still time-consuming and physically challenging. It does not leave her too tired to do her schoolwork, but her team has to decide when it is appropriate for her to leave a class early or arrive late in order to make driving a priority. Rhiannon's team will try having a peer, rather than her paraprofessional, accompany her for some transitions to see if she will drive more quickly to keep up with a friend. A younger child might roll on the floor as another form of mobility at home and school (for example, while playing on the floor). For Rhiannon, rolling on the floor is not appropriate at school, but it would be an important addition to her home routine so she could change her own position in bed at night. Because of Rhiannon's disability and size, transferring her requires either two people to lift her or use of a hydraulic lift with a sling seat, which an adult can manage alone (see Figure 12.3). At home, her lift is part of an overhead tracking system that also allows her to walk. Rhiannon is expected to participate actively in these transfers by staying relaxed, which requires considerable effort on her part.

Daniel uses "bunny hopping" as his primary form of independent mobility. His team is starting to teach him reciprocal crawling when playing on the floor (see Figure 12.4a) and walking with a rolling walker for transitions at school and home (see Figure 12.4b). These alternatives to bunny hopping will challenge Daniel, improve his coordination and endurance, and increase his independence. For transfers, Daniel is learning to stand up from and sit down in a chair and to stand up from the floor using a reciprocal pattern, which reinforces his mobility skills (see Figure 12.5.) For now, Daniel will use a wheelchair pushed by an adult in the community and during some transitions at school. Knowing that walking takes more time and energy at first, Daniel's team needs to determine when it is appropriate for Daniel to walk from one area in the school to another and when he will travel in his wheelchair. A paraprofessional or special education teacher usually pushes

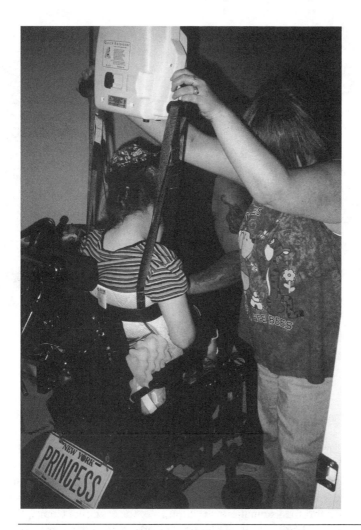

FIGURE 12.3 *Rhiannon in her lift, being transferred into her wheelchair.*

Daniel in his wheelchair and, with training from Daniel's physical therapist, also will assist him with walking.

Occupational and physical therapists are usually involved in teaching transfer and mobility skills and bring specialized knowledge and skills to this area of instruction. Too often, however, teachers assume that teaching mobility and transfers is the sole responsibility of therapists and/or that teachers cannot also learn to teach these skills. Studies of athletes, musicians, and handworkers (for example, knitters) suggest that a movement must be practiced frequently and repeated at least one million times to develop "skillful coordination" (Kottke, Halpern, Easton, Ozel, & Burrill, 1978). These findings show that the traditional approach to providing therapy services (for example, 30 minutes twice a

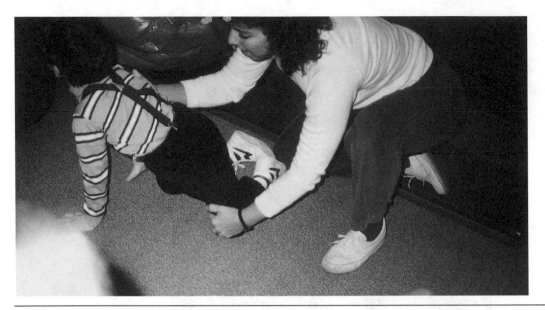

FIGURE 12.4A *Daniel crawling during free play in kindergarten, with prompting to use reciprocal movement.*

week) cannot come close to providing the practice children need to develop new motor skills. Especially when children have disabilities that interfere with independent movement, educational teams, including teachers, must ensure frequent physical activity for both learning and physical fitness.

An effective approach to teaching transfer and mobility skills is to do a task analysis of a movement like rolling or walking and then teach the steps through the prompting and fading strategies central to systematic instruction (see, for example, Campbell & Stewart, 1986; Horn, Jones, & Warren, 1999). Thorough understanding of the *processes* of normal motor development is important to planning effective intervention, and this is an important contribution from occupational and physical therapists. When children have severe physical disabilities, however, programs based on normal developmental sequences have not proven to be an effective means of teaching mobility skills (Bidabe, 1990). One alternative to developmental programs is the MOVE Curriculum, which consists of 16 categories of functional motor skills (listed in Table 12.1), which are further divided into 74 foundation skills. For example, the category of Stands has six subskill, (see Table 12.2), starting at points that students with the most severe disabilities can achieve. Within a category, skills are taught in sequence, but skills related to sitting, standing, and walking are taught simultaneously. For many children, new experiences in upright positions elicit immediate improvement in head control.

The MOVE manual includes detailed instructions to assess and teach each skill and addresses generalization to home, school, and community settings. Longitudinal data on

FIGURE 12.4B *Daniel learning to walk as he travels to the cafeteria.*

15 students (ages 6 to 16) with significant cognitive and motor disabilities document considerable achievement during a three-year period (Bidabe, Barnes, & Whinnery, 2001). In another study, three children (ages 3 to 9) with severe disabilities who did not walk during baseline received instruction in the MOVE curriculum during natural routines for one school year. During maintenance checks two years later, two children were walking more than 500 feet independently, and the third was walking at least 100 steps in a gait trainer (Barnes & Whinnery, 2002). Because the author of MOVE is a special educator, the manual is written in the language that other educators will understand. Having a special educator develop this powerful curriculum also demonstrates that teachers can acquire the knowledge and skills for and take a leadership role in teaching mobility to students with significant disabilities.

Teaching Hand Use

Hand use, often thought of as fine motor skills, involves several types of grasp, as well as the abilities to rotate the wrist (from palm down to palm up), use both hands together, and release objects. Information about fine motor skills usually is illustrated through student

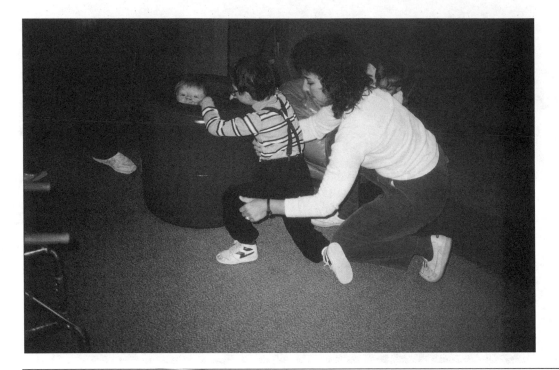

FIGURE 12.5   *Daniel rising to stand during free play in kindergarten, with prompting to use a reciprocal pattern.*

performance on a selection of tasks. Unfortunately, the underlying motor skills may not be evident, and the tasks often are inappropriate for school-age children. For example, the classic task of stacking three 1-inch cubes is not important for an eight-year-old with significant disabilities. Successful performance of the task does demonstrate important motor skills, however, including a three-point grasp, precise placement, and controlled release in space. These skills also could be demonstrated through a variety of other tasks. Table 12.3 lists important aspects of hand use, in approximate order of difficulty, with examples of applications for children in inclusive schools and classrooms. (For detailed delineation of hand-use skills, as well as impact of motor disabilities, see Erhardt, 1999).

Analysis of the motor skills required for these tasks illustrates that hand use requires consideration of more than just the hand. For example, many teachers have experienced the difficulty of teaching a student with poor motor skills to feed himself with a spoon. A task analysis includes only six simple steps: grasp the spoon, scoop food, bring spoon to mouth, insert spoon, remove spoon, and return spoon to dish. The gross grasp used to hold the spoon is the least difficult form of grasp, and a splint can assist the student with this. Completing the task successfully requires the hand and forearm to stay level, however, so the student must constantly adjust the position of his elbow and shoulder, requiring considerable motor control. The student's trunk and head must be stable to move the arm this

TABLE 12.1   *Categories of Skills Addressed in the MOVE Curriculum*

Functional Motor Skills in the MOVE Curriculum

Maintains a sitting position
Moves while sitting
Stands
Transitions from sitting to standing
Transitions from standing to sitting
Pivots while standing
Walks forward
Transitions from standing to walking
Transitions from walking to standing
Walks backward
Turns while walking
Walks up steps
Walks down steps
Walks on uneven ground
Walks up slopes
Walks down slopes

Source: from Bidabe, D. L. (1990). *Mobility opportunities via education (MOVE) curriculum.* Bakersfield, CA: Kern County Superintendent of Schools.

way and to put the spoon in the mouth. This example illustrates that successful hand use requires numerous motor skills. Once again, the foundation is good positioning.

Although sitting is the most appropriate position for eating, some students with significant motor disabilities have better control of their arms and hands in other positions. Sidelying, for example, offers far more support for the head, trunk, and arms than sitting does, so it may allow a student with significant motor disabilities to concentrate on using

TABLE 12.2   *Example of Skill Broken into Component Skills from the MOVE Curriculum*

Component Skills for Standing

C.6 Can tolerate being placed in a vertical position.
C.5 Can tolerate fully prompted extension of hips and knees.
C.4 Can tolerate bearing weight on feet for a minimum of 45 minutes per day when knees, hips, and trunk are held in alignment by a mobile stander or similar standing device.
C.3 Can maintain hip and knee extension to allow weightbearing for a minimum of three minutes while another person keeps participant's body in alignment.
C.2 Can stand in one place with one or both hands held for a minimum of five minutes.
C.1 Can stand in one place without support for a minimum of 60 seconds.

Source: from Bidabe, D. L. (1990). *Mobility opportunities via education (MOVE) curriculum.* Bakersfield, CA: Kern County Superintendent of Schools.

TABLE 12.3   *Hand-use Skills and Examples of Applications by School-Age Children*

	Skill	*Applications*
Grasp	Gross/palmar (fingers hold object in palm, thumb not used in immature grasp)	Hold toothbrush, handle of lunch box, small cup, telephone, swing
	Three-point (thumb and two or more fingers hold object)	Hold book, pen, computer disk; take cap off glue stick
	Pincer (thumb and index finger hold object)	Hold paper clip, coin, zipper tab
Wrist position	Prone (palm down)	Press microswitch button on table, touch picture on communication page
	Neutral (palm vertical)	Hold cup, tray/bin, pen; hold phone to ear
	Supine (palm up)	Bring tissue to nose, pull up back of pants
Bilateral coordination	Two hands hold together	Carry ball, wastebasket, cafeteria tray
	One hand stabilize, other hand manipulate	Hold paper while writing, spread butter on toast
	Both hands manipulate	Take wrapper off straw, zip backpack, cut with scissors
	Surface firm, wrist supported	Not typical (add firm surface, wrist support to improve performance)
Stabilization (to point at or release object)	Surface firm, no wrist support	Put cup on table, stick date on wall calendar, touch symbol on communication system
	Surface not firm, wrist supported	Use computer mouse, type
	Surface not firm, no wrist support	Hand materials to peer, put coin in vending machine, throw ball

her hands (rather than keeping her head and trunk upright) and to experience success that is impossible in other positions. Therefore, when planning instruction on hand use, it is important to consider the student's motor abilities, the demands of the task, and the position(s) usually used by classmates without disabilities, and seek the best possible match among the most critical factors.

Another consideration in teaching hand use is whether a splint or adaptation would reduce the motor demands of the task, so the student can concentrate on fewer movements. When Rhiannon drives her power wheelchair, for example, the wheelchair stabilizes her trunk and arm so she can concentrate on holding the joystick with a palmar grasp and moving her wrist. When Rhiannon tries to use a standard keyboard, she hits several keys at once because she has difficulty stabilizing her arm and isolating one finger to point. A keyguard helps her direct her finger to the desired key, while it allows her to stabilize her hand on the keyboard for better control of her fingers. When students are just starting to develop hand-use skills, microswitches allow them to concentrate on goal-directed movement of the arm or hand (for example, touch switch), rather than grasp. Several ideas for adaptations that maximize participation of students who are developing hand skills are illustrated in York-Barr, Rainforth, and Locke (1996) and the Ablenet catalogue (available from *www.ablenetinc.com*).

When teaching hand use, prompts at the hand or wrist are usually best to facilitate grasp, release, and wrist rotation, while prompts at the elbow or upper arm are usually best to facilitate reach and other alignment of the arm in space. Research indicates that children with disabilities also achieve better quality of movement when skills such as reaching are learned in meaningful tasks rather than practiced as isolated movements (Beauregard, Thomas, & Nelson, 1998). Daniel uses a palmar grasp and is starting to use a three-point grasp to feed himself and play with toys. When Daniel eats with a spoon, an adult gently guides his elbow to direct the spoon to his mouth; when he drinks from a cup, he is guided at the wrist to keep the cup upright as he puts it on the table. When he eats a sandwich, a small splint across his palm holds his fingers open so he can use the three-point grasp (and not crush the sandwich in his palm) without intrusion of an adult to prompt his hand. When Daniel plays in the block area, an adult prompts him at the forearms so he can both hold cardboard blocks with two hands and reach out to place them on a stack he is building with other boys. In all these situations, adults try to balance Daniel's opportunities to experience "correct" movements with his opportunities to practice and refine independent movement.

Teaching Motor Participation

Motor participation is a broad category that refers to using combinations of several motor skills. For example, carrying a bin of materials in a classroom requires mobility and hand use and is more complex than either mobility or hand use alone, especially when the student must anticipate and negotiate furniture and moving peers. Playing kickball requires a student to stand, kick, and run, all in quick succession. Students with motor-planning problems often have difficulty with changes in type, direction, or tempo of movement, especially when those changes are quick or unexpected.

Sometimes it is appropriate to simplify demands of an activity, like having a novice kickball player only kick or only run. In other situations, the student may rise to the demands of the activity. For example, Riccardo is a middle school student with significant cognitive disabilities who has difficulty walking on uneven ground, stepping off a curb, and standing still while using his hands. After lunch, he helps the janitor in the cafeteria by putting chairs up on the tables. A special education teacher analyzed the task and physically guided Riccardo through turning each chair upside down, lifting it, and placing the seat securely on the table. After several days of instruction and no apparent improvement in Riccardo's performance, the teacher briefly left Riccardo's side. On his own, Riccardo picked up a chair, adjusting how he held it, how he balanced his body and the chair in space, and the order of the steps in the task until he found his own way of placing the chair on the table. Although the teacher's instruction undoubtedly helped Riccardo understand the task, solving this motor-planning problem on his own was an important part of his learning.

When considering motor participation, it is important to consider the student's overall physical fitness as well as motor skills in the areas of postural control, mobility, and hand use. It is also important to consider other dimensions of task difficulty, which are outlined in Table 12.4. Students learn the most when they are challenged, but not frustrated.

TABLE 12.4 *Considerations in Determining Difficulty of Motor Tasks*

Dimension	Characteristics	Examples and Implications for Teaching
Body in space	Stable	Sitting, standing
	In motion	Walking, climbing stairs, riding a bike
Hand use	Balance (or no required use)	Listening to directions, watching a demonstration, playing kickball
	Manipulation	Cutting with scissors, putting storage bin on shelf, playing computer games, turning pages of a book; Requires good head and trunk stability, from internal and/or external support
Task continuity	Discrete trials	Activating microswitch, regrouping math manipulatives, printing spelling words; Requires preparation to execute movement
	Continuous	Walking, driving power wheelchair to cafeteria; Requires error detection during movement, ongoing adjustments, time to rest between
	Serial (discrete and continuous)	Eating with a spoon, playing kickball
Predictability	Predictable	Opening carton of milk, printing name on paper; Allow preparation to execute movement
	Variable	Playing on playground, transitions with other children (e.g., changing centers in classroom, going to another classroom); Requires learning and adjusting to irregularities
Complexity	Simple	Using microswitch, playing board game; Requires less coordination and fewer body parts, high arousal needed to motivate repetition
	Complex	Putting on backpack, carrying tray in cafeteria; Requires preparation to execute movement (more body parts and/or coordination), keep arousal low

Source: Adapted from Larin (2000).

When a student struggles, being aware of these dimensions can help teachers determine why a motor task is too difficult and how it can be modified for an appropriate challenge.

Theoretical Considerations in Teaching Motor Skills

When students have motor delays or disabilities, their special education team is likely to include an occupational therapist and/or a physical therapist. To address students' movement needs effectively, therapists need to be full participants in the education team so that services can be well-coordinated and integrated, and so knowledge and skills can be exchanged through role release (Rainforth & York-Barr, 1997). Achieving these ends is easier when teachers understand the perspectives that therapists bring to educational settings. Parents, teachers, and administrators also may assume that all occupational therapists would bring certain expertise to a team, while all physical therapists would bring other types of expertise. Although there is a core of knowledge associated with each discipline, there is also great variation in therapists' expertise, depending upon preservice education, work experience, inservice education, and personal interests (Rainforth, 2002). Thus teams must learn what expertise each individual therapist brings. At the same time, effective practice requires therapists to a) develop competence in several frames of reference so they can choose the treatment approach that best addresses an individual's disability and current goals (Hinojosa & Kramer, 1999), and b) articulate their rationale and continually reassess whether selected strategies elicit the desired results (Embry, Yates, Nirider, Hylton, & Adams, 1996). Many pediatric therapists have embraced three frames of reference for students with motor delays and disabilities: neurodevelopmental treatment, sensory integration, and motor learning. Each of these will be discussed briefly.

Neurodevelopmental Treatment (NDT)

NDT was developed for children with cerebral palsy and now is used for children with a variety of motor delays and disabilities. It was based on the belief that sensory input could change motor output, which also would change the central nervous system. NDT involves techniques to a) inhibit abnormal muscle tone and reflex activity and b) facilitate normal movements and equilibrium reactions (Bobath, 1980; Schoen & Anderson, 1999). If a student has spasticity in the arms, for example, slow, rhythmic movement, like rocking the child or slowly moving the child's arms back and forth, can reduce spasticity. As the child's arms relax, reach can be facilitated by guiding the arm from above the elbow (rather than pulling on the hand). When techniques of this type were added to a program of systematic instruction for a 13-year-old student with very limited motor abilities, her success at pressing a microswitch for leisure tasks increased significantly (Giangreco, 1986).

NDT has been criticized for overuse of passive movement and for treatment in isolated contexts. For example, a therapist might believe that, after giving full physical assistance to reduce the child's tone and guide reaching in the therapy room, the child eventually would be able to reach for objects in the classroom. A therapist might also believe that exercises sitting on a therapy ball in a therapy room eventually would improve coordination during walking. Recently, NDT has been influenced by motor learning theory (discussed later in this chapter), resulting in increased concern for student motivation and active participation in functional tasks. This emphasis on active participation and practice has decreased emphasis on passive techniques intended to normalize tone. The Giangreco (1986) study demonstrated that incorporating NDT strategies, even passive strategies, into systematic instruction can improve performance. In a student's educational routine, it may be most appropriate to use passive movement (full physical assistance) as a warm-up or rehearsal, followed immediately by use in a motivating task.

Sensory Integration (SI)

SI was developed for children with learning disabilities with the belief that sensory input to the vestibular, proprioceptive, and tactile systems would improve performance of the auditory and visual systems for academics (Kimball, 1999). This approach is now used with children with many types of disabilities. Hanschu (1997) used the broader term, "sensory processing," to refer to four types of disabilities:

1. **Sensory modulation:** Difficulty becoming and staying alert enough to learn, causing lethargy or high levels of activity
2. **Sensory defensiveness:** Intolerance for normal environmental stimuli, causing physical avoidance or shutting down (neurological withdrawal)
3. **Sensory registration:** Disregard for stimuli that don't register or intensification of stimuli to make them register (self-stimulation)
4. **Sensory integration:** Difficulty using normal (concurrent) stimuli to all sensory systems

Like NDT, sensory processing has been criticized for techniques being used in isolated contexts too often, with hope that they would influence routine performance in natural settings. For example, a student may swing in a net swing or ride on a scooter board in therapy, but it may not be clear how these activities should influence class participation or could be reinforced in class routines. There are also limited data on, and disagreement about, effectiveness of sensory-processing techniques for students with significant disabilities (see, for example, Case-Smith & Bryan, 1999; Dawson & Watling, 2000). Anecdotal reports suggest that some children benefit from sensory interventions like firm pressure down through the shoulders; traction of joints; or scrubbing arms, legs, and back with a nylon brush, which can be provided as part of daily routines (Grandin, 1996; Hanschu, 1997). Even if more published research were available, student needs and responses vary widely, so ongoing data collection and careful monitoring of individual student benefits are essential. Like NDT, sensory-processing interventions seem best as preparation for educational tasks, rather than in isolated episodes.

Motor Learning Theory

Motor learning theory and the corresponding motor teaching strategies (Kaplan & Bedell, 1999; Larin, 2000) are based on learning theory and are, therefore, highly consistent with best practices in systematic instruction. Motor learning is enhanced when the student is actively engaged in challenging and meaningful tasks in stimulating environments. In contrast, Norman Kunc, a man with cerebral palsy, expressed considerable frustration with his endless practice on the "stairs to nowhere" in a therapy room as a child (Giangreco, 1996). Although education team members need to recognize symptoms of overstimulation (for example, irritability and withdrawal), often it is the special education teacher and therapist who are distracted or overstimulated in the general education classroom, or they are frustrated that the student with a disability is more interested in rich classroom activities than an isolated parallel task. Reciprocity with peers has proven to be particularly motivating for children working on motor skills (Brady, Martin, Williams, & Burta, 1991), and classmates without disabilities are helpers, models, and encouragers when teaching motor skills in general education contexts.

Prompting must strike a balance between giving needed guidance and support and allowing the student to experiment with varied forms of movement that fulfill a desired function. Feedback also must strike a balance between preventing incorrect performance and allowing self-correction. Although continuous feedback (given at every step) may be needed during early skill acquisition, summary or intermittent feedback (at the end of a task or a "chunk" of the task) is better for improving performance (McEwen & Shelden, 1995). These principles were illustrated in the earlier description of Riccardo, who devised new motor strategies when guidance and support were inadvertently stopped, thereby allowing opportunities for independent practice and self-correction. Research has substantiated these principles. After students with significant cognitive and motor disabilities were physically guided through complex routines in inclusive schools, and then the physical guidance was interrupted, the students performed new motor skills in order to continue their routines (Gee, Graham, Goetz, Oshima, & Yoshioka, 1991).

Motor skill learning is enhanced by cognitive mediation strategies, including verbal rehearsal of movements required to complete a task, visualization of oneself performing desired movements and tasks, student prediction of how well he or she will perform a task, and self-assessment of actual performance. Some students will not understand these strategies, but cognition is hard to assess accurately when students have multiple disabilities. Therefore, it is appropriate to see how each student responds to these suggestions. It can also be hard to judge how much feedback a student needs. When intrinsic feedback (for example, how a movement feels or whether a goal is attained) is adequate, extrinsic feedback (for example, praise) can actually hinder skill acquisition (Larin, 2000).

When teaching motor skills, it is important to consider whether the goal is motor learning (that is, initial skill acquisition, maintenance over time, and generalization to other tasks or settings) or motor performance (that is, improved accuracy, fluency, speed, timing, adaptability, and economy of effort) (Larin, 2000). It is better to develop a broad foundation of motor skills before focusing on quality of motor performance. Thus, a child would be taught to handle a spoon, dab a glue stick, and pull velcroed pictures off a schedule page before being expected to develop the precision needed to print his name. In the same way, performance at one level of motor development (for example, creeping on hands and knees) is refined only after work on more advanced skills (for example, pulling to stand and walking), so it is important to teach motor skills at multiple levels concurrently.

Motor learning theory is related closely to systematic instruction, offering teachers and therapists some common ground from which to start developing more integrated services. Although NDT and sensory processing have their roots in neurophysiological theory, they may serve as important adjuncts to systematic instruction. To use these neurophysiological approaches effectively in inclusive schools, however, it is critical to determine if specific methods have a positive effect on performance of specific students and, if so, to identify how strategies can be incorporated into daily routines.

Summary

Physical activity and fitness are important components of education for all students. Many students with significant disabilities need explicit instruction on motor skills as a foundation for further learning and participation. Rather than use typical developmental sequences as the framework to assess and teach basic motor skills, it is more useful to think about the functions of motor skills: postural control, mobility, hand use, and participation in motor activities. Students with physical disabilities need many opportunities to learn and practice motor skills, and the daily routines and classroom activities of general education offer these opportunities. Careful planning and a commitment to instruction are needed to ensure that teaching and practice occur frequently. Occupational and physical therapists are important resources for planning and providing motor instruction. Their knowledge and skills in the areas of NDT, sensory processing, and motor learning complement special education teachers' knowledge and skills in systematic instruction. Providing motor skill instruction to students with significant disabilities in the context of general education settings and activities improves the quality and quantity of their participation.

References

Barnes, S. B., & Whinnery, K. W. (2002). Effects of functional mobility skills training for young students with physical disabilities. *Exceptional Children, 68*(3), 313–324.

Beauregard, R., Thomas, J. J., & Nelson, D. L. (1998). Quality of reach during a game and during rote movement in children with cerebral palsy. *Physical and Occupational Therapy in Pediatrics, 18*(3/4), 67–84.

Bidabe, D. L. (1990). *Mobility opportunities via education (MOVE) curriculum*. Bakersfield, CA: Kern County Superintendent of Schools.

Bidabe, D. L., Barnes, S. B., & Whinnery, K. W. (2001). MOVE: Raising expectations for individuals with severe disabilities. *Physical Disabilities: Education and Related Services, 19*(2), 31–48.

Bobath, K. (1980). *A neurophysiological basis for the treatment of cerebral palsy*. Philadelphia: J. B. Lippincott Co.

Brady, M. P., Martin, S., Williams, R. E., & Burta, M. (1991). The effects of fifth graders' socially directed behavior on motor and social responses of children with severe multiple handicaps. *Research in Developmental Disabilities, 12*(1), 1–16.

Campbell, P., & Stewart, B. (1986). Measuring changes in movement skills with infants and young children with handicaps. *Journal of The Association for Persons with Severe Handicaps, 16*(3), 153–161.

Campbell, S. K. (2000). The child's development of functional movement. In S. K. Campbell, D. W. Vanderlinden, and R. J. Palisano (Eds.), *Physical therapy for children* (2nd ed., pp. 3–44). Philadelphia: W. B. Saunders Company.

Case-Smith, J., & Bryan, T. (1999). The effects of occupational therapy with sensory integration emphasis on preschool-age children with autism. *American Journal of Occupational Therapy, 53*(5), 489–497.

Dawson, G., & Watling, R. (2000). Interventions to facilitate auditory, visual, and motor integration in autism: A review of the evidence. *Journal of Autism and Developmental Disorders, 30*(5), 415–421.

Embry, D. G., Yates, L., Nirider, B., Hylton, N., & Adams, L. S. (1996). Recommendations for pediatric physical therapists: Making clinical decisions for children with physical therapy. *Pediatric Physical Therapy, 8*(4), 165–170.

Erhardt, R. P. (1999). *Developmental hand dysfunction: Theory, assessment, treatment* (2nd ed.). San Antonio, TX: Psychological Corporation.

Franks, C. A., Palisano, R. J., & Darbee, J. C. (1991). The effect of walking with an assistive device and using a wheelchair on school performance in students with myelomeningocele. *Physical Therapy, 71*(8), 570–577.

Gee, K., Graham, N., Goetz, L., Oshima, G., & Yoshioka,

K. (1991). Teaching students to request the continuation of routine activities by using time delay and decreasing physical assistance in the context of chain interruption. *Journal of The Association for Persons with Severe Handicaps, 16*(3), 154–167.

Giangreco, M. F. (1986). Effects of integrated therapy: A pilot study. *Journal of The Association for Persons with Severe Handicaps, 16*(3), 205–208.

Giangreco, M. F. (1996). "The stairs didn't go anywhere!" A self-advocate's reflections on specialized services and their impact on people with disabilities. *Physical Disabilities: Education and Related Services, 14*(2), 1–12.

Grandin, T. (1996). *Thinking in pictures: And other reports from my life with autism.* New York: Vintage Books.

Hanschu, B. (1997). *Autism and attention deficit disorder/ hyperactivity: A sensory perspective.* Phoenix, AZ: Bonnie Hanschu.

Hinojosa, J., & Kramer, P. (1999). Frames of reference in the real world. In P. Kramer, & J. Hinojosa (Eds.), *Frames of reference for pediatric occupational therapy* (2nd ed., pp. 519–532). Baltimore, MD: Williams and Wilkins.

Horn, E. M., Jones, H. A., & Warren, S. F. (1999). The effects of a neurobehavioral intervention on motor skill acquisition and generalization. *Journal of Early Intervention, 22*(1), 1–18.

Hunt, P., Farron-Davis, F., Beckstead, D., Curtis, D., & Goetz, L. (1994). Evaluating the effects of placement of students with severe disabilities in general education versus special classes. *Journal of The Association for Persons with Severe Handicaps, 19*(3), 200–214.

Jensen, E. (2000). Moving with the brain in mind. *Educational Leadership, 58*(3), 34–37.

Kaplan, M. T., & Bedell, G. (1999). Motor skill acquisition frame of reference. In P. Kramer, & J. Hinojosa (Eds.), *Frames of reference for pediatric occupational therapy* (2nd ed., pp. 401–430). Baltimore, MD: Williams and Wilkins.

Kimball, J. G. (1999). Sensory integration frame of reference: Theoretical base, function/dysfunction continua, and guide to evaluation. In P. Kramer, & J. Hinojosa (Eds.), *Frames of reference for pediatric occupational therapy* (2nd ed., pp. 119–168). Baltimore, MD: Williams and Wilkins.

Kottke, F., Halpern, D., Easton, J., Ozel, A., & Burrill, C. (1978). The training of coordination. *Archives of Physical Medicine and Rehabilitation, 59*(11), 567–572.

Larin, H. M. (2000). Motor learning: Theories and strategies for the practitioner. In S. K. Campbell, D. W. Vanderlinden, and R. J. Palisano (Eds.), *Physical therapy for children* (2nd ed., pp. 170–197). Philadelphia: W. B. Saunders Company.

McEwen, I., & Shelden, M. L. (1995). Pediatric therapy in the 1990s: The demise of the educational versus medical dichotomy. *Physical and Occupational Therapy in Pediatrics, 15*(2), 33–45.

National Association for Sport and Physical Education (1995). *Moving into the future: National standards for physical education.* Reston, VA: American Alliance for Physical Education, Recreation, and Dance.

Ott, D. D., & Effgen, S. K. (2000). Occurrence of gross motor behaviors in integrated and segregated preschool programs. *Pediatric Physical Therapy, 12*(4), 164–172.

Park, E. S., Park, C. I., & Kim, J. Y. (2001). Comparison of anterior and posterior walkers with respect to gait parameters and energy expenditure of children with spastic diplegia cerebral palsy. *Yonsei Medical Journal, 42*(2), 180–184.

President's Council on Physical Fitness and Sports. (1999, March). Physical activity and fitness for persons with disabilities. *Research Digest, 3*(5), 1–10.

President's Council on Physical Fitness and Sports. (1999, September). Physical activity promotion and school physical education. *Research Digest, 3*(7), 1–11.

Rainforth, B. (2002). The primary therapist model: Addressing challenges to practice in special education. *Physical and Occupational Therapy in Pediatrics, 22*(2), 29–51.

Rainforth, B., & York-Barr (1997). *Collaborative teams for students with severe disabilities: Integrating therapy and educational services* (2nd ed.). Paul H. Brookes Publishing Co.

Schoen, S. A., & Anderson, J. (1999). Neurodevelopmental treatment frame of reference. In P. Kramer, & J. Hinojosa (Eds.), *Frames of reference for pediatric occupational therapy* (2nd ed., pp. 83–118). Baltimore, MD: Williams and Wilkins.

Sents, B., & Marks, H. (1989). Changes in preschool children's IQ scores as a function of positioning. *American Journal of Occupational Therapy, 43*(10), 685–688.

Tardieu, C., Lespargot, A., Tabary, C., & Bret, M. D. (1988). For how long must the soleus muscle be stretched each day to prevent contracture?

Developmental Medicine and Child Neurology, 30(1), 3–10.

Tremblay, F., Malouin, F., Richards, C. L., & Dumas, F. (1990). Effects of prolonged muscle stretch on reflex and voluntary muscle activations in children with spastic cerebral palsy. *Scandinavian Journal of Rehabilitation Medicine, 22*(4), 171–180.

York, J. (1989). Mobility methods selected for use in home and community environments. *Physical Therapy, 69*(9), 736–747.

York-Barr, J., Rainforth, B., & Locke, P. (1996). Developing instructional adaptations. In F. Orelove and D. Sobsey (Eds.), *Educating students with multiple disabilities: A transdisciplinary approach* (3rd ed., pp. 119–159). Baltimore: Paul H. Brookes Publishing Co.

13

Application of the Process to Ecological Domains

Sandra Alper

Objectives

After completing this chapter, the reader will be able to:

1. Discuss similarities between the ecological curriculum domains and curriculum for students without disabilities.
2. Identify skills in the domestic, community access, vocational, and recreation/leisure domains in which the students may receive instruction in inclusive settings.
3. Describe three approaches to teaching recreation/leisure skills.
4. Apply the curriculum content identification process to the functional skill domains.
5. Discuss options for providing instruction in natural settings in the school and community.

Key Terms

Community access	Domestic skills	Recreation/leisure domain
Community-based instruction	Ecological domains	Supported employment
Criterion of ultimate functioning	Job analysis	Transition
Discrepancy analysis	Next future environment	Work domain

Certain aspects of day-to-day life are shared by all people. These include activities that occur at home, in the community, at work, and during free time. Brown et al. (1979) referred to these areas as ecological domains. They recommended a systematic analysis of these four basic life domains to develop functional curricula for students with disabilities, an approach that was described in detail in Chapter 5.

The purpose of this chapter is to discuss the development of curriculum for inclusive settings in the areas of domestic, community access, vocational, and recreation/leisure skills. First, each of the four ecological domains will be briefly reviewed with examples of skills included. Second, an explanation of the importance of teaching skills within each of these domains will be provided. Third, the curriculum content identification process will be applied to the recreation/leisure skills domain. Fourth, strategies for grouping students to facilitate instruction in natural settings in the community will be discussed.

Ecological Domains Common to General and Special Education

Teaching skills that students with disabilities require to participate fully in the community (that is, to live, work, enjoy leisure time, and have access to a variety of community settings) affords many opportunities for participation in the same activities with persons without disabilities. This is because the ecological domains share some similarities with the general education curriculum. The general education curriculum often includes courses that emphasize job skills (for example, business and industrial education classes). Students without disabilities may take courses in home economics that emphasize managing and maintaining a home, social-sexual information, and consumer skills. Many students are required or elect to take courses in physical education (PE) that emphasize skills used in leisure time such as sports activities. Finally, students without disabilities obtain information in a variety of different classes that enables them to be participating, contributing members of their community. They acquire skills necessary to be informed consumers and good citizens.

Although many students with and without disabilities learn skills that fall under the four broad life domains of home, community, work, and leisure, the specific skills taught must match the individual needs of each student. Falvey (1989) and Browder (2001) identified several considerations for targeting skills for instruction. First, one should analyze the particular settings and skill requirements of the student's home community. This is necessary because skills necessary to maintain a home, obtain and maintain a job, or engage in some leisure-time activity vary across settings within the same community, as well as across communities. Second, one should consider the individual strengths and weaknesses of the student. Any adaptations for skill performance or materials that a particular individual may require receive special attention. Third, consistent with person-centered planning, one should explore preferences of the parents and student. It is important for parents, teachers, and the student to agree on what skills become targets for instruction. Fourth, one should identify the skills that chronological age peers who do not experience disabilities perform in a number of natural settings. This maximizes opportunities available for interaction between students with and without disabilities. Fifth, one should carefully consider the question of what the student's next least restrictive environment might be and the skills necessary to transition to that setting.

Domestic Skills

Traditionally, the curriculum in domestic skills for students with disabilities has emphasized grooming, dressing, self-feeding and toileting, and basic housecleaning tasks, such as making a bed or washing dishes (cf., Eshilian, Haney, & Falvey, 1989; Snell, 1993; Snell & Brown, 2000). As more and more people with disabilities have prepared to live in the community in their natural homes, group homes, or foster homes, educators have become aware that a broader spectrum of skills is necessary to function successfully in domestic environments. Currently, the emphasis is on skill areas in the domestic domain including social-sexual skills, home management, home care, and personal health care and hygiene (Eshilian et al., 1989; Snell, 1993). Figure 13.1 includes an array of skills typical in the domestic domain.

Educational programs designed to result in acquisition, maintenance, and generalization in domestic skills are important for all students. These programs are particularly critical for persons with disabilities for several reasons. First, if people with disabilities grow up without competence in this area, they are very likely to place heavy burdens on their family members, or they may have to move to more restrictive and costly settings. This problem worsens in situations in which the person with disabilities is an adult and the primary caregivers are elderly parents.

Second, competence in the domestic domain can maximize an individual's chances of not only living in his or her home community, but in the least restrictive domestic environment within that community. For example, a person with disabilities who cannot perform simple household chores, interact appropriately with roommates or neighborhoods, or completely care for all his or her own personal hygiene needs may live in a group home with several paid professional staff. An individual who has learned to care for all personal care needs and, in addition, can clean, shop, cook, and interact appropriately with others is far more likely to live more independently, have fewer supervisors, and exercise more choice in day-to-day activities.

Third, competence in the domestic domain projects a positive image of persons with disabilities to those who are not challenged by disabilities (Eshilian et al., 1989; Falvey, 1989). The more frequently persons with disabilities openly perform normal day-to-day activities in their homes and communities means the more capable they are perceived by the general public. Gold (1972) referred to this phenomenon as the competence-deviance hypothesis. Gold maintained that, when an individual with disabilities is observed performing a functional, normalized activity competently, the public tends to focus on that person's competence and deemphasize the disability.

Community Access Skills

Having learned skills that allow people with disabilities to live in normalized homes in the community is a necessary, but not sufficient, condition to become fully participating

FIGURE 13.1   *Sample Skills in Domestic Domain*

Social Interaction	Home Care	Home Management

1. Family/Roommates
  Appropriate greetings
  Communication skills
  Sharing space and appliances
  Sharing responsibilities
  Following house rules
  Making decisions together
  Respect of others belongings
  Respect of privacy
  Acknowledgment of personal
    space
  Knowing emergency
    procedures
  Social skills/manners
2. Neighbors/Visitors
  Appropriate greetings
  Respect of property and
    privacy
  Social skills/manners
  Acknowledgement of skills
  Communication skills
  Borrowing and lending skills
3. Friends
  Telephone skills
  Communication skills
  Invitations to come over,
    meet
  Social skills/manners
  Planning foods/activities
  Transportation
  Time skills
4. Service Providers
  Social skills/manners
  Communication skills
  Acknowledging personal
    space
  Money skills
  Time Skills
	1. Meals
	  Planning what to eat
	  Purchasing
	  Locating items
	  Storage
	  Preparation
	  Clean up
	2. Eating skills
	  Table manners
	  Social skills
	  Communication skills
	  Basic skills
	3. House Cleaning
	  Appropriate usage of
	    materials
	  Acceptable level of
	    performance
	  How to perform each given
	    task (i.e., dust, make bed,
	    vacuum)
	4. Laundry
	  Storage of clean clothes
	  Storage of dirty clothes
	  Using washer
	  Using dryer
	  Sorting clothes
	  Use of detergents and bleach
	  Ironing skills
	5. Clothing
	  Daily care
	  Storage (hang, fold)
	  Choice of what to wear
	    (matching)
	  Purchasing
	  Size
	  Sewing
	  Repair
	6. Yard maintenance
	  Basic care (i.e., mowing,
	    trimming hedges)
	  Removal of trash
	  Knowing where to store tools
	  Trash-collection day
	7. Household appliances
	  Appropriate use of safety
	    measures
	  Storage
		1. Choices
		  Decisionmaking skills
		  Natural consequences
		2. Schedules/Routines
		  Following a schedule
		  Following through on tasks:
		    responsibility ownership
		  Cleaning/maintenance
		    sequence
		  Public vs. personal space
		  Natural consequences
		3. Time
		  Reference to schedule
		  Concept of
		  Use of
		  Management of
		4. Materials
		  Appropriate use of and
		    following directions
		  Purchase of
		  Storage of
		  Maintaining and replacing
		5. Organizations
		  Location of items
		  Sharing responsibilities
		  Establishing routines
		  Following a determined
		    schedule
		6. Use of home space
		  Safety and placement of
		    items
		  Accessibility
		  Personal taste

members of the community. These individuals need to have access to the same resources, facilities, and programs as persons without disabilities.

Snell (1993) identified two major areas of community access skills: mobility around the community and the use of community facilities. Traveling from place to place around the community involves a number of different means of transportation, depending on the size of the community. Riding a bus, taxi, or subway; walking from one location to another; crossing intersections and obeying traffic signs; and riding a bicycle are all examples of activities that fall in the mobility skill category. In addition, students with disabilities need to know what to do in the event that they become lost, need to ask directions, or require some type of assistance.

The age of the individual dictates use of facilities in the community. In general, the objective is to teach the student with disabilities to use the same generic community facilities as do chronological age peers without disabilities. These facilities include parks, wellness centers, playgrounds, restaurants, stores, banks, grocery and convenience stores, video arcades, public transportation, and health care services. Figure 13.2 lists many of the skills on which a student with disabilities may require instruction within the community access domain.

FIGURE 13.2   *Sample Skills Included in Community Access Domain.*

A. Mobility
   Bus: routes, times, payment/money skills, social skills
   Taxi: phone skills, dialing and telephone book skills, payment/money skills
   Friends: social skills, phone skills

B. Usage of generic community resources
   Skills used in all domains: communication, money, transportation, social, time
   1. Physician's office
   2. Dentist's office
   3. Public library
   4. Post office
   5. Public school
   6. Grocery store
   7. Convenience store
   8. Public telephone
   9. Shopping mall
   10. Public school bus
   11. Restaurants
   12. Hotels
   13. Laundromat
   14. Gymnasium
   15. Swimming pool
   16. Extracurricular activities
   17. Theaters
   18. Bowling alley
   19. Gas stations

Teaching students with disabilities to use generic resources in the community is critical if they are to remain in the least restrictive setting. This is particularly important as more and more people with disabilities either remain in their home communities or return to the community from institutional settings. Gothelf (1987) pointed out that "an important component of successful community living is a flexible network of community resources consisting of educational, social, vocational, medical, commercial, and recreational resources" (p. 146). In order for students to fully participate in their schools and communities, they should be able to use the same facilities in the same ways as people without disabilities.

The use of community resources is one indicator of participation in the neighborhood. Although use of generic community resources does not guarantee social integration with those who do not have disabilities, it is one important measure of integration in the community (Sherman, Frenkel, & Newman, 1984).

Keul, Spooner, Grossi, and Heller (1987) described a program in North Carolina for teaching people with mental retardation to use community resources. The Community Resources Training (CRT) program researchers developed three major components: (a) teaching skills necessary for independent living in the community, (b) training people with mental retardation to use generic resources in the community, and (c) involving parents and other family members in the instructional program. The Assessment of Independent Living Skills (AILS) developed by Keul, Spooner, Test, Heller, and Grossi in 1985 is the basis of the curriculum of the CRT program. This scale consists of eight clusters of skills including appropriate public behavior, grooming, social skills, use of transportation, use of sources of information in the community, leisure, time and money management, and use of generic community resources.

Vocational Skills

A number of follow-up studies of students with disabilities who have graduated from special education revealed consistently disappointing results in terms of postschool outcomes (Frank & Sitlington, 1993; Frank, Sitlington & Carson, 1992; Halpern, 1990; Halpern & Benz, 1987; Hasazi, Gordon, & Roe, 1985; Mithaug, Horiuchi, & Fanning, 1985). These studies indicated that the majority of special education graduates were not adequately prepared to work and live successfully in the community. Rather, they have moved from school to sheltered and restrictive settings with little contact with persons without disabilities. They experienced exceedingly low wages that foster dependence on welfare, long periods of inactivity, few friends, and little opportunity for training that could lead to less restrictive settings (Bishop & Falvey, 1989; Frank & Sitlington, 1993; Halpern & Benz, 1987).

Several researchers in special education and rehabilitation have developed models of transition to result in meaningful outcomes for special education graduates, including remunerative work in competitive employment (Rusch, 1986; Rusch, Destefano, Chadsey-Rusch, Phelps, & Szymanski, 1992; Wehman, 1982; Wehman & Moon, 1988; Wehman, Moon, Everson, Wood, & Barcus, 1988). Meaningful work is a valued aspect of life for most adults (Turkel, 1972). Work provides the economic ability to acquire desired items, provides outlets for meeting people and developing social interactions, structures our daily lives, helps us to formulate self-concepts, and allows us to become contributing members of society (Rusch, 1986).

The goal of teaching students with disabilities vocational skills is the same as that for their peers without disabilities. Vocational skill training should lead to competitive employment. At least three factors drive the goal of employment in competitive, rather than sheltered, job sites for people with disabilities according to Bishop and Falvey (1989). First, the results of follow-up studies, such as those cited previously, led many special educators to the conclusion that traditional sheltered employment was a costly dead end, with few opportunities for productivity. Second, researchers in the 1970s demonstrated that students, including those with severe disabilities, were capable of learning complex vocational tasks when appropriately trained (Gold, 1972; 1976; Bellamy, Horner, & Inman, 1979). Third, the trends toward normalization, social integration, and full inclusion are consistent with competitive employment.

Supported employment is the service delivery model through which students with disabilities are trained in competitive jobs. The Office of Special Education and Rehabilitative Services in 1985 launched a federal initiative to make supported employment the primary job training model for people with mental retardation. Since then, people with learning disabilities, closed head injuries, mental illness, physical disabilities, and hearing and visual impairments have received services from supported employment programs. Supported employment has the following features (Rusch, 1986; Wehman & Moon, 1988):

- Work produces valued goods or services.
- Remuneration for work is minimum wage or more.
- The job site employs workers without disabilities.
- Opportunities for advancement exist.
- A job coach accompanies the student to the actual job site in the community and provides training and support services as needed.
- Ongoing support is readily available for as long as needed.
- Interagency collaboration between special education, employers, vocational rehabilitation, and other adult service providers (case managers) is crucial.
- An emphasis is on parent and family involvement.

The following components are common to supported employment programs:

- Potential employment options in the job market in the local community are identified, including jobs that are likely to exist in a number of different locations and that have a demand for new workers.
- Specific jobs are task-analyzed into on-the-job skills; social skills; and any functional, academic, or other job-related skills necessary to obtain and maintain the job.
- Community-based training sites open at the workplace. The student receives employment skills training from a job coach.
- After training, the student works in either the training site or a similar job site.
- The employee receives ongoing training and support to ensure that he or she maintains the job and learns any new skills that might be required if the demands of

the job change in any way (for example, new equipment changes the way in which the work is performed or a new supervisor has different standards and expectations of employees).

Implications for Inclusive Educational Settings

The emphasis on supported employment programs that result in competitive employment for students with disabilities has several implications for inclusive education settings. First,

---

FIGURE 13.3   *Sample Job Analysis Format*

Job Tasks (in prioritized order)

1. Punch in at time clock in office.
2. Get job list from supervisor.

Pick Up Grounds Daily Routine

1. Get black trash bags from storage house.
2. Place trash bags in hip pocket.
3. Get pick from storage house.
4. Begin at entrance gate to apartment complex.
5. Pick up trash around buildings A-Z in order.
6. Take full trash bag to nearest dumpster.
7. Tie bag.
8. Place in dumpster.

Trim Bushes

1. Get trimming list from supervisor, who will tell which buildings' bushes need trimming.
2. Get hedge trimmers from storage house.
3. Get trash bags from storage house.
4. Go to apartment building on list, i.e., Building C.
5. Place trash bags in a pile in the grass.
6. Take trimmers and trim bush so that new growth is cut off. New growth will be a lighter green than rest of bush.
7. Continue trimming until bush is completely finished.
8. Place trimmers by trash bags on the ground.
9. Pick up trash bag.
10. Open trash bag.
11. Place trimmings in bag.
12. Fill trash bag with all trimmings until bag is full.
13. Take out list given by supervisor.
14. Check off tasks that have been completed, i.e., Building C.
15. If bag is full, tie and place in nearest dumpster.
16. Continue trimming until all bushes on the given list are completed and checked off.
17. Make sure that every building is completed and is checked off.

---

vocational curriculum has to be functional. The skills taught are those that workers actually perform on the job. The job analysis, or task analysis of a specific job, provides the basis for the curriculum. Classroom skills must be functional and directly related to the demands of competitive employment. Figure 13.3 presents a sample job analysis format.

Second, community-based training sites are critical. Students with disabilities (and many individuals without disabilities) can most effectively learn job skills only at the actual job site. Community-based training should occur on a regular basis, preferably every day. In addition to job skills, teaching skills that involve shopping, banking, social interactions, and use of public transportation should occur in the community as frequently as possible.

Third, direct and systematic instruction is necessary for teaching on-the-job and job-related skills. This includes behavioral objectives that are task-analyzed into measurable and observable responses; procedures for data collection; and instructional strategies that include shaping, prompting, reinforcement, and correction procedures.

Fourth, and perhaps most important, the collaboration of professionals from a variety of disciplines is necessary, including those in general education. It is extremely unlikely that any one discipline can achieve the outcome of competitive employment for students with disabilities. Professionals must begin to plan collaboratively for effective vocational training for students with disabilities long before graduation. The expertise of general educators needed in this process should focus on the social, functional, academic, and other job-related skills necessary to maintain employment.

Cavin, Alper, Sinclair, and Sitlington (in press) analyzed published reports of transition programs for youth with mild, moderate, and severe disabilities. Unfortunately, they found very few published program descriptions that included all four of these characteristics.

Recreation and Leisure Skills

Recreation/leisure time has been one of the most neglected areas of curriculum for students with disabilities until recently. This area has been underemphasized for several reasons. First, academic, social, and communication needs of these students were given a much higher priority than recreational skills. Some educators took the position that recreation/leisure skills could be part of the curriculum only if time permitted. Second, because some students with disabilities have physical and motor difficulties, educators often assumed them to be unable to participate in many sports activities students without disabilities enjoy. Third, during the years in which students with disabilities primarily attended separate schools and classes, there were few opportunities for recreation/leisure activities. The exception to this situation was the Special Olympics program that the Kennedy family originated in the 1960s. While this program has many advantages, including numerous opportunities for students with disabilities to participate in sports, it has not included opportunities for the participation of many students without disabilities.

Recently, there has been increased recognition of the importance of teaching students with disabilities to participate in integrated recreation/leisure activities at school and in the community. This awareness has been the result of at least two factors (Falvey & Coots, 1989). First, researchers have established that students with severe disabilities are able to learn and participate in functional and age-appropriate recreational activities (Bates

& Renzaglia, 1982; Datillo, 1991; Schleien & Meyer, 1988; Schloss, Smith, & Kiehl, 1986; Voeltz, Wuerch, & Wilcox, 1982). Second, there is value in teaching students with disabilities appropriate behaviors to replace inappropriate responses. Recreation/leisure skills can serve as acceptable replacement behaviors.

Schleien, Green, and Heyne (1993) recommended that recreation/leisure curricula have a basis in best professional practices. According to these authors, best practices in integrated recreation are "founded on the belief that every individual has the basic human right to be fully included in typical recreational activities. The community has been identified as the least restrictive environment for recreation participation" (p. 536). Recreational activities in the community afford students with disabilities opportunities for social interaction as well as development of recreation skills. The authors identified the following best professional practices:

- Individual needs assessments
- Individual preference assessments
- Activity selection guidelines
- Collateral skill development
- Environmental analyses
- Adaptations
- Ability awareness orientations and friendship training
- Cooperative grouping arrangements
- Behavioral teaching methods
- Program evaluation

Approaches to Recreation and Leisure Programs

Schleien and Green (1992) described three approaches to developing integrated, community-based recreation/leisure skills programs for students with disabilities. They contended that, although recreation programs that serve only students with disabilities are preferable to no recreation/leisure program at all, the development of socially integrated programs is most desirable.

Integration of Generic Recreation Programs

Within this approach, a student who has disabilities indicates preferences for recreation activities from among the traditional, age-appropriate activities that already exist in the community. Next, special education and general education professionals work together to identify any discrepancies between the skill requirements and environmental constraints of the activity and the capabilities of the student. Finally, the educators develop and use strategies to accommodate student participation in the activity despite the skill deficits and environmental demands. Examples of such strategies are partial participation (that is, the student participates in some, but not all, steps involved in the activity), adaptation of materials or equipment, peer tutoring, cooperative learning groups, or revision of the way in which the activity is performed.

The integration of generic recreation programs approach has several advantages over segregated programs according to Schleien et al. (1993). These include the opportunity for social contact, use of generic programs that exist within the community, and development of skills required for participation in age-appropriate recreation activities that many students without disabilities enjoy. A major disadvantage is that the very strategies designed to enable the student with disabilities to participate in the activity may call undue attention to his or her differences and attract negative attention from others.

Reverse Mainstreaming

The second approach to developing integrated recreation programs in the community is reverse mainstreaming. Within this approach, which some Special Olympics programs have adopted, educators make efforts to attract students without disabilities to activities originally established for students with disabilities. First, they identify the needs and interests of students without disabilities relative to recreation/leisure activities. Then, they make modifications to the program to attract the interest of and maintain participation by individuals without disabilities.

Advantages of this approach include opportunities for social interactions and friendships. Students with disabilities stay in the same programs to which they may have grown accustomed and in which they feel comfortable. Schleien et al. (1993) noted several disadvantages to the reverse mainstream approach. Among these are the sporadic, rather than ongoing, nature of the program and the difficulty in attracting large numbers of students without disabilities into programs originally designed for those with disabilities.

Zero Exclusion

The newest approach to developing integrated, community recreation/leisure-time programs that serve all students is the zero exclusion approach (Schleien & Green, 1992). Within this approach, special and general education professionals collaborate to design, develop, and implement new programs that will attract and serve all interested students regardless of ability level. This is the most inclusionary of the three approaches Schleien and Green (1992) describe.

The zero exclusion approach to recreation programs requires a commitment from educators, as well as the larger community, to serve all students within one program. It avoids more costly duplication of services often found in dual-service delivery systems, that is, separate services for different groups of people. The need for programs using this approach grows as more and more students with disabilities are enabled to live, go to school, and work in the same community settings as those without disabilities.

Schleien et al. (1993) observed that zero exclusion programs are not free of disadvantages. These programs typically have higher initial start-up costs. In addition, they may generate fears among some parents and professionals that segregated programs will be either eliminated or watered down as a result of decreasing revenues.

I have reviewed the areas of domestic, community access, vocational, recreation/leisure skills, and the ecological curriculum domains that have parallels in the general education curriculum. The content of each of these domains was described along with the critical need for these skills to be learned by students who have disabilities. A detailed description of specific instructional strategies for each curriculum domain is beyond the scope of this text. The interested reader is referred to the excellent and comprehensive discussions of teaching strategies found in Cipani and Spooner (1994), Falvey (1989), Snell (1993), Snell and Brown (2000), and Westling and Fox (2000). In the next section of this chapter, the curriculum content identification process is applied to the recreation/leisure skill domain.

Application of the Curriculum Content Identification Process to the Recreation and Leisure Domain

Several key characteristics of activities should be stressed when developing curriculum for students with disabilities in the recreation/leisure domain. First, activities must be functional. Schleien et al. (1993) recommended that to develop the palmar grasp, for example, the student should engage in functional activities such as riding a bicycle or throwing a Frisbee.

Second, recreational activities should be age appropriate and attractive to peers without disabilities. As in all areas of curriculum for students with disabilities, there must be many opportunities for social interaction and friendship. The recreation/leisure domain offers many naturally occurring opportunities in which students with and without disabilities may share mutually enjoyable activities.

Third, recreational activities students with disabilities learn should be readily accessible and ongoing. Activities that occur infrequently (for example, a skiing trip or a float trip) are enjoyable, but unlikely to be part of a regular routine due to cost or availability. If they are the only recreational activities available, there will be few opportunities for participating in recreation and interacting with peers.

Finally, selection of recreation/leisure activities should be based on the student's choice of activities. By definition, leisure time is freedom from activities of which the individual has little or no choice. Having the freedom to engage in the activity makes it enjoyable and increases the probability that it will become part of a regular routine. Some students with disabilities have limited choice repertoires due to lack of exposure or experience with certain activities. Nevertheless, educators should make every effort to allow students to express preferences for leisure pursuits.

The first step in the curriculum content identification process is to gather information to identify functional recreation/leisure needs of the student. Information from a variety of sources, including community and family, is necessary (Browder, 2001). Table 5.3 in Chapter 5 (Community Inventory Worksheet) is useful to survey the community and determine what generic recreational opportunities are available. Figure 13.4 illustrates how this format can assess the availability of community recreational activities for a 12-year-old student with mental retardation and challenging behaviors, such as verbal and physical aggression.

The next step in the curriculum content identification process is to gather information to identify general education curriculum needs. The General Education Curriculum Content Worksheet can be helpful here. The activities and objectives in the general

FIGURE 13.4 *Community Inventory Worksheet Domain: Leisure Skills*

A. Resource: Bowling Alley-Oakland Lanes

   Location: 2116 Vandiver

   Activities: Bowling, roller skating, pool tables, video games, snack bar

   Clientele: Older adults, middle-aged adults, younger adults, college students, teenagers, children

   Dress code and
   average dress: Shirt and shoes required, pants/shorts, socks, shoes (either own bowling shoes or rental for bowling participation)

   Hours: M-F, Saturday, and Sunday hours open 10:00 a.m., closed between hours of 11 p.m. and 2 a.m.

   Travel: Approximately 15 miles round trip

   Accessibility: Ramp to the door, level flooring, ramp to bowling lanes, no automatic doors

B. Resource: Albert-Oakland Swimming Pool

   Location: 1900 Blue Ridge Road

   Activities: Swimming, diving boards, laying out in the sun, bring own games from home, pool games (i.e., tag, Marco Polo)

   Costs: Youth
                        Teen
                        Adult

   Clientele: High to low SES, older adults, middle-aged adults, younger adults, college students, teenagers, youth, infants

   Dress code and
   average dress: Bathing suits, wraps, (change to casual clothes, sandals or tennis shoes, bathing cap, goggles, floatation devices)

   Hours: Monday-Sunday

   Travel: Approximately 10 miles to and fro

   Accessibility: Ramps, level concrete to pool (has reservoir along edges), steps and ladders to get in and out of pool from edge, ladders to reach diving board, changing and shower and restroom area is accessible

C. Resource: Wellness Center

   Location: UNI campus

   Activities: Indoor track for walking, jogging, running, wheelchair accessible, basketball, volleyball, racquetball, tennis, weight lifting, stationary bike and stepper, aerobics, mats available for exercise (i.e., sit ups, push ups, warm-up exercises, wall exercises), spectator area for sitting and watching games, badminton, paddle ball, handball

   Locker rooms: Showers, restrooms, saunas, lockers, changing area

   Cost: $5.00 for pass, students enrolled use student ID

   Clientele: students, professors, teenagers, youths

   Dress code and
   average dress: Sweats, tee shirt, shorts, socks, tennis shoes

FIGURE 13.5   *General Education Curriculum Content Worksheet*

| | | Settings and Activities for Application | | |
Expected Outcomes	Components Relevant	General Education	Home	Community
Skill: Putting models together Integration: Work with peers Can be an individual or small group activity that can facilitate use of communication skills	Eye-hand coordination Age-appropriateness Shopping skills Money skills Social skills Communication skills Decisionmaking skills	Math skills Communication skills	Communication skills Time to spend by self Quiet leisure time Social skills	Interaction with peers without disabilities Shopping skills Money skills Social skills Transportation skills
Skill: Video/arcade games Integration: Interaction with peers without disabilities Can be performed in home setting	Transportation to arcade in community Eye-hand coordination Money skills Social skills Communication skills Age-appropriate activity	Social skills Communication skills Money skills Problem-solving techniques	Communication skills Social skills engaged individually or with family member	Interaction with peers without disabilities Social skills Money skills Communication skills
Skill: Swimming Integration: Lessons with peers without disabilities	Swimming skills learned and developed in swimming lessons: floating, kicking	Extracurricular activities Swim team	Communication with family and peers Exercise/fitness routine Parties (birthday)	Oakland Pool Twin Lakes Camping or float trips Vacationing

education curriculum and other settings are entered on the inventory. An example of a completed worksheet for the 12-year-old student is Figure 13.5.

After one identifies the functional and general education goals, a blending of both content areas may occur to establish the final annual goals and the education settings. Schleien et al. (1993) described a discrepancy analysis procedure that blends functional and general education recreational skills content. This process first analyzes recreational activities in which students without disabilities engage at school and in the community into the component steps necessary to complete the task. Then, discrepancies in performance between students with and without disabilities are noted. Finally, any necessary adaptations of the task or materials that will allow the student with disabilities to participate in the task are identified. Figure 13.6 describes the completion of this procedure for a student with disabilities.

Facilitating Community-Based Instruction

This text emphasizes the importance of teaching functional skills in the settings in which they naturally occur. Teaching in natural settings is necessary because many students with disabilities have difficulties in performing skills learned in one setting in other, untrained settings. Because of these generalization difficulties, there is no guarantee that students will be able to perform skills learned in the classroom in any other setting.

The natural setting for many skills includes the classroom and other environments within the school. School settings provide many naturally occurring opportunities for students to perform social interaction skills; functional money, time, and measurement skills; and functional reading tasks. Many skills in the domestic, vocational, community access, and recreation/leisure domains, however, normally occur outside of school settings. Educators are then faced with the need to provide instruction in nonschool settings, while, at the same time, meeting the needs of students remaining in the classroom. Two examples follow.

Austin is a ten-year-old student with severe mental retardation. He is able to communicate verbally using short phrases and can feed himself. His mother is a working single parent who has two younger children. The family usually has dinner at a fast-food restaurant two nights each week. Austin's mother would like him to learn how to order his meal, find a place to sit down, and eat dinner without assistance.

Alicia is 16 years old and has moderate mental retardation and a seizure disorder. Her family wants Alicia to be able to work in competitive employment. There is a job-training site for Alicia in the kitchen of the local hospital. Alicia will need to spend two hours each school day at the hospital kitchen with her job coach. The hospital is located approximately three miles from her school.

Targeting Settings for Instruction

Selecting appropriate settings for instruction is as important as identifying the necessary functional and age-appropriate skills. Instruction for some skills (for example, writing

FIGURE 13.6 *Discrepancy Analysis*

Name: Jasper L.
Domain: Leisure
Environment: Community
Subenvironment: Skate town
Activity: Roller skating and
appropriate interaction with
people in the community

Directions: Read the steps in the ecological inventory on the left and use the System of Least Prompts to collect data on which steps can be done: I (Independently), M (through Modeling the behavior), V (with Verbal assistance), T (with a Tactile cue), or H (with Hand-over-Hand assistance). Mark the level of assistance needed to perform the step in the middle column. Identify a teaching procedure, adaptation, or strategy to increase the independence level or partial participation of the individual when performing that step in the right column.

1. Enter the skating rink.	I	1. No adaptations needed.
2. Wait in line to pay for admittance.	I	2. No adaptations needed.
3. Give the cashier the correct amount of money using the next dollar strategy.	V	3. Needs practice on using the next dollar strategy across all situations/settings.
4. Smile and use appropriate gestures.	I	4. Good greeting skills, needs practice saying "Thank you" and "excuse me" when necessary.
5. Remove shoes and give to counter attendant.	V	5. Practice going to the skating rink more.
6. Take skates and find appropriate skate size.	I	6. No adaption needed.
7. Put on and lace up skates.	I	7. Motor problems make this time consuming, but he can still do independently.
8. Skate over to rink on carpet.	H	8. Just needs practice skating and prompting.
9. Enter rink appropriately.	H	9. Needs practice entering rink. Holds onto rails and staff.
10. Skate on rink appropriately.	H	10. Practice skating and encourage to let go of wall.
11. Remain calm during falls.	V	11. Stick to behavior plan, practice skating, and leave rink, if necessary.
12. Interact appropriately with others.	V	12. Model and practice.
13. Get off skating rink appropriately.	H	13. Practice skating and getting off rink without staff assistance.
14. Unlace skates and return to attendant. Receive shoes from attendant.	V	14. Practice routine to follow at rink.
15. Put on shoes.	I	15. No adaptations needed.
16. Exit skating rink.	I	16. No adaptations needed.
17. Follow staff instructions at all times.	V	17. Follow behavior plan. Make clear to student that he will have to leave for inappropriate behavior.

a name) can be provided almost entirely within the classroom. Instruction in other skills may occur in both classroom and community settings. Austin may work on using money in the classroom and school cafeteria, as well as in fast-food restaurants. Still other skills are appropriately taught only in the natural community setting in which they occur, as in the case of operating a dish-washing machine in a hospital cafeteria. These skills are difficult or impossible to re-create or simulate in the school setting. The stimulus conditions (for example, supervisors, coworkers, and materials) present in the work site will not be present at school.

Determining the Amount of Time Allotted for Community Training

Brown et al. (1979) and Sailor et al. (1986) argued that time spent in community-based training settings should increase as students with disabilities become older. This is because, as chronological age increases, there is more emphasis on performing functional skills necessary to work and live in the community and less emphasis on academic skills. Although elementary students may spend most or all of the school day in school, secondary students may be in community training sites for the majority of their instructional time.

In many secondary programs, the goal is for students to be working full time in a competitive job site and have well-developed plans for living arrangements by the time they are high school seniors. This makes the transition from school to adult life in the community easier for students with disabilities and their families. Young adults with disabilities often require services that professionals from a variety of agencies offer. Many families find that these services are easier to access and coordinate while the student is still in school.

Shared Responsibilities

Community-based instruction requires teamwork and cooperation. All involved must meet the needs of students remaining in the classroom and those receiving instruction in community sites. Educators must carefully consider how to group students for instruction in nonschool settings and who will provide instruction.

Most authorities agree that instruction in any one community-based setting should be provided to small groups of students or, in some cases, on an individual basis (Snell, 1993). Two to four students may receive instruction from one adult. Small, heterogeneous groups of students may be formed. One student who requires a great deal of the teacher's time may be part of a group in which all the other students require less of the instructor's time. Many teachers stagger community-based instruction so that a few students are in the community with a teacher while another teacher or aide stays in the classroom.

A number of different individuals may provide instruction in community-based sites. Teachers and related services personnel such as physical therapists, paraprofessionals, peer tutors, volunteers, practicum students, and student teachers may provide instruction. Individuals without disabilities who are normally in the community setting (for example, a coworker on a job site, a child in the playground, or a clerk in a store) sometimes spontaneously provide assistance. It is extremely important to specify exactly who is responsible for providing instruction to the student before implementing community-based training.

Jorgensen (1992) and Browder (2001) presented formats for systematically analyzing instructional periods in inclusive schools and specifying activities that normally occur, what the student with disabilities is expected to do during the activity, and the exact responsibilities of any individual who provides support to the student. These formats would be appropriate for use in community-based and school settings.

Transportation

The availability of reliable transportation is a major consideration in selecting training sites. Transportation between the school and community training sites may be provided in a number of different ways. Snell (1993) discussed the use of teachers' and paraprofessionals' private automobiles, assuming adequate insurance coverage; school bus or van; public transportation; and walking.

Safety Issues

Parents and school officials often express concerns in the planning phases of community-based instruction. Concerns about students getting lost or approached by strangers, insurance coverage in case of injury in the community, and how the general public will treat students with disabilities are common. Students can get instruction on what to do if lost or in need of assistance. Students with disabilities may receive training in how to ask for assistance, call 911, and show a laminated ID card. Staff involved in community-based instruction can be trained in emergency medical procedures. Some teachers have shadowed their students in the community by having them unobtrusively observed by individuals unknown to the students. This can be a very effective method to assess periodically the degree of safety and capabilities of students in the community.

Snell (1993) suggested that school personnel check their insurance coverage before implementing instruction in the community. Parents must have complete information about community instruction, and they must give permission in writing.

Although the general public may, at times, ridicule or tease students with disabilities, the reverse situation is also true. Educators involved in community-based instruction often observe many individuals who are helpful and friendly to students with disabilities.

Summary

The emphasis in this chapter has been on developing curriculum content for students with disabilities in ecological domains. These areas, or domains, are domestic, community access, vocational, and recreation/leisure. These areas of the curriculum are important for several reasons. First, they include the functional skills that are necessary for students with disabilities to learn to live, work, and recreate in normal community-based settings. Second, they increase the level of competence of students with disabilities in many of the same life activities that all people perform. Viewing students with disabilities perform competently can result in more positive attitudes held by people without disabilities. Finally, because these curriculum domains contain skills and activities performed by all people, they offer increased opportunities for social interaction between those with and without disabilities.

References

Bates, P., & Renzaglia, A. (1982). Language instruction with a profoundly retarded adolescent: The use of a table game in the acquisition of verbal labeling skills. *Education and Treatment of Children, 5*(1), 13–22.

Bellamy, G. T., Horner, H., & Inman, D. (1979). *Vocational habilitation of severely retarded adults: A direct service technology.* Baltimore: University Park Press.

Bishop, K. D., & Falvey, M. A. (1989). Employment skills. In M. A. Falvey (Ed.), *Community-based curriculum: Instructional strategies for students with severe handicaps.* (2nd ed., pp. 165–187). Baltimore, MD: Paul H. Brookes Publishing Co.

Browder, D. (2001). *Alternate assessment for students with moderate to severe disabilities.* Boston: Allyn and Bacon.

Brown, L., Branston, M., Hamre-Nietupski, S., Pumpian, I., Certo, N., & Gruenwald, L. (1979). A strategy for developing chronological age appropriate and functional curricular content for severely handicapped adolescents and young adults. *Journal of Special Education, 13*(1), 81–90.

Cavin, M., Alper, S., Sinclair, T., & Sitlington, P. (in press). School to adult life: An analysis of transition programs serving youth with disabilities between 1986 and 1999. *Journal of Vocational Special Needs Education.*

Cipani, E. C., & Spooner, F. (1994). *Curricular approaches for persons with severe disabilities.* Boston: Allyn & Bacon.

Datillo, J. (1991). Mental retardation. In D. Austin & M. Crawford (Eds.), *Therapeutic recreation: An introduction* (pp. 163–188). Englewood Cliffs, NJ: Prentice-Hall.

Eshilian, L., Haney, M., & Falvey, M. A. (1989). Domestic skills. In M. A. Falvey (Ed.), *Community-based curriculum: Instructional strategies for students with severe handicaps,* (2nd ed., pp. 115–140). Baltimore: Paul H. Brookes Publishing Co.

Falvey, M. A. (1989). *Community-based curriculum: Instructional strategies for students with severe handicaps,* (2nd ed.). Baltimore, MD: Paul H. Brookes Publishing Co.

Falvey, M. A., & Coots, J. (1989). Recreation skills. In M. A. Falvey (Ed.), *Community-based curriculum: Instructional strategies for students with severe handicaps* (2nd ed., pp. 141–163). Baltimore, MD: Paul H. Brookes Publishing Co.

Frank, A. R., & Sitlington, P. L. (1993). Graduates with mental disabilities: The story three years later. *Education and Training in Mental Retardation, 28,* 30–37.

Frank, A., Sitlington, P., & Carson, R. (1992). Adult adjustment of persons with severe/profound mental disabilities: A longitudinal study. *Journal of Developmental and Physical Disabilities, 4,* 37–50.

Gold, M. (1972). Stimulus factors in skill training of the retarded on a complex assembly task: Acquisition, transfer, and retention. *American Journal of Mental Deficiency, 76,* 516–526.

Gold, M. W. (1976). Task analysis of a complex assembly task by the retarded blind. *Exceptional Children, 43,* 78–84.

Gothelf, C. R. (1987). The availability of community resources to group homes in New York City. In R. F. Antonak & J. A. Mulick (Eds.), *Transitions in mental retardation: The community imperative revisited* (Vol. 3, pp. 146–164). Norwood, NJ: Ablex.

Halpern, A. (1990). A methodological review of follow-up and follow-along studies tracking school leavers from special education. *Career Development for Exceptional Individual, 13*(1), 13–27.

Halpern, A., & Benz, M. (1987). A statewide examination of secondary special education for students with mild disabilities: Implications for the high school curriculum. *Exceptional Children, 54,* 122–129.

Hasazi, S., Gordon, L., & Roe, C. (1985). Factors associated with the employment status of handicapped youth exiting high school from 1979 to 1983. *Exceptional Children, 51,* 455–469.

Jorgensen, C. M. (1992). Natural supports in inclusive schools. In J. Nisbet (Ed.), *Natural supports in school, at work, and in the community for people with disabilities* (pp. 179–215). Baltimore: Paul H. Brookes Publishing Co.

Keul, P. K., Spooner, F., Grossi, T. A., & Heller, H. W. (1987). The community resources training program: A collaborative program between the University of North Carolina at Charlotte and Goodwill Industries of the Southern Piedmont. In R. F. Antonak & J. A. Mulick (Eds.), *Transitions in mental retardation: The community imperative revisited* (Vol. 3, pp. 183–201). Norwood, NJ: Ablex.

Keul, P. K., Spooner, F., Test, D. W., Heller, H. W., & Grossi, T. (1985). *Assessment of Independent Living Skills* (AILS). Unpublished manuscript, University of North Carolina at Charlotte, College of Education and Allied Professions, Charlotte, NC.

Mithaug, D., Horiuchi, C., & Fanning, P. (1985). A report on the Colorado statewide follow-up survey of special education students. *Exceptional Children, 51*, 397–404.

Rusch, F. R. (1986). *Competitive employment issues and strategies.* Baltimore, MD: Paul H. Brookes Publishing Co.

Rusch, F. R., Destefano, L., Chadsey-Rusch, J., Phelps, L. A., & Szymanski, E. (1992). *Transition from school to adult life.* Sycamore, IL: Sycamore Publishing Co.

Sailor, W., Halvorsen, A., Anderson, J., Goetz, L., Gee, K., Doering, K., & Hunt, P. (1986). Community intensive instruction. In R. Homer, L. Meyer, & B. Fredericks (Eds.), *Education of learners with severe handicaps* (pp. 251–288). Baltimore: Paul H. Brookes Publishing Co.

Schleien, S., & Green, F. (1992). Three approaches for integrating persons with disabilities into community recreation. *Journal of Park and Recreation Administration, 10*(2), 51–66.

Schleien, S. J., Green, F. R, & Heyne, L. A. (1993). Integrated community recreation. In M. E. Snell (Ed.), *Instruction of students with severe disabilities*, (4th ed., pp. 526–555). New York: Charles E. Merrill.

Schleien, S., & Meyer, L. (1988). Community-based recreation programs for persons with severe developmental disabilities. In M. Powers (Ed.), *Expanding systems of service delivery for persons with developmental disabilities* (pp. 93–112). Baltimore: Paul H. Brookes Publishing Co.

Schloss, P. J., Smith, M. A., & Kiehl, W. (1986). Rec club: A community centered approach to recreational development for adults with mild to moderate retardation. *Education and Training of the Mentally Retarded, 21*(4), 282–288.

Sherman, S., Frenkel, E., & Newman, E. (1984). Foster family care for older persons who are mentally retarded. *Mental Retardation, 6*, 302–308.

Snell, M. E. (1993). *Instruction of students with severe disabilities* (4th ed.). New York: Charles E. Merrill.

Snell, M. E., & Brown, F. (2000). *Instruction of students with severe disabilities* (5th ed.). New York: Charles E. Merrill.

Turkel, S. (1972). *Working.* New York: Pantheon.

Voeltz, L. M., Wuerch, B. B., & Wilcox, B. (1982). Leisure and recreation: Preparation for independence, integration, and self-fulfillment. In B. Wilcox & G. T. Bellamy (Eds.), *Design of high school programs for severely handicapped students* (pp. 175–209). Baltimore: Paul H. Brookes Publishing Co.

Wehman, P. (1982). *Life beyond the classroom: Transition strategies for young people with disabilities.* Baltimore: Paul H. Brookes Publishing Co.

Wehman, P., & Moon, M. S. (1988). *Vocational rehabilitation and supported employment.* Baltimore, MD: Paul H. Brookes Publishing Co.

Wehman, P., Moon, M. S., Everson, J. M., Wood, M., & Barcus, M. (1988). *Transition from school to work: New challenges for youth with severe disabilities,* Baltimore: Paul H. Brookes Publishing Co.

Westling, D. L., & Fox, L. (2000). *Teaching students severe disabilities* (2nd ed.). Upper Saddle River, NJ: Merrill Prentice Hall.

Acknowledgement

The author acknowledges the contributions made by Nicole Werner and Michelle Meenahan in developing the figures presented in this chapter.

14

Promoting the Self-Determination of Students with Severe Disabilities

Martin Agran and Michael Wehmeyer

Objectives

After completing this chapter, the reader will be able to:

1. Discuss the importance of self-determination.
2. Define self-determination.
3. Identify the component elements of self-determination.
4. Describe strategies to assess preferences and to promote choice-making for students with severe disabilities.
5. Describe the student-directed learning strategies associated with self-determination.
6. Discuss the importance of teaching students to problem solve.
7. Discuss how student-directed learning strategies can promote access to the general curriculum for students with moderate to severe disabilities.

Key Terms

Goal setting
Problem solving
Self-determination
Self-determined learning model
   of instruction

Self-evaluation
Self-instruction
Self-monitoring

Self-regulation
Self-reinforcement
Student-directed learning

Promoting Self-Determination

Best practice in the education of students with disabilities since 1990 has included a focus on promoting and enhancing self-determination, but what do we mean when we use this term (Agran & Hughes, 1998; Wehmeyer, 1998)?

There is no question that self-determination is a complex construct with meanings, at least within the field of disability, that are intertwined. A number of models or theories of self-determination have emerged during the last decade that either implicitly or explicitly address people with severe disabilities (Wehmeyer, 2001; Wehmeyer, Abery, Mithaug, Powers, & Stancliffe, in press). Suffice it to say, it means teaching *people or peoples ways to control their lives and their destinies*. It is both that simple and that complex.

Most definitions of self-determination in the educational literature focus on the specific behaviors or actions in which people engage that, in turn, enable them to exert control over their lives. We suggest, however (Sands & Wehmeyer, 1996; Wehmeyer 1996a; 1998), that one cannot define self-determination only as a set of skills or behaviors, but instead must look at the function of that behavior in the person's life. People who are self-determined act in ways that enable them to achieve desired goals and to enhance their quality of life. Virtually any action or behavior can be applied to achieve that end. Reflecting this emphasis, Wehmeyer (1996b) defined self-determination as *"acting as the primary causal agent in one's life and making choices and decisions regarding one's quality of life free from undue external influence or interference"* (p. 24). Broadly defined, *causal agency* implies that it is the individual who makes or causes things to happen in his or her life. A *causal agent* is someone who makes or causes things to happen in his or her life. Self-determined people act as the causal agent in their lives. They act with intent to shape their futures and their destiny.

Self-determination emerges across the life span as children and adolescents learn skills and develop attitudes that enable them to become causal agents in their own lives. These attitudes and abilities are the component elements of self-determination, and it is this level of the theoretical framework that drives instructional activities. As they acquire these component elements, individuals become increasingly self-determined. Figure 14.1 lists these elements.

FIGURE 14.1   *Component Elements of Self-Determined Behavior*

Choice-making skills
Decision-making skills
Problem-solving skills
Goal-setting and attainment skills
Self-observation, self-evaluation, and self-reinforcement skills
Self-instruction skills
Self-advocacy and leadership skills
Internal locus of control
Positive attributions of efficacy and outcome expectancy
Self-awareness
Self-knowledge

A complete discussion of each of these component elements is not feasible within the context of this chapter (see Wehmeyer, Agran, & Hughes, 1998). However, describing the component elements is important for two reasons. First, it is this level at which instruction occurs, that is, instructional strategies, methods, materials, and supports enable educators to teach self-determination by enhancing student capacity in each of these areas. Wehmeyer, Agran, and Hughes (1998) identified literally hundreds of methods, materials, and supports to promote these component elements. Second, each of these component elements has a unique developmental course or is acquired through specific learning experiences. It is by describing the development of each of these component elements that we can describe the development of self-determination (Doll, Sands, Wehmeyer, & Palmer, 1996; Wehmeyer, Sands, Doll & Palmer, 1997). The development and acquisition of these component elements is lifelong and begins when children are very young. Some elements have greater applicability for secondary education and transition, while others will focus more on elementary years. As such, promoting self-determination as an educational outcome will require not only a purposeful instructional program, but one that coordinates learning experiences across the span of a student's educational experience.

Efforts to promote self-determination for all students, whether they have a disability or not, focus on skills and knowledge enhancement in these component elements and on providing opportunities to exert control in one's life, as depicted in Figure 14.2. There are several issues to consider in relation to promoting self-determination for students with severe disabilities. First of all, it is safe to say that people with severe disabilities learn fewer and less complex skills than their nondisabled peers and may not be able to acquire the knowledge or skills that would enable them to make complex decisions or solve complex problems independently. Nevertheless, there are portions of the decision-making process or the problem-solving process in which students with severe disabilities can participate, thus maximizing their participation in these activities and making them *more* self-determined. Second, one important component of self-determined behavior is expressing preferences and acting according to those preferences. All people, independent of the level or severity of their disability, can express preferences and make choices, and promoting self-determination for students with severe disabilities must include a focus on choice-making and preferences. Third, there is a broad literature with robust findings on the use of self-management strategies by people with severe disabilities to promote greater productivity and enhanced independence. We have reframed these strategies as student-directed learning strategies (as opposed to teacher- or other-directed instructional strategies) and have shown that teaching students with severe disabilities how to self-direct learning and task performance is a powerful means of promoting self-determination for this population (Agran, 1997).

Assessing Interests and Preferences and Promoting Choice Making

More than any other component element of self-determined behavior, choice making, and the right of people with disabilities to make choices, has been a focal point in the self-determination movement. Like all of us, people with disabilities have preferences (Benz & McAllister, 1990; Brown, Belz, Corsi, & Wenig, 1993). Unlike most citizens,

A functional model of self-determination.

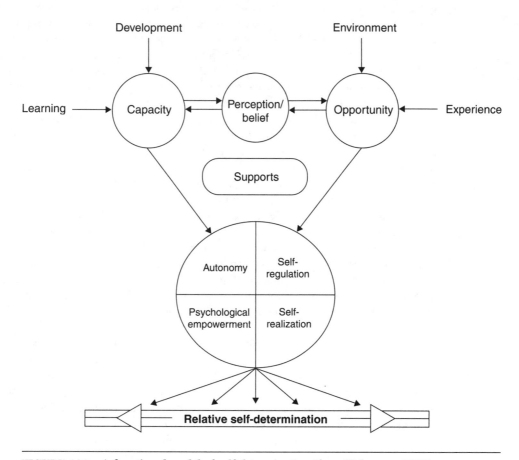

FIGURE 14.2   *A functional model of self-determination (from Wehmeyer, 1998).*

however, people with disabilities too frequently do not have the opportunity to make choices and decisions based on their own preferences (Stancliffe & Abery, 1997; Stancliffe & Wehmeyer, 1995; Wehmeyer & Metzler, 1995). The reasons that individuals do not make choices based on individual preferences vary, but the experience of lacking choice-making opportunities appears to be universal (Wehmeyer & Metzler, 1995).

For individuals with more significant disabilities, there are multiple barriers to choice making. Because many individuals with severe disabilities have too few opportunities, they do not know how to make choices and need targeted, systematic instruction on this skill. Other individuals with severe disabilities do not express their preferences though conventional means and also have limited opportunities to express their choices

(Brown et al., 1993; Dattilo & Rusch, 1985). The essence of the problem is not that people with disabilities do not have preferences, but that professionals, family members, and others are not always able to recognize the problematic behavior as an expression of preferences (Dattilo & Mirenda, 1987). Unwittingly, teachers may believe that they are protecting students by preventing them from the risks resulting from experiencing the consequences of poor choices (Bannerman, Sheldon, Sherman, & Harchik, 1990; Brown et al., 1993; Ficker-Terrill & Rowitz, 1991; Perske, 1972).

Preference and choice, although related, are not synonymous. The latter, choice-making, consists of two distinct components: (a) the identification of a preference and (b) the act of communicating that preference (Parsons & Reid, 1990). Typically, the means by which individuals express preferences are by verbally identifying the preferred option. However, for individuals with more significant disabilities and limited communication skills, preference must often be inferred from the act of choosing. People, places, or things that are chosen consistently over time typically are considered to be preferred or more highly valued by an individual than other options (Newton, Horner, & Lund, 1991).

Because of limited verbal or communication skills or lack of experience or practice in expressing themselves, students with severe disabilities often cannot tell important others what their preferences are (Hughes, Pitkin, & Lorden, 1998). Sometimes, practitioners must infer preferences from a student's behavior when a student responds to situations in which choices are presented. However, several methods have been found effective. These include the activation of a microswitch; approach toward an object; verbalizations, signing, gestures, vocalizations, or affect; physical selection of an item; task performance; and time engaged with an item. The next section of this chapter provides an overview of strategies that have been proven effective at (a) assessing the preferences and choices of students with disabilities and (b) teaching choice-making skills.

Activation of a Microswitch

A strategy that is gaining attention is to teach people with limited use of their bodies to use whatever physical movement they can make to activate a microswitch to indicate a choice among one or two items or activities. Dattilo (1986) taught three students with severe mental retardation, sensory and motor impairments, and no expressive verbal communication skills to activate microswitches connected to a computer software program. Activation of a microswitch by a slight movement of a student's body (for example, raising arm) resulted in the activation of a choice of one of two options (for example, video scenes, vibrating pad, or taped music).

Approach Toward an Object

Assessing preferences using the approach strategy may easily be used with any student, with or without a disability. A teacher simply needs to note, across time, which items, activities, materials, or events students tend to approach in a situation in which all choices are equally and readily available (for example, free time).

Verbalizations, Gestures, and Affect

For students who have expressive communication skills, indications of preferences and choices may include a variety of expressive behavior, including verbalizations, manual signing, physical gestures, vocalizations, or physical affect. Needless to say, these responses are highly individualistic. However, an advantage of using verbal responses as an indication of a preference is that the preferred item need not always be present in the environment in order to query a student regarding a preference (for example, asking a student if she would like to go swimming at the lake).

Physical Selection of an Item

The preferences of students with disabilities also can be assessed by observing whether they physically select (for example, pick up) an item when it is presented. This strategy requires that the item be present in the environment for the student to select, which may limit the variety of choices that can be offered. However, the range of options can be expanded by presenting items representational of an activity, event, or situation. For example, a ticket to a baseball game could represent the opportunity to see a game, or a book of coupons could represent the opportunity to go grocery shopping.

Task Performance

Another strategy for measuring preference that requires the physical presence of a choice item is observing a student's performance of a specific task. The task-performance strategy is based on the principle of positive reinforcement, which indicates that people are more likely to perform a behavior if the consequence of the behavior is an activity, event, or item that they prefer. Preference for a particular consequence is inferred from its reinforcing effect on an individual's performance. For example, by observing the performance of any student in class, with or without disabilities, a teacher could determine if getting good grades is a reinforcing (preferred) consequence for the student.

Time Engaged with an Item

Preference for items or activities also has been inferred from the amount of time that a student has continued to be engaged with a particular item in comparison to time spent with other items or activities. Kennedy and Haring (1993) used a time-engagement strategy when they assessed the preferences of four students with profound multiple disabilities. The amount of time the student was engaged with the item during a one-minute opportunity was noted and compared with time spent with other items. Engagement with an item was defined as a student physically touching the item with his or her hand or arm or facing the item. Findings showed that each student had definite preferences for interacting more with some items than others.

The time-engagement strategy for assessing preferences could be used with all students. For example, a teacher or parent could observe the amount of time a student spends on different leisure activities during periods of free time across several weeks. If a student spends considerable time talking with peers on the phone instead of conversing with family members or watching television during his or her free time, one could assume that talking to peers is a preferred activity for that student.

Observing Students' Responses over Time

In assessing a student's preferences, it is important to observe the choices a student makes across an extended period of time. For example, a student may prefer to listen to rock music for several weeks in a row and then change to a preference for country music. Shifts in preference should not be surprising when one considers that, after recent access to one type of event or activity, a student may become bored or disinterested and want a change. Consequently, preferences may not be evident immediately. In order to get a true picture of a student's preferences, it is important to observe the choices a student makes across an extended period of time.

Promoting Self-Determined Behavior

The following section of this chapter presents an overview of strategies used to teach students with severe disabilities to self-regulate learning and task performance and their role in promoting access to the general curriculum. Teaching students to use such self-directed learning strategies provides, we believe, a powerful mechanism to promote self-direction and self-determination. Most important, performance of these strategies may modify teachers' and parents' expectations about students, and this, in turn, may increase opportunities, both in school and at home, to promote student self-determination.

Student-Directed Learning Strategies

Student-directed learning strategies, alternatively referred to as self-regulated learning or self-determination strategies, involve teaching students to modify and regulate their own behavior (Agran, 1997). Such strategies enable students to regulate their own behavior, independent of external control, and allow students to become active participants in their own learning, a valued outcome of the school reform movement. Indeed, to advance the participation of students with disabilities into general education, Fisher, Sax, and Jorgensen (1998) suggest that students need to be taught to become self-directed learners. To do so, they need to learn strategies that will allow them to problem-solve; retrieve, process, and synthesize information; and manage their own behavior; in other words, student-directed learning strategies.

Student-directed learning strategies have demonstrated educational efficacy across a wide age range of learning and adaptive skills and students with a variety of disabilities and have been well-validated and supported in the literature (see Agran, 1997; Agran & Wehmeyer, 1999; King-Sears & Carpenter, 1997; Wehmeyer, et al., 1998). Among the strategies that have been extensively investigated are goal-setting, self-monitoring, problem solving, self-instruction, self-reinforcement, permanent prompts, and self-evaluation. A description of each follows.

Goal Setting.   Goal setting is an essential skill for self-directed learning. Inherent in goal setting is understanding that there is a discrepancy between "where I am" and "where I want to be." The anxiety created by this discrepancy has been shown to motivate people toward change. Although many students with disabilities, especially those with severe disabilities, have not had an opportunity to learn how to set their own goals, or lack the skills associated with goal setting, evidence strongly suggests that implementing the procedures in this strategy will enhance positive student outcomes.

Although only a few studies have examined the effects of goal setting on task performance in inclusive settings for students with moderate to severe disabilities, the findings to date are promising. Copeland, Hughes, Agran, Wehmeyer, and Fowler (2002) taught four high school students with mental retardation who were enrolled in general education classes (cosmetology and hairdressing) to assist in setting performance goals for themselves. Improved performance for all participants was reported. Wehmeyer, Hughes, Agran, Bolding, and Yeager (2002) taught four high school students with mental retardation participating in general education to select performance goals for themselves. Among the target behaviors were holding head upright, increasing eye contact, and increasing attendance. Improvements were reported for all students. Last, Agran, Blanchard, Hughes, and Wehmeyer (in press) taught four students labeled as having autism, intellectual disabilities, or multiple disabilities to set their own goals. The students participated in general education life skills, science, and English classes. The participating students were taught to identify a target behavior he or she wanted to improve. Two students selected social skills: to refrain from inappropriately touching others and following directions, respectively. Two other students selected the goal of contributing more in their English class. Immediate and dramatic changes were reported for all students. The students indicated that they appreciated having a goal-setting role.

Goal setting ultimately allows students both to establish performance standards for themselves, a task traditionally done by teachers, and to evaluate how well they are progressing relative to the standards. Goal setting has great utility in putting responsibility for learning where it belongs—with the student.

Self-monitoring.   Self-monitoring consists of a student's self-observation of a target behavior followed by recording the behavior's occurrence. The strategy requires that a student understand and successfully implement two functions: (1) the student recognizes that the desired or goal behavior was or was not performed, and (2) the student accurately records the occurrence on a card or chart. A variety of recording forms can be used to meet the needs of the specific student and the target behavior. Essentially, any discrete behavior (that is, a response that has a distinguishable beginning and end) that can be operationally defined can be self-monitored.

Recommended target behaviors may include any behavior that the student would like to increase or decrease, essentially any behavior for which frequency of occurrence can be observed. For example, Gilbert, Agran, Hughes, and Wehmeyer (2001) taught five middle school students with severe intellectual disabilities, served in general education classrooms, to monitor a set of classroom survival skills; additionally, peer tutors recorded the occurrence of these skills. The survival skills included being in class and in their seat when the bell rings, having appropriate materials, greeting the teacher and other students, asking and answering questions, sitting up straight, looking at the teacher when addressed, acknowledging teacher and student comments, and using a planner. Positive changes were reported for all students, with behavior maintaining at 100 percent for all students.

Common methods of self-monitoring include the use of golf counters, grocery store counters, or wrist counters (Agran, 1997). In effect, paper and a pencil (or marking pen) are all that are required to use this strategy successfully. Because the supplies for self-monitoring are simple, the cost of the strategy is minimal. As long as the target behavior is easily discriminated, instruction is straightforward and takes little time.

Self-monitoring produces behavior change because it may serve as a discriminative stimulus and, thus, cues the desired response. The self-monitoring process allows the student to recognize the specific target behavior, as well as to remind the student of the present and future contingencies that exist in the environment (that is, "If I perform this response, this will happen"). The target behavior is more likely to occur when this information is available to the student.

Self-evaluation. Self-evaluation involves the comparison of the behavior being monitored with the student's desired goal. It is an important component of self-determination because it keeps the student aware daily of whether she or he is meeting a desired goal. The experience of monitoring and evaluating is potentially a reinforcing event.

Self-evaluation provides the student with a standard to assess his or her behavior (Agran, 1997). If the standard is not being met, the comparison may serve a corrective function. If it is being met, it serves as a reinforcing event and promotes the likelihood of the behavior being performed in the future. Of practical significance is the fact that the student provides him- or herself with the feedback and is not dependent on a teacher or other individual. For example, in one application of self-evaluation conducted by the authors, a student was taught to give herself the correct amount of insulin at lunch time (Agran, Blanchard, & Wehmeyer, 2000). Information was collected from the student, her mother, and doctor to develop a list of steps that guided her through the process. The decision to teach the student to self-evaluate was based on the medical implications of making an error. The goal was to become 100 percent proficient in following the procedures outlined; anything less than that could have life-threatening consequences. The strategy proved to be successful.

Essentially, the same procedure to teach self-monitoring is used to teach self-evaluation. However, the student is taught to discriminate and record the occurrence of the target behavior and to discriminate whether the frequency of occurrence of the target behavior as reflected in the recordings meet or are higher or lower than the specified criterion. As with self-monitoring, this is done through the presentation of examples and nonexamples. First, the student is reinforced for self-monitoring and then is reinforced for self-evaluation, followed by self-monitoring and self-evaluation. Also, as with self-monitoring, the self-evaluations are reviewed by the student and teacher to assess progress in goal attainment.

Self-reinforcement. Self-reinforcement represents a major component of most conceptualizations of self-determination. Because the aim of self-determination is to promote student independence and control of their learning and development, self-reinforcement can be an important strategy in student learning and life functioning. Self-reinforcement involves a system in which students can reinforce their own behavior immediately (Wehmeyer, Agran, & Hughes, 1998). Students are always present to administer their own consequences or feedback, so the possibility of lost reinforcement is greatly minimized. Students may often have difficulty acquiring desired outcomes because the natural consequences are too delayed, too small, or not achievable. Self-reinforcement essentially fills in the deficit by providing immediate feedback (Malott, 1984).

Two operations are involved in self-reinforcement: discrimination and delivery. A student must discriminate that the target behavior has occurred before he or she can reinforce him- or herself. It has also been suggested that self-reinforcement has stimulus properties that may cue appropriate responding. In any case, the essential element of the strategy is that the student determines and provides the consequences for his or her own behaviors.

As with self-monitoring and self-evaluation, self-reinforcement is not acquired automatically. Most individuals, with or without disabilities, are not experienced in overtly reinforcing themselves. However, individuals with the most extensive support needs can systematically be taught to reinforce themselves. For example, Lagomarcino and Rusch (1989) taught a student with profound mental retardation to reinforce himself by placing a coin into an empty slot in a board after completing a work task. The intervention increased the student's productivity.

When teaching students to reinforce themselves, the following sequence is recommended. First, the target behavior is identified by the student and teacher. Second, a criterion is set for the behavior (that is, the desired level of performance). Third, a reinforcer is identified by the student. Next, as described previously, the student is taught to discriminate the behavior, record its occurrence, and compare the frequency to the goal standard. Following, the student is taught to deliver to him- or herself the reinforcer after the response is completed and the recording matches the goal set. Last, the student's performance is monitored to ensure that the self-reinforcement is being correctly performed, the target behavior is performed at the desired level, the reinforcer is still effective, and the criterion is appropriate.

Self-instruction. Self-instruction involves teaching students to make task-specific statements out loud prior to their performance of a task, that is, they are taught to tell themselves what they need to do. Because many students with disabilities have difficulty relating to problem solving and short-term memory retention, self-instruction provides students with additional information (verbal cues) to promote desired responding. It allows students to rehearse verbally what they need to do and to engage in meaningful problem solving. Because our behavior is largely controlled by language, self-instruction allows students to control their own behavior—clearly, a valued skill if someone is to become more self-determined. Self-instruction involves a two-step process: teaching the student to produce the self-instructions and then to complete the task. An assumption is made that, as long as the target behavior can be operationally described, a self-instruction can be identified and subsequently taught.

Self-instruction can be used to teach a wide variety of skills (Agran & Moore, 1994). As indicated previously, if you can define the target behavior, the relevant self-instruction can be easily identified. Typically, self-instruction applications have followed a problem-solving approach in which the student is first taught to identify a problem. Such a problem may be a condition that prevents the student from completing a task (for example, "I don't answer in class. What am I doing wrong?") or the realization the student lacks some knowledge relevant to completion of the task (for example, "My teacher wants me to finish the worksheet, but I don't know how long that should take"). Following, the student is taught to identify a solution to the problem (for example, "I'll find out how much time I have and set a timer"). Then, the student is taught to tell him- or herself what to do (for example, "Now, I'll set the timer and work on the worksheet"). An example appears in Figure 14.3.

Self-instruction can also be used to teach complex task sequences. A "Did-Next-Now" strategy teaches the student to learn how to complete a complex sequence by stating what response he or she just completed and what responses need to be done next and then to direct him or her to perform the response. Additionally, a "What-Where" strategy can be used to help establish stimulus control and is suitable for a response the student performs inconsistently. The strategy involves teaching the student to repeat what he or she must do and where the response is to be performed. It has been used to teach instruction-following skills.

When teaching self-instruction, a rationale is first presented to the student on the value of using self-instruction. Following, the instructor models the self-instruction strategy while completing the task. Next, the student is asked to repeat the self-instructions and to perform the desired response. As mastery in both is achieved, the student is reinforced when he or she both self-instructs and completes the task appropriately.

FIGURE 14.3 *Self-instruction Example*

Training Sequence	Verbalization
Problem:	
Runs out of instructional materials	"I ran out of _____."
Solution	"I need to get up and get more _____." (Or "I need to ask _____ for more _____.")
Planned Response	"I'll get up and ask for more _____."

Typically, self-instructions are comprised of complete phrases or sentences. They need to contain sufficient information so that the student can attend to the salient dimensions of the task. For students with limited language capacity, it may be necessary to shorten the self-instructions and use only a word or two. For example, if the student has difficulty saying, "I need to set the calculator out of the supply closet," it may be necessary to teach the student only to say "calculator in closet."

Permanent Prompts.   The use of permanent prompts—for example, picture cues—is highly recommended. (Note: A prompting system such as recorded messages on a cassette player is also considered to be a permanent prompt strategy.) They provide students—particularly students with severe learning needs—with an easy-to-use learning strategy and memory aid.

From symbols designating special parking areas to restroom signs to computer icons, we are surrounded by many picture cues and symbols. Unlike verbal cues that may be vague or confusing, picture cues are less ambiguous. They portray or illustrate exactly what one needs to do. Independent of teacher assistance, the student can literally cue or prompt his or her behavior and determine his or her own success.

It is safe to say that picture cues are the easiest educational support strategy to teach to students with disabilities. In contrast to the other support strategies, the student does not need to monitor or evaluate his or her performance or respond to verbal stimuli, but only perform the response pictured. Consequently, the instructional time needed to teach this strategy may be quite short. In essence, two skills are involved in picture-cue-use instruction: learning to refer to the appropriate picture in the appropriate sequence (and match the picture to the actual task to be completed) and performing the responses illustrated.

Picture cues may include a variety of presentation formats: graphic symbols, simple line drawings, published instructional materials, magazine pictures, single photographs, and detailed photographic sequences, among others. Some students may respond better to one method than another. For example, line drawings are less costly to produce, but are more abstract than photographs. Consequently, it is recommended that the visual method the student responds to best be determined.

Instruction involves two phases. First, the student needs to be taught to identify the picture and to follow the picture sequence correctly if more than one picture is shown. It is assumed that the student will be able to match the picture to the actual stimulus condition or task, but this level of instruction may also need to be provided. Second, the student is taught to refer to the picture and perform the response pictured. In the second phase, the student is reinforced for following the picture cues and performing the illustrated pictures.

Problem Solving

Functioning successfully at school and in the community requires the ability to determine multiple solutions to multiple problems (Agran & Hughes, 1997), and, regrettably, youth with disabilities have considerable difficulty in this area. When confronted with problems at school, work, or community, they often respond impulsively and do not weigh the consequences of their actions, or do not respond at all. Without problem-solving skills, there is little likelihood that these students will achieve any true true sense of autonomy or self-determination. Fortunately, similar to the other strategies discussed, problem solving can be systematically taught. The model described next presents a model to teach these skills.

The Self-Determined Learning Model of Instruction

Wehmeyer and colleagues (Mithaug, Wehmeyer, Agran, Martin & Palmer, 1998; Wehmeyer, Palmer, Agran, Mithaug, & Martin, 2000) developed a model of teaching that enables teachers to, in essence, teach students to problem-solve. This model, called the *Self-Determined Learning Model of Instruction* and derived from an earlier instructional model, the *Adaptability Instruction Model* forwarded by Mithaug, Martin, and Agran (1987) and Mithaug, Martin, Agran, and Rusch (1988), incorporates principles of self-determination and self-regulated learning.

Implementation of the model consists of a three-phase instructional process. Phase I is presented in Figure 14.4. Each instructional phase presents a problem to be solved by the student. The student solves each problem by posing and answering a series of four *Student Questions* per phase that students learn, modify to make their own, and apply to reach self-selected goals. Each question is linked to a set of *Teacher Objectives*. Each instructional phase includes a list of *Educational Supports* identified that teachers can use to enable students to self-direct learning. In each phase, the student is the primary agent for choices, decisions, and actions, even when actions are teacher directed.

To answer the questions in this sequence, students must regulate their own problem solving by setting goals to meet needs, constructing plans to meet goals, and adjusting actions to complete plans. Thus, each instructional phase poses a problem the student must solve (What is my goal? What is my plan? What have I learned?) by, in turn, solving a series of problems posed by the questions in each phase. The four questions differ from phase to phase, but represent identical steps in the problem-solving sequence. Students answering the questions must (1) identify the problem, (2) identify potential solutions to the problem, (3) identify barriers to solving the problem, and (4) identify consequences of each solution. The model allows a student to learn a self-regulated problem-solving strategy. Concurrently, teaching students to use other student-directed learning strategies provides students with another layer of skills that enables them to become the causal agent in their lives.

Wehmeyer, Palmer, Agran, Mithaug, and Martin (2000) conducted a field test of the model with teachers responsible for the instruction of 40 adolescents with mental retardation, learning disabilities, or emotional or behavioral disorders. Students identified a total of 43 goals they wanted to address (three students chose two goals). The field test indicated that the model was effective in enabling students to attain educationally valued goals. Also, Gilbert, Agran, Hughes, and Wehmeyer (2001) taught students with severe disabilities to use the model and reported an increase in classroom survival skills (for example, bringing appropriate materials to class and asking questions) for all participants.

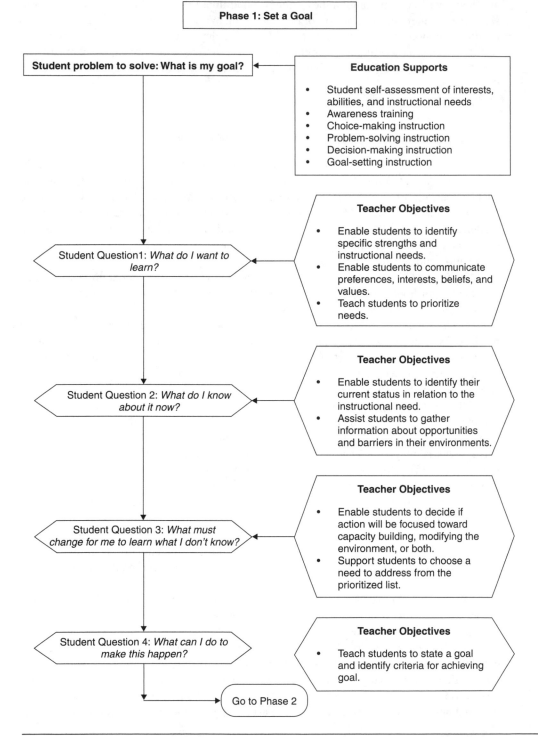

FIGURE 14.4 *Instructional Phase 1 of Self-Determined Learning Model of Instruction*

Self-Determination and Access to the General Curriculum

Ensuring that all students with disabilities have access to the general curriculum was a key feature of the 1997 amendments to the Individuals with Disabilities Education Act (IDEA). Those amendments included statutory and regulatory language pertaining to providing such access. However, despite a growing number of efforts to conceptualize how to gain access to the general curriculum for students with disabilities, few of these have addressed the needs of learners with mental retardation and other cognitive disabilities. Wehmeyer and colleagues (Wehmeyer, Lance, & Bashinski, in press; Wehmeyer, Lattin, & Agran, 2001; Wehmeyer, Sands, Knowleton, & Kozleski, 2002) introduced a multilevel model to promote such access for students with mental retardation and severe disabilities. Such access is achieved through a five-step process, depicted in Table 14.1, which begins with setting standards that provide the opportunity for all students to show progress. The process implements a decision-making model that encourages IEP teams to consider both the

TABLE 14.1 *Steps to Gaining Access to the General Curriculum for Students with Mental Retardation*

Action Step	Description
Standard setting and curriculum design	Standards are written as open ended and the curriculum is planned and designed using principles of universal design that ensure that all students can show progress.
Individualized educational planning	The individualized planning process ensures that a student's educational program is designed based on the general curriculum, taking into account unique student learning needs.
Schoolwide materials and instruction	There is schoolwide use of universally designed curricular materials and high-quality instructional methods and strategies that challenge all students.
Partial school and group instruction	Groups of students who need more intensive instruction are targeted and building and classroom instructional decisionmaking activities focus at the lesson, unit, and classroom level to ensure students can progress in the curriculum.
Individualized interventions	Additional curricular content and instructional strategies are designed and implemented to ensure progress for students with learning needs not met by schoolwide efforts or partial school efforts.

general curriculum and unique student learning needs in making decisions about the students' formal education program (Wehmeyer, Lattin, & Agran, 2001). The process also implements schoolwide, partial school, and individualized strategies to promote progress in the general curriculum (Wehmeyer, Sands, et al., 2002).

Among the strategies that can be implemented schoolwide to promote access to the general curriculum for students with severe disabilities are the student-directed learning strategies described previously. Instruction in strategies like self-monitoring or self-instruction provide all students with skills they can apply to learning a wide array of knowledge and skills within the general curriculum. Such strategies are important for all students and, by ensuring that teachers across the campus are teaching all students to use such skills, educators can ensure that students with disabilities, including students with severe disabilities, are being provided with skills they need to progress in the general curriculum and also can reduce the need for more highly individualized instruction.

Summary

Self-determination represents, arguably, one of the most dynamic changes in special education in the last decade and has had a pervasive impact on the delivery of educational strategies and teacher and parent expectations regarding learning outcomes for students with extensive support needs. Increasingly, students are learning to assume meaningful responsibility for determining what they want to learn, as well as strategies to achieve these outcomes. By doing so, they are no longer relegated to a passive recipient role in the learning process, but are provided opportunities to have a dynamic and active role in their own learning and development. There is no question that, as student roles change, so will those of teachers. Many of the activities traditionally performed by teachers are now being assumed by students (for example, goal setting, delivery of reinforcement, and evaluation). For teachers receptive to this change, mutually beneficial outcomes result. Regrettably, for teachers resistant to this shift, the converse will occur. As we seek to promote the self-determination of our students, we, as educators, must understand that, as mentioned earlier in the chapter, self-determination is not just something a student "does," but represents a concentrated effort by all involved in the student's development. Like us, students with disabilities have the right to control and design their own lives, and we, as educators, must ensure that they know how to do this.

References

Agran, M. (1997). *Student-directed learning: Teaching self-determination skills.* Pacific Grove, CA: Brooks/Cole.

Agran, M., & Hughes, C. (1997). Problem solving. In M. Agran (Ed.), *Student-directed learning: Teaching self-determination skills* (pp. 171–198). Pacific Grove, CA: Brooks/Cole.

Agran, M., & Hughes, C. (1998). Introduction to the special issue on self-determination. *Journal of The Association for Persons with Severe Handicaps, 23,* 1–4.

Agran, M., & Moore, S. (1994). *How to teach self-instruction of job skills.* Washington D.C.: American Association on Mental Retardation.

Agran, M., & Wehmeyer, M. (1999). *Teaching problem solving to students with mental retardation.* Washington, D.C.: American Association on Mental Retardation.

Agran, M., Blanchard, C., & Wehmeyer, M. (2000). Promoting transition goals and self-determination through student self-directed learning: The self-determined learning model of instruction. *Education and Training in Mental Retardation and Developmental Disabilities, 35*, 351–364.

Agran M., Blanchard, C., Hughes, C., & Wehmeyer, M. (in press). Increasing the problem-solving skills of students with developmental disabilities participating in general education. *Remedial and Special Education.*

Bannerman, D. J., Sheldon, J. B., Sherman, J. A., & Harchirk, A. E. (1990). Balancing the right to habilitation with the right to personal liberties: The rights of people with developmental disabilities to eat too many donuts and take a nap. *Journal of Applied Behavior Analysis, 23*, 79–89.

Benz, M. R., & McAllister, M. (1990). Occupational and leisure preferences of older adults with mental retardation. *Australia and New Zealand Journal of Developmental Disabilities, 16*, 233–244.

Brown, F., Belz, P., Corsi, L., & Wenig, B. (1993). Choice and diversity for people with severe disabilities. *Education and Training in Mental Retardation, 28*, 318–326.

Copeland, S., Hughes, C., Agran, M., Wehmeyer, M., & Fowler, S. E. (2002). An intervention package to support high school students with mental retardation in general education classrooms. *American Journal on Mental Retardation, 107*, 32–45.

Dattilo, J. (1986). Computerized assessment of preference for severely handicapped individuals. *Journal of Applied Behavior Analysis, 19*, 445–448.

Dattilo, J., & Mirenda, P. (1987). An application of a leisure preference assessment protocol for persons with severe handicaps. *Journal of The Association for Persons with Severe Handicaps, 12*, 306–311.

Dattilo, J., & Rusch, F. (1985). Effects of choice on leisure participation for persons with severe handicaps. *Journal of The Association for Persons with Severe Handicaps, 10*, 194–199.

Doll, B., Sands, D. J., Wehmeyer, M. L., & Palmer, S. (1996). Promoting the development and acquisition of self-determined behavior. In D. J. Sands & M. L. Wehmeyer (Eds.), *Self-determination across the life span: Independence and choice for people with disabilities* (pp. 63–88). Baltimore,: Paul H. Brookes Publishing Co.

Ficker-Terrill, C., & Rowitz, L. (1991). Choices. *Mental Retardation, 29*, 63–64.

Fisher, D., Sax, C., & Jorgensen, C. M. (1998). Philosophical foundations of inclusive, restructuring schools. In C. M. Jorgensen (Ed.), *Restructuring high schools for all students* (pp. 29–47). Baltimore,: Paul H. Brookes Publishing Co.

Gilberts, G. H., Agran, M., Hughes, C., & Wehmeyer, M. (2001). The effects of peer-delivered self-monitoring strategies on the participation of students with severe disabilities in general education classrooms. *Journal of The Association for Persons with Severe Handicaps, 26*, 25–36.

Hughes, C., Pitkin, S., & Lorden, S. (1998). Assessing preferences and choices of persons with severe and profound mental retardation. *Education and Training in Mental Retardation and Developmental Disabilities, 33*, 299–316.

Kennedy, C., & Haring, T. (1993). Teaching choice making during social interactions to students with profound multiple disabilities. *Journal of Applied Behavior Analysis, 26*, 63–76.

King-Sears, M. E., & Carpenter, S. L. (1997). *Teaching self-management to elementary students with developmental disabilities.* Washington D.C.: American Association on Mental Retardation.

Lagomarcino, T., & Rusch, F. R. (1989). Utilizing self-management to teach independence on the job. *Education and Training in Mental Retardation, 24*, 139–148.

Malott, R. C. (1984). Rule-governed behavior, self-management, and the developmentally disabled. *Analysis and Intervention in Developmental Disabilities, 4*, 199–209.

Mithaug, D. E., Martin, J. E., & Agran, M. (1987). Adaptability instruction: The goal of transitional programming. *Exceptional Children, 53*, 500–505.

Mithaug, D. E., Martin, J. E., Agran, M., & Rusch, F. R. (1988). *Why special education graduates fail: How to teach them to succeed.* Colorado Springs, CO: Ascent.

Mithaug, D., Wehmeyer, M. L., Agran, M., Martin, J., & Palmer, S. (1998). The self-determined learning model of instruction: Engaging students to solve their learning problems. In M. L. Wehmeyer & D. J. Sands (Eds.), *Making it happen: Student involvement in educational planning, decision-making and instruction* (pp. 299–328). Baltimore: Paul H. Brookes Publishing Co.

Newton, J. S., Horner, R. H., & Lund, I. (1991). Honoring activity preferences in individualized plan development: A descriptive analysis. *Journal of The Association for Persons with Severe Handicaps, 16*, 207–212.

Parsons, M., & Reid, D. (1990). Assessing food preferences among persons with profound mental retardation: Providing opportunities to make choices. *Journal of Applied Behavior Analysis, 23,* 183–195.

Perske, R. (1972). The dignity of risk: In W. Wolfensberger (Ed.), *The principle of normalization in human service* (pp. 194–200). Toronto, Ontario, Canada: National Institute on Mental Retardation.

Powers, L., Sowers, J., Turner, A., Nesbitt, M., Knowles, E., & Ellison, R. (1996). TAKE CHARGE: A model for promoting self-determination among adolescents with challenges. In L. E. Powers, G. H. S. Singer, & J. Sowers (Eds)., *Promoting self-competence in children and youth with disabilities* (pp. 291–322). Baltimore: Paul H. Brookes Publishing Co.

Sands, D.J., & Wehmeyer, M.L. (1996). *Self-determination across the life span: Independence and choice for people with disabilities.* Baltimore: Paul H. Brookes Publishing Co.

Stancliffe, R.J., & Abery, B.H. (1997). Longitudinal study of deinstitutionalization and the exercise of choice. *Mental Retardation, 35,* 159–169.

Stancliffe, R., & Wehmeyer, M. L. (1995). Variability in the availability of choice to adults with mental retardation. *The Journal of Vocational Rehabilitation, 5,* 319–328.

Wehmeyer, M. L. (1996a). Self-determination as an educational outcome: Why is it important to children, youth and adults with disabilities? In D. J. Sands & M. L. Wehmeyer (Eds.), *Self-determination across the life span: Independence and choice for people with disabilities* (pp. 15–34). Baltimore, MD: Paul H. Brookes Publishing Co.

Wehmeyer, M. L. (1996b). A self-report measure of self-determination for adolescents with cognitive disabilities. *Education and Training in Mental Retardation and Developmental Disabilities, 31,* 282–293.

Wehmeyer, M. L. (1998). Self-determination and individuals with significant disabilities: Examining meanings and misinterpretations. *Journal of The Association for Persons with Severe Handicaps, 23,* 5–16.

Wehmeyer, M. L. (2001). Self-determination and mental retardation. In L. M. Glidden (Ed.), *International review of research in mental retardation* (Vol. 24, pp. 1–48). Hillsdale, NJ: Lawrence Erlbaum and Associates.

Wehmeyer, M. L., & Metzler, C. (1995). How self-determined are people with mental retardation? The National Consumer Survey. *Mental Retardation, 33,* 111–119.

Wehmeyer, M. L., Abery, B., Mithaug, D., Powers, L., & Stancliffe, R. (in press). *Theory in self-determination: Foundations for educational practice.* Springfield, IL: Charles C. Thomas.

Wehmeyer, M. L., Agran, M., & Hughes, C. (1998). *Teaching self-determination to youth with disabilities: Basic skills for successful transition.* Baltimore: Paul H. Brookes Publishing Co.

Wehmeyer, M. L., Hughes, C., Agran, M., Bolding, N., & Yeager, D. (2002). Promoting self-directed learning of adolescents with mental retardation in regular education classrooms: Goal setting and self-monitoring. Manuscript submitted for publication.

Wehmeyer, M. L., Lance, G. D., & Bashinski, S. (in press). Promoting access to the general curriculum for students with mental retardation: A multilevel model. *Education and Training in Mental Retardation and Developmental Disabilities.*

Wehmeyer, M. L., Lattin, D., & Agran, M. (2001). Promoting access to the general curriculum for students with mental retardation: A decision-making model. *Education and Training in Mental Retardation and Developmental Disabilities, 36,* 329–344.

Wehmeyer, M. L., Palmer, S., Agran, M., Mithaug, D., & Martin, J. (2000). Promoting causal agency: The self-determined learning model of instruction. *Exceptional Children, 66,* 439–453.

Wehmeyer, M. L., Sands, D. J., Doll, B., & Palmer, S. (1997). The development of self-determination and implications for educational interventions with students with disabilities. *International Journal of Disability, Development and Education, 44,* 305–328.

Wehmeyer, M. L., Sands, D. J., Knowlton, H. E., & Kozleski, E. B. (2002). *Teaching students with mental retardation: Providing access to the general curriculum.* Baltimore: Paul H. Brookes Publishing Co.

15

The Adult Lifestyles Planning Cycle: A Continual Process for Planning Personally Satisfying Adult Lifestyles

Lori A. Garcia and Bruce M. Menchetti

Objectives

After completing this chapter, the reader will be able to:

1. Describe the Individuals with Disabilities Education Act's (IDEA's) age 14 and age 16 transition-planning requirements.
2. Discuss curricular opportunities for transition-aged students with severe disabilities.
3. Identify graduation criteria and diploma options for high school students.
4. Describe the components and function of the Adult Lifestyles Planning Cycle.
5. Define quality of life in terms of its subjective and objective dimensions.
6. Identify quality of life domains.
7. Describe common elements within and examples of person-centered planning techniques.
8. Identify the steps and applications of an ecological inventory.
9. Identify formal supports typically available at the federal, state, and local levels.
10. Describe the purpose of accreditation organizations and their relationship to formal support providers.
11. Describe concept of and steps for building natural support networks.
12. Identify dimensions within the working definition of social inclusion.

13. Discuss the relationship between quality of life and the four components of the Adult Lifestyles Planning Cycle: Person-Centered Planning, Ecological Approach, Formal Supports, and Natural Support Networks.

Key Terms

Accreditation	Ecological approach	School-sponsored work
Adult Lifestyles Planning	Ecological inventory	experience
Cycle	Eligibility	Social inclusion
Commission on Accreditation of	Formal supports	Social Security Administration
Rehabilitation Facilities	IDEA	(SSA)
(CARF)	Job shadowing	Task analysis
Community connections	National Association on	Transition planning
Consumer movement	Developmental Disabilities	U.S. Office of Vocational and
Council on Quality and	Council (NADDC)	Adult Education (OVAE)
Leadership in Supports for	Natural supports	Vocational education
People with Disabilities (The	Personal career plan	Vocational Rehabilitation (VR)
Council)	Person-centered planning	
Decisionmaking	Quality of life	
Developmental Disabilities	Readiness model	
Waiver Program		

For a society in which the majority of youth go to college (Blackorby & Wagner, 1996), it is sometimes difficult to remember that higher education is not the only avenue leading to a personally satisfying lifestyle. Given access to an array of adult opportunities and the support needed to benefit from these opportunities, individuals with and without disabilities may attain personally satisfying goals and a sense of well-being without graduating from high school. All people, however, will need help in identifying opportunities and planning adult life supports. For people with disabilities, this may be more difficult, not because of their differences, but because society has developed a broad array of formal services and programs designed specifically for those with disabilities. Further complicating the transition from school to adult life is the finding that availability of and access to formal supports for individuals with disabilities has become a national crisis. According to Wehman (1996), there were more than 186,000 people with disabilities awaiting some type of formal support, with the majority of these people being youth with severe disabilities.

Another dilemma faced by those attempting to access formal programs arises when they try to establish eligibility for service. Cozzens, Dowdy, and Smith (1999) have pointed out that, following high school exit, people must qualify for services based on their disability and the specific eligibility criteria established by the agency involved. In some cases, there are differences in eligibility criteria and policies from school to adult agencies, potentially meaning that a person who was previously receiving special education services may not be eligible for an adult program. There may also be differences in policies between various adult agencies and programs, which add to the confusion (Cozzens et al., 1999).

Given the challenges inherent in accessing the adult service system, the important questions become these:

1. How do we assist people in identifying and securing the supports they want and need to attain personally satisfying adult outcomes?
2. Further, what formal programs and agencies are available in typical communities, and what services do they offer to people?
3. Finally, how can these programs and services be augmented by natural support networks and community connections to ensure that a person's entire quality of life is addressed?

In response to these questions, the purposes of this chapter are to (a) describe the adult planning opportunities presented by the transition requirements of the Individuals with Disabilities Education Act (IDEA), (b) suggest a model for facilitating the development of personally satisfying adult lifestyles, and (c) suggest ways to make formal systems responsive to personal outcomes.

Transition Planning: An Opportunity for a Bright Future

One important opportunity for meaningful adult lifestyle planning occurs during adolescence while a student is still in school. Since 1990, IDEA has required that schools work together with families and adult agencies to plan high school curriculum, future goals, and comprehensive services that facilitate the successful transition from school to adult life. The IDEA transition requirements recognize the critical importance of a strong secondary education foundation, early planning during adolescence, and interagency collaboration for the attainment of desired adult goals.

Decisions that students and their families make during adolescence often have lifelong impact. Choices about which high school courses and extracurricular activities to engage in, and what social relationships to form, can shape the future in many important ways. Timely information and an individualized support plan can assist students and families in making appropriate decisions about high school and beyond. The transition-planning requirements of IDEA represent an opportunity to provide adolescents with disabilities and their families with just such information, planning, and support.

One purpose of this section is to describe the IDEA transition-planning requirements and the information that is needed to support informed decisionmaking. Another purpose is to suggest ways that teachers, counselors, families, and students can work together to make transition planning a launching pad to a bright adult future.

IDEA Transition-Planning Requirements

For more than a decade, IDEA has offered a collaborative process for professionals and families to share information and to plan for a student's future. Transition planning, at its most fundamental level, represents an opportunity for people to discuss an individual student's interests, goals, and abilities and then to use this information to plan for the future. Transition planning provides families and professionals with a process for selecting secondary education curricular programs, formal adult services, and natural, community supports that will assist a student in achieving his or her goals.

Transition planning beginning at age 16 was first incorporated into the Individualized Education Program (IEP) under IDEA of 1990 (P.L. 101-476). Later amendments, specifically that of 1997 (IDEA, P.L. 105-17), strengthened transition requirements by mandating that planning begin at age 14. The current IDEA transition-planning requirements provide two important opportunities for meaningful futures planning, first when a student reaches age 14 and again at age 16, with annual revisions thereafter.

Consequently, age 14 and age 16 represent critical milestones for professionals, students, and families. Teachers, counselors, school administrators, and adult agency personnel must be prepared to provide information about curriculum, programs, and services to students and their families at these critical transition ages. These transition team members must be prepared to use this information to plan services and supports that best match the student's interests, goals, and needs. The Western Regional Resource Center (WRRC) has provided a comprehensive guide to IDEA 1997 transition planning requirements. The WRRC Web site is listed in Table 15.1 (Resources for Transition Planning).

Planning the High School Curriculum at Age 14.   IDEA requires that schools involve students and their families in transition planning beginning at age 14. For many students,

TABLE 15.1 *Resources for Transition Planning*

Secondary Services	Source	Web site Address
Accommodations, graduation requirements, and alternative assessment	National Center on Educational Outcomes	*www.coled.umn.edu.nceo/*
Career and vocational education	University of Wisconsin, Center on Education and Work Incentives	*www.cew.wisc.edu*
Diploma decisions	Florida Department of Education, Bureau of Instructional Support and Community Services	*www.firn.edu/doe/commhom/pub-home.htm*
School to work	University of Minnesota, All Means All School-to-Work Project	*ici.coled.umn.edu/NCEO/*
Transition planning	Western Regional Resource Center, Transition Guide	*interact.uoregon.edu/wrrc/trnfiles/ trncontents.htm*

age 14 coincides with their eighth grade year of school. Students of this age are typically preparing to make the transition from junior high or middle school to high school. Transition planning at age 14 requires schools to provide families with information about the various high school curricular options or courses of study and the variety of graduation credentials that students may earn.

There are a number of courses of study and high school credentials available to students with disabilities. Each of these offers different preparation opportunities and outcomes to students. As a result, decisions about the high school curriculum made at age 14 can have longterm, lifestyle consequences for students. Choices made about a student's courses of study during high school should be meaningful to the student's future and should augment, but not replace, the separate age 16 IEP transition statement.

Curricular Options. For example, the college preparatory curriculum has specific course credit requirements and academic standards that should be discussed with students and their families during age-14 transition planning. At age 14, decisions can be made about whether a college prep curriculum best meets the future goals of the student. In most Florida school districts, for instance, students must earn at least 24 credit hours in specified coursework, including 15 hours in required subjects (for example, algebra, English, science, and so forth) and 9 credits of electives. Florida high school students in a college prep curriculum must also earn a minimum grade point average (for example, 2.0 on a 4.0 scale). Finally, in order to complete the college prep curriculum successfully, students in most states will have to earn passing scores on standardized assessments to document their academic proficiency. It is important to note, however, that IDEA 1997 required accommodations be provided as necessary to allow students with disabilities to participate in high school exit examinations and other statewide assessments. The National Center on Educational Outcomes (see Table 15.1) has reported that, although all states now allow accommodations, there is great variability in the specific types of accommodations allowed. Age-14 transition planning provides an opportunity to discuss a student's interests, goals, abilities, needs, and available accommodations to determine whether a college prep curriculum best meets the student's plans for the future.

If a college preparatory curriculum does not appropriately meet the future goals of students, the age-14 transition planning/IEP team may want to discuss secondary vocational education options. The requirements and benefits of vocational programs designed to prepare individuals in a specific occupational area (for example, agriculture, automotive, and culinary) should be explained. Cobb and Neubert (1998) described the three typical components of the secondary vocational education curriculum. These were in-school skills instruction, out-of-school work experience, and participation in vocational student organizations. Although enrollment in vocational education curricula usually is reserved for junior and senior high school students, vocational education options and accommodations should be discussed early with students and their families to ensure that there is a match between the student and the program.

Cobb and Neubert (1998) suggested that there was an overrepresentation of students with special needs in three curricular areas: agriculture, occupational home economics, and trades. Conversely, few students with special needs were enrolled in business, health, and technical education programs. For this reason, it is important to use the age-14 transition-planning opportunity to discuss students' interests, goals, abilities, and accommodations, as well as the school-based and secondary vocational curriculum that best meets their plans for the future.

Hagner and Vander Sande (1998) described a hierarchy of common types of school-sponsored work experiences based upon the intensity of the experience offered by each option. Field trips involving on-site visits to a variety of workplaces that allow students to learn about the practical applications of academic skills are often available as part of the high school curriculum. Another work experience option is job shadowing, which involves students being matched with an employee in a field of interest to spend a short period of time observing and assisting. Field trips and job shadowing represent less intensive forms of school-sponsored work experience and are often available to freshman (9th grade) and sophomore (10th grade) high school students. More intensive work experiences, usually available to high school juniors and seniors, are work study, part-time job placements (that is, supported employment), tech-prep programs, and career academies consisting of a sequence of academic classes linked to an occupational area (Hagner & Vander Sande, 1998). The age-14 transition-planning meeting represents an opportunity to provide information about all such curricular offerings and to determine which levels of work experience match the future goals of the student.

High School Credentials.   In addition to considering secondary curricular programs and courses of study, it is also important to discuss high school credential options during age-14 transition planning. The completion of high school has been an important indicator of positive adult outcomes for all people. Obviously, high school graduation is one condition necessary for access to higher education, and completing high school has also been associated with earning power. For students with disabilities, high school completion has been associated with enrollment in postsecondary education and training, employment, and higher wages (Blackorby & Wagner, 1996). In a recent report to Congress, the United States (U.S.) Department of Education (2000) indicated that most states offer alternate or modified diplomas and certificates of completion, as well as regular high school diplomas, to students with disabilities.

Given the importance of high school completion, it is useful to examine how many youth with disabilities obtain the various credentials now available. In the 1997–98 school year, the U.S. Department of Education (2000) reported that 25.5 percent of all students with disabilities ages 17 and older obtained a standard high school diploma. Further, the rate of earning a standard diploma varied greatly by disability type and by state. For example, youth with learning disabilities, speech or language impairments, visual impairments, and those who were deaf-blind were most likely to leave high school with a standard diploma in 1997–98. The groups least likely to earn a standard diploma in the same year were youth with autism, multiple disabilities, and mental retardation, with standard graduation rates of 8.4, 10.3, and 13.8 percent, respectively.

Whatever the reasons, the variance in standard graduation rates among students with disabilities has important implications for adult life. The different modes of high school completion will determine the types of postsecondary education and training options available to youth and young adults. These education and training options, in turn, will provide different adult outcome opportunities to individuals with disabilities. A clear example of the relationship between high school graduation and opportunities is higher education. Most institutions of higher education, including both two-year and four-year colleges and universities, require a standard diploma or its equivalent (for example, Graduation Equivalency Diploma [GED]) for admission. According to the 2000 U.S. Department of Education's graduation data, approximately 75 percent of all students with disabilities may be denied an opportunity for higher education because they have not earned a standard diploma. Opportunities for higher education are even more limited for youth with developmental disabilities because about 87 to 92 percent of these students do not obtain a standard diploma.

Planning Adult Outcomes and Community Linkages at Age 16.   Since 1990, IDEA has required that each student's IEP, beginning at age 16 (or younger, if appropriate), include a statement of needed transition services. This transition statement, at its most basic level, is an opportunity to include adult lifestyle goals as part of the IEP and to identify the formal services and other sources of support needed to help the student attain their desired quality of life. In this context, the IEP transition statement becomes a kind of accountability measure for documenting the outcomes of the free, appropriate public education promised to students in IDEA.

The age-16 IEP transition statement should refine and clarify the student's postschool goals or future plans articulated earlier at age 14. Because these goals must be based on the student's needs, preferences, and interests, age-16 transition planning provides another opportunity for students to engage in self-advocacy and to develop self-determination skills. Strategies for developing self-determination have been described in Chapter 14 of this book, but it is important to note that transition planning (at both age 14 and 16) can add context, relevance, and meaning to self-determination instruction. Consequently, schools must take steps to actively involve the student in his or her IEP development at this stage of transition planning. Similarly, students and families should be prepared to express their preferences and interests and engage in a dialogue with professionals about instructional opportunities, related service needs, community experiences, and development of employment and other adult living outcomes. This dialogue should be based on the concepts and principles of quality of life presented in this chapter.

Linkages with postsecondary education, vocational rehabilitation, developmental services, or local adult service agencies (for example, supported employment or supported living providers) should be explored and, if appropriate, actively arranged during this stage of transition planning. These linkages should support attainment of the student's desired postschool goals as expressed during transition planning. The school should invite a representative of any agency that is likely to be responsible for providing transition services. If the invited representative does not attend the meeting, steps must be taken to involve other agencies in transition planning. These may include the identification of another source of transition services, referral to another agency, the identification of community resources the school could use to meet the student's needs, or a combination of these approaches.

Summary.   Effective transition planning (at any age) requires the involvement and support of many people. Often it necessitates an ongoing effort beyond the constraints of the IEP process. Transition plans and strategies must be implemented, evaluated, and revised on a continuous basis to ensure lifestyle enhancement. Consequently, we offer the Adult Lifestyles Planning Cycle as a model to support the ongoing coordination and collaboration that must occur to support personally satisfying decisions and choices for individuals with severe disabilities.

The Adult Lifestyles Planning Cycle

We begin this section by presenting a *continual and cyclical process* for facilitating the development of a personally satisfying adult life. We recommend that this cycle be used to support planning and to identify relevant curriculum for individuals with disabilities. Planning for a satisfying adulthood can begin at an early age, especially if the focus begins with the development of such necessary skills as self-determination. Students, parents, and educators can use the Adult Lifestyles Planning Cycle (see Figure 15.1) to facilitate the transition-planning process (beginning at age 14 or 16), which is required by IDEA to assist students with disabilities as they transition from school to their communities. Further, individuals, parents, advocates, support staff, and programs can use the Adult Lifestyles Planning Cycle to assist people with disabilities of any age as they progress throughout life. Consequently, the cycle will require collaboration and involvement of a variety of people and agencies.

The Adult Lifestyles Planning Cycle is comprised of four components operating together and continuously in a cyclical fashion with the central focus on enhancing quality of life. The cycle, illustrated in Figure 15.1, begins with a consideration of quality of life issues. *Quality of life* issues, as identified and prioritized by the individual and his or her natural support network, *must be the central concern* when planning for a personally satisfying adult lifestyle and is at the heart of our planning cycle. Identification of essential quality of life areas for development can be achieved through person-centered planning. Depending upon the quality of life areas and personal needs conveyed through person-centered planning, an ecological approach to establishing specific supports and services could be used. Finally, identification of and linkage to both formal and natural supports are coordinated in this process.

It is paramount to note that the Adult Lifestyles Planning Cycle is proposed as a *continual and cyclical process*, and *not* as a one-time approach for satisfying unnaturally imposed, time-limited benchmarks or other such requirements. As we all naturally progress throughout life, we are constantly growing and changing as a result of our experiences. As we mature, our views, expectations, interests, dreams, and even our abilities transform. It is no different for an individual with a disability. What may vary, however, is the amount of support a person with a disability may need in order to make this natural progression. This level of support will vary across individuals and may increase or decrease depending upon the situation in which the individual finds him or herself. As a result, the Adult Lifestyles Planning Cycle is recommended as a continual and ongoing process to assist individuals with disabilities as they progress throughout their life. For agencies providing coordination of such services as supported employment, community inclusion, and supported living, the individual and his or her support network would continually be operating within the Adult Lifestyles Planning Cycle.

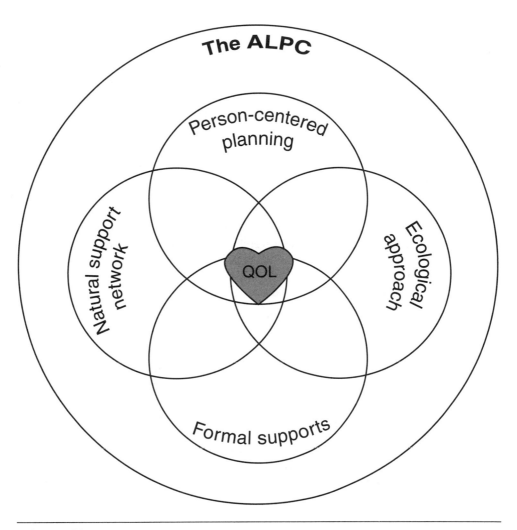

FIGURE 15.1

As illustrated in our cycle, efforts to enhance quality of life begin with person-centered planning and continue with an ecological approach, as both formal and natural supports based upon an individual's interests and needs are established and maintained. We propose that the Adult Lifestyles Planning Cycle can assist people with disabilities as they encounter major life changes or as they engage in daily efforts of lifestyle enhancement. Consequently, we offer the Adult Lifestyles Planning Cycle as a model to support the continual coordination and collaboration that must occur to support personally satisfying decisions and choices for people with severe disabilities. In the sections that follow, each area of the Adult Lifestyles Planning Cycle will be discussed in greater detail.

Importance of Quality of Life in Planning for a Satisfying Adult Lifestyle

A major development during the 1990s in the field of developmental disabilities was the increased attention to the quality of life of people with disabilities (McVilly & Rawlinson, 1998). As stated by Taylor and Bogdan (1996), ". . . the concept of quality of life directs attention to the human needs of people who have developmental disabilities. Although it is important that service systems and schools help children and adults . . . to learn and develop, it is more important that they contribute to the quality of life of the people they serve" (p. 11).

Consequently, when assisting people with disabilities in planning for a personally satisfying lifestyle, it is necessary to consider the many areas that comprise what most would consider as essential to establishing a quality adult life. It is vital to state that our intention is not to delineate several skill areas for assessment and training, but rather to give the reader a context for understanding the breadth and depth of quality of life. We believe that a broad understanding will help professionals assist people with the type of self-directed decisionmaking needed to contribute to quality of life.

A Quality of Life Model

Many professionals have attempted to define, conceptualize, and determine the nature of quality of life and how it applies to people with disabilities. According to Goode (1994). ". . . quality of life is seen as the product of the person consciously acting on situations that confront his [or her] own needs with that of society" (p. 160). He further stated that quality of life ". . . is experienced when a person's basic needs are met and when he or she has the opportunity to pursue and achieve goals in major life settings" (Goode, 1994, p. 148). In the sections that follow, we present one example of how quality of life has been conceptualized and how a model of quality of life can provide a framework upon which to assist people with disabilities in identifying personal goals and planning for a satisfying adult life.

In a model suggested by Felce and Perry (1995) quality of life is a multidimensional concept, which incorporates subjective indicators (for example, personal and internal) and objective indicators (for example, social and external). After an extensive review of the literature, Felce and Perry (1995) identified five domains of life, which should be ranked in importance according to the individual: (a) physical well-being, (b) material well-being, (c) social well-being, (d) development and activity, and (e) emotional well-being. Examples of these five domains are provided in Table 15.2.

According to Felce and Perry (1995), three major elements affect the overall assessment of well-being and quality of life: (a) objective life conditions, (b) subjective feeling of well-being, and (c) personal values and aspirations, all of which are constantly affected by external influences such as social, economic, and political variables.

Quality of Life from a Personal Perspective

In addition to Felce and Perry (1995), others have addressed the personal or self-defined aspect of quality of life. According to Butterworth, Steere, and Whitney-Thomas (1997),

TABLE 15.2 *Quality of Life Domains and Examples*

Domain	Example
Physical well-being	Health, fitness, mobility, personal safety
Material well-being	Finance, income, stability, tenure, security, housing quality, neighborhood, privacy, transportation, possessions, meals, food
Social well-being	Interpersonal relationships, family and household life, relatives, friends and social life, community involvement, activities and events, acceptance and support
Development and activity	Competence, independence, choice, control, employment, home life, housework, leisure, hobbies, education, productivity, contribution
Emotional well-being	Positive affect, satisfaction, status, respect, fulfillment, self-esteem, faith and belief, self-determination

Source: Adapted from Felce & Perry (1995), Domains Relevant to Quality of Life, p. 61.

". . . quality of life is a subjective concept that has meaning only as experienced and expressed by the individual" (p. 20). Taylor and Bogdan (1996) stated that quality of life ". . . has no meaning apart from what a person feels and experiences. It is a question of how people view or what they feel about their lives and situations and not what others attribute to them" (p. 16). Undeniably, however, quality of life is also influenced by more objective, external, and social factors, such as social status, employment, earnings, and housing. Consequently, an in-depth process that personalizes quality-of-life decisions is needed to assist people with formal support planning and natural support network development. In addition, it is precisely because of the considerations identified previously that we have made quality of life the heart of our Adult Lifestyles Planning Cycle.

Quality of Life and Person-Centered Planning

According to Perrin (1999), the most influential movement in the developmental disabilities field during the 1990s was the consumer movement, which was characterized by consumers becoming increasingly involved in making decisions about the services directly affecting their quality of life. This consumer-driven approach to formal support and service provision has required the development of nontraditional planning techniques that place the individual at the center of the planning process (for example, Gardner & Nudler, 1997; Inge, 1997; Smith, 1994). Person-centered planning is one such approach, and it has been used for planning in a variety of life areas.

As previously discussed, quality of life is a multidimensional construct in which determination is influenced by objective, external factors, but, more importantly, by the subjective evaluation of the person for whom quality of life is being determined. Further, quality of life, as a personal and unique experience, can be difficult to address for people with the most severe disabilities. As pointed out by Hatton (1998), determining subjective satisfaction with quality of life for people with severe disabilities and limited communication skills can be challenging, making it necessary to rely on the interpretations, judgments, and expectations of others (for example, family, friends, support personnel, and interviewers). Further, reliable and valid measures for ascertaining quality of life for this group are limited (Hatton, 1998). However, excluding people with the most severe disabilities from subjective assessments of quality of life is neither morally nor ethically appropriate. Relying solely on objective measures could exclude meaningful personal experiences and lead us back to a service-driven model of supports for people with disabilities (Hatton, 1998).

Consequently, person-centered planning has been recommended as a method of identifying personal interests, desires, and needs for people with severe disabilities, through the support of caring and knowledgeable people in the person's life (Everson, 1996; Mount & Zwernik, 1988). Person-centered planning has also been identified as a means for increasing participation in life planning and decisionmaking (Marone, Hoff, & Helm, 1997), and, consequently, a method for enhancing a person's quality of life (Butterworth, Steere, & Whitney-Thomas, 1997).

According to Butterworth and his colleagues (1997), person-centered planning overcomes the restrictions of typical adult service systems by honoring the uniqueness of each person and emphasizing personally satisfying quality of life issues. Butterworth et al. (1997) pointed out that "... person-centered approaches emphasize quality of life, as defined by each unique individual, as the only justifiable outcome of supports individuals receive from both systems and community resources," as they advocated for lifestyle changes that are unrestricted by the typical boundaries of human service structures (p. 20). For these reasons, we have identified person-centered planning as the beginning of our Adult Lifestyles Planning Cycle (see Figure 15.1).

Person-Centered Planning Techniques

There are a variety of person-centered planning techniques described in the literature, such as Essential Lifestyle Planning (Smull & Harrision, 1992); Personal Futures Planning (Mount & Zwernick, 1988; O'Brien, 1987); McGill Action Planning System (MAPS; Vandercook, York, & Forest, 1989); Whole-Life Planning (Butterworth, Hagner, Heikkinen, Faris, DeMellow, & McDonough, 1993); and the Personal Career Plan (Menchetti & Piland, 1998, 2001). These person-centered planning strategies share some common elements, because all the strategies focus on the person for whom the planning is taking place.

Such planning, then, centers on the preferences, interests, strengths, and abilities of the focus person, or the individual for whom a natural support network has gathered. The network members assist the focus person in exercising personal choices and developing a future vision. The natural support network also helps the individual develop an action plan and identify responsible parties, as well as participate in evaluation and follow-up efforts. The goals of person-centered planning include helping a person with disabilities to be as involved as possible in his or her life planning and the decision-making process.

Applications of Person-Centered Planning

Person-centered planning techniques have been used by professionals to assist individuals with disabilities in a variety of life areas. For example, Artisani and Mallar (1998) took a person-centered approach to functional assessment of challenging behaviors, while Reid, Everson, and Green (1999) applied a person-centered approach to preference assessments. In the school system, person-centered planning has been used as a method for facilitating the successful inclusion of students with disabilities in general education settings (Perlroth, Pumpian, Hesche, & Campbell, 1993). Further, person-centered planning has been used to enhance student and family participation in developing the IEP (Getzel & deFurs, 1997) and transition plan (Miner & Bates, 1997). Person-centered planning has also been used as a method for ensuring interagency collaboration (Knoster, 1995) and guiding program implementation (Hagner, Helm, & Butterworth, 1996; Roberts, Becker, & Seay, 1997). Finally, person-centered planning has been used to assist individuals with disabilities in developing and exercising self-determination (Cross, Cooke, Wood, & Test, 1999) and planning for later life (Heller, Factor, & Sterns, 1996), as well as for career planning and supported employment (Abrams, DonAroma, & Karan, 1997; Everson & Reid, 1997; Inge, 1997; Menchetti & Piland, 1998, 2001; Wehman, 1998).

The Personal Career Plan

The Personal Career Plan (Menchetti & Piland, 1998, 2001) was developed to assist people with career decisionmaking. It has five major steps, including (a) assembling a natural support network (for example, friends, family, employment consultant, and vocational rehabilitation counselor), (b) facilitating a planning meeting with an employment consultant serving as facilitator, (c) developing action plans comprised of steps and identification of responsible parties for meeting career goals, (d) reviewing efforts through a meeting between the employment specialist and individual, and (e) writing a résumé based on information gathered in the planning meeting. In Case Study 1, we will see how the Personal Career Plan (Menchetti & Piland, 1998, 2001), operating within the Adult Lifestyles Planning Cycle, was used to assist Andy with career decisionmaking.

As demonstrated in Case Study 1, Andy had some very specific ideas about the type of worklife he wanted, yet had a difficult time getting others to listen to him or respect his wishes. By respecting Andy's personal wishes about the quality of life areas most important to him, person-centered planning became the start of a cycle leading to a new career and better quality of life. The cycle consisted of person-centered planning (for example, the Personal Career Plan), ecological approach (for example, inventory of job tasks), coordination of formal supports (for example, GH staff, behavior analyst, support coordination), and development of natural supports (for example, manager and coworkers). With the guidance and structure of the Adult Lifestyles Planning Cycle proposed in this chapter, and the support of many people who shared his goal of a better life, Andy was able to leave the sheltered workshop and get "a real job."

It is important to recognize that person-centered planning approaches can become ineffective and nonresponsive when used in isolation. As pointed out by Mount (1994), person-centered planning runs the risk of becoming ". . . a quick fix without appreciation

CASE STUDY 1 • *Working at a "real job" (Andy)*
HIGHLIGHT: *Person-Centered Career Planning*

Andy is a 25-year-old young man who has been attending a local sheltered workshop since he finished high school 4 years ago. Andy had been telling his mom, friends, group home (GH) staff, and support coordinators that he wanted "a real job." However, the workshop (WS) manager and staff always told him he wasn't ready yet. When Andy got a new support coordinator (SC), he talked again about wanting to get out of the workshop and get "a real job." This time, Andy was listened to, and the SC began gathering information. According to Andy, he was ". . . sick of the same old stuff," (for example, collating calendars, shrink-wrapping CDs, and assembling flyers), and ". . . wanted to make some real money." According to the GH manager, "Andy is more than capable of getting a job. The reason he's not doing well at the workshop is because he's bored and just plain sick of the place." According to the WS manager, however, "Andy's not ready, he's off task, he doesn't finish his contracts . . . until he can show he can work, he can't do a real job." Although Andy was put on the waiting list for supported employment, each month Andy and his support staff were told that ". . . there are a lot of people waiting for jobs . . . we're doing the best we can." Rather than wait any longer, however, Andy's GH manager suggested using the Personal Career Plan. Andy would wait no more. First, Andy identified who he wanted to attend his meeting (for example, mother, friend, GH manager, SC, and certified behavior analyst) as well as whom he didn't want there (for example, sheltered workshop staff). At the meeting, the natural support network listened to Andy and helped him identify his skills, interests, preferences, and steps he would need to take to actualize his vision statement: "I want to work at a real job." Andy talked about a friend who was working and got free meals. He told the network members he wanted to work at the restaurant up the street so he could get free meals and make his own money. As a team, the natural support network identified different tasks they would complete. After a few visits to the nearby restaurant, the GH manager presented them with Andy's résumé and was able to convince them to give Andy a part-time job washing dishes at the exact restaurant he wanted to work.

for the complex tasks of changing environments, enhancing respect and decision-making, and creating a context for friendships" (p. 97). Person-centered planning is not a one-time meeting, but is an ongoing process. As presented in our model, it is a step in a continuous Adult Lifestyles Planning Cycle. We now take a closer look at another strategy or step suggested in our planning cycle for helping people attain satisfying adult lifestyles: an ecological approach.

Quality of Life and an Ecological Approach

As we saw in Andy's case, person-centered planning only represents the beginning of a process for enhancing quality of life. After the person and his or her natural support network have identified goals and future visions, it is important to identify what types and levels of support are needed in order for the person to maximize his or her participation. This can be achieved through an ecological approach or inventory, which provides a holistic look at both the environment and the skills a person brings with him or her (Thurlow & Elliott, 1998).

As a part of a holistic approach to life planning, and as suggested in our Adult Lifestyles Planning Cycle, an ecological approach can bring many advantages. According to Alper (1996b), an ecological inventory can generate information about types and levels of support a person needs to achieve independence in specific adult life areas. In addition, ecological inventories ensure that skills are (a) learned in the natural setting, (b) referenced directly to the person's local community, (c) socially validated by the person and others who participated in the planning process, (d) learned among age-appropriate peers and settings, and (e) learned in an inclusive, normalized setting (Alper, 1996b). These are important reasons why ecological inventories should be a part of any Adult Lifestyles Planning Cycle.

Steps in an Ecological Inventory

According to Alper (1996b), an ecological inventory is a hierarchical analysis of the many settings comprising the larger ecology. When conducting an ecological inventory, one analyzes the (a) domain (for example, domestic, vocation, and leisure), (b) environment (for example, home, work, and recreation), (c) subenvironment (for example, kitchen, break room, and movie theater), (d) skill (for example, cook microwave food, use time clock, and watch selected movie), and (e) tasks (for example, list of tasks required to complete skill in particular environment/subenvironment) needed for participation and inclusion in any activity (Alper, 1996b).

Applications of an Ecological Approach

Ecological inventories have been used to enhance various quality of life areas, including community living (Dymond, 1997) or living at home (Steere & Burcroff, 1997), teaching personal care and hygiene skills (Spooner & Wood, 1997), social inclusion (Chadsey & Shelden, 1998), and career development (Szymanski, 1998). Ecological inventories also have been recommended as an alternative assessment (Thurlow & Elliott, 1998; Silberman & Brown, 1998; Wolffe, 1998); a method for adapting environments, materials, and instruction to facilitate inclusion (Ryndak, 1996); and a technique for identifying curricular content for inclusive settings (Alper, 1996a). Finally, ecological inventories have been used as a process for teaching skills for successful participation in a variety of daily activity environments, including home, community, work, and leisure (Alper, 1996a). For these reasons, we have included ecological inventories in the Adult Lifestyles Planning Cycle. In Case Study 2, we will see how an ecological approach, operating within the Adult Lifestyles Planning Cycle, was used to assist Shari to participate in personally relevant activities.

As demonstrated in Case Study 2, Shari had some very clear ideas on what she wanted for herself. Further, we again see how all areas of the Adult Lifestyles Planning Cycle are demonstrated. For example, through person-centered planning, Shari was able

CASE STUDY 2 • *Living in "my own place and cooking my own food" (Shari)*
HIGHLIGHT: *Ecological Approach*

Shari is a 27-year-old young woman who had informed various people around her that she was tired of living in the group home. A person-centered planning meeting was held, and Shari told her natural support network she wanted a person like her job coach to help her live in "her own place . . . [and] someone to help me when I'm cooking my own food." Shari talked about a friend at work that has her own apartment and a roommate that she cooks with weekly. Members of Shari's natural support network helped Shari create vision statements, "I want to live in an apartment" and "I want to cook." These vision statements helped Shari and her network members prioritize the domain (domestic) that would enhance Shari's quality of life and identify the environment (home) in which she would learn to do those things she wanted to do for herself (for example, cook), versus those things with which she would like help (for example, budgeting and shopping). Consequently, Shari's support coordinator helped her schedule meetings with various supported living counselors (SLCs), and Shari picked the one she liked best: a woman who introduced Shari to other people using SLCs to help them live in their own apartment. The SLC knew of a college-aged girl who previously had worked as a paid companion and was looking for a roommate. Shari was very excited about this prospect. Shari's support coordinator helped her access money for supported living from Developmental Service's Medicaid Waiver funding, and shortly after she met the college student, Shari moved out of the group home and into her own apartment. The SLC used an ecological approach, including a task analysis, to help Shari cook her own meals. Eventually, Shari and her roommate cooked for each other, friends, and family. Shari, as well as those who knew her before she moved out of the group home, still talk about how much she has changed since getting out of the group home. She is happier, more outgoing, and just plain excited about her life, the people in it, and the things she is doing.

to express her priorities and gather a natural support network that could help her make her dreams a reality. By using ecological inventories, Shari and the network members were able to prioritize important domains, environments, and subenvironments. Using task analyses, Shari and her natural support network were able to identify steps that she could take to participate in the activities that were important to Shari. Through the coordination of a variety of formal adult services and natural supports, Shari was able to realize a number of quality of life goals (for example, own home, friendship, independence, life satisfaction, belongingness, and happiness).

When used in conjunction with a holistic planning process, such as that proposed in our Adult Lifestyles Planning Cycle, an ecological approach can broaden visions and expectations for community participation and can foster fuller collaboration for all those involved in the person-centered process (Alper, 1996a, 1996b). As pointed out by Chadsey and Shelden (1998), an ecological perspective proposes an alternative to the deficit-remedial approach so often used with people with disabilities because the ecological perspective suggests that the environment and others in the environment can be changed in addition to an individual's behaviors and skills. Consequently, people with even the most severe disabilities naturally are viewed as capable of community participation, as well as realizing other quality of life goals. In the next section, we will take a closer look at some of the formal supports available at the federal, state, and local levels for which people with disabilities may be eligible and from which they may choose.

Quality of Life and Formal Supports

Thus far, we have seen how the person-centered and ecological components of the Adult Lifestyles Planning Cycle can assist the individual in addressing his or her most important quality of life areas. Another critical step in this ongoing lifestyle planning cycle is identifying and accessing the formal supports and services that enhance those quality of life areas most important to the person. As pointed out by Nisbet (1992), "people with disabilities need support, instruction, and assistance" (p. 7) from professional service providers. Quality of life areas typically addressed by formal support providers include material well-being (for example, income, employment, and residential), physical well-being (for example, recreation, healthcare, and mobility), social inclusion (for example, community integration and participation); emotional well-being (for example, mental health); and rights (for example, access). Consequently, we have included formal supports as a necessary element in our Adult Lifestyles Planning Cycle.

Formal Supports, Services, and Agencies

When assisting people in selecting formal supports and services from various agencies, it is important to understand that programs exist at the federal, state, and local levels. Most individuals with disabilities will benefit from formal supports combining some arrangement of federal, state, and local resources. In the sections that follow, we will explore some typical programs that provide a variety of services and funding for people with disabilities.

Developmental Disabilities Waiver Program

At the federal level, such programs as the developmental disabilities waiver program are available to eligible individuals. Although eligibility requirements may vary from state to state, services typically are provided to a person who has a severe chronic disability that is attributed to a mental or physical impairment that was manifested before age 22; is expected to last indefinitely; and requires extended treatment, supports, and services. Further, this severe chronic disability must result in substantial limitations in three or more areas of major life activity, such as self-care, receptive and expressive language, learning, mobility, self-direction, capacity for independent living, and economic self-sufficiency (Palley & VanHollen, 2000).

The waiver program has been used in many states to fund a variety of formal services, including (a) assisted, supported, or supervised living; (b) supported employment; (c) case management; (d) nutritional counseling; (e) behavior management; (f) physical, speech, and occupational therapies; (g) day habilitation; (h) companion or home-based services; and (i) respite, personal, and nursing care (Cozzens et al., 1999). For more information about how specific states use the developmental disabilities waiver program, the interested reader can contact his or her local, state, or national Developmental Disabilities office. Table 15.3 provides contact information for the National Association on Developmental Disabilities Council, as well as a variety of other national agencies and organizations offering support for people with disabilities.

TABLE 15.3   *National Program Contact Information, Including Web site and Email Addresses*

Program/Telephone	National Contact Information/Details	Web sites and Email Addresses
Association for Retarded Citizens (ARC)	National Headquarters Office 1010 Wayne Ave., Suite 650 Silver Spring, MD 20910 Voice: (301) 565-3842 Fax: (301) 565-5342	*www.thearc.org* email: Info@thearc.org
Commission on Accreditation of Rehabilitation Facilities (CARF)	4891 E. Grant Road Tucson, AZ 85712 Voice/TYY: (520) 325-1044 Fax: (520) 318-1129	*www.carf.org* How to Choose a Provider Guide, Available at *www.carf.org/CARF/Consumer.htm* email: webmaster@carf.org
Council on Quality and Leadership in Supports for People with Disabilities (The Council)	100 West Road, Suite 406 Towson, MD 21204 Voice: (410) 583-0060 Fax: (410) 583-0063	*www.thecouncil.org* email: info@thecouncil.org
Easter Seals	230 West Monroe Street Suite 1800 Chicago, IL 60606 Toll Free: 1-800-221-6827 TTY: (312) 726-4258 Fax: (312) 726-1494	*www.easter-seals.org* email: info@easter-seals.org
Florida Department of Education, Bureau of Instructional Support & Community Services	Room 614 Turlington Bldg. Tallahassee, FL 32399-0400 Ph: (850) 488-1879 Suncom: 278-1879 Fax: (850) 487-2679	*www.firn.edu/doe/cgi-bin/horne/menu.pl* email: cicbiscs@mail.doe.state.fl.us
Goodwill Industries International, Inc.	9200 Rockville Pike Bethesda, MD 20814 Toll Free: 1-800-664-6577	*www.goodwill.org* email: contactus@goodwill.org

TABLE 15.3 *Continued*

National Association of Developmental Disabilities Council	1234 Massachusetts Ave., NW, Suite 103 Washington, DC 20005 Ph: (202) 347-1234 Fax: (202) 347-4023	*www.naddc.com* email: mgray@naddc.org
Office of Vocational and Adult Education (OVAE)	400 Maryland Avenue, SW Washington, DC 20202 Toll Free: 1-800-872-5327 Fax: (202) 205-8748	*www.ed.gov/offices/OVAE/* email: ovae@ed.gov
Social Security Administration (SSA)	6401 Security Blvd. Baltimore, MD 21235-0001 Toll Free: 1-800-772-1213 TTY: 1-800-325-0778	Home page: *www.ssa.gov* Desktop guides available at: *www.ssa.gov/work/ ResourcesToolkit/pubsnforms.html* *see specific states for email address
State Vocational Rehabilitation Offices	Links to state voc rehab offices provided by State Rehabilitation Advisory Council for BVS of Pennsylvania	*www.parac.org/srac.html* *see specific states for email address
United Cerebral Palsy (UCP)	1660 L Street, NW, Ste 700 Washington, DC 20036 Toll Free: 1-800-USA-5-UCP TTY: (202) 973-7197 Fax: (202) 776-0414	*www.ucpa.org* email: national@ucp.org

Social Security Administration (SSA)

Many people with disabilities may be eligible for Social Security (SS) or Supplemental Security income (SSI) benefits. Though available benefits may differ across states, several basic eligibility requirements typically apply. SS and SSI are federal programs that make monthly payments to people who have limited income and resources if they are 65 or older *or* if they are blind *or* if they have another disability (SSA, 2001).

For people who are already receiving SS or SSI benefits, concerns may arise (for example, loss of benefits) when planning for employment. Fortunately, there are a variety of programs that support people receiving SS or SSI benefits who want to work without experiencing considerable loss of benefits (SSA, 2001). These Social Security work incentive programs include the continuation of SSI payments and medical insurance and the option to set aside income and resources to achieve self-support (Plan for Achieving Self-Support [PASS]). For more information, see Table 15.3 for details on contacting the SSA. Finally, the SSA also can assist in connecting people with state and local agencies, such as vocational rehabilitation (SSA, 1997).

Vocational Rehabilitation (VR)

Although VR has been conceptualized as a federal and state partnership, it usually is administered at the state level and is generally considered a state agency. Again, though access and eligibility criteria may vary from state to state, VR typically provides services to individuals who have a significant disability. Therefore, the disability must be characterized by a severe physical or mental impairment that limits one or more functional capacities, such as mobility, communication, self-care, self-direction, interpersonal skills, and work tolerance or work skills (Cozzens et al., 1999).

VR provides a variety of services and/or funding at the state level to assist people with disabilities to become employed for the first time or return to work. Their services include (a) testing and assessments; (b) counseling; (c) wheelchairs, specially modified vans, prosthetics, and other devices; (d) training; (e) transportation; (f) job placement; (g) postplacement services; and (h) other goods and services necessary to achieve the planned job goals of the person's rehabilitation program (Social Security Administration, 1997).

As contracted through such funding agencies as Developmental Disabilities and VR, programs such as the Association for Retarded Citizens, United Cerebral Palsy, Goodwill, and Easter Seals provide employment services, residential support, and opportunities for community inclusion. With a variety of formal supports and providers available at the local level, the question becomes "How do I know who is qualified to provide these services?" Consequently, a brief discussion on accreditation is provided.

Accreditation

According to The Council on Quality and Leadership in Supports for People with Disabilities (The Council, 2001), accreditation is an ongoing process that supports organizations in their efforts at quality enhancement. This process includes evaluation of performance, as well as a review process, which provides participating organizations with benchmarks and ways to strengthen internal practices (The Council, 2001). According to Gardner and Nudler (1997), successful programs are moving away from a product focus (for example, develop a service and search for customers) to a market focus, where they identify what the person wants and then customize the services they provide. Two types of accreditation are relevant to formal support providers and are discussed in the following sections.

The Council on Quality and Leadership in Supports for People with Disabilities (The Council).

The Council is an international organization that provides a variety of services in an effort to promote quality improvement in services and supports for people with disabilities. Their services include accreditation, research, training, and consultation. In the early 1990s, The Council "redefined quality as a responsiveness to people rather than compliance with organizational processes" (The Council, 2001, p. 1). The Council developed a set of Personal Outcome Measures as the basis for the services they provide, with the intent of emphasizing "the outcomes that people with disabilities identified as being most important. . . . through a person-centered focus to life planning and service delivery" (The Council, 2001, p. 1).

These outcome-based performance measures include the following: (a) realization of personal goals; (b) choices in home, leisure, and work; (c) community inclusion and participation; (d) naturally developing friendships and intimacy; (e) rights and due process; (f) dignity, respect, privacy, and possessions; (g) safe and inclusive environments; (h) security and resources; and (i) personal satisfaction with life and services (The Council, 1998).

Agencies and organizations serving individuals with disabilities can use the personal outcome measures or quality indicators proposed by The Council for program evaluation and improvement. Most important, however, these quality of life indicators can assist the individual and his or her family in choosing the agencies that match their needs and preferences.

The Commission on Accreditation of Rehabilitation Facilities (CARF)

CARF is a private, not-for-profit organization that accredits programs providing employment services, medical rehabilitation, assisted living, adult day services, behavioral health, and community services (CARF, 2000). CARF develops and maintains practical and relevant standards of quality for such programs as Association for Retarded Citizens (ARC), Easter Seals, and Goodwill Industries. According to CARF, a quality organization illustrates the following:

> (1) service design and delivery [are] focused on the needs of the persons receiving services and its other stakeholders; (2) the persons receiving services are partners in the individual service planning process; and (3) an outcomes management system is used to improve individual services and organizational design (CARF, 2000, p. 2).

Agencies and organizations that seek accreditation and adhere to the outcomes and standards discussed previously recognize the importance of providing supports that reflect various quality of life areas (for example, choice, control, inclusion, employment, home life, and so forth). Consequently, individuals with disabilities and their families are encouraged to seek formal supports provided by agencies that are accredited and adhere to the outcomes and standards reflective of a high quality of life. Interested readers can contact the various national organizations and agencies discussed in the chapter (see Table 15.3) to obtain information about the formal supports and services these entities are accredited to provide at the state and local levels.

Quality of Life and Natural Support Networks

Formal supports alone will not necessarily enhance an individual's overall quality of life. In fact, many advocates have discussed the limitations of formal supports and services (for example, Cozzens et al., 1999; Inge, 1997; Klein, 1992; Menchetti & Piland, 1998; Murphy & Rogan, 1994; Nisbet, 1992; Wehman, 1996). For these reasons, natural support networks must be a part of a process for the enhancement of an individual's quality of life. According to Nisbet (1992), "the concept of natural supports is based on the understanding that relying on typical people and environments enhances the potential for inclusion more effectively than relying on specialized services and personnel" (p. 5).

Ideas for Building Natural Support Networks

As stressed by Amado (1993), creating natural support networks through community connections and friendships is not a linear process because each person, relationship, and situation is unique. Further, we should avoid the readiness model (for example, requiring a prerequisite set of skills) when planning supports and services for people with disabilities (Amado, 1993; Klein, 1992). While keeping these tenets in mind, strategies can be employed as part of a holistic approach to establishing a natural support network for an individual during the Adult Lifestyles Planning Cycle. Four steps for building natural support networks have been suggested by Amado (1993) and are presented in Table 15.4.

As indicated by Amado (1993), the first step involves exploring and discovering what the person's interests, gifts, and contributions are, which is also one of the key steps in person-centered planning. Members of the natural support network also can be of great assistance with the next step, which involves identification of people with whom connections can be made by exploring and developing their own community networks. After possible community connections are established, natural support network members, hosts, or sponsors can facilitate either one-to-one or group introductions. A final step for developing a natural support network for an individual in the Adult Lifestyles Planning Cycle involves providing continued assistance and encouragement to those involved in the relationship (Amado, 1993).

When developing a natural support network, it is important to determine all the places in which the person's interest can be expressed (Amado, 1993). To assist with this process, Amado (1993) suggests several areas for exploration, which include the following: (a) personal businesses, (b) leisure and recreation, (c) hobbies, (d) continuing education and personal development, (e) clubs and organizations, and (f) volunteerism.

It is important to stress that the steps and locations identified by Amado (1993) are suggested as a part of a holistic process within the Adult Lifestyles Planning Cycle, when using a natural support network to enhance an individual's quality of life. Consequently, through person-centered planning, an ecological approach, and formal supports, as well as through the development of a natural support network, a person can achieve his or her goals and attain satisfaction in personally valued quality of life areas.

Applications of Natural Support Networks

Natural support networks have been identified as a life-enhancing approach to assisting individuals with disabilities plan for personally satisfying lifestyles (Forest & Pearpoint, 1992). Network members can help establish and maintain opportunities to develop such quality of life areas as socialization (O'Brien & O'Brien, 1992), inclusion and friendship (Strully & Strully, 1992), employment (Hagner, 1992; Murphy & Rogan, 1994; Wehman, 1996), and home life (Klein, 1992). Natural support networking can also serve as a means for identifying curriculum and teaching strategies (Jorgensen, 1992), as well as influencing public policy (Gerry & Mirsky, 1992). In Case Study 3, we will see how a natural support network helped Kathy, an elderly woman, to develop hobbies and friendships in her local community.

TABLE 15.4 *Steps for Building Natural Support Networks*

Steps for Building Natural Supports	*Examples/Guidelines*
1. Identify interests, gifts, and contributions	(a) People should not have to wait until they learn more skills or their behavior is fixed before they can have relationships. (b) Identifying mutual interests and gifts while considering physical proximity are critical components of the process. (c) Listening carefully to the person, as well as those who know him or her best, to identify interests and gifts is essential. (d) It may be necessary to explore and discover interests when people have had limited experiences.
2. Explore and identify possible connections	(a) Identify opportunities for community relationships. (b) Remember that seeing the same people over time is important, and some basis for exchange is needed, e.g., teams or clubs. (c) Look for potential welcoming places, e.g., local, family-owned, neighborhood groups, clubs, and church. (d) Explore the local community, e.g., local history, leaders, and association life. (e) Look for interested people, e.g., explore natural support network's social connections.
3. Make introductions	(a) One-to-one introductions: The facilitator should know the individual well and speak personally about the person's gifts and interests. (b) Introductions of individual to groups: A host or sponsor is identified to facilitate the person joining formal or informal groups or clubs.
4. Continue to support the relationship	(a) Check on the relationship from time to time. (b) Informally ask people in the setting how things are going. (c) Verify that the person is really being included, especially if he or she belongs to a club or group. (d) Remember that relationships go up and down over time. (e) People may need space and time to work problems out, or they may need assistance.

Source: Adapted from Amado (1993), Steps for Supporting Community Connections, pp. 313–323.

As demonstrated in Kathy's situation (Case Study 3), members of her natural support network greatly facilitated the development of the activities Kathy identified as most important to her during person-centered planning (for example, social inclusion, friendship, hobbies, and belongingness). Clearly, ecological inventories were helpful in facilitating Kathy's access to and participation in the programs in which she wanted to be a part. For example, in establishing the hobby of craft making, the ecological domain was leisure, the environment was the craft store, the subenvironment was the craft

CASE STUDY 3 • *Having friends and "doing things with people my own*
                        age" (Kathy)
HIGHLIGHT: *Building a Natural Support Network for Social Inclusion*

Kathy is a 76-year-old woman who had lived the first 56 years of her life with her parents. When they died, Kathy moved in with her younger brother and sister-in-law. Kathy's brother became ill and Kathy eventually moved into a small community-based group home, where she has lived for the past eight years. A new resident manager was instrumental in broadening the social connections of Kathy and the other women living at the group home. The process began by holding a person-centered planning meeting for Kathy. At her meeting, Kathy and her natural support network explored various interests of Kathy's, such as looking at books and magazines, working on crafts, and painting. They helped Kathy develop several vision statements, including "I would like friends" and ". . . to do things with people my own age." Next, the network members explored their own social connections. For example, one of the members suggested a publication called Active Lifestyles, designed for members of the older adult community and available at their local newspaper's Web site. Kathy and her group learned that a variety of activities were available (for example, senior clubs and centers, advocacy groups, caregivers, education, financial issues, health-related resources, help lines, housing, transportation, and volunteer programs). Kathy and her natural support network identified three community connections and divided up their roles as facilitators for each one. The first connection was a painting club, created by and for senior citizens and taught by a professor from a nearby university. The second was a craft club, which was forming at a local fabric and craft supply store. The third was a literacy volunteer program at the local library. The SC worked out funding for transportation, while the GH manager obtained assistance in performing several ecological inventories for participation in the activities that were important to Kathy. After the facilitators made introductions, some one-on-one relationships were fostered through naturally occurring activities and continued support. Interestingly, the literacy program at the local library proved to be the most meaningful connection of all because Kathy was afforded the opportunity to develop a lasting friendship with another senior citizen who met with Kathy twice weekly at the library to read a chapter book together. Occasionally, they went to lunch, and, eventually, Kathy became a member of her friend's church.

area, and the activity was arranging a floral centerpiece. Although some formal supports were used at the beginning (for example, funding for transportation), the naturally forming friendships that Kathy and her network members developed were instrumental in helping her achieve personally satisfying and meaningful relationships and social supports. As pointed out by Gerry and Mirsky (1992), ". . . most individuals with severe disabilities will be integrated into the community best through a strategy of natural supports . . ." (p. 345).

Several researchers have stressed the importance of socialization when establishing a natural support network. As pointed out by Forest and Pearpoint (1992), *people* are "the ultimate natural support resource" (p. 65). According to O'Brien and O'Brien (1992), "good lives for people with severe disabilities depend on whether they are recognized as members of the social networks and associations that constitute community" (p. 18). Consequently, developing a natural support network for an individual with disabilities must include opportunities for social inclusion that are based upon the desires of the person.

According to Blaney and Freud (1994) it is also important to provide meaningful and relevant opportunities for social inclusion, which can be described according to five dimensions: (a) *frequency*, that is, activities that occur often enough; (b) *duration*, that is, over a considerable amount of time; (c) *intensity of interaction*, that is, with deliberate concentration, as demonstrated between friends; (d) *proportion*, that is, are connected to the local community; and (e) *symmetry*, that is, recognize the person as an equal member of society. Consequently, this working definition of social inclusion, as proposed by Blaney and Freud (1994), can guide natural support networks in helping a person expand his or her recreational and leisure activities, as well as serve as a model for evaluating the quality and nature of such activities.

When viewing the various community connections developed for Kathy (Case Study 3) with these dimensions in mind, we can see how the literacy program at the local library resulted in the most meaningful natural support and opportunity for social inclusion. This connection afforded more frequently scheduled activities (for example, twice weekly), for an extended duration (for example, one hour), with interactions that were more intense (for example, meeting with her friend for two hours a week), within proportion (for example, inclusive setting, and age-appropriate activity with friend), and with eventual symmetry (for example, Kathy started as recipient, but the connection developed into a true peer relationship). Clearly, then, Blaney and Freud's (1994) working definition can assist natural support networks, working within the Adult Lifestyles Planning Cycle, to establish and foster meaningful connections and opportunities for social inclusion.

Summary

As evidenced in the case studies presented in this chapter, planning an adult lifestyle for individuals with disabilities that reflects a commitment to personally satisfying quality of life issues is a continual and cyclical process. This process requires discovering, accessing, facilitating, and maintaining a variety of formal and natural supports. This can be achieved through person-centered planning and expansion of an individual's natural support network, as well as through an ecological approach to an individual's participation in a variety of settings and activities. It is important to stress that we are advocating for a continual and cyclical process and not a readiness or skill acquisition program. Inherent in the latter approaches is the risk that programs become a stringent method for teaching a set of subskills, which are taken out of the personal context and taught in isolation. Rather, person-centered planning techniques focus on the interests and capacities of the individual, instead of limitations or deficits (Getzel & deFurs, 1997; Menchetti & Piland, 1998; Mount & Zwernick, 1988). As pointed out by Everson (1996), "all person-centered planning approaches begin with the belief that all individuals, regardless of the type or severity of their disabilities, not only benefit from services provided in their communities, but also offer their communities many gifts and capacities" (p. 8).

For most people, it takes coordination of all five of the areas proposed in the Adult Lifestyles Planning Cycle. Consequently, we propose that, in order to assist an individual with disabilities to achieve a personally satisfying adult lifestyle, planning must be:

1. Based on personal determination of quality of life areas
2. Developed through a person-centered planning process (not a one-time meeting)
3. Facilitated through an ecological approach that supports people in the activities that are important to them
4. Supported through access and coordination of formal services
5. Accentuated through meaningful opportunities for development of natural support networks and social inclusion

At no time do we suggest that any component of the Adult Lifestyles Planning Cycle be used in isolation, nor any of its components to be taken out of the context of personal values.

In addition to being consistent with those best practices identified in a plethora of current research, our Adult Lifestyles Planning Cycle is consistent with the principles and philosophy of major accreditation organizations (for example, CARF and The Council). Further, our Adult Lifestyles Planning Cycle reflects the policies and practices proposed by a variety of advocacy agents. For example, the ARC also advocates for person-centered planning and support for quality of life outcomes, which are based on those personal values and outcomes deemed important to the individual.

The Adult Lifestyles Planning Cycle is also reflective of the five basic organizing principles proposed by Gerry and Mirsky (1992): (a) Services for people with disabilities should be based on the needs and wishes of the individual themselves and, as appropriate, their families; (b) services for people with disabilities must be inclusive to empower consumers and flexible to reflect the differing and changing needs of people with disabilities; (c) every person with a disability must have a real opportunity to engage in productive employment; (d) public and private collaborations must be fostered to ensure that people with disabilities have the opportunities and choices that are to be available to all Americans; and (e) social inclusion of people with disabilities in their neighborhoods and communities must be a major focus of the overall effort.

As discussed at the beginning of this chapter, an important opportunity for meaningful adult lifestyle planning occurs while a person is still in school. Therefore, understanding the requirements and implications of age-14 and age-16 transition planning, which is mandated by IDEA, is critical for all parties involved. Collaboration between the student, parents, special and general educators, and other school and community professionals is imperative. Further, it is vital that all parties involved in the collaborative process are not only aware of, but also *make use of* the plethora of school- and community-based curricular opportunities available to assist students as they approach adulthood. Finally, it is essential that everyone involved in the transition process recognize that decisions made at the age-14 and age-16 milestones can have longterm lifestyle consequences for all students. As a result, students, parents, educators, and other professionals are strongly urged to use the Adult Lifestyles Planning Cycle to assist in ensuring a bright and successful transition from adolescence into adulthood for students with severe disabilities.

In conclusion, we propose that the Adult Lifestyles Planning Cycle reflects the ongoing nature of a continual and cyclical process in which the central tenets are to support a personally satisfying quality of life and self-directed decisionmaking for all people. We will not engage in debate of whether people are capable of making decisions. Rather, the issue is how we can support people in making decisions that result in a quality of life that is based upon the person's values, interests, and desires. We suggest that the Adult Lifestyles Planning Cycle achieves this essential goal and more.

References

Abrams, K., DonAroma, P., & Karan, O. C. (1997). Consumer choice as predictor of job satisfaction and supervisor ratings for people with disabilities. *Journal of Vocational Rehabilitation, 9,* 205–215.

Alper, S. (1996a). Application of the process to ecological domains. In D. L. Ryndak & S. Alper (Eds.), *Curriculum content for students with moderate and severe disabilities in inclusive settings* (pp. 155–176). Boston: Allyn & Bacon.

Alper, S. (1996b). An ecological approach to identifying curriculum content for inclusive settings. In D. L. Ryndak & S. Alper (Eds.), *Curriculum content for students with moderate and severe disabilities in inclusive settings* (pp. 19–31). Boston: Allyn & Bacon.

Amado, A. N. (1993). Steps for supporting community connections. In A. N. Amado (Ed.), *Friendships and community connections between people with and without developmental disabilities* (pp. 299–326). Baltimore, MD: Paul H. Brookes Publishing Co.

Artisani, A. J., & Mallar, L. (1998). Positive behavior supports in general education settings: Combining person-centered planning and functional analysis. *Intervention in School and Clinic, 34*(1), 33–38.

Blackorby, J., & Wagner, M. (1996). Longitudinal postschool outcomes of youth with disabilities: Findings from the national longitudinal transition study. *Exceptional Children, 62*(5), 399–413.

Blaney, B. C., & Freud, E. L. (1994). Trying to play together: Competing paradigms in approaches to inclusion through recreation and leisure. In V. J. Bradley, J. W. Asbaugh, & B. C. Blaney (Eds.), *Creating individual supports for people with developmental disabilities: A mandate for change at many levels* (pp. 237–254). Baltimore, MD: Paul H. Brookes Publishing Co.

Butterworth, J., Hagner, D., Heikkinen, B., DeMello, S., & McDonough, K. (1993). *Whole life planning: A guide for organizers and facilitators.* Boston, MA: Children's Hospital, Institute for Community Inclusion.

Butterworth, J., Steere, D. E., & Whitney-Thomas, J. (1997). Using person-centered planning to address personal quality of life. In R. L. Schalock (Ed.), *Quality of life, Volume II: Application to persons with disabilities* (pp. 5–23). Washington, D.C.: American Association on Mental Retardation.

Chadsey, J., & Shelden, D. (1998). Moving towards social inclusion in employment and postsecondary school settings. In F. R. Rusch and J. G. Chadsey (Eds.), *Beyond high school: Transition from school to work* (pp. 406–437). Belmont, CA: Wadsworth Publishing Co.

Cobb, R. B., & Neubert, D. A. (1998). Vocational education: Emerging vocationalism. In F. R. Rusch and J. G. Chadsey, *Beyond high school: Transition from school to work* (pp. 101–126). Belmont, CA: Wadsworth Publishing Co.

Commission on Accreditation of Rehabilitation Facilities, The. (2000). *Managing outcomes: Employment and community services.* Tuscon, AZ: Author.

Council on Quality and Leadership in Supports for People with Disabilities, The. (1998). *Personal outcomes: Advancing the future . . . person by person.* Retrieved March 13, 2001 from *www.thecouncil. org/pom.htm.*

Council on Quality and Leadership in Supports for People with Disabilities, The. (2001). *Welcome to the council on quality and leadership in supports for people with disabilities home page.* Retrieved March 13, 2001 from *www.thecouncil.org.*

Cozzens, G., Dowdy, C. A., & Smith, T. E. C. (1999). *Adult agencies: Linkages for adolescents in transition.* Austin, TX: Pro-ED, Inc.

Cross, T., Cooke, N. L., Wood, W. M., & Test, D. W. (1999). Comparison of the effects of MAPS and ChoiceMakers on student self-determination skills. *Education and Training Mental Retardation and Developmental Disabilities, 34*(4), 499–510.

Dymond, S. K. (1997). Community living. In P. Wehman & J. Kregel (Eds.), *Functional curriculum for elementary, middle, and secondary aged students with special needs* (pp. 197–226). Austin, TX: Pro-ED, Inc.

Everson, J. M. (1996). Using person-centered planning concepts to enhance school-to-adult life transition planning. *Journal of Vocational Rehabilitation, 6,* 7–13.

Everson, J. M., & Reid, D. H. (1997). Using person-centered planning to determine preferences among people with the most severe developmental disabilities. *Journal of Vocational Rehabilitation, 9,* 99–108.

Felce, D., & Perry, J. (1995). Quality of life: Its definition and measurement. *Research in Developmental Disabilities, 16*(1), 51–74.

Forest, M., & Pearpoint, J. (1992). Families, friends, and circles. In J. Nisbet (Ed.), *Natural supports in school, at work, and in the community for people with severe disabilities* (pp. 65–86). Baltimore, MD: Paul H. Brookes Publishing Co.

Gardner, J. F., & Nudler, S. (1997). Beyond compliance to responsiveness: Accreditation reconsidered. In R. L. Schalock (Ed.), *Quality of life, Volume II: Application to persons with disabilities,* (pp. 135–148). Washington, D.C.: American Association on Mental Retardation.

Gerry, N. H., & Mirsky, A. J. (1992). Guiding principles for public policies on natural supports. In J. Nisbet (Ed.), *Natural supports in school, at work, and in the community for people with severe disabilities* (pp. 341–346). Baltimore, MD: Paul H. Brookes Publishing Co.

Getzel, E. E., & deFurs, S. (1997). Transition planning for students with significant disabilities: Implications for student-centered planning. *Focus on Autism & Other Developmental Disabilities, 12*(1), 39–48.

Goode, D. (Ed.). (1994). *Quality of life for persons with disabilities: International perspectives and issues.* Cambridge, MA: Brookline Books, Inc.

Hagner, D. C. (1992). The social interactions and job supports of supported employees. In J. Nisbet (Ed.), *Natural supports in school, at work, and in the community for people with severe disabilities* (pp. 217–240). Baltimore, MD: Paul H. Brookes Publishing Co.

Hagner, D., Helm, D. T., & Butterworth, J. (1996). "This is your meeting:" A qualitative study of person-centered planning. *Mental Retardation, 34*(3), 159–171.

Hagner, D., & Vander Sande, J. (1998). School-sponsored work experience and vocational instruction. In F. R. Rusch and J. G. Chadsey (Eds.), *Beyond high school: Transition from school to work* (pp. 341–366). Belmont, CA: Wadsworth Publishing Co.

Hatton, C. (1998). Whose quality of life is it anyway? Some problems with the emerging quality of life consensus. *Mental Retardation, 36*(2), 104–115.

Heller, T., Factor, A., & Sterns, H. (1996). Impact of person-centered later life planning training for older adults with mental retardation. *The Journal of Rehabilitation (62),* 77–83.

Individuals with Disabilities Education Act of 1990, 20 U.S. C. 1401 (a)(19).

Individuals with Disabilities Education Act Amendment of 1997, 20 U.S. C. 1414 (d)(1).

Inge, K. J. (Ed.). (1997, Winter). A customer-driven approach to supported employment. *Rehabilitation Research and Training Center at Virginia Commonwealth University,* 1–4.

Jorgensen, C. M. (1992). Natural supports in inclusive schools: Curricular and teaching strategies. In J. Nisbet (Ed.), *Natural supports in school, at work, and in the community for people with severe disabilities* (pp. 179–216). Baltimore, MD: Paul H. Brookes Publishing Co.

Klein, J. (1992). Get me the hell out of here: Supporting people with disabilities to live in their own homes. In J. Nisbet (Ed.), *Natural supports in school, at work, and in the community for people with severe disabilities* (pp. 277–340). Baltimore, MD: Paul H. Brookes Publishing Co.

Knoster, T. (1995). Understanding the difference between "rap around" and "run around" interagency collaboration under the Kordero court order. *TASH Newsletter, 21*(11,12), 25–26.

Marone, J., Hoff, D., & Helm, D. T. (1997). Person-centered planning for the millennium: We're old enough to remember when PCP was just a drug. *Journal of Vocational Rehabilitation, 8,* 285–297.

McVilly, K. R., & Rawlinson, R. B. (1998). Quality of life issues in the development and evaluation of services for people with intellectual disabilities. *Journal of Intellectual & Developmental Disability, 23*(3), 199–218.

Menchetti, B. M., & Piland, V. C. (1998). The personal career plan: A person-centered approach to vocational evaluation and career planning. In F. R. Rusch and J. G. Chadsey (Eds.), *Beyond high school: Transition from school to work* (pp. 319–339). Belmont, CA: Wadsworth Publishing Co.

Menchetti, B. M., & Piland, V. C. (2001). Transition assessment and evaluation: Current methods and emerging alternatives. In S. Alper, D. L. Ryndak, & C. N. Schloss (Eds.), *Alternate assessment of students with disabilities in inclusive settings* (pp. 220–255). Boston: Allyn & Bacon.

Miner, C. A., & Bates, P. E. (1997). The effects of person-centered planning activities on the IEP/transition planning process. *Education and Training in Mental Retardation and Developmental Disabilities, 32*(2), 105–112.

Mount, B. (1994). Benefits and limitations of personal futures planning. In V. J. Bradley, J. W. Asbaugh, & B. C. Blaney (Eds.), *Creating individual supports for people with developmental disabilities: A mandate for change at many levels* (pp. 97–108). Baltimore, MD: Paul H. Brookes Publishing Co.

Mount, B., & Zwernick, K. (1988). *It's never too early, it's never too late: An overview of personal futures planning*. St. Paul, MN: Governor's Planning Council on Developmental Disabilities.

Murphy, S. T., & Rogan, P. M. (1994). *Developing natural supports in the workplace: A practitioner's guide*. St. Augustine, FL: Training Resource Network, Inc.

Nisbet, J. (Ed.). (1992). *Natural supports in school, at work, and in the community for people with severe disabilities*. Baltimore, MD: Paul H. Brookes Publishing Co.

O'Brien, J. (1987). A guide to life-style planning: Using the activities catalog to integrate services and natural support systems. In B. Wilcox & G. T. Bellamy (Eds.), *A comprehensive guide to the activities catalogue: An alternative curriculum for youth and adults with severe disabilities* (pp. 175–189). Baltimore, MD: Paul H. Brookes Publishing Co.

O'Brien, J., & O'Brien, C. L. (1992). Members of each other: Perspectives on social support for people with disabilities. In J. Nisbet (Ed.), *Natural supports in school, at work, and in the community for people with severe disabilities* (pp. 17–63). Baltimore, MD: Paul H. Brookes Publishing Co.

Palley, H. A., & VanHollen, V. (2000). Long-term care for people with developmental disabilities: A critical analysis. *Health & Social Work, 25*(3), 181–189.

Perlroth, P., Pumpian, I., Hesche, S., & Campbell, C. (1993). Transition planning for individuals who are deaf and blind: A person-centered approach. *OSERS News in Print, 5*(3), 24–30.

Perrin, B. (1999). The original "Scandinavian" normalization principle and its continuing relevance for the 1990s. In R. J. Flynn & R. A. Lemay (Eds.), *A quarter-century of normalization and social role valorization: Evolution and impact* (pp. 181–196). Ottawa (Ont.), Canada: University of Ottawa Press.

Reid, D. H., Everson, J. M., & Green, C. W. (1999). Systematic evaluation of preferences identified through person-centered planning for people with profound multiple disabilities. *Journal of Applied Behavior Analysis, 32*(4), 467–477.

Roberts, G., Becker, H. A., & Seay, P. C. (1997). A process for measuring adoption of innovation within the supports paradigm. *The Journal of the Association for Persons with Severe Handicaps, 22*(Summer), 109–119.

Ryndak, D. L. (1996). Adapting environments, materials, and instruction to facilitating inclusion. In D. L. Ryndak & S. Alper (Eds.), *Curriculum content for students with moderate and severe disabilities in inclusive settings* (pp. 97–124). Boston: Allyn & Bacon.

Silberman, R. K., & Brown, F. (1998). Alternative approaches to assessing students who have visual impairments with other disabilities in classroom and community environments. In S. Z. Sacks & R. K. Silberman (Eds.), *Educating students who have visual impairments with other disabilities* (pp. 73–98). Baltimore, MD: Paul H. Brookes Publishing Co.

Smith, G. (1994). Paying for supports: Dollars, payments, and the new support paradigm. In V. J. Bradley, J. W. Ashbaugh, & B. C. Blaney (Eds.), *Creating individual supports for people with developmental disabilities: A mandate for change at many levels*. Baltimore, MD: Paul H. Brookes Publishing Co.

Smull, M. & Harrison, S. (1992). *Supporting people with severe reputations in the community*. Alexandria, VA: National Association of State Directors of Developmental Disabilities Services, Inc.

Social Security Administration. (1997). *How we can help with vocational rehabilitation*. Retrieved March 13, 2001 from *www.ssa.gov/pubs/10050.html*.

Social Security Administration. (2000). *A desktop guide to social security and SSI work Incentives*. Retrieved March 13, 2001 from *www.ssa.gov/pubs/11002.html*.

Social Security Administration. (2001). *A desktop guide to SSI eligibility requirements*. Retrieved March 13, 2001 from *www.ssa.gov/pubs/11001.html*.

Spooner, F., & Wood, W. M. (1997). Teaching personal care and hygiene skills. In P. Wehman & J. Kregel (Eds.), *Functional curriculum for elementary, middle, and secondary aged students with special needs* (pp. 251–281). Austin, TX: Pro-ED, Inc.

Steere, D. E., & Burcroff, T. L. (1997). Living at home. In P. Wehman & J. Kregel (Eds.), *Functional curriculum for elementary, middle, and secondary aged students with special needs* (pp. 227–249). Austin, TX: Pro-ED, Inc.

Strully, J. L., & Strully, C. F. (1992). The struggle toward inclusion and the fulfillment of friendship. In J. Nisbet (Ed.), *Natural supports in school, at work, and in the community for people with severe disabilities* (pp. 165–178). Baltimore, MD: Paul H. Brookes Publishing Co.

Szymanski, E. M. (1998). Career development, school-to-work transition, and diversity. In F. R. Rusch & J. G. Chadsey (Eds.), *Beyond high school: Transition from school to work* (pp. 127–145). Belmont, CA: Wadsworth Publishing Co.

Taylor, S. J., & Bogdan, R. (1996). Quality of life and the individual's perspective. In R. L. Schalock (Ed.), *Quality of life, Volume I: Conceptualization and measurement* (pp. 11–22). Washington, D.C.: American Association on Mental Retardation.

Thurlow, M., & Elliott, J. (1998). Student assessment and evaluation. In F. R. Rusch & J. G. Chadsey (Eds.), *Beyond high school: Transition from school to work* (pp. 265–296). Belmont, CA: Wadsworth Publishing Co.

United States Department of Education (2000). *The twenty-second annual report to Congress on the implementation of the Individuals with Disabilities Education Act*. Washington, D.C.: U.S. DOE, Office of Special Education and Rehabilitative Services.

Vandercook, T., York, J., & Forest, M. (1989). The McGill action planning system (MAPS): A strategy for building the vision. *Journal of the Association for Persons with Severe Handicaps, 14*(3), 79–87.

Wehman, P. (1996). *Life beyond the classroom: Transition strategies for young people with disabilities* (2nd ed.). Baltimore, MD: Paul H. Brookes Publishing Co.

Wehman, P. (1998, Fall). How are we doing? *The National Supported Employment Consortium,* 1–5.

Wolffe, K. (1998). Transition planning and employment outcomes for students who have visual impairments with other disabilities. In S. Z. Sacks & R. K. Silberman (Eds.), *Educating students who have visual impairments with other disabilities* (pp. 339–365). Baltimore, MD: Paul H. Brookes Publishing Co.

16

"We Want to Go to College Too": Supporting Students with Significant Disabilities in Higher Education

Mary Beth Doyle

Objectives

After completing this chapter, the reader will be able to

1. Describe the current status of high school graduation for students with significant disabilities.
2. Describe the higher education options for students with significant disabilities who do not have a high school diploma or a Graduation Equivalency Diploma (GED).
3. Describe how students with significant disabilities can participate in college experience.
4. Describe the role of high school special education teachers in facilitating the inclusion of students with significant disabilities in a college experience.

Key Terms

Audit option	Inclusion in the college experience	Natural supports
Higher education		Support facilitator

The college experience is, for many young adults, a rite of passage into adulthood. It is a time of continued academic, social, and personal growth. It is a time of movement toward independence, with certain types of support. Young adults learn how to balance responsibilities such as studies, work, and leisure, but do not have to worry about providing for spouses and children. Some students learn to live away from their families in a dormitory, yet not have the full responsibilities of paying monthly bills, making daily meals, or maintaining a home. For approximately 15.3 million young adults, college is the intermediate step between high school and the full responsibilities of adulthood (U.S. Department of Education National Center on Education Statistics, 2001).

Historically, young adults with significant disabilities have not had the same college opportunities available to them as they transition between high school and the full responsibilities of adulthood. Students within this population more typically attend high school until they are 21 years old and then transition into a variety of types of adult services, including supported work, supported living, day treatment facilities, and sheltered workshops (Agran, Snow, & Swaner, 1999; Certo, Pumpian, Fisher, Storey, & Smalley, 1997). However, as increasing numbers of students with significant disabilities are included as members of their local public school communities, it is not surprising that some of these students question the possibility of joining their nondisabled classmates in a college or university experience (Doyle, 1997; Grigal, Neubert, & Moon, 2001; Hall, Kleinert, & Kearns, 2000). Actually, this choice can be an ideal transition between high school and adulthood for some students with significant disabilities. Although there has been movement in this direction, it is on a very small scale (Page & Chadsey-Rusch, 1995; Tashie, Malloy, & Lichtenstein, 1998). The numbers of examples that describe truly inclusive programs, as opposed to high school programs meeting on college campuses, are few. There are examples where students with significant disabilities are included into the very fabric of the community that have become part of the emerging conversation, but not part of the written professional literature.

The purpose of this chapter is to offer suggestions and strategies to move the conversation forward. Because the conversation is so new, the primary knowledge and experience base used to inform this chapter stem from the first-hand experiences of the author, who was a member of an inclusive college community. Additional information from the emerging professional literature on the topic will be woven throughout the chapter.

This chapter is divided into four major sections. The first section is a description of the inclusive program at the former Trinity College of Vermont. The second section highlights legal issues that impact this topic both directly and indirectly. The third section focuses on the role of high school special educators in exploring the process within the local community. The focus of the final section provides suggestions for the future.

Program Description of Trinity College of Vermont

Trinity College of Vermont closed its doors in June of 2000. However, between 1989 and 2000, students with moderate and severe disabilities were members of the community. Referred to as the ENHANCE program, it was an early example of supporting students with moderate and severe disabilities on a college campus. Through the years, the program evolved from being a separate post–high school program hosted on a college campus to a completely inclusive program. The lessons learned from those experiences can be applied to the current thinking related to exploring participation in higher education as yet another option for students with significant disabilities.

In the early 1980s, a key administrator at Trinity College of Vermont recognized that young adults with significant disabilities were not given the option to participate in the college experience. She examined the core values of the college and recognized that welcoming students with significant disabilities to the college would be in alignment with those values. The core values that drove this decision were the following:

1. Trinity College values the preparation of students who will treasure diversity among people and who will base their valuation of others on a respect for the inherent worth of the human person.
2. Trinity College values itself as a place that calls each of its members to be accountable for her/his gifts that serve the community and work toward the betterment of society.

Given such clearly articulated core values, the administration decided that it was appropriate to make college experiences available for persons with developmental disabilities. Such a program would be beneficial for students with and without disabilities, as well as for the college community as a whole. In 1989, the College launched the ENHANCE Program.

Students who enrolled in the ENHANCE program had received either Individualized Education Program (IEP) diplomas or certificates of attendance from their high schools. None of the students had earned a high school diploma or GED. None of the students could read or write on a high school level. In fact, many of the students could not read or write at all. All of the students received special education services throughout their academic careers. Most relied heavily on paraprofessional supports and spent 50 percent or more of their time in self-contained special education classes prior to enrolling at Trinity College.

Initially, the program consisted of self-contained classes on the college campus. The curriculum was a functional curriculum that included content around maintaining a budget, filling out job applications and interpersonal skills. Students without disabilities volunteered to help in the self-contained classes, but rarely established friendships that extended beyond those classes. The self-contained classes were taught and advised by a Trinity College staff member who was not given faculty status. Students with significant disabilities enrolled in typical college classes on a very limited scale.

In 1996, the program became fully inclusive in response to a comment made by one of the ENHANCE students. Ken casually remarked, "When you're retarded you always have to take these courses in banking and shopping. I've been taking the same class since I was a kid. I'm still not very good at it, so I keep taking classes. It doesn't matter anyway because I don't have much money to worry about." No need for analysis or explanation, Ken's thoughts became the impetus for an immediate and significant program change. The following September all students with significant disabilities were (a) enrolled in typical college classes, (b) taught and advised by college faculty, and (c) received support from their nondisabled classmates. The special education pullout courses were completely eliminated, and the program was no longer referred to as a separate program. Rather, students were referred to by name and how they were connected with the academics of the institution (for example, Peter, the student who is auditing the class).

Enrollment Option

Students with significant disabilities enrolled as nonmatriculating students through the audit option at Trinity College. The audit option is a registration structure available at most institutions of higher education. This option provides any community member the opportunity to participate in college-level classes without enrolling as a degree-seeking student in the college. When auditing a course, the student does not have to meet the same curricular outcomes as the rest of the class. At Trinity College, we took curricular advantage of the audit option because it afforded an enormous amount of flexibility within which we developed rigorous, individualized coursework for the students with significant disabilities. When auditing, the student does not receive academic credit. In most situations, courses that are audited appear on a transcript without grades or credits attached.

At Trinity College, the audit option provided a legitimate front door approach for students with significant disabilities to enroll in college courses. The registration process was already established and record keeping was done through the registration office at the college, just like everyone else. Special or separate systems did not have to be created.

Curriculum and Instruction

Beginning in 1996, the primary approach to the design of curriculum and instruction was the use of multilevel curriculum and instruction. Multilevel curriculum and instruction refers to teaching a diverse group of students within a shared activity in which students have individually appropriate learning outcomes within the same curriculum area (Giangreco & Doyle, 2000). The use of multilevel curriculum and instruction gave us the opportunity to adapt instruction, but, because the curriculum was in the context of shared activities, we also had many opportunities to be surprised. Students with significant disabilities were frequently energized and excited to learn interesting and new information. As Peter once said about an advanced history course, "This is the first time I'm able to learn interesting stuff. When you're in special ed. in high school they make you do baby stuff like brushing your teeth in school. In college I get to learn a lot of really cool stuff" (Hunton & Doyle, 1999). Multilevel curriculum and instruction enabled faculty to design interesting and engaging curricular content for all learners while offering the opportunity to be surprised. Giangreco (1997) described it as follows:

> This core of curricular content should be reasonably attainable based on the student's current level of functioning and characteristics, but a quality curriculum should also provide ample opportunities for students to surprise us with their capabilities. Therefore, we should never presume to know the upper limits of a student's abilities, especially if they have never been exposed to something or received competent instruction. We should expose them to, and instruct them in, a full range of general education curricular activities to complement more traditional functional life skills. Too often we artificially limit curricular opportunities for students with severe disabilities based on our own preconceived notions (p. 56).

At Trinity College, after professors understood the concepts of multilevel curriculum and instruction as the guiding pedagogical framework, the concept of inclusion became more clear, and we were all more open to the surprises of students surpassing initial expectations. As individual students expressed their excitement for learning, professors experienced a new excitement for teaching.

Two key tools were developed and used to assist professors in understanding the application of multilevel curriculum. These tools created a structure within which professors understood the concepts and could engage in a common language about curricular inclusion. The tools were *Syllabi Adaptation and Negotiation* and *Contract of Participation* (refer to Tables 16.1 and 16.2). The *Syllabi Adaptation and Negotiation Plan* was completed by the student with disabilities, a faculty advisor, and the student's nondisabled peers (refer to Table 16.1). Professors reported that the plans provided necessary practical bridges between a theoretical understanding of inclusion and multilevel instruction to the actual day-to-day technical management of both within the context of typical classes. They appreciated the clarity of expectations, as well as the teaching tips that were often helpful for students without disabilities as well.

The second form, the *Contract of Participation* (refer to Table 16.2), provided the student with significant disabilities the opportunity to self-advocate *how* s/he would participate in common routines of college classes. Professors reported that the course contract helped them to be comfortable with the actual class implementation and process.

Experiences related to issues of curriculum and instruction were both interesting and challenging. As described by Giangreco, Baumgart, and Doyle (1995), the inclusion of students with disabilities fundamentally changes and improves instruction for all students in the class. That was certainly the case at Trinity College. In some cases, classroom instruction had to change in order to support the learning styles and characteristics of a new, more diverse community. Lectures, notes, papers, and exams were no longer adequate. Perhaps they never were. As a result of the inclusion of undergraduates who had significant disabilities, active engagement with students around interesting content using activity-based instruction and cooperative learning became part of the cultural norms in many courses. Although these instructional approaches might not sound unusual to an elementary or middle school teacher who regularly uses such approaches, they can be very uncommon in higher education. The participation of students with significant disabilities had a positive impact on the curriculum and instruction for all of the undergraduate students.

Social Aspects of College

Being a college student means more than just attending classes. The social life is, for many students, at the very core of college/university life. The impact of relationships established during college/university should never be underestimated. Many students share experiences and make friendships that provide the material for fond memories that last for the rest of their lives.

Fostering relationships between students with and without significant disabilities was perhaps the most difficult aspect of the program at Trinity College. It was challenging for two reasons. First, prior to attending college, students with significant disabilities had a history of constant adult proximity (that is, paraprofessionals and special educators), so

TABLE 16.1 *Syllabi Adaptation and Negotiation*

Student: **Peter**	*Peer Partner(s):* **Danielle P. (in class), Jennifer**
Class: **Western Civilization**	*Professor:* **Pat H.** *Third* **Semester at Trinity**

Adapted Course Goals for Peter:
Peter will be focusing on fewer goals (i.e., 3 of the 6 listed).

1. To trace (via pictures) the development of Western Civilizations through remembered, recovered, and invented history.
2. To nurture memory of the past in order to develop attachments to abiding concerns and perspectives on human existence.
3. To become familiar with the geography of our planet (i.e., identify the seven continents on a picture of planet).

Course-Related Strengths
1. Peter is very interested in history.
2. Peter has a lot of previous knowledge related to a variety of topics within history.
3. Peter works hard to understand the content and is responsible in completing his assignments.
4. Peter's family is interested in the study of history.
5. Peter has been in class with P. Habif and enjoys her teaching style a great deal. He has said, She uses humor and isn't boring.

Course-Related Needs
1. Peter does not read or write well.
2. Although Peter wants to learn academic content, he is reluctant to tell the professor when he does not understand the content that is presented.

Assignments
1. Daily participation

Modifications
1A. A peer will summarize the reading for Peter.
B. Peter will bring in index cards with content and picture prompts that he has prepared for class.
C. Pat can ask a question related to the index card.
D. Peter will raise his hand to participate in content-related questions.
E. Peter will watch the videotapes listed on the syllabi and discuss the content with a peer or family member.

Assignment
2. Quizzes (4)

3. Midterm and final exams
This assignment will be handed in twice.
Sept.–Oct. travels will be handed in on Oct. 21.
The Oct.–Dec. travels will be handed in on Dec. 16.

Modification Suggestions
2A. Peter will have an adapted verbal quiz. The content will be taken from the index cards and notes that he has taken throughout the semester. A peer or Mary Beth will transcribe Peter's thoughts.
3. Throughout the course Peter will travel around the world using cyberspace. This journey will be taken using the Internet and books. He will visit each continent and stop at points of particular interest (i.e., those studied in class). Peter will document his journey by creating a picture travel log (e.g., poster, picture book) that includes material from the Internet, scanned onto and printed from the computer and xeroxed.
Note: Extra credit will be earned if Peter learns how to incorporate the use of PowerPoint presentation software.

Teaching Tips
1. Please do not ask Peter to read in front of the class.
2. Peter might benefit from tape recording class.
3. Peter is learning to respond to a delayed questioning technique. This technique involves the professor posing a question to Peter. Peter, why is humankind on this planet? I want you to think about that for a minute, and I'll come back to you for your response. During this interim, Peter has several choices:
   a. Construct an answer.
   b. Refer to his notes or pictures.
   c. Ask a peer (e.g., Danielle).
   d. Make a mistake.

TABLE 16.2 *Contract of Participation*

Student: _____ *Faculty:* _____

Class: _____

Class Participation

☐ I can volunteer.
☐ Allow me a few seconds to think about my response.
☐ Allow me to make note of what I want to say.
☐ Before class, I will give you a notecard with a question on it that I have prepared. Then you can ask me that question during class.
☐ Allow me to pass.
☐ I need you to use a *delayed questioning strategy*. This is how it works. You ask me a question, and, then, before I answer, you go on to ask a question(s) to another student. Then come back to me for my answer.
  ☐ During the delay time, I will either find the answer in my materials or ask another student.
☐ Would you like to discuss other possibilities?

Reading
In class

☐ I would be comfortable reading during class.
☐ Please do not ask me to read in front of the class.

Homework

☐ I can read all of the text (e.g., book, articles) independently.
☐ Someone else will read them to me.
☐ I can use CLIFF notes.
☐ I can listen to the book on tape.
☐ I can read parts of the text. Specifically: _____
☐ Someone else will read portions of the text to me. Specifically: _____
☐ I am not able to read the text, but someone else (e.g., classmate, family member) can summarize the information for me.

Papers
Short Papers (1–3 pages)

☐ I can write all required short papers.
☐ I can write _____ short papers.
☐ I can receive assistance from a friend or family member.
☐ I can dictate my papers to someone else who will write down my thoughts.
☐ In lieu of a paper(s) I will _____.
☐ I cannot write papers.

Long Papers (3 or more pages)

☐ I can write all required long papers.
☐ I can write _____ papers.
☐ I can receive assistance from a friend or family member.
☐ I can dictate my papers to someone else who will write down my thoughts.
☐ I can write a short paper instead.
☐ In lieu of a paper(s) I will _____.

Tests

☐ I can take the same tests as all of the students.
☐ I can make arrangements with the Advising Center to take the tests in a different location.
☐ _____ can adapt the test for me. I can take either a written or an oral (circle one) version of the test.
☐ I am unable to take the tests.

Grading

☐ Although I am auditing this course, I would like to receive a grade on all of my work. I realize that this grade is adapted.
☐ I would not like to receive a grade on any of my work.
☐ I can work with _____ to grade my own work.

they were unfamiliar with how to interact with their same-age peers. Second, students with and without disabilities lacked shared experiences (for example, attending classes, sporting events, or clubs), so they had few common high school experiences to refer to in common conversation. This became painfully clear during freshmen orientation activities. When asked "What were your favorite high school clubs or sports," students with significant disabilities often responded, "I wasn't in any."

Recognizing the complexities of facilitating friendships, the college did not automatically adopt support strategies that are commonly used in elementary, middle, and high schools (for example, friendship groups or circles). Instead, as a community, we remained open to problem solving individual situations based on the strengths of members of the community. For example, when a student with significant disabilities did not know how to hang out, several nondisabled students provided the natural supports to teach the student how to hang out at the coffee bar, eat in the cafeteria, and attend sporting events. When another student spoke too loudly in the student union, several nondisabled students intervened and modeled appropriate volume. Inappropriate social behaviors (for example, babytalk, hugging, or demanding to be the center of attention) were shaped or eliminated very quickly. When students with or without disabilities were behaving in an unusual or inappropriate manner, other members of the community (for example, professors, students, or staff) would simply provide feedback as a natural course of the day. For example, it was not unusual for a faculty member to say to a student, "No, please don't hug me. You can shake my hand." As a community who cared deeply for the success of all of the members, we were able to support students who had significant disabilities in similar ways to students without disabilities.

Welcoming students with significant disabilities into the fabric of the Trinity College community provided an opportunity to operationalize the mission of the college: Trinity College valued the preparation of students who would treasure diversity among people and base their valuation of others on a respect for the inherent worth of every human being.

The experiences at Trinity College of Vermont provide one lens with which to consider the multifaceted issue of the inclusion of students with significant disabilities in higher education. Many of the structures, strategies, and processes were similar to those used by public schools across the country. However, because this is such a new area of thinking, it is important that we all think creatively and outside of the box. This is an opportunity for higher education to experience the contributions that are realized when students with significant disabilities are indeed members of the academic community.

In the following section, the legal requirements associated with the inclusion of students with significant disabilities in higher education will be highlighted. This section will be followed by practical suggestions for special educators who are interested in pursuing this line of work in their own communities. Finally, rather than offering concluding thoughts, I will offer thoughts for the future.

Legal Requirements and College

As a special education teacher with an interest in expanding post–high school options for students with significant disabilities, it might be helpful to have a working knowledge of the legal obligations of higher education in this area. First, higher education does not fall under all of the same legislation as public elementary, middle, and high schools. Specifically, the legal protections of IDEA (1997) apply to school-age students prior to high school graduation, which occurs between 18 and 21, depending on the needs of the student. Section 504 of the Rehabilitation Act (1973) applies to post–high school options. Section 504 stipulates that "no otherwise qualified handicapped individual . . . shall, solely by reason of his/her handicap, be denied the benefits of, or be subjected to discrimination, under any program or activity receiving Federal financial assistance" (Rehabilitation Act of 1973, Section 104.44 (c)). Subpart E of Section 504 stipulates that higher education cannot impose discriminatory academic requirements or assessments on students with disabilities. However, they are also *not* required to augment the aspects of academic programs that are directly related to licensing requirements of any particular field (Section 104.44 (c)).

For the population referred to throughout this text (that is, students with significant disabilities), significant augmentation in programming is typically necessary in order for the students to actively participate in higher education. These students would not, even with supports and accommodations, meet the entrance requirements of most institutions of higher education. Most are not able to read and write at a high school level and have not earned a high school diploma or GED. For these students, the goal would not be to earn a college diploma, but to partially participate in a wide variety of college academic and cocurricular experiences.

The Role of a Special Education Teacher in Initiating the Process

This section highlights several ways that a high school special education teacher can initiate the process of creating bridges between high school and college-level experiences for students with significant disabilities. An important place to begin is the acknowledgement that this is an entirely new area of thinking. As with all systems change efforts, it takes time to clarify the vision, as well as to understand the issues. Because this is such a significant undertaking, begin by establishing a task force with the intention of exploring the issues together. Membership on the task force might include high school teachers, parents, young people with significant disabilities and their friends, and guidance counselors. Invite higher education faculty members who teach their undergraduate and graduate students about issues of diversity and inclusive education. Faculty members with this type of focus are often found in the education, social work, or multicultural departments of colleges or universities.

Create a Clear Working Agenda

The initial responsibility of the task force is to understand the available literature on the following topics: inclusive education, friendship facilitation, and creative problem solving. Rather than including lists of references at this point, refer to the previous chapters of this textbook for each of the topics. Specifically explore the literature related to successful inclusion at the high school level. As a task force, read and discuss everything that you can find related to building inclusive communities. Adopt a common definition of "inclusion" (Giangreco, Baumgart, & Doyle, 1995) to ensure that there is a common understanding and language.

Next the task force should become well-informed about the three "Cs" of higher education: culture, cost, and curriculum. Each of these areas will be discussed in the following sections.

Understand the Culture.   Members of the task force can engage in a variety of fact-finding activities in order to understand the unique culture of the higher education institutions in the area. Although the number of students with significant disabilities who have participated in higher education is limited, learn from their experiences. Read their stories (Doyle, 1997; Grigal et al., 2001; Hunton & Doyle, 1999; Ryndak, Morrison, & Sommerstein, 1999). Contact the students, as well as their high schools and colleges/universities. Ask them to share their most significant learning. Visit as many examples as possible, with the intention of finding out what has worked well and what has not. Explore the challenges and opportunities. Remain open to new ideas and the possibility of being influenced.

Next, members of the task force can become familiar with the two- and four-year colleges in your area. Read the college literature, especially the mission statements. Become familiar with the curricular and co-curricular opportunities available at each institution. Familiarize yourselves with the cultures of the colleges by attending open houses, lectures, and sporting events and eating lunch in the student union. A task force member might even audit a class or two.

Understand the Cost.   Next it is important to be very familiar with the costs and funding of higher education. Examine the financial issues associated with each higher education institution. What is the tuition for matriculating students? Is there an audit option available? What are the costs associated with auditing? Keep in mind that, typically, students who are not matriculating do not qualify for student aid (for example, grants or student loans). Gather financial information related to nontraditional funding sources. For example, if an IEP team decides that the student's individualized learning objectives can best be addressed on a college campus, in regular college classes, would the high school pay for tuition? Would the student placement be similar to the high school advanced placement (AP) option?

Lay out a mock financial plan. Who will pay for tuition and fees? If people supports are needed (for example, paraprofessionals, faculty, and personal care attendants), who will pay for those costs? Generate ideas and proposals instead of definitive answers. As you fact-find, it is important to remain open to the suggestions and input from others. For example, district-level special education administrators will have a good deal of information about certain types of available funding, while financial aid officers from higher education will have information from another vantage point.

Understand the Curriculum.   Given all of your new study, as a special education teacher you might find it helpful to get back to the familiar. Conduct ecological assessments (refer to Chapter 5 of this book) of several campuses. Be certain to focus on locations on the campuses that are often busy with students (for example, classroom buildings, student union, bookstore, or sports complex). Keep these assessments on file to be used at an instructional level at a later point. Gather examples of a few syllabi as well. During a task force meeting, actually mock up how the syllabi could be adapted to meet the needs of a student with significant disabilities. Move from adapting one syllabi to envisioning implementation for the entire semester (refer to Table 16.1). Engaging in this type of practical application provides members of the task force with the opportunity to examine the details of the daily experiences that lie ahead. The more often the task force engages in this type of activity means the more efficient and creative members become with the practical followthrough of their vision.

Proposal Development

Work with the task force to combine all of the information into a short proposal to be presented to an institution of higher education (that is, community colleges and four-year colleges and universities). Highlight (a) what you want, (b) how the college will benefit, and (c) how you propose to move forward. Include brief explanations of inclusive education, multilevel instruction, and a description of how this opportunity is in alignment with the mission of the institution. Share brief articles of successful experiences, such as Hunton and Doyle (1999) (refer to Figure 16.1).

Generate examples (i.e., videotapes or student portfolios) of how your high school includes students with significant disabilities in curricular and cocurricular opportunities. Such examples increase your credibility as you communicate that you do understand the challenges and opportunities associated with building inclusive communities, because you have done this in your own high school.

After the proposal is developed and the materials are gathered, it is time to approach higher education. Members of the task force should decide whether it makes more sense to invite higher education representatives (for example, dean of students and faculty members) to a task force meeting or if it is better to go to the individual colleges or universities. At this point, the goal is to invite them into the creative thinking process so that they can become connected with the issues, challenges, and opportunities.

Initial Meeting with Higher Education

The initial meeting with higher education is an important opportunity to share the vision and opportunities associated with building diverse communities. Share your contextual knowledge of the college and create bridges between what is and what could be. One way to do this is to help them to see how their individual school could benefit by welcoming students with significant disabilities. Keep in mind that the benefits will vary per institution. In one institution, it could provide an opportunity to increase diversity; for another it might be a good way to actualize the mission; in another, it could provide practical academic support for social work or education programs.

During this initial meeting, briefly explain your initial thoughts regarding curriculum, participation in classes, and co-curricular experiences. Have one or more students

FIGURE 16.1   *Peter's Story*

I'm Not Special Ed. Anymore:
My Name is Peter

By: Peter Hunton

I am a tall, handsome, single guy. I am 22 years old. I am a college student and I'm NOT a special ed. student anymore. I like playing basketball. I like exercising. I like hanging out in downtown Burlington. I like being with my friends. I like jazz and rock and roll music. I like school too because now I am taking very interesting classes. I especially love my History of the '60s class. I've gotten more out of that class than out of any other class that I've ever taken. I never liked any other class before. I like that class because the teacher has a sense of humor and teaches a lot of She teaches about women, Vietnam War, and the Civil Rights Movement. It's all really powerful stuff. The class is outgoing and busy.

I don't like boring teachers. Boring teachers teach slowly and don't have a sense of humor. I had a lot of boring teachers in high school because I was special ed. In high school if you're special ed. they make you do stupid things like brushing your teeth in school. That isn't good because that stuff you do in kindergarten. I don't think the other special ed. kids like it either. They also give you stupid kindergarten contracts when you're special ed. in high school. It is a good thing that I had a good case manager, Mari Jo Reesee because she said I didn't have to do stuff that I thought was baby stuff.

I was in high school for 6 years. That's a long time to be at a place that you don't like. I didn't like high school much at all because the kids were mean. They would pick on special ed. kids and call us retards. I think they didn't care because they were with their friends and they weren't friends with special ed. kids. Some of the other special ed. kids would pick on special kids too. I don't quite get why, but I think it was because they were being jealous because they didn't want to be picked on either.

In high school my teacher always had someone on my back. The person was like a tour guide. There was always a teacher or aide hanging on my back like I was a baby. Now I don't have people hanging out on my back because I'm not a special ed. kid anymore.

I couldn't do sports or anything in high school. I wasn't in any clubs because I didn't have any friends.

I hated being special ed. because when people talk they talked to me like a baby. They talk very slow and very loud as if I were deaf. I wish they would have talked to me like they do to other adults. They talk to them like adults.

I hated being special ed. because I didn't have any friends. Now I dream about having friends. I'm not special ed., so I can make friends now. People take me seriously now.

Now I'm not special ed. and I have a friend whose name is Chuck. Chuck goes to college too. We exercise and play basketball.

I'm not special ed. anymore, my name is Peter I'm a college student. I like college because it is open and people like to talk to you. The other kids don't care if you were special ed. or not when you were in high school. I'm a lot happier now because I have friends. Mostly the other college kids don treat me like a baby. But sometimes, the other adults do treat me like a ten year old kid. Maybe it is because the adults never grew up with special ed. kids. Those adults grew up in the sixties and then the special ed. kids were put away.

I learn a lot more stuff now too. I get to learn stuff I never learned before. The most important things that I learned this year are how to speak more clearly and to share my ideas. I've also learned how to joke around with people. I'm really liking college. Now people call me by my name . . . they don't call me names. My name is Peter and I am not a special ed. kid anymore.

Source: Reprinted with permission from Hunton, P., & Doyle, M. B. (1999, October). I'm not in special education anymore: My name is Peter. *TASH Newsletter, 25*(10), p. 22.

with significant disabilities share their portfolio work and résumés. Be prepared to answer questions regarding people support, training, and finance. As a task force, be very clear about the response to a likely question. Ultimately, whose student is this? Is the student with significant disabilities a member of the college community with all of the rights, privileges, and responsibilities or a student enrolled in another program receiving services on the college campus? Or is this student a college student with supports from a variety of noncollege resources?

Invite their questions and concerns as part of the problem-solving process. It is likely that some of the questions have been considered by the task force, while others have not. Respond honestly. Do not hesitate to say, "Those are important questions that we haven't considered yet. Would you be interested in helping us to think about the implications related to your questions?" Invite members of higher education into the problem-solving process.

Beginning with One Student at a Time

After a student with significant disabilities is identified to enroll at a local college, work as a task force to develop a capacity-focused transition plan with the student and a staff member from the admission office at the college. Highlight the student's strengths, interests, and abilities. Following are several suggestions to incorporate into the transition plan.

The student should attend college events prior to beginning of year (for example, lectures, lunch in the cafeteria, and orientation) as a way to become familiar with the settings and atmosphere. Refer back to the ecological assessments that were conducted and use them as the task force prepares for the student's participation on campus. Clarify roles and responsibilities of all involved parties (that is, task force members, professors, and peers). What are the student's goals, and how will they be determined? Who will modify the curriculum and instruction? Who will support the student, and how will that be carried out? What is the role of higher education faculty? How will higher education faculty be brought into the process (for example, individually, per department, or through the whole college)? What is the expectation regarding student ownership? Who will provide support to the faculty, and what form will that support take?

Plan the Student's Schedule.   Strategically plan a weekly schedule that balances classes, hanging out, participation in campus clubs, and attending college-sponsored events (for example, sports games, plays, or evening lectures). In order to encourage membership and connection between the student with significant disabilities and other college students, faculty, and staff, it is important that the student is on campus during nonclass hours as well. One way to increase the likelihood of this happening is to plan the schedule so that the student arrives on campus before class to have a cup of coffee with a classmate and goes to class with a classmate, followed by a second class or a club meeting.

Help the student to fit in socially by wearing similar clothes and carrying a similar bag or backpack as the other college students do. Every campus has a different sense of "what's in" among traditional students. Perhaps the student with significant disabilities should go on a precollege shopping spree before going to school. Better yet, s/he could go with other college students.

Plan Interesting Content.   Students with significant disabilities who were college students at Trinity College taught their professors an important lesson related to curriculum content. Professors were taught to be careful not to underestimate the importance of rich and interesting content. Each of the students with significant disabilities who was fully included in the typical college courses between 1996 and 2000 was very excited by the new and interesting information that they were exposed to. These students demonstrated time and again that they wanted to learn and that they understood the value of content information. They also reminded their professors of the importance of a liberal arts education by the reasons behind some of their course selections. When Mary was asked why she wanted to take a course entitled *Women's Spirituality*, she responded, "Because I'm a woman so I must have spirituality so I better learn about it" (Doyle, personal communication). When Peter, a student with significant disabilities who was interested in history and very much enjoyed a specific professor's entry-level history course was asked "Peter, why don't you take Dr. Habif's advanced history course," Peter's response was, "She might figure out that I'm not really so smart." Further discussion led to a conversation with Dr. Habif. In all of her wisdom, Dr. Habif not only shared her delight in having such an interested history student, but she brought out many adaptations and accommodations that she had already been working on to support Peter in her next course. Both Peter and Mary offer first-person perspectives of the importance of having the opportunity to engage with interesting content that may not be tied directly to functional work. That is the type of information that becomes the basis for our connections and conversations with the larger world.

Plan for Peer Support Outside of the Classroom.   As described earlier in this chapter, supporting students in establishing friendships is, perhaps, the most important aspect of the college experience. Given the lack of shared experiences prior to college, many young adults with and without disabilities are likely to need a bridge. This is a delicate task in friendship facilitation. Following are a few suggestions when navigating this area.

If the student with significant disabilities needs assistance with establishing social relationships with other college students, be honest and clear with the students without disabilities. Identify a few students from one of the student's classes. Explain the situation in a clear manner. Then ask if the student could hang out with them before or after class for awhile. It is likely the students without disabilities will say "yes." After the students agree, it is critical to introduce the students to each other and get out of the way. Try to create this as a time when the students have the opportunity to create friendships without support staff in the picture.

Tips on Course Selection.   Given the flexibility of the audit option and the variety of course topics, class selection is relatively simple. One tried-and-true method is simply ask the other students. Another is to build a program based on the student's interests. Whatever courses are selected, think in broad terms and be creative. Initially, be certain that students are encouraged to participate in classes that are in alignment with their skills and interests. However, as the student gains confidence in his/her membership in college, it is very important that s/he has the opportunity to expand personal experiences in new areas. Also, select courses that lend themselves to activity-based instruction and are offered at a time that allows the student to be on campus for at least half-day increments of time. For example, rather than taking one class that meets on Monday, Wednesday, and Friday and one class that meets on Tuesday and Thursday, take two classes on either set of days. This allows the student to have more of a real presence on campus. The student would be more visible.

Plan for Graduation Exercises.   At the very beginning of the process, discuss the end (that is, participation in senior class activities, including graduation ceremonies). It is important for the whole community to celebrate the successes of all members of the community. The student with significant disabilities must participate in graduation activities and ceremonies along with other members of the class. It is likely that this would be discussed with the entire faculty so that everyone is clear about the expectations.

Thoughts for the Future

The inclusion of students with significant disabilities into the fabric of a college community is not just about a particular type of student, nor is it about doing "something nice to do for people with disabilities." Rather, it is an opportunity for all involved to experience both community and learning because everyone becomes influenced by the range of people who live, work, and play in our communities. Lifelong learning becomes a concept that should be encouraged for everyone, not just an elite few. Clearly, there is much to do in this arena. Most importantly, we need to listen and respond to the voices of young adults with significant disabilities and their families when they choose higher education as a post-high school option. We need to think creatively and plan well for their supported participation in higher education.

We must study the social and cultural differences between high schools and colleges, simultaneously examine the perceptions of individual personal supports. Examination of curricular content and attitudes about adaptations and accommodations in higher education are also key concepts.

Ultimately, when considering college as a viable option for young adults with significant disabilities, higher education is being given an opportunity to be influenced in amazing ways.

References

Agran, M., Snow, K., & Swaner, J. (1999). A survey of secondary level teachers' opinions of community-based instruction and inclusive education. *Journal of The Association of Persons with Severe Disabilities, 24*, 58–62.

Americans with Disabilities Act of 1990, Pub. L. No. 101-336. (ERIC Document Service Reproduction No. ED 359-365).

Certo, N. J., Pumpian, I., Fisher, D., Storey, K., & Smalley, K. (1997). Focusing on the point of transition: A service integration model. *Education and Treatment of Children, 20*, 68–84.

Doyle, M. B. (Fall, 1997). College life: The new frontier. *IMPACT: Feature Issue on Social Inclusion.* Minneapolis: University of Minnesota, Institute on Community Integration and the Research and Training Center on Residential Services and Community Living.

Giangreco, M. F. (1997). Responses to Nietupski et al. *The Journal of Special Education, 31*(1), 56–57.

Giangreco, M. F., & Doyle, M. B. (2000). Curricular and instructional considerations for teaching students with disabilities in general education classrooms. In. S. Wade (Ed.), *Inclusive education: A case* book of readings for prospective and practicing teachers (Volume 1) (pp. 51–69). Hillsdale, NJ: Lawrence Erlbaum.

Giangreco, M., Baumgart, D., & Doyle, M. B. (1995). Including students with disabilities in general education classrooms: How it can facilitate teaching and learning. *Intervention in School and Clinic, 30*(5), 273–278.

Giangreco, M. F., Dennis, R., Cloninger, C., Edelman, S., & Schattman, R. (1993). I've counted Jon: Transformational experiences of teachers educating students with disabilities. *Exceptional Children, 59*(4), 359–372.

Grigal, M., Neubert, D. A., & Moon, M. S. (2001). Public school programs for students with significant disabilities in post-secondary settings. *Education and Training in Mental Retardation and Developmental Disabilities, 36*(3), 244–254.

Hall, M., Kleinert, H. L. & Kearns, F. L. (2000). Going to college! Post-secondary programs for students with moderate and severe disabilities. *Teaching Exceptional Children, 32*(3), 58–65.

Hunton, P., & Doyle, M. B. (1999, October). I'm not in special education anymore: My name is Peter. *TASH Newsletter, 25*(10), p. 22.

Individuals with Disabilities Education Act of 1990 (IDEA), Pub. L. no. 101–476, 602a, 20 U.S.C., 1401. (ERIC Document Service Reproduction No. ED 321 513).

National Center on Education Statistics (2001). *Record enrollments at elementary and secondary schools, colleges, and universities expected this fall.* Washington, D.C.: U.S. Department of Education. (*www.ed.gov/PressReleases/08-2001/08162001. html*).

Page, B., & Chadsey-Rusch, J. (1995). The community college experience for students with and without disabilities: A viable transition outcome? *Career Development for Exceptional Individuals, 18*, 85–95.

Ryndak, D., Morrison, A., & Sommerstein, L. (1999). Literacy before and after inclusion: A case study. *Journal of The Association of Persons with Severe Handicaps, 24*, 5–22.

Tashie, C., Malloy, J. M., & Lichtenstein, S. J. (1998). Transition or graduation? Supporting all students to plan for the future. In C. J. Jorgensen (Ed.), *Restructuring high schools for all students: Taking inclusion to the next level* (pp. 234–259). Baltimore: Paul H. Brookes Publishing Co.

17

Individualized Positive Behavior Intervention and Support in Inclusive School Settings

Tim Knoster

Objectives

After completing this chapter, the reader will be able to:

1. Define student-centered positive behavior support (PBS).
2. Define school-wide PBS.
3. Describe the relationship between student-centered and schoolwide PBS.
4. Define and describe the problem-solving process known as functional behavioral assessment (FBA).
5. Describe and outline the various elements of a comprehensive, student-centered behavior support plan.
6. Describe important aspects of monitoring an individual student's progress.
7. Describe an efficient process to design student-centered behavior support plans based on hypotheses generated through an FBA.
8. Describe strategies to address two primary factors that can inhibit application of student-centered PBS.

Key Terms

Antecedents (fast triggers)
Array of tools/procedures
Aversive interventions
Behavior intervention/support
  plan
Collaboration
Child-centered
Community-based
Consequence strategies
Contextual fit
Continuum of approaches
Coping and tolerance skills
Crisis management
Culturally competent
Databased decision-making
Durable behavior change
Experimental analysis

Family-centered
Focus student
General skills
Global hypothesis
Individual student system
Informant method
Integrated assessment
  procedures
Intervention and support
Least restrictive/intrusive
Long-term prevention
Life style enhancements
Monitoring student progress
Multi-component behavior
  support plan
Normal deviance
Observation

Person-centered planning
Positive behavior support
Prevention
Quality of life
Reactive strategies
Reinforcement
Replacement skills
School-wide PBS
Setting events (slow triggers)
Specific hypothesis
Student-centered behavior
  support team
Student-centered PBS
Systems change
Teaching alternative skills
Wraparound process

One of the more perplexing challenges that schools face today is effectively educating students with problem behavior in typical school, work, and community settings. In particular, students with disabilities who have histories of problem behavior often find themselves at great risk for exclusion and devaluation at school and by society at large. Further, students with significant disabilities and problem behavior are typically the last group of students in even the most progressive schools to receive a Free Appropriate Public Education (FAPE) within the Least Restrictive Environment (LRE). Although there are many reasons as to why this occurs, one clear inhibitor to providing inclusive educational programs for this population of students is the capacity of school systems to support teachers in providing student-centered, positive behavior support (PBS).

This chapter will highlight the core component parts and processes associated with providing student-centered PBS within inclusive school settings. In particular, the practices highlighted will describe an approach to designing interventions and supports that is portable to general education settings. The chapter begins by providing definitions of a) school-wide PBS and b) student-centered PBS. Next, the PBS process is described using practical terms and illustrations that are relevant to inclusive schools. In a larger sense, student-centered programs are contextualized within broader schoolwide prevention and early intervention approaches highlighting the application of the problem-solving process known as functional behavioral assessment (FBA). Assessment and intervention procedures are presented as occurring along a least-to-most intrusive continuum. Further, FBA procedures are reviewed in concert with a description of a process for designing comprehensive, student-centered behavior support plans for particular students. Specifically, key components of student-centered behavior support plans are described (that is, prevention, teaching alternative skills, consequence strategies, lifestyle intervention and support). Further, practices relevant to monitoring student progress are highlighted, along with a description of an efficient process to design student-centered programs in general education settings. Finally, strategies are provided to facilitate application of student-centered PBS within inclusive settings.

PBS

PBS is an applied science that places emphasis on changes in practice to enhance the quality of life of stakeholders and to reduce problem behaviors. As Carr et al. (2002) notes, PBS initially evolved within the field of developmental disabilities and emerged from three major sources: applied behavior analysis, the normalization and inclusion movement, and person-centered values. Although components of PBS may be found in other approaches, PBS uniquely interweaves a number of key features, including a comprehensive lifestyle perspective, stakeholder participation and social validity, flexibility in application, and implementation of evidence-based practice with individual students and entire schools.

An Overview of Schoolwide PBS

In addition to being successfully employed across a broad range of individual students and settings, PBS has been extended to a systems-level intervention approach for entire schools (Colvin, Kameenui, & Sugai, 1993; Taylor-Green et al., 1997; Todd, Horner, Sugai, & Sprague, 1999). Acknowledging the fact that many children (and specifically not just students with disabilities) come to school with learning histories that set the stage for increasing behavioral problems, schools (in general) have responded to student problem behavior in a variety of ways. Unfortunately, evidence suggests that many aspects of traditional school discipline practices exacerbate and, in some instances, contribute to children and youth's patterns of problem behavior (Lewis & Sugai, 1999). In response to this dilemma, efforts to build schoolwide PBS have been gaining national attention (Dwyer, Osher, & Warger, 1998). Schoolwide PBS is, first and foremost, a teaching approach. As such, emphasis is placed primarily on identifying and defining behavioral expectations, teaching those expectations, and systematically reinforcing performance of the behavioral expectations with all students in the school (not just those who have a history of problem behavior). For example, a given school might identify three school expectations, such as, be on time, be respectful, and be responsible. They would next define those expectations across routines/settings (for example, classroom, cafeteria, or playground). In turn, a system for acknowledging student performance of these expectations would be put in place and implemented by a majority (if not all staff) to "catch kids being good." Data would be collected relevant to student behavior over time and used to design, adapt, or modify strategies to further reinforce acquisition and demonstration of the behavioral expectations by all students.

Although variation exists among schools implementing schoolwide PBS, they share a number of essential features (key themes according to Horner & Sugai, 2000) that enable them to realize positive changes in school environments accompanied by sustainable reductions in student problem behavior (for example, reductions in discipline referrals). Applying a systems approach (that is, broadening the focus from a given student's program to programs for all students) supports the application of positive prevention and early intervention in schools with the entire student body that emphasizes teaching and acknowledges appropriate student behavior. A systems approach at the school-building level provides for a continuum of PBS practices (see Figure 17.1) in which prevention is emphasized and intensity of problem behavior and context are considered.

Introduction to Student-Centered PBS

PBS is a general term that refers to the application of positive behavioral interventions and systems to achieve socially important behavior change (Sugai et al., 2000). Socially important behavior change for an individual student includes skills that are necessary to increase the likelihood of success and personal satisfaction in typical school, work, home, and community settings. The primary goal of student-centered PBS is to assist a student's lifestyle to evolve in a direction that enables all relevant stakeholders (for example, teachers, employers, parents, friends, and the focus student) to have the opportunity to perceive and to enjoy an improved quality of life (Carr et al., in press). An important, but secondary, goal of this approach is to decrease a student's problem behavior by helping students to learn to meet their needs in a socially acceptable manner (for example, asking for help or a break as opposed to crying and screaming in the classroom) and through environmental changes (for example, making changes in how we teach). Student-centered PBS initially emerged in practice as an alternative to aversive interventions used with students with significant disabilities. More recently, the approach has been successfully used with a wide range of students in a variety of school settings (Carr et al, 1999; Horner, Albin, Sprague, & Todd, 1999). PBS represents the application of a behaviorally-based systems approach to building the capacity of schools, families, and communities to design conducive environments for learning that improves the match between research-proven practices and naturally occurring routines. Interventions and supports that are designed through the process reflect culturally competent approaches that take into account the unique and personal learning experiences (histories) of all relevant stakeholders (for example, the student with problem behavior, his/her family and friends, and teachers).

PBS and Student-Centered Programs

The process of designing and implementing comprehensive student-centered behavior support is comprised of five major steps that include: 1) conducting a functional behavioral assessment, 2) developing hypothesis statements, 3) designing and implementing the behavior support plan, 4) monitoring student progress and evaluating the effect of the behavior support plan, and 5) modifying the support plan as needed. This five-step process places great emphasis on determining the function of student problem behavior and identifying factors that may be contributing to the student's problem behavior in order to develop and provide effective intervention and support. The five-step process

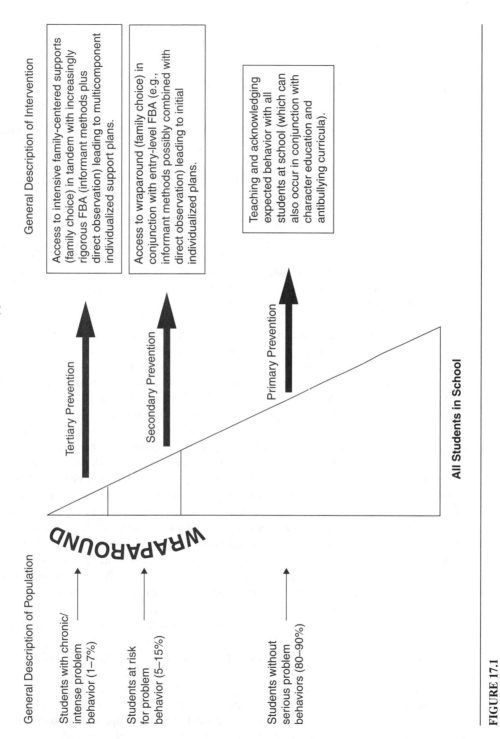

Continuum of behavior support

General Description of Intervention

Access to intensive family-centered supports (family choice) in tandem with increasingly rigorous FBA (informant methods plus direct observation) leading to multicomponent individualized support plans.

Access to wraparound (family choice) in conjunction with entry-level FBA (e.g., informant methods possibly combined with direct observation) leading to initial individualized plans.

Teaching and acknowledging expected behavior with all students at school (which can also occur in conjunction with character education and antibullying curricula).

Tertiary Prevention

Secondary Prevention

Primary Prevention

WRAPAROUND

All Students in School

General Description of Population

Students with chronic/ intense problem behavior (1–7%)

Students at risk for problem behavior (5–15%)

Students without serious problem behaviors (80–90%)

FIGURE 17.1

Source: Adapted from Eber, in press; and Sugai et al., 2000.

of designing and providing student-centered behavior support is most effective when employed by student-centered teams.

Step One: Conducting a Functional Behavioral Assessment (FBA)

FBA serves as the foundation for the design and delivery of positive behavior support. In particular, student-centered, school-based teams educating students with disabilities who present behavior that impedes learning have the responsibility of conducting FBAs as stipulated in the Individuals with Disabilities Education Act (IDEA). The regulations state the following:

> Either before or no later than 10 business days after either first removing the child for more than 10 school days in a school year or commencing removal that constitutes a change in placement under section 300.519 . . . . If the LEA did not conduct a functional behavioral assessment and implement a behavioral intervention plan that resulted in the suspension described in subparagraph (a), the agency shall convene an IEP meeting to develop an assessment plan.

Acknowledging this requirement coupled with an understanding of the IDEA (in total), a case can be made for the application of FBA in a proactive manner by Individualized Education Plan (IEP) teams in providing educational services and programs. In light of the practical utility of FBA coupled with legal requirements, it is important to understand that the true utility of FBA is not simply the adoption and documentation of its use, but as a process that leads to desired outcomes (Reid, 2000).

FBA is a problem-solving framework that leads to student-centered intervention and support (Knoster & McCurdy, 2002; Repp, Karsh, Munk, & Dahlquist, 1995; Tilly et al., 1998). The process of coming to an understanding about why a student engages in problem behavior and how student behavior relates to the environment (both internal to the student and external in terms of settings and routines) is referred to as FBA. There are three common approaches to collecting functional assessment information, the first two of which are very applicable in general education settings. The first commonly employed approach in general education classrooms is referred to as informant methods, which involve record reviews and talking with the student of concern as well as people who have direct contact with the student. The second approach that can also be efficiently used in typical classrooms is direct observation (in its various forms), which involves systematic observation of the student within typical settings and routines over time. The third approach, which is not typically required or employed in general education classrooms, is experimental analysis (that is, analog functional analysis), which involves the manipulations of variables that are hypothesized as being related to the student's problem behavior.

The process of FBA can best be understood as a continuum of integrated assessment procedures that may involve an array of data collection tools and procedures (Tilly et al., 1998, 2000). In this sense, the continuum for FBA is consistent and analogous to the array of integrated assessment procedures that general education teachers use in assessing aca-

demic progress of students. Student-centered teams, in determining the amount of resources and precision necessary to design an effective behavior support plan, should make
decisions on a case-by-case basis (for example, initial use of informant methods alone or
in combination with some form of direct observation). Decisions should be made in relation to the need for immediate behavior change (for example, urgent behaviors, such as
self-injury versus what has been described as excessive or nuisance behaviors that reflect
"normal" deviance as described by Meyer & Evans, 1989). In addition, it is important to
also consider resource and capacity issues in the school program (for example, available
time and competencies of staff).

After a student-centered team decides to conduct an FBA, these information-
gathering approaches are used in a least-to-most resource intensive manner to collect two
types of information that is ultimately summarized into hypothesis statements (Bambara &
Knoster, 1995, 1998). First, the team gathers broad contextual information about the student: skills and abilities, preferences and interests, general health, and quality of life. Next,
the team gathers specific information that pinpoints the conditions that are regularly associated with occurrence and nonoccurrence of problem behavior. When viewed together, these
two types of information can enable the team to see the proverbial "forest and the trees" as
it pertains to the student of concern.

To illustrate, most mild problem behaviors in general education classrooms can be
efficiently assessed through informant methods (for example, infrequent acts such as one
child occasionally raising his/her voice toward other children during activities to resolve
conflicts). Contrarily, an educational team confronted with a student who engages in extreme problem behavior will likely need to combine informant methods with direct observation (for example, a student who frequently bites his hands and scratches his face in a
variety of settings when upset). In addition, this may require a comprehensive record review, which could lead to a medical assessment concerning physical health factors (for example, history of a dry skin condition) that may be contributing to the student's problem
behavior. Further, the team may see fit to conduct this record review within the context of
a person-centered planning process (Kincaid, 1996; Knoster, 2000) and/or in tandem with
a wraparound approach (Eber, in press).

Person-centered planning describes a range of techniques for identifying a person's
wants and needs (Kincaid, 1996). The team-facilitated process helps team members learn
more about the student and emphasizes planning for a more positive future as defined by
the student and his or her family. Person-centered planning processes include Lifestyle
Planning (O'Brien, 1987), Personal Futures Planning (Mount, 1987; Mount & Zwernick,
1988), the McGill Action Planning System (Forrest & Lusthaus, 1987; Vandercook, York
& Forest, 1989), Framework for Accomplishment/Personal Profile (O'Brien, 1987), and
Essential Lifestyle Planning (Smull & Harrison, 1992). Each of these processes can result
in gaining a deeper understanding of the student with a disability and can help guide the
student-centered team to design interventions and supports that facilitate the realization of
self-determined life goals and objectives.

The wraparound process has emerged from the system of care concept that uses a
community-based approach to provide comprehensive and integrated services and supports in collaboration with families. More specifically, wraparound is a philosophy of care
with a defined planning process that results in a uniquely designed individual plan through

a partnership with the child and family to achieve a set of outcomes that reflect the voice and choices of the child and his or her family (Eber, in press).

Step Two: Generating Hypothesis Statements

The culminating activity of an FBA is the team developing hypothesis statements. Hypotheses summarize assessment results by offering a logical explanation for problem behavior (O'Neill et al., 1997; Tilly et al., 1998, 2000). Specifically, hypotheses summarize the function of and factors identified as contributing to the student's problem behavior. Specific and global hypotheses serve as the foundation from which student-centered interventions and supports are designed (Bambara & Knoster, 1995, 1998). An example of a specific and global hypothesis is provided in Table 17.1.

As shown in Table 17.1, important information is contained in both the specific and global hypotheses. The support team in this example would design interventions and supports for Joshua in his general education classes based on the specific hypothesis (for example, teaching him how to get a break in a more socially acceptable manner) as well as

TABLE 17.1 *An Example of Specific and Global Hypotheses*

Joshua

Specific Hypothesis Statement
When Joshua is presented with instructions of more than a few words that are not paired with pictures/symbols, passive and/or independent tasks that last more than three minutes, and/or he did not get an ample amount of sleep the night before (i.e., less than six hours), he disrupts the classroom through verbal outbursts (e.g., making shrieking sounds), destroying property (e.g., flipping the desk at the workstation), or leaving his work area and invading the physical space of the teaching staff (e.g., sometimes grabbing the teacher's arm when ignored) in order to stop the task and/or activity (i.e., get a break).

Global Hypothesis
Joshua is a 12-year old student who is identified as having a significant language delay and mental retardation. He appears interested in social relationships with peers his own age and enjoys listening to country music (especially with other kids). Joshua is a physically active boy who loves gym class. Joshua uses a picture communication system (limited to about 20 key words/phrases). He enjoys physical activities. His greatest difficulties have been increasingly noted in traditional academic settings. As Joshua started attending his local middle school this year (he previously attended a special education class in a neighboring school district), he is familiar with some of the students at school who live in his neighborhood. He has not (to date) established what might be viewed as any real close friendships. Joshua's mother and brother both report that Joshua wants and needs some friends to "hang around with." Joshua lives with his mother and older brother John. His father moved to another state following a divorce three years ago, and Joshua rarely sees his father (about one time per year when he comes back to town). John goes to visit his father about three times a year. Joshua's mother reports that Joshua tends to be irritable when his brother is away visiting his father.

keep looking forward into the future with the student and his or her family (for example, person-centered plans can help guide the team in their endeavors to modify support plans in a manner consistent with long-range personal goals).

An Efficient Process to Design Student-Centered Programs

It is not uncommon for student-centered teams to be composed of people with diverse perspectives. In reality, this diversity is natural and can be helpful to providing PBS for an individual student. In order to increase the likelihood of successful outcomes, a structured process should be used to identify and select strategies and interventions across component parts of the support plan in light of the student-centered team's hypotheses (Knoster, 1998, 1999, 2000). The student's support team may proceed in the following manner repeating the process across the four components of the support plan as depicted in Figure 17.2 (that is, prevention, teaching alternative skills, consequence strategies, and lifestyle intervention and support). First, the team brainstorms possible interventions and supports with the goal being to generate the greatest number of potential options for strategies within a set time frame (for example, within four minutes). Second, team members clarify strategies should questions arise at the end of the set time for brainstorming. Third, the team discusses the appropriateness of interventions and supports in terms of the match with the hypotheses and feasibility of implementation. Fourth, the team prioritizes interventions and supports. Next, the top two to four priorities per program component are selected along with identifying the types of supports that team members will need to implement the selected interventions and supports. Finally, the selected interventions and supports (including the necessary supports for team members) are documented in the student's support plan (and/or IEP).

Factors that Can Inhibit Student-Centered PBS

Effective student-centered teams accomplish two primary objectives: 1) They accomplish important tasks, and 2) they maintain relationships among team members. These two objectives are particularly important for student-centered teams working with students who have histories of problem behavior. In particular, collaborative problem solving concerning the problem behavior of a student with disabilities in a general education classroom may be inhibited by a number of factors. Specifically, a sense of helplessness or hopelessness on the part of team members as a result of past adverse experiences coupled with the personal (emotional) stress that can be created when confronted with the need to change practice can essentially freeze some teams in space and time.

Factor One: Past Experiences

We are all influenced by our past experiences. This can be a particular problem in the instance in which team members have experienced prolonged negative interactions with the student as well as among stakeholders in team meetings (for example, faculty, staff, and

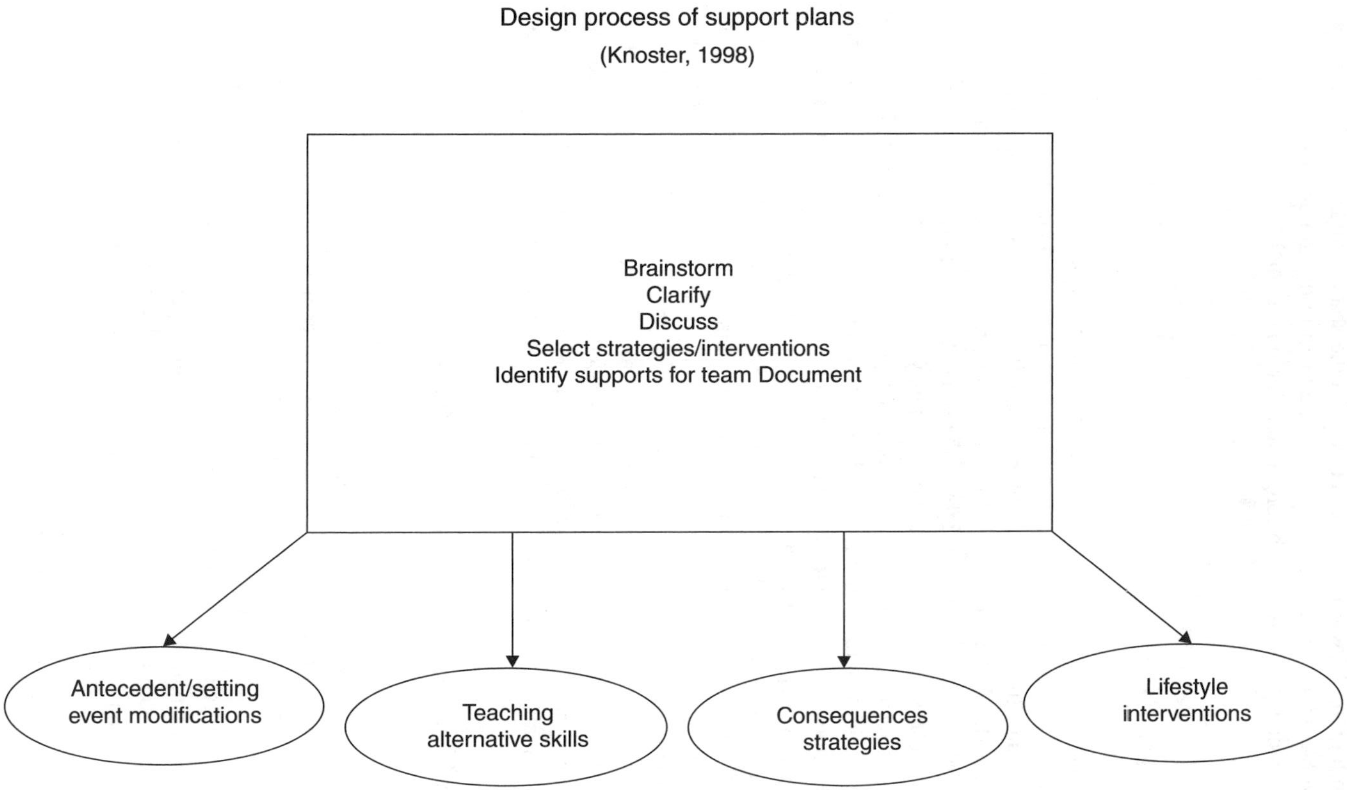

Design process of support plans
(Knoster, 1998)

Brainstorm
Clarify
Discuss
Select strategies/interventions
Identify supports for team Document

Antecedent/setting
event modifications

Teaching
alternative skills

Consequences
strategies

Lifestyle
interventions

FIGURE 17.2

Source: Adapted from Knoster, 1998.

family). In Joshua's example, this could include numerous class disruptions over the course of the school year coupled with negative experiences among the team members in failed attempts to problem-solve (for example, emergency team meetings in response to problem behavior). In light of the potential impact that past experiences will likely have on team functioning, it is important to proactively structure collaboration by 1) establishing a common set of ground rules for meetings; 2) attending to the process of interactions so that all team members feel that their perspective is heard; 3) using conversational language to the greatest extent possible, and where impossible, defining terms and jargon; 4) agreeing to a shared set of goals and objectives prior to rushing headstrong into identifying interventions and supports; 5) reaching consensus (not majority voting) on which interventions and supports to employ; and 6) documenting a plan of action to which all team members commit.

Factor Two: Personal (Emotional) Aspects of Change

Volumes upon volumes of helpful books, articles, videotapes, and audiocassettes have been published on the process of change in schools and other organizations. One common theme (a common denominator, so to speak) throughout these resources is the realization that change is a highly personal experience that can be emotionally unsettling. This can be particularly the case when confronted with the need to change our operating assumptions and procedures under highly stressful circumstances, such as being confronted by a student who engages in serious problem behavior (for example, Joshua uses increasingly disruptive behavior in his general education classes). Such circumstances can be even further compounded when the problem behavior of concern can become dangerous to the safety of the child or others in the classroom. In order to address this inhibiting factor effectively, student-centered teams are encouraged to attend to the support needs of individual team members as a part of the process of designing and implementing behavior support plans. The need for support by each team member will likely vary over time and may include different forms of support. In the case of Joshua, supports for team members may include providing in-service training for his teacher, altering staffing patterns for a short time frame in the general education classrooms where Joshua is experiencing greatest difficulty, or simply providing team members with a sympathetic ear to listen to their story or a shoulder to cry on after a really tough day.

Summary

Successfully including students with significant disabilities that include problem behavior can be challenging. The focus of this chapter has been on the approach known as positive behavior support (PBS). The chapter provides a description of student-centered and school-wide PBS. In particular, a team process to designing and implementing individualized student-centered support plans based on functional behavior assessment is described. In addition, guidance is provided concerning factors (practical matters) that can inhibit initiation and sustained implementation of student-centered PBS within inclusive school settings.

References

Albin, R. W., Lucyshyn, J. M., Horner, R. H., & Flannery, K. B. (1996). Contextual fit for behavior support plans. In L. K. Koegel, R. L. Koegel, & G. Dunlap (Eds.), *Positive behavioral support: Including people with difficult behavior in the community* (pp. 82–98). Baltimore: Paul H. Brookes Publishing Co.

Bambara, L. M., & Knoster, T. (1995). *Guidelines: Effective behavior support.* Harrisburg, PA: Pennsylvania Department of Education, Bureau of Special Education.

Bambara, L. M., & Knoster, T. (1998). *Designing positive behavior support plans.* Washington, D.C.: American Association on Mental Retardation.

Bambara, L. M., Mitchell-Kvacky, N. A., & Iacobelli, S. (1994). Positive behavioral support for students with severe disabilities: An emerging multicomponent approach for addressing challenging behaviors. *School Psychology Review, 23,* 263–278.

Carr, E. G., Dunlap, G., Horner, R. H., Koegel, R. L., Turnbull, A. F., Sailor, W., Anderson, J., Albin, R. W., Koegel, L. K., Fox, L. (2002). Positive behavior support: Evolution of an applied science. *Journal of Positive Behavior Interventions, 4,* 4–16.

Carr, E. G., Horner, R. H., Turnbull, A. P., Marquis, J. G., McLaughlin, D. D., AcAtee, M. L., Smith, C. E., Ryan, K. A., Ruef, M. B., & Doolabh, A. (1999). *Positive behavior support for people with developmental disabilities: A research synthesis.* Washington, D.C.: American Association on Mental Retardation.

Colvin, G., Kameenui, E. J., Sugai, G. (1993). Reconceptualizing behavior management and school-wide discipline in general education. *Education and Treatment of Children, 16,* 361–381.

Dunlap, G., & Kern, L. (1996). Modifying instructional activities to promote desirable behavior: A conceptual and practical framework. *School Psychology Quarterly, 11,* 297–312.

Dwyer, K. P., Osher, D, & Warger, W. (1998). *Early warning, timely response: A guide to safe schools.* Washington, D.C.: U.S. Department of Education.

Eber, L. (in press). Blending process and practice to maximize outcomes: Wraparound and positive behavioral interventions and supports in the schools. *Journal of Emotional and Behavioral Disorders.*

Forrest, M., & Lusthaus, E. (1987). The kaleidoscope: Challenge to the cascade. In M. Forrest (Ed.), *More education/integration* (pp. 1–16). Downsview, Ontario, Canada: G. Allan Roeher Institute.

Hansen, M. (1999). *Writing effective treatment plans: The Pennsylvania CASSP model.* Harrisburg, PA: Pennsylvania CASSP Training and Technical Assistance Institute, Pennsylvania Department of Education.

Horner, R. H., & Day, H. M. (1991). The effects of response efficiency on functionally equivalent competing behaviors. *Journal of Applied Behavior Analysis, 24,* 719–732.

Horner, R. H., & Sugai, G. (2000). School-wide behavior support. *Journal of Positive Behavior Interventions, 2,* 231–232.

Horner, R. H., Day, H. M., & Day, J. R. (1997). Using neutralizing routines to reduce problem behaviors. *Journal of Applied Behavior Analysis, 30,* 601–614.

Horner, R. H., Albin, R. W., Sprague, J. R., Todd, A. W. (1999). Positive behavior support. In M. E. Snell and F. Brown (Eds.), *Instruction of students with severe disabilities (5th ed., pp. 207–243). Upper Saddle River, NJ: Merril/Prentice-Hall.*

Kincaid, D. (1996). Person-centered planning. In L. Kern-Koegel, R. L. Koegel, & G. Dunlap (Eds.), *Positive behavioral support: Including people with difficult behavior in the community* (pp. 439–465). Baltimore: Paul H. Brookes Publishing Co.

Knoster, T. (1998, Spring). Positive behavior support in schools. *Tri-State Consortium on Positive Behavior Support Newsletter, 1,* 1–3.

Knoster, T. (1999). Effective support for students with dual diagnoses who have histories of challenging behavior at school. *Journal of Positive Approaches.* 15–20.

Knoster, T. (2000). Practical application of functional behavioral assessment in schools. *The Journal of The Association for Persons with Severe Handicaps, 4,* 201–211.

Knoster T., & McCurdy, B. (2002). Best practices in functional behavioral assessment. In A. Thomas & J. Grimes (Eds.), *Best practices in school psychology: Vol. 4.* (pp. 1007–1028). Bethesda, MD: National Association of School Psychologists.

Lewis, T. J., & Sugai, G. (1999). Effective behavior support: A systems approach to proactive school-wide management. *Focus on Exceptional Children, 31*(6), 1–24.

Meyer, L. H., & Evans, I. M. (1989). *Non-aversive intervention for behavior problems: A manual for home and community.* Baltimore, MD: Paul H. Brookes Publishing Co.

Mount, B. (1987). *Personal futures planning: Finding directions for change* (Doctoral dissertation,

University of Georgia). Ann Arbor, MI: UMI Dissertation Information Service.

Mount, B., & Zwernick, K. (1988). *It's never too early. It's never too late: A booklet about personal futures planning.* St. Paul, MN: Metropolitan Council.

O'Brien, J. (1987). A guide to lifestyle planning: Using The Activities Catalog to integrate services and natural support systems. In B. Wilcox & G. T. Bellamy (Eds.), *A comprehensive guide to The Activities Catalog: An alternative curriculum for youth and adults with severe disabilities* (pp. 175–189). Baltimore: Paul H. Brookes Publishing Co.

O'Neill, R. E., Horner, R. H., Albin, R. W., Sprague, J. R., Storey, K., & Newton, J. S. (1997). *Functional assessment and program development for problem behaviors: A practical handbook.* Pacific Grove, CA: Brookes/Cole.

Reid, D. H. (2000). Enhancing the applied utility of functional assessment. *Journal of The Association for Persons with Severe Handicaps, 4,* 241–244.

Repp, A. C., Karsh, K. G., Munk, D., & Dahlquist, C. M. (1995). Hypothesis-based interventions: A theory of clinical decision-making. In W. O'Donohue & L. Krasner (Eds.), *Theories of behavior therapy: Exploring behavior change* (pp. 585–608). Washington, D.C.: American Psychological Association.

Smull, M. W., & Harrison, S. B. (1992). *Supporting people with severe retardation in the community.* Alexandria, VA: National Association of State Mental Retardation Program Directors.

Sugai, G., Horner, R. H., Dunlap, G., Hieneman, M.,

Lewis, T. J., Nelson, C. M., Scott, T., Liaupsin, C., Sailor, W., Turnbull, A. P., Turnbull, H. R., Wickham, D., Wilcox, B., & Ruef, M. (2000). Applying positive behavior support and functional behavioral assessment in schools. *Journal of Positive Behavior Interventions, 2,* 131–143.

Taylor-Green, S., Brown, D., Nelson, L., Longton, J., Gassman, T., Cohen, J., Swattz, J., Horner, R. H., Sugai, G., & Hall, S. (1997). School-wide behavior support: Starting the year off right. *Journal of Behavioral Education, 7,* 99–112.

Tilly, W. D., Knoster, T. P., & Ikeda, J. J. (2000). Functional behavioral assessment: Strategies for positive behavior support. In C. Telzrow & M. Tankersley (Eds.), *IDEA amendments of 1997: Practice guidelines for school-based teams.* Bethesda, MD: National Association of School Psychologists Publications.

Tilly, W. D., Knoster, T. P., Kovaleski, J., Bambara, L., Dunlap, G., & Kincaid, D. (1998). *Functional behavioral assessment: Policy development in light of emerging research and practice.* Alexandria, VA: National Association of State Directors of Special Education.

Todd, A. W., Horner, R. H., Sugai, G., & Sprague, J. R. (1999). Effective behavior support: Strengthening school-wide systems through a team-based approach. *Effective School Practices, 17*(4), 23–37.

Vandercook, T., York, J., & Forrest, M. (1989). The McGill Action Planning System (MAPS): A strategy for building the vision. *Journal of The Association for Persons with Severe handicaps, 14,* 205–215.

18

Planning Instruction for the Diverse Classroom: Approaches that Facilitate the Inclusion of All Students

Linda Davern, Roberta Schnorr, and James W. Black

Objectives _____

After completing this chapter, the reader will be able to:

1. Describe the importance of the team's *active* knowledge of Individualized Education Plan (IEP) objectives when doing general classroom planning.
2. Distinguish between planning for disciplinary (for example, Science)/interdisciplinary units and planning for foundation skills such as literacy.
3. Identify how individual goals are determined during unit planning.
4. Offer examples of instructional methods that can be effective in student groupings which present a wide range of learner characteristics.
5. Describe how a student with a significant disability can maintain membership in a classroom "literacy community" while having her or his individual needs met as well.

Key Terms _____

Disciplinary/interdisciplinary planning
Foundation skills planning

Instructional approaches
  Activity-based; Cooperative;
  Interactive; Product-oriented

Learning standards
Specific unit outcomes
Modified unit outcomes

Whether a student with a significant disability is successfully included as a full member of her or his educational community depends largely on the philosophy and instructional practices of the general classroom team. This chapter focuses on planning and instructional approaches for the diverse classroom.[1] Classrooms can be diverse along multiple dimensions such as culture, race/ethnic heritage, language, and socioeconomic class. This chapter focuses primarily on the types of diversity that result in a special education classification (for example, learning, emotional, and physical characteristics), although many of the instructional practices overviewed are beneficial to a wide range of learners. The teaching methods in this chapter are not instituted by the classroom team due to the presence of a student(s) with significant disabilities. They are simply good instructional practices, which by their nature, allow multiple opportunities for all students to participate in meaningful ways.

The Foundation for Success is Teamwork

The focus of this chapter is on the people who design instruction week to week, day to day and moment to moment based on their expertise with curriculum, effective teaching strategies, and knowledge of human development. These people can be considered the classroom team. Members will include the classroom teacher, special educator, and other professionals who work directly with students in the classroom (for example, related service providers, reading teachers, and curriculum specialists). Paraprofessionals and parent volunteers may also be members of the classroom team. In addition, parents/caregivers of individual children will often offer ideas that provide invaluable insight as to how their child or teenager can best be educated.

Teaming is a powerful approach because the skills of members often complement each other. Teaming can result in a richer instructional environment for all students. However, this outcome only occurs when the skills of all team members are *fully* used. For example, in addition to supporting the success of individual students with disabilities, a range of active coteaching strategies can be used when a special educator joins a classroom teacher for all or part of the day. Some are planned in advance, and others can be demonstrated on the spot. Examples include offering mnemonic (memory) devices for linking information, preparing visuals, teaching/modeling notetaking for the large group, teaching goal setting, constructing cooperative groups, and teaching social skills (Davern, 2000).

Team Decisionmaking for the Diverse Classroom

The classroom team brings its collaborative attitudes and skills to the creation of a successful learning environment for all students. Team planning typically reflects two types of decisionmaking:

1. Planning for disciplinary (or interdisciplinary) topics (for example, units in science, social studies, health, and the arts)

2. Planning that focuses on the development of *foundation skills*,[2] such as language arts and literacy

Depending on the age of students (that is, elementary or secondary), a greater emphasis on one of these two types of curriculum planning may exist. For example, planning in developmental literacy and language arts will likely be the dominant focus in primary grades, with some planning for disciplinary topics. In intermediate and secondary schools, there is increasing emphasis on planning disciplinary or interdisciplinary units.

Team planning must acknowledge and address the individual needs of students with disabilities for *both* types of curricular decisionmaking. This chapter will offer a decisionmaking framework for planning disciplinary or interdisciplinary units. In addition, some considerations will be provided to guide team planning for students with disabilities in the foundation skill area of literacy.

A Decisionmaking Framework for Diverse Groups: Planning Disciplinary/Interdisciplinary Units

A framework such as the following can be helpful in planning for a learning environment that meets all students' needs. This framework consists of four steps:

1. Start with the general education curriculum for all students as well as an *active* awareness of individual priorities.
2. Identify student outcomes (both group and individual) for the unit being planned.
3. Design instructional activities.
4. Compile and communicate assessment information.

Step 1. Start with the General Education Curriculum for All Students as Well as an Active Awareness of Individual Priorities

The starting place for planning for a diverse classroom is the general curriculum. In addition, as team members plan for their week, month, and year, they often must consider district or state *learning standards*. A growing number of teachers must also consider how best to prepare students for standardized assessments mandated by their district or state.

As teachers consider these factors in their planning at the start of each new school year, they need to bring to this process an active awareness of learning priorities for individual students with disabilities in their classes. (Of course, students without disabilities may also have some individual priorities that need to be carefully considered.) Awareness of individual priorities determined on students' Individualized Education Plans (IEPs) is sometimes lacking in schools. One reason for this dilemma is the fact that the average IEP is often a lengthy document where the critical information that a classroom teacher (for example, fourth grade teacher, art teacher, or high school English teacher) needs may not be easily accessible. No one is to blame for this. The numerous decisions of the IEP team need to be documented, as well as the sources of information for making those decisions. However, the outcome of this process is typically not a concise delineation of the information teachers need *day to day*.

One response to this challenge is a tool called a Program-at-a-Glance. This tool was originally proposed by Giangreco, Cloninger, and Iverson in an earlier edition of their 1998 work *Choosing Outcomes and Accommodations for Children: A Guide to Educational Planning for Students with Disabilities*. This tool is a concise one-to-two-page document outlining the most essential information on an individual student. The format for such a tool is not rigid, but rather can be determined by teams.

A defining feature of the Program-at-a-Glance is that it presents the student through what Thomas Armstrong calls a *growth paradigm* (2000, p. 104). This can also be called a strength paradigm. Special education has typically functioned in a *deficit paradigm*, that is, the focus has been on students' deficiencies. Although it is obviously important to have clarity on a student's characteristics, achievement levels, and areas of challenge, it is equally important to be able to articulate a student's strengths. Strengths can be a vehicle for making progress in areas with which the student struggles.

In Table 18.1, you will find a Program-at-a-Glance for an example student, Michael, who is a member of a fourth grade class. Michael has a significant disability. This Program at-a-Glance includes some of his educational priorities as determined by the IEP team. This can be shared with every teacher who interacts with the student on a regular basis (for example, fourth grade general educator, speech therapist, or physical education [PE] teacher). Often, teachers do not feel well-informed about the individual student. This type of document can be particularly helpful for the secondary teacher who sees a large number of students every day.

Another advantage to this document is that it can include the related service objectives that should be known by the entire team. For example, a student may have several objectives recommended by the speech therapist (for example, speak clearly at slower rate; initiate words/phrases). For a student to make the maximum progress possible, all teachers need to be aware of these priorities. This allows teachers to plan instructional opportunities, as well as to take advantage of teachable moments that arise throughout the day. In this way, general communication goals are addressed by the entire instructional team—not just the speech therapist. The power of one person to influence a student's development cannot be compared to the power of a team. The same is true for objectives related to areas such as social development and organizational skills. Regardless of the particular system used by teams, it is necessary that a discussion of individual priorities become a part of the overall planning process for the class.

Step 2. Identify Student Outcomes (Both Group and Individual) for the Unit Being Planned

The second step in this framework is identifying student outcomes for the particular unit being designed. This process is illustrated in Table 18.2 for an elementary unit on plants. The level of written detail in this table is for purposes of illustration. Teams may or may not write out this level of detail for each unit.

TABLE 18.1   *Program-at-a-Glance: Michael Grade 4*

Profile
Enjoys computer activities
Enjoys music
Interested in sports
Very social

General Supports/Management
Seated in proximity to teacher
Peer partners/small groups increase participation
Tires in afternoon
Responds well to visual cues

Learning Priorities
Social/Communication
   Attend to peers during small group/partner activities

   Stay with group for routine class activities

   Initiate words/phrases with familiar people (peers/adults)

   Respond to requests or comments from peers/adults

   Make choices/indicate preferences when presented with 2–3 choices (visual/graphic form)

Academic
   Follow picture schedule with minimal prompts for activity closure and to prepare for transitions

Attend to stories read aloud by adults or peers in partnerships/small groups

Use combinations of graphics and print to represent ideas and create messages (e.g., greeting cards, content assignments)

Copy key words and phrases for routine activities (e.g., language experience stories)

Use familiar combinations of coins to purchase lunch

Count out (up to 6) from groups of objects as skill is needed throughout day

Tell time for a few major transitions on or near the hour (11:00=lunch)

Participate for 5–10 minutes on select steps/activities

Physical Development
   Demonstrate increased stamina for school schedule and routines (e.g., walking within school building, maintaining attention throughout day with short breaks)

Test Accommodations
Content is modified. Format for assessment is determined by team according to modified content and ability to communicate understanding/skill.

Source: Adapted from Giangreco, M. F., Cloninger, C. J., & Iverson, V. S. (1998). *Choosing outcomes and accommodations for children: A guide to educational planning for students with disabilities* (2nd ed.). Baltimore: Paul H. Brookes Publishing Co.

Learning Standards to be Addressed.   This plant unit example is linked to students' achievement of the New York State Learning Standards, several of which are listed at the top of Table 18.2. Learning standards are broad outcome statements that "represent the core of what all people should know, understand and be able to do as a result of their schooling" (New York State Academy for Teaching and Learning). An example of a learning standard in English Language Arts is "Students will read, write, listen and speak for information and understanding." Students who are successful with this unit on plants are demonstrating progress in reaching specific standards in the areas of English Language Arts, as well as Mathematics, Science, and Technology.

Specific Outcomes for Disciplinary (for example, Science) or Interdisciplinary Units (Integrated English/Social Studies).   Unit outcomes include key ideas, concepts,

TABLE 18.2   *Elementary Unit Plan: Plants (Grades 4–5)*

New York State Learning Standards to be Addressed:
English Language Arts #1: Students will read, write, listen, and speak for information and understanding.

Math/Science/Technology #1: Students will use mathematical analysis, scientific inquiry, and engineering design, as appropriate, to pose questions, seek answers, and develop solutions.

Math/Science/Technology #4: Students will understand and apply scientific concepts, principles, and theories pertaining to the physical setting and living environment. . . .

Plants: Unit Outcomes for Most Students	*Unit Outcomes for Students with IEPs*

1. Describe the process of photosynthesis.
2. Name and describe the functions of plant parts (e.g., xylem, phloem, blade, epidermis, stomata).
3. Apply knowledge of plants to make predictions based on observations of a "bottle biome."
4. Apply knowledge of plants to provide and justify explanations for observations of changes in "bottle biome."
5. Explain how plant features in different biomes (e.g., desert, rainforest) relate to local climate and geography.
	Elaine,* Daniel,* Jarrod,* Jamika, Juan:
	
	SAME UNIT OUTCOMES AS REST OF CLASS—with adaptations/accommodations throughout learning and assessment activities (e.g., peer or adult reading partner, short answers, scribe, oral responses, increased visuals, study guides, extended time).
	
	Michael*:
	
	MODIFIED OUTCOMES—with adaptations/accommodations throughout learning and assessment activities.
	
	   Identify basic parts of plant (i.e., stem, roots, leaves).
	   Sequence three pictures of stages of plant development.
	   Communicate changes in "bottle biome."
	
	See ADDITIONAL OUTCOMES for these students.

and/or skills that teachers derive from the curriculum development process. These are outcomes or goals for the class (for example, describe the process of photosynthesis and name and describe the functions of plant parts).

Unit outcomes may be pursued during the course of several weeks. In pursuing these outcomes, the classroom team considers class members who have IEPs and asks the following question. For *this* student with an IEP, which of the following appears to be the wisest approach based on assessment and achievement information, as well as the team's current knowledge of the student:

- Same curriculum outcomes as classmates (no unique accommodations and/or supports)
- Same curriculum outcomes *with* accommodations and/or supports
- Different/modified curriculum outcomes

Same curriculum outcomes as classmates (no unique accommodations and/or supports). In alignment with an educational philosophy that sets high expectations for every student, *most* students with IEPs will have the same unit outcomes as their classmates without IEPs. In addition, team members should never assume that a student with an IEP needs unique accommodations to achieve those outcomes. Team members consider the tasks and provide support *only as special as necessary* (Giangreco, 1996). Sometimes, nothing special is needed.

Same curriculum outcomes with accommodations and/or supports. On the right side of Table 18.2, notice that Elaine, Daniel, Jarrod, Jamika, and Juan are expected to have generally the same unit outcomes as their classmates without IEPs, that is, the team expects them to meet the outcomes related to plants listed on the left. They may need accommodations to learn and participate successfully. Several examples are offered such as reading partners and extended time on tests. Four of these students have characteristics of learning disabilities, and one has an IEP due to emotional difficulties.

Different/modified curriculum outcomes. A *very* small number of students with IEPs will have modified unit outcomes, that is, the outcomes as delineated for the rest of the students would not appear to be reachable given the information the team has at this time about this student. The word "appear" is quite intentional. Teams can never be fully confident that they understand what a student is experiencing or comprehending. This is particularly true for students who struggle with communication. Teams make the best decisions they can day to day based on wise consideration of the information at hand.

Although Michael has different plant unit outcomes, he still participates in the *same* rich unit activities as his peers. There is not a *parallel* modified or special lesson for him.

Michael is a student with a significant disability who has modified outcomes for this unit. Michael represents how the field of education has changed in the past decade or so. In the past, Michael would likely have been placed in a special class. His current school is committed to providing full membership and has placed Michael in a fourth grade class. The planning team has determined outcomes related to plants that appear obtainable by Michael (i.e., identify basic parts of plant: stem, roots, leaves; sequence three pictures of stages of plant development; communicate changes in "bottle biome").

Changing Expectations Regarding Outcomes.   Determinations such as *same curriculum outcomes* and *modified curriculum outcomes* should be fluid in the sense that, at any time in the process, if it becomes apparent that a child can achieve *more* than the modified outcomes imply, expectations should be immediately altered to reflect this.

Yet, this immediate response is not wise in the opposite situation: when a child is expected to achieve the same curriculum outcomes and does *not* do so. Moving a child from the same outcomes to modified outcomes can significantly alter the likelihood that a child will eventually obtain a regular high school diploma. In such situations, teams (including, of course, parents) should consider a wide range of responses (for example, changes in level of support, use of technology, or testing modifications) in order to maintain the highest expectations. These decisions are life altering.

Additional Individual Outcomes for Students (Embedded in Unit Activities).   In addition to unit-related outcomes, there are additional individual outcomes that the classroom team will want to be cognizant of when planning. The IEP is the team's guide for determining these outcomes. Such individual outcomes are shown in the right column in Table 18.3. These are priorities that may be addressed during unit activities that are *not* directly related to the science topic under focus (that is, plants). Additional outcomes include

TABLE 18.3   *Elementary Unit Plan: Additional Outcomes*

Plants: Unit Outcomes for Most Students	*Additional Outcomes for Some Students With IEPs*
1. Describe the process of photosynthesis. 2. Name and describe the functions of plant parts (e.g., xylem, phloem, blade, epidermis, stomata). 3. Apply knowledge of plants to make predictions based on observations of a "bottle biome." 4. Apply knowledge of plants to provide and justify explanations for observations of changes in "bottle biome." 5. Explain how plant features in different biomes (e.g., desert, rainforest) relate to local climate and geography.	Elaine: Interact positively with peers in structured learning activities. Daniel, Jarrod: Use system to organize and manage unit materials. Michael: Attend to peer(s) during partner/group work. Respond to requests or comments from peers and adults. Participate for 5–10 minutes on select steps/activities. Use words/phrases. Make choices/indicate preferences when presented with 2–3 choices. Use combinations of graphics and print to represent ideas and create messages. Copy key words and phrases. Demonstrate increased stamina.

many curricular areas that are addressed throughout this book. These outcomes can be categorized in various ways, such as Language and Literacy; Personal/Social Development; School, Community, and Work Participation; and Mathematics and Technology (Ford, Davern & Schnorr, 2001, p. 218).

This approach to planning and teaching has also been referred to as curriculum overlapping, which has been defined as "teaching a diverse group of students within a shared activity in which students have different, individually appropriate learning outcomes that come from two or more curriculum areas" (Giangreco, Cloninger & Iverson, 1998, p. 12).

Michael's high priority *additional outcomes* that will be focused on during this plant unit relate to communication/literacy (e.g., respond to requests or comments), social skills (e.g., attend to peer(s) during partner/group work), and physical development (e.g., increase stamina). If we were to go back to his IEP and Program-at-a-Glance, we would find these skills listed as priorities for Michael. They are priorities because the team felt that his progress in these areas was critical to his participation and success both now and in the future. These skills carry as much importance as the plant-related information/understanding he achieves.

Step 3. Design Instructional Activities

After clarifying outcomes, the team begins the process of instructional design. As they design activities, they plan for individual goals to be addressed. In addition, some opportunities (or teachable moments) will arise unexpectedly, and, because team members have an active awareness of students' priorities, they will take advantage of these moments.

Instructional Design: Where To Start?   The "one size fits all" type of instructional design is quickly fading from practice. But where does the team start in terms of instructional design for diversity? When planning activities for the diverse classroom, the starting place is clear: excellence in *overall* curriculum and instructional design. Sophisticated understanding of good teaching is the foundation for planning for diversity in learning characteristics. The best teachers (general or special education) have this foundation.

In addition, the principle of *universal design* is changing the ways in which teachers think about learning resources. "As a new paradigm for teaching, learning, assessment and curriculum development, Universal Design for Learning (UDL) draws upon and extends principles of universal design as used in architecture and product design" (CAST Universal Design for Learning, 2002). The Center for Applied Special Technology (CAST) reminds teachers that curriculum materials should be varied and diverse. Materials should accommodate the many ways that students differ. Versatility in instructional materials can be achieved by computer technology which can emulate "a book, an audio CD player . . . , a phone, a VCR, a spreadsheet, a drafting table, an editing studio" (CAST Universal Design for Learning, 2002). This expansion of instructional methodology and materials, if used wisely, enhances all students' opportunities to participate in meaningful ways.

An Expansive Repertoire of Instructional Approaches. A successful classroom is characterized by rich, active, and varied learning experiences. Good teachers demonstrate a range of instructional practices throughout the day and typically use more than one format in any given learning session. For example, the teacher may have student partners brainstorm to review key ideas from the unit in progress. Next, the teacher may provide a full group presentation or demonstration before students carry out a small group task. Finally, groups may share their observations/conclusions with the large group.

Some methods, although helpful at times, have traditionally been *overused*, for example, extended lecture format. This does not mean that lecture does not have its place in a teacher's repertoire. The problem occurs when the teacher overuses this instructional technique because it is hard for students to sustain their attention for long periods of time on one speaker.

As noted by Wiggins and McTighe (1998), "the challenge is to *expand* a teaching repertoire to make sure that a greater diversity of appropriate methods for instruction are used than are typically found in most classrooms" (p. 6). This expansion is just as critical for the student who is considered uniquely gifted, as it is for the student who struggles with learning.

It is encouraging to learn that the often-stated belief that "good teaching is good teaching" is supported by research. Vaughn, Gersten, and Chard (2000) in their discussion of findings from research syntheses on interventions with students with learning disabilities delineated particular interventions that had positive effects. What is of great interest is that these same interventions were shown to have positive effects on students *without* disabilities as well. The types of instructional approaches they discuss include "making instruction visible and explicit" (such as the explicit teaching of steps or demonstrations with examples), "systematic feedback" through dialogue (teacher with student or student with student), "small interactive groups and pairs" (including tutoring), and "strategies used to enhance task persistence" (pp. 108–109).

Many experienced teachers would argue that these same approaches lend themselves to the inclusion of students with very significant disabilities. The reason for this is because instructional design, which is based on interactions between students and active engagement with varied materials, creates rich opportunities for participation. Participation can result in progress on priority areas, such as communication skills, social skills, working with others, and following routines. These types of goal areas tend to be widely represented in the IEPs of students with significant disabilities.

Curricular Approaches and Teaching Methods for Heterogeneous Groupings. The section that follows focuses on teaching approaches drawn from integrated thematic instruction, differentiated instruction, multiple intelligences theory, activity-based and product-oriented approaches, and instructional design that is interactive and cooperative.

Each method will be paired with an example of how such an approach might be used during the plant unit and how Michael might participate during the use of the approach. In *each* of these examples, there are multiple opportunities for Michael to benefit from curriculum overlap. He is able to make progress on a range of social, communication, literacy, school routines, and organizational skills, and other areas of priority from his IEP. In addition to the approaches discussed in the following sections, see

"Additional Resources on Instructional Design and Inclusive Practices" at the end of this chapter for further study.

Integrated Thematic Instruction.   Kovalik (1997) discusses the different types of input teachers can use when designing learning activities around themes. She argues that a powerful type of input is having a "being there" experience with the "real thing" (p. 80), for example, leaving the school to examine plant life in natural settings. She suggests that powerful curriculum uses print and other forms of second-hand information to supplement learning.

How does Michael participate?

> Students visit a national forest in their region to explore plant life with an outdoor educator who hosts student groups. Michael participates without the need for any adaptations.

Differentiated Instruction.   Tomlinson, author of *The Differentiated Classroom* (1999), also acknowledges the importance of excellence in overall design. She describes good differentiated teaching as starting with "a clear and solid sense of what constitutes powerful curriculum and engaging instruction" (p. 2) and then proceeding as needed to "modify content, process or product" (p. 11). The *content* is "what the students will learn." The *process* is the particular activity "through which students make sense of key skills," and the *product* is the way that students "demonstrate and expand what they understand and can do as a result of . . . learning" (p. 48).

How does Michael participate?

> When Michael builds a bottle biome with his small group, the *content* is differentiated for him, that is, he has *different* content goals related to plants. The *process* remains essentially the same (building the bottle biome), although he may require additional support in participating. The *product* is also the same (the completed bottle biome).
>
> During other activities in Michael's day, *process* and *product* may be quite differentiated for him. For example, Michael's product for writing in his science journal will look quite different from others in his fourth grade class.

Multiple Intelligences Approaches.   Howard Gardner's Theory of Multiple Intelligences states that each person has many areas of intelligence (1983). Thomas Armstrong has written a very accessible book, *Multiple Intelligences in the Classroom* (2000), which describes the eight areas of intelligence and the theory's application to planning educational activities. The goal is to draw on a range of areas of intelligence when designing activities in order to capture students' interests and highlight their unique areas of strength. Here is an example of some varied activities based on bringing the multiple intelligences approach to the plants unit.

- **Logical-Mathematical**: Graph and compare data related to plant growth and rainfall.
- **Linguistic**: Write predictions and observations in science journal; create a Hyperstudio presentation that relates plant features to climate and geography.
- **Bodily kinesthetic**: Create a model of an ecosystem (for example, desert, tundra, grasslands, or rainforest).
- **Spatial**: Draw and label a plant in different stages of growth.
- **Musical**: Compose a song linking plant parts to their functions.
- **Intrapersonal**: Discuss how the stages of a plant's life are like the stages in your life.
- **Interpersonal**: Turn to a partner and interview that classmate about whether she or he has ever worked in a garden. Which factors appeared to influence plant growth?
- **Naturalistic**: Plan the content for a self-guided tour brochure on plant life in the school courtyard garden.

How does Michael participate?

Naturalistic: Plan the content for a self-guided tour brochure on plant life in the school courtyard garden.

Michael takes digital pictures of plants in the courtyard with a partner. Later, he and his partner (with adult support) use the class computer to print each picture. Selections from this collection of photos will be used in the brochure students develop for the self-guided tour.

Activity-Based and Product-Oriented Approaches. Good teachers offer students varied ways to explore the topic under focus. This will often lead to a higher level of engagement on the part of students. Renzulli, Leppien, and Hays (2000) offer an extensive array of possible instructional products. In the example that follows, a product category that they offer is matched to the objectives for the plant unit.

- **Spoken products**: Record a five-minute simulation of a radio segment on plant features and local climate.
- **Construction products**: Build a bottle biome.
- **Written products**: Write a research report describing plants for a specified biome (for example, rainforest or desert).
- **Leadership products**: Design an awareness campaign to address practices that disrupt biome conditions required for plant and animal life (for example, destruction of wetlands).
- **Artistic products**: View examples of works of art based on scenes in nature and then produce an illustration of a biome (for example, wetlands, desert). Students can create an original or re-create a famous work of art. Written statements accompany their artwork and describe the features of the plant life.
- **Performance products**: Develop a song/skit that focuses on the theme of photosynthesis.

How does Michael participate?

Construction products: Students build a bottle biome.

Michael and his partner collect materials for the upper half of their group's bottle biome, which is the terrestrial ecosystem. They collect two precut (2-liter) soda bottles, a square of cheese-cloth, stones, potting soil, grass seed, and any combination of six animals from the selection of earthworms, slugs, and beetles. Other group members collect another precut bottle, pond water, duckweed, and a small snail for the bottom half of their project, which will be the aquatic ecosystem.

Instructional Design that is Interactive and Cooperative.   Research reviews have reported the effectiveness of cooperative learning methods with students with disabilities (Johnson & Johnson, 1989; Slavin, 1990). Cooperative methods use face-to-face interaction, positive interdependence, individual and group accountability, teaching of interpersonal and small group skills, and group processing (that is, leading students in a discussion on how they performed on both the task and the social skills) (Johnson, Johnson & Holubec, 1993).

Positive interdependence and individual accountability have been shown to be critical components of cooperative approaches (Slavin, 1990). Positive interdependence is "successfully structured when students perceive that they are linked with each other in a way that one cannot succeed unless everyone succeeds" (Johnson, Johnson & Holubec, 1993, p. 9). In the following example, one method of positive interdependence is the use of roles. Students have specific responsibilities in contributing to the group outcome.

How does Michael participate?

Students gather data, create graphs, and prepare a presentation that compares annual precipitation in two different biomes (for example, desert and grasslands). Although each member contributes in various ways throughout the task, members also have specific roles in which they take leadership:

- The Reader/Leader reads guiding questions and leads the group through the steps of the task.
- The Recorder writes responses and data on group guide sheet.
- The Illustrators use the computer to create a graph that represents the data.
- The Reporter takes the lead in presenting the group's product to the class.

Michael is one of the Illustrators for his group. With assistance from an adult (and paired with a peer), he uses the computer and spreadsheet software to contribute to entering data and printing the graph for his group.

Active, High-Engagement Daily Instructional Routines.   High-engagement, active strategies tend to benefit a range of learners. Many such strategies are offered by Harmin (1994) in his compilation, *Inspiring Active Learning*. For example,

1. *"Outcome sentences"* (p. 25). Outcome sentences are used as a summary to activities. The teacher provides a sentence starter to the large group, and each student is expected to formulate a quick written response (e.g., I learned . . .; I'm wondering . . .).

How does Michael participate?

Michael is prompted to refer to his science notebook, which includes relevant pictures and key words. An adult or peer guides him to choose from several options that would be appropriate responses to the sentence starter.

2. *"Paired reading"* (p. 101). In paired reading, students read aloud in partnerships determined by the teacher. This can be used with any type of text. As noted by Harmin, this tends to engage more students, more of the time, than having one student at a time read to the large group.

How does Michael participate?

In partnership with a peer, an adult determines that Michael will participate in "reading" the opening paragraph and the summary paragraph of the assigned reading. A few key words (nouns) recur in both passages and are linked with images in advance of the activity. When it's Michael's turn to read, an adult (or peer) reads the passage, but stops when these key words arise. Michael is prompted to verbalize the words drawing on information from the images.

Adaptations.   Even in settings where effective teaming and innovative instructional design exist, a small number of students will still need individualized supports. As noted by Tomlinson (1999), students learn best with "moderate challenge" (p. 19). This means that adaptations that lead to success must be offered if students are to learn and enjoy their learning. A task that far exceeds the current abilities of the student is likely to lead to withdrawal or problematic behaviors used to escape the task.

Supports may include additional visuals, changes in how the information is expressed, assistive technology, or additional adult or peer assistance. Extensive guidelines for individualized adaptations are offered in other chapters. Adaptations are created through the collaboration of general and special educators. Related service providers, parents, and paraprofessionals will also generate many ideas for adaptations. In addition, the student may be able to share preferences regarding adaptations.

Students do not like to stand out as different. Adaptations should use age-appropriate images and materials. Preschool and early elementary images should be avoided for older students. Magazines, catalogs, clip art, and the World Wide Web, as well as specialized commercial products, are good sources of age-appropriate images for instructional adaptations.

Step 4. Compile and Communicate Assessment Information

The fourth step of the process is compiling and communicating assessment information. As is usual with assessment, the team considers the outcomes that were determined for the plant unit. They also consider some of the individual objectives from students' IEPs.

Effective teams use multiple forms of assessment throughout the year. Of course, teachers can never afford to lose sight of the assessments their students will be required to take (district or state), so creative teachers infuse examples of how skills and information explored through creative methods might be assessed in the standardized form. Making this connection in an *embedded, ongoing* fashion ensures that students can demonstrate their knowledge when formal assessments are administered.

For teacher-created assessments, teams may need to provide alternative ways for students to demonstrate their understanding. If the team depends solely on reading and writing activities to assess knowledge of plants, they will receive an inaccurate picture of what has been learned by some students. For this reason, teachers consider many sources of information in reporting assessment data.

Modified outcomes for the plant unit are reflected on assessment summaries for Michael (for example, identify basic parts of plant). The team is also going to report on Michael's progress on Additional Individual Outcomes (for example, respond to requests or comments).

A Decisionmaking Framework for Diverse Groups: Considerations for Foundation Skills and Students with Significant Disabilities

In addition to planning for all students' participation in disciplinary/interdisciplinary units, teams must also plan to facilitate the development of foundation skills, such as language arts. All students who have disabilities must have access to typical literacy opportunities with peers. According to Erickson and Koppenhaver (1998), "People with severe disabilities can learn to read and write. At the very least, they can benefit linguistically, cognitively and communicatively from regular and predictable interactions with others around print" (p. 63). It is important that teams maintain attention to all students' opportunities to fully develop abilities to communicate and access print throughout school years. For students with disabilities, this requires valid membership in the class literacy community—that is, participation in age-appropriate language arts and literacy activities with peers who are proficient speakers, listeners, readers, and writers. In addition to this participation, many students with significant disabilities will need individualized instruction as well.

Although learners' characteristics and general education settings will vary, the following considerations can guide planning for meaningful literacy development for all students:

- Literacy is viewed as authentic communication and a means for connecting students within (and beyond) their classroom community (not just a set of hierarchical sub-skills) (Kliewer, 1998).
- Children need not demonstrate specific skills as a condition of membership in the classroom literacy community (Erickson & Koppenhaver, 1995; Kliewer, 1998).
- Teachers are problem solvers who explore and develop alternatives (for example, "tools") to allow students to access the range of rich literacy opportunities afforded their peers. Individualized supports are provided to enhance participation and to provide high quality instruction (Erickson and Koppenhaver, 1998; Kliewer & Biklen, 2001).

In implementing these considerations, several steps will be critical to success. These are discussed in the following sections.

Step 1. Create a Team/Class Literacy Program that Promotes Membership for All Students

Fundamental to team planning is creating a schedule that will facilitate a sense of community for all class members through *shared* experiences with language and print, as well as a focus on individual growth and development of all members. To accomplish both, the schedule must allow for sustained blocks of time devoted to literacy, flexible grouping, varied materials, multilevel activities, and, for some learners, *additional* time and focused experiences. One strategy is to organize sessions according to the four blocks: guided reading, self-selected reading, writing, and working with words (Allington & Cunningham, 1996; Fountas & Pinnell, 2001). This type of framework allows for (a) full group instruction and activities (for example, teacher read-aloud of age-appropriate books, teaching strategies for unknown words or comprehension, a minilesson on revising a piece of writing, or sharing/listening to a piece of writing during "author's chair"); (b) small group, teacher-facilitated instruction (for example, guided reading with small groups of students with materials that match instructional levels); and (c) partner or individual activities with or without adult support (for example, "making words," doing self-selected reading, developing a piece of writing on a self-selected topic or related to a personal experience). Within this framework, individuals can participate in shared activities at various levels (for example, writers' workshop pieces may range from lengthy, narrative stories to a picture booklet with captions generated by the student author).

The "readers' workshop" and "writers' workshop" approach can also be very effective for supporting the literacy development of middle school learners. Within this structure, students select materials for reading (with teacher guidance) to match abilities and interests (Atwell, 1998, p. 49). In writers' workshop, students choose and develop pieces on their interests and first-hand experiences. Teachers provide minilessons to the full group and closely monitor student progress in reading and writing through conferences that focus on individual goals. There are frequent opportunities for students to reflect on and interact with peers and teachers about what they are reading and writing (for example, through reader-response journals, book talks, peer conferences, group meetings). Emphasis is on reading and writing for authentic purposes within an accepting and supportive class community. This structure can allow students with a wide range of literacy characteristics to participate as valued members and to pursue individual learning goals.

Step 2: Engage in Team Planning to Maximize Participation of Individual Students (Through Adaptations when Necessary)

Individual students with moderate and severe disabilities should be supported to participate in both formal and informal literacy activities within their general education classes with classmates who are proficient readers, writers, listeners, and speakers. Team members (for example, general educator, special educator, reading teacher, or speech and language therapist) can share responsibilities for planning, teaching, and adapting various components of the individual, small group, or full group activities. Paraprofessionals may also participate in supporting student involvement.

The classroom team supports Michael's participation in structured literacy activities within the fourth grade classroom (for example, partner reading during self-selected reading; adult support to create captioned "picture stories" during writer's workshop; providing character pictures to accompany teacher read-aloud; "working with words" activities, such as adding labeled pictures and a few key words to his portable word wall folder (Cunningham, 2000).

Step 3. Create Opportunities for Individualized Instruction to Ensure Ongoing Development in Language and Literacy

It is likely that most students with significant disabilities will require some structured, individualized instruction to facilitate the development of skills needed to become better communicators, and, to whatever degree possible, readers and writers. This will require receiving daily individual or small group instruction from the classroom teacher, special educator, speech therapist, or reading teacher. This may occur as one of the flexible grouping arrangements within the class literacy and language block. Some learners may need additional instructional or practice opportunities (that is, more time and more instruction than their same-age peers). The purpose of additional sessions is to augment (not replace) the typical language and literacy opportunities in the general education classroom. Consider the following examples that highlight individualized instructional sessions. (Individual teachers maintain responsibility for particular guided reading groups in order to plan effectively and to monitor student progress.)

Michael's fourth grade team uses the four-block schedule on a daily basis during a 90-minute morning block. Every day Michael participates in a small group guided reading session. The other student in this group is an emergent-level reader/writer. Materials and learning activities are geared to the instructional level of these students (for example, picture books with familiar words and predictable text, shared reading that emphasizes the print-language connection and the reading process, and sight word development). Two other guided reading groups occur routinely whose members read at other instructional levels (Cunningham & Allington, 1999, p. 222).

Daniel's speech therapist sponsors a small lunch group twice a week with Daniel (age 7) and five of his classmates. She plans and facilitates semistructured conversations around topics that reflect shared experiences. This provides instruction and practice for Daniel to use his augmentative communication device for social communication.

Serena (age 13) is a middle school student whose English teacher uses Atwell's Readers and Writers workshop as the foundation for the class schedule. The class meets for 80 minutes every other day and is cotaught with a special educator. Serena participates with support, using reading materials that match her current abilities (teacher-made books, books on tape, CD-ROM books, and other books at approximately first-grade level). During writing, she sequences four to six pictures from a file reflecting some of her interests and experiences and writes key words as captions from a word bank. In addition to these experiences, Serena receives small group instruction in guided reading at her instructional level from the special educator on alternate days. This session occurs at the end of the school day during a 40-minute, schoolwide study and support time.

Team planning should include literacy program structures that build community and support the participation of all learners *and* allow sufficient flexibility to address individual learner needs.

Summary

The emphasis of this chapter has been on the importance of instructional design that meets the needs of all students. Meeting student needs requires an active awareness of student priorities. Instructional design will vary depending on whether the focus is building foundation skills or exploring a disciplinary/interdisciplinary topic. As teaching teams increase their instructional repertoires for both of these areas of planning, they create greater opportunities for the active and meaningful participation of students with the most significant disabilities. The successful diverse classroom is based on a strength paradigm in relation to all students (Armstrong, 2000).

Children and teenagers generally want what we want: to feel valued and acknowledged for our accomplishments, to feel safe, and to be presented with tasks that are challenging, but doable. Teamwork, creative instructional design, and thoughtful adaptations create the right type of challenge, and the climate we create ensures that students see their value.

TABLE 18.4   *Secondary Unit Plan: U.S. Immigration*

New York State Learning Standards to be addressed:
English Language Arts #1: Students will read, write, listen and speak for information and understanding.

English Language Arts #3: Read, write, listen and speak for critical analysis and evaluation.

Social Studies #1: Use a variety of intellectual skills to demonstrate their understanding of major ideas, eras, themes, developments, and turning points in the history of the U.S. and New York State.

U.S. Immigration: Unit Outcomes for Most Students	*Unit Outcomes for Students with IEPs*
1. Describe causes and effects of changes in U.S. immigration policies from 1840 to present. 2. Describe immigration (immigrants, origins, language, culture, reasons, participation/assimilation, effect) for three major time periods between 1840 and present. 3. Demonstrate increased knowledge and appreciation of many contributions to American culture by past/current immigrants from diverse backgrounds.	Anna, Jessica,* Ed,* Dave, Jamal:* SAME UNIT OUTCOMES AS REST OF CLASS—with adaptations/accommodations throughout learning and assessment activities (e.g., audiotaped readings or reader, scribe, oral responses, extended time) Maria:* MODIFIED OUTCOMES—with adaptations/accommodations throughout learning and assessment activities. Contribute to partner/group activities to explore contributions of past/current immigrants (e.g., gather relevant resources/images to contribute to group projects). *See ADDITIONAL OUTCOMES for these students

TABLE 18.5 *Secondary Unit Plan: Additional Outcomes*

U.S. Immigration: Unit Outcomes for Most Students	Additional Outcomes for Some Students with IEPs
1. Describe causes and effects of changes in U.S. immigration policies from 1840 to present. 2. Describe immigration (immigrants, origins, language, culture, reasons, participation/assimilation, effect) for three major time periods between 1840 to present. 3. Demonstrate increased knowledge and appreciation of many contributions to American culture by past/current immigrants from diverse backgrounds.	Jessica, Ed, Jamal: Use planner and folder system to organize and manage materials and meet due dates. Apply strategies for note taking and developing written products. Demonstrate self-advocacy skills by seeking clarification and assistance/ accommodations from teachers as needed. Ed: Demonstrate self-monitoring strategies in group activities to maintain positive/neutral tone. Maria: Use vocalizations and augmentative systems to communicate choices, share information and socialize. Use communication boards to demonstrate understanding of what others say. Use touch screen to make selections in activities. Demonstrate self-advocacy by expressing preferences and seeking assistance when needed.

References

Allington, R. L., & Cunningham, P. M. (1996). *Schools that work: Where all children read and write*. New York: Addison-Wesley Longman.

Armstrong, T. (2000). *Multiple intelligences in the classroom*. Alexandria, VA: Association for Supervision and Curriculum Development.

Atwell, N. (1998). *In the middle: New understandings about writing, reading and learning*. Portsmouth, NH: Boynton-Cook.

CAST Universal Design for Learning (2002, March 28). Summary of universal design for learning concepts. Retrieved from *http://www.cast.org/udl/index.cfm?i=7*

Cunningham, P. M. & Allington, R. L. (1999). *Classrooms that work: They can all read and write*. (2nd ed.) New York: Longman Publishing.

Davern, L. (2000). Complementary roles and mutual benefits: Strategies for active teaming between general and special education. In *1999 TASH conference yearbook* (pp. 73–76). Baltimore, MD: TASH.

Erickson, K. A., & Koppenhaver, D. A. (1995). Developing a literacy program for children with severe disabilities. *The Reading Teacher, 48*, 676–684.

Erickson, K., & Koppenhaver, D. (1998). Using the "Write talk-nology" with Patrik. *Teaching Exceptional Children, 31*(2), 58–64.

Ford, A., Davern, L., & Schnorr, R. (2001). Learners with significant disabilities: Curricular relevance in an era of standards-based reform. *Remedial and Special Education, 22*(4), 214–222.

Fountas, I. C., & Pinnell, G. S. (2001). *Guiding readers and writers (Grades 3–6): Teaching comprehen-*

sion, genre and content literacy. Portsmouth, NH: Heinemann.

Gardner, H. (1983). *Frames of mind: The theory of multiple intelligences*. New York: Basic Books.

Giangreco, M. F. (1996). *Vermont interdependent services team approach (VISTA): A guide to educational support services*. Baltimore: Paul H. Brookes Publishing Co.

Giangreco, M. F., Cloninger, C. J., & Iverson, V. S. (1998). *Choosing outcomes and accommodations for children: A guide to educational planning for students with disabilities* (2nd ed.). Baltimore: Paul H. Brookes Publishing Co.

Harmin, M. (1994). *Inspiring active learning*. Alexandria, VA: Association for Supervision and Curriculum Development.

Johnson, D. W., & Johnson, R. T. (1989). *Cooperation and competition: Theory and practice*. Edina, MN: Interaction Book Co.

Johnson, D. W., Johnson, R. T., & Holubec, E. J. (1993). *Circles on learning: Cooperation in the classroom* (4th ed.). Edina, MN: Interaction Book Co.

Kliewer, C. (1998). *Schooling children with Down syndrome: Toward an understanding of possibility*. New York: Teachers College Press.

Kliewer, C., & Biklen, D. (2001). "School's not really a place for reading": A research synthesis of the literate lives of students with severe disabilities. *Journal of The Association for Persons with Severe Handicaps, 26*(1), 1–12.

Kovalik, S. (1997). *ITI: The model: Integrated thematic instruction* (3rd ed.). Kent, WA: Books for Educators/Susan Kovalik and Associates.

New York State Academy for Teaching and Learning (n.d.). *New York State learning standards.* Retrieved October 3, 2001 from *www.nysatl. nysed.gov/standards.html.*

Renzulli, J. S., Leppien, J. H., & Hays, T. S. (2000). *The multiple menu model: A practical guide for developing differentiated curriculum*. Mansfield Center, CT: Creative Learning Press.

Slavin, R. E. (1990). *Cooperative learning: Theory, research and practice*. Englewood Cliffs, NJ: Prentice-Hall.

Tomlinson, C. A. (1999). *The differentiated classroom: Responding to the needs of all learners*. Alexandria, VA: The Association for Supervision and Curriculum Development.

U.S. Department of Labor. (1991). *What work requires of schools: A SCANS report for America 2000*. Washington, D.C.: Author.

Vaughn, S., Gersten, R., & Chard, D. J. (2000). The underlying message in LD intervention research: Findings from research syntheses. *Exceptional Children, 67*(1), 99–114.

Wiggins, G., & McTighe, J. (1998). *Understanding by design*. Alexandria, VA: Association for Supervision and Curriculum Development.

Additional Resources on Instructional Design and Inclusive Practices _____

Apacki, C. (1991). *Energize! Energizers and other great cooperative activities for all ages*. Granville, OH: Quest International.

Castagnera, E., Fisher, D., Rodifer, K., & Sax, C. (1998). *Deciding what to teach and how to teach it: Connecting students through curriculum and instruction*. Colorado Springs, CO: PEAK Parent Center.

Cohen, E. (1994). *Designing groupwork* (2nd ed.). New York: Teachers College Press.

Giangreco, M. F. (Ed.). (1997). *Quick-guides to inclusion: Ideas for educating students with disabilities*. Baltimore: Paul H. Brookes Publishing Co.

Giangreco, M. F., & Doyle, M. B. (2000). Curricular and instructional considerations for teaching students with disabilities in general education classrooms. In S. Wade (Ed.), *Inclusive education: A case book of readings for prospective and practicing teachers* (Volume 1) (pp. 51–69). Hillsdale, NJ: Lawrence Erlbaum.

Janney, R., & Snell, M. E. (2000). *Modifying schoolwork*. Baltimore: Paul H. Brookes Publishing Co.

Johnson, D. W., Johnson, R. T., & Holubec, E.J. (1994). *The new circles of learning: Cooperation in the classroom and school*. Alexandria, VA: Association for Supervision and Curriculum Development.

Kagan, S. (1994). *Cooperative learning*. San Clemente, CA: Kagan Cooperative Learning.

Kagan, S., & Kagan, M. (1998). *Multiple intelligences: The complete MI book*. San Clemente, CA: Kagan Cooperative Learning.

Kronberg, R., & York-Barr, J. (1998). *Differentiated teaching and learning in heterogeneous classrooms: Strategies for meeting the needs of all students*. University of Minnesota: Institute on Community Integration.

McGregor, G. & Vogelsberg, R. T. (1998). *Inclusive schooling practices: Pedagogical and research foundations: A synthesis of the literature that informs best practices about inclusive schooling*.

University of Montana: Rural Institute on Disabilities.

Putnam, J. W. (1993). *Cooperative learning and strategies for inclusion: Celebrating diversity in the classroom.* Baltimore: Paul H. Brookes Publishing Co.

Salend, S. J. (2001). *Creating inclusive classrooms: Effective and reflective practices* (4th ed.). Upper Saddle River, NJ: Prentice-Hall.

Sapon-Shevin, M. (1999). *Because we can change the world: A practical guide to building cooperative,* *inclusive classroom communities.* Boston: Allyn and Bacon.

Schniedewind, N., & Davidson, E. (2000). Differentiating cooperative learning. *Educational Leadership, 58* (1), 24–29.

Wheelock, A. (1992). *Crossing the tracks: How untracking can save America's schools.* New York: The New Press.

Endnotes

1. The framework for the process described in this chapter was developed in partnership with the New York State Education Department, Office of Vocational and Educational Services for Individuals with Disabilities. The authors would like to extend their thanks to Charlene Gurian, Elaine Gervais, and Barbara Miller for their insight and contributions to this work.

2. We have borrowed the term *foundation skills* from the Secretary's Commission on Achieving Necessary Skills (SCANS; U.S. Department of Labor, 1991). This phrase captures the essence of identifying priorities, although we use it in a somewhat different way than used in the SCANS report.

19

Principles and Practices for Instructing Students with Significant Needs in Inclusive Settings

Felix Billingsley

Objectives

After completing this chapter, the reader will be able to:

1. Discuss contextual considerations in selecting instructional strategies for application in inclusive settings.
2. Discuss the role played by consequent events, natural cues, and prompts in instructional programs, as well as the importance and nature of practices to promote generalization and maintenance.
3. Discuss methods for assessing the preferences of students and identifying potential reinforcers for their behaviors.
4. Discuss the importance of using instructional methods that promote high levels of successful performance by students.
5. Discuss the importance of, and methods for, fading prompts and contrived consequences.

Key Terms

Consequences	Intermittent reinforcement	Respondent conditioning
Constant time delay	Maintenance	Response prompt
Continuous reinforcement	Natural cue	Secondary reinforcer
Contrived reinforcer	Negative reinforcer	Self-monitoring
Discriminative stimulus	Operant learning	Shaping
Extinction	Positive reinforcer	Simultaneous prompt and test
Fading	Preference assessment	Stimulus prompt
Generalization	Punishment	System of least prompts

The contents of this chapter reflect the position that the principles underlying effective teaching and learning do not change as a function of placement. That is, those principles of behavior that have proven successful in teaching a broad range of skills to a broad range of students with and without disabilities should not be considered applicable only within restrictive environments. They are equally valuable when applied where students with disabilities learn side-by-side with their typically developing peers in inclusive settings. Using those principles in inclusive settings, however, requires careful attention to some issues that may not have been obvious within segregated contexts (Jackson, Ryndak, & Billingsley, 2000).

One such issue is the recognition that quality of life is a multidimensional concept. A satisfactory quality of life, for example, depends on the nature of our jobs, the characteristics of our residences, the activities available in our leisure time, the social relationships and friendships that we form, and the supports provided by our communities. Likewise, the outcomes that can be achieved by students with severe disabilities in inclusive environments are multidimensional and contribute to increased participation in those roles and activities that characterize the lives of typically developing individuals.

As noted by Billingsley, Gallucci, Peck, Schwartz, and Staub, D. (1996) and Schwartz, Staub, Gallucci, and Peck (1995), at least three major outcome domains can be identified for students in inclusive settings: relationships, membership, and skill development. In other words, students with disabilities form a variety of relationships with their peers, participate as members of the classroom and school in various roles, and develop both functional and academic skills. Further, those outcomes are transactional, each affecting the development of the other. When one domain is positively effected, positive influences are noted in other domains; when a domain is negatively effected, negative influences are noted in the others. The implication is that we must consider the impact of instructional methods on social relationships and membership (Jackson, Ryndak, & Billingsley, 2000). It is possible, for example, that the teacher might select a perfectly sound method, based on empirically validated principles of behavior, for increasing a skill, but that its use as planned in an inclusive setting would interfere with important relationship or membership outcomes. It is also possible that a method that would be appropriate for an elementary school student might produce unforeseen, collateral negative effects (for example, ridicule from peers) for a student in high school.

Because the use of instructional methods may have an undesirable spread of effect across outcome domains, and because those methods are not context independent, you should consider the following questions in relation to the principles and associated practices described in the sections that follow:

- Is the method likely to stigmatize the student in the setting where it will be applied?
- Is the method likely to stigmatize students of a certain age?
- Is the method likely to interfere with the formation or maintenance of social relationships with typically developing peers?
- Is the method likely to be detrimental to the student's classroom or school membership?
- Will it be difficult to implement the method correctly in the setting where it will be applied?
- Are any components of the method undesirable to the student's family or within the student's culture?

If the answer to any of the previous questions is yes, consider whether another method might be used to promote positive outcomes. The most favorable results will, of course, be obtained where instructional practices are culturally acceptable and correctly implemented without making students stick out, and where improvements are observed in skill development as well as in relationships and membership.

Three Decisions

Any instructional arrangement constructed for learners with severe disabilities requires that educators make at least three major decisions. They must determine (a) what consequences should be used and how they will be applied to promote learning, (b) what steps should be taken to ensure that desired behaviors occur in order that consequences can be applied, and (c) what steps should be taken to promote generalization and maintenance. The following sections should help you make those decisions.

Consequences

A great deal of basic and applied research suggests that the behaviors we attempt to teach are a function of their consequences. However, some behavior changes occur as a result of *respondent* conditioning (also known as classical or Pavlovian conditioning) in which the presence of previously neutral objects or events (stimuli) evoke reflexive behaviors because those objects or events have systematically preceded other stimuli that elicited those behaviors. The consequence of the behavior, in such cases, may not be responsible for the behavior change. Think, for example, of Pavlov's dogs salivating when they heard a tone that had previously preceded the presentation of meat powder, or of a child who becomes upset upon seeing men with beards after having had unpleasant experiences with a bearded man in the past. The result of respondent conditioning, then, amounts to *stimulus substitution*, in that a new stimulus comes to exert control over an existing behavior. Extended discussions of respondent conditioning may be found in such sources as Baldwin and Baldwin (1998), Miltenberger, (2001) and Rescorla (1988).

Because respondent conditioning involves reflexes that are not typically under voluntary control, and because educators are primarily concerned with voluntary behaviors, the focus here will be on *operant* learning, where individuals act on their environment (behave) in the presence of certain stimuli and incur a consequence. In operant learning, it is the impact of consequences that determines whether a behavior will be more or less likely to occur in the future. The arrangement of appropriate consequences should, therefore, be given an extremely high priority in the process of planning and implementing instruction.

Positive Reinforcers

Although educators should be familiar with the effects of other consequences, much of their work will involve developing ways for students to achieve access to *positive reinforcers*. A positive reinforcer is a stimulus (object or event) that increases the future probability of the behavior it follows. Positive reinforcers, then, are defined by their effect, and they strengthen behavior. The term *positive* here has no relationship to the desirability of outcomes or to perceived inherent qualities of stimuli. Positive reinforcers may, for example, be encountered (and inadvertently delivered by teachers) that result in the development of highly undesirable behaviors. If Tony's teacher doesn't use instructional strategies that make it highly probable that Tony will be successful, she may find that she has to use many correction procedures. It is then possible that the attention provided by the correction procedures will act as a reinforcer, and Tony's failure to follow directions, complete tasks, or behave in generally acceptable ways will increase rather than decrease. In addition, although ice cream might be perceived by many of us to possess inherently positive attributes, it may not be a positive reinforcer for some children and in some contexts. Similarly, most of us would probably agree that receiving corrections as used by Tony's teacher in the previous example does not seem to be a positive experience. However, the corrections may turn out to be positive reinforcers for Tony's undesirable behavior, perhaps because the teacher provides little in the way of praise or other recognition for his successful and desirable behaviors or because her instruction does not give Tony many opportunities to perform successfully.

Note that it is nonsensical to say "I tried positive reinforcers, but they didn't work." If "they didn't work," the stimuli were not positive reinforcers. By definition, positive reinforcers work. This underscores the fact that they can be highly individual; what may be a reinforcer for Dimitri under a given set of circumstances may not be a reinforcer for Luann in the same circumstances. Therefore, those items frequently considered to be rewards (free time, stickers, high fives, fish crackers, attention from a peer or the teacher, and so forth) may or may not be reinforcers at a given moment for a particular student. A number of methods exist, however, to identify what *might* act as positive reinforcers. Those methods, which may be either informal or formal, fall under the general heading of *preference assessments*.

Preference Assessments.   Informal methods to assess preferences include asking parents, teachers, or other caregivers to identify activities that the student likes to engage in, toys he or she likes to play with, or food items that he or she likes, or asking the student to identify such preferred stimuli. Information of this nature often may emerge during the process of personal futures planning or be found in ecological inventories that have been conducted to aid in Individualized Education Program (IEP) development. We also may observe students during their free time in order to determine what appear to be preferred activities or items. However, many students with the most significant disabilities may have acquired the skills to engage in few leisure activities and may have very limited experiences with toys, games, or other items compared to their peers who are typically developing. As a result, their choices of items or activities may be severely restricted and not reflect the broad range of stimuli for which students might display preferences had opportunities and accommodations been available that would have allowed them to sample those stimuli. In addition, teachers often observe children during their free time in order to apply the Premack principle (Baldwin & Baldwin, 1998) that states that high probability behaviors can be used to reinforce lower probability behaviors (for example, "You can make brownies in home economics class and eat them [high probability behavior] if you measure the ingredients correctly [lower probability behavior]").

The principle may, indeed, be useful, but educators should keep in mind that opportunities to perform the high probability behavior (eating brownies) will not act as a reinforcer if the student has access to all the brownies he or she wants without performing the target behavior (correct measuring). Using the "measure correctly-eat a brownie" contingency right after a snack time or lunch in which brownies were served, then, would not be a good way to employ the Premack principle.

Formal methods for assessing preferences involve arranging for children to have some degree of familiarity with items or events and then presenting them one at a time, or in paired or group arrangements, for the student to select. A possible advantage of paired or group arrangements can be the ability to identify a hierarchy of preferences. It is possible, however, to sample some activities or settings only one option at a time (for example, going swimming) (Lohrmann-O'Rourke, Browder, & Brown, 2000). If the student can respond to symbols, pictures or line drawings can be used to represent stimuli; otherwise, actual objects or participation in activities should be used. Items selected for presentation often may be based on the results of the informal methods discussed previously.

Whether stimuli are presented alone, in pairs, or in groups, educators must be alert to idiosyncratic and subtle behaviors that may indicate positive and negative responses to these stimuli. In addition, Lohrmann-O'Rourke et al. (2000) have noted that, "for some individuals, it may be necessary to shape an existing response or teach a new response (e.g., symbol identification) to promote preference expression" (p. 46).

Because preferences may change frequently, it is desirable to employ assessment methods that can be used often and with minimal intrusion into instructional time. Such a method was described by Roane, Vollmer, Ringdahl, and Marcus (1998) who gave children and adults with moderate to profound disabilities five minutes of free access to an array of items suggested by teachers and other caregivers as possible reinforcers. The items in the array included food, drinks, leisure and play items, tactile stimuli, auditory stimuli, and social attention. The participants were permitted to interact with each item at any time and for as long as they desired during the brief assessment period, and data were collected on the percentage of 10-second intervals in which the participants interacted with an item. Items with which the participants interacted most of the time were identified as highly preferred and were found to act as reinforcers for simple responses. The method also was found to be associated with fewer behavior problems and required less time to complete than an assessment procedure using paired stimuli. However, given the caution regarding the use of the Premack principle outlined earlier, when using this assessment method, it "may be necessary to wait for a period of time following assessment before beginning sessions using identified reinforcers" (Roane et al., 1998, p. 618).

Although the preference assessments have been discussed as a method for identifying potential reinforcers, be aware that they also can serve broader purposes for improving quality of life. Among these are (a) selecting activities that students with disabilities may enjoy participating in with their typically developing peers; (b) selecting items and activities to be used when offering choices in everyday contexts and routines; and (c) using preferred materials, activities, or settings as antecedents, rather than consequences, during instruction. Using preference assessments for the latter purpose could, perhaps, reduce the need to use contrived reinforcers (see the following section) during instruction. Reviews of issues and methods relevant to the assessment of preferences among students with severe disabilities may be found in Lohrmann-O'Rourke and Browder (1998) and Lohrmann-O'Rourke et al. (2000).

Natural and Contrived Reinforcers.   Potential reinforcers can be employed as consequences in two ways. First, they can occur as natural outcomes of skills and skill routines (that is, sequences of skills that result in some important outcome). Second, they can occur as *contrived reinforcers* (that is, reinforcers that are not a natural outcome of a skill or skill sequence, but that are used during instruction to strengthen a particular skill or sequence). An example of the former would be teaching a secondary student who seems to prefer the smell and tactile sensations provided by clay to make clay pottery during art class. Another example would be teaching a student to carry his or her own tray in the school lunch line where the natural reinforcer could be getting to eat and/or interact with peers at the cafeteria table. An example of the latter would be putting a "happy face" sticker on a journal entry that was prepared with the assistance of a peer, or giving a student who seems to prefer social stimuli a high five when getting to class on time. The problem with such contrived reinforcers is that, unless they have been faded out carefully and systematically, the student may cease responding when the reinforcers are withdrawn or not perform the be havior in situations in which they are not available. Further, when the provision of structional reinforcers is obvious, it could tend to make the student with disabilities out in undesirable ways. Few 15-year-olds, for example, receive a small carrot st' getting dressed after gym class.

As a rule of thumb, always seek ways that potential reinforcers can be u' ural outcomes for educationally important skills. When skills selected for in' naturally followed by reinforcers or possess intrinsically reinforcing char' example, desirable sensory input), they will be reinforced frequently ? strengthened. Such skills also are likely to be reinforced across settin' time, which should enhance generalization and maintenance.

Some educationally important behaviors may not be followed by consequences that will be reinforcing for a particular student. For example, the social interaction or positive attention from peers that may naturally follow a variety of desirable behaviors may be highly reinforcing for many students with severe disabilities. However, those same consequences may not be reinforcing for many others, particularly children and youth with autism. If it is important for students to perform skills for which natural reinforcers do not exist, educators will need to use stimuli that *will* serve a reinforcing function, even though those stimuli will not be naturally available. The good news is that stimuli that are paired with established reinforcers, or are part of a sequence of behaviors that allows individuals to obtain them, can acquire reinforcing qualities themselves. Such stimuli or behaviors are referred to as *secondary reinforcers*. For example, money may not have acted as a reinforcer for a student's performance in a job-training program until the use of money on a number of occasions allowed the student to obtain items that already were reinforcing; money then became a secondary reinforcer. Similarly, if the recognition from teachers and peers that follows participation in class discussions by an elementary student using a speech synthesis communication device is not reinforcing, the teacher might provide the student with a contrived reinforcer in the form of a preferred sticker following participation. The teacher's aim here is to develop the typical level of recognition that follows discussion participation as a secondary reinforcer.

When contrived reinforcers are used, they should be faded out (that is, systematically eliminated or reduced in frequency) in such a manner that the desired behaviors are maintained. Typically, reinforcers applied for instructional purposes are first provided on a *continuous schedule* in which each performance of the skill is reinforced. Continuous schedules help build response strength and ensure the most frequent pairing of the reinforcer and the natural events that are intended to gain reinforcing qualities. When behaviors are occurring reliably when the contrived reinforcers are provided, educators then should move to an *intermittent schedule* in which they provide contrived reinforcers less frequently, either by requiring the student to demonstrate more behaviors to obtain the reinforcer or by increasing the time behaviors must occur. Finally, the contrived reinforcers may be removed altogether. Occasionally, however, those natural stimuli that have become reinforcing through the pairing process once again must be paired with the original contrived, but effective, reinforcer or with some other potent reinforcer to prevent *extinction* (the reduction in frequency of behavior that occurs when the reinforcer is no longer available). It is unlikely, for instance, that money could act as a secondary reinforcer indefinitely if it could not be used to obtain other reinforcers.

Additional Important Practices.   Some additional practices that are important in the use of positive reinforcers include the following:

At least initially, the interval between desired behaviors and the acquisition of reinforcers should be very brief (Alberto & Troutman, 1999). If Jessica is being taught to request desired toys from peers, the peers should be instructed to provide toys *immediately* following Jessica's request in the beginning stages of the program. This immediacy is critical because, the further removed in time the reinforcer is from the behavior being taught, the more difficult it will be to ensure that the reinforcer follows the target behavior and not some other behavior. This confusion will have the effect of delaying skill acquisition. In addition, it is possible that some undesirable behavior will occur in the interval between the target behavior and the reinforcer. The undesirable behavior, then, might be strengthened rather than the target behavior. Later in the instructional process, the temporal interval between target behaviors and reinforcers can be increased, if necessary.

Be consistent in the provision of consequences (Alberto & Troutman, 1999). Once again, this is particularly critical in the early stages of a program. It is also a guideline that requires close attention in environments in which the student may receive instruction on the same target behaviors from general and special education teachers, instructional assistants, peers, parents, and volunteers. Where consequences are not applied consistently from time to time or from individual to individual, the students may learn only that their behavior has no predictable effect on their environment. As a result, they may acquire skills slowly, if at all, or they may learn that the behavior should be performed in the presence of only a small and insufficient number of individuals. As in the case of immediacy of reinforcement, the provision of reinforcers can occur on an intermittent basis (if appropriate) after the behavior has become established in the individual's skill repertoire.

Vary reinforcers where variation makes sense (Egel, 1981). Satiation, a decrease in behavior as a function of continued exposure to reinforcement, may occur if students constantly receive the same reinforcer. When you use praise, for example, vary your praise statements and voice inflection. If you are teaching Kiet to activate a personal CD player, it will probably be useful to ensure that she can listen to a variety of CDs. A good way to vary reinforcers is to give a choice, where possible (for example, let Kiet select the CD she would like to hear). Not only will this provide variation, but the act of choice-making itself can result in improvements in performance and reductions in challenging behaviors (Bambara, Koger, Katzer, & Davenport, 1995; Dyer, Dunlap, & Winterling, 1990: Lancioni, O'Reilly, & Emerson, 1996).

Negative Reinforcers and Punishment

Although both negative reinforcers and punishment are consequences that result in behavior change and both involve stimuli that many of us might consider unpleasant, do not confuse them. Negative reinforcers, like positive reinforcers, increase the future probability of behaviors in ways that will be explained in the following sections, whereas punishers decrease the future probability of the behaviors they follow. Although we typically avoid the use of negative reinforcers and punishers because of their aversive qualities, educators should be aware of their effects because of the outcomes of their use and because of their omnipresence in our society.

Negative Reinforcers.   Negative reinforcers are stimuli that increase the probability of behaviors that allow one to escape or avoid them. Rain can be a negative reinforcer for coming indoors or putting on a raincoat (those behaviors allow one to escape or avoid getting wet, respectively); a teenager may perform household chores reliably to avoid or escape the nagging of a parent; a student may increase the speed with which he or she walks to the classroom to avoid penalties associated with being tardy; and so forth.[1]

In the previous examples, negative reinforcement was responsible for strengthening adaptive behaviors; however, the results of such reinforcement also can be responsible for some rather insidious outcomes in the classroom. Of particular danger is a circular pattern of positive and negative reinforcement that can result in highly undesirable interactions between students and classroom staff or their peers. Consider, for example, a general education classroom that serves Spencer, a child with severe disabilities. Unfortunately, Spencer, who has some physical disabilities and spends considerable time in a wheelchair, does not receive much attention. Although he generally is well-behaved, he engages in stereotypic hand flapping from time to time. The general education teacher considers the hand flapping inappropriate and distracting to the other students; therefore, she asks Mr. Evans, an instructional assistant, to intervene to reduce the undesired behavior. Mr. Evans's method is to correct Spencer each time he flaps his hands with the stage-whispered comment, "Spencer, have quiet hands." When he does this, Spencer always stops flapping for a while. Over time, however, the hand flapping increases in frequency with a concurrent increase in Mr. Evans's correction attempts. In fact, the corrections become much more intrusive and emphatic over time.

What may be going on here is that Spencer's hand flapping is being positively reinforced by the attention provided by Mr. Evans, so he flaps more often in order to increase access to that reinforcer. Concurrently, because Spencer *does* stop flapping when corrected, Mr. Evans can escape the perceived disturbance produced by those behaviors and avoid the displeasure of the teacher by providing the correction. In other words, both the hand-flapping disturbance and the displeasure of the teacher negatively reinforced Mr. Evans's corrections, and, as a result, the correction behaviors increased in strength.

After they are established, such circular patterns can be extremely hard to abolish. Be on the lookout for situations in which they might occur and attempt to use practices that will preclude them. By way of illustration, a better intervention method in the current example would be to modify Spencer's curriculum so that he receives reinforcement for participating in activities that require meaningful hand use. Further, the general classroom environment should be enriched so that he receives increased levels of attention when he isn't flapping.

Punishers.   As in the case of positive and negative reinforcers, punishers are defined by their effect on behavior. In contrast to reinforcers, however, punishers decrease the frequency of the behaviors they follow, either as a result of the presentation of aversive conditions or of the loss of reinforcers. Punishments applied to decrease the inappropriate behaviors of persons with severe disabilities have run the gamut from extremely intrusive and aversive events to those that are far less intrusive. Some punishers in the former category have been electric shock, aromatic ammonia, slaps, and water sprayed in the face. Some examples of the latter include brief periods of ignoring (a form of *time out*, that is, a period in which the opportunity to obtain reinforcers is removed) or response-cost procedures in which privileges, items, or points are taken away contingent on undesired behavior. Currently, most education professionals reject the use of punishers that are highly aversive and try to minimize the use of even those that are on the less aversive end of the continuum. In addition to posing serious ethical questions, the use of punishment may produce a variety of detrimental side effects including lying, cheating, aggression, avoidance, fear, and so forth (Alberto & Troutman, 1999). Further, because punishment teaches students what not to do rather than what they can do to achieve their goals, teachers who use punishment may see the punished behavior decrease only to see another, equally unwanted, behavior take its place. As a result of such considerations, punishment is largely being replaced in educational settings with functional, positive approaches that focus on teaching acceptable useful behaviors to replace the unwanted ones. Knoster provides a comprehensive discussion of such approaches in Chapter 17 of this text.

One effect of punishment that often goes unrecognized is its possible impact on classroom staff. When punishment is used, its impact on the environment is frequently immediate; the student is likely to stop hitting, screaming, throwing, or engaging in other disruptive or disturbing behaviors, at least for a while. As discussed earlier, this immediate reduction in disruption may reinforce, and thereby increase in frequency, the future punishing behavior of the staff member. In addition, punishing behavior may generalize to new situations and new students. In contrast, providing positive reinforcers for desired behavior may not make such immediate and dramatic changes in the environment. The resulting reinforcing effects on staff, then, may be relatively weak compared to those obtained through the delivery of punishment. It is easy to see how the classroom climate could deteriorate rapidly under such conditions. Special educators in inclusive settings have a particularly serious responsibility to model techniques that will demonstrate to general education colleagues and other classroom staff how to manage what may be unusual and perplexing inappropriate behaviors in ways that are effective and that contribute to a positive, humane classroom atmosphere.

Evoking Desired Behaviors and Building Independence

When consequences are provided for desired behaviors, they are not provided in a vacuum, that is, they are provided in a context and various elements (stimuli) within that context come to set the occasion for responding. When behaviors occur reliably in the presence of certain stimuli because the behaviors have been reinforced in the presence of those stimuli, we say that the behaviors are under *stimulus control* and that the controlling stimuli are *discriminative stimuli* (S^Ds). A major part of the educational enterprise involves providing instruction that leads to students' maximally independent performance in the presence of an appropriate and natural S^D. The configuration of words in a story should act as S^Ds for correct reading, while the characteristics of pictures in a picture recipe book for making a salad should act as S^Ds for the actions necessary to make the salad; a greeting from a peer should act as the S^D for a greeting in reply; the elements of an algebra problem should act as the S^D to undertake the procedures necessary to solve for X; a direction from the teacher should be the S^D to perform the requested task; putting on one's sock should generally be the S^D for putting on one's shoes. In fact, our lives are full of examples of stimulus control where natural S^Ds, which I will refer to as "natural cues" for the remainder of this chapter, include traffic lights, price tags, signs on stores and roads, appointment calendars, characteristics of problem situations, computer icons, verbal and nonverbal behaviors of others, steps in behavioral chains (for example, showering, or dressing) where completion of one step acts as the cue for the next, and so on. Because stimulus control is established when consequences reliably follow specific behaviors, it is important that we consider ways that (a) desired target behaviors can be evoked (b) in the presence of the natural cues that should set the stage for the behaviors so that (c) the desired target behaviors can be reinforced. This often is accomplished through shaping and/or prompting.

Shaping

When *shaping* is used, teachers first reinforce some behavior that is already in the student's repertoire. When that behavior occurs reliably in the presence of the natural cue, the teacher withholds reinforcement until the student emits a behavior that more closely approximates the target behavior. The approximation is then reinforced. This movement through successive approximations continues until the student eventually performs the target behavior. In teaching a student to expand his or her communicative repertoire, for example, the teacher might first reinforce single word responses to the question (that is, the natural cue) "What do you want?" Later, the teacher might reinforce two-word responses, such as "Want help." Still later, reinforcement might follow only responses of three or more words (for example, "I want help"). As noted by Miltenberger (2001), "shaping can be used to generate a novel behavior (language in a young child . . .), to reinstate a previously exhibited behavior (walking, which Mrs. F was refusing to do), or to change some dimension of an existing behavior (the time between urination . . .)" (p. 159). Although shaping can be an extremely useful technique, it also can be excruciatingly slow when complex behaviors are involved. For example, waiting for the emergence of all of the behaviors necessary for a student to dress him or herself or play a game of soccer so that those behaviors could be differentially reinforced would almost certainly be an exercise in frustration for both student and teacher. Often, then, shaping is used as an adjunct to programs that also include various types of prompts and systems for fading those prompts.

Prompting

Prompts can be thought of as auxiliary S^Ds that are used to increase the probability that the target behavior will occur and be reinforced in the presence of the natural cue. A student, for example, might not initially hand a communication card to a teacher or peer (the natural cue) in order to obtain some desired item. In this case, the student would never have the opportunity to make requests that would be reinforced by receiving desired items from the teacher or peer, and the skill would not be learned. The instructor, therefore, might assist the student to move the hand holding the card toward the appropriate person in order that the request could be completed and reinforced. Because the assistance is not intended to be present when the skill is mastered, it acted as a prompt. Prompts can be either response prompts or stimulus prompts.

Response Prompts.   Response prompts are behaviors of other persons that assist the student to make correct responses (Billingsley, 1998; Miltenberger, 2001). Of the possible response prompts, physical assistance such as that used in the previous example generally is considered to be the most intrusive. However, physical prompts can vary along a continuum from full assistance (in which the learner's movements are completely guided through the desired behavior) to partial assistance (in which only a portion of the response is assisted) to a simple touch. In addition, physical prompts can vary on a continuum of placement; for example, a hand movement could be guided by providing the assistance at the hand (over the hand or under the hand), at the forearm, or at the bicep. The precise nature of the physical prompt, or of other types of prompts, is best determined by assessing the type of assistance that is needed to ensure that the learner successfully achieves the reinforcer (Neel & Billingsley, 1989; Wolery, Ault, & Doyle, 1992). With too little assistance, the student is likely to make many errors; if too much assistance is provided, the student may react by emitting challenging behavior, and teachers can lose time as they attempt to reduce unnecessary levels of assistance.

Although physical prompts may be the only way to evoke responses from some students for some behaviors, they should be used judiciously because many students may vigorously resist physical manipulation. Further, they may draw negative attention to students with disabilities (Billingsley & Kelley, 1994). For example, an adolescent receiving physical assistance in learning to play golf would probably not draw much attention; however, that same adolescent would probably draw considerable attention if equivalent degrees of physical assistance were provided during a shopping program in a community grocery store. For such reasons, less intrusive types of assistance should be used if they are adequate to ensure student success. Some possibilities include demonstrations, gestures, and verbal instructions.

Like physical assistance, gestures and verbal instructions can impart varying amounts of information. The amount of information in verbal directions can be varied according to the extent to which they are directive. A highly directive prompt, for example, would be "It's time to take your turn"; a less directive prompt could be "Whose turn is it now?"; "What next?" would be still less directive. Similarly, gestures in a "Please come here" program could be varied from a wide sweep of the arm to a movement of the hand to simply a crooked finger. Once again, select a prompt that is least obvious while still occasioning the desired behavior.

Demonstrations, provided in person or using video, can be a highly effective and desirable method of providing prompts. Not only do they impart instruction efficiently, but they also are used often by teachers and caregivers of typically developing students and, therefore, should not make students with disabilities stick out. Some guidelines for using demonstrations (also referred to as modeling) include the following (see sources such as Baldwin and Baldwin [1998)], Miltenberger [2001], and Schoen [1989] for discussions):

- The best person to provide the demonstration is likely to be someone who is similar to, and held in high regard by, the student who is receiving instruction. This, of course, suggests the desirability of including peers as models, both formally and informally.
- The student receiving instruction should observe the demonstrator receiving reinforcement for performing the behavior.
- The demonstration should be provided from the student's visual orientation.
- Behaviors should be demonstrated in real situations or in simulations (for example, role plays) of real situations.

- If the student can benefit from verbal input, a verbal description of the demonstrator's behavior should accompany the demonstration.
- The student should have the opportunity to imitate the modeled behavior as soon as possible following the demonstration and receive immediate reinforcement for performing the behavior correctly.

Fading Response Prompts.   Each of the response prompts described previously is used only to get the behavior started and to ensure reinforcement in the presence of the natural cue. This means that, eventually, the prompts must be withdrawn and stimulus control transferred to the natural cue. This process is known as *fading*. Many methods to successfully fade prompts have been described in detail in other sources (for example, Billingsley, 1998; Demchak, 1990; Schoen, 1986; Wolery et al., 1992). This discussion, therefore, will be limited to only three methods, chosen because they are frequently recommended in the instructional literature and/or because of their ease of use and demonstrated effectiveness. Those methods are (a) the system of least prompts ("least to most" fading), (b) constant time delay, and (c) simultaneous prompt and test.

The *system of least prompts* involves moving sequentially through a presumed hierarchy of prompts from those that are considered least intrusive to those that are considered most intrusive. Although the types of prompts included in the hierarchy may vary, the teacher always begins by giving the student an opportunity to perform the behavior independently when the natural cue is present. If the student fails to initiate the behavior or makes an error response during some predetermined time interval (say, 5 seconds), a typical sequence of events might be the following.

- The teachers gives a directive verbal prompt.
- If, after the given time period, the correct response still is not initiated, the teacher repeats the directive prompt and provides a demonstration or a gesture.
- Finally, if the student does not emit the correct behavior, the teacher gives full physical assistance along with the directive prompt to evoke the correct behavior, and the student is provided with the reinforcer.

Although, as noted previously, most descriptions include the delivery of the directive verbal prompt concurrent with other types of prompts, it has been suggested that this may slow down transfer of stimulus control (Billingsley, 1998). The findings of recent research do, in fact, indicate that it may be desirable to eliminate the verbal prompt completely if it does not initially control the target behavior (West & Billingsley, 2001). The system of least prompts has been considered to be self-fading in the sense that "prompts considered to be more intrusive ideally will be eliminated without procedural modification as learning progresses" (Billingsley, 1998, p. 159).

The *constant time delay* procedure consists of providing several trials of instruction in which the controlling prompt and the natural cue are provided simultaneously so that the learner has no opportunity to make an error. Subsequently, only the natural cue is provided initially, and the prompt is delayed for a predetermined amount of time (3–5 seconds is common). If the student initiates the correct response during that time period (an "anticipation" correct), the reinforcer is delivered. If the student fails to initiate during that time or makes an error response, the teacher provides the controlling prompt followed, typically, by a reinforcer. For example, in teaching sight word recognition, several trials might be conducted in which the teacher requests that the student point to specific words within an array. At the same time he or she makes a request for a given word, the teacher demonstrates by pointing to that word, and the student receives praise following a correct response. Following those trials, the teacher provides the prompt only if the student fails to point to the target words within the designated time interval. The student is praised for both anticipation responses and responses that follow the prompt.

The *simultaneous prompt and test* procedure is very similar to constant time delay in that it starts with several trials in which the natural cue and the controlling prompt are provided simultaneously. It differs, however, in that the simultaneous presentation occurs during each instructional session, and each instructional session is preceded by a test session in which the student has the opportunity to perform independently within a designated time interval, as in the case of the delay trials in the time delay method. Assessment of mastery is based on student performance during these test trials.

Although the system of least prompts is easy to use and is widely described and recommended, it has the disadvantage of producing relatively high rates of errors during the instructional process. This can have a number of undesirable outcomes, including the possibility of reducing the efficiency of stimulus control transfer (Billingsley, 1998). Both constant time delay and the simultaneous prompt and test procedure are also easy to use; further, they result in relatively low error rates and are efficient methods for transferring stimulus control. Those methods, therefore, are considered more suitable for most purposes than the system of least prompts. Where those methods fail to achieve desired outcomes, other low error methods are available, such as progressive time delay (for example, Schuster & Griffen, 1990) or most-to-least (that is, decreasing assistance) prompting (for example, Wolery et al., 1992).

Although response prompts have many advantages (for example, they are free, they are easily transportable, and they require no preparation of materials), some learners may tend to become dependent on teacher assistance. Others may attend only to the prompt and not to the natural cue, in which cases transfer of stimulus control may not occur. Where such problems are noted, it may be possible to promote successful performance by using stimulus prompts.

Stimulus Prompts.   When stimulus prompts are used, the natural cue is changed in some way, or something is added to, or removed from, the context in which it occurs. Its color may be modified, its size or proximity might be changed, and so forth. The idea is to make the natural cue more noticeable or conspicuous (Miltenberger, 2001) and thereby increase the probability that the student will respond correctly in its presence. Changes in the natural cue are known as *within-stimulus prompts*, whereas additions to or subtractions from the context are known as *extrastimulus prompts*. Previously, I briefly described how constant time delay (a response prompting technique) might be used to teach sight word recognition. If one were to use within-stimulus prompts to teach the skill, the target sight word within an array could be placed closer to the learner than the other words, or the lettering of the correct word could be made larger. If extrastimulus prompts were used for the same purpose, a distinctive color could be added to the correct word, or a circle could be drawn around it. Other examples of extrastimulus prompts are picture or written schedules, directions, or scripts used to encourage students' participation in classroom routines, completion of self-help and vocational tasks, or performance of social skills.

As in the case of response prompts, stimulus prompts usually must be faded out so that the learner comes to respond to the natural cue for the target behavior. There are some exceptions. For example, a pictorial schedule to help a student with disabilities organize his or her daily activities might be employed as a lifelong accommodation, just as written or electronic schedules have become a lifelong accommodation for many typically developing individuals. Generally, however, stimulus prompts are temporary. When within-stimulus prompts have been used, fading involves "gradually changing the S^D from its altered state to its natural form" (Miltenberger, 2001, p. 183). In our sight word example, the target word would be made to more closely approximate the size of the other words in the array across instructional trials or would be moved closer to those words and farther away from the student. To fade extrastimulus prompts where some additional stimulus has been added, "fading would involve gradually removing that additional stimulus as the response began occurring reliably in the presence of the S^D" (Miltenberger, 2001, p. 183). Therefore, if a distinctive color had been added to the sight word, the hue might be systematically modified until it is no longer visible. If a circle had been drawn around the word, the solid line of the circle might be changed to a series of dashes that, in turn, could be reduced in number until they were eliminated.

Extrastimulus prompts, like response prompts, are additions to the context in which the natural cue exists. Therefore, some learners may pay attention to the prompt itself rather than to the critical characteristics of the natural cue. In such cases, when extrastimulus prompts are faded, desired behaviors may become less, rather than more, probable. For that reason, within-stimulus prompts should be used where it seems likely that both types of stimulus prompts will ensure skill performance.

Promoting Generalization and Maintenance

Usually, it is not enough for a student to learn to perform skills only in the instructional environment in the presence of those who provided instruction. By the same token, it is not enough for a learner to retain skills for a period that does not extend beyond the demonstration of skill acquisition. A student who is taught to give compliments to peers in his or her elementary school classroom almost surely would reap a small number of social benefits from performing the skill only within that classroom and only for a limited period of time. More extensive benefits, however, would be derived if he or she learned to give compliments appropriately to others in the school and community (generalization) and if he or she retained this ability for an extended period of time (maintenance). Many examples of the need for generalization and maintenance are more dramatic. A failure to generalize and maintain street-crossing skills, for instance, can result in dire consequences. The major point to be made here is that instruction cannot be considered successful until the student can perform skills in those natural situations in which the skills are valued or required.

A number of basic principles are found in the literature regarding those situations that are most likely to promote generalization. A number of those principles, based upon the work of Haring (1988), Koegel, Koegel and Parks (1995), Stokes and Baer (1977), and Stokes and Osnes (1988) follow.

Select skills for instruction that will be reinforced naturally. In other words, teach skills that routinely will lead to reinforcement outside of the instructional environment. It may be beneficial to think about this procedure as teaching children behaviors that will help them achieve their goals that serve a purpose from the student's point of view. By way of illustration, Haring (1988) states that "teaching a student to communicate `yes' and `no' might allow the student to access a whole new set of reinforcers, since this skill fosters natural interactions with others. If the student had no means of acceptable expressive language prior to learning to answer yes/no, generalization might be almost immediate and at a level which accesses sufficient reinforcement to ensure maintenance" (p. 8). In contrast, teaching a child with severe disabilities to point to specific body parts may fail to generalize and to be maintained because that skill is seldom requested and reinforced outside of instructional contexts.

Select skills that can be used frequently in many situations. Skills that serve a function (that is, skills that are demanded by or useful in natural environments and/or that are enjoyable to the learner) are typically those that the student will have the chance to practice frequently and within a broad range of contexts. This means that the student will have the chance to receive frequent and sustained reinforcers and considerable opportunities to recognize appropriate natural cues for his or her behaviors. A variety of social and communication skills are good examples.

Write IEP objectives for generalization. In the past, it was common for IEP objectives to require performance only in the instructional context (Billingsley, Burgess, Lynch, & Matlock, 1991). However, as Stokes and Baer (1977) noted, generalization is not a passive process; educators, therefore, need to plan for generalization. By indicating the need for generalized outcomes in IEP objectives, education teams will establish the basis for a plan to promote student success across environments and time (Billingsley et al., 1991; Westling & Fox, 2000; Wolery, Bailey, & Sugai, 1988).

Assess generalization before instructing. It is entirely possible that skills selected for instruction are already in the learner's repertoire and performed adequately in at least some circumstances outside of the classroom. If such performances are unknown to the education team, they may waste time in unnecessary instruction or inappropriately select instructional strategies that are designed to promote skill acquisition, instead of strategies that are likely to further enhance generalization.

Avoid instructional strategies that may interfere with generalization. Remember that any reinforcers or prompts that are used in instruction, but that will not be present under the natural conditions under which the skill should be used, must be faded to effectively transfer stimulus control to those conditions. For example, a helpful peer seated with a student at lunch may routinely, and without being aware of the possible consequences, prompt the student to "take a bite" throughout the lunch period. The student may later sit quietly in a restaurant waiting for someone to give him or her the prompt (Haring, 1988). In addition, the student may have been taught to perform skills under conditions of extremely limited stimulus and response variation with the result that he or she fails to learn to use the skills under the range of variations that exist in natural environments. Hence, if a student learns purchasing skills in a student-managed snack bar in the school, he or she may be befuddled when he or she attempts to make purchases in the community where the environment and routine are different, where individuals may not automatically make accommodations offered at the student store, and where the communication demands differ. It is, therefore, critical that stimulus and response demands be varied in instruction to the extent that stimuli and responses vary in the environment. In other words, use multiple examples of when and how the skill should be performed, as well as examples of when and how it should not be performed. The method known as general case programming provides a highly systematic and effective method for designing appropriate variations (for example, Albin & Horner, 1988).

Teach children to manage their own behavior. Self-management has been considered to be a pivotal behavior in that, when a person learns to self-manage behavior "that person learns a skill that will facilitate generalization to an infinite number of behaviors across an infinite number of environments and people" (Koegel et al., 1995, p. 70). Although self-management may include a number of elements, helping students to acquire self-management skills often consists of teaching them to record (or *self-monitor*) the occurrence or absence of instructed behaviors, a technique that often seems sufficient to generate behavior change. Students could be taught to self-monitor a wide range of target skills, such as social and communication behaviors (for example, asking or answering questions, initiating or responding to greetings, or sharing items), activities of daily living (for example, completing household chores or getting to class on time), and vocational tasks (for example, completing assemblies).

In any self-monitoring program for students with severe disabilities, it will be necessary to (a) choose a particular monitoring method or device, (b) teach the student to discriminate appropriate (or inappropriate) behavior on his or her part and use the selected monitoring method or device, and (c) fade prompts or consequences that have been used during the foregoing instruction. Specific methods and issues in self-management are discussed in such sources as Browder and Shapiro (1985), Koegel et al. (1995), and Liberty and Paeth (1990).

Use systematic guidelines and rules to help select appropriate generalization strategies. In 1977, Stokes and Baer discussed eight methods designed to facilitate generalization. Since that time, the number of strategies and tactics available to educators has grown enormously (see, for example, Westling and Fox [2000]), and their challenge is to choose an appropriate procedure from these large numbers. When failures in generalization and maintenance occur, it may be tempting to simply select what appears to be the easiest or most familiar method to achieve the desired outcome. Generalization and maintenance failures may occur for several reasons, however, and the method chosen should address the specific nature of the problem. Liberty, Haring, White, and Billingsley (1988), for example, identified seven distinct types of generalization problems and suggested appropriate interventions for each. In order to pinpoint the type of problem that has produced the failure and, thereby, select a suitable method to promote generalization, one can use guidelines and rules to help identify potentially effective strategies. Guidelines and rules can be found in such sources as Horner, Bellamy, & Colvin (1984), Horner and Billingsley (1988), and Liberty et al. (1988).

Summary

The basic principles presented in this chapter have been selected from a much larger body of research-based knowledge and practice. They can, nonetheless, form the foundation of effective instructional programs for children and youth with significant disabilities in inclusive settings. They can help you to plan instruction that will help students learn new behaviors and increase the sophistication and utility of behaviors they already possess. Peers, volunteers, paraprofessionals, and others often can successfully implement practices based on these principles when the teacher provides appropriate training and oversight. They can be applied in programs that are teacher-directed as well as in child-directed, incidental teaching programs and can promote students' performance and maintenance of skills in complex, natural environments. However, they also can be used in ways that result in undesirable behaviors on the part of educators and students, and that may stigmatize people with disabilities, reduce students' opportunities to make meaningful choices, and lead to students' acquisition of trivial behaviors that can be performed only in decontextualized settings. Educators, therefore, must continue to develop their knowledge of instructional principles and techniques throughout their careers and, as they apply that knowledge, be keenly aware that their practices will have a profound impact on the dignity of, and lifestyle outcomes for, their students.

References

Alberto, P. A., & Troutman, A. C. (1999). Applied behavior analysis for teachers (5th ed.). Columbus, OH: Merrill.

Albin, R. W., & Horner, R. H. (1988). Generalization with precision. In R. H. Horner, G. Dunlap, & R. L. Koegel (Eds.), *Generalization and maintenance: Life-style changes in applied settings* (pp. 99–120). Baltimore, MD: Paul H. Brookes Publishing Co.

Baldwin, J. D., & Baldwin, J. I. (1998). *Behavior principles in everyday life.* Upper Saddle River, NJ: Prentice-Hall.

Bambara, L. M., Koger, F., Katzer, T., & Davenport, T. (1995). Embedding choice in the context of daily routines: An experimental case study. *Journal of The Association for Persons with Severe Handicaps, 20,* 185–195.

Billingsley, F. F. (1998). Behaving independently: Current practices and considerations in fading instructor assistance. In A. Hilton and R. P. Ringlaben (Eds.), *Best and promising practices in developmental disabilities.* (pp. 157–168). Austin, TX: Pro-ED, Inc.

Billingsley, F. F., & Kelley, B. (1994). An examination of the acceptability of instructional practices for students with severe disabilities in general education settings. *Journal of The Association for Persons with Severe Handicaps, 19,* 75–83.

Billingsley, F., Burgess, D., Lynch, V., & Matlock, B. (1991). Toward generalized outcomes: Considerations and guidelines for writing instructional objectives. *Education and Training in Mental Retardation, 26,* 351–360.

Billingsley, F. F., Gallucci, C., Peck, C. A., Schwartz, I. S., & Staub, D. (1996). "But those kids can't even do math": An alternative conceptualization of outcomes for inclusive education. *Special Education Leadership Review, 3,* 43–55.

Browder, D. M., & Shapiro, E. S. (1985). Applications of self-management to individuals with severe handicaps: A review. *Journal of The Association for Persons with Severe Handicaps, 10,* 200–2008.

Demchak, M. A. (1990). Response prompting and fading methods: A review. *American Journal on Mental Retardation, 94,* 603–615.

Dyer, K., Dunlap, G., & Winterling, V. (1990). Effects of choice making on the serious problem behaviors of students with severe handicaps. *Journal of Applied Behavior Analysis, 23,* 515–524.

Egel, A. (1981). Reinforcer variation: Implications for motivating developmentally disabled children.

Journal of Applied Behavior Analysis, 14, 345–350.

Haring, N. G. (1988). A technology for generalization. In N. G. Haring (Ed.), *Generalization for students with severe handicaps: Strategies and solutions* (pp. 5–11). Seattle: University of Washington Press.

Horner, R. H., & Billingsley, F. F. (1988). The effects of competing behaviors on generalization and maintenance of adaptive behaviors in applied settings. In R. H. Horner, G. Dunlap, and R. L. Koegel (Eds.), *Generalization and maintenance: Lifestyle changes in applied settings* (pp. 197–220). Baltimore, MD: Paul H. Brookes Publishing Co.

Horner, R., Bellamy, G. T., & Colvin, G. T. (1984). Responding in the presence of non-trained stimuli: Implications of generalization error patterns. *Journal of The Association for Persons with Severe Handicaps, 9,* 287–295.

Jackson, L., Ryndak, D. L., & Billingsley, F. (2000). Useful practices in inclusive education: A preliminary view of what experts in moderate to severe disabilities are saying. *Journal of The Association for Persons with Severe Handicaps, 25,* 129–141.

Koegel, R. L., Koegel, L. K., & Parks, D. R. (1995). "Teach the Individual" model of generalization: Autonomy through self-management. In R. L. Koegel & L. K. Koegel (Eds.), *Teaching children with autism: Strategies for initiating positive interactions and improving learning opportunities* (pp. 67–77). Baltimore, MD: Paul H. Brookes Publishing Co.

Lancioni, G. E., O'Reilly, M. F., & Emerson, E. (1996). A review of choice research with people with severe and profound developmental disabilities. *Research in Developmental Disabilities, 17,* 391–411.

Liberty, K., & Paeth, M. A. (1990). Self-recording for students with severe and multiple handicaps. *Teaching Exceptional Children, 22(3),* 73–75.

Liberty, K. A., Haring, N. G., White, O. R., & Billingsley, F. F. (1988). A technology for the future: Decision rules for generalization. *Education and Training in Mental Retardation, 23,* 315–326.

Lohrmann-O'Rourke, S., & Browder, D. M. (1998). Empirically based methods to assess the preferences of individuals with severe disabilities. *American Journal on Mental Retardation, 103,* 146–161.

Lohrmann-O'Rourke, S., Browder, D. M., Brown, F. (2000). Guidelines for conducting socially valid systematic preference assessments. *Journal of The*

Association for Persons with Severe Handicaps, 25, 42–53.

Miltenberger, R. G. (2001). *Behavior modification: Principles and procedures* (2nd ed.). Belmont, CA: Wadsworth.

Neel, R. S., & Billingsley, F. F. (1989). *IMPACT: A functional curriculum handbook for students with moderate to severe disabilities.* Baltimore, MD: Paul H. Brookes Publishing Co.

Rescorla, R. A. (1988). Pavlovian conditioning: It's not what you think. *American Psychologist, 43,* 151–160.

Roane, H. S., Vollmer, T. R., Ringdahl, J. E., & Marcus, B. A. (1998). Evaluation of a brief stimulus preference assessment. *Journal of Applied Behavior Analysis, 31,* 605–620.

Schoen, S. F. (1986). Assistance procedures to facilitate the transfer of stimulus control: Review and analysis. *Education and Training of the Mentally Retarded, 21,* 62–74.

Schoen, S. F. (1989). Teaching students with handicaps to learn through observation. *Teaching Exceptional Children, 22(1),* 18–21.

Schuster, J. W., & Griffen, A. K. (1990). Using time delay with task analyses. *Teaching Exceptional Children, 22(4),* 49–53.

Schwartz, I., Staub, D., Gallucci, C., & Peck, C. A. (1995). Blending qualitative and behavior analytic research methods to evaluate outcomes in inclusive schools. *Journal of Behavioral Education, 5,* 93–106.

Stokes, T. F., & Baer, D. B. (1977). An implicit technology of generalization. *Journal of Applied Behavior Analysis, 10,* 349–367.

Stokes, T. F., & Osnes, P. G. (1988). The developing applied technology of generalization and maintenance. In R. H. Horner, G. Dunlap, and R. L. Koegel (Eds.), *Generalization and maintenance: Lifestyle changes in applied settings* (pp. 5–19). Baltimore, MD: Paul H. Brookes Publishing Co.

West, E., & Billingsley, F. (2001, May). *Assessing the effects of two prompting procedures on skill acquisition.* Poster presented at the 27th Annual Convention of the Association for Behavior Analysis, New Orleans, Louisiana.

Westling, D. L., & Fox, L. (2000). *Teaching students with severe disabilities* (2nd ed.). Columbus, OH: Merrill.

Wolery, M., Ault, M. J., & Doyle, P. M. (1992). *Teaching students with moderate to severe disabilities: Use of response prompting strategies.* New York: Longman.

Wolery, M., Bailey, D. B., Jr., & Sugai, G. M. (1988). *Effective teaching: Principles and procedures of* *applied behavior analysis with exceptional students*. Boston: Allyn and Bacon.

Endnote

1   In each of the examples, positive reinforcers also can play an important role. For instance, the teenager may perform household chores in order to obtain reinforcers, such as an allowance, privileges, feelings of satisfaction, and so forth.

20

Adapting Environments, Materials, and Instruction to Facilitate Inclusion

Diane Lea Ryndak and Theresa Ward

Objectives

After completing this chapter, the reader will be able to:

1. Define adaptation, and describe how an adaptation can facilitate the participation of a student with moderate or severe disabilities in activities in general education settings.

2. Define the terms adaptation, accommodation, and modification, and explain their importance in relation to the standards movement.

3. Give a hierarchy of decision rules for determining appropriate adaptations for a student, and provide a rationale for its use.

4. Explain why an education team begins the consideration of adaptations with a student's needs rather than available adaptations.

5. Describe various ways an education team could divide responsibilities for determining, developing, providing instruction on the use of, monitoring the instruction of the use of, and evaluating the effectiveness of an adaptation.

6. Describe ways in which an education team can adapt general education environments to facilitate the participation of a student with moderate or severe disabilities.

7. Describe ways in which general education activities can be adapted through materials, devices, and/or equipment to facilitate the participation of a student with moderate or severe disabilities.

8. Describe ways in which instruction can be adapted during general education activities to facilitate the inclusion of a student with moderate or severe disabilities.

9. Describe ways in which an education team can identify appropriate adaptations for a student prior to general education activities beginning.

10. Describe ways in which an education team can identify appropriate adaptations for a student after a general education activity has begun.

Key Terms

Accommodation	Decision hierarchy	Modification
Adaptation	Ecological analysis	Peer partners
Adapting environments	Friendship facilitation	Routine activity analysis
Adapting instruction	General education activity	Standards
Adapting materials	analysis	Unit plan
Assistive technology	Generic instructional plan	Weekly plan
Cooperative learning		

Adaptations in General Education

During the 1990s, schools across the nation experienced a flurry of activity that focused on rethinking, restructuring, and reforming education. Simultaneously, the inclusion of students with disabilities in the standards-based assessments gained increasing attention. Ysseldyke, Thurlow, and Shriner (1992) state that students with disabilities were initially ignored with regard to the development and dissemination of standards and assessments. Gradually, federal laws helped focus the efforts of the larger educational community on the need to include students with disabilities in the standards and assessment movement (for example, Goals 2000: Educate America Act, Improving America's Schools Act, and the Individuals with Disabilities Act [IDEA] [PL105-17]). Although there has been debate concerning the benefits and pitfalls of the standards movement, the convergence of accountability for higher student achievement in both general and special education has had a significant impact on building-based education teams that serve students with disabilities (Hock, 2000).

By definition, students with moderate and severe disabilities have learning characteristics that hamper their ability to learn the same amount of information, in the same amount of time, and in the same manner as their peers without disabilities. In addition, students with moderate and severe disabilities do not participate in all activities in the same manner as their peers without disabilities. These aspects of individuals with moderate and severe disabilities should be kept in the forefront when discussing involvement in and progress within the general education curriculum because of the Amendments to the IDEA in 1997.

The amendments of particular interest to the discussion of curriculum adaptations and decisionmaking contain language that indicates the preference for all students with disabilities to be involved in and progress in the general education curriculum. Specifically, the law states the following:

- The Individualized Education Program (IEP) must indicate "how the child's disability affects involvement in the general education curriculum" {Section 614(d)(1)(a)}.
- Special education and related services include those supports necessary for the child to be involved and progress in the general education curriculum" {Section 614(d)(2)(b)}.
- Assessments should include "information related to enabling the child to be involved in and progress in the general education curriculum" {Section 614(b)(2)(1)}.
- The IEP team include a general education teacher if the child is or might be participating in the general education environment {Section 614(d)(1)(B)(iii)}.
- State education agencies establish performance indicators that aid in monitoring and implementing the IDEA. Further, these indicators must be "consistent with other goals and standards for children established by the State," and that children with disabilities must be "included in general State and district-wide assessment programs, with appropriate accommodation, when necessary" {Section 612(a)(16)}.
- Alternative assessments must be provided when participation in general assessments, even with accommodations, is not appropriate.

High expectations under one standard curriculum have become common policy and practice in our nation's schools. The educational team for a student, regardless of the severity of the disability, must decide the extent of participation in the general education environment and the types of supports that are necessary for involvement and progress (DeStafano, Shriner, & Lloyd, 2001). Clearly, the language in the IDEA and the accountability standards dictate the types of discussions occurring around the issues of adaptations. According to Webster's Third World Dictionary, to adapt is "to make fit or suitable by changing or adjusting" and an adaptation is "a thing resulting from adapting; a change in structure, function, or form that improves the chance of survival . . . within a given environment." During the past ten years many professionals have come to characterize adaptation as a broad term that describes various types of supports provided to students with disabilities in order to gain access to the general education curriculum (Beech, 1998; Fisher & Frey, 2001).

Common in the discussion of adaptations are the terms "accommodation" and "modification." Generally, most students with disabilities require accommodations in order to participate and be successful within the general education curriculum. An accommodation is a change made to teaching or testing procedures in order to provide a student with access to information and to create an equal opportunity to demonstrate core knowledge and skills. Accommodations do not change the content or performance criteria for meeting the standards. Some examples of accommodations are preferential seating, enlarged print, providing extra time for a test, and using a calculator.

Many students with moderate and severe disabilities may require accommodations and additional modifications in order to demonstrate mastery of a skill. A modification is a change in what the student is expected to learn and demonstrate. Often, a student may work within the same content, but the expectations are modified from those of peers without disabilities within the classroom. If the educational team determines that a student is in need of a modification, this implies that the student may have less content, alternative or embedded content that stems from the IEP, or a significant alteration to the materials used during the lesson. Generally, if a student is in need of modifications, the performance expectations under the standards are altered. The educational team must determine when a modification is needed, during what activity, and to what extent based on each individual child (Beech, 1998; Fisher & Frey, 2001; Udvari-Solner, 1996).

Within the framework of this chapter, the term "adaptations" shall be used as the broader term encompassing both accommodations and modifications. Although terminology is critical to the discussion of curriculum standards and individual performance outcomes, it is more critical that every member comprehend how, when, and to what extent adaptations should be used with each individual child with a moderate or severe disability.

When education teams focus on increasing the participation of a student with moderate or severe disabilities in both functional and general education activities that occur in inclusive settings, they systematically identify activities in which that student requires an adaptation, develop and initiate the use of the adaptation, and evaluate its effectiveness in meeting the student's need in that activity. This chapter discusses each of these tasks and provides examples of how education teams have addressed these tasks through determining adaptations in advance of activities and determining adaptations within the general education curriculum.

Deciding to Use an Adaptation in General Education Settings

As with augmentative communication systems (Reichle, 1997; Sigafoos & Iacono, 1993), deciding whether to use an adaptation, and which adaptation to use, can be complex. Education teams first must agree that a problem exists in a student's ability to participate in a given general education activity (Cohen & Lynch, 1991). Second, the team ascertains that instruction in specific skills cannot quickly meet the student's need, because the student's disability prohibits the completion of the task in the same manner as the other students. This could occur for both functional activities throughout the day and general education activities across settings. After determining the need for an adaptation, education teams clarify the precise nature of the student's problem by reaching consensus on the component of the task that the student cannot complete. The team analyzes the student's strengths and weaknesses in relation to that task component. With this information, team members identify an adaptation that would accentuate the student's strengths, while compensating for weaknesses, and allow the student to complete the task or participate in the activity with classmates.

When possible the team identifies an adaptation that not only meets the student's immediate need and allows participation at the moment, but that also can have a lasting role in the student's life. For instance, instead of identifying an adaptation for one math class or unit on multiple digit addition, a better use of the education team's time and the student's instructional time would be to identify an adaptation that the student *also* can use long term. This adaptation should be usable, or adaptable for use, across time (that is, as the student matures) and across activities and settings (that is, general education activities, activities in the community, and self-management activities at home). In addition, this adaptation should be (1) portable for use across environments, (2) appropriate for the student's age, (3) durable for frequent use or use over time, (4) least intrusive during activities and the natural flow of events, (5) within the student's financial limitations, and (6) accessible within the time and resource parameters of the education team. Although all of these variables may not be relevant for the specific activity for which a student initially requires an adaptation, their consideration will prevent the development of multiple adaptations when fewer or better planned adaptations would suffice. Not only do more adaptations mean more intrusion into the flow of activities as they are retrieved, set up, used, and removed, but they also mean the team members take more time in developing and maintaining each adaptation, and the student needs more instructional time to learn effective use of each adaptation.

After the team carefully conceives the adaptation, they then develop the adaptation and initiate instruction on its use during activities. Every education team handles the responsibilities involved in development and instruction differently, each focusing on the strengths of team members in terms of expertise, interest, time, and resources available. The key to a student's successful use of an adaptation does not lie in which team member fulfills which responsibility; rather, it lies with the collaborative efforts of team members in conceptualizing the most appropriate adaptation, providing consistent instruction to the student on the use of that adaptation, and consistently facilitating the student's continued use of that adaptation across all relevant activities. Collaborating to facilitate instruction on, and use of, the adaptation results in team members collectively evaluating the appropriateness and effectiveness of the adaptation in meeting the student's identified need. These evaluation efforts may result in modifying the adaptation to better meet that student's need across activities and time.

Types of Adaptations

There are many ways to adapt general education environments, materials, and instructional activities to meet the needs of a student with moderate or severe disabilities (Giangreco, 1997; Udvari-Solner, 1996). When selecting which type of adaptation to provide for a student, the education team prefers those that allow the student to participate in the activity without the need for another person's assistance and that minimize differences between the student and classmates. This type of adaptation (1) encourages independent completion of activities, thus making the student less dependent on others, and (2) maintains the general education curriculum content, thus maximizing the complexity of the content of instruction for the student.

Some adaptations modify the environment. Environmental adaptations (Cohen & Lynch, 1991; Udvari-Solner, 1997) could be as simple as changing the location of a student (for example, closer to the focus of an activity and minimal distractions) or changing the student's physical position (for example, side lying, standing, and seated with support from positioning equipment). To maintain the focus of instruction in inclusive general education settings, however, removing the student to another environment that is not being used by nondisabled classmates does not constitute an environmental adaptation.

The education team can make adaptations to materials, devices, or equipment that is currently used in the student's general education settings, or by adding materials, devices, or equipment to those settings (Cohen & Lynch, 1991; Nevin, 1993; Schulz, Carpenter, & Turnbull, 1991). Again, the team prefers adaptations that meet a specific need of a student and that allow the student to participate in the activity independently. They must be careful to refrain from identifying a new or innovative adaptation and identifying when or where it could be used. Rather, the impetus for selecting an adaptation is a difficulty that a specific student is experiencing in participating in an already existing activity, and the purpose is to best meet that student's need. Adaptations in materials, devices, or equipment range from simple modifications in existing curriculum worksheets (for example, simplifying language or decreasing number of response options), to adding low-tech devices to existing materials (for example, a grip to a pencil or a finger guide to a keyboard), and adding high-tech equipment to the learning environment (for example, electronic communication device or automated page turner). For example, there are a number of both low- and high-tech devices available to meet the needs of students with moderate or severe disabilities, allowing their participation in general education activities. Areas in which assistive technology can meet a student's needs include:

1. Positioning (Campbell, 1993; Gearheart, Weishahn, & Gearheart, 1996; Rainforth & York, 1997; Utley, 1994)
2. Mobility (Gearheart et al., 1992; Rainforth & York, 1997; Trefler, 1992)
3. Augmentative communication systems (Miller, 1993)
4. Use of computers for instruction (Ellis & Sabornie, 1988)
5. Access to devices, such as computers or communication devices (Campbell & Forsyth, 1993; Hill & Romich, 1999)
6. Control of the immediate environment (Campbell & Forsyth, 1993; Rainforth & York, 1991)
7. Hearing or listening (Gearheart et al., 1996; Schulz et al., 1991; Sobsey & Wolf-Schein, 1991)
8. Seeing or looking (Gearheart et al. 1996; Schulz et al., 1991; Sobsey & Wolf-Schein, 1991)
9. Recreation, leisure, or play (Schleien, Green, & Heyne, 1993; York & Rainforth, 1997)
10. Self-care and self-management activities (Browder & Snell, 1993; Orelove & Sobsey, 1991; Snell & Farlow, 1993; York & Rainforth, 1997)

The education team also can make adaptations in the manner in which instruction is presented or in the manner in which students are expected to respond to instruction (Borich, 1992; Nevin, 1993; Schulz et al., 1991; Udvari-Solner, 1996). For instance, the size and composition of instructional groups can be modified (Cohen & Lynch, 1991; Post, 1984). In presenting instruction or directions, there may be visual materials, color-coded materials, outlines, mnemonic devices, or shortened directions (Borich, 1992; Post, 1984). Each of these adaptations draws little attention to a student with moderate or severe disabilities. Their use may be appropriate whether the curriculum content for that student is the same as, or different from, nondisabled classmates. Although a peer or an adult can provide personal assistance (Udvari-Solner, 1996; Villa & Thousand, 1993), such support is more intrusive than the previously mentioned adaptations. When used, the level of intrusiveness should be kept to a minimum by removing the support whenever it is not necessary during an activity (Villa, Udis, & Thousand, 1994).

When a student with moderate or severe disabilities is able to complete some, but not all, of the work presented to classmates, other instructional adaptations are possible. Work structure can be such that all students work at their own pace, receive cues that assist them in answering questions, or have different rules for completing their tasks (Borich, 1992; Post, 1984). For instance, the number of problems to be solved may be fewer, the time for task completion may be longer, the student may ask questions, or the concepts of the task may be minimal for a student. Such adaptations may allow a student to perform a task more independently while working on the same curriculum content as nondisabled classmates, and receiving instructional emphasis on the curriculum components that are most relevant.

Finally, the education team can make adaptations to the actual curriculum content presented to a student. Changes in curriculum content can take many forms, including modification in (1) the skill sequence or task presented to peers without disabilities (Cohen & Lynch, 1991; Giangreco, Cloninger, & Iverson, 1993), (2) the size of steps in the same task (Giangreco et al., 1993; Post, 1984), (3) the level of skill being taught in the same task or required to complete the task (Fisher & Frey, 2001; Giangreco et al., 1993; Post, 1984), and (4) the curriculum content area itself (Cohen & Lynch, 1991; Giangreco et al., 1993). The more that curriculum content presented to a student with moderate or severe disabilities remains the same as that presented to classmates means the more the targeted student will participate in general education activities and gain acceptance as a peer (Schnorr, 1990, 1997).

Team Member Support Related to Adaptations

When identifying, developing, and providing instruction on the use of an adaptation, team members rely on each other for various types of support (Giangreco et al., 1993; Janney & Snell, 2000; Rainforth, York, & Macdonald, 1993; Snell & Janney, 2000). Written information from team members may assist in identifying or developing an adaptation, and team members have access to different materials that may be helpful in developing an adaptation (Rainforth et al., 1993). Team members may divide the responsibility for actually developing an adaptation (Hamre-Nietupski, McDonald, & Nietupski, 1992), depending upon the expertise and time required. For example, instead of requiring additional time to implement, many instructional adaptations require a modification in the manner in which the primary instruction is presented to the entire class. The general education teacher most easily implements this type of adaptation. Other adaptations, however, require development by the special education teacher or a related service provider.

Team members also can provide each other support in identifying, developing, and providing instruction on the use of an adaptation through human resources. This type of support occurs whenever an adult must help prepare the environment in which instruction will occur, assist a student or group of students during instruction, or clean up after instruction has occurred, thus allowing another team member time to develop an adaptation. Although often overlooked, human resource support can ease a tremendous amount of pressure for any team member at critical times. Careful scheduling of this type of support will ensure the team maximal benefit from human resources and maximal time to develop and provide instruction on the use of adaptations.

Perhaps most important, however, is the support team members provide each other, not only so adaptations are developed, but also so they are both effective and efficient at allowing a student to participate in general education activities. To accomplish this, team members provide support as they collaboratively strategize about different types of adaptations and how each potentially could meet the student's need (York & Vandercook, 1991). The expertise and perspective of every team member is invaluable in this process because each sees the student and the situation differently. Throughout the strategizing and development process, technical support from each team member is essential, whether the identified adaptation is related to the environment, materials, or instruction. Finally, team members provide support in evaluating the effectiveness of an adaptation in meeting the student's need, both in the initial situation for which it was required and in other situations where the adaptation may be helpful. In addition to evaluating the effectiveness of the adaptation itself, the evaluation process allows team members to monitor how consistently and correctly the team is providing instruction on its use and how appropriately the student is using the adaptation across settings.

Making Decisions About Adaptations

The use of a decisionmaking process in relation to identifying the most appropriate adaptation has had the support of many authors for a number of years (Baumgart et al., 1982; Cohen & Lynch, 1991; Filbin & Kronberg, undated; Giangreco et al., 1993; Hamre-Nietupski et al., 1992; Janney & Snell, 2000; Kronberg & Filbin, 1993; Sailor, Gee, & Karasoff, 1993; Thousand et al., 1986). Inclusion of students with moderate or severe disabilities in general education settings has made additional considerations relevant in these processes. There are various suggested hierarchies of considerations, however. Though specific levels of each hierarchy differ, they are consistent in four ways. First, they all demonstrate a preference for a student with moderate or severe disabilities participating in the same activity as nondisabled classmates, rather than removal from the general education activity. Second, the hierarchies demonstrate a preference for adapting the environment and instruction before adapting curriculum content. Third, the hierarchies emphasize first devising adaptations that allow a student to participate in activities independently, rather than immediately creating a situation in which the student cannot participate without the support of another person. Finally, the hierarchies demonstrate a preference for maintaining the student with nondisabled classmates before considering removal from the general education setting. Figure 20.1 summarizes suggested levels of hierarchies of considerations when identifying the most appropriate adaptation for a student with moderate or severe disabilities in inclusive settings. With each level, if the education team responds affirmatively, they either refrain from identifying an adaptation, as in the first level of the hierarchy, or they identify the problem that exists for the student and strategize on the adaptations that could meet the student's need. If the team responds to a level negatively, they progress to the next level in the hierarchy. All team members must be cautious not to respond negatively to a certain level when a new or previously unconsidered adaptation at that level would facilitate the student's participation.

FIGURE 20.1 *Decisionmaking Hierarchy for Identifying Adaptations in Inclusive Educational Programs*

Level	References

1. Can the student participate in the class activity just like other classmates?
    If yes, do not adapt.
    If no, go on to level 2.
	Baumgart et al., 1982; Filbin & Kronberg, undated; Giangreco et al., 1993; Kronberg & Filbin, 1993; Sailor et al., 1993

2. Can the student participate in the same class activity if the environment is adapted?
    If yes, identify the student's need and strategize on adaptations for the environment.
    If no, go on to level 3.
	Baumgart et al., 1982; Cohen & Lynch, 1991; Filbin & Kronberg, undated; Giangreco et al., 1993; Kronberg & Filbin, 1993; Sailor et al., 1993; Udvari-Solner, 1994

3. Can the student participate in the same class activity if instruction is adapted?
    If yes, identify the student's need and strategize on instructional adaptations.
    If no, go on to level 4.
	Cohen & Lynch, 1991; Filbin & Kronberg, undated; Giangreco et al., 1993; Kronberg & Filbin, 1993; Sailor et al., 1993; Udvari-Solner, 1994

4. Can the student participate in the same class activity but with adapted materials?
    If yes, identify the student's need and strategize on adapted materials.
    If no, go on to level 5.
	Baumgart et al., 1982; Cohen & Lynch, 1991; Filbin & Kronberg, undated; Giangreco et al., 1993; Kronberg & Filbin, 1993; Sailor et al., 1993; Udvari-Solner, 1994

5. Can the student participate in the same class activity but with adapted expectations or rules?
    If yes, identify the student's need and strategize on adapted expectations or rules.
    If no, go on to level 6.
	Baumgart et al., 1982; Filbin & Kronberg, undated; Giangreco et al., 1993; Kronberg & Filbin, 1993; Sailor et al., 1993; Udvari-Solner, 1994

6. Can the student participate in the same class activity but with personal assistance?
    If yes, identify the student's need and strategize on personal assistance; train peer or adult.
    If no, go on to level 7.
	Baumgart et al., 1982; Filbin & Kronberg, undated; Giangreco et al., 1993; Kronberg & Filbin, 1993; Hamre-Nietupski et al., 1992; Sailor et al., 1993; Udvari-Solner, 1994

7. Can the student participate in the same class activity but with goals on a different level of the same content?
    If yes, identify the student's need and strategize on adaptations to incorporate different level.
    If no, go on to level 8.
	Filbin & Kronberg, undated; Giangreco et al., 1993; Kronberg & Filbin, 1993

8. Can the student participate in the same class activity but with goals from a different curriculum content area?
    If yes, identify the student's need and strategize on adaptations to incorporate goals from a different curriculum content area?
    If no, go on to level 9.
	Filbin & Kronberg, undated; Fisher & Frey, 2001; Giangreco et al., 1993; Kronberg & Filbin, 1993; Sailor et al., 1993

FIGURE 20.1 *Continued*

9. Can the student work in the room on a logical different activity related to IEP goals?
 	
    If yes, identify the student's need and strategize on incorporating a different activity least intrusively.
    If no, go on to level 10.
	Demchak, 1997; Fisher & Frey, 2001; Giangreco et al., 1993; Hamre-Nietupski et al., 1992; Sailor et al., 1993

10. Can the student work in the building on a logical different activity related to IEP goals?
 	
    If yes, identify the student's need and strategize on incorporating change of location least intrusively.
    If no, go on to level 11.
	Giangreco et al., 1993; Hamre-Nietupski et al., 1992; Sailor et al., 1993

11. Can the student work on a logical community-based activity related to IEP goals? Identify the student's need and strategize on incorporating change of location least intrusively.	Giangreco et al., 1993; Hamre-Nietupski et al., 1992; Sailor et al., 1993

IEP = Individualized Education Program.

Determining Adaptations in Advance

There are a number of ways in which an education team can determine in advance the adaptations a student with moderate or severe disabilities will need to participate fully in specific general education activities. Although adaptations determined in advance may need modification as more information is available about the student's needs during specific activities, they are preferable because they allow the student to participate as soon as general education activities begin.

Determining Adaptations Based on IEP Content

An IEP offers a wealth of information about a student's strengths, weaknesses, current level of performance, and projected level of performance at the end of the year in the content identified as most important for that student. Frequently, adaptations that are essential to the student's independent participation in general education activities also appear on the IEP. For instance, an IEP may indicate the student's need to use an assistive device (for example, calculator for math activities or computer for writing activities) or have instructional adaptations (for example, extended time for completing assignments and tests and decreased amount of work). Each of these comments can assist an education team in having appropriate adaptations available for a student prior to related activities.

In addition, an education team systematically could review the instructional content on a student's IEP and compare this content with current performance levels. Teams can perform this task for both functional and general education curriculum content included on the IEP and for functional needs not included as goals on the IEP. For example, the matrix in Figure 20.2 lists areas of functional curriculum content frequently found on traditional

FIGURE 20.2 *Determining Adaptations for Functional Curriculum Content in Advance*

Adaptations	Decision Hierarchy Level	Functional Curriculum Content						
		Communication		Choice Making	Postural Control & Manipulation of Objects	Mobility	Eating	Hygiene/ Appearance
		Receptive	Expressive					
Accomodations	1. Participate as classmates							
	2. Adapt environment							
	3. Adapt instruction							
	4. Adapt materials							
Modifications	5. Adapt rules/ expectations							
	6. Personal assistance							
	7. Different content level							
	8. Different content							
	9. Different activity in room							
	10. Different activity in building							
	11. Different activity in community							

IEPs for students with moderate or severe disabilities. On the left hand side of this matrix are the levels in the adaptation-decision hierarchy previously described. An education team can discuss the student's level of performance in each of the functional curriculum content areas and determine the levels and types of adaptations the student may require before general education activities begin. Though the adaptations identified in advance may require refinement or modification once more, the initial adaptations at least will allow the student to participate more fully in the functional aspects of general education activities from the beginning.

	Social Interactions	Socially Appropriate Behavior	Problem Solving	Performance Quality	Performance Tempo	Activity Completion			
						Initia-tion	Prepa-ration	Core	Termi-nation

Similarly, an education team can determine adaptations in advance for the general education curriculum content included on a student's IEP. The matrix in Figure 20.3 provides space for team members to list up to ten components of the IEP's general education content and systematically consider the levels and types of adaptations the student may require in general education activities by using the decision hierarchy per area. Again, the team may modify or refine these adaptations as it learns more about the student's needs during activities in general education settings. The initial adaptations, however, will allow the student to participate more fully in the general education activities upon entering those settings.

FIGURE 20.3 *Determining Adaptations for General Education Curriculum Content in Advance*

Decision Hierarchy Level	General Education Curriculum Content									
	#1.	#2.	#3.	#4.	#5.	#6.	#7.	#8.	#9.	#10.
1. Participation as classmates										
2. Adapt environment										
3. Adapt instruction										
4. Adapt materials										
5. Adapt rules/ expectations										
6. Personal assistance										
7. Different content level										
8. Different content										
9. Different activity in room										
10. Different activity in building										
11. Different activity in community										

Determining Adaptations from Unit Plans

Education teams also can determine adaptations throughout the academic year in advance of activities when there is a change in instructional units in general education classes. Figure 20.4 is an example of an eighth-grade team's identification of adaptations for

FIGURE 20.4 *Determining Adaptations per General Education Unit: An Example*

Grade: ___8th___   Subject: ___Math___   Unit: ___Pythagorean Theorem___

Student: ___Maureen___   Date: ___Oct.___   Teacher: ___Brown___

General Education Curriculum Content	General Education Content Identified for the Student	Adaptations
1. Evaluate exponents $2^3+5^2-1^9$	1. Decimals $(+, -, x, \div)$; exponents to 5^2	Calculator
2. Name square, square root of given number	2. Use chart to find square	Chart of squares
3. Name legs, hypotenuse of right triangle using proper geometric notation	3. Name legs and hypotenuse by labeling leg and hypotenuse on diagram	Diagram of example
4. Given legs of triangle, find hypotenuse using $a^2+b^2+c^2$	4. Use $a^2+b^2+c^2$ and substitute all 3 numerals into a formula—are they equal?	Calculator and chart
5. Given leg and hypotenuse, find either leg using $a^2+b^2+c^2$	5. As above	Calculator and chart
6. Word problem applications	6. Directional problems only	Calculator and chart

	Embedded Functional Content	Adaptation
Preparation for Class	Have materials ready	
	Homework ready to hand in	
During Class	Ask for assistance when needed	
	With prep time, answer questions when called on	Asked question during class in advance of requesting a response
Terminating Class	Write down homework assignment	Work organizer/notebook
	Organize materials to carry out of room	Backpack
	Exit room with the flow of classmates	Prompting from peer

Maureen, a student with moderate mental retardation (see Appendix B). The adaptations are for a math unit on the Pythagorean theorem. The first part of this example identifies the general education curriculum content for the entire class, the components of that general education content most relevant for Maureen, and the adaptations most appropriate for her. The second part of this example identifies functional curriculum content, only some of which is from her IEP, for which there is instruction embedded throughout math class. Maureen's education team determined the adaptations that would best facilitate her participation throughout the class.

Determining Adaptations from Weekly Lessons Plans

When a general education teacher develops detailed weekly lesson plans, education teams can use these plans to determine the adaptations that will facilitate participation in activities of a student with moderate or severe disabilities. By using the general education teacher's traditional lesson plans, team members can discuss every activity scheduled for the week and identify the levels and types of adaptations the student will require throughout the week. For example, in a 15-minute meeting per week, one education team clarifies information on a kindergarten teacher's weekly lesson plans, indicating the adaptations required for a student with severe disabilities to participate per activity (see Figure 20.5). Using a code, notations alongside each activity on the lesson plans delineate the level and type of adaptation the student requires throughout the week. In addition, the team adds notations on (1) the general education curriculum content emphasized in the student's instruction during each activity, (2) the functional curriculum content for which instruction will be embedded into each activity, and (3) the best position to facilitate the student's participation. Copies of this teacher's notated lesson plans are available to each team member before these activities occur the following week.

Determining Adaptations when Limited or No Weekly Plans Exist

When general education teachers write lesson plans that include little or no detail about instructional contexts, team members have difficulty determining in advance adaptations specifically designed to allow a student with moderate or severe disabilities to participate in each activity. One approach to this situation is to identify the instructional contexts the general education teacher frequently uses and determine ways in which the student can participate in each of those contexts. Tony's education team (see Appendix A, Student Profiles) used this approach to develop generic instructional plans (see Figure 20.6) for use in his fourth-grade class. For these generic plans the teacher developed only global units per subject area, with no specific activities delineated per day or even per week. This flexibility allowed the fourth-grade teacher to synthesize content across subject areas, but the lack of specific activities created difficulty in planning adaptations that allowed Tony, a student with severe disabilities, to participate with his classmates. To deal with this situation, the team used a generic instructional plan that identified the subject area and corresponding instructional contexts the teacher frequently used for the entire class. For example, during language arts, the class frequently engaged in independent work using

FIGURE 20.5   *Determining Adaptations with Weekly General Education Lesson Plans*

Teacher: _____ *Mary P.* _____   Week of: _____ *5-28* _____   Grade: _____ *K* _____

Monday	Tuesday	Wednesday	Thursday	Friday
8:50–9:03 Quiet play; journal writing	8:50–9:03 Quiet play; journal writing	8:50–9:03 Quiet play; journal writing	8:50–9:03 Quiet play; journal writing	8:50–9:03 Quiet play; journal writing
9:03–9:10 Clean-up; attendance[4]	9:03–9:10 Clean-up; attendance[4]	9:03–9:10 Clean-up; attendance[4]	9:03–9:10 Clean-up; attendance[4]	9:03–9:10 Clean up; attendance[4]
9:10–9:45 Art seed pictures[OT]	9:10–9:30 Opening read "H"; sound box book[A,P]	9:10–9:30 Opening read "Hippo Sandwich"[A,P]	9:10–9:30 Opening Discuss hippos with zoo book[A,P]	9:10–9:30 Catch up day: finish any weekly activities
				9:30–9:50 If time, terrarium lecture
	9:30–9:50 Letter H; intro. sound; practice Hh; brainstorm H words; review A,C,G,O[F]	9:30–9:50 Letter H; practice Hh; write a few Hh; write A,C,G,O[F]	9:30–9:50 Blending writing on board; write on lined paper	
10:25–11:00 Science: pop bottle terrarium (demo & lecture); read "A Seed is a Promise"				9:50–10:20 Library
	9:55–10:35 Gym[PT]	9:55–10:35 Music	9:55–10:35 Gym[PT]	10:25–11:00 Shared reading: "Hairy Bear"
11:06–11:36 Lunch[3,P]	10:40–11:00 Hh ditto	10:40–11:00 finish AM work on Hh	10:40–11:00 finish AM work on writing	
11:40–12:00 Story or movie				11:06–11:36 Lunch[3,P]
	11:06–11:36 Lunch[3,P]	11:06–11:36 Lunch[3,P]	11:06–11:36 Lunch[3,P]	11:40–12:30 Movie; Rhythm Band; Craft
	11:40–12:00 Story or movie	11:40–12:00 Story or movie	11:40–12:00 Story or movie	12:00–12:30 Movie; Rhythm Band; Craft
12:00–12:30 Craft: May baskets[OT]				
	12:00–12:30 Science readiness: Color Hh ditto	12:00–12:30 Shared reading: "A House is a House for Me"	12:00–12:30 Craft: blow indian ink into shape of tree[OT]	

Underlined = constant entry from week to week.
Not underlined = entry added per week.
Number = objective on IEP.
   2. independently propel wheelchair
   3. use napkin appropriately
   4. locate locker and insert/remove backpack
   5. remove and care for eyeglasses
   6. coat on
   7. say "bye" to classmates without prompting
Supporting team member during instruction:
   A = aide
   P = peer(s)
   F = facilitating/special education teacher
   OT = occupational therapist
   PT = physical therapist

FIGURE 20.6 *Generic Instructional Plan Based on Instructional Contexts*

Student: ___*Tony*___   Start Date: ___*4–1*___   Review Date: ___*5–1*___   Subject: ___*Language Arts*___

General Education Activity	Generic Instructional Activity
1. Spelling: individual workbooks	a. Use letters from worksheets, and identify letters on flashcard b. Range of motion, then pass out papers to classmates, using wrist adaptation c. Throw out paper towels, put away other materials from groups
2. Spelling: on overhead	See 1a through 1c above
3. Journal writing	a. Ask Tony yes or no questions about activities at home or school, enter responses in his journal b. Have Tony match letters in his journal to his letter flashcards
4. Reading aloud	a. Range of motion and position, then use taped stories to read preselected segments for the class b. Ask yes or no questions related to the material read aloud in class
5.	

spelling workbooks, group work with the teacher orchestrating from the front of the room with the aid of an overhead projector, journal writing, and oral reading. For each possible instructional context, the team determined adaptations that would enable Tony to participate with his classmates and work on his IEP objectives.

A second approach to determining adaptations in advance when a general education teacher does not develop detailed lesson plans is a generic instructional plan developed around the student's IEP goals (see Figure 20.7). The team can implement such generic plans regardless of the instructional context the general education teacher uses. All team members share this information, and the student also carries copies that are available upon request. Instruction based on these generic instructional plans is embedded into both instructional and noninstructional class activities.

Determining Adaptations in Current General Education Activities and Settings

After a student with moderate or severe disabilities enters general education activities, team members may find it necessary either to modify an adaptation that they already have

FIGURE 20.7 *Generic Instructional Plan Based on IEP Content*

Student: _Tony_   Start Date: _4–1_   Subject: _Routine Activities_   Review Date: _5–1_

IEP Goal	Generic Instructional Activity Across General Education Activities
1. Responding correctly to yes or no questions	a. Attend to instructor, and answer yes or no questions when asked in large group; reinforce verbal approximation, while accepting physical responses (yes = smile plus look to left, no = look to right) b. Respond to peers' yes or no questions related to activities
2. Indicating the desire for "more"	a. When Tony finishes a preferred activity and time remains, ask if he wants to do "more," reinforce raising his arm for "more" b. Provide only some of the required materials for Tony; when he finishes with them, ask if he needs "more"
3. Letter and object identification	a. Ask Tony to identify letters (those used during class activities) by getting light from head light on the correct card b. Have Tony use head light to identify objects used during activities, and objects in pictures (textbooks/worksheets)
4.	

developed or to develop an adaptation for a need that they did not identify in advance. The following sections describe strategies for analyzing how a student currently is participating in general education activities and determining relevant adaptations to meet the student's needs during those activities.

Analysis of Current General Education Activities

One strategy for determining a relevant adaptation that allows a student to participate more fully in a current general education activity is to analyze that activity (Demchak, 1997; Downing & Eichinger, 1990; Halvorsen & Neary, 2001; York, Doyle, & Kronberg, 1992). As demonstrated in Figure 20.8, the education team completes an analysis of the instructional strategy implemented during the activity (for example, cooperative learning strategy or lecture format with overhead projector), the configuration of student participation in the activity (for example, small group or independent work), and the general education materials being used during the activity. With this information, an education team can determine more accurately the aspect of the activity with which the student is having difficulty and

FIGURE 20.8 *Analysis of Current General Education Activities to Determine Adaptations*

Decision Hierarchy Level	General Education Activity #1 Instructional Strategy: Student Configuration: General Education Materials:	General Education Activity #2 Instructional Strategy: Student Configuration: General Education Materials:	General Education Activity #3 Instructional Strategy: Student Configuration: General Education Materials:
1. Participation as classmates			
2. Adapt environment			
3. Adapt instruction			
4. Adapt materials			
5. Adapt rules/ expectations			
6. Personal assistance			
7. Different content level			
8. Different content			
9. Different activity in room			
10. Different activity in building			
11. Different activity in community			

develop an adaptation that focuses on the appropriate component of the activity using a decision hierarchy.

Analysis of Participation in Specific General Education Settings

A second strategy useful when determining relevant adaptations for a student with moderate or severe disabilities is an analysis of the student's participation in specific general education settings. For example, some student responsibilities are specific to a particular general education setting (for example, obtaining and paying for lunch). If a student is having difficulty completing such an activity independently, an education team can complete an ecological analysis of that setting (Browder & Snell, 1993; Halvorsen & Neary, 2001; Sailor et al., 1993; York & Vandercook, 1991) by observing students in the subenvironment in which the task is completed and listing the steps used by nondisabled classmates to complete the activity. As illustrated in Figure 20.9, the team then can delineate the steps on which the performance of the student with moderate or severe disabilities differs from classmates. To allow independent performance of the activity, the team identifies the least intrusive adaptations the student needs by progressing through the levels of the adaptation hierarchy.

Analysis of Participation in Routines in General Education Settings

A third strategy useful when determining relevant adaptations for a student with moderate or severe disabilities is an analysis of the student's participation in the routines that occur regularly across general education settings (Halvorsen & Neary, 2001; Macdonald & York, 1989; York et al., 1992). Completion of some responsibilities, such as being prepared for class activities and following classroom rules is subject to analysis across general education settings (see Figure 20.10). The education team may be required to conduct an ecological analysis if a student is able to participate independently in some general education settings, but is having difficulty in others.

Instructional Strategies that Facilitate Inclusion

There are several instructional strategies already in use in general education settings that facilitate the inclusion of students with moderate or severe disabilities. Although including a student in the class of a general education teacher who already uses such strategies is possible, other general education teachers can be encouraged to use such strategies to increase the effectiveness of their instruction for *all* students.

Cooperative Learning Strategies

Cooperative learning strategies promote the interdependence of students in their acquisition and use of knowledge. Although cooperative learning strategies require small

FIGURE 20.9   *Ecological Analysis of General Education Settings to Determine Adaptations*

Setting: Subenvironment:		Decision Hierarchy Level			
Responsibility or Skill	**Discrepancy with Peers**	**1. Participate as classmates**	**2. Adapted environment**	**3. Adapted instruction**	**4. Adapted materials**

groups of two to six students, the mere placement of students in groups for instruction or activities does not constitute a cooperative learning situation, for such groups also can engage in competitive and independent learning activities (Davidson, 1994; Johnson & Johnson, 1994; Putnam, 1993; Villa & Thousand, 1993). Johnson and Johnson (1994) stated that there are five components required for a group activity to be a cooperative learning experience: (1) clearly perceived positive interdependence, (2) considerable face-to-face interaction, (3) clearly perceived individual accountability and personal responsibility to achieve the group's goals, (4) frequent use of interpersonal and small-group skills, and (5) frequent and regular group processing of current group functioning to improve the group's future effectiveness.

Davidson (1994) describes several cooperative learning strategies that have been used in general education settings, including the following:

1. Student Team Learning Strategies, such as Student Teams Achievement Divisions, Teams-Games-Tournaments, Jigsaw II, Team Assisted Individualization, and Cooperative Integrated Reading and Composition (Slavin, 1983, 1990)

Decision Hierarchy Level						
5. Adapted rules/ expectations	6. Personal assistance	7. Different content level	8. Different content	9. Different activity in room	10. Different activity in building	11. Different activity in community

2. Learning Together (Johnson & Johnson, 1987, 1989)
3. Group Investigation (Sharan & Hertz-Lazarowitz, 1980, 1982; Sharan & Sharan, 1992)
4. Structural Approach Strategies, such as Think-Pair-Share, Roundtable, Numbered Heads Together, Three-Step Interview, Jigsaw, Pairs Check (Kagan, 1992)
5. Complex Instruction (Cohen, 1986)
6. Collaborative Approach (Barnes, Britton, & Torbe, 1990; Barnes & Todd, 1977; Britton, 1970; Brubacher, Payne, & Rickett, 1990; Reid, Forrestal & Cook, 1989)
7. Simple Cooperation Model (McCabe & Rhoades, 1990; Rhoades & McCabe, 1992)

These cooperative learning strategies are effective to varying degrees across different variables; however, Putnam (1993) summarized the positive effects of cooperative learning strategies in the following manner:

1. Academic achievement was most likely to occur with an incorporation of the components of positive interdependence and individual responsibility.

FIGURE 20.10 *Analysis of Participation in Routines in General Education Settings to Determine Adaptations*

Settings For Routines: a) b) c)	Decision Hierarchy Level			
	1. Participate as classmates	2. Adapted environment	3. Adapted instruction	4. Adapted materials
1. Arrives at class on time				
2. Brings required materials to class				
3. Is in seat, with materials ready, as class begins				
4. Completes transitions between activities in response to situational cues				
5. Begins tasks with situational cues				
6. Stays on task throughout activity				
7. Terminates tasks with situational cues				
8. Puts away instructional materials after use				
9. Uses instructional materials for intended purposes				
10. Uses classroom materials and equipment safely				
11. Shares materials when appropriate				
12. Works cooperatively with one partner				
13. Works cooperatively with small group				
14. Tolerates changes in classroom routines				
15. Follows classroom rules and class directions				
16. Readily accepts correcton and uses assistance to modify performance				

2. Students' self-esteem increased with students learning to value and perceive themselves positively.
3. Students became more actively involved in the learning process.
4. Students accepted peers to a greater extent, despite their weaknesses.
5. Students, especially those with moderate or severe disabilities, developed more social skills.

	Decision Hierarchy Level					
5. Adapted rules/ expectations	6. Personal assistance	7. Different content level	8. Different content	9. Different activity in room	10. Different activity in building	11. Different activity in community

General education activities that incorporate cooperative learning strategies are ideal for effective instruction of students with moderate or severe disabilities (Halvorsen & Neary, 2001; Putnam, 1993; Thousand, Villa, & Nevin, 1994).

Small-Group Instruction

Not all small-group activities incorporate cooperative learning strategies, but other small-group instruction also can be effective for students with moderate or severe disabilities in general education settings (Post, 1984). Udvari-Solner (1994) described a small-group arrangement as one in which "students are allowed to work together to complete a project . . . or to socialize and share ideas while completing individual work" (p. 61). Support provided by peers who are working independently on their own activities is the least intrusive form of personal assistance possible in inclusive settings. Although peers are available for support, their focus is on their own work, rather than on the work of their classmate. Because of this, small groups provide natural situations for students with moderate or severe disabilities to work independently when possible, and yet unobtrusively request assistance from a peer when needed.

Peer Partnering

Partnering classmates with and without disabilities is an effective instructional strategy that education teams frequently use in inclusive general education settings under numerous titles. Jenkins and Jenkins (1988) stated that peer tutors can be effective in increasing the skill acquisition of classmates when partnering includes several critical components, including the following:

1. Highly structured lesson formats
2. Instructional content focused on extra practice, repetition, or clarification of concepts covered in class
3. Daily instruction until the concept is mastered
4. Continuous or daily programs of moderate duration
5. Training for tutors on appropriate interpersonal behaviors
6. Class climate of mutual respect and concern, coupled with high expectations for everyone
7. Active supervision of tutors
8. Supportive teachers and administrators who advocate with program participants
9. A program manager for schoolwide programs
10. Measurement of student progress
11. Careful selection and pairing of partners

Study buddies play a different role for students with moderate or severe disabilities. They provide support by performing tasks that the targeted student cannot do. For instance, if a student is not able to write down information provided in class, a study buddy might provide copies of written materials (for example, class notes or homework assignments) (Jakupcak, 1993). If a student is not physically able to complete preparation and clean up tasks for class activities or requires so much time that it interferes with the activity itself, a study buddy might complete part or all of those tasks. On the other hand, instructional buddies can assist in setting up learning situations (for example, for social interactions) and reinforcing a student's appropriate participation (Hamre-Nietupski et al., 1992).

Through these various roles, nondisabled classmates contribute significantly to the educational experiences of students with moderate or severe disabilities. Ideally, they will become members of students' natural support networks and be involved long-term in both their educational programs and lives outside of school.

Summary

Students with moderate or severe disabilities frequently are unable to participate in functional and general education activities in the same manner as their nondisabled classmates and require adaptations to facilitate maximally independent participation. Adaptations may be made to general education environments, materials, and instruction, depending upon the component of an activity during which the student demonstrates a need for assistance that cannot be addressed adequately and quickly enough through direct instruction. Rather, the student's overriding disability requires an adaptation.

The education team selects an adaptation with consideration to its (1) usefulness over time and across activities; (2) appropriateness in relation to the student's age, financial resources, and importance of participation in the activity; and (3) degree of intrusiveness in general education settings and the community. In addition, preferred adaptations allow the student to perform the same activity as nondisabled classmates without relying on another person and without changing the curriculum content. A hierarchy of decisions assists team members in determining the least intrusive adaptation to meet a student's need.

References

Barnes, D., Britton, J., & Torbe, M. (1990). *Language, the learner and the school* (4th ed.). Portsmouth, NH: Boynton/Cook.

Barnes, D., & Todd, F. (1977). *Communicating and learning in small groups*. London: Routledge, Kegan Paul.

Baumgart, D., Brown, L., Pumpian, I., Nisbet, J., Ford, A., Sweet, M., Messina, R., & Schroeder, J. (1982). The principle of partial participation and individualized adaptations in educational programs for students with severe handicaps. *Journal of The Association for Persons with Severe Handicaps, 7*(2), 17–27.

Beech, M. (1998). *Accommodations*. Tallahassee, FL: Florida Department of Education.

Borich, G. D. (1992). *Effective teaching methods* (2nd ed.). New York: Charles E. Merrill.

Britton, J. (1970). *Language and learning*. Portsmouth, NH: Boynton/Cook.

Browder, D., & Snell, M. E. (1993). Daily living and community skills. In M. E. Snell (Ed.), *Instruction of students with severe disabilities* (4th ed.) (pp. 480–525). New York: Charles E. Merrill.

Brubacher, M., Payne, R., & Rickett, K. (1990). *Perspectives on small group learning: Theory and practice*. Oakvale, Ontario: Rubicon Publishing.

Campbell, P. H. (1993). Physical management and handling procedures. In M. E. Snell (Ed.), *Instruction of students with severe disabilities* (4th ed.) (pp. 248–263). New York: Charles E. Merrill.

Campbell, P. H., & Forsyth, S. (1993). Integrated programming and movement disabilities. In M. E. Snell (Ed.), *Instruction of students with severe disabilities* (4th ed.) (pp. 264–289). New York: Charles E. Merrill.

Cohen, E. (1994). *Designing groupwork: Strategies for the heterogeneous classroom* (2nd ed.). New York: Teachers College Press.

Cohen, S. B., & Lynch, D. K. (1991). An instructional modification process. *Teaching Exceptional Children,* summer, 12–18.

Davidson, N. (1994). Cooperative and collaborative learning: An integrative perspective. In J. S. Thousand, R. A. Villa, & A. I. Nevin (Eds.), *Creativity and collaborative learning: A practical guide to empowering students and teachers* (pp. 13–30). Baltimore, MD: Paul H. Brookes Publishing Co.

Demchak, M. (1997). *INNOVATIONS: Teaching students with severe disabilities in inclusive settings*. Washington, DC: American Association on Mental Retardation; Research to Practice Series number 12.

DeStefano, L., Shriner, J. G., & Lloyd, C. A. (2001). Teacher decision-making in participation of students with disabilities in large scale assessments. *Exceptional Children, 68*(1), 7–22.

Downing, J., & Eichinger, J. (1990). Instructional strategies for learners with dual sensory impairments in integrated settings. *Journal of The Association for Persons with Severe Handicaps, 15*, 98–105.

Ellis, E. S., & Sabornie, E. J. (1988). Effective instruction with microcomputers: Promises, practices, and preliminary findings. In E. L. Meyen, G. A. Vergason, & R. J. Whelan (Eds.), *Effective instructional strategies for exceptional children*. Denver: Love.

Filbin, J., & Kronberg, R. (undated). *Ideas and suggestions for curricular adaptations at the secondary level*. Denver: Colorado Department of Education.

Fisher, D., & Frey, N. (2001) Access to the core curriculum: Critical ingredients for student success. *Remedial and Special Education 22*(3), 148–157.

Gearheart, B. R., Weishahn, M. W., & Gearheart, C. J. (1996). *The exceptional student in the regular classroom* (6th ed.). New York: Charles E. Merrill.

Giangreco, M. F. (1997). Persistent questions about curriculum for students with severe disabilities. *Physical Disabilities: Education and Related Services, 15*(2), 53–56.

Giangreco, M. F., Cloninger, C. J., & Iverson, V. (1993). *Choosing options and accommodations for children: A planning guide for inclusive education*. Baltimore, MD: Paul H. Brookes Publishing Co.

Halvorsen, A. T., & Neary, T. (2001). Building inclusive schools: Tools and strategies for success. Boston: Allyn & Bacon.

Hamre-Nietupski, S., McDonald, J., & Nietupski, J. (1992). Integrating elementary students with multiple disabilities into supported regular classes: Challenges and solutions. *Teaching Exceptional Children*, spring, 6–9.

Hill, K., & Romich, B. (1999). Choosing and using augmentative communication, Part 3: Assessment, intervention, and resources. *Exceptional Parent, 29*(12), 45–49.

Hock, M. (2000). Standards, assessments, and individualized education programs: Planning for success in the general education classroom. In R. A. Villa & J. S. Thousand (Eds.), *Restructuring for caring and effective education* (pp. 210–211). Baltimore, MD: Paul H. Brookes Publishing Co.

IDEA 1990 & 1997

Individuals with Disabilities Education Act (IDEA) Amendments of 1997, PL 105-17, 20 U.S.C. §§ 1400 et seq.

Jakupcak, J. (1993). Innovative classroom programs for full inclusion. In J. W. Putnam (Ed.), *Cooperative learning and strategies for inclusion: Celebrating diversity in the classroom* (pp. 163–179). Baltimore, MD: Paul H. Brookes Publishing Co.

Janney, R., & Snell, M. (2000). *Modifying schoolwork*. Baltimore, MD: Paul H. Brookes Publishing Co.

Jenkins, J., & Jenkins, L. (1988). Peer tutoring in elementary and secondary programs. In E. L. Meyen, G. A. Vergason, & R. J. Whelan (Eds.), *Effective instructional strategies for exceptional children* (pp. 335–354). Denver: Love.

Johnson, D. W., & Johnson, R. (1987). *Creative conflict*. Edina, MN: Interaction Book Company.

Johnson, D. W., & Johnson, R. (1989). *Cooperation and competition: Theory and research*. Edina, MN: Interaction Book Company.

Johnson, R. T., & Johnson, D. W. (1994). An overview of cooperative learning. In J. S. Thousand, R. A. Villa, & A. I. Nevin (Eds.), *Creativity and collaborative learning: A practical guide to empowering students and teachers* (pp. 31–44). Baltimore, MD: Paul H. Brookes Publishing Co.

Kagan, S. (1992). *Cooperative learning: Resources for teachers*. San Juan Capistrano, CA: Resources for Teachers.

Kronberg, R., & Filbin, J. (1993). *Ideas and suggestions for curricular adaptations at the elementary level*. Denver: Colorado Department of Education.

McCabe, M., & Rhoades, J. (1990). *The nurturing classroom*. Sacramento, CA: ITA Publications.

Macdonald, C., & York, J. (1989). Instruction in regular education classes for students with severe disabilities: Assessment, objectives, and instructional programs. In J. York, T. Vandercook, & S. Wolff (Eds.), *Strategies for full inclusion*. Minneapolis: University of Minnesota, Institute on Community Integration.

Miller, J. (1993). Augmentative and alternative communication. In M. E. Snell (Ed.), *Instruction of students with severe disabilities* (4th ed.) (pp. 319–346). New York: Charles E. Merrill.

Neufeldt, V., & Guralnik, D. B. (1994). *Webster's new world dictionary of American English* (3rd college ed.). New York: Prentice-Hall.

Nevin, A. (1993). Curricular and instructional adaptations for including students with disabilities in cooperative groups. In J. W. Putnam (Ed.), *Cooperative learning and strategies for inclusion: Celebrating diversity in the classroom* (pp. 41–56). Baltimore: Paul H. Brookes Publishing Co.

Orelove, F. P., & Sobsey, D. (1991). *Educating children with multiple disabilities: A transdisciplinary approach* (2nd ed.). Baltimore, MD: Paul H. Brookes Publishing Co.

Post, L. M. (1984). Individualizing instruction in the middle school: Modifications and adaptations in curriculum for the mainstreamed student. *The Clearing House, 58*, 73–76.

Putnam, J. W. (1993). The process of cooperative learning. In J. W. Putnam (Ed.), *Cooperative learning* and strategies for inclusion: Celebrating diversity in the classroom (pp. 15–40). Baltimore, MD: Paul H. Brookes Publishing Co.

Rainforth, B., & York, J. (1991). Handling and positioning. In F. P. Orelove & D. Sobsey, Educating children with multiple disabilities: A transdisciplinary approach (2nd ed.) (pp. 79–117). Baltimore, MD: Paul H. Brookes Publishing Co.

Rainforth, B., York, J., & Macdonald, C. (1992). Collaborative teams for students with severe disabilities: Integrating therapy and educational services. Baltimore, MD: Paul H. Brookes Publishing Co.

Reichle, J. (1997). Communication intervention with persons who have severe disabilities. Journal of Special Education, 31, 110–136.

Reid, J., Forrestal, P., & Cook, J. (1989). Small group learning in the classroom. Scarborough, Australia: Chalkface Press. Portsmouth, NH: Heinemann.

Rhoades, J., & McCabe, M. (1992). Outcome-based learning: A teacher's guide to restructuring the classroom. Sacramento, CA: ITA.

Sailor, W., Gee, K., & Karasoff, P. (1993). Full inclusion and school restructuring. In M. E. Snell (Ed.), Instruction of students with severe disabilities (4th ed.) (pp. 1–30). New York: Charles E. Merrill.

Schleien, S. J., Green, F. P., & Heyne, L. A. (1993). Integrated community recreation. In M. E. Snell (Ed.), Instruction of students with severe disabilities (4th ed.) (pp. 526–555). New York: Charles E. Merrill.

Schnorr, R. F. (1990). "Peter? He comes and goes . . . ": First graders' perspectives on a part-time mainstream student. Journal of The Association for Persons with Severe Handicaps, 15, 231–240.

Schnorr, R. F. (1997). From enrollment to membership: "Belonging" in middle school. Journal of The Association for Persons with Severe Handicaps, 22(1), 1–15.

Schulz, J. B., Carpenter, C. D., & Turnbull, A. P. (1991). Mainstreaming exceptional students: A guide for classroom teachers (3rd ed.). Boston: Allyn & Bacon.

Sharan, S., & Hertz-Lazarowitz, R. (1980). A group investigation method of cooperative learning in the classroom. In S. Sharan, P. Hare, C. Webb, & R. Hertz-Lazarowitz (Eds.)., Cooperation in education (pp. 14–46). Provo, UT: Brigham Young University Press.

Sharan, S., & Hertz-Lazarowitz, R. (1982). Effects of an instructional change program on teachers' behavior, attitudes and perceptions. Journal of Applied Behavioral Science, 18, 185–201.

Sharan, Y., & Sharan, S. (1992). Expanding cooperative learning through group investigation. New York: Teachers College Press.

Sigafoos, J., & Iacono, T. (1993). Selecting augmentative communication devices for persons with severe disabilities: Some factors for educational teams to consider. Australia and New Zealand Journal of Developmental Disabilities, 18(3), 133–146.

Slavin, R. (1983). Cooperative learning. New York: Longman.

Slavin, R. (1990). Cooperative learning: Theory, research and practice. Englewood Cliffs, NJ: Prentice-Hall.

Snell, M. E., & Farlow, L. J. (1993). Self-care skills. In M. E. Snell (Eds.), Instruction of students with severe disabilities (4th ed.) (pp. 380–441). New York: Charles E. Merrill.

Snell, M., & Janney, R. (2000). Collaborative teaming. Baltimore, MD: Paul H. Brookes Publishing Co.

Sobsey, D., & Wolf-Schein, E. G. (1991). Sensory impairments. In F. P. Orelove & D. Sobsey, Educating children with multiple disabilities: A transdisciplinary approach (2nd ed.) (pp. 119–153). Baltimore, MD: Paul H. Brookes Publishing Co.

Thousand, J., Fox, T. J., Reid, R., Godek, J., Williams, W., & Fox, W. (1986). The homecoming model. Burlington, VT: Center for Developmental Disabilities.

Thousand, J. S., Villa, R. A., & Nevin, A. I. (1994). Creativity and collaborative learning. Baltimore, MD: Paul H. Brookes Publishing Co.

Trefler, E. (September, 1992). Positioning, access, and mobility module. Technology in the classroom: Applications and strategies for the education of children with severe disabilities. ERIC Document #ED384147.

Udvari-Solner, A. (1994). A decision-making model for curricular adaptations in cooperative groups. In J. S. Thousand, R. A. Villa, & A. I. Nevin (Eds.), Creativity and collaborative learning: A practical guide to empowering students and teachers (pp. 59–77). Baltimore, MD: Paul H. Brookes Publishing Co.

Udvari-Solner, A. (1996). Examining teacher thinking: Constructing a process to design curricular adaptations. Remedial and Special Education, 17, 245–254.

Utley, B. L. (1994). Providing support for sensory, postural, and movement needs. In L. Sternberg (Ed.), Individuals with profound disabilities: Instructional and assistive strategies (3rd ed.,)(pp. 258–287). Austin, TX: PRO-ED.

Villa, R. A., & Thousand, J. S. (1993). Redefining the role of the special educator and other support personnel. In J. W. Putnam (Ed.), *Cooperative learning and strategies for inclusion: Celebrating diversity in the classroom* (pp. 57–91). Baltimore, MD: Paul H. Brookes Publishing Co.

Villa, R. A., Udis, J., & Thousand, J. S. (1994). Responses for children experiencing behavioral and emotional challenges. In J. S. Thousand, R. A. Villa, & A. I. Nevin (Eds.), *Creativity and collaborative learning: A practical guide to empowering students and teachers* (pp. 369–390). Baltimore, MD: Paul H. Brookes Publishing Co.

York, J., Doyle, M. B., & Kronberg, R. (1992). A curriculum development process for inclusive classrooms. *Focus on Exceptional Children, 25*(4).

York, J., & Vandercook, T. (1991). Designing an integrated program for learners with severe disabilities. *Teaching Exceptional Children*, winter, 22–28.

Ysseldyke, J. G., Thurlow, M. L., & Shriner J. G. (1992). Outcomes are for special educators too. *Teaching Exceptional Children, 25*, 35–50.

21

Accommodating Motor and Sensory Impairments in Inclusive Settings

June E. Downing

Objectives

After completing this chapter, the reader will be able to:

1. State some common physical and sensory impairments.
2. Recognize the impact of a motoric impairment on the student with significant disabilities.
3. Recognize the impact of a sensory loss, whether hearing or visual impairment, on the student who has significant disabilities.
4. Recognize behavioral characteristics of students who have sensory impairments and the purpose those behaviors hold for the student.
5. Understand the concept of partial participation and identify several ways for students with motoric and sensory impairments to actively participate in general education classrooms.
6. Make accommodations that facilitate the learning of students with physical and sensory impairments within general education classrooms.
7. Recognize the value of integrated service delivery on the student's educational program.
8. Understand the teacher's role in identifying potential sensory impairments.

Key Terms

Assistive technology	Hearing impairments	Sensorineural hearing loss
Cerebral palsy	Integrated service delivery	Spina bifida
Conductive hearing impairment	Legal blindness	Spasticity
Cortical visual impairment	Partial participation	Tactile sensitivity
Deafness	Physical or motoric impairments	Visual impairments
Hard-of-hearing	Saliency	

Students with significant disabilities frequently have additional impairments, such as a visual loss, hearing impairment, and/or motoric impairment, which can compound the challenges of providing effective educational programs (Hoon, 1996; Sobsey & Wolf-Schein, 1996; Wesson & Maino, 1995). This chapter will provide information regarding certain types of motoric and sensory impairments that students with significant disabilities could have as additional disabilities and their potential impact on learning. Suggestions will be provided to accommodate their unique needs and to support these students as they learn in general education classrooms. Successfully including these students requires a collaborative team effort and a willingness and ability to work in an integrated manner within natural environments for the student. The role that teachers play in this collaborative effort will be emphasized as they strive to meet the unique needs of their students who have significant and multiple disabilities.

Motoric Impairments of Students with Significant Disabilities

Students with significant disabilities may have physical disorders that complicate the learning process. Physical disabilities can range from mild to severe and can have varying impacts, depending on the severity. Some students may be able to ambulate, albeit slowly, and often with the aid of a walker or personal support. Other students will not be able to stand unaided and will use a wheelchair for mobility purposes. A fewer number of students may have such significant physical disabilities that using their hands to manipulate items is extremely challenging as well. The more complex and limiting the disability means the greater will be the need to aid the student with assistive technology, such as switches, head pointers, adapted keyboards, and control units. Regardless of the accompanying physical impairment or label attached to a child, the critical element to remember is that each student is a unique learner with interests, strengths, and goals that define him or her far more than any label or impairment.

Perhaps the most common physical disability of students with significant disabilities is cerebral palsy (Nelson, 1996; Pellegrino, 1997). This impairment refers to damage to the motor cortex of the brain and results in an inability for the individual to control physical movements (Batshaw & Perret, 1992; Nelson, 1996). Students can have mild to severe forms of cerebral palsy, which can impact different parts of the body to a greater or lesser degree. Overall muscle tone could either be tense (hypertonic) or limp (hypotonic). Taut and rigid tone that restricts movement is referred to as spastic cerebral palsy, while more uncontrolled and fluctuating movement is called athetoid cerebral palsy. Of course the individual student could have a combination or mixed type of both spastic and athetoid cerebral palsy affecting different parts of the body.

Other common causes of physical disabilities with additional impairments include spina bifida (a failure of the spinal column to close properly) and a range of brain trauma that can occur after birth (for example, asphyxiation from near drowning, ingestion of poisons, and car accidents). Regardless of the cause or label given to the disability, what is of greater importance is the impact it has on the student's ability to move and manipulate items. Some students may have greater involvement in their legs, but have quite functional use of their hands. Other students may find it difficult to use their hands and manipulate items without adaptive aids or switches. Simply labeling a student with a specific physical disability tells little about the students—their abilities, motivation, or goals. It is always necessary to look beyond the physical disability to know the student.

The Impact of a Physical Disability on Learning

Physical movement allows the student to explore the environment, follow others to observe what they are doing, and experiment first-hand with different items. Physical movement offers a way for the student to have some direct impact on the environment. The sense of mastery is achieved through such exploration when the student recognizes the relationship between one's behavior and the resulting consequences (MacTurk & Morgan, 1995). When this ability to move freely in space and manipulate items is limited, acquiring information becomes more difficult and can be further complicated if additional disabilities are present (for example, intellectual, or sensory) (Dunn, 1996).

Physical impairments also make it difficult for a student to demonstrate acquired knowledge. Students who are unable to speak often resort to demonstrating what they know. For students with significant disabilities who are unable to use speech to express themselves, being unable to physically act on their environment further complicates their ability to demonstrate understanding. Assistive technology in its many forms is needed to allow this learner to demonstrate what is known. For example, a student with significant disabilities that include a severe physical impairment may not be able to write her name. However, she can identify her name from three or four name stamps, grasp the adapted handle of her name stamp, and press it onto her papers to turn in to the teacher. As another example, a young child with significant disabilities may not be able to handle building materials while in play with peers. However, this child uses a rotary scanner with the colors and shapes of the different building blocks on it. By using a switch, this child tells a playmate what block should be used next in the structure. When students are unable to physically control their environment, the emphasis should be on teaching them how to exert control over their social environment. Regardless of the severity of the physical and cognitive disabilities, all students communicate (Downing, 1999a). Teaching students to convey their intent using alternative and augmentative communication provides students with some control over their lives and with a means of sharing what they know.

Meeting the Needs of the Student with Physical Impairments in the General Education Classroom

The student who has physical impairments often requires additional equipment, such as equipment needed to maintain a given position (for example, wheelchair, stander, sidelyer or adapted chairs) and assistive technology (for example, adaptive keyboards, control units, augmentative communication devices, and switches), which will all require space. The classroom teacher will need to make sure that room is available for this equipment and that aisles are clear and wide enough for a wheelchair and/or walker. Obviously, all classrooms and school facilities will need to be physically accessible (for example, ramps, elevators, and fountains at wheelchair level) and safe (for example, safety rails and nonslip walking surfaces). With the aid of the physical therapist, the team will determine how often the student will need to be physically positioned, where, and what equipment will be necessary. Such decisions will help to determine where equipment will be kept when not being used.

If the student has difficulty making effective use of his or her hands, adaptations will be needed to help the student handle and make use of various items. A variety of sources exist to help teachers obtain the necessary equipment, which would include both light technology and high technology. Examples of light technology to support students with physical disabilities include mitts that allow the student to grasp items; adapted handles to ease grasping; elevated surfaces for easier access; mouth or head sticks; magnetic backings on items; page fluffers to make turning pages easier; and an array of simple switches to control toys, appliances, and other equipment. Materials of this nature can be purchased or made by teachers, occupational therapists, volunteers, parents, or students without disabilities (see Campbell & Truesdell, 2000; Elder & Goossens, 1996). Higher technology would involve complex switches, control units, and computer adaptations, such as specialized keyboards, Touch Windows, and switch-activated software. The intent of all assistive technology of this nature is to increase the participation level of the student and to enhance opportunities to learn (Inge & Shepherd, 1995; Parette, 1997).

The concept of partial participation plays a critical role in ensuring accessible education for students with physical disabilities in general education classrooms. Partial participation refers to the notion that full involvement in all steps of an activity is not necessary for meaningful participation (Ferguson & Baumgart, 1991). Although students with significant disabilities, which include a physical disability, may not be able to perform many steps in a given activity, depending on the physical requirements, these students do not need to be excluded from participation. They can be encouraged to engage in the steps that are accessible, and activities can be modified to meet their needs. Assistive technology can play a major role in increasing their ability to participate successfully. For example, during her foods class, Stephanie cannot use her hands to measure or pour ingredients, stir, put on baking trays, or put the item into the oven. However, she does follow a pictorial recipe, and, when asked what to do next, she looks at one of two pictorially depicted steps to indicate the correct answer. She also is asked several questions related to the proper kitchen tool to use to perform a step (for example, do we use a spoon or a cup to measure fi T. vanilla?). She responds by looking at the appropriate tool. Stephanie also uses her head switch to turn on the blender when directed by a peer. When dropping cookie dough onto baking sheets, she is asked if there is room to put more. Through these modifications in the activity, Stephanie plays an active role in her cooking group despite her inability to make use of her hands. Suggestions for improving the environment to facilitate the learning of students with severe physical disabilities can be found in Figure 21.1. Various team members, such as an occupational therapist, physical therapist, and speech-language pathologist can provide considerable input regarding a variety of accommodations and assistive technology to best support this student and allow for active participation.

Visual Impairments of Students with Significant Disabilities

Although a teacher of students with visual impairments on the team can provide information concerning visual impairments, some basic knowledge can be helpful for all team members to have. The following section presents general information on visual impairments of students who have significant disabilities.

A student is considered legally blind when the degree of remaining visual acuity in the best eye is measured at 20/200 or worse (compared to 20/20 or "perfect" vision). The other way to be categorized as legally blind is to have a remaining visual field of 20° (from 360°) or less. The student could have considerable visual acuity if the 20° of visual field includes central vision or very limited visual acuity if the 20° is in the peripheral visual field. Despite the label of legal blindness, most students with this disability have functional vision (Barraga & Erin, 1992; Orel-Bixler, 1999). Sometimes the remaining central vision allows the student to see facial expressions, print, pictures, and anything with considerable detail. This student probably learns a great deal from the visual sense as long as items are brought sufficiently close to the eyes and remain within the visual field, despite the label

FIGURE 21.1 *Considerations for Improving the Physical Environment*

1. Is there sufficient room for a student using a walker or wheelchair to maneuver easily around the classroom?
2. Are tables high enough for a student's wheelchair to fit under?
3. Are chairs and tables low enough to allow students to have their feet flat on the floor?
4. Are materials kept at a level easily accessible from a wheelchair?
5. Is the student's work environment sufficiently large to hold adapted materials while still allowing room for the student to work?
6. Is positioning equipment readily available to allow the child to be in as similar a position as possible as classmates?
7. Is assistive technology available and in use throughout the day to enhance access to the curriculum?

of blindness. Other students will detect some colors, movement, and large shapes, but will be unable to see detail (for example, print or pictures). A few students will only be able to detect the presence or absence of light and use that information for mobility purposes (for example, to head toward the open door for recess). A very small number of students will have no usable vision at all and require a completely nonvisual approach to learn.

One of the most common visual impairments seen in learners with significant disabilities has little to do with the actual functioning of the eye itself, but refers more to the ability of the visual cortex in the brain to interpret the information that is received visually. Students who have cortical visual impairment (CVI) often have fluctuating vision, which means that sometimes under certain conditions at different times of day, they can detect visual information much more readily than at others (Crossman, 1991). This characteristic of CVI is frustrating to learner and teacher alike. Visual responses can vary significantly from day to day. However, some information concerning this particular impairment can be helpful to teachers. Usually this group of learners sees things up close and slightly to the side. There may be a preference for one or more bright colors that aid in visual recognition. Students with this type of visual impairment typically can detect movement and bright objects better than detail. Therefore, these aspects of vision can be used to gain visual attention when presenting information. Furthermore, they need time to visually examine the information and try to interpret its meaning.

Impact of a Visual Loss on Learning

Vision plays a critical role in learning for most students. The visual sense allows us to obtain information at a distance, sometimes at great distances, making it possible to form concepts without having to come in direct contact with what we observe. Experts in this field have stated that as much as 90 percent of what is learned occurs through the visual sense (Barraga & Erin, 1992; Gee, 1994). For students with multiple disabilities who struggle with basic communication and who may have an extremely difficult time understanding their world, a severe visual loss can compound the difficulty they experience (Chen, 1995; Prickett & Welch, 1995; Topor, 1999). Instead of relying on visual information to help with understanding, they must rely on auditory and tactile information, which may only provide partial information at best. For teachers accustomed to providing instruction using highly visual means, the student with a visual loss in addition to other significant disabilities can present an incredible challenge. Most teachers have not been prepared to adjust their teaching strategies to such children. Furthermore, students with significant disabilities may have visual impairments that have not yet been identified (Mamer, 1999; Wesson & Maino, 1995). Teachers not trained to look for possible visual impairments can ignore this critical characteristic of the student.

The process of learning is slowed when the sense of vision is severely impaired. Students must piece together or synthesize pieces of information into an understandable whole, versus seeing and understanding the whole at once and later analyzing its parts. An analogy of putting together a large jigsaw puzzle may help clarify the difference. With vision, the end product can be seen on the jigsaw puzzle cover and can be used to organize and eventually complete the puzzle. Without vision, the jigsaw puzzle must be put together with no guiding picture on the box cover. Although not impossible, the amount of time required for such a task will be considerably longer than with the use of vision.

What to Look for if a Visual Loss Is Suspected

Because vision is so critical to learning, it is imperative that all students receive as much visual information as possible. Therefore, detection of a visual loss is an important aspect of providing quality services to students with significant disabilities. Unfortunately, these students do not typically respond appropriately to traditional assessment procedures to measure vision. Furthermore, when a student has significant disabilities, the effort to assess vision and visual functioning may not be as seriously undertaken as with students who respond to traditional vision-testing procedures. However, there exist both clinical and informal assessment procedures to obtain excellent information on whether a student is obtaining visual information and how much (Jacobsen, Grottland, & Flaten, 2001; Orel-Bixler, 1999; Topor, 1999). For best results, clinical examinations by ophthalmologists who are experienced with working with individuals who have severe and multiple disabilities are imperative.

Informal, observational procedures performed by members of the education team can provide quality information regarding a particular student's visual abilities that can aid optometrists and ophthalmologists in obtaining more accurate clinical information. Documentation of student behavior in response to visual information can be collected in natural environments during daily activities by those most familiar with the student. Such documentation should include the student's reaction, the visual item, the distance of the item to the student, and the peripheral field in which the item was presented (Topor, 1999; Utley, Roman, & Nelson, 1998). For example, while Lori is considered to be functionally blind, she has been noticed by different team members (for example, support teacher and paraeducator) to occasionally reach for a very bright yellow cup when presented to her at snack time in the lower-left peripheral range of her right eye. Although this amount of visual information may preclude tasks that require detection of detail, it still provides useable vision that can aid learning and interacting with the environment.

Teachers should look for behaviors from students that indicate that there is a consistent response to visual stimuli. Knowing what visual information the student can detect can help determine how best to teach the student uses of this information. Visual behaviors of a student with significant disabilities might include the following: startling to a bright light or movement, reaching toward items, flicking hand or an item in front of eyes, turning the head toward a bright light source, bringing an item up very close to one or both eyes, or avoiding large items when traveling. This information may conflict with a more clinical vision assessment, but certainly is more helpful to teaching staff than a given label (for example, blind).

Equally important as recognizing visual behaviors is recognizing when a student may be having difficulty obtaining visual information. Such observations are particularly important if there is no visual impairment noted and, therefore, no attempt to correct the potential loss. The following behaviors may indicate a visual problem that could lead to clinical intervention that could help the student see better: rubbing eyes extensively, poking eyes, excessive squinting outdoors or in response to light, and holding items very close to the eyes. Figure 21.2 provides a list of behaviors that teachers should consider when trying to decide if a student has a visual impairment and needs a more formal and clinical assessment. Observations should be shared with the family, who will be able to confirm or deny such behaviors at home. In turn, the information should be shared with an ophthalmologist to aid that professional in a diagnosis and prescription for correction as needed.

Addressing Visual Needs in General Education Classrooms

Having a visual loss, regardless of the severity, does not mean that the student with significant disabilities cannot be taught effectively in general education classrooms. However, certain strategies must be in place to make the intervention most effective. Certain team members with specialized information regarding visual impairments can help guide the team to determine the best ways to provide instruction and support. The teacher trained in visual impairments and blindness, as well as the orientation and mobility instructor, may be able to obtain specialized equipment, improve environmental factors, and provide instruction to others on the team concerning how best to present information and what factors to consider. For example, Lilly, a 15-year-old high school student, uses an adapted push cane that the orientation and mobility instructor recommended because Lilly was not using a standard cane in the correct manner. With the adapted cane, she did not need to hold the cane in one hand, cross her midline, or move the cane back and forth across her path to detect potential barriers. Instead she used both hands and simply pushed the cane in front of her. This was easier for her to do, provided her greater stability, and still gave her cues as to what lay in front of her path.

Orientation and Mobility (O&M)

Students who have very limited or no vision will require specific instruction in moving safely and efficiently within their classroom and school environments. This type of

---

FIGURE 21.2 *Behaviors Indicating a Potential Visual Loss*

- Student frequently trips over items on the floor.
- Student typically moves very close to view items or holds items very close to the eye.
- Student rubs and/or pokes one or both eyes frequently.
- Student frequently bumps into large objects.
- Student often has red and runny eyes.
- Student squints excessively, especially inside.
- Student's eyes do not appear to be balanced and do not move together.
- Student does not appear to use vision.
- Student frequently covers one or both eyes.
- Student responds inconsistently to visual information.

instruction, called O & M, is designed to meet the individual needs of the student, who may also have a hearing impairment, physical impairment, and/or medical considerations. The O & M instructor plays a critical role in helping to determine important travel routes for the student (based on student goals and daily routines) and in determining how to teach the student these routes. Despite the importance of this skilled professional, all members of the team and the student's classmates need to be familiar with orientation and mobility strategies. The O & M instructor can assume responsibility for educating everyone who interacts with the student who is blind on how and when to provide appropriate sighted guide; encourage more independent travel (for example, trailing a wall with one's hand); and what to do in different situations such as stairs, ramps, and narrow aisles. A recommended practice for O & M instruction for students with significant disabilities is that it occurs within natural and typical routines of the day and not in an isolated and unfamiliar context (Bailey & Head, 1993). In this way the student does not have to learn certain skills in an unfamiliar time or setting and then learn to apply them where and when needed. Relevance for the student is much more immediate when skills are taught within a natural context. For more specific information on orientation and mobility for students with visual impairments, see Hill and Snook-Hill (1996).

Instructional and Material Accommodations for a Visual Loss

Depending on whether the student can make use of remaining vision or must rely on the sense of touch to obtain information, different strategies and materials will be needed. Considerable information exists to guide the education team on adaptations to consider for enhancement of the learning environment (Ashley & Cates, 1992; Downing, 1999b; Utley et al., 1998). In general the student should be seated close to the teacher or where the teacher has easy access to the student. Information typically provided at a distance needs to be replicated and brought closer to the student for up-close viewing. Information also may need to be enlarged and can be made clearer when extraneous visual information is deleted and the critical information is made more salient. Bold, dark lines and highlighters help to draw visual attention to the most important aspects. The effective use of color also can help the student recognize and understand the information. Ensuring a clear contrast between important information and background aids visual recognition. Visual information that is the focus of interest needs to be bright, clear, and visually uncluttered, while the background should be of a contrasting, solid and dull color. For example, if a student is to recognize the picture of a glass to request a drink, the glass is bright yellow in color and is on a solid dark gray background. In contrast, some symbols like this drink symbol are sometimes of pale color and put on bright neon colors as the background, making the background of greater visual interest than the symbol. Therefore, careful attention should be paid to how materials are modified to be more visually salient.

Lighting is of critical importance when adapting to meet the visual needs of the learner (Barraga & Erin, 1992). Sufficient light needs to be on the student's work, not in his or her eyes. High-intensity lights can be clamped onto a student's desk or wheelchair to provide the necessary lighting. In addition, flickering fluorescent light bulbs should be fixed immediately (for all students), and every effort should be made to prevent glare or keep it to a minimum. Positioning in the classroom should be away from windows that allow in excess sunlight. The student's seat should be placed so that the student is not facing these windows, and the teacher should avoid standing in front of them. Glare-free acetate sheets can be used on top of paper products that produce glare, such as magazine pages. Glare can be a particular problem for students with cataracts, glaucoma, albinism (lack of pigment), or aniridia (lack of an iris). Of course, lighting needs will vary per student depending on the visual disorder and other unique needs, which the teacher certified in visual impairments should be able to discern. Figure 21.3 provides some guidelines for improving the learning environment of students who have visual impairments.

In general visual adaptations involve increasing the visual saliency of the available information so that it is easier to detect and interpret (Smith & Levack, 1996). The teacher of students with significant disabilities that include a visual impairment needs to remember that it is not enough to make the information more visually accessible. They also must encourage the student to use remaining vision, and they must teach the student what the visual information means. In general, this means that a close association must be made between what the student perceives and what it means. Greatly simplified visual information followed by the immediate presentation of (or involvement in) what it represents helps to establish this association. For example, when trying to teach a fourth grader with significant disabilities and a severe visual loss that a photograph means "time for recess," the photograph of a single red wrist band she wears for this activity against a plain beige table is presented to her. When the student brings the photograph to her face to look more closely, she also is shown the actual red wristband, which she is helped to match to the photograph. Finally, she is helped to put the wristband on before going outside for recess. This representation is much more visually salient than a photograph of her playing with her friends, which would be much more visually cluttered and confusing. Of course repetition and consistency across different individuals using this symbol are critical if the student is to make the desired association.

When students have extremely limited vision and cannot access visual information, the education staff must use information that is nonvisual in nature. Auditory information

IGURE 21.3 *Considerations for Improving the Environment for Students with Limited or no Vision*

1. Is lighting sufficient for the task and strong enough for the student?
2. Is glare on work eliminated or greatly reduced?
3. Does important visual information stand in sharp contrast to the background field?
4. Is important visual information made larger with bold lines and/or highlighted?
5. Is color used to draw visual attention and add important information?
6. Is the student sitting close to the teacher?
7. Is sufficient time allowed for the student to explore visual information?
8. Are appropriate tactile and auditory materials used to compensate for limited vision?
9. Does the student have access to corrective lenses and other optical aids and use these for appropriate tasks?

(for example, speech) is an obvious way to bypass the visual mode and still provide considerable information, as long as the student can access auditory information and understand it. For students who are deaf-blind or who have limited understanding of linguistic output, tactual information is the best alternative. However, obtaining information through the tactile sense is considerably different than through the visual sense (see Downing & Chen, in press). Instead of obtaining reliable information at a distance, the individual must feel it with one or both hands. The greater the ability to feel the entire object with the hands and not just parts of the object at a time means the easier it is to gain an understanding of size, shape, and function. Therefore, exploring an apple will be considerably easier than exploring a table. Parts of the table that are felt at any one time will have to be synthesized together with other parts as they are felt. Without a visual image of the table as a whole, this process can become quite laborious. Larger items and things that move (for example, water fountain or animals) will be harder for the child to tactually understand than items that fit under the hands. In addition, very small items or very delicate items (for example, spider web or ant) are also difficult to capture tactually. Of course, some things are purely visual (for example, rainbow, sunrise, or landscape) and cannot be realistically presented tactually. The education team will need to determine the relevance of such information to the student and make appropriate adjustments as needed (for example, instead of trying to convey what a rainbow is, the focus could be on rain and preparation when it rains).

The teacher trained in visual impairments can be a good resource for obtaining or producing appropriate tactile information to convey important concepts. A general guideline when developing tactile materials is to adopt the perspective of the student who does not have usable vision and feel the item that is to be represented. The most salient tactile information will be material that most closely *feels* (not looks) like its referent. Therefore, though miniatures can be easily felt by one hand, they are often not tactilely salient and require vision to determine what they represent. As a result, the most meaningful tactile symbol may represent only a part of the referent (for example, handlebars to represent going for a bike ride). The following example demonstrates the use of tactile information for a high school student with significant disabilities.

Nela is a 15-year-old sophomore attending her local high school. She has a terrific smile and a great sense of humor. Nela is functionally blind (sees light and movement only) and uses a wheelchair due to spastic quadriplegia cerebral palsy. Nela takes physical education (PE) (swimming), keyboarding, band, ceramics, woodshop, and drama. She uses a tactile daily schedule throughout her day (a notebook with representative items for each period affixed with HandiTak to different pages). Nela has the ability to grasp each item and hands it to each teacher to represent "Hi, I'm here" at the beginning of each class period. When the bell rings and the period ends, the teacher hands the item back to Nela and says goodbye. Nela grasps the item and drops it into her finished bag attached to her wheelchair. This entire process helps put a definite beginning and end to each period and helps her to anticipate what period is next. For the 20-minute schoolwide nutrition break, Nela has an empty granola bar wrapper attached to this page in her schedule. She gives this to the person supporting her at the time (classmate, peer tutor, or paraeducator) in exchange for the granola bar snack in her backpack. At lunch there will be a plastic baggy on her schedule if she brings her lunch, and she will give this baggy to the special education support person (paraeducator or teacher) to request her lunch. If she will be buying her lunch, there will be a small change purse on her schedule with sufficient funds to cover her lunch costs. She will hand this to the cashier when she goes through the lunch line. Age-appropriate written messages on these items in her schedule make her intent clear to anyone with whom she is interacting.

Encouraging students of different abilities to work together and cooperate on common tasks can be a very successful adaptation for a student with significant disabilities and combined visual loss. The benefit of a general education classroom is the availability of numerous and competent peers who can provide an appropriate model to follow, encouragement, and a variety of support as needed. Working with others who have different abilities encourages interdependence and allows individual students to contribute to the learning process in their own unique way.

Hearing Impairments of Students with Significant Disabilities

As with visual impairments, it is not uncommon for a student with significant disabilities to also have hearing impairments (Chen, 1999; Schildroth & Hotto, 1996). Perhaps the greatest difficulty presented by a hearing impairment is that of accessing verbal information from others and the deleterious impact on language development. In general, there are two major types of hearing impairments: conductive losses and sensorineural losses. Depending on the severity of loss, the impact on learning can be quite challenging. A student is considered deaf when speech cannot be understood with or without a hearing aid. In contrast, a student is considered hard of hearing when speech can be heard, although with distortion. Hearing losses are classified according to the intensity or volume of sound as measured by decibels (dB) and frequency of sound or pitch as measured by hertz (Hz). Speech ranges from approximately 500 Hz to 2,000 Hz. Therefore, hearing losses occurring within this range are particularly problematic. Following are some of the most common hearing impairments that the teacher of students with significant disabilities may encounter.

Conductive Hearing Loss

A hearing impairment that involves the inability to obtain sufficient volume of sound is called a conductive loss. Such a hearing impairment can range from mild (15 dB to 30 dB) to profound (90 dB or greater) and can result from a variety of problems, such as atresia (no opening to ear canal), otitis media (middle ear infection), excessive wax, and damage to the eardrum or any part of the outer and middle ear. Conductive losses usually can be mediated by increasing the volume of the auditory information through the use of hearing aids. Conductive losses also may be corrected medically or surgically.

Sensorineural Loss

Many students with significant disabilities have a type of hearing impairment that involves the inner ear and the auditory cortex of the brain. This type of impairment impacts the detection of the various frequencies of sound (pitch) and the interpretation of the sounds detected. Such impairments are less amenable to correction with the use of a standard hearing aid or to surgical intervention. Even when the auditory information can be detected (for example, it is loud enough), it is still unclear, and the relationship between the sound detected and what it represents is not understood. The neural cells responsible for clarity of sound may be damaged, which results in distorted and vague auditory input. Damage to the auditory cortex where the brain interprets auditory information received may make it very difficult for the individual to understand the sounds despite minimal or no damage to the ear itself. This type of hearing impairment can be caused by maternal infections (for example, rubella, cytomegalovirus [CMV], or a hereditary condition) or childhood diseases (for example, meningitis, anoxia, and drugs known to be harmful to hearing, or ototoxic). Hearing impairments also can result in a combination of both conductive and sensorineural loss.

Impact of a Hearing Loss on Learning

Even a mild hearing loss can have a profound impact on the development of effective communication and learning, especially if the child has additional disabilities (Batshaw & Perret, 1992; Chen, 1999). The age of onset of the impairment, the actual damage to the ear and/or auditory cortex, prognosis, presence of additional disabilities, as well as factors such as motivation to hear and familial expectations will all play a role in how well a student is able to use auditory information. Connecting items and actions with words is the basis of learning and greatly eases effective interactions. As the young child attempts to create meaning to his or her world, words help to label items and activities. Without this access to verbal information, the student, especially one with a severe cognitive impairment, will struggle to create a foundation on which to develop a clearer understanding of the world.

In addition, sounds in our environment alert us to potential dangers and provide many cues that allow us to anticipate upcoming events. For example, hearing the bell ring means it is time to go to the next class, a barking dog can signal danger or just someone coming, a whistling teapot lets us know when water has boiled, the ping of a microwave oven signals that the food is ready, and the clank of keys dropping alerts us to stop and retrieve them. We use sounds throughout each day to interpret what is happening around us. The absence of this distance sense means less information and the need to use other information to compensate (for example, visual information).

What to Look for if a Hearing Loss Is Suspected

Hearing loss can be an invisible disability, especially if the student presents with more obvious impairments, such as physical disabilities and cognitive limitations. Furthermore, students with significant disabilities may not perform well under traditional assessment procedures for determining a hearing loss (Abdala, 1999; Sobsey & Wolf-Schein, 1996). The decision may be not to pursue this avenue of determining the presence of a hearing loss and focus on more apparent needs. Unfortunately, such a decision places the student at increased risk for learning difficulties. Every effort should be made to ensure that the student has access to auditory information that is as clear as possible. Furthermore, both clinical and informal assessment procedures exist that can determine the student's ability to detect sound and make use of it (Abdala, 1999; Chen, 1999; Sobsey & Wolf-Schein, 1996).

Members of the education team may be in an excellent position to be on the alert for and collect information pertaining to a student's ability to detect and recognize auditory information. Observations can be made within the student's typical routine (both at home and at school) and should document the student's reactions to sound, the type of sound, and the distance of the student from the sound source. Figure 21.4 provides a list of behaviors to consider if a hearing loss is suspected. Knowing the stimuli to which the student responds (for example, the type of sound, volume, and distance from the sound source) will enable instructional staff and family members to make use of similar auditory information within various activities. For instance, although Derrick is considered to have a profound hearing impairment, his family reported to the school staff that he did seem alert and excited when he attended a traditional Japanese drum demonstration on an outing with his family. Given this information, Derrick was enrolled in a band class at his middle school to see how he would like it. As with the Japanese drums, Derrick seemed to pull his head up and orient toward the bass drums when they were played. Given adaptations to hold drum sticks (due to his severe physical disabilities), a goal for Derrick was to hit the drums when he heard others in his class doing this. Without the information from home, Derrick's education team might not have considered band as an appropriate class for Derrick.

Supporting the Needs of Students with Hearing Loss/Deafness in General Education Classrooms

Recognizing that some students with significant disabilities have difficulty receiving auditory information challenges the education team to adjust instructional strategies and the learning environment. Because so much information is presented verbally in most classrooms, the student who cannot access this information will face considerable challenges to

---

FIGURE 21.4 *Behaviors Indicating a Potential Hearing Loss*

- Failure to respond to auditory information or substantial delay in response time
- Withdrawal from social situations
- Interested in very loud noises, but not more normal sounds
- Responds only when the TV, CD, radio, or VCR is very loud
- Speech is difficult to understand (not due to physical limitation)
- Seems confused by auditory information
- Has difficulty attending when there is background noise or seems more interested in background noise
- Has frequent colds or ear infections
- Pulls on ears or puts hands over ears
- Consistently cocks head to one side

---

learn. Team members trained in the area of deafness and hard of hearing impairments can contribute their expertise to enhance the auditory environment, while also making suggestions to compensate for the loss of auditory information.

To enhance auditory input, efforts should be made to reduce background and extraneous noise so that it does not interfere with auditory reception (Prickett & Welch, 1995). Drapes, wall hangings, and rugs around the room can absorb such sounds, and the use of acoustic tiles is recommended. Noise made by chairs scrapping against the floor can be greatly reduced by adding tennis balls to the end of each chair leg. In addition to reducing background noise, it is critical to amplify and highlight the relevant and meaningful sound (for example, the teacher's voice, voices of classmates, or sound from a film being shown). Highlighting the important auditory information can be achieved by means of a frequency modulation (FM) system, which sends the speaker's voice through radio waves directly to the ear of the receiver and blocks extraneous noise. Reducing the distance between speaker and listener (for example, the student with significant disabilities) is another way to amplify the important sound. It is also helpful to have a class rule that only one person speak at a time, and that every effort be made to face the student who has a hearing impairment and make effective use of facial expressions and gestures. This will help the student who is deaf or hard of hearing focus on one relevant source, and, of course, is also a good rule for all class members.

Appropriate hearing aids can be very helpful to students with certain hearing losses, depending on the environment and expectations. Those individuals working with a student with significant disabilities who also has a hearing impairment and wears hearing aids should make sure that the hearing aid is on and is turned to the right setting and volume level. Batteries should always be checked so that the hearing aid is functioning properly. Furthermore, the mold that is attached to the aid should be clean and excess wax (cerumen) should be removed so that it does not block sound. The teacher trained in the area of deafness and hearing losses and/or audiologist can help other team members set up a routine to check for the proper fit and functioning of the hearing aid.

After the environment is made as acoustically salient as possible, it is still up to teachers to help the student understand what sounds are and what they mean. Helping the student receive auditory information is the first step. The more difficult step may be teaching that student what sounds mean and what the student is to do as a result. Although much auditory stimulation targets the student's ability to detect sound, the important next step may not be addressed—teaching the student how to use that information. We do not respond the same way to all sounds. When we hear the fire alarm, we leave the area and go to safety. When we hear the sound of something dropped, we stop and look for it. When we hear someone calling our name, we stop and turn toward that person. When we hear the sound of a large truck backing up, we stop, locate the truck, and get out of the way. Teaching the student one way to respond (for example, look at the sound source) fails to help the student differentiate the different sounds that are possible and the different responses that are expected. Teaching such behavior within the context of the natural learning environment would make the most sense if generalization of skills is to occur (Dote-Kwan & Chen, 1999; Sacks, 1998).

Besides highlighting auditory information and masking irrelevant background noise, adding clear visual information is essential, especially for students unable to make use of speech sounds. Using visual information such as pictures, photographs, logos, and graphic organizers to clarify teacher expectations is a recommended practice for students with no or limited hearing (Downing, 1999b; Luckner, Bowen, & Carter, 2001). Teachers may be more comfortable adjusting to the increased needs of the student for visual information. Teachers typically show students what they want them to do by presenting models, diagrams, and samples of desired work. Students unable to hear can still gain valuable information from the Internet, pictures or photographs in books, maps, and a host of other visual material. Given the technology available in the form of scanners, digital cameras, and CDs with graphic information, increasing or supplementing the information through visual means is not overly challenging to the average teacher. Furthermore, such additional information benefits all students, not just the student with significant disabilities, which include a hearing impairment. Figure 21.5 provides guidelines for enhancing the learning environment for students who are deaf or hard of hearing.

However, the addition of pictorial information should not just be passively provided for the student. Creative use of pictorial information can allow the student to write by sequencing pictures or photographs, to add simple words to pictures using color coding, to read pictorial/written directions, and to match the American Sign Language (ASL) sign to the correct picture from a choice of two or three. Regardless of the age of the student or subject matter, the effective use of pictorial information can provide the student with a very active way to partially participate in typical classroom activities. For example, in a tenth grade earth science class, the class is studying the effects of extreme weather conditions. Guillermo is learning to pair signs for DRY with drought pictures, WATER with flood pictures, and SHAKE with earthquake pictures during the lecture/discussion. The entire class also learns these signs as well, and, when the teacher signs one of these weather extremes, Guillermo is to select the appropriate picture and show it to the class while a classmate provides information regarding its cause. For additional examples of curricular modifications for students with significant disabilities and deafness, see Downing (2002).

Of course, the use of a visual communication system such as ASL is certainly recommended for students who are deaf. Although students with significant disabilities,

---

FIGURE 21.5   *Considerations for Improving the Auditory Environment*

1. Has every effort been made to reduce extraneous background noise (for example, tennis balls on chair legs, carpets, and drapes used)?
2. Has important auditory information been highlighted (for example, increased volume and FM system in use)?
3. Is the student sitting close to the main speaker?
4. Are other students relatively quiet when the teacher is talking?
5. Are visual aids in use to compensate somewhat for loss of auditory information?
6. Is the student's hearing aid on the right setting, and are the batteries charged?
7. Are gestures, body language, facial expressions, and mime used to enhance communication interactions?
8. Is American Sign Language (ASL) or ASL vocabulary used as much as possible by everyone in the class (for example, teachers, classmates, and related service providers)?

especially those who are also severely visually impaired and physically disabled, may not acquire fluency with ASL, they may benefit receptively from the information, and they may learn some signs or adapted signs to express certain needs. Even minimal use of signs to receive or express information should be encouraged to facilitate more effective communication. In general, students without disabilities seem interested in learning signs (Heller, Manning, Pavur, & Wagner 1998), and teachers can make effective use of this skill for all students. Teachers can add this kinesthetic element to spelling and vocabulary learning through fingerspelling and signs. Some high schools recognize ASL as a foreign language requirement, and several high schools have sign language clubs (ASL or a signed English system).

Integrated Service Delivery

A recommended practice for students with significant disabilities is the integration of all service delivery into a typical daily routine (Downing, 2002; Giangreco, Edelman, & Nelson, 1998; Orelove & Sobsey, 1996; Silberman, Sacks, & Wolfe, 1998). Instead of removing students from their general education classroom to work with a specialist on specific skills, those specialists integrate their expertise into the student's day. Advantages of such an approach have been articulated in the literature (see Chapter 8 in this text on collaborative teamwork) and include the following: (a) The student does not have to miss what is being covered in class and then play catch up upon return; (b) the problem of having to transfer skills learned in one environment to the setting where they are needed is avoided; (c) other students can benefit from the attention of another adult in the room; (d) the classroom teacher and paraeducators, as well as other members of the education team, can see what skills are being targeted within their natural context, and they can more easily implement the same strategies when the specialist is not there; and (e) work on important skills does not just happen during the limited time that the specialist is available to work directly with the student, but these skills can be addressed by a number of people as they naturally occur throughout each day.

Following an integrated model of service delivery, the teacher trained in visual impairments would work directly with the student at various times during the school day, but also would work with team members to ensure that the accommodations and adapted instructional techniques were occurring at all times. For example, during a science lesson, Nolan's fifth grade class is studying the planets. They are working in groups to build replicas of the planets and are doing research on the Internet to find information regarding the planet they have been given to research. The teacher trained in visual impairments is in the classroom working with Nolan and his group. She makes sure that the materials used to make the planets are organized in such a manner that Nolan has easy access to them and they will not scatter everywhere when he moves his hands. Nolan dislikes getting his hands sticky with glue, so they are using HandiTak to hold pieces together. When a peer asks Nolan for a piece of material, this teacher helps him to recognize that material by touch, to pick it up, and to hold it out in the direction of the peer's voice. He is not to let go of the item until he feels his classmate's hand under his. When the model is complete, this teacher helps him to feel the model without breaking it and to recognize that there are nine planets after she's helped him tactually feel nine glue dots on a card. Several of these skills are skills that Nolan uses throughout all of his activities during the day. The teacher trained in visual impairments gets to work directly with Nolan on these skills so she can identify problems that may result and make suggestions for other situations. Others in the room can see how she is working with Nolan (that is, how information is given to him) and can replicate similar strategies when she is not in the room.

Although this particular teacher originally was trained to remove students from the classroom and work with them in a small room on either tactile or visual skills, she recognized that this was potentially confusing for Nolan. His routine was interrupted a couple of times each week to leave his classroom and receive services from her in a special room. This teacher recognized that instruction in this manner did not have any meaning for him in terms of what is expected in his fifth grade class. The materials used in this special room were different than those experienced in his class, as were the activities. Furthermore, the stimulus level in the room was considerably different from his typical classroom. Because he needs to use his hands to learn in his fifth grade class, it made more sense for the teacher trained in visual impairments to infuse her expertise and experience into the fifth grade class. By doing so, she could see where Nolan had trouble and what he could do to compensate for his lack of vision. She also can assist his classmates as questions emerge and as they need some added guidance, thus helping the classroom teacher to support all students.

Keeping Everyone Informed

When students with significant disabilities have additional sensory and motoric impairments, interactions with others may be more difficult to maintain (Downing, 2002; Haring, Haring, Breen, Romer & White, 1995). Without prior experience, teachers, related service providers, administrators, and, certainly, classmates may have limited knowledge of how to interact most effectively with a student who is blind, or deaf, or both. Without eye contact, being able to use facial expressions or gestures, or show pictorial information, interacting with a student with significant disabilities who is also blind may seem somewhat daunting. Presenting information to this same student in a tactile format may seem exceptionally challenging. If the student is deaf and unable to benefit from speech, not knowing ASL or even some ASL vocabulary may discourage interactions. Specific information and some reliable general strategies to enhance and support interactions are needed.

Sharing information concerning various impairments and compensatory strategies that a particular student has can be done in a number of ways, depending on family and student preference, teacher and classmate needs, type of disability, and expected outcome. Simulating the impairment so others can experience it first hand (as much as possible) is one good way to help others better understand the sensory impairment. For example, classmates can be blindfolded and then asked to complete a tactual task that is novel for them. To complicate the task and make it relate more closely to a student who does not use formal language, no verbal information or instructions can be given. Very hard-to-understand speech can be recorded or spoken and classmates asked to write the words they hear to simulate the effects of being hard of hearing. A teacher also can give simple directions to follow, but without voicing them to simulate deafness and its potential impact. Students without disabilities can experience using a wheelchair and be allowed to confront curbs, getting a drink from a water fountain, and going through doors. They also can don heavy and overly large gloves and attempt to perform some fine motor tasks, such as turning pages in a book, tying their shoes, or picking up a pin. Simulations of this nature can't replicate what a given student experiences, but they can help others gain an appreciation for the challenges encountered, as well as the potential to meet these challenges. Whenever simulations are enacted, the abilities of students should always be stressed, not the disability.

The most direct way to share information concerning a given student's experience with a disability is to ask questions in a neutral and nonjudgmental manner with which the student feels comfortable. For many students with significant disabilities, responding to such questions may be overly difficult given minimal language skills. When this is the issue, family members can respond for the student, explaining the condition and how the student interacts and learns. Other less direct strategies might include having guest speakers with certain disabilities come to the class to discuss in a very personal way their disability and the obstacles they have overcome to learn and grow. Some teachers incorporate ability and disability awareness into the curriculum by having students study individuals with certain disabilities and their many accomplishments (for example, Helen Keller, Beethoven, or Stephen Hawking). Several commercially available books present the concept of differences and ability using a variety of formats and targeting differently aged children. When helping everyone understand about a specific disability, it is always imperative to emphasize the naturalness of the condition as part of the human experience, the similarity with others, and the unique gifts that a student possesses.

Summary

This chapter has focused on physical and sensory impairments of the student with significant disabilities in the inclusive general education classroom. Despite the additional challenges that are created by impairments to the distance senses of vision and hearing, as well as to the student's ability to move well in space, creative accommodations to the curriculum, materials, and instructional strategies can provide the necessary support to enable the student to learn. The use of assistive technology, both light and high technology, plays a critical role in meeting the unique learning needs of each student. The primary purpose of all accommodations and modifications is to increase the student's access to critical information and to ensure that the student has a means of indicating what has been learned. Such accommodations also add to the learning of classmates who do not have disabilities and, thus, benefit all students when they are educated together.

References

Abdala, C. (1999). Pediatric audiology: Evaluating infants. In D. Chen (Ed.), *Essential elements in early intervention: Visual impairment and multiple dis-* *abilities* (pp. 246–286). New York: American Foundation for the Blind Press.

Ashley, J., & Cates, D. (1992). Albinism: Educational

techniques for parents and teachers. *RE:view,* *24*(3), 30.

Bailey, B. R., & Head, D. R. (1993). Providing O & M services to children and youth with severe multiple disabilities. *RE:View, 25*(2), 57–66.

Barraga, N. C., & Erin, J. (1992). *Visual handicaps and learning.* Austin, TX: Pro-ED, Inc.

Batshaw, M. L., & Perret, Y. M. (1992). *Children with disabilities: A medical primer.* Baltimore, MD: Paul H. Brookes Publishing Co.

Campbell, M., & Truesdell, A. (2000). *Creative constructions: Technologies that make adaptive design accessible affordable, inclusive and fun.* Cambridge, MA: Campbell & Truesdell.

Chen, D. (1995). Who are young children whose multiple disabilities include visual impairment? In D. Chen & J. Dote-Kwan (Eds.), *Starting points: Instructional practices for young children whose multiple disabilities include visual impairment* (pp. 1–14). Los Angeles: Blind Childrens Center.

Chen, D. (1999). Understanding hearing loss: Implications for early intervention. In D. Chen (Ed.), *Essential elements in early intervention: Visual impairment and multiple disabilities* (pp. 207–245). New York: American Foundation for the Blind Press.

Crossman, H. L. (1991). Visual improvement in the multi-handicapped child with cortical visual impairment. *Transactions of the VIIth International Orthoptic Congress* (pp. 2.6–6.6). Nuremberg, Germany.

Dote-Kwan, J., & Chen, D. (1999). Developing meaningful interventions. In D. Chen (Ed.), *Essential elements in early intervention: Visual impairment and multiple disabilities* (pp. 287–336). New York: AFB Press.

Downing, J. E. (1999a). *Teaching communication skills to students with severe disabilities.* Baltimore, MD: Paul H. Brookes Publishing Co.

Downing, J. E. (1999b). Critical transitions: Educating young children in a typical preschool. In D. Chen (Ed.), *Essential elements in early intervention: Visual impairment and multiple disabilities* (pp. 378–419). New York: American Foundation for the Blind Press.

Downing, J. E. (2002). *Including students with severe and multiple disabilities in the typical classroom: Practical strategies for teachers* (2nd ed.). Baltimore, MD: Paul H. Brookes Publishing Co.

Downing, J. E., & Chen, D. (in press). Tactile strategies: Interacting with students who are blind and have severe disabilities. *TEACHING* Exceptional Children.

Dunn, W. (1996). The sensorimotor systems: A framework for assessment and intervention. In F. P.

Orelove & D. Sobsey (Eds.), *Educating children with multiple disabilities: A transdisciplinary approach* (pp. 35–78). Baltimore, MD: Paul H. Brookes Publishing Co.

Elder, P. S., & Goossens, C. (1996). *Engineering training environments for interactive augmentative communication: Strategies for adolescents and adults who are moderately/severely developmentally delayed.* (2nd ed.). Birmingham, AL. Southeast Augmentative Communication Conference Publications Clinician Series.

Ferguson, D. L., & Baumgart, D. (1991). Partial participation revisited. *Journal of The Association for Persons with Severe Handicaps, 16,* 218–227.

Gee, K. (1994). The learner who is deaf-blind: Constructing context from depleted sources. In K. Gee, M. Alwell, N. Graham, & L. Goetz (Eds.), *Facilitating informed and active learning for individuals who are deaf-blind in inclusive schools* (pp. 11–31). San Francisco: California Research Institute.

Giangreco, M. F., Edelman, S. W., & Nelson, C. (1998). Impact of planning for support services on students who are deaf-blind. *Journal of Visual Impairment and Blindness, 92*(1), 18–29.

Haring, T., Haring, N. G., Breen, C., Romer, L. T., & White, J. (1995). Social relationships among students with deaf-blindness and their peers in inclusive settings. In N. G. Haring & L. T. Romer (Eds.), *Welcoming students who are deaf-blind into typical classrooms: Facilitating school participation, learning, and friendships* (pp. 231–248). Baltimore, MD: Paul H. Brookes Publishing Co.

Heller, I., Manning, D., Pavur, D., & Wagner, K. (1998). Let's all sign! Enhancing language development in an inclusive preschool. *Teaching Exceptional Children, 30*(3), 50–53.

Hill, E. W., & Snook-Hill, M. (1996). Orientation and mobility. In M. C. Holbrook (Ed.), *Children with visual impairments: A parent's guide* (pp. 260–286). Bethesda, MD: Woodbine House.

Hoon, A. H., Jr. (1996). Visual impairments in children. In A. J. Capute & P. J. Accardo (Eds.), *Developmental disabilities in infancy and childhood. Vol. II: The spectrum of developmental disabilities* (2nd ed., pp. 461–478). Baltimore, MD: Paul H. Brookes Publishing Co.

Inge, K. J., & Shepherd, J. (1995). Assistive technology applications and strategies for school system personnel. In K. F. Flippo, K. J. Inge, & J. M. Barcus (Eds.), *Assistive technology: A resource for school, work, and community* (pp. 133–166). Baltimore, MD: Paul H. Brookes Publishing Co.

Jacobsen, K., Grottland, H., & Flaten, M. A. (2001). Assessment of visual acuity in relation to central nervous system activation in children with mental retardation. *American Journal on Mental Retardation, 106*, 145–150.

Luckner, J., Bowen, S., & Carter, K. (2001). Visual teaching strategies for students who are deaf or hard of hearing. *Teaching Exceptional Children, 33*(3), 38–44.

MacTurk, R. H., & Morgan, G. A. (1995). *Advances in applied developmental psychology: Vol. 12. Mastery motivation: Origins, conceptualizations, & applications.* Norwood, NJ: Ablex.

Mamer, L. (1999). Visual development in students with visual and additional impairments. *Journal of Visual Impairment and Blindness, 93*, 360–369.

Nelson, K. B. (1996). Epidemiology and etiology of cerebral palsy. In A. J. Capute & P. J. Accardo (Eds.), *Developmental disabilities in infancy and childhood. Vol. II: The spectrum of developmental disabilities* (2nd ed., pp. 73–79). Baltimore, MD: Paul H. Brookes Publishing Co.

Orel-Bixler, D. (1999). Clinical vision assessments for infants. In D. Chen (Ed.), *Essential elements in early intervention: Visual impairment and multiple disabilities* (pp. 107–156). New York: American Foundation for the Blind Press.

Orelove, F. P., & Sobsey, D. (1996). *Educating children with multiple disabilities: A transdisciplinary approach* (3rd ed.).Baltimore, MD: Paul H. Brookes Publishing Co.

Parette, H. P. Jr. (1997). Assistive technology devices and services. *Education and Training in Mental Retardation and Developmental Disabilities, 32*, 267–280.

Pellegrino, L. (1997). Cerebral palsy. In M. L. Batshaw (Ed.), *Children with disabilities* (4th ed., pp. 499–528). Baltimore, MD: Paul H. Brookes Publishing Co.

Prickett, J. G., & Welch, T. R. (1995). Adapting environments to support the inclusion of students who are deaf-blind. In N.G. Haring & L.T. Romer (Eds.), *Welcoming students who are deaf-blind into typical classrooms: Facilitating school participation, learning, and friendship* (pp. 171–193). Baltimore, MD: Paul H. Brookes Publishing Co.

Sacks, S. Z. (1998). Educating students who have visual impairments with other disabilities: An overview. In S. Z. Sacks & R. K. Silberman (Eds.), *Educating students who have visual impairments with other disabilities* (pp. 3–38). Baltimore, MD: Paul H. Brookes Publishing Co.

Schildroth, A., & Hotto, S. (1996). Annual survey of hearing impaired children and youth: 1991–92 school year. *American Annals of the Deaf, 138*(2), 163–171.

Silberman, R., K., Sacks, S. Z., & Wolfe, J. (1998). Instructional strategies for educating students who have visual impairments with severe disabilities. In S. Sacks & R. K. Silberman (Ed.), *Educating students who have visual impairments with other disabilities* (pp. 101–138). Baltimore, MD: Paul H. Brookes Publishing Co.

Smith, M., & Levack, N. (1996). *Teaching students with visual and multiple impairments: A resource guide.* Austin, TX: Texas School for the Blind and Visually Impaired.

Sobsey, D., & Wolf-Schein, E. (1996). Children with sensory impairments. In F. P. Orelove & D. Sobsey (Ed.), *Educating children with multiple disabilities: A transdisciplinary approach* (3rd ed., pp. 411–450). Baltimore, MD: Paul H. Brookes Publishing Co.

Topor, I. (1999). Functional vision assessments and early interventions. In D. Chen (Ed.), *Essential elements in early intervention: Visual impairment and multiple disabilities* (pp. 157–206). New York: American Foundation for the Blind Press.

Utley, B. L., Roman, C., & Nelson, G. L. (1998). Functional vision. In S. Z. Sacks & R. K. Silberman (Eds.), *Educating students who have visual impairments with other disabilities* (pp. 371–412). Baltimore, MD: Paul H. Brookes Publishing Co.

Wesson, M. D., & Maino, D. M. (1995). Oculovisual findings in children with Down syndrome, cerebral palsy, and mental retardation without specific etiology. In D. M. Maino (Ed.), *Diagnosis and management of special populations* (pp. 17–54). St. Louis, MO: Mosby Year Book

22

Managing the Needs of Students with Physical and Health Challenges in Inclusive Settings

Donna H. Lehr, Jill Greene, and Stephanie Powers

Objectives

After completing this chapter, the reader will be able to:

1. Describe the population of students considered to have physical and health challenges.
2. Describe the unique needs to be considered in providing educational programs for students with physical and health challenges.
3. Discuss considerations in providing physical access for students.
4. Discuss methods for ensuring the health and safety of students.
5. Describe the unique considerations related to accommodations and modifications of curriculum and instruction for students with physical and health challenges.
6. Describe types and purposes of low and high technology assistive devices for communication and environmental control.
7. Describe approaches to increase students' social and emotional access to general education programs.

Key Terms

Assistive technology
Emergency care
Health care access
Health care plan

Hygienic care
Instructional access
Physical access
Routine care

Social/emotional access
Specialized care
Universal precautions

The general focus of this textbook is on curriculum and instruction of students with significant disabilities in inclusive settings. As such, most of the chapters have included information useful to readers in the process of decisionmaking and program planning in specific areas of instruction for this population of students. This chapter differs in some important ways. Unlike the other chapters, it is not focused on the entire population of students with significant disabilities, but instead on a subgroup within the population: students with physical and health challenges. The information on educational program planning presented by authors in other chapters in this book is relevant for this subpopulation of students, but there are some unique areas that must be addressed to ensure that these students receive appropriate inclusive educational programming. This chapter includes a description of this population of students and a discussion of their needs. Also presented are considerations critical for meeting their needs within inclusive school settings.

Students with Physical and Health Challenges

Abby is an eight-year-old third grade student with severe mental retardation, low vision, profound deafness, asthma, and the need to obtain her primary nourishment through four gastronomy tube feedings each day, one while at school. Abby wears glasses and communicates using a combination of gestures, approximately 20 signs, and communication boards with Mayer-Johnson pictures and symbols. Due to her asthma, she uses her inhaler periodically during the day.

Troy is a twelve-year-old sixth grade student with Osteogenesis Imperfecta, also known as Brittle Bone disease. He weighs only 30 pounds and is quite short in stature. Troy is nonambulatory and uses a motorized wheelchair because his arms and legs have orthopedic deformities as a result of numerous bone fractures. Generally, his endurance is fair, but he often tires easily. Due to his short statue and small rib cage, Troy has difficulty breathing at times, particularly in warm environments. Other associated health issues include recurrent bronchitis in addition to chronic constipation with intermittent rectal prolapse.

Abby and Troy are just two examples of students with physical and health challenges. Others who might also be described as having physical and health challenges may present markedly different profiles; consequently, it is difficult to develop general descriptions of this population of students. There are two categories of disabilities described in the Individuals with Disabilities Act (IDEA) into which students with physical and health challenges are likely to fall. These include orthopedic impairments and other health impairments and are described in the following paragraphs:

(8) **Orthopedic impairment** means a severe orthopedic impairment that adversely affects a child's educational performance. The term includes impairments caused by congenital anomaly (e.g., clubfoot, absence of some member, etc.), impairments caused by disease (e.g., poliomyelitis, bone tuberculosis, etc.), and impairments from other causes (e.g., cerebral palsy, amputations, and fractures or burns that cause contractures).

(9) **Other health impairment** means having limited strength, vitality or alertness, including a heightened alertness to environmental stimuli, that results in limited alertness with respect to the educational environment, that

(i) Is due to chronic or acute health problems such as asthma, attention deficit disorder or attention deficit hyperactivity disorder, diabetes, epilepsy, a heart condition, hemophilia, lead poisoning, leukemia, nephritis, rheumatic fever, and sickle cell anemia; and

(ii) Adversely affects a child's educational performance.

(20 U.S.C. 1401(3)(A) and (B); 1401(26))

As a review of these categories reveals, there is tremendous diversity among the students who may be included. Additionally, conditions vary across and within students on a number of variables. That is to say, an individual's condition may be variable over time, and manifestation of the same condition may vary across individual students in terms of severity, chronicity, and multiplicity. For example, one student with cerebral palsy may be mildly affected by the disability, and the only accommodations necessary for the student to benefit from instruction are the use of a computer for note taking and preparation of written responses while another student, also with cerebral palsy, requires a full-time aide to assist the student with personal care needs, including toileting. A student with sickle cell anemia may experience relatively long periods of time in which the condition is in remission and episodic periods of intense pain. A student who eats through a gastrointestinal tube may experience long periods of time with good health and other periods of time in which infections may develop at the site of the stoma where the feeding tube is inserted. One student with Down syndrome may experience only reoccurring ear infections, common in students with Down syndrome, while others may have serious congenital heart defects, also commonly coexisting with Down syndrome. Bigge, Best and Heller (2001) pointed out one additional way in which students' physical and health challenges may differ: visibility of the disability to others that can affect the way in which the student and his or her family adjust to the presence of the disability and the ways in which others interact with the student.

What is in common among students with physical and health challenges is that the conditions "adversely affect child's educational performance" (20 U.S.C. 1401(3)(A) and (B); 1401(26)). This requires that educational program-planning teams engage in careful decisionmaking regarding service delivery to ensure each individual student's full access to education. Although public schools in the United States have had a long history of educating students with physical disabilities and health challenges, it has been only fairly recently that there has been an increase in the number of students with physical and health conditions served in general education settings; and an increase in the complexity of the needs of the students who are being educated (Lehr & Noonan, 1989; Heller, Fedrick, & Rithmire, 1997). This difference is attributed to the federal laws requiring education be provided to all students with disabilities; the increasing trend toward educating students with disabilities in least restrictive settings; the survival of children who in the past would not have survived periods of critical illness (Lehr & Noonan, 1989); and litigation that has clarified, and increased, school districts' roles in providing necessary health care services to students (Lehr, 1999; Cedar Rapids Community School District v. Garrett F, 1999). The consequence of these increases is that school district personnel have been facing considerable challenges as they develop comprehensive plans for providing appropriate educational programs in inclusive settings for students with physical and health challenges.

Access to Education for Students with Physical and Health Challenges

Full access to an inclusive education for students with physical and health needs requires that teams of school personnel, in collaboration with the student and his and her family, address four areas of need. These include physical access, health care access, instructional access, and social/emotional access. Planning in the area of physical access requires that considerations be given to the location of the delivery of educational services, transportation, and physical accessibility within the school building. In the area of health care, programs must include the delivery of safe, hygienic care and for the provision of specialized care specific to the needs of the students. Instructional access is facilitated through careful planning for the provision of technological supports and specialized instructional and curricular modifications necessary due to the unique physical and health needs of the students. Social/emotional access is facilitated through attention to the impact of physical or health disability on the students and the perception of others interacting with the students. Specific planning considerations for each of these areas will be addressed in greater detail later in this chapter.

Key to successful educational programs for students with physical and health challenges is the presence of knowledgeable personnel who work closely together with each student and his or her family to develop comprehensive plans for the students' instructional and related service needs. It is not always the case that the needed expertise is present among the team members. Because, as previously mentioned, the number of students with physical and health challenges has increased in recent years and the complexity of their needs have likewise increased, additional information and training must be secured by the team to enable them to meet the unique need of the students. This may be accomplished by either team members obtaining additional training or by adding people to the team. For example, during the past ten years, many school district teams have had to learn, for the first time, how to configure services for students who receive their nutrition through feeding tubes such as was the case for Abby. Other teams' members have had to learn how to provide clean intermittent catheterization for students with spina bifida who are unable to control the flow of urine from their bladders. District personnel have had to focus on the receipt of both general training designed to provide basic background information about specific physical and health conditions and specific training resulting in the acquisition of competence in the delivery of specific health care services (Porter, Haynie, Bierle, Caldwell, & Palfrey, 1997).

Special training is provided to Abby's team prior to the start of each school year. The district nurse, who supervises health care support for students with special health care needs in the system, provides this mandatory training to designated team members on how to administer the g-tube feedings and asthma medication. Additionally, the team is trained and certified in first aid and cardiopulmonary resuscitation (CPR).

Physical Access to Education

Although inclusion in general education settings is the most desired placement option for all students, including those with physical and health conditions, it is recognized that, at times, for some students with physical and health challenges attendance at school is not appropriate. A student with an acute illness and unstable medical condition may need constant and intensive medical care that can be provided only in a hospital facility. For a student with a compromised immune system, attendance at school during an outbreak of a disease such as chicken pox can be life threatening, and education at home is safest for the student.[1] With the exception of students in acute periods of illness, methods for the student to continue to be a part of the class to which he or she is assigned, even if the student must be in the hospital or at home for a period of time, can be arranged. Inclusion is defined by many as not just a placement in general education classroom, but rather an attitude related to a sense of belonging for all students. School personnel can work to create a sense of belonging for the student by having the student connected to the classroom through technology, including email, video cameras, and closed circuit television systems. For example, Troy must be at home for periods of time. During those times, he receives home tutoring for 2 hours each day, and, for the rest of the time, he can see and be seen in his classroom though the use of video cameras that are set up in his room and in the classroom. When Troy is able, he can watch and listen in to the classroom instruction, and he can participate in the discussions taking place.

Safe Transportation.   When it is appropriate to their health, students with physical and health challenges should be attending the school they would if they did not have a disability. To make this happen requires important decisions related to transportation and physical building access. To transport students with physical and health needs to school, consideration must be given to safety, access, and inclusion. The most desired option among programs that support inclusive practices is to apply the same principle regarding school attendance: Students with physical and health challenges should ride the same bus that they would if they did not have a disability. Safe transportation of students with physical disabilities and health conditions, however, requires taking into consideration the needs of the student and those of others. At times, it becomes difficult for school districts to make the necessary adaptations to multiple buses needed by students throughout the district and, consequently, may chose to equip specialized vans to transport those students. The preference, however, as previously stated, is to transport students in vehicles where they will have opportunities to interact with their nondisabled peers.

Some students are able to transfer or be transferred from their wheelchairs to bus or van seats. For other students, different decisions may need to be made regarding the use of "restraints, positioning students into them, and securing the restraints into vehicles" (American Academy of Pediatrics, 1999, p. 1). Methods for securing specialized equipment must also be arranged, so in the event of an accident, walkers, oxygen tanks, and so forth, do not become dangerous projectiles (American Academy of Pediatrics, 1999).

Additional considerations in the safe transport of students focus on the provision of routine and emergency care during the period of time that the student is on board. In addition to general first aid training, drivers typically receive additional training and information regarding procedures to follow in the event of medical emergencies for specific students for whom they have responsibility transporting. During their bus ride, some students are also accompanied by school personnel trained to provide routine care and emergency medical care. For example, Troy is transported to school on a wheelchair-accessible van. The driver has been trained to secure his wheelchair, which features a specially designed harness. The driver has also been trained in procedures for carrying him off the bus in the case of an accident.

Accessible School Buildings. When ensuring physical access for students with physical and health challenges, movement into and around the school building must also be considered. Specific requirements that must be met by school districts are specified in the Americans with Disabilities Act (ADA) of 1990. Regulations focus on architectural structures, including exterior routes of travel, ramps, lifts, entrances, lobbies and corridors, elevators, classrooms, toilet facilities, assembly rooms, cafeterias, libraries, and other locations within the school. Specifications are also made regarding the heights of tables, door handles, drinking fountains, and so forth. (Office of Civil Rights, 1998). Figure 22.1

FIGURE 22.1 *A sampling of questions taken from the Office of Civil Rights'* **Self-Evaluation Guide for Public Elementary and Secondary School (1998)** *designed for school-district use to determine their compliance with the ADA.*

Passenger Loading Zone
Is there an access aisle 60 inches wide by 20 feet long adjacent and parallel to the vehicle
   pull-up space?
Is the slope of the access aisle and the pull-up space no more than 1:50?

Exterior Route of Travel
Is there at least one accessible route of travel from public transportation stops, accessible
   passenger loading zones, public streets, and sidewalks to the accessible entrance?
Is the surface of the curb ramp stable, firm, and slip resistant?

Ramps
Do ramps and landings with dropoffs have walls, railings, projecting surfaces, or curbs at least 2
   inches high to prevent people from slipping off the ramp?

Stairs
Are stair treads no less than 11 inches?

Lifts
Are controls between 15 and 48 inches high (up to 54 inches if each side is possible)?
Are the controls operable with one hand and without tight grasping, pinching, or twisting of
   the wrist?

Entrances
Can accessible doors be opened without too much force (maximum is 5 pounds for interior
   doors)?

Rooms and Spaces
Are at least 50 percent of drinking fountains, but at least one, on each floor accessible?

includes a sampling of the questions taken from a guide that can be used by school districts to determine their compliance with regulations based on the ADA.

Physical access for this population of students also goes beyond the obvious arrangements that must be made for students to get in and around the building and to reach tables and cafeteria food. For students dependent upon electrical equipment, such as suctioning pumps to clear their airways or ventilators to aid their breathing, structural modifications to school facilities may be necessary. Additional electrical outlets may need to be installed, and electrical systems may need to be upgraded so that fuses are not blown. Easier access to water for care providing may be necessary, as may be the ability to adjust room temperature and classroom design (Wadsworth & Knight, 1999).

Accommodations for Troy's access to his school building include a temperature-regulated classroom, use of the elevator, and specially designed adapted desks and tables allowing full use of all classroom resources. Occasionally, after a severe fracture, a hospital bed has been set up in his classroom so Troy can safely return to school when he is unable to remain seated in his wheelchair for an extended period of time.

One more area that must be addressed related to physical access for students with physical and health challenges is that of appropriate physical positioning in specialized equipment. As Bigge, Best, and Heller (2001) stated, "the importance of positioning cannot be understated. The individual's position will always effect [sic] the quality and precision of the individual's movement and the ability to accomplish tasks. That effect is either positive or negative, depending on its appropriateness" (p. 197). Readers are referred to Chapter 21 in this book for more information regarding positioning and handling procedures for students with motor impairments.

Health Care Access

While the safety and health of all students should be of utmost concern to school personnel, when the students for whom they are responsible have physical and health challenges, additional attention must be pay to their general and specific healthcare needs. In the follow sections, both the areas of needs and recommended practices are reviewed.

Routine Health Care.   Students with physical and health challenges require school district personnel to be more stringent in providing what should be routine health care and a greater range of health care services than that which is typically provided in school settings. Although general first aid and CPR skills should be within the repertoire of all school personnel, it is not a general requirement for certification or employment as a teacher or administrator. However, there is an increased chance that educators working with students with physical and health challenges will need these skills. Consequently, the presence of students with health challenges in inclusive schools necessitates comprehensive training for all school personnel in these important areas.

Similarly, although hygienic care practices should be followed in all settings in which children are congregated for care and education, there are several reasons why more careful attention must be paid to effective practices where students with physical and health challenges are educated (Lehr & Noonan, 1989; Orelove & Sobsey, 1996). Some students have compromised respiratory systems that make them particularly vulnerable to diseases, even the common cold. Some students, as a result of their disabilities, lack control of their body functions and must receive assistance in such care, including nose blowing and bowel and bladder elimination. To prevent transmission of diseases such as the common cold and more serious diseases such as hepatitis B, extra attention must be paid to the handling of body secretions. The American Academy of Pediatrics (1999) has emphasized the importance of hand washing in school settings to prevent the transmission of diseases. In addition, they recommend the use of gloves when contact with blood or blood-containing body fluids may occur. Guidelines focus on procedures to use when toileting or changing diapers of students, when feeding students, when dealing with nasal hygiene, and when providing first aid. Specific procedures for hygienic care providing can be found in resources, such as the one on the Web site of the United States (U.S.) Department of Public Health (1996). An example of the recommendations provided for hand washing can be viewed in Figure 22.2.

The Centers for Disease Control (CDC) and the American Academy of Pediatrics recommend the use of universal precautions to prevent the transmission of diseases in school settings.

> "Universal precautions," as defined by CDC, "are a set of precautions designed to prevent transmission of human immunodeficiency virus (HIV), hepatitis B virus (HBV), and other blood borne pathogens when providing first aid or health care. Under universal

FIGURE 22.2   *Hand Washing Instructions*

How To Wash Hands

- Always use warm, running water and a mild, preferably liquid, soap. Antibacterial soaps may be used, but are not required. Premoistened cleansing towelettes do not effectively clean hands and do not take the place of hand washing.
- Wet the hands and apply a small amount (dime to quarter size) of liquid soap to hands.
- Rub hands together vigorously until a soapy lather appears and continue for at least 15 seconds. Be sure to scrub between fingers, under fingernails, and around the tops and palms of the hands.
- Rinse hands under warm running water. Leave the water running while drying hands.
- Dry hands with a clean, disposable (or single use) towel, being careful to avoid touching the faucet handles or towel holder with clean hands.
- Turn the faucet off using the towel as a barrier between your hands and the faucet handle.
- Discard the used towel in a trash can lined with a fluid-resistant (plastic) bag. Trash cans with foot-pedal operated lids are preferable.
- Consider using hand lotion to prevent chapping of hands. If using lotions, use liquids or tubes that can be squirted so that the hands do not have direct contact with container spout. Direct contact with the spout could contaminate the lotion inside the container.
- When assisting a child in hand washing, either hold the child (if an infant) or have the child stand on a safety step at a height at which the child's hands can hang freely under the running water. Assist the child in performing all of the above steps and then wash your own hands.

Source: From U.S. Department of Public Health and Centers for Disease Control and Prevention [1996]. *The ABCs of safe and healthy childcare: A handbook for child care providers*: Washington, D.C.: author.

precautions, blood and certain body fluids of all patients are considered potentially infectious for HIV, HBV and other blood-borne pathogens" (*www.cdc.gov/ncidod/hip/Blood/ UNIVERSA.HTM*).

Specialized Healthcare.   General hygienic care practices are but one part of the process of creating a safe and healthy environment for students with physical and health challenges. For some students, more specialized care must be planned for and provided, such as tube feeding, ventilator care, and tracheostomy suctioning. What follows are brief descriptions of some of the care procedures increasingly being provided in school to familiarize the reader with these types of health care services.

- **Clean intermittent catheterization (CIC)**: Involves the insertion of a tube (catheter) through the urethra into the bladder to reduce bladder pressure and to drain urine. It is necessary for those students unable to control the flow of urine from their bladder.
- **Tube feeding**: The provision of nutrition through a tube that goes directly into a student's stomach. It is necessary when oral feeding is unsafe or insufficient for adequate nutrition.
  Gastronomy tubes (g-tubes) are inserted into a stoma on the abdomen, and nasogastric tubes are inserted through a student's nose into the throat and down to the stomach; and jejunostomy tubes (j tubes) are inserted into the student's small intestines.
- **Respiratory care**: The provision of a range of procedures necessary to support a student's breathing. Care providing includes respiratory monitoring, the administration of oxygen, and monitoring and maintenance of equipment, including suctioning machines, nebulizers, and ventilators (respirators).
  Supplemental oxygen is provided through a nasal cannnula or oxygen mask to the student's nose and mouth or through a tracheostomy, a surgical opening directly into a student's windpipe.
  Mechanical ventilation is provided to students who are limited in their ability to, or are unable to, breathe independently. Different types of ventilators are used that provide various amounts of support for the student.

Provision of these health care procedures requires that educational planning teams develop comprehensive health care plans for each individual student that typically becomes a part of the student's Individualized Educational Program (IEP). Specified in the plans are the nature of the services to be provided, including a detailed description of the procedure protocol; the frequency with which the services should be provided; identification of persons responsible for providing the health care services; records of dates for staff training and monitoring; and indicators of need for emergency care. A sample health plan for Abby can be viewed in Figure 22.3.

It must be noted that there is great variability throughout the country regarding who (school nurse, teachers, health care aide, paraprofessional, and therapist) provides different health care services to students. Decisions are based on a number of factors, including state laws regarding licensing required for implementation of procedures, professional preferences, family preferences, and, ideally, students' preferences (Lehr, 1996).

FIGURE 22.3   *Sample Health Care Plan*

Health Care Plan
Name   Abby   *Date*   8/25/02

Health Care Need   Gastrostomy tube feeding, breathing monitoring for asthma

Protocol   Attached

Plan developed by   Mother, teacher, school nurse, in consultation with physician

Frequency   Tube feeding during scheduled lunch; breathing monitoring-ongoing

Responsible Staff
    Feeding: school nurse, special education teacher, aide
    Breathing monitoring: all

Training
    Dates 8/28   *Trainer* school nurse   *Topic* general first aid
        Trainees special education teacher, general education teacher, aide
    Dates 8/29   *Trainer* school nurse   *Topic* CPR
        Trainees special education teacher, general education teacher, aide
    Dates 8/30   *Trainer* school nurse   *Topic* general first aid
        Trainees special education teacher, aide

Monitoring
    Dates 9/15   *Trainer* school nurse   *Topic* general first aid
        Trainees special education teacher, general education teacher, aide
    Dates 10/4   *Trainer* school nurse   *Topic* CPR
        Trainees special education teacher, general education teacher, aide
    Dates 9/4, 10/4   *Trainer* school nurse   *Topic* general first aid
        Trainees special education teacher, aide

Emergency Indicators: labored breathing, diarrhea, g-tube comes out

Emergency Procedures: See Emergency Care Plan

    Prior to Troy starting sixth grade, his mother was concerned that his middle school only had one nurse for the 1,400 students who attend the school and that this nurse may not be available at times when Troy needed specialized health care assistance. The school district addressed his mother's concerns by hiring a registered nurse (RN) to work directly with him. The RN assists Troy with toileting, dispensing his medications, transferring and positioning him in and out of his wheelchair, and providing general medical monitoring.

Additionally, the RN assists Troy with setting up class materials, preparing his lunch, and navigating the school building by operating the elevator and opening doors as needed. In order to maximize staff resources in the school, the RN assists in the school nurse's office when Troy is absent.

Emergency Care.   Plans to be implemented in the event of an emergency are also important to students' safety in schools. Most schools have in place procedures for providing emergency medical care, and, when students with physical and health challenges attend these schools, the plans must be reviewed with each individual student in mind. The American Academy of Pediatrics' "Guidelines for Emergency Medical Care in School" (American Academy of Pediatrics, 2001) includes recommendations that procedures for addressing emergencies include the following:

- Identification of people responsible for making decisions regarding emergency care that should be provided.
- Emergency plans should specify who should be responsible for contacting that person(s).
- Design of individual emergency plans for those students for whom it is anticipated might need them.
- Education of all appropriate personnel about emergency response guidelines.
- Education of all school personnel in the use of universal precautions.

Specific plans must also be designed for the evacuation of students unable to walk down stairs in the event of an emergency; plans must be in place for emergency generators in the event of an electrical outage for students who are dependent on electrical equipment, such as suctioning machines and ventilators to aid their breathing; and plans must be in place for the safe evacuation of students who use oxygen in the event of a fire. Collaboration with fire departments to design specific emergency plans for individual students have proven to be very helpful for school districts.

Instructional Access

After arrangements are made to ensure that (a) students are able to physically access education and (b) the students' routine and specialized health care needs will be met while at school and plans are in place in the event of an emergency, attention can shift to ensuring that instructional access is arranged. The focus of many of the other chapters in this book is on the topic of curriculum content, adaptations, and accommodations for students with severe disabilities; what is included in this section are special considerations relevant to students with physical and health challenges. Specifically, the focus is on the use of technology and accommodations necessary due to periods of time in which students miss educational opportunities.

Assistive Technology.   Both the Technology-Related Assistance for Individuals with Disabilities Act of 1988 and IDEA encourage schools to provide assistive technology services to students with disabilities. Assistive technology devices are defined in IDEA as being "any item, piece of equipment or product system, whether acquired commercially off the shelf, modified, or customized, that is used to increase, maintain, or improve the functional capabilities of a child with a disability" (US U.S.C., 1401 § 602[1]). Assistive technology can enable or enhance the learning process, communication, mobility, and environmental control. A great array of technological devices are available to aid students, ranging from what some call "low tech" devices, such as padded pencil grips that help a student hold a pencil correctly and Post-it® notes attached to pages to make them easier to turn to "high tech" devices including highly sophisticated computers that "read" eye movements directed toward a screen on which words are displayed, which is then translated into synthesized speech.

A number of variables must be considered when determining if a student should use assistive technology. In the Wisconsin Assistive Technology Initiative Consideration Guide (Reed & Best, 2001) planning teams are asked to consider the following questions:

- What task is it that we want this student to do that s/he is unable to do at a level that reflects his or her skills/abilities?
- Is the student currently able to complete the task with special strategies or accommodations?
- Is there available assistive technology (either devices, tools, hardware, or software) that could be used to address this task?
- Would the use of assistive technology help the student perform this skill more easily or efficiently, in the least restrictive environment, or perform it successfully with less personal assistance? (p. 156)

Two important cautions regarding the use of assistive technology are that of being wary of technology seduction and being mindful of normalization. Technology seduction refers to the lure of sophisticated technology and the selection of that technology when a much simpler, lower tech, and often much less expensive, option would be as, or possibly more, effective than the higher tech option. Normalization, in this context, refers to the use of materials that are most like those to be used by others or those that are the most natural in appearance. For example, mechanical page turners and rubber thumbs can both aid a person in turning pages of a book, yet the cost differential is great. Additionally, it is much more normal looking to turn a page with a rubber thumb than with a page turner, and the use of the higher tech option can serve to further differentiate a student from his or her peers. Another example is the use of a computer display on which there are two items from which a student can make a selection when the same selection can be made from a communication board that can be moved within the room and throughout the school. Obviously, the computer is a more complex and expensive option, and having methods of communication available wherever the student is located is much more typical, or normal, than having a means of communication only when positioned in front of a computer.

With careful decisionmaking resulting in a match between technology and students' needs, both low and high tech devices can support instruction in many ways. Through the use of a scanner and a computer with a speech synthesizer, written materials can be changed from text to speech, changing the requirements from reading to listening and markedly modifying the skills necessary on the part of the learner to access the information being presented.

In the past two decades, numerous options have been developed to aid students with physical and health challenges who also have communication challenges. Students with motor impairments whose speech is also affected can use voice output devices that can "speak for them." Students who have difficulty holding a pencil can be provided with low tech adaptive grips or high tech computers that enable them to dictate their messages into a microphone attached to a computer that then translates the spoken words into written text.

Students who are unable to use a keyboard to enter information into a computer can use a mouth stick to touch on-screen keyboards or a switch with an on-screen scanner, and select desired words as they appear. Students, for whom typing is physically exerting, can use word prediction programs that reduce the amount of keystrokes necessary to compose text.

Advances in technology have also improved mobility options for students with physical and health challenges in several significant ways. For students who are dependent on electrical equipment like a suctioning machine and mechanical ventilator, technological advances have resulted in smaller, lighter weight, portable, battery-operated equipment that has permitted students to move about their environments untethered by electric cords. Inclusion prior to these improvements was greatly restricted. For example, Abby's entire g-tube feeding takes approximately 90 minutes. During lunch, she sits at a cafeteria table with her peers. Abby does not need to sit in a designated area, only near an electrical outlet where her pump can be plugged into for the 30-minute lunch period. After the designated lunch period, Abby is able move about the school with her peers while she continues with her g-tube feeding because her pump can be battery operated. Two fully charged sets of batteries are readily available so Abby can be mobile and walk throughout the school.

Mobility aids for students with physical and health challenges include walkers, strollers, wheelchairs, and scooters, both manual and powered by a variety of switches operated by hand, head, or mouth. According to Best, Bigge and Reed (2001) they are designed to "provide a means of movement with the greatest amount of independence, using the best quality of movement patterns in the most efficient manner" (p. 195).

Assistive devices designed to enable a student to interact with objects in his or her environment can also be considered critical to a student's inclusive education. Independence in holding objects is facilitated through the use of adaptations such as handles and padding, designed to make objects easier to hold. Materials such as Dycem or clamps can be used to stabilize objects making it easier for students to manipulate them. A variety of switches, including those operated by students' hands, arms, elbows, heads, and feet by pulling, pushing, puffing, and squeezing (Best, Bigge & Reed, 2001) can be used to aid a student in operating electrical equipment including lights, televisions, stereos, blenders, and so forth.

Curriculum Compacting.   For some students with physical and health care challenges, planning teams must make adjustments to students' programs due to intermittent absences from their classrooms throughout the school day or from school for extended periods of time. Reduced endurance or recurring illness may disrupt the flow of learning for those students. Health care treatments may need to be scheduled at times that conflict with the scheduled time for instruction in specific subjects. Maintaining continuity of curriculum becomes a challenge to educational planning teams. Decisions must be made about how to extract critical components from the curriculum, compact, and deliver them in a manner that enables the student to keep up with the curriculum. In some schools, before or after school tutoring or between times are used as catch-up time.

Social Emotional Access

Strong and Sandoval (1999) pointed out that there is a misconception that removal of physical barriers is the only thing that has to be addressed to enable the inclusion of students with physical and health care challenges into general education settings. What they refer to as non-physical barriers may also need to be overcome if inclusion is to be successful for these students.

Knowledge, skills, and attitudes on the part of individual students and their peers can all influence the acceptance of students with disabilities by their nondisabled peers. Chapter 11 in this text includes a general discussion of methods for facilitating interactions with peers during general education activities. Included in this chapter are some unique things to consider that may affect the nature of the interactions when students have physical and health challenges.

Both the student with physical and health challenges and his or her peers need information about the cause of the disability, the characteristics, implications and treatment, and reasons for the treatments. That information should be provided through a variety of means. These may include informational sessions, discussions, and through infusion of information about disabilities into the ongoing curriculum. Regardless of what information is provided to the students, however, it is likely that the behaviors they observe in others will have the greatest impact on their attitudes about the nature of physical and health challenges. Consider, for example, the different impression that may be formed when a student's ongoing need for nasal suctioning is treated as routine care as contrasted with treatment provided as though it is a medical emergency. Consider the potential impact of the difference between considering a student as being *sick because they are fed with a feeding tube* as contrasted with the notion of a student being *healthy and thriving because of being fed through a feeding tube* that permits the student to receive sufficient nutrition. For many students, the feeding tube results in the students maintaining good health, and they are able to receive adequate nutrition and not be subjected to pneumonia due to aspiration. Last, consider the potential influence of students viewing a nurse in the classroom with the sole responsibility of responding to an individual's health care needs in contrast to a staff member whose primary responsibility it is to monitor a students' health status and provide necessary care, but also provide instructional support to all students in the classroom. These impressions that students and staff form have the potential for greatly influencing the acceptance of a student as a part of the class.

A lack of maintaining a student's sense of presence in the classroom when he or she is absent for period of time, as previously mentioned, can also be a barrier to inclusion. As Brown et al. (1989) pointed out some time ago, it is the longitudinal interactions between students with and without disabilities that affect the extent to which students without disabilities get to know students with disabilities. Maintaining the student's presence as a classmate can be key.

Many students with physical and health challenges must be provided with either routine care related to eating and toileting, or specific care of tube feeding, respiratory care, or catheterization. School personnel must take into consideration the effect of this care on the student's own perception of competence and the perception of others. Independence and dignity are associated with personal care. Students who have all procedures done to them are likely to be perceived differently than a student who provides his or her own care, at least partially participates in his or her own care, or directs his or his own care, if he or she is physically able to provide the care themselves.

The Division of Physical and Health Disabilities of the Council for Exceptional Children (1999) stated their position that

> "specialized health care procedures should be viewed as self-help skills or independent living skills which students should be taught to promote their independence. Specialized health care procedures and other health management skills should be considered for IEP goals and objectives. These IEP objectives could target independent performance, partial participation, directing someone else in performance or knowledge of the task" (p. 1).

Summary

Students with physical and health challenges are increasingly being provided with education in general education settings. For this population of students, as for others, successful inclusion will be the result of teams of school personnel collaborating closely with students and their families to plan, implement, and evaluate IEPs. Unique to this population of students are the comprehensive plans that must also be designed to address physical, health care, instructional, and social emotional access for these students.

References _____

American Academy of Pediatrics. (1999). Transporting children with special health care needs. *Pediatrics, 104*(4), 988–992.

American Academy of Pediatrics. (2001). Guidelines for emergency medical care in schools. *Pediatrics, 107*(2), 435–436.

Americans with Disabilities Act (ADA). (1990). (PL 101-336), 42, U.S.C. § 12101, et. seq.

Best, S., Bigge, J., & Reed, P. (2001). In Bigge, J. L., Best, S., & Heller, K. W. (Eds.). *Teaching individuals with physical, health or multiple disabilities* (pp. 195–228). Upper Saddle River, NJ: Prentice-Hall.

Bigge, J. L., Best, S., & Heller, K. W. (2001). *Teaching individuals with physical, health or multiple disabilities*. Upper Saddle River, NJ: Prentice-Hall.

Brown, L. Long, E., Udvari-Solner, L., Van Deventer, P., Ahlgren, C., Johnson, F., Gruenwald L., & Jorgensen, J. (1989). The home school: Why students with severe intellectual disabilities must attend the schools of their brothers, sisters, friends, and neighbors. *JASH, 14*(1), 1–7.

Brown, R. T., & DuPaul, G. J. (1999). Introduction to the mini-series: Promoting school success in children with chronic medical conditions. *The Journal of School Psychology Review, 28*(2), 175–181.

Centers for Disease Control. (*www.cdc.gov/ncidod/hip/Blood/UNIVERSA.HTM*).

Cedar Rapids Community School District v. Garrett F., No. 96-1793 (1999).

Division of Physical and Health Disabilities Critical Issues and Leadership Committee. (1999).

Position statement on specialized health care procedures. *Physical Disabilities: Education and Related Services, 18*(1), 1–2.

Heller, K. W., Fedrick, L., & Rithmire, N. M. (1997). Special health care procedures in the schools. *Physical Disabilities: Education and Related Services, 14*(2), 5–22.

Individuals with Disabilities Education Act (IDEA), 20 U.S.C. 140o et. seq.

Lehr, D. (1996). People with complex health care needs. In D. H. Lehr & Brown, (Eds.), *Persons with disabilities who challenge the system.* Baltimore, MD: Paul H. Brookes Publishing Co.

Lehr, D. (1999). U.S. Supreme Court requires school district to pay for nursing services for student with complex health care needs. *TASH Newsletter,* 25(3) 28–30.

Lehr, D. H., & Noonan, M. (1989). Issues in the education of students with complex health care needs. In F. Brown & D. Lehr (Eds.). *Persons with profound disabilities: Issues and practices.* (pp. 139–158). Baltimore, MD: Paul H. Brookes Publishing Co.

Orelove, F. P., & Sobsey, D. (1996). *Educating children with multiple disabilities: A transdisciplinary approach.* Baltimore, MD: Paul H. Brookes Publishing Co.

Office of Civil Rights (1998). *Compliance with the Americans with Disabilities Act: A self-evaluation guide for public elementary and secondary schools.* Washington, D.C.: U.S. Department of Education.

Porter, S., Haynie, M., Bierle, T., Caldwell, T.H., & Palfrey, J.S. (1997). *Children and youth assisted by medical technology in educational settings: Guidelines for care.* Baltimore, MD: Paul H. Brookes Publishing Co.

Reed, P., & Best, S. (2001) Assessment for assistive technology. In Bigge, J. L., Best, S., & Heller, K. W. (Eds.). *Teaching individuals with physical, health or multiple disabilities* (pp. 149–194). Upper Saddle River, NJ: Prentice-Hall.

Strong, K., & Sandoval, J. (1999). Mainstreaming children with a neuromuscular disease: A map of concerns. *Exceptional Children, 65*(3), 353–366.

Technology-Related Assistance for Individuals with Disabilities Act of 1988, PL 100-407.

U.S. Department of Public Health and Centers for Disease Control and Prevention. (1996). *The ABCs of safe and healthy childcare: A handbook for child care providers*: Washington, D.C.: Author.

Wadsworth, D. E., & Knight, D. (1999). Preparing the inclusion classroom for students with special physical and health needs. *Intervention in the School and Clinic, 34*(3), 170–175.

Endnote

1. There is a difference between an acute illness and chronic illness. An acute illness is marked by a period of intense discomfort and medical instability with an accompanying need for intensive medical care. A chronic illness is one that persists for a long period of time, which may be marked by periods of acute illness and/or periods of medical stability.

Appendix A

Student Profiles

Diane Lea Ryndak

Including Mark in Kindergarten

Student Description Before Inclusion in Kindergarten

Mark, a five-year-old boy with severe autistic behaviors, had been in a self-contained preschool program for three years. At the end of his preschool experiences, Mark was described as avoiding physical contact with others, especially resisting any contact adults made to assist him in participating in structured activities. He preferred to play alone, usually looking at picture books or manipulating objects in a stereotypic manner. Mark tended to continue the same activity until repeatedly given directions to change activities. During attempts to interact, Mark avoided eye contact with both adults and peers. While he was capable of verbal communication in one word utterances, Mark expressed his wants and needs through gesturing and pointing. When asked a question, Mark either gave no response or repeated the last phrase he heard. At times, Mark attended well to some classroom activities, particularly coloring and music. Mark's family seldom took him into the community because of his inappropriate behavior, lack of attending to directions, and resistance to physical guidance to ensure appropriate and safe behaviors.

Upon transitioning from preschool services to kindergarten, the education team decided that he would be included in an all-day general education kindergarten with assistance from a classroom aide, as well as special education and related services support. The team completed the curriculum content identification process and yielded the following results.

Prioritized Results from Inventories

Family Inventory
1. Allow for physical contact when in need of assistance
2. Initiate activities of preference instead of waiting for parental cues
3. Increase use of current verbal communication skills, and expand both vocabulary and use of new skills

4. Increase the time attending to tasks the instructor identified
5. Use the toilet independently instead of needing occasional assistance
6. Express feelings verbally or in an appropriate physical manner

Community Inventory.   The education team looked only at the school and Mark's home environments when completing the community inventory. The education team wanted to focus initial instruction on school and home environments because (1) five-year-old children spend the majority of their day and week in those environments, and (2) Mark's family life limited his current interaction with other community environments. The team hoped that demonstration of skill acquisition at school and home would result in a higher probability of his family allowing him to interact with the community.

1. Increase expression of needs and wants across environments through verbal language, rather than pointing and gesturing
2. Initiate play across environments and play with peers in school
3. Across environments, verbalize to an adult his need to use the bathroom and use it independently

Peer Inventory
1. Interact with classmates throughout the day
2. Initiate and engage in conversation with peers, teachers, and significant others
3. Listen to the kindergarten teacher when she is reading a story
4. Socialize after school with friends

General Education Settings Inventory
1. Attend to instructional activities with reminders when in large (more than ten) and small (less than ten) groups
2. Perform a classroom job (e.g., take attendance to the office, clean erasers)
3. Go through the lunch line, select desired items, pay, and sit with friends in the cafeteria

General Education Curriculum Inventory
1. Speak in complete sentences
2. Cut, color, and paste when given step-by-step instruction
3. Write, pronounce, and say the sounds associated with letters of the alphabet
4. Write and name the numerals zero through ten

Annual Goals Derived from Inventories
Goal 1   Mark will increase communication skills *from* the use of gestures and one-word utterances *to* verbally expressing himself in complete sentences across kindergarten activities, by the end of the school year.

Goal 2   Mark will increase social interaction skills across kindergarten activities *from* (1) avoiding eye contact, (2) not responding, and (3) resisting physical assistance *to* (1) initiating interactions, (2) responding to directions and questions, and (3) participating in activities with adults and peers, by the end of the school year.

Goal 3   Mark will increase toileting skills *from* occasionally wetting himself *to* using bathrooms independently during waking hours, by the end of the school year.

Summary of Progress on Goals During First Year of Inclusion

Goal 1   Increase communication skills
                Mark uses fragmented sentences in response to peer and adult conversation during structured and unstructured classroom activities.

Goal 2   Increase social interaction skills
                Mark reaches for the hand of an adult or peer when he needs assistance. He sings with the class, makes cards for classmates' birthdays, and performs assigned classroom jobs with peer partners. When an adult or peer initiates interaction with him, Mark usually makes eye contact and responds appropriately to the interaction.

Goal 3   Independent toileting skills
                Mark uses the bathroom during scheduled times throughout the school day, rarely having toileting accidents.

Student Description After Inclusion in Kindergarten

After completion of kindergarten, Mark often interacts independently with his peers during lessons and free time. Mark has begun to express his desires without prompting and to respond to questions using short phrases or fragmented sentences, although a large amount of his communication still involves gesturing and pointing. He initiates physical contact with others in a socially appropriate manner and does not resist when teachers and peers who are known to him make purposeful physical contact. When he needs assistance, Mark reaches for the hand of an adult or peer. He continues to attend to classroom activities, and he has increased dramatically his active participation in those activities. Because of his more appropriate behaviors, increase in following directions, and acceptance of physical contact, Mark's family takes him into the community on a regular basis to participate in family activities. Table A.1 summarizes Mark's changes.

Including Tony in Fifth Grade

Student Description Prior to Inclusion in Fifth Grade

Tony, a ten-year-old with spastic quadriplegic cerebral palsy, scoliosis, and profound mental retardation, had received no educational services until he was eight years old due to family issues and medical concerns. He cried about 90 percent of the day, wore a body jacket, received a great deal of physical and occupational therapy, had very little volitional movement in only one arm, was not toilet trained, and was fed through a gastrointestinal

TABLE A.1   *Mark's Summarized Changes*

Skill Area	Before Inclusion	After Inclusion
Physical contact with peers and adults	Avoided contact; resisted physical assistance	Initiates physical contact in socially acceptable manner; initiates hand touching for assistance; accepts physical assistance from known adult or peer
Involvement with peers in play and class activities	Played alone; looked at books and objects stereotypically	Independently interacts with peers; actively participates in classroom activities
Latency	Continued in same activity; did not respond to directions	Responds to directions; attends to class activities as they occur
Communication	Avoided eye contact with adults and peers; could verbally communicate in one-word utterances but usually used gestures or pointing; did not respond to questions; repeated last phrase	Makes eye contact with adults and peers; uses short phrases, along with gestures and pointing, when initiating requests; responds to questions with short phrases; sings
Attention	Attended to classroom activities at times, especially coloring and music; did not attend to directions	Performs classroom jobs with peer partners; follows directions most of the time; attends to tasks for up to ten minutes
Community involvement	Seldom taken into community	Participates in family activities in community on regular basis
Self-care	Occasionally wet self	Rarely has accident; follows schedule

tube. When initially receiving educational services, Tony's school district had placed him in a self-contained class with periodic opportunities for him to participate in third grade activities. His IEP goals had consisted of (1) reducing crying, (2) responding correctly to yes-or-no questions, and (3) beginning oral motor control for sucking and chewing.

Tony entered a fourth grade general education class, in spite of his lack of progress on IEP goals, almost constant crying, and numerous physical and medical needs. His educational program now focused on decreasing crying, increasing communication skills through visual responses to yes-or-no questions or object identification, improving tolerance of community-based instruction, and addressing health issues. Upon transitioning to fifth grade, Tony's education team implemented the curriculum identification process. It yielded the following results.

Prioritized Results from Inventories

Family Inventory
1. Increase communication skills
2. Increase use of adaptive switches
3. Partially participate in daily living activities
4. Express need to use the bathroom
5. Improve lip and mouth closure for eating and drinking

Community Inventory
1. Partially participate in community activities
2. Increase amount of time spent in the community

Peer Inventory
1. Collect and trade sports cards with peers
2. Increase interactions with peers through an Introtalker

General Education Settings Inventory
1. Participate as fully as possible in gym, art, music, and library
2. Partially participate in cooking activities with a peer during home and careers class
3. Take daily medication without resistance

General Education Curriculum Inventory
1. Recognize numbers 0 to 9
2. Indicate need for attention and make choices through eye gaze or switch use
3. Decrease crying and increase listening skills
4. Attend to filmstrips and movies
5. Answer concrete yes-or-no questions

Goals Derived from Inventories

Goal 1   Tony will participate as fully as possible in all fifth grade activities, including all academic areas and specials, by the end of the school year.

Goal 2   Tony will increase expressive communication skills *from* using zero symbols on his Introtalker *to* using four symbols, by the end of the school year.

Goal 3   Tony will increase the amount of time he tolerates community-based instruction without crying *from* an average of fifteen minutes *to* an average of sixty minutes, by the end of the school year.

Goal 4   Tony will operate electronic equipment (i.e., pencil sharpener; blender; tape player; computer) with an adaptive switch, *from* using it once a day *to* using it three times a day, by the end of the school year.

Summary of Progress on Goals

Goal 1   Increase participation in fifth grade activities
Tony is actively engaged in fifth grade activities, without crying, for 70 percent of the day. In addition to decreased crying and apparent listening to class activities, Tony's classroom "jobs" include passing out papers to classmates. He accomplishes this with a sticky band attached to his wrist, which he lowers to a stack of papers on his wheelchair tray. As he raises his arm, one paper stays attached to the band for a classmate to grasp. He then lowers his arm for the next paper. Tony's participation in fifth grade activities also consists of him responding to yes-or-no questions on concrete content.

Goal 2   Increase expressive communication skills with the Introtalker
Tony shows a great interest in communicating with both peers and adults through his Introtalker. Encouragement from his peers reinforces this. Tony consistently uses four symbols on his Introtalker to indicate his needs across the day through an eye gaze, and he indicates his desire to use the Introtalker by ringing a classroom bell positioned at midline. The education team found that Tony's crying was frequently accompanied either by his wetting or soiling himself, or by his body jacket fitting uncomfortably, leaving red marks on his trunk. Of particular interest is his use of symbols to identify his need to go to the bathroom and his desire to have his body jacket checked. By responding to his use of these two symbols, Tony's crying has decreased to occurring for only 30 percent of the school day.

Goal 3   Increase time spent in community-based instruction
Tony gradually increased the time he spends in community-based instruction without crying. Because of the education team's inability to predict when he needs to go to the bathroom or when his body jacket will begin to be uncomfortable, however, he still cries periodically in the community excessively, necessitating an early return to school.

Goal 4   Increase use of adaptive switches
Tony uses adaptive switches during home and careers class, computer class, and within his fifth grade classroom. His classroom "jobs" include running the electric pencil sharpener at specified times of the day for classmates. Tony's family has also expressed interest in using switches at home.

Student Description After Inclusion in Fifth Grade

Tony is able to follow one-step directions, operate adaptive switches with one hand when they are positioned either at midline or under the hand at his arm's length, and use an Introtalker to indicate four of his needs. He continues to increase the amount of time he spends with peers, frequently requesting to be with his friends. Tony's crying has decreased to situations when his Introtalker is not available to him or when an appropriate symbol is not available on the Introtalker.

Tony is strongly motivated to participate in activities with his peers. They provide him support, encouragement, and reinforcement for his efforts. During fifth grade the team observed Tony (1) visually attending to his fifth grade teacher passing out papers, (2) moving his arm to midline to ring the classroom bell for attention, and (3) moving his arm up and down, indicating to his support person that he wanted to do his classroom "job," which the teacher was doing. While not appearing to be important, it must be remembered that upon entering fourth grade, Tony was considered to be profoundly retarded, have little volitional movement, and no manner of communicating beyond crying. The intellectual processes Tony required to recognize that somebody (i.e., the fifth grade teacher) was completing an activity that was "his" (i.e., passing out papers), realizing that he needed to get somebody's attention (i.e., through the use of the bell) to create the opportunity for him to do his own "job" (i.e., getting them to realize what was happening by moving his arm as if he were doing the "job"), were beyond expectations that education team members had for Tony. In addition, the fact that Tony chose

TABLE A.2   *Tony's Summarized Changes*

Skill Area	Before Inclusion	After Inclusion
Behavior	Cried 90% of the day	Actively involved in fifth grade activities without crying 70% of the day; cries 30% of the day when Introtalker or correct symbol not available
Volitional movement	Limited movement of one arm; no use of switches	Uses vertical movement to pass out papers; uses movement to midline to ring bell for attention; runs electric pencil sharpener for classmates
Communication	Cried 90% of the day; no other communication (e.g., yes-or-no responses; eye gaze; Introtalker)	Responds to yes-or-no concrete questions on class activities; uses four symbols on Introtalker; uses bell to indicate desire to use Introtalker
Socialization	Cried 90% of day; no other consistent responses to others or situations	Interested in communicating with peers; frequently requests to be with peers
Self-care	Fed through gastrointestinal tube; not toilet trained	On toileting schedule; chewing and sucking instruction terminated due to frequent pneumonia; fed through gastrointestinal tube
Community	Cried after fifteen minutes	Cries less frequently, after longer periods

to demonstrate these abilities at this time indicated the degree to which he is motivated to participate in class activities. Table A.2 summarizes Tony's changes.

Including Dave in Ninth Grade

Student Description Prior to Inclusion in Ninth Grade

Dave, a seventeen-year-old identified with moderate autistic behaviors, previously received educational services in self-contained classes in a segregated building. Dave responded to verbal cues from adults and peers and engaged in both appropriate and inappropriate interactions with classmates in the self-contained classroom. Interactions between Dave and nondisabled peers, however, were frequently more inappropriate, unnatural, and repetitive, presumably because of his limited exposure to them and the characteristics of his disability. Interactions were characterized by echolalic responses or initiating discussions on irrelevant and inappropriate topics. Academically, Dave was strongest in mathematics. He solved math problems independently, using a calculator to check his answers. Dave was reading at a sixth grade comprehension level and was learning the aspects of compositional writing (e.g., paragraph formation, spelling, punctuation, capitalization). Vocationally, Dave had limited prevocational experience and no vocational experiences on actual jobs.

Dave's education team decided to change his services and place him in general education classes in his home high school. While receiving services in the self-contained settings, however, Dave had become accustomed to a highly structured school environment with consistent routines and guidelines. These and other factors were taken into consideration by his education team, and they believed that Dave's best chances for success were at the ninth grade level.

Prioritized Results from Inventories

Family Inventory
1. Express his feelings and emotions more clearly
2. Initiate hygiene routine at home when getting ready for school, before meals, etc.
3. Participate in after-school activities
4. Explore vocational opportunities
5. Stay with his family when in the community and keep to the schedule when given time on his own

Community Inventory
1. Go to and use the library
2. Go to fast-food restaurants with friends, order, and pay for a meal
3. Go to a book store and buy a book
4. Go to a video store and rent a preferred video

Peer Inventory
1. Participate in school-based extracurricular activities (e.g., sports, clubs)

2. Go to a mall to shop and socialize with peers
3. Cope with his feelings about sexuality
4. Get a part-time job after school

General Education Settings Inventory

1. Take notes in class
2. Move between classes within four minutes

General Education Curriculum Inventory

1. Display problem solving behaviors
2. Increase reading comprehension during high school course work
3. Write complete sentences and paragraphs
4. Improve math computation and application skills

Annual Goals Derived from Inventories

Goal 1   Dave will increase social interaction skills with peers *from* relying on verbal cues during conversation *to* engaging in reciprocal conversations during social situations at school and extracurricular activities, within one year.

Goal 2   Dave will increase his independence during activities in and out of school *from* relying on adult assistance *to* engaging in activities either independently or by requesting assistance from peers, within one year.

Goal 3   Dave will increase his reading and writing skills *from* sixth-grade level *to* seventh-grade level across all academic courses, within one year.

Goal 4   Dave will increase expression of his emotions *from* not discussing his feelings *to* discussing them with adults in structured situations, within one year.

Summary of Progress on Goals During First Year of Inclusion

Goal 1   Social interaction skills
           Dave initiates conversations with peers and adults at appropriate times throughout the school day. He is a member of the track team and an active member in a school club. During interactions, however, his conversation often is repetitive and lacks spontaneity and flexibility. While he periodically continues to be echolalic, this behavior has decreased dramatically, especially with peers. In the structured settings of general education classes, Dave's language skills usually are adequate. He continues, however, to have great difficulty in unstructured situations.

Goal 2   Increase independence
           On the track team, Dave participates in both practice and competitions with support only from his peers. To increase his independence in academic tasks, Dave independently uses a personal computer to take notes during classes.

Goal 3   Increase reading and writing skills
           Dave demonstrates comprehension of short reading passages of ninth grade

course material (e.g., sentences, paragraphs). His comprehension difficulties continue to be apparent, however, when reading longer passages (e.g., short stories, novels). Dave participates in all written classroom assignments, focusing on both reading and writing content appropriate for each topic. He writes answers to questions involving facts found in his textbooks. Creative writing, however, is still a challenge for him.

Goal 4   Increase expression of emotions

Teachers, family, and friends address this goal with Dave, explaining and practicing appropriate social behavior with him. He has demonstrated tremendous growth in identifying others' feelings, following the social amenities for high school students, and using body language. When faced with new situations, however, Dave continues to need assistance and feedback.

Student Description After Two Years of Inclusion

At nineteen years of age Dave has been included in general education classes for two years and is completing the tenth grade. His classes include U.S. Government, English, Introduction to Occupations, Physical Education, and Business Math, during which Dave independently uses a lap-top computer to take notes. Dave's education team identifies the general education content per class that would be most useful for him in his current and future life and focuses instruction on that content. Because of this, he is responsible for less content than his peers. His instruction focuses mainly on reading, writing, increasing independent work, and interacting appropriately with adults and peers across all settings, both in school and in the community. In spite of this, however, he has learned much more of the academic content than the education team expected.

In addition to taking class notes with a computer, Dave has used his computer skills during his summer job experiences. He has held part-time jobs filing, entering information into a computer, and shelving library books. The education team expects that his employment training will continue across different types of jobs, leading to an after-school job.

Socially, Dave continues to be a member of the track team, and his teammates report that he is well-liked by both male and female members of the team. His social interaction skills have improved dramatically, with Dave initiating interactions at appropriate times with both adults and peers. His communication skills during those interactions are much more understandable to strangers and more extensive in content. Table A.3 summarizes Dave's changes.

Note: After five years of being included in general education classes, Dave has progressed dramatically. He gradually became responsible for more of the general education content so that now he is responsible for *all* of it. He is receiving his high school diploma because he has met *all* of the academic requirements for graduation. His language and interactions with others are much more appropriate, although he still is noticeably different from his peers. Dave has shown some ability with computers and recently completed an introductory course on microcomputers at a local community college.

TABLE A.3 *Dave's Summarized Changes*

Skill Area	Before Inclusion	After Inclusion
Behavior	Used echolalic responses constantly; relied on adults for assistance; refused to discuss emotions, especially when angry or frustrated	Periodically is echolalic; participates in school activities with support only from peers; uses personal computer for class notes; identifies others' feelings; follows high school social amenities; uses body language appropriately
Social interactions	Interactions were frequently inappropriate, unnatural, stifled; echolalic responses to overtures from others; initiated interactions on irrelevant and inappropriate topics; needed verbal cues to respond appropriately	Initiates interactions at appropriate times; actively participates in school clubs and teams; interactions often lack spontaneity and flexibility and are repetitive
Math	Solved problems independently; used calculator to check answers	
Reading and writing	Comprehended sixth grade material; learning compositional writing	Comprehends ninth grade material in sentences and paragraphs (not books); does assignments where answers are in texts; has difficulty with creative writing
Community	No independent use of the community	Independently attends school functions held on evenings or weekends
Vocational training	Limited prevocational experiences; no vocational experience	Part-time summer jobs

Portrait of Maureen Before and After Inclusion

Diane Lea Ryndak

Maureen Prior to Inclusion

When the education team first considered inclusion for Maureen, she was fifteen years old and labelled as having moderate mental retardation and speech delays. She had received special education and related services for the last ten years from seven different teachers in self-contained classes, each class located in a different school district within one hour of her home school. Maureen's most recent self-contained classroom was comprised of twelve students, a special education teacher, a full-time classroom aide, and a part-time aide available to Maureen for academic reinforcement. She also received one-to-one speech and occupational therapy on a pull-out basis.

Overall Performance Levels

The progress report the education team wrote at the end of the previous year in a self-contained class stated that Maureen had low social maturity but displayed appropriate social interactions with nondisabled peers. Her speech and language records indicated that Maureen had a receptive vocabulary of six years ten months but an oral vocabulary of only three years five months. Maureen's speech delay resulted in numerous difficulties with conversational skills, both with adults and nondisabled peers. Few people (e.g., family members, peers from neighborhood) could understand Maureen's verbalizations, though her vocabulary was extensive enough for her to participate in lengthy conversations. In addition, Maureen demonstrated what appeared to be a difficulty with word retrieval. When faced with situations where she anticipated being misunderstood, Maureen responded with contrived phrases that quickly extricated her from further interactions. Her speech services consisted of one-to-one speech therapy for thirty minutes, five times a week. During these sessions Maureen received therapy for articulation, vocabulary expansion, and role playing interactions during games.

Academically, Maureen's records indicated that she performed at a third grade level in math. While Maureen's reading test scores indicated a comprehension performance of second grade fourth month, she behaved in a manner that was inconsistent with that score and that educational personnel could not explain. For example, at night Maureen frequently was under the covers of her bed with a flashlight and an adolescent love story. Though these novels did not include pictures and were not from a high interest–low vocabulary series, Maureen answered global questions about these stories. She refused, however, to read any section of these novels or other reading materials either silently in front of an adult or aloud to any person. To extricate herself from adults' requests for her to read or situations which required reading, Maureen consistently resorted to a repertoire of coping behaviors. This especially occurred when Maureen was in a one-to-one instructional setting, a testing situation, or any situation in which she expected that she would perform poorly. In addition, when Maureen became aware that she did not understand a concept required in a desired activity, she would refuse any assistance and use her coping strategies to bluff her way through the situation. When pressed to (1) read or complete an academic task (e.g., use math functionally), (2) perform a task or activity in which she expected that she would do poorly, or (3) accept assistance to complete a desired activity, Maureen usually "tantrummed" by yelling, walking away angrily, or sitting down and refusing to acknowledge anyone. Interpreting them as noncompliance and behavior management problems, Maureen's education team addressed these behaviors by developing behavior management programs and goals for responding appropriately to authority figures.

In relation to physical development, Maureen exhibited generalized hypotonia, poor balance, and a variety of visual motor, motor planning, and visual perception problems. In addition Maureen fatigued easily, so that during activities that required strength or endurance from either fine or gross motor muscles (e.g., writing; physical education activities; walking quickly or for a long distance) she would perform much better at the beginning of the activity than at the end. Physical fatigue also was a factor during afternoons. Maureen frequently arrived home after school exhausted and unable to participate in family activities without a rest.

Pre-Inclusion Program and Performance

Behaviors and Social Interactions. Though the objectives on her individualized education program (IEP) included adding appropriate comments to conversations with adults and peers (see Figure B.1), Maureen's education program provided limited opportunities for her to develop the skills necessary to hold a conversation with nondisabled peers. For instance, while she and her classmates ate in the school cafeteria at the same time as nondisabled peers, the self-contained class was assigned to a separate table. In addition, there were no strategies for facilitating either interactions or conversations between the students from the self-contained class and their nondisabled peers. This resulted in Maureen and her classmates eating lunch in isolation from nondisabled peers and with limited conversations even among themselves. Maureen's main opportunities to interact with nondisabled peers came daily when she left her self-contained class to attend either sixth grade girls' chorus or sixth grade physical education class (see Figure B.2).

Maureen demonstrated differentiated behaviors between situations which did and did not include nondisabled peers, as between her self-contained special education room

FIGURE B.1 *Maureen's IEP Objectives Before Inclusion*

1. Improve proper behavior
2. List ways of contributing to her family and community
3. Verbally express her feelings
4. Add appropriate comments to conversations with adults and peers
5. Improve her understanding of her location in space and other spatial relations
6. Improve the organization of work on her paper
7. Read, spell, and use in sentences new vocabulary from a phonics book and basal reader
8. Improve phonics and comprehension skills to the second grade fifth month level
9. Write complete sentences
10. Improve leisure skills by reading materials (e.g., newspapers, magazines) during free time in the self-contained classroom
11. Read and write dollar amounts
12. Solve three- and four-digit addition and subtraction problems from a workbook or teacher-made worksheets
13. Demonstrate knowledge of body parts
14. Improve work skills by alphabetizing ten words within fifteen minutes

and the sixth grade music and physical education classes. When in the self-contained room, Maureen (1) refused to complete her work, (2) yelled across the room at classmates and adults, (3) kicked other students, especially boys, when seated together, (4) refused to follow directions, and (5) avoided eye contact with nondisabled peers as they passed in the hallway. As soon as Maureen crossed the threshold into the hallway on her way to sixth

FIGURE B.2 *Maureen's Schedule Before Inclusion*

Time Period	Monday	Tuesday	Wednesday	Thursday	Friday
9:05–9:50	M-T-TH-F: Language in self-contained room W: One-to-one occupational therapy				
9:50–10:35	Reading in self-contained room				
10:35–11:20	Odd days: sixth grade girls' chorus Even days: sixth grade physical education				
11:20–12:00	Math in self-contained room				
12:00–12:35	Lunch in cafeteria				
12:35–1:20	Home and careers with self-contained classmates				
1:20–2:05	M: One-to-one occupational therapy T-W-TH-F Odd days: Seat work in self-contained room T-W-TH-F Even days: Functional skills in self-contained room				
2:05–2:30	Science and social studies in self-contained room				
2:30–3:00	Seat work in self-contained room				
3:00–3:30	One-to-one speech therapy				

grade music or physical education, however, she became quiet and observant while moving to her assigned room. During those classes, Maureen attended to the teacher and quietly followed directions to the best of her ability.

For instance, before chorus began, Maureen obtained her folder of music (which she could not read), moved to her assigned seat, opened her folder, and alternated between surreptitiously observing her nondisabled peers and pretending to read the music. Once class started Maureen followed the teacher's directions by participating in the warm-up exercises, opening her materials to the named sheet of music (by modeling her neighbor's behaviors), and singing with the group when she knew the words of the song. When she did not know the words, Maureen "faked it" by moving her mouth while not producing any sound. To assist her in learning the songs, the music teacher made an audio tape of every song she presented to the class, both with and without full accompaniment. Maureen independently used these tapes at home to memorize the songs.

At no time outside of special education settings did Maureen demonstrate inappropriate social behaviors, refuse to follow directions or complete her work, or resort to her coping behaviors. In spite of these differentiated behaviors and Maureen's demonstrated ability to act appropriately when with nondisabled peers, her IEP included an objective to improve proper behavior (see Figure B.1).

Reading and Math.   For her math and reading instruction, Maureen received either teacher-made worksheets or copies of pages from elementary workbooks. Because the education team based Maureen's educational program on her learning developmental skills in these areas, she was not allowed to use a calculator or other adaptive devices when doing her work (see Figures B.3 through B.6). When faced with tasks or activities in her daily life which required academic skills she did not have, Maureen found numerous ways of either getting out of doing the work, or getting somebody else to do it for her.

Therapeutic Services.   Maureen received one-to-one occupational therapy services for thirty minutes, two times a week, on a pull-out basis. When observed, Maureen's therapy consisted of her (1) walking forward, backward, and sideways on a line made with masking tape on the floor of a small equipment room off the school stage, and (2) walking toward a poster with the parts of a business letter labelled in their proper place and attaching a card with the label of each part in the proper place. The occupational therapist explained that these activities were selected "to help Maureen develop better balance . . . a better sense of spatial relationships . . . and better organization skills."

Program Structure.   Upon observing Maureen's education program throughout the school day, it became clear that both her IEP objectives and the delivery of educational and related services to meet those objectives were both disjointed and fragmented. Staff members never met as a team except for the annual review of Maureen's IEP, and there was no communication system to replace periodic team meetings. This resulted in each staff member providing services related to one or more IEP objective in isolation from the other objectives. Education team members did not solicit from the parents or other support network members information about relevant instructional content. In fact, when the education team developed the last IEP, the parents requested therapy support to assist Maureen in

FIGURE B.3   *Sample of Maureen's Math Work on Time after Ten Years of Special Education and Before Inclusion*

acquiring the skills necessary to complete two activities with which she had great difficulty: (1) walking on icy pavements without falling, and (2) riding a two-wheel bicycle as a potential means of future community mobility. The remainder of the education team translated these requests into the need to acquire balance skills, and the requests resulted in the occupational therapy services described in the Therapeutic Services section. In addition to

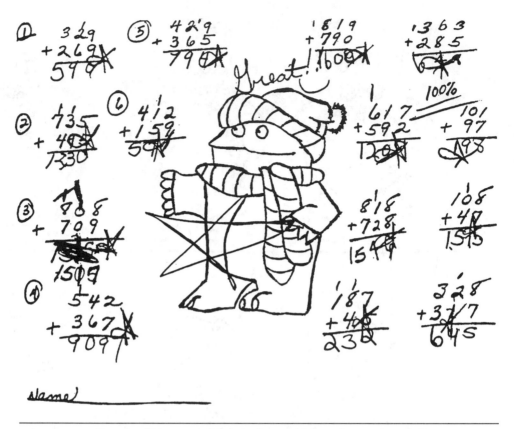

FIGURE B.4 *Sample of Maureen's Math Work on Addition after Ten Years of Special Education and Before Inclusion*

these concerns, the parents frequently questioned the lack of age-appropriate materials and activities in the self-contained class. These types of experiences resulted in a serious lack of communication both among education staff members and between the education staff members and the family.

Maureen Immediately After Inclusion

Reluctantly, Maureen's home school district "included" her on a trial basis in seventh grade classes (see Figure B.7) for the last month of the school year and modified her IEP objectives to reflect Maureen's use of skills in situations that naturally occurred for seventh graders (see Figure B.8). While the district did not provide special education support for the seventh grade teachers whose classes Maureen attended or for her participation during class activities, Maureen did receive pull-out services from a resource room teacher one period per day for support with language development. In addition, there was a great

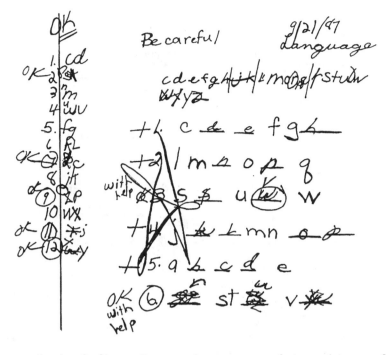

FIGURE B.5 *Samples of Maureen's Writing Work after Ten Years of Special Education and Before Inclusion*

deal of confusion and discussion about how Maureen would receive speech and occupational therapy services without the therapists isolating her from nondisabled peers in a separate room. For this reason, Maureen received few, if any, therapy services during this month, even though services were part of her schedule (see Figure B.7). Despite the lack of well-structured special education and related services support, Maureen flourished during this month and the next full year of inclusion, demonstrating more progress than anticipated across a number of areas.

Write a Summary

Read these sentences about the story you just read. Some of the sentences give the big events that happened in the story. Others give the small things. The sentences are all in order. Write a summary of the story. Find 3 sentences that give the big events. Write them in order below.

You are a good chimp.

1 Mr. Homer is mad about the 2 nights of open cages, but he lets Jay work one more day.

2 This time Jay doesn't go home after he closes the cages.

Maybe that's why he didn't hear.

3 Jay finds the chimp taking off the catches on all the cages. She is flashing her teeth.

Mr Homer is mad about the 2 nights of open cages, but let jay work one day. This time jay doesn't go home after he closes the cages Jay finds the chimp taking off the catches on all the cags.

good

Remembering Small Things

Find the words that answer the questions. Write the words in the right spaces in the game below. Some of the words go across, and some of them go down.

Across

1. What animal is hitting the window and screaming when Mr. Homer walks in?

2. What animals besides cats are happily running around the room?

Down

1. What must be closed tight before Jay can go home?

3. What animals are flying around the shop when Nick walks in?

chimp / cages / dogs

FIGURE B.6 *Samples of Maureen's Reading Work after Ten Years of Special Education and Before Inclusion*

Behaviors and Social Interactions

Maureen never exhibited inappropriate behaviors (i.e., yelling, refusing to work, kicking classmates) in general education settings. When speaking she focused on articulating so that her classmates and teachers could understand her. When in classes, Maureen attended to the instruction presented, and acquired a great deal of the general education curriculum content. She completed both classwork and homework, some of which her education team

FIGURE B.7 *Maureen's Schedule While Included in Seventh-Grade Classes in the Last Month of School Year*

Time Period	Monday	Tuesday	Wednesday	Thursday	Friday
8:55–9:05	Seventh grade homeroom				
9:05–9:50	Seventh grade library				
9:50–10:35	Computer lab				
10:35–11:20	Odd days: seventh grade physical education Even days: seventh grade girls chorus				
11:20–12:05	Resource room: language development				
12:05–12:35	Lunch				
12:35–1:20	Technology				
1:20–2:05	M: occupational therapy in natural situations with nondisabled peers T-TH: seventh grade science W-F: resource room science				
2:05–2:50	Seventh grade math				
2:50–3:00	Study hall				
3:00–3:30	Speech therapy in natural situations with nondisabled peers				

had adapted to challenge her while allowing mostly independent performance, and some of which did not require adaptation (see Figures B.9 through B.12). Maureen earned the nickname "Mayor" of her middle school because of her friendly and enthusiastic social interactions with schoolmates and adults throughout the school. Despite this honorary title, during her first year of inclusion Maureen consistently stated that her nondisabled peers did not like her. After receiving detention as a disciplinary measure that was consistent with school policy for all students, Maureen quickly learned the school rules about being on time, using hallway passes, and accessing restrooms at appropriate times—all rules she previously never had had a reason to know because of the logistics of her self-contained classes. Maureen spent her lunch break talking and eating with nondisabled classmates, though her lunches consisted mainly of french fries! After observing Maureen in a local grocery store, a woman from the community asked Maureen's mother what she "had done to Maureen"—that she looked "entirely different." Upon considering these comments, Maureen's mother realized that her daughter's physical appearance had changed. She now walked with her head up, body erect, and with a spring in her step, instead of using the "special education shuffle" she had used for a number of years. Nondisabled classmates congratulated her for "graduating from that [special education] room."

Academic Performance

When observed in her seventh grade classes, two interesting facts were found in relation to Maureen's time-in-instruction and time-on-task during instruction. First, when

FIGURE B.8   *Maureen's IEP Objectives While Included in Seventh-Grade Classes in the Last Month of School Year*

1. Verbally communicate in social, vocational, academic, and stressful situations
2. Verbally request assistance of adults and peers when a stressful situation occurs in which support is needed
3. Improve use of articulation skills throughout the day so adults and peers understand
4. Display age-appropriate behaviors by interacting with nondisabled peers in seventh grade classes
5. Develop coping mechanisms in life situations where balance is uncertain
6. Ride a two-wheel bicycle
7. Apply life skills to academics
8. Complete activities independently by using a systematic approach
9. Apply reading skills to adapted seventh grade social studies, geography, and science curriculum
10. Improve current reading skills through recreational reading, use of the computer, and life situations
11. Improve writing skills through use of the computer
12. Apply math skills to life activities

comparing Maureen's time-in-instruction and time-on-task during instruction between the self-contained and general education settings, it was found that Maureen was both in-instruction and on-task during instruction significantly more in general education settings. When comparing Maureen's time-in-instruction and time-on-task during instruction with her nondisabled peers in general education settings, it was found that Maureen was in-instruction, and on-task during that instruction, the same amount of time as her classmates. In fact, Maureen's performance on these variables was differentiated across seventh grade teachers in the same manner as her nondisabled classmates' performance. That is, when her classmates had a high rate of time-in-instruction and time-on-task during instruction throughout a class period with one teacher, so did Maureen; when they had a low rate with another teacher, so did Maureen.

Maureen after Five Years of Inclusion

At the age of twenty, Maureen "graduated" from high school with classmates she had since the last month of seventh grade. She and her family made plans for her to be included in a college program and live in a dormitory. During the years she received special education and related services in inclusive settings, Maureen had grown in many ways. Some of her growth occurred in areas that were targeted by her education teams, which finally included her family. Some, however, occurred in areas that the entire education team never considered for Maureen due to her disabilities, her lack of prerequisite skills, or the perceived lack of importance of the skills for Maureen's life.

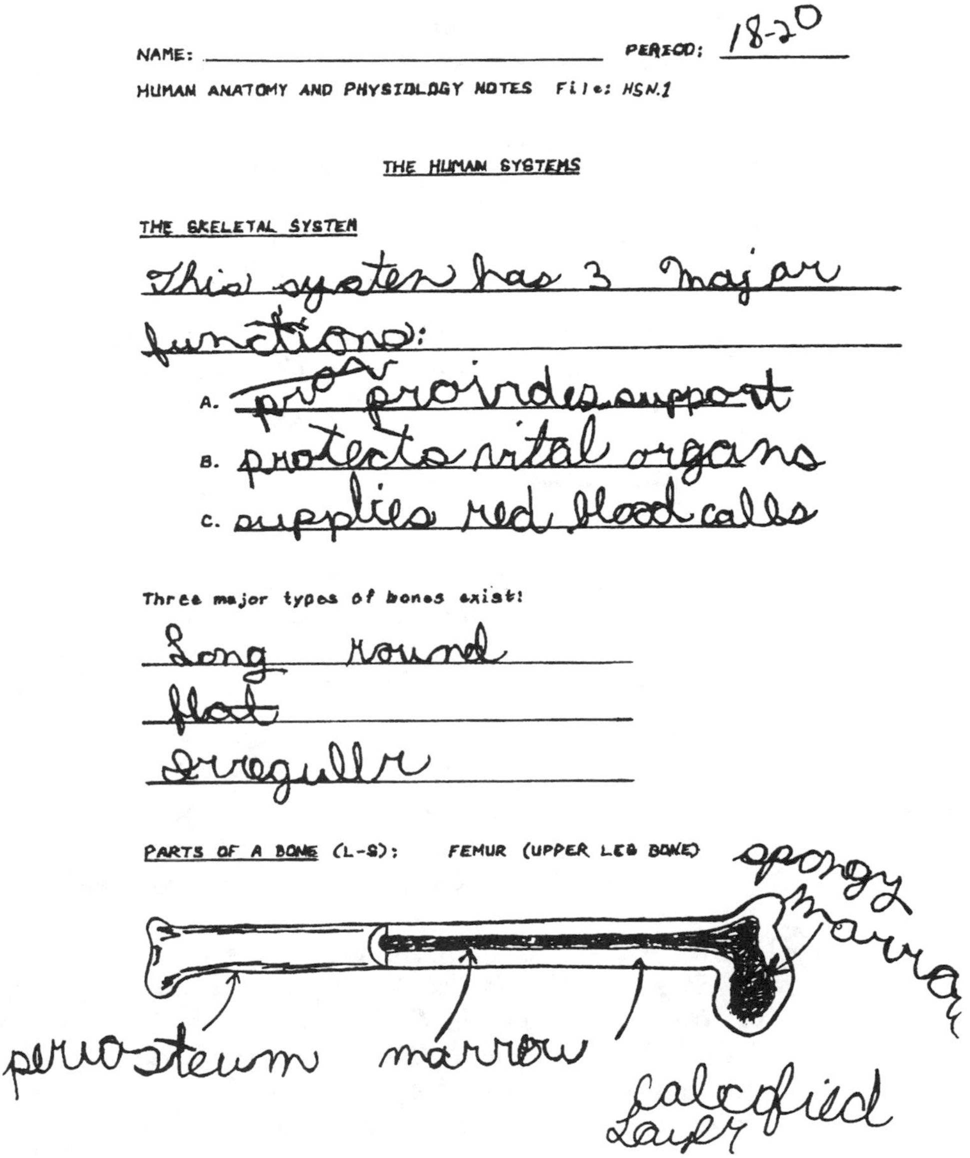

NAME: _____   PERIOD: 18-20

HUMAN ANATOMY AND PHYSIOLOGY NOTES   File: HSN.1

<u>THE HUMAN SYSTEMS</u>

<u>THE SKELETAL SYSTEM</u>

This system has 3 major functions:

A. ~~pro~~ *proivdes support*

B. *protects vital organs*

C. *supplies red blood cells*

Three major types of bones exist:

Long   round

flat

Irregular

<u>PARTS OF A BONE</u> (L-S):   FEMUR (UPPER LEG BONE)   *spongy marrow*

periosteum   marrow   calcified layer

FIGURE B.9 *Sample of Maureen's Science Work Immediately after Inclusion*

Behaviors and Social Interactions

In relation to the coping behaviors Maureen had used to extricate herself from difficult situations in inclusive settings, Maureen developed good problem solving skills and more appropriate coping behaviors. She still, however, encountered situations for which she did

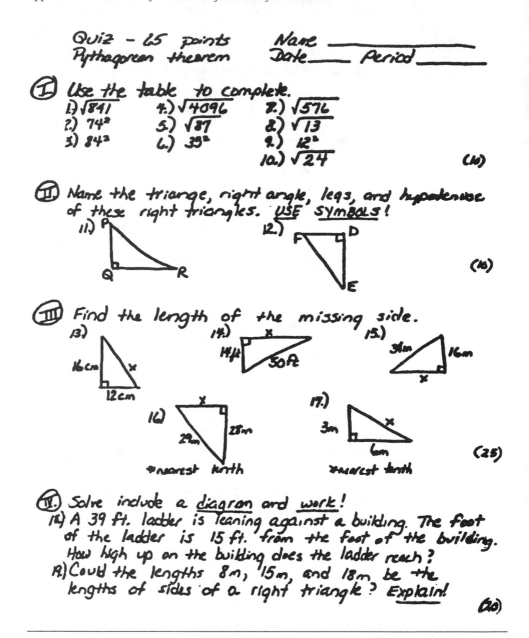

FIGURE B.10   An Eighth-Grade Math Test on Pythagorean Theorem

not have all the necessary skills to cope appropriately. In these situations, Maureen still periodically refused assistance, though she usually accepted assistance from familiar adults who understood her resistance to help and applied strategies that accommodated for this resistance. Maureen did best when assistance was paired with praise and when people explained how she could do things by herself, rather than relying on other people. When

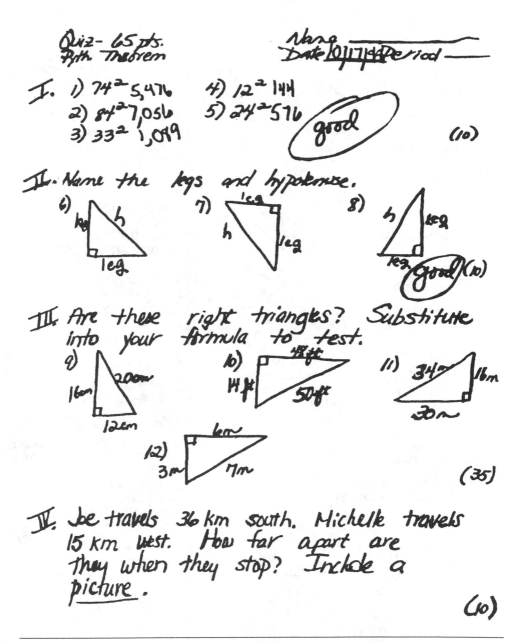

Quiz— 65 pts.   Name _____
Pyth Theorem   Date 10/17/9? Period ____

I. 1) 74² 5,476   4) 12² 144
    2) 84² 7,056   5) 24² 576   *good*   (10)
    3) 33² 1,089

II. Name the legs and hypotenuse.
    6)   7)   8)   *good* (10)

III. Are these right triangles? Substitute
     into your formula to test.
     9)   10)   11)

     12)

                                          (35)

IV. Joe travels 36 km south. Michelle travels
    15 km west. How far apart are
    they when they stop? Include a
    picture.

                                          (10)

FIGURE B.11 *Maureen's Adapted Math Test on Pythagorean Theorem Shortly
after Inclusion*

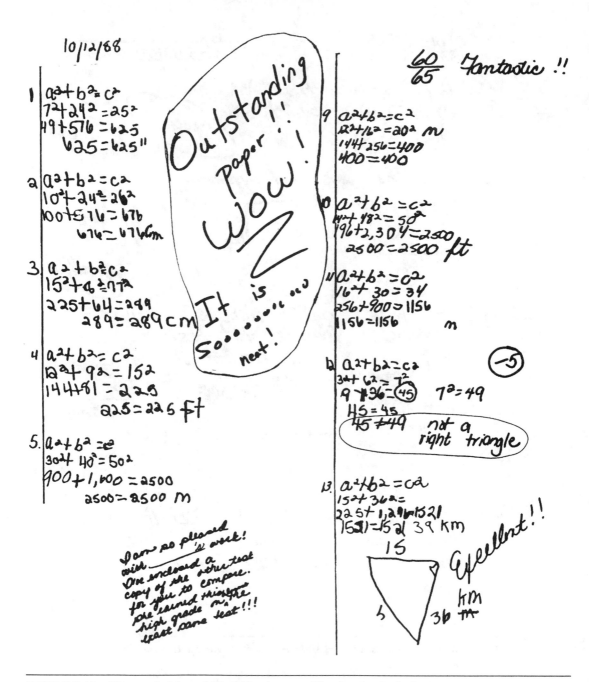

10/12/88

$\frac{60}{65}$ Fantastic !!

1 | $a^2 + b^2 = c^2$
$7^2 + 24^2 = 25^2$
$49 + 576 = 625$
$625 = 625$ "

2 | $a^2 + b^2 = c^2$
$10^2 + 24^2 = 26^2$
$100 + 576 = 676$
$676 = 676$ cm

3 | $a^2 + b^2 = c^2$
$15^2 + 8^2 = 17^2$
$225 + 64 = 289$
$289 = 289$ cm

4 | $a^2 + b^2 = c^2$
$12^2 + 9^2 = 15^2$
$144 + 81 = 225$
$225 = 225$ ft

5 | $a^2 + b^2 = c^2$
$30^2 + 40^2 = 50^2$
$900 + 1,600 = 2500$
$2500 = 2500$ m

Outstanding paper !! WOW !

It is Sooooooooo neat!

9 | $a^2 + b^2 = c^2$
$12^2 + 16^2 = 20^2$ m
$144 + 256 = 400$
$400 = 400$

10 | $a^2 + b^2 = c^2$
$14^2 + 48^2 = 50^2$
$196 + 2,304 = 2500$
$2500 = 2500$ ft

11 | $a^2 + b^2 = c^2$
$16^2 + 30 = 34$
$256 + 900 = 1156$
$1156 = 1156$ m

12 | $a^2 + b^2 = c^2$
$3^2 + 6^2 = 7^2$ $7^2 = 49$ (-5)
$9 + 36 = $ (45)
$45 = 45$
$45 \neq 49$ not a right triangle

13 | $a^2 + b^2 = c^2$
$15^2 + 36^2 =$
$225 + 1,296 = 1521$
$1521 = 1521$ 39 km

Excellent!!

15
5   36 km m

I am so pleased with ___'s work! I've enclosed a copy of the other test for you to compare. She earned the same high grade on a least same test!!!

faced with the realization that she did not understand a concept, Maureen had begun to request assistance. For instance, when discussing the score from one of the girls' soccer team games, Maureen was able to recite the final score but, when asked, could not explain what the score meant (i.e., which score correlated with which team and, therefore, which team won). Upon realizing she did not understand, Maureen asked her mother to explain how to interpret the scores. This was a major change in Maureen's acceptance of her lack of understanding, as well as her willingness to admit that lack to another individual and request assistance. It resulted in much less frequent use of her contrived phrases and coping behaviors to extricate herself from difficult situations.

Socially, Maureen had been involved in numerous extracurricular activities during her high school years. Initially she had become involved with the girls' soccer and field hockey teams as a team manager. In this capacity she had attended every practice and game, assisting the coach and team members in a variety of tasks. She had participated in school musicals and been involved in school sponsored clubs (e.g., Volunteers Interested in People, Distributive Education Clubs of America). Because of her involvement in school activities, Maureen left home at 7:15 A.M. and did not return from school before 6:00 P.M. When participating in night games she did not return home until 8:30–9:00 P.M. Despite this more extensive schedule, Maureen quickly adjusted to the physical demands and did not exhibit fatigue beyond that of other high school students.

In her interaction with nondisabled peers, Maureen's initial growth had been in the areas of articulation and vocabulary. As she became more intelligible to classmates and adults, Maureen developed behaviors that demonstrated a heightened awareness of her nondisabled peers and their reactions to her, although she still had difficulty interacting maturely with boys. For instance, Maureen participated in disability awareness sessions in each of her high school classes. During these sessions she helped explain her disability, the things with which she had difficulty, and the most effective manner in which to respond to her when she "fell apart" (e.g., when she was angry or frustrated and unable to cope) (see Figure B.13). Through these continued discussions and observing classmates' responses to her, Maureen became aware of her reactions to difficult situations and learned to identify when she was "falling apart." Once she had the ability to identify these situations, Maureen began to tell people when she was "falling apart" and request that they "give her a minute." In addition, as she began to cope with these situations more effectively the frequency with which she actually "fell apart" decreased dramatically, and she began to use humor to defuse her own anger.

Maureen also recognized two important facts about herself. First, she learned that she could learn; that she was a capable individual who just needed instruction and repetition provided in specific manners in order to learn more efficiently. Maureen also recognized a tendency she displayed to focus so intently on something that she was unable to respond to changes by restructuring her thoughts and expectations. This inflexibility, or hyperfocusing, kept her from participating in many activities and presented situations in which she "fell apart." With information about this inflexibility, Maureen was able to modify her own behavior and learn to "go with the flow" of life.

Maureen also learned inappropriate behaviors from her nondisabled classmates, as well as the societal consequences that result from those behaviors. For instance, when Maureen realized that a lot of her classmates smoked cigarettes between classes in the

People think that I can't do a lot of things, but I really can. I Just need Someone to tell me what to do and do it with me once or twice then I am ready to work myself.

I like to be busy. when I finish my work, I like to help others.

I like to be treated like a high School person. I am almost an adult.

If I don't understand you, say it again, or show me what you mean. Sometimes I get crabby when things get too confusing. Please stay away for a couple of minutes and then say, are you ready?"

FIGURE B.13   *Maureen's Disability Awareness Statement after Five Years of Inclusion*

restrooms, even though it was not permitted, she joined them. The embarrassment of being caught by a teacher and the ensuing detention that forced her to miss one of her team's field hockey games resulted in no recurrence of this behavior.

Reading, Math, and Other Academic Performance

During the five years in which Maureen received special education and related services in general education settings, she developed a number of decoding skills that assisted her in reading new material. In addition, she learned numerous functional vocabulary words and developed a "word bank" from which she could retrieve words for a first draft of written work (see Figure B.14). With this draft Maureen worked with a peer or adult who would facilitate the development of her thoughts into complete sentences and assist Maureen in

October Tuesday 20,92

I help manager field hocey and keep score, take out equpent keep time,

The Coach is Mrs. Baker.
we won the championship last year is very good. The teams is sue jones and Jeanie Boss,
sue Black, the use slicks cleats shin pads the hurt the self.

FIGURE B.14   *Sample of Maureen's Independent Writing after Five Years of Inclusion*

writing them either on the computer or by hand. The combination of these strategies allowed Maureen to develop written material and read it at will. For instance, using these
strategies Maureen wrote and read testimony for the Education Committee of the State
Assembly related to her State's implementation of the least restrictive environment component of the Individuals with Disabilities Education Act (see Figure B.15). In addition,
Maureen used these strategies to participate in high school class activities. When her
English class was studying Shakespearean plays, Maureen participated by reading study
versions of the plays that summarized the stories, practiced reading aloud specific sections
of the play to facilitate her participation in class readings, watched videotapes of the plays,
and used the library to prepare six posters about the author and his plays. She also took
adapted tests (see Figure B.16).

In relation to math, Maureen learned systematic approaches to problem solving and
applying math formulas to real life situations. Specifically, Maureen learned to apply formulas to work-related issues (e.g., wages, depositing pay-checks) and budgeting the use of
her funds for life activities (see Figure B.17).

Therapeutic Services

During her high school experiences, the education team determined that Maureen's speech
impairment partially was due to an inability to hear and reproduce all the syllables in some
words. Speech therapy then expanded from articulation and vocabulary training to focusing on syllables and practicing words that were particularly problematic. For instance,
Maureen could not differentiate the syllables in the word *iron*, but she could pronounce the
word correctly by thinking about articulating and blending the words *I* and *earn*. While
practicing her testimony for the State Assembly Education Committee (see Figure B.15),
Maureen had similar problems with the word *economics*. She could say it correctly however, if she first thought of the word *echo* and then added *nomics*. During her actual testimony Maureen read her statement smoothly up to the word *economics*. She then paused
and said *echo nomics*, paused again and smiled at her mother. She then continued reading
the remainder of her testimony smoothly.

Through her occupational therapy Maureen accomplished several tasks with which
she previously had had a great deal of difficulty, such as opening the lock on her locker

I was in special class for ten years. I was very Angery. I used to put my head Down On the Desk and Look out the door and see the Kids. I want to be with Them.

Now I have a Locker And take government, Journalssm, marketing, economics and Health. The Kids I used to Look at are my friends now.

I Learn Better in the regular class. I watch my friends and Do what they Do. Sometines my friends help me and teach me Stuff. Sometines I help them. my Special Eductions teacher, my Spech teacher and my ot. help me, too. I am very 600d In School. I also have a new Job. I have a Lot of friends there. I Get paid. I pay texes.

if Someone Said That I Could Go back to the Special class I would say "no" I will never Go back.

Please change the Lans to help kids Like me be in Regular classes with Their friends.

February 12, 1993

FIGURE B.15 *Maureen's Testimony on Least Restrictive Environment to the Education Committee of the State Assembly*

and walking up and down the stairs between high school classes with the other 900 students in her school. Maureen also was able to accomplish class-related tasks with the assistance and training provided through occupational therapy. For instance, because Maureen demonstrated difficulty with visual perception skills, organization skills, and coordination, the development of six large posters on Shakespeare for English class required the integration of occupational therapy into her work. Visual perception skills,

Name _____ Date 10/22/97

Choose the best meaning for the following terms:

✓ 1. plot   (a) the list of characters
                  b) events that make up the story
                  c) the place where the story happens

    2. moral   a) lesson
✓   b) events that happened in the past
                  (c) world as it is

70

    3. flashback   a) world as it is
+   (b) showing events that happened in the
                     past
                  c) time and place where the story happens

    4. idealism   a) world as it is
+   (b) world as the author would like it to
                     be
                  c) the main idea of the story

✓ 5. climax   (a) unusual events, characters, or
                     situations
                  b) highest point of interest or emotion
                  c) the lesson

    6. setting   (a) time and place where the story takes
                     place
+   b) lesson to be learned
                  c) list of characters

    7. theme   a) stage set
                  b) main idea
+   (c) way the author sees the world

    8. realism   (a) the way the world is
                  b) the lesson of the story
+   c) the props the director uses

    9. fantasy   a) the way the world is
+   (b) unusual events, situations, or
                     characters: not real.
                  c) realism

   10. antagonist   a) the main character
                  b) the hero
+   (c) the character who is against the
                     main character.

Use the word setting in a sentence:

+   The Setting is where the story takes place.

FIGURE B.16 *Sample of Maureen's Adapted Tests after Five Years of Inclusion*

"Review" (40) (36) good work! Name _____

Find your total wages for a week: HOURS × Wage = Total Wage

(a) You work   10 hours   at $4.65 an hour. $46.50 ✓

(b) You work   15 hours   at $4.65 an hour. $69.75 ✓

(c) You work   20 hours   at $4.65 an hour. $93.00 ✓

How much money do you have to spend?

Ex: Total Wages $ 80.00
  −   Taxes   − 22.00
                          58.00
  −   Bus Tickets   − 11.00
                         $ 47.00

(a) Total Wages $71.25   (b) Total Wages $95.00

  − Taxes $17.80   − Taxes   23.75
                    53.45 (2)   (7) $71.25

  − Bus Tickets   11.00   − Bus Tickets   11.00
                  $42.45   60.25

*Bonus Points: Which is less expensive?

        Riding the Bus   Taking a taxi

                                    $60.25

MAUREEN   0104
                                           10-2/220
                        Sept. 21, 92
PAY TO THE
ORDER OF Lynne | $61.44
sixty-one and 44/100 ～～～   DOLLARS
☺
FOR Sony wm   M
⑇:0 2 2000 0 20⑇: 7 288 27 31 0⑇' 0104
© HARLAND 1991

FIGURE B.17   *Samples of Maureen's Math Work after Five Years of Inclusion*

478

organization skills, and coordination were critical when visually locating appropriate material for the posters and preparing materials through photocopying, cutting, placing materials in a coordinated manner, and gluing materials in place. In addition, Maureen developed some materials on the computer, which required the incorporation of occupational therapy into keyboarding skills. Finally, Maureen's occupational therapy became part of the components of the jobs for which she received instruction during part of her last two years of high school and over those summers.

Note

Portions of Appendix B are adapted from Ryndak, D. L., Morrison, A. P., & Sommerstein, L. (1999). Literacy prior to and after inclusion in general education settings: A case study. *Journal of the Association for Persons with Severe Handicaps, 24*(1).

Name Index

Subject Index